Major League Baseball
Transactions, 1946

To Annette, wife and partner, my best friend;
to Alan Berger and Chuck Partington;
all for their constant encouragement and support in finishing this work.

To the late Eddie Stanky, who gave me my first autograph;
to the late Harry Walker, who gave me kindness
and always remembered my name.

(The Brat and The Hat, if not exactly enshrined at Cooperstown,
are, nonetheless, the stuff of baseball's mythic past.)

And to John Carden, who would never get the chance.

Major League Baseball Transactions, 1946

Bob Levy

McFarland & Company, Inc., Publishers
Jefferson, North Carolina, and London

Library of Congress Cataloguing-in-Publication Data

Levy, Bob
Major league baseball transactions, 1946 / Bob Levy.
p.   cm.
Includes bibliographical references (p.   ) and index. ∞
ISBN 0-7864-0947-9 (softcover : 50# alkaline paper)
1. Baseball players—Trading of—United States—History—20th century. 2. Baseball draft—United States—History—20th century. 3. Baseball players—United States—Registers. I. Title.
GV880.3.L48   2001
796.357'64'0973—dc21   2001030339

British Library cataloguing data are available

©2001 Robert J. Levy. All rights reserved

No part of this book may be reproduced or transmitted in any form or by any means, electronic or mechanical, including photocopying or recording, or by any information storage and retrieval system, without permission in writing from the publisher.

Manufactured in the United States of America

Cover images ©2001 PhotoSpin

*McFarland & Company, Inc., Publishers
Box 611, Jefferson, North Carolina 28640
www.mcfarlandpub.com*

Contents

Preface 1

The 1946 Season, Day by Day 3

Daily Player Grids 117
The American League 119
The National League 208

Appendix: Annotated 1946 Team Rosters 297
Bibliography 319
Index 321

Preface

The research that has led to this book began a quarter-century ago, part of a lifelong fascination with World War II and its effects upon major American sports. Those effects lingered into the late 1940s, most keenly felt in baseball during the 1946 season. Many pressures were being brought to bear on the game that year. Many careers were ending, others were in limbo, others just beginning. New powers were building, old ones reshaping themselves. In its way, 1946 was the closing of the prewar era. The game and its prewar stars tried mightily to be the way they were before. More accurately, though, it was the introduction to a new era, starting in 1947 and lasting until the Dodgers and Giants moved west, followed by Major League Baseball's first expansion of the century.

Those who were active in 1946—the players, managers and executives who fashioned its dynamics—have now either passed away, or become old men whose numbers diminish with increasing pace. Knowing this, how haunting are the words of a man I never met, a retired military officer and war historian, Jay B. Smith. In a 1974 letter, Captain Smith cautioned, through a mutual friend at the Navy Department, that, while many of 1946's players remained with us, life's clock had already wound down, for "…others, who unhappily would have to testify these days from the Elysian Fields. Levy had better hurry before we're real gone."

Their small corner of baseball's Valhalla has grown in the quarter-century since he penned those words. Of the 633 major league players in 1946, at least 413 have passed on as I write this (by my cursory count, 65 percent of the participants; there could be more). In 1999 and early 2000, at the Millennium, the toll added, among others, Joe DiMaggio, Birdie Tebbetts, Early Wynn, the Dodgers' 1946 keystone combination of Eddie Stanky and Pee Wee Reese, Pat Mullin, Harry Walker, Whitey Kurowski and Bob Lemon. Their deaths tug on very personal heartstrings. They were among my earliest idols, demigods to a boy growing up, just learning their names, regarding them as a boy does, larger than life. They were *big leaguers*, stars and one-gamers alike (there are no class distinctions in the Elysian Fields; they rest there, those already gone, side by side, in our mind's eye, waiting). To illustrate my point, here are a representative few of them.

Bobby Adams of the Reds, rookie at 24 in 1946, died in 1997, at 75. Veteran pitcher Ernie Bonham of the 1946 Yankees, big man called "Tiny," dead of complications from appendicitis in 1949, just 35. Hank Greenberg of the 1946 Tigers, first prominent big leaguer to be drafted into the Army, the spring before Pearl Harbor, whose home run won the pennant for the 1945 Tigers, died in 1986, at 75. Coach Red Kress of the Giants, once a top shortstop who played a final game in 1946, as a pitcher, and passed away at 55, in 1962.

Future star outfielder Dale Mitchell of the Indians reached the big leagues near the end of the 1946 season. He died in 1987, aged 65. Established star outfielder Terry Moore of the Cardinals, a civilian again in 1946 after three years of soldiering and playing ball in Panama, died in 1993, aged 83.

The legendary Bobo Newsom, of the 1946 Athletics and Senators, died in 1962 at 52, having pitched for Brooklyn, the Cubs, the Browns, Washington, the Red Sox, the Browns, Detroit, Washington, Brooklyn, the Browns, Washington, the A's, Washington, the Yankees, the Giants, Washington and the A's. Pitcher Johnny Podgajny of the Indians made a half-dozen appearances in 1946, final season of an undistinguished career. He died in 1971, at 51.

Mel Ott, great slugger, "Master Melvin, the Little Giant," manager of the Giants, who hit a solitary home run in 1946, last of his National League record 511, died young in 1958, at 49. Paul Rapier Richards, sage of Waxahachie, Texas, veteran Detroit catcher, soon to be an influential manager and executive, died old in 1986, age 77. Vin Smith, long-forgotten Pittsburgh catcher and umpire, died in 1979, at 63. Phil Marchildon, Canadian ace of the A's pitching staff before and after he flew as a tail-gunner on bombing missions in the RCAF, having survived prisoner-of-war camp and Connie Mack as well, died in 1997, aged 83 (the tight-fisted Mister Mack was already 84, the year after the war, with four more seasons to go in his long, long time as owner-manager of the Philadelphia Athletics).

Pitcher Ralph McCabe of the Indians, whose major league career lasted one game, died in 1974, aged 55. Pitcher John Carden of the Giants, also a one-game big leaguer, died in early 1949, not yet 28.

The grand, star-crossed Dodger outfielder, Pete Reiser, who might have been better than anyone, died in 1981, at 62. The now-obscure catcher, Hugh Poland of the Braves, died in 1984 at 71. The still-famous pitcher, Hal Newhouser of the Tigers, died in 1998 at 77, having finally received long-denied membership at Cooperstown. It meant he was more than just a *wartime* pitcher.

This is written in their memory.

The 1946 Season, Day by Day

It was the first season after the War, when all the "Boys" were back. Though some didn't return till after Opening Day. A few, very late into military service, were away most or all of the season. The point is, *all* the Boys weren't back, not all. And a good many of those in major league dugouts were months from really being big leaguers again, the way they were before. Some not till next year; some never.

Nineteen forty-six was pivotal, a season of transition, immense changes taking place. The two major league pennant races were significant — one for its unprecedented intensity, the other for its Yankee-like domination by a team *not* the Yankees. Interest was higher than ever before. In 1945, while our boys still fought in the Pacific, big league baseball had enjoyed record crowds. Yet, 1946's attendance explosion made the previous season's gains easily forgotten.

In 1945, *The Sporting News* had reported 3,541 minor leaguers on active duty in military service. By 1946, returning players were virtually a glut on the market, making possible a terrific minor league growth, generating an upward spiral which continued till the next decade. (Because of the war, there had been just 10 leagues in 1944, 12 in 1945; the number burgeoned to 43 in 1946, and would total 59 in 1949, with teams in 438 cities.)

Some who came back didn't care much about baseball any more. Many prewar and wartime players no longer could compete at the intense level of the big leagues. Many didn't even make it to Opening Day. Of those marginal ones who did, it was often the last gasp in a career gone bad. There were many quickly-gulped cups of coffee for many would-be big leaguers in 1946, some who would enjoy only a handful of games Up There.

It was a landmark year, the year Jackie Robinson broke organized baseball's color line; of Country Slaughter's mad dash home. It was the year Bob Feller did or didn't set a new strikeout record, the year Ted Williams happily knocked Rip Sewell's elusive blooper ball over the fence for a homer in the All-Star Game, his second four-bagger of the day. It was the year Stan Musial, just 25 and a wartime batting champion, returned from the Navy, won another title and firmly established himself on the very upper strata reserved for the game's brightest stars. It was Joe DiMaggio's worst year yet. His fans expected, daily, that he'd snap out of it and lead the Yankees back to the pennant. Their hopes were premature.

Mickey Vernon found his batting touch this year; it was the year righthanded Bob Lemon, 25 years old, began as Cleveland's center fielder, ended as a pitcher, winning the first four of his 207 career victories; it was the year unknown lefty Warren Spahn, late of the battlefields of Europe, appeared out of nowhere in midseason, also 25 and without a single major league win to his name.

It was the year Ralph Kiner hit so hard in spring training that the Pirates couldn't farm him to the minors for seasoning, as they'd planned. Nineteen forty-six was the year Del Ennis wasn't supposed to be a major leaguer, either. But his reputation playing ball on islands in the Pacific created such support for him among his contemporaries that he finally got into a game for his hometown Phillies, couldn't be dislodged and became Rookie of the Year.

Before detailing next season's player transactions (the intended purpose of this document), I've included some random notes from the 1945 postseason and the 1946 preseason. They include some player movement prior to Opening Day 1946, deals which seem particularly important or of special interest, or which help set the scene.

From a historical context, there are obvious, glaring omissions in the following pages: there's little of pennant races, except in a broad sense, till the final days of the season. This is a sort of *anti-record* of the season. You won't read much of the men who provided the bulk of 1946's heroics and timeless memories, the regulars, everyday guys, the stars, the big hitters and dazzling pitchers, prominent from start to finish, who didn't change teams, didn't get optioned out or released. They stayed in one place, throughout the season, and don't receive much mention herein. Their accomplishments are in the record books, already there to see.

You'll read a minimum, in this venue, of the abortive attempt at a players' guild, or the early grudging, unenthusiastic concessions by big league owners to set a minimum wage and establish a pension plan. I take too many tangents already, in this volume.

A good story is out there, of increasing violence on minor league playing fields this year. Minor league umpires became, as they hadn't since the nineteenth century, targets of fists, bottles, overflowing grandstands, over-aggressive managers and apathetic club owners who, by turning a deaf ear to discord, watched their coffers fill faster than ever, with the dollars of patrons who enjoyed a little extra violence. One theory holds that men in the grandstands, just back from killing other men, savored a little more mayhem after the war than before, to help them adjust to a world of peace: whatever the reason, it awaits further investigation.

There's little attention paid, in this document, to life outside baseball, though this is one of the more compelling, pivotal years of the twentieth century. The Nuremburg war crimes trials in Germany were conducted, of Nazi leaders held responsible for their acts, or their complicity in the acts of others. In Japan, two years of similar trials began in 1946, prosecuted by 11 Allied nations.

There's nothing here about the monolith of world Communism, other than to repeat Winston Churchill's solemn declaration in March 1946 to a Missouri college audience that "from Stettin in the Baltic to Trieste in the Adriatic, an iron curtain has descended across the Continent" of Europe, giving our generations a half-century descriptive for the line separating "us and them."

I've included minimal discussion of racial integration, outside or inside sports, though it's impossible not to recognize that, in this century, it first arrived in organized baseball in 1946. It heralded the social future of America forever after. Jackie Robinson's signing and brief reports on his season at Montreal are mentioned, with little embellishment.

This is about major league baseball transactions from the end of the 1945 to the end of the 1946 seasons. It is written, as much as possible, in the present tense, as if the events are unfurling for the first time. All statistical records, from a historical standpoint, are noted as of the day in 1946 when they were accomplished (unless described otherwise).

A primary source of this text is the weekly publication *The Sporting News*, self-styled "Bible of Baseball," so regarded for its comprehensive coverage of the game in those days. Yet this important source, authoritative as it is, contains errors. It is, like any other newspaper, written and typeset by real people, on deadline, who make mistakes and follow sometimes confusing policies and have sometimes conflicting opinion. Its published box scores, invaluable and necessary as they are to research, do have typos and wrong names or wrong positions shown — not many, but some. So do those of the *New York Times*. They do occasionally omit a player from a box score who should have been there, or sometimes give him one game too many. It causes one to pause and attempt to analyze what's happening or, often, to get it even more wrong.

There's the matter of timing, in its way far more a problem to contend with. For a glimpse at how it works, or doesn't, here's an excerpt from *The Sporting News*, issue of July 10, 1946. It's important in ascertaining days and dates, and things. It's included so you, too, will have a clearer, firmer grasp on essentials, same as me.

> In carrying out plans originally made when the publication date was changed from Thursday to Wednesday, *The Sporting News* effective with the issue of July 17, will be printed on the Friday preceding the date of issue…
> There will be no change in the policy of dating each issue, which will continue to bear a Wednesday dateline. Heretofore, the paper has been printed seven days in advance of the date of issue; under the new arrangement, copies will be printed only five days in advance of date of issue, making possible later, more up-to-the-minute news coverage.

That should clear up any questions you might have. (There seemed to be a firm editorial policy, there, to omit specific transaction dates in the paper's weekly reports. To commit to inclusion of dates might only emphasize the delay between getting a story and printing it. Dates might mislead a reader, who might question how current a publication could be, reporting "news" datelined two or three weeks earlier. Or, perhaps, no one thought it important. Maybe, they might have rationalized, those deals are done, who cares about dates?)

This in mind, we proceed to the waning days of 1945, in preparation for 1946.

October 2, 1945

The Athletics sell pitcher Don Black to Cleveland. Though a starter for the A's (8–11) in 1945, he'll be limited to 18 games with the Indians in 1946 (1–2) and spend the last half of the season at Milwaukee. Coming back in 1947, he'll pitch a no-hitter for Cleveland. Through it all, he'll fight a protracted and agonizing extracurricular battle, against alcohol.

October 16, 1945

The Browns trade first baseman George McQuinn to the Athletics, for first baseman Dick Siebert. Both are good fielders, once good hitters, now getting along in years.

It's a deal which indicates A's owner-manager Connie Mack has lost his once-magical touch: McQuinn, who has a bad back, will hit only .225 for him in 1946. Then, Mister Mack will slip up even more, letting McQuinn go a year too soon, making it possible for the first baseman, bad back and all, to help propel the Yankees to a World Championship in 1947.

The Browns are equally short-sighted, having sentenced McQuinn to the A's in the first place. He was a meaningful factor in St. Louis' only American league pennant, just over a year ago and, despite his age (36), disposing of him is premature.

In fact, slipping it up themselves, Browns management thoughtlessly delivers a financial slap in the face to the incoming Siebert (also given up for dead by the astute Mack, remember). Siebert is offered a cut in salary by his new team, from $12,000 in 1945 to $10,000 in 1946, claiming poverty (true; the Browns, through a succession of owners, were always one step from folding). Siebert, acting preemptively, declares he's through playing and, rather than slave for St. Louis at what he considers coolie wages, he retires, to become a radio broadcaster.

The Browns then demand McQuinn's return to St. Louis, since they have received what amounts to nothing in the exchange. McQuinn *there* would be lots better as a first baseman than Dick Siebert *not there.*

It will take till April for a decision, when Baseball Commissioner A.B. "Happy" Chandler rules the deal stands. The Browns, he says, had the opportunity to reach an agreement with Siebert and didn't. Unhappy, near broke, vindictive, the team then insists Siebert be placed on the dread *ineligible* list, in effect banning him from the game forever, like the eight "Black" Sox charged with throwing the 1919 World Series. The player, understandably incensed, wants simply to be classified "voluntary retired," which is how it all seems to play out.

Siebert will later coach the University of Minnesota for three decades, guiding his baseball teams to 11 Big Ten titles and three NCAA championships, contributing much more than he ever did as a player.

October 23, 1945

In Montreal, it's announced that Jack Roosevelt Robinson, shortstop for the Kansas City Monarchs of the Negro American League, has signed a contract to play with the Brooklyn farm club in the Canadian city, the Royals, of the International League. It's almost two months since an initial, secret talk, in Brooklyn, August 28th, with Dodgers president Branch Rickey. That day, Mr. Rickey informed Robinson he hadn't been scouted for a fictional Brooklyn *Brown* Dodgers baseball team, as he'd been led to believe, but for the *real* Dodgers.

It is, of course, loudly applauded by black leaders and citizens (and the black press, mostly ignored by their white contemporaries, which had been vigorously campaigning for integration of sports for years, though apparently beaten to it, as early as 1936, by Lester Rodney, sole sports writer of the Daily Worker. This, according to Tom Gallagher, writing in the 1999 *National Pastime,* a publication of SABR—the Society for American Baseball Research).

Mr. Rickey quickly incurs the wrath of most everyone else, including millions of white Americans, whose daily lives haven't included fellow countrymen of African descent. It is not altogether a benign ignorance. Other big league club owners are opposed, without exception. Many white players, who don't want to appear on the same field with black men, are opposed, some because they feel racially superior, others opposed to being seen on the field with a Negro, they claim, because the folks "back home" just wouldn't understand or accept it.

They grumble for the present, not so loudly this year as next, when Robinson is at last promoted to the parent club, to the Brooklyn Dodgers. For now, for players on the Dodgers, it's something to be considered at some other time. "If he isn't on our club right now, today, it's not my worry" is the attitude frequently attributed to team leader Fred (Dixie) Walker and adhered to by several of his white teammates.

Negro League owners are fearful. They see ominous portents in Robinson's signing. If they can lose him, they can lose all their stars, their best players, to organized baseball. It's the death knell of their business. More, since theirs is a business, like any other, they decry being given no compensation for the loss. Major League club owners, recognizing how morally, legally and financially at risk are their actions, will begin compensating those who lose players, but Rickey doesn't in Robinson's case. Robinson says he has no contract with the Monarchs, there's no hold on him; he's free to join the Royals and Rickey, never one to part with money needlessly, takes Robinson at his word.

Some Negro League players are sure Robinson is simply the wrong man to break the color line, which has been in place since the 1880s. Jackie's not good enough, they say, not experienced enough; he won't make it. They say there are many Negro Leaguers more experienced and more qualified than Robinson. His arm isn't strong enough for third base or shortstop (his position with the Monarchs); he's never before played second base professionally, where he might best be suited. First base is out of the question.

Attributed to Rickey are all sort of odious motives: greed, avarice, divisiveness, even a hidden docket to *deliberately* create a situation in which this first Negro to play in organized ball in over 80 years will fail miserably, thus setting the movement of baseball integration back by years, or even decades.

It is possible Rickey acts out of genuine concern for racial equality, or, at the very least, the conviction that a significant and untapped player pool waits out there, and whoever taps it first, and best, can build his team into a baseball power for years to come, reaping scads of money (Rickey himself says it, when he isn't being overly sanctimonious on the subject).

Never mind the why and wherefore (to borrow a phrase from W. S. Gilbert). It makes no difference. The signing of Jackie Robinson by Branch Rickey changes the course of American history; no motive need be ascribed. It sets nothing back, heralds things to come. As Leo Durocher says to his players in the spring of 1947, when there are mumblings about a petition against Robinson joining the Dodgers, "It's only the beginning, boys, only the beginning."

Pitcher John Wright, who's had Negro League experience and compiled a fine record in service baseball at Great Lakes Naval Training Station, is signed as a "companion" for Robinson, so he won't be the only member of his race on the Royals. Wright, sadly, is but a footnote to history.

October 23, 1945

A trusted reference, the 1946 *Baseball Register*, says White Sox pitcher John Rigney is discharged from the Navy today. One assumes it's today, after his serving since May 8, 1942. Only problem is, the book says Rigney, born in 1914, was discharged on October 23, *1915* (it's corrected by the next edition, 1947).

November 6, 1945

Billy Southworth resigns as manager of the Cardinals, takes over as manager of the Braves. Southworth, who led St. Louis to consecutive pennants in 1942, 1943 and 1944, took them to World Championships in 1942 and 1944. He's replaced by Eddie Dyer, a superb and patient teacher of young players, who's spent many years in the St. Louis farm system as a manager and supervisor. His last managing job, in 1942, earned him *The Sporting News* "Minor League Manager of the Year" award, for his leadership of the Cards' American Association farm club in Columbus. In 1946, he'll win the major league award.

December 7, 1945

The White Sox sell pitcher John Humphries, 6–14 in 1945, to the Phillies. Back in 1941, Humphries won four games for Chicago, all shutouts, three of them in a row, all within a month. A starter throughout the war, he went 12–12 in 1942 and 11–11 in 1943, but that 4–2 season in 1941 was his best for the Chisox.

December 10, 1945

Cincinnati trades first baseman Frank McCormick to the Phillies for $30,000 and unnamed players. McCormick, once (1940) NL MVP, is slowing down, but he'll be around through a 1948 pennant with the Braves.

December 12, 1945

Cleveland trades pitcher Jim Bagby, Jr., to the Red Sox for pitcher Vic Johnson and cash. Bagby's biggest day came when he helped stop Joe DiMaggio's 1941 hitting streak, but he won 17 games twice during the war for the Indians. Johnson pitched in 1944 and 1945 and will wind up his big league career with nine final games for the Indians in 1946.

The Red Sox sell infielder Skeeter Newsome (real name, *Lamar* Newsome) to the Phillies. He hit .290 last season, will hit .232 the next.

December 14, 1945

The Indians trade outfielder Jeff Heath to the Nationals ("official" name of the Senators) for outfielder George Washington Case. Case, five-time American League leader in stolen bases, considered the fastest man in baseball, will add a sixth title next summer, but except for his speed afoot, he's pretty much over the hill. Heath has had some very good seasons, for instance 1941, when, to go with a .340 batting average, he hit 32 doubles, 20 triples and 24 homers.

January 3, 1946

The Red Sox, staying busy, trade infielder Eddie Lake to Detroit for first baseman Rudy York. Lake missed out on a World Series check by not being with the Tigers last year and will miss another by not being with the Red Sox this year. He's in the wrong place, at the wrong time, again (by this measure, York will be in the right place, at the right time, again). Lake will play all of Detroit's games, the only Tiger to do so in 1946. York, legendary power hitter and legendary un-fielder, once (August 1937) hit 18 home runs in a month, a record which will last 60 years. He's nearing the end of the line, but he'll hit .276 and play a key role in helping the Bosox to the Series this year.

January 5

Walker Cooper, captain and All-Star catcher of the Cardinals before he entered the Navy last May, is sold, while still a sailor, to the New York Giants, for $175,000. He and his older brother, Mort (pitcher and 1942 National League MVP, with three consecutive 20-win seasons at St. Louis) were the greatest "brother battery" ever seen in baseball, vital members of pennant winners in 1942, 1943 and 1944. Mort was traded to Boston last May, somewhat damaged goods after blowing out his elbow, for pitcher Red Barrett. Each brother eased his way out of St. Louis by publicly and loudly fighting with team owner Sam Breadon about salary.

The younger Cooper will remain in the Navy till April 4th. True to the respect he commands with his work behind the plate and at bat, he'll be named captain of the Giants. That's a mark of high regard, by management and his peers.

In addition, the Cardinals sell infielder Jimmy Brown to Pittsburgh today, for a reported $30,000. Brown, himself a former captain of the Cards, lost almost three full seasons to the Army, which discharged him last fall. In 1941, he hit .306 as St. Louis almost caught Brooklyn in the NL pennant race. In 1942, he was batting star of the Cards as they beat the Yankees in the Series. But Brown is pushing 34 and well past his prime, though he'll see plenty of duty in the coming season for the Pirates.

Time away in military service, it will become increasingly evident, has taken a heavy toll on many players.

January 12

Ted Williams is released by the Marines, after three seasons away. The Red Sox left fielder will hit a home run on the first pitch thrown to him in spring training. Early in March, he'll reportedly receive a $500,000 offer from the Mexican League, but Ted stays North of the Border. Time, in his case, has taken no toll on his performance, though he'll say it takes great effort to regain his physical fitness for the game. Where time has mattered most in Williams' case, and others' who are among baseball's greatest players of the period, is in the loss of whole years out of their careers. Ted and Stan and the others can regain their edge, but they can't get back those lost years. Bob Feller says he might have won a hundred more games, had the war not taken three and a half years from his career. No one will ever know.

January 21

The Cubs sell infielder Roy Hughes to the Phillies. Hughes, eight-year big league vet, was Chicago's starting shortstop in the World Series last fall, but a knee injury had hampered him during the 1945 season. He's just turned 35, will hit .236 for Philadelphia, get injured again and play less than a hundred games, again.

January 22

The Red Sox sell third baseman Jim Tabor to the Phillies for an undisclosed sum. Tabor, in the Navy last year, hit .285 with 13 homers in 1944. This season he'll bat .268, with 10 home runs. *The Ballplayers,* a very good reference book, says Tabor, nicknamed "Rawhide," is "rough hewn."

February 1

The government has passed a "G.I. Bill of Rights," guaranteeing former soldiers and sailors certain job-related security. Commissioner Chandler has taken it upon himself to modify its provisions, in response to pleas from team owners for relief from the letter of the law, which would require them to guarantee many players a year's salary when they may not be in their club's plans. Chandler decrees a player must have a 30-day chance in spring training, or 15 days during the season, before he can be released or assigned to the minor leagues.

Brooklyn's special early camp for players returning from military service opens today, giving the Dodgers a head start on getting in shape. It also allows large numbers of returning war vets a better chance to demonstrate whether or not they might be able to play ball at the major league level. The Yankees hold a similar camp for returning servicemen, in Panama. Washington plans some of its training for Havana. The Cubs, as they used to do pre-war, are going back to Catalina Island, which team owner Phil Wrigley also happens to own.

This year, the whole time-honored process of spring training is returning to Florida, California and the Caribbean, after three years of government-dictated camps up north, nearer home, to reduce wartime train travel. *The Sporting News* says over a thousand men are on major league spring rosters, swelled by those back home from war duty. That's 62 and a half players per team.

February 2

At their annual joint meeting, major league owners vote to extend the 1946 roster cutdown day from May 15th to June 15th. The purpose is to accommodate many returning servicemen who might be discharged till the early stages of the season and may not be in playing shape till later than their contemporaries. After June 15th, the player limit will be 25, and five service returnees. That will stand, too, in the World Series this fall.

February 4

The Cardinals sell pitcher Al Jurisich and outfielder Johnny Wyrostek to the Phillies. Just out of the Army, Wyrostek was with the Pirates part of 1942 and 1943, then spent 1944 as an outfielder for the St. Louis farm team at Columbus, Ohio, in the American Association (he's never played a regular-season game for the Cards). He'll bat .281 for the Phillies and prove a valuable contributor for them and, later, the Reds, into the mid–1950s. Jurisich, 10–12 over the last two years with the Cards, will go 5–10 over the next two for the Phils.

February 5

The Cardinals sell first baseman-outfielder Johnny Hopp to the Braves for $40,000. He's yet another St. Louis star peddled away, one of many Cardinals unloaded to other teams during the early- and mid 1940s. The deals aren't generally made to acquire new talent (the St. Louis farm system has been funneling top-notch replacement recruits upward for years and, with the coming of peacetime, it's loaded with prospects), but to acquire operating capital and unload rising salaries. Hopp, himself, once enabled St. Louis to dispose of first baseman Johnny Mize, unceremoniously sent to the Giants for $50,000 and two players late in 1941.

Last year, Hopp hit .289; this year, in new surroundings, he'll bat .333. Also included in the deal for St. Louis is "a player to be named later." He turns out to be shortstop Eddie Joost, light-hitting former regular with the Reds and Braves, transferred to the Cardinal farm club at Rochester of the International League. He is instructed to learn to be a power hitter, after 16 years in baseball. Joost, who hasn't enjoyed great rapport with management, later claims he's been "blacklisted" from the majors because of his continual money haggling with a succession of club owners. But he'll return in 1947 with the Athletics and, in Philadelphia, Joost will enjoy a half-dozen solid seasons as their hard-hitting shortstop, having learned to hit home runs in a year at Rochester. Then he'll suffer through a last-place finish in a one-season trial as manager of the A's.

Late in April, there will be 90 former Cardinals players or farmhands on major league teams, including four managers and seven coaches. It attests to St. Louis' success and influence. Not yet fully grasped, the man who created the Cardinal colossus, Branch Rickey, is back at even more empire building, in Brooklyn. When Sam Breadon let Rickey walk away after the 1942 season, the owner had convinced himself it was *he* who had built the Cardinal dynasty, not that old fool Rickey, who got all the credit — and a cut of the money when he sold players, money that should have remained in Breadon's pockets.

February 8

Outfielder–first baseman Joe (Ducky) Medwick, an earlier Cardinal star traded away back in 1940, once the most feared hitter in the National League, is released today by the Braves.

About now, the frightful spectre of the Mexican League publicly arises, as a threat to baseball on this side of the border. Concocted, from an independent league already in place, by the multi-millionaire Pasquel family of businessmen and political king makers, they claim their circuit will soon be the equal of the major leagues in the U.S.A. The Mexican League's president is Jorge Pasquel, most visible of the clan. Their teams, they say, will boast many big league ball players, who are encouraged to come down and enjoy huge salaries and instant adulation of the *beisbol*-crazy population of Mexico. Organized baseball's immediate reaction is to brand the Mexican League an "outlaw." Soon, a minimum five-year ban is placed on players going there who are already bound by contract. Commissioner Chandler says the ban applies to any man who "jumps" his contract and doesn't report to his O.B. team by the end of spring training.

Some ex–big leaguers have already been playing in Mexico. Tomas de la Cruz, ex–Reds pitcher, and Roberto Ortiz, once a Washington outfielder, spent the 1945 season down there. In their case, it had much to do with their being Cuban nationals. To return to the United States would have made them liable to be drafted into the U.S. Army, which they didn't relish. De la Cruz left the Reds during the 1944 season, ostensibly to serve in the Cuban Army.

Among those who'll jump to Mexico is outfielder Danny Gardella of the Giants, a little guy from the New York docks, who somehow hit 18 home runs last season (perhaps a fluke; we'll never know). Gardella is as well-known for bursting into impromptu operatic arias as he is for his questionable skills. His fate with the Giants is sealed February 14th, when team manager Mel Ott casts him out, following a loud public argument with staid club secretary Eddie Brannick. Ott vows Gardella will never again play with the Giants.

On the 18th, Gardella declares he's signed with the Pasquels. Since New York released him, he claims, he should not be subject to Section 10(a) of Baseball's Uniform Player's Contract, the *reserve clause*, which can effectively bind a player to one team forever. After the riches and promise of Mexico wear away and many players want to come back but aren't allowed, Gardella will file the lawsuit that finally breaks the ban. Turned down, appealed and finally settled out of court for $29,000, his is the wedge that opens the way for everyone to return in 1949. It's the only successful court challenge ever to be made to the reserve clause. Settlement notwithstanding, Gardella will play only one more game in the big leagues, with the Cardinals in 1950.

In his pronouncement of February 18th, Gardella brags, correctly, that New York teammates Adrian Zabala, a pitcher, and Napoleon Reyes, infielder, have also agreed to play in Mexico. Other defectors include infielder Murray Franklin of the Tigers, pitcher Alejandro (Alex) Carrasquel of the White Sox and outfielders René Monteagudo of the Phillies, Luis Olmo of the Dodgers (who hit .313 last season), and Roberto Estalella of the Athletics, whose grandson, Bobby, will play major league ball, some fifty years ahead.

It's hoped, in Brooklyn, that Johnny Rizzo, back from three seasons in military service, can step into Olmo's slot. At the moment, he's the only experienced righthanded hitter in Brooklyn's outfield.

The most prominent big leaguer to go to Mexico is former Dodger catcher Mickey Owen, just returning from the Navy. He appears to quickly grow disenchanted down there. According to him, he's supposed to be manager of the Torreon club, but isn't. In April, Owen contacts Brooklyn manager Leo Durocher about rejoining the Dodgers. Leo's boss, Branch Rickey, declares there's no way Owen will ever be welcomed back. At the end of May, Owen is appointed interim manager of the Vera Cruz Blues, during a 30-day suspension leveled against incumbent manager Ramon Braganza. Braganza will be tabbed for throwing easy-to-hit balls to the visiting Babe Ruth, on hand as a publicity stunt, allegedly lobbing them to the great slugger (despite which, the Babe only manages foul balls).

In August, Owen again will seek reinstatement, again will be rebuffed by Rickey, who loudly supports Happy Chandler's prior edict. Owen repairs to his Missouri farm, complaining of broken Mexican promises and a generally lousy time. He seems to be willing to sit out his five-year suspension from organized baseball at home, though he feels Chandler's ban is heavy-handed. A lawsuit by the Pasquels is soon threatened, seeking to reclaim the money Owen has been paid so far, plus $100,000 in damages.

Hard-hitting holdout shortstop Vernon Stephens of the Browns, AL home run champ in 1945, joins the Mexican League and even plays some, but has second thoughts and scurries home before the American League season starts, thus avoiding Chandler's suspension deadline. He and the Browns settle his contract dispute and the Stephens episode goes away, for now. Later, Pasquel will also threaten to sue him, but the shortstop repays his $5,000 signing bonus check, thereby putting a lid on his misadventure.

The Mexican League won't go away. Pete Reiser, Brooklyn center fielder, is reportedly offered a $100,000 package for three years in Mexico, including $50,000 down, but he refuses it. Throughout the summer, rumors abound that many big name stars, for instance Stan Musial, are on the brink of jumping. He doesn't go, however, nor does Ted Williams. Bob Feller claims he, Williams and Joe DiMaggio are offered $120,000 a year for three years, the entire $360,000 guaranteed. There are rumblings from Mexico that, next year, they'll raid major league rosters with even more ferocity and money. *The Ballplayers* reports that 23 major league regulars do jump, but most of them have already gone.

February 28

Today's *Sporting News* quotes Jorge Pasquel, lashing back at organized baseball, bragging he has $30 million to fight this war, in which his league will emerge triumphant. "Joe Medwick," Pasquel trumpets, "has been made an attractive offer and I hope he sees fit to play." Babe Ruth, who still smarts over never being tendered a big league managing job, "has done a lot for baseball and the sport should have a place for him. I believe he definitely would be a big drawing card as a manager in our league." Pasquel is often full of hot air, but no one has caught on, yet.

March 3

Medwick, just released by the Braves, signs with the Browns.

March 17

Detroit center field prospect Walter (Hoot) Evers, whose return from the Army has been keenly anticipated, breaks an ankle and a thumb in an exhibition game against Cleveland. Hoot, who played one game for the Tigers in 1941, will see action only 81 times this season, batting .266. His first regular-season game won't be till May 21st.

March 20

The Braves release veteran infielder Billy Jurges, who was cut by the Giants in October and signed by Boston in December.

March 21

Opening Day in the Mexican League. At Mexico City, Gen. Manuel Avila Camacho, president of the country, is one of a reported 33,000 on hand in a stadium seating only 23,000. Jorge Pasquel claims a new park, seating 52,000, will be built there. Mexico City has two clubs, the Mexico City Reds and Vera Cruz Blues, because the weather is too uncomfortable in Vera Cruz for the Blues to actually play in that city.

March 23

Billy Jurges, free agent for three days, is signed by the Cubs, for whom he played eight years in the 1930s. He'll later be named a coach, as well, serving in dual capacities.

March 26

Paul O'Dea, wartime Cleveland outfielder, is released. Once a top prospect whose right eye was injured in batting practice by a foul tip in 1940, O'Dea did bat .318 as a part-timer in 1944. Today, he got the Indians' only hit in an exhibition game against Detroit. But it's not enough for the 25 year old. He'll never return to the major leagues.

The Yankees sell catcher Rollie Hemsley to the Phillies. *Rollickin' Rollie*, once known for fast living but somewhat reformed, went into the Navy in August 1944 and got out last October. This will be his 18th season in the big leagues. He will play again in 1947, before becoming a successful minor league manager.

March 31

Giants owner Horace Stoneham orders first baseman Roy Zimmerman, second baseman George Hausmann and pitcher Sal Maglie out of camp, after rumors surface they're negotiating with the Mexican League. The team claims they're excess baggage anyway, but New York is doomed to finish dead last and could use every hand that might have helped. Of all the Mexican League jumpers, the loss of Maglie for the next three-plus years will, in retrospect, be felt most. He was only five-and-four in his rookie season of 1945, but after he returns in 1950 "Sal the Barber," by then an accomplished pitcher, will enjoy a lifetime 119–62 record in the majors, one of the best pitchers of the following decade.

April 4

Tom Gorman, getting another chance with the Giants after five years away at war, is released by New York. He pitched four games for them in 1939. Gorman goes to the Mexican League, too, as a free agent, but hurts his arm. In 1947, unaffected by the ban on contract jumpers, Gorman begins a new life, as an umpire, in the New England League. Umping his way up to the National League by late 1951, he'll spend 25 years there. This is Thomas David Gorman, "Big Tom," not his contemporary, Thomas Aloysius Gorman, a few years younger and pitcher for the Yankees and A's in the 1950s. Apparently unrelated, both are natives of New York City.

April 5

Joe Medwick, just signed by the Browns, is released today. Despite his reputation as most menacing NL slugger of the 1930s, he's way over the hill. Yet Medwick will hang on a while more. In a couple of months, he'll sign with one of his former teams, the Dodgers. Ducky Wucky and the Mexican League never do get together.

April 11

Two Dodgers, center fielder Pete Reiser and third baseman Harry (Cookie) Lavagetto, are nursing sore arms. Today, they consult Dr. George E. Bennett, at Johns Hopkins in Baltimore. Lavagetto is advised he should have surgery for elbow chips, but if he insists on playing, while the problem might not get worse, the pain will. Cookie opts for surgery and won't play again till early May.

Reiser is told he'll be fine if he throws sidearm for a while, prompting the team to move him to third base while Lavagetto's out. That'll last till the first week of May, when Reiser moves back to center and Billy Herman takes over at third, filling in until Lavagetto returns.

Van Lingle Mungo of the Giants, once Brooklyn's best pitcher and 14–7 for New York last season, is suspended indefinitely when he's found "in no condition to pitch" inside the clubhouse at Richmond, where the Giants are to play an exhibition game. It appears to be the last straw in a career laden with straws. Mungo will receive his unconditional release on the 23rd, his 14 years in the big leagues over.

Indians first baseman Mickey Rocco, a regular since 1943, has a broken bone in his right foot and will be out till the 28th. This is the final season of his big league career. He'll end it, not by choice, at Nashville.

The Cubs sell catcher Bennie Warren to the Giants on waivers. Warren's last season was 1942, with the Phillies. They sold him to Chicago in November that year, two months before he went into the Navy. The Big Giants want to send him to their Little Giants farm club in Jersey City now, but the rules demand players claimed on waivers get a 21-day trial by the team buying them. In mid–June, Warren does briefly join Jersey City, to shore up a temporarily-depleted catching staff. Warren pinch-hits a solitary time for the Triple-A club, on the 18th of that month, between New York appearances June 16th and June 30th. He plays in 39 games altogether for the parent club over the course of 1946, filling in for periodic depletion of the Big Giants' catching staff.

"Deals of the Week," selected transactions, *Sporting News* issue of April 11

This week's list is published before Opening Day, mostly assignments to the minor leagues. Some involve players who were in the big leagues before or during the war, or will be big leaguers in the future, or are otherwise meaningful to the game's history. With some exceptions, many players who receive mention but don't ever play in the major leagues are excluded below. "Deals," as explained earlier, generally carry only the paper's issue date, which is either seven or five days after printing. Thus, depending on when a transaction notice reaches *TSN*'s offices in relation to press time, reporting it could be a week late, or as many as two, or more.

Included this week: the Giants sell veteran second baseman Hugh Luby to San Francisco. Pitcher Bob Barthelson is optioned to Minneapolis, pitchers Marv Grissom, Roy Lee and Don Fisher to Jersey City. Of the bunch, Grissom alone will return and play in the majors. The others have already used up their big league lives. Also announced, the Giants have purchased left-handed pitcher Montia (Monte) Kennedy from Richmond.

The Red Sox return catcher Fred Walters to Louisville, where he played half of last season. Third baseman Don Lang is assigned to Louisville; pitcher George (Pinky) Woods is sold to Indianapolis. Lang, who played for the Reds in 1938, won't be back in the big leagues till 1948, with the Cardinals. Walters and Woods, wartime Bosox, are done. Walters will become interim manager of the Colonels in July, when the incumbent, Nemo Leibold, assaults an umpire and draws a lengthy suspension.

The Senators sell pitcher–first baseman Bill Lefebvre to Minneapolis. Outfielder Bruce Campbell and pitcher Pete Appleton (who played under his real name, *Jablonowski*, from 1927 to 1933) are released. None of the three will return to the majors. All have recently been released from the Armed Forces. Campbell threatens to sue the team for violating the G.I. Bill and not paying him for a full year's service. He served 38 months in the Army and was given a $9,000 contract when he returned, same as he got in 1942. He claims, having been away so long and not given ample time to get in shape (the fault of Happy Chandler's 30-day limit on returning servicemen getting ready to play), he should be paid in full. It will be settled out of court, on August 1.

The Reds sell outfielder Eric Tipton to St. Paul. A memorable pre-war football player at Duke and a .300 hitter for Cincinnati two years ago, his seven seasons in the bigs are completed. We'll hear about him once more, later this month.

The Indians option outfielder Cliff Mapes to San Diego. From there, he'll be demoted to Wilkes-Barre. His big league career begins in 1948 with the Yankees.

The Athletics option outfielder Ray Poole to Savannah. A pinch-hitter twice in 1941, he'll return to pinch-hit 13 times more next year. Philadelphia options third baseman Don Richmond, pitcher Bill McCahan and catcher Joe Astroth to Toronto. Richmond played a handful of games for the A's in 1941, Astroth ten games last year; McCahan none yet. All three will return in early September. A's outfielders Frank Demaree and Eddie Collins, Jr., are released. Demaree spent a lot of time in the big leagues in the 1930s and early 1040s, but he's through. Collins spent parts of three seasons with the A's before wartime military duty. His only real claim to fame is that he's the son of Hall-of-Fame second baseman Eddie Sr., now general manager of the Red Sox.

The Braves send first baseman Joe Mack to Chattanooga. Mack's only year in the majors was 1945, when he split the position with Vince Shupe, whose only year was also 1945.

The Cubs sell pitcher Hy Vandenberg to Oakland. His seven years in the big leagues, during which he never won more than seven games in a season, are now completed.

The Cardinals assign infielder George Fallon to Mobile. Fallon was a regular substitute during the war, but that was then. St. Louis pitcher Art Lopatka is waived to the Phillies, where he'll appear in four games.

The White Sox release pitcher Lee (Buck) Ross, returned by the Phillies, to whom they'd dealt him in the offseason. Ross was in the majors for ten years and in 1943 went 11–7 for the Sox.

The Dodgers assign pitchers Clyde King and Leroy Pfund to Mobile. King, with Brooklyn in 1944 and 1945, came out of the University of North Carolina and straight onto the mound for the Dodgers. The war over, he won't be back till next season. Reaching 14–7 in 1951, he'll have a long career as a manager and front office guy. Pfund, on the other hand, had his only chance last year.

The Phillies option pitcher Wes Hamner (*aka* Garvin Hamner) to Atlanta. His only big league season was 1945. He's Granville Hamner's older brother (more, much later, on Granville, *aka* Granny Hamner).

April 12

Significant in a historical sense, the Giants purchase the Minneapolis Millers of the American Association. Minneapolis is where they'll send Willie Mays, to start his second season of organized ball, in 1951. Mays will play 35 games for the Millers, hit .477 and come to New York on his way to baseball glory.

Tickets for Minneapolis' April 23rd home opener this year, bear the outdated legend, "boost the home-owned Millers."

April 13

White Sox third baseman Dario Lodigiani rejoins the team after breaking a thumb. He's on his way to Johns Hopkins Hospital in Baltimore for an operation on his elbow, but that won't happen till next month, at Chicago's Mercy Hospital. It occurs just after he relinquishes an early lead in the AL batting race. He'll finish at only .245 in 44 games for Chicago. Next year, Lodigiani will go back out to Oakland (where he hit .327 in 1937). He was, according to Coast League authority Dennis Snelling, Joe DiMaggio's double play partner in their junior high school infield.

Pitcher Si Johnson of the Phillies suffers a broken nose when hit by a misjudged fly ball in fielding practice.

Myron (Red) Hayworth, catcher for the Browns in 1944 and 1945, signs with Torreon of the Mexican League. He won't play in organized ball again till 1949 (and never again in the majors). His older brother, Ray, former Tiger, caught for 15 seasons in the big leagues, finishing with last year's Dodgers.

April 14

Cleveland releases pre-war pitcher Harry Eisenstat, who worked in the big leagues for eight years through 1942. His best season was 8–9 in 1939, split between the Tigers and Indians.

April 15

The Cardinals sell first baseman Ray Sanders and pitcher Max Surkont to the Braves. The price, it's reported, is $40,000, plus Boston infielder Tommy Nelson, who'll report to the St. Louis farm at Columbus, Ohio. (Nelson's only chance in the big leagues came last year, when he hit .165 in 40 forgettable games for the Braves.)

Surkont, 23 and just out of three and a half years in the Navy, is injured. He won't pitch for Boston and will quickly be returned to St. Louis. Sanders, regular first baseman for the Cards throughout the war, in late August will run into physical problems that virtually end his productive career. Although record books say this deal takes place tomorrow, it is made at 11 P.M. tonight.

Surkont, who doesn't play big league ball till 1949, is the source of an interesting war story. According to SABR's Kit Crissey, in his entertaining and informative booklet on wartime Navy baseball, *Athletes Away*, Surkont was a gunner's mate on a landing craft, taking part in American landings on eight Pacific islands and in the Philippines. That's a lot of places to visit in a lifetime, and not even a big leaguer, yet.

While having little to do with the playing of a baseball season, such matters add an unusual historical perspective to go with often-faceless names. For example, pitcher Bob Savage of the Athletics carries shrapnel fragments in his right side, which are "souvenirs," the *New York Times* says, of North Africa, Italy and Germany. Teammate Jack Wallaesa, young shortstop, spent 40 straight days passing ammunition to others, at the Anzio beachhead.

With increasing frequency, the press speculates this or that player is considering the Mexican League. Prewar A's second baseman Benny McCoy is said to be negotiating with the Pasquels. The *New York Times* notes McCoy hasn't made the grade upon trying to rejoin the

A's. He'd gone away, a .271 batter, after the 1941 season. Returning only to be cut loose this spring, he'll never play pro baseball again. But instead of Mexico, his 1946 will be spent playing for the semipro St. Joseph Autos, back home in Michigan. It's not a total waste, as McCoy's team does win the annual National Baseball Congress nonprofessional tournament in Wichita, baseball's biggest semipro event of the year. Besides the honor, the Autos receive $10,000, which, it appears, will be divided among members of the team.

Speaking, again, of the Mexican League, here's a trade that never happens. According to *The Sporting News*, Mickey Owen was to have been part of a three-way deal between the Dodgers, Cardinals and Braves. He was to have gone to St. Louis for first baseman Dick Sisler, pitcher Blix Donnelly and catcher Del Rice. Then, packaged with third baseman Whitey Kurowski, Owen would go to Boston, for catcher Phil Masi and cash. But Mickey went to Mexico and there was no deal. St. Louis owner Sam Breadon denies it was ever considered, nor was another phantom trade, that would have sent Kurowski to the Pirates for catcher Al Lopez, infielder Frankie Gustine and cash.

Pitcher Bob Muncrief of the Browns, who suffered a broken toe when hit by a line drive in spring training, won't pitch in the regular season till May 25.

The White Sox have offered a season pass to anyone who provides information that results in housing for 20 team members. What with the end of the war and so many troops coming home, lodging is at a premium. It will remain so, in most cities, until building restrictions are relaxed. Contractors can then catch up with the demand by America's returning service personnel, millions of whom, having once left home, want now to live alone, or with a new spouse, or go off to school and take up residence there, under the generous, unprecedented support of the G.I. Bill. But it will take time. This year, a ball player sleeping the night in his clubhouse is not an unusual scene. And there is, already, early evidence of a mushrooming population: the baby boom is about to explode.

April 16

OPENING DAY IN THE MAJORS. Washington third baseman George Myatt trips when his spikes catch on the dugout steps before today's game, resulting in a chipped ankle bone. He'll pinch-run May 19th but won't return to the starting lineup until May 30th. Myatt, who hit .296 in 1945, will play only 15 times this season.

Tigers catcher Bob Swift is out of action the first two weeks of the season, with a pulled left ankle tendon. It happened yesterday, in Detroit's final exhibition game, played in Louisville. His first appearance won't be till May 1.

Giants manager-outfielder Mel Ott, whose playing career is winding down, hits his 511th and last home run for New York, a National League record. Tomorrow, unfortunately, he'll hurt his knee. Ott will spend most of the season on the bench, playing only 31 times in 1946. He'll make his final four appearances in 1947.

Pitcher Andy (Swede) Hansen of the Giants, recently discharged after seven months in the Army, has asked for voluntary retirement status from baseball, due to the illness of his father. Hansen won't play at all this season, but is listed in *"Who's Who in Baseball"* and the first volume of Macmillan's *"Baseball Encyclopedia"* (back when the encyclopedia gave reasons for extended absences) as spending the year in the military, which appears mistaken.

Brooklyn catcher Ferrell Anderson, just purchased from Montreal, makes his major league debut today, as do Dodger first baseman Jack Graham and outfielders Carl Furillo and Dick Whitman. Anderson will hold down the regular job till midseason, when Bruce Edwards arrives from Mobile. Other debuts: Cincinnati second baseman Bobby Adams, outfielder Bob Usher and third baseman Grady Hatton; Giants third baseman Billy Rigney; and Phillies shortstop John O'Neil, who plays 46 times in 1946, hits .266 and nevermore appears in the majors.

Outfielder Ralph Kiner of the Pirates debuts on his road to the Hall of Fame today. Not to become a baseball immortal because of his skill with the glove, Kiner nevertheless is Pittsburgh's center fielder till late July, when he moves to left (curiously, manager Frankie Frisch not only plays Kiner in center, but often bats him seventh).

Dick Sisler, first baseman of the Cardinals, also debuts. Others include third baseman Ernie Andres of the Red Sox who, as a highly-regarded minor leaguer, spent a considerable amount of time on crack Navy all-star teams throughout the war. He only gets this one shot at the major leagues, however, playing 16 games for Boston before going back to the minors.

Gene Handley of the A's makes his first big league appearance today, too. In pro ball since 1935, Handley was in the Pacific Coast League, with Sacramento, during the war. He spends just this season and next in the majors. He's the younger brother of Lee Handley, Pittsburgh infielder, who is in his ninth of ten seasons in the major leagues.

It's also debut day for third baseman Bob Dillinger of the Browns, called "The Player of the Pacific" in service baseball during the war. Dillinger is one of the fastest men in baseball and will lead the AL in steals from 1947 to 1949, but he's already 27 and left some potentially fine seasons behind him, while out in the islands playing ball. St. Louis manager Luke Sewell isn't all that taken with Dillinger. The third baseman spends a lot of time on the bench. He'll play third today and tomorrow, then won't return to the hot corner till May 25th.

Danny Murtaugh of the Phillies, back from three years in the war, has a solid Opening Day. He gets two hits, including a homer, and handles six chances flawlessly at second base. Murtaugh clinched his leadoff spot yesterday, starring in Philadelphia's 8–7 exhibition win over Villanova College. By May 4th, about two weeks from now, Murtaugh will be playing for the Rochester Red Wings, a Cardinals farm club.

Rookie center fielder Bob Lemon saves a 1–0 shutout over the White Sox for Cleveland's Bob Feller today. Lemon makes a diving catch of Jake Jones' would-be Texas League single, then doubles runner Bob Kennedy off second base with a great throw to end the game. Lemon was in a couple of games at third base for the Indians in 1941-42, but is still in search of a position. Problem is, he won't hit a lick, only .180 all season.

Of the 633 players in the big leagues this year, 105 will make their debuts in the majors. Of those, 34 will play just this one season in the majors. A further 145 men with multiple-year careers are in their final year. All together, 1946 marks the end of 179 big league careers, nearly 30 percent of those who play.

The Yankees, as might be expected, have the most players returning who were in their 1941 Opening Day starting lineup. Phil Rizzuto, Tom Henrich, Joe DiMaggio, Charley Keller, Joe Gordon, Bill Dickey and pitcher Marius Russo are the returning seven. The first baseman of 1941, Johnny Sturm, won't play again in the big leagues, while third baseman Red Rolfe is a Yankee coach now.

Out of action today is shortstop Rizzuto, who has leg problems. Rizzuto can't play until April 24th. Pitcher Ruffing is sidelined with leg problems, too, till May 1st. To complicate things, Frankie Crosetti, the man Rizzuto replaced at short in 1941, replaces Rizzuto today, pulls *his* calf muscle and won't be able to return to the infield till June. Between Crosetti and Rizzuto, Oscar Grimes is New York's fill-in shortstop.

On the Dodgers' bench is Brooklyn first baseman Ed Stevens, sidelined by a bad tooth, which his dentist pulls. Stevens will miss the first two games, before he replaces Jack Graham and Howie Schultz in the lineup. Stevens and Schultz will share first base this season and Graham will be shunted off to the Giants toward the end of the month.

April 17

Brooklyn pitcher Hank Behrman makes his major league debut, just four days after promotion from Montreal. Behrman's previous pro experience was at Valdosta and Durham, back in 1941 and 1942, before he went to Europe with the Air Force. Though he lasts four years in the majors, this is his best, 11–5 in 47 games. Today is also debut day for Detroit outfielder Anselm "Anse" Moore, who spends only this season in the majors. Pitcher Bill Wight debuts for the Yankees, but his best years are ahead, with the White Sox, between 1948 and 1950 (in 1948, he'll go 9–20). Today, he has a terrible introduction, pitching to three batters in a 7–1 loss to Philadelphia, getting no one out.

The Yankees send wartime outfielder Russ Derry to Newark. Rumors had Derry headed for the Mexican League, but after first balking at his demotion, he winds up with the A's, playing his first game for them on May 1st. Somewhat delayed, Philadelphia obtains Derry in exchange for pitcher Porter Vaughan (whose only big league game this year will be on April 21st), sent on to Kansas City, and outfielder Ford Garrison, assigned to Newark.

Vaughan, after four years in the military, is through in the majors with his upcoming token 1946 appearance, first since 1941. He makes his initial showing for the Blues a month from now, on May 18th.

Playing nine games for Philadelphia in 1946, concluding the 28th, Garrison's four years in the big leagues are over, too, when the deal is done.

April 18

Jackie Robinson plays second base for Montreal in the Royals' International League opener at Jersey City. He makes an out in his first at-bat, then collects four straight hits, including a home run. He steals two bases, scores four times and drives in four runs, leading Montreal to a 14–1 victory before a huge minor league crowd of 25,000.

Having appeared as a pinch-runner yesterday in his only big league game of 1946, today utility infielder Sebastian (Sibby) Sisti is optioned by the Braves to Indianapolis, along with orders to Indy manager Bill Burwell to teach Sisti to be a shortstop. An early wartime regular third and second baseman before he spent three seasons in the Army, Sisti will hang around into 1954, but won't ever get much steady work in the majors again.

Sisti will be named Minor League Player of the Year for 1946, as designated by *The Sporting News*. It's difficult, in retrospect, to see why. Sisti does win the American Association batting championship, but slugger Jerry Witte of Toledo, not Sisti, will be the AA's *official* Most Valuable Player. Over in the International League, Jackie Robinson will lead his loop with a higher batting average than Sisti, .349 to .343. Robinson will also steal 40 bases for Montreal, leading the Royals to victory in the Junior World Series. Yet Baltimore's hard-hitting Eddie Robinson will be *that* loop's MVP.

"Deals of the Week," *Sporting News* issue of April 18

Though the season began April 16, this week's list is also of late preseason transactions, involving former or future big leaguers, etc.

The Dodgers sell first baseman Jack Bolling to Mobile, option pitcher Johnny Van Cuyk to Fort Worth, option infielder Gene Mauch to St. Paul and pitcher Erv Palica to Meridian. Catcher Herman Franks is assigned to Montreal, catcher Gil Hodges to Newport News.

Bolling, just out of the Service, played only 1939 and 1944 in the big leagues, never again. Van Cuyk and his little brother, Chris, will each pitch a few games in the majors, but not yet. Next year, Chris will have a 25–2 record in the Eastern Shore League. This year, Johnny will be 18–8 in the Texas League.

Mauch has an indifferent nine seasons as a big league player ahead, but spends 1946 in the minors. In 1960, he'll begin 26 years as a manager in the major leagues and should be in the Hall of Fame but isn't. Palica will pitch nine seasons in the majors, starting next year. Franks, who sandwiches six big league years around wartime military service, won't play up here in 1946. He'll manage the Giants and Cubs in later decades. Hodges, who should also be in the Hall of Fame, plays 18 seasons in the majors, but not 1946. He got into one game in 1943 and will play 17 years more, beginning in 1947.

The Reds option outfielder Ted Kluszewski to Columbia. Muscular football star at Indiana University, this is his first year in pro baseball. He hits .352 in the Sally League (South Atlantic League, or Sally League, Class A in the minor league hierarchy) and will be back for a long stay in the majors later in the 1940s and the 1950s. But he won't start till next year.

The Yankees option third baseman Eddie Bockman to Kansas City, assign first baseman Johnny Sturm, pitcher Marv Breuer and outfielder Milt Byrnes to Kansas City, return outfielder Harry Craft to Kansas City, and assign infielder Bobby Brown to Newark.

Bockman, late in the season, will return to break into the big leagues. Five years ago, in 1941, Sturm replaced Babe Dahlgren, who had replaced Lou Gehrig as Yankee first baseman, but it was his only big league season. He wasn't a big league hitter, went into the Army early in the war and that, pretty much, was that. Breuer's big league career is over, too. So is Byrnes's, so is Craft's. Craft, a superior defensive center fielder, will be back as a coach and manager in years to come.

Brown, 21, one of the most highly-sought amateurs of the late war period, got a $35,000 signing bonus from the Yankees, one of the highest ever awarded. Fifteen of the sixteen big league clubs tried to make a deal with him. A rare combination of gifted athlete and brilliant student, he studies at Tulane University's medical school in the off-season, and will continue to do so till he earns his M.D., becoming the first big leaguer ever to accomplish it while remaining an active player.

Brown spends most of this season at Newark, but does return for seven games with the Yankees in September, start of an eight-year stint with New York. After the season, he'll attend med school till next Opening Day. After serving with a M*A*S*H unit in the Korean War and making a brief return to the Yankees in 1954, he'll retire from baseball, take an internship in San Francisco, then complete training at Tulane. In 1984, after decades as a noted Fort Worth cardiologist, he'll become president of the American League for ten years.

While sending the above players down, the Yankees have purchased pitcher Randy Gumpert from Newark, where, in 1942, he won 10, lost 5. Three years in the Coast Guard, Gumpert last appeared in the majors in 1938, with the Athletics. Good move for the Yanks: though being blown out of a game by Philadelphia yesterday, Gumpert will go 11–3 this season, with a 2.31 ERA (that's according to the Barnes Official Baseball Guide, but later records modify it down a hundredth of a run, to 2.30). Writing in SABR's 1999 "National Pastime," Victor Debs, Jr., relates that Gumpert himself took the initiative in his promotion from Newark after the war, by writing New York vice-president George Weiss. He reminded Weiss of his work at Newark and told him he'd remained in shape by pitching for his USCG base team on weekends and, occasionally, weeknights. Weiss told him to report to spring training. At the end of it, after a string of scoreless innings pitched, manager Joe McCarthy offered him a contract, for $4,000. Gumpert lost no time in signing.

The Tigers option rookie pitcher Lou Kretlow to Buffalo, where he loses all three of his decisions, being somewhat batted about. In July, he'll filter further down, to the Williamsport, Pennsylvania, Tigers, of the Eastern League, where he's 10–7. He'll pitch once for Detroit this season, on September 26th. Kretlow was voted the outstanding prospect coming out of the war by the National Baseball Congress, governing body of semipro ball. Pitching three years for the Enid, Oklahoma, Army Air Force Base, he won 10 of 11 decisions in NBC play and was 48–16 overall with his AAF team. All that hasn't quite prepared him for the high minors, let alone the Tigers, but he'll win 21 games in 1948 at Williamsport and finally achieve full-time status in the majors in 1950.

The Browns option outfielder–first baseman Boris (Babe) Martin to Oakland, with the idea of converting him to catcher. Martin played 54 games with St. Louis in 1945 and will return in the season's waning days. He'll also appear between 1948 and 1953 for the Browns and Red Sox.

Browns pitchers Chet Johnson and Fred Sanford are optioned to Toledo. Sanford, who pitched three games for the St. Louis Americans in 1943, will pitch in three more later this season. Johnson, whose brother, Earl, is with the Red Sox, will pitch five times later this season, his sole year in the majors. Good career in the minors: Chet will win 204 games (but lose 215) in the minor leagues, striking out over 2,000.

The Pirates option pitcher Lee Howard to Hollywood. Returning to pitch for the Pirates in September, he'll work three games.

The Red Sox sell catcher Bill Conroy to Sacramento, without playing a game. Boston's first-string catcher for part of 1942, he's returned from a year in the service and ended a half-dozen seasons of bouncing up and down from the minors. Anxious about their catching staff, the Bosox had ten candidates on their spring roster.

Debuts today include those of outfielder Jesse Pike and pitchers Monte Kennedy and Mike Budnick of the Giants and outfielder Ray Goolsby of Washington.

April 19

The Reds send pitcher Jim Konstanty and cash to the Braves for outfielder Max West. A Boston regular for the five seasons prior to his Army service, West has batted just once for the Braves. Konstanty had not pitched for Cincinnati since 1944. In 1946, he'll appear on the mound 10 times for Boston, 20 more for Toronto. After extended obscurity, Konstanty will emerge to become NL MVP in 1950 for the Phillies, the first relief pitcher ever to win the award in the majors. This 1946 deal took place on April 18 according to *The Sporting News*. But the Commissioner's Office gives the date as April 19.

Herb Karpel, in his one big league season, pitches the first of his two games for the Yankees.

April 20

Washington pitcher Emil (Dutch) Leonard hurts a leg while on the mound against the Yankees today, will have to rest till his next start on May 5.

Pitcher Alpha Brazle, released by the Army at Jefferson Barracks, near St. Louis, rejoins the Cardinals. Eight and two in 1943 before he went away, he'll go 11–10 in 1946. Understandably, it'll take him a while to get back in shape: Brazle won't make an appearance till May 16.

Catcher Al Lopez of the Pirates, nursing an injured finger, is out of action. Later, the injury will be described as a broken hand, attributed to a preseason mishap, and he won't appear this season until May 19. It's a painful summer for Lopez: another finger injury will finish his year prematurely.

Debuts today: infielder Bob Ramazzotti and outfielder Johnny Corriden of the Dodgers, and catcher Sherman Lollar of the Indians. Ramazzotti's contract was just acquired from Brooklyn's farm team at Montreal, on the 18th.

The Cubs sell outfielder Mizell (Whitey) Platt across town to the White Sox, on waivers. Out of the Navy, Platt, who hadn't played for the Cubs since brief stints in 1942 and 1943, will get into 84 games with the Chisox.

April 21

Pitcher Joe Hatten makes his major league debut for the Dodgers (14–11 this year). Pittsburgh pitcher Jim Hopper debuts, the first of two appearances in his only big league season. Pittsburgh outfielder Ben Guintini debuts, too, one of a pair of games he plays for the Pirates in 1946. Other debuts: catcher Del Wilber, outfielder Bill Endicott and pitcher Freddie Martin of the Cardinals; and pitcher Mel Deutsch of the Red Sox.

Pitcher Ray Prim of the Cubs hurts his elbow today, won't reappear till May 4.

April 22

Debuting today is outfielder Otis (Scat) Davis of Brooklyn. Davis has just been sold to the Dodgers by the Cardinals, for whom he didn't play. Pinch-running, he scores, in the first and last big league game of his life. He'll soon be sent down to the International League, play four times for Montreal, then step down another minor league notch, to the Fort Worth Cats, Dodger farm team in the Texas League. That's noted in the June 5th issue of *The Sporting News*, in its "Deals" column.

Another one-game big leaguer, outfielder Johnny Corriden, is sent to Montreal by the Dodgers today. He'll end up at Mobile in the Southern Association, Double-A ball, batting .263 in 98 games, an indication of the difference between wartime and peacetime baseball. Last season, in a few more games, Corriden hit .313 for Montreal, Triple-A. Now, with baseball full of talented wartime returnees, he's not considered good enough to play at that level.

Brooklyn infielder Al Campanis, whose only major league season was 1943, is sent outright to Montreal. He'll play short for the Royals, teaming with Jackie Robinson as the team's "keystone combination."

Reds pitcher Clay Lambert debuts, in his first of two major league seasons (23 games, 2–2 in 1946). Lambert was a whiz in 1942 with Syracuse, but then the Army Air Force got him and the middle of his career went out the window.

Lastly, today is Red Sox infielder Eddie Pellagrini's first major league game. He's been around baseball a while, but, like thousands of others, lost time to the war. Pellagrini was first signed off Boston sandlots in 1938, but his career since then won't always be documented correctly. In the annual "Who's Who in Baseball," a quick, dependable reference for tracing careers, Pellagrini's five previous seasons in the minors and three in the Navy will inexplicably be left out, until someone catches the mistake and corrects it in the 1954 issue.

He'll play only 22 times for Boston this year, mostly at third base. But this afternoon, after Washington's Sid Hudson beans regular shortstop Johnny Pesky, Pellagrini makes history with his bat, not his glove. He hits a home run in his first at-bat, the 20th man in big league history to accomplish it. Not only that, it wins the game, 5–4. A banjo hitter, it's one of two homers he hits all year, one of just 20 during the eight seasons he spends in the big leagues.

White Sox manager Jimmie Dykes, ill the past month, is released from Cedars of Lebanon Hospital in Hollywood after stomach surgery. He's expected to rejoin the team shortly. Till then, coach Mule Haas, Dykes' longtime teammate and friend, is acting manager.

Outfielder Pat Mullin of the Tigers dislocates a finger while chasing a fly ball against the White Sox. He only misses four days, pinch-hitting on the 27th.

Old pro outfielder Mike McCormick of the Reds makes his first appearance since early in 1943, when he entered the Navy. He was injured on April 4, during spring training. He pinch-hits today and will return to his usual center field post on the 24th.

April 23

Brooklyn's Ed Head pitches the big leagues' first no-hitter of 1946, against the Braves, winning 5–0. It's his first regular-season appearance since he went into the Army in July of 1944. Head's total time in the big leagues is stretched over a scant five seasons between 1940 and this year, which unfortunately, is as far as it goes. Three and two in 13 games, including the no-hitter, Head falls victim to a sore arm.

As unfortunate as it is, his career might not have come even this far, were it not for the steadfast determination he displayed over the past decade. Back in 1935, as a left-handed 15-year-old traveling with a semipro team down home in Louisiana, Head almost lost his pitching arm in a bus accident. He had to learn to pitch righty, as he never recovered full use of his left arm. With all that, compared to Bob Feller, whose second career no-hitter is due next week, Head is one of the least-remembered of postwar no-hit pitchers.

Giants outfielder Sid Gordon returns to the lineup after a week's absence, due to a painful blood clot on his right thigh, result of a torn muscle.

The Giants purchase pitcher Jack (Tex) Kraus from the Phillies. Kraus didn't appear for Philadelphia this season, though he did in 1943 and 1945, sandwiching the two seasons around military service. Earlier this spring, the Phils thought they'd sold Texas Jack to Brooklyn, but the pitcher held out and wouldn't report. So, with Tex back on their hands but unwanted, Philadelphia moved him again, to the Giants. This time, it takes. Kraus will pitch 17 games for New York, winning two, losing one. His first appearance as a Giant won't be till May 18th.

Four Cubs players are ill and unable to make today's trip from Chicago to Pittsburgh. They are pitchers Vern Olsen, Russ Meers and Red Adams, and infielder Billy Jurges. Olsen, winner of 13 and 10 games in 1940 and 1941, respectively, is back from three years in the Navy. He won't be seen in a Cubs game till a doubleheader on June 23. Meers, another Navy vet, will spend much of late summer down at Nashville, without contributing much either here or there. Adams, trying to recover from a skull fracture suffered in spring training, will make his big league debut on May 5. Jurges, slowly rounding into shape, isn't feeling well, either, but he'll play more than half the Cubs' games, even though he turns 38 next month. Pitcher Ray Prim, whose arm injury was noted on the 21st, will also be absent from Forbes Field today.

The Indians option first baseman Eddie Robinson to Baltimore. Robinson, who broke in with eight games back in 1942 before Navy service, plays another eight this September for the Indians, after being recalled at the end of the Orioles' season ("Mac I" will say it's seven, but the number is corrected in later editions).

First Baseman Babe Dahlgren is sold by the Pirates to the Browns, for his twelfth and last big league season. He didn't play for Pittsburgh, will appear 28 times for St. Louis, but quickly loses the regular's job to good-field-not-much-hit Chuck Stevens. Dahlgren is best remembered as the man whom the Yankees tabbed to replace Lou Gehrig in 1939. He won't be much of a replacement for George McQuinn with the Browns, either.

Though the Baseball Writers Association of America fails to vote anyone into the Hall of Fame this spring, a special committee, named by Judge Kenesaw Mountain Landis, the game's first commissioner, picks 11 old-timers for Cooperstown. They include Jesse (Crab) Burkett, three-time .400 hitter; Joe Tinker, Johnny (Crab) Evers and Frank Chance (the "Peerless Leader"), famed double-play combination of the Cubs in the first decade of the century; early American League pitcher-turned-manager Clark Griffith (the "Old Fox"), now owner of the Washington Nationals; Tommy McCarthy, outfielder on Boston's great teams of the 1890s; pitchers "Iron Man" Joe McGinnity, "Gettysburg Eddie" Plank, George "Rube" Waddell, "Big Ed" Walsh and "Happy Jack" Chesbro. It's remarkable, reporting this from afar, how many of the above had such well-remembered, colorful nicknames. By the way, committee members are Hall of Fame treasurer Paul Kerr, Yankees chairman Ed Barrow, Athletics owner-manager Connie Mack, Bob Quinn of Wilson Sporting Goods and Mel Webb, baseball writer of the Boston Globe. A second writer, Harry Cross, passed away on April 3. His position will be taken, on May 7, by syndicated New York columnist Grantland Rice, best-known sportswriter in the nation, whose timeless prose and poetry make a lasting impact on generations of American sports writers.

April 24

Rookie Indians catcher Sherman Lollar is Cleveland's backstop today, ending the major league record of 312 consecutive games caught, by teammate Frank Hayes. For Hayes, just 31 years old, it's the beginning of the end. Still an All-Star catcher this year, by next year he'll be gone from the scene.

Cincinnati's Ray Mueller is winding down on his National League mark of 233 straight games caught, which will end on May 5. Mueller's string began in 1943, with time out for Army duty in 1945. Mueller won't be penalized by the year-long lull in his streak. The decision is made by none other than good old Ford Frick, NL president, who, as baseball's commissioner in 1961, makes the historic unpopular decision to append an asterisk (or some similar mark) to Roger Maris' 61 home runs because Maris plays in a lengthier season than Babe Ruth did. In Mueller's case, no asterisk is even considered.

These are remarkable streaks: Hayes and Mueller will still be in the record books, more than fifty years later.

Clarence "Cuddles" Marshall of the Yankees debuts. He'll pitch 23 games, with a 3–4 record. *The Sporting News* shows a profile photo of Marshall in a later issue, next to one of lookalike movie star Tyrone Power.

Jake Caulfield, Athletics shortstop, also debuts. This is his only season in the majors, though he does pretty well offensively, batting .277 in 44 games. He doesn't get compared to movie stars.

Indians infielder Vern Freiberger reports upon his discharge from the Army, but the only two games of his major league career were back in 1941. *The Sporting News* says at one point there were almost 300 American Leaguers in the military during the war; there are still 37 serving.

Montreal pitcher John Wright is batted about in his organized baseball debut today. In three and two-thirds innings, he surrenders three walks, five hits and four runs to the Syracuse Chiefs. The Royals lose, 11–3. The premise which says Jackie Robinson's confidence must be buoyed by the presence of another African American on the team will steadily lose meaning.

April 25

Catcher Walker Cooper of the Giants fractures his right little finger, a day after going 5-for-5. He's optimistic he can be back within a week, but his doctors say it could be four, at best. Splitting the difference historically, he pinch-hits in two weeks, but it'll be more than a month, May 30, before he catches again.

Reds pitcher Gene (Junior) Thompson, who injured his knee during spring training, is released without making an appearance for Cincinnati. He'll surface with the Giants, signing May 14, pitching in 39 games. (*The Baseball Register* says Cincinnati doesn't let him go till April 30; interestingly, the 1946 version names him Eugene Earl [Gene] Thompson, while the 1942 version said he was Junior Eugene [Gene] Thompson; *Mac X* says Eugene Earl is his real given name, but lists him as Junior Thompson, by which he's most commonly known.)

The Cubs' front office claims a loss of $2,700 a year since 1928, in response to a proposed bill that would tax professional sports in Illinois. The tax would benefit a state soldiers' bonus.

The Pirates send pitcher Bill Clemensen to Columbus (American Association), after pitching one game, back on the 20th. He had other trials with Pittsburgh in 1939 and 1941, before spending four years away in the war. Now, he disappears from the majors for all eternity.

The Yankees assign pitcher Ken Holcombe to Kansas City, for whom he pitches tomorrow. Holcombe, who worked 23 games as a rookie last season, won't be back in the majors till 1948, when he appears with the Reds. The Yanks option pitcher Rinaldo "Rugger" Ardizoia to Oakland, where he'll post a 15–7 record. His major league record totals 10 games pitched, all of them next season.

"Deals of the Week," *The Sporting News* issue of April 25

The Tigers option pitchers Joe Orrell and Bob Hogue to Dallas, and outfielder-first baseman Ed Mierkowicz to Milwaukee. None sees major league action in 1946. Orrell's big league career is done; Hogue's won't begin till next year with the Braves; Mierkowicz, who plays most of the season with Buffalo, is between engagements in the majors.

The Dodgers assign pitcher Eddie Chandler to Fort Worth (his big league career will span only 1947).

The White Sox assign pitcher Doyle Lade to Shreveport. He doesn't play for the Chisox in 1946, but does pitch three times for the Cubs.

The NL Bostons sell first baseman Johnny McCarthy to Minneapolis. He played the first two games of the season, apparently till Ray Sanders was ready to take over the position for the Braves. A "prospect" ever since he played 12 games for the Dodgers in 1934, McCarthy's now 36 and has ridden a two-stop elevator during his career: minors to majors, majors to minors. His best year could have been 1943 with the Braves, but he broke an ankle. Once mended, the Navy got him. Down in the American Association, McCarthy is now property of the Giants, for whom he played in the late thirties. He delays his arrival, due to the illness of his wife. His first game for the Millers is April 30. True to form, he'll bat .333, second in the Association. Next time his elevator goes up, it'll be 1948, when he takes a final ride to the major leagues.

Boston also assigns outfielder Frank Lamanna to Hartford (his last big league games were in 1942, so don't look for him again) and pitcher Lou Tost to Seattle (last a major leaguer in 1943; he'll pitch once for the Pirates in 1947). Boston returns Max Surkont to the Cardinals (he's also identified in print as "Matt" till later in the season). He arrived in Boston with arm problems.

Cleveland options outfielder Clarence Campbell to Baltimore. "Soup" Campbell's two-season big league career ended in spring training 1942, when he enlisted in the Army. Another outfielding Campbell, Bruce, 13-year American Leaguer nicknamed "Soupy," is also returning from the war this season, but he plays ball at Buffalo and Minneapolis and is through in the majors. A decade ago, he recovered from a near-fatal two-season bout with spinal meningitis, batting .376 the last half of 1936 with Cleveland. A third Campbell, Paul, first baseman and pinch-hitter with the Red Sox, will be around all summer and, though he plays just 28 games, appears in the World Series.

The Phillies have optioned first baseman-outfielder Vance Dinges to Utica. He'll be back in late June.

April 26

Giants pitchers Harry Feldman and Ace Adams jump the club to play in the Mexican League. Feldman was 0–2 in three games for New York. Adams also pitched three times, with an 0–1 record. During the war, Adams was one of the game's great relief specialists— one of the first — appearing in 61, 70, 65 and 65 games from 1942 to 45. Though their abbreviated five-year bans are lifted in 1949, neither will ever make it back to the big leagues.

On the other hand, Red Sox catcher Eddie McGah plays his first major league game today, highly regarded as a prospect by no less than Ted Williams, who saw McGah play in the Navy. Unfortunately, he's only an afterthought in history, with 15 games for Boston in 1946 and another nine in 1947.

Catcher George Armstrong of the A's also debuts today. Coming off a strong 1945, when he hit .290 for Lancaster, he'll play just eight games for Connie Mack this year, then never be seen again in the big leagues.

On April 23, the Cardinals sold outfielder Earl Naylor to Brooklyn, for whom he pinch-runs today. He'll pinch-hit twice, then be sent to Montreal on May 18. He didn't play for St. Louis, was a Phil in 1942 and a Blue Jay in '43 (both *Phillies* in disguise), before he went into the Service.

April 27

Reds pitcher Howie Fox has an emergency appendectomy and will be lost till June 9.

Convalescent White Sox manager Jimmie Dykes is on hand to see his team for the first time this season. They're shut out by the Browns, 2–0, on the strength of Sam Zoldak's pitching and a Vern Stephens home run. "I thought that guy was in Mexico," Dykes grumbles. He'll take the team's reins, personally, on April 30, when his Chisox lose to Washington on their first trip east.

If you're unfamiliar with the structure of major league baseball in these years before expansion, each eight-team league has four "eastern" and four "western" cities, but it's for scheduling, exclusively. Everybody plays everybody else in the league 22 games, 11 at home, 11 away, over the course of a 154-game season. This season began with eastern and western teams playing within their own geographical divisions. Then, in each league, one division's teams will travel to play the other division's teams. The schedule often calls for an off-day when traveling to the other division, as it's a long, overnight train ride from the East Coast to Chicago or St. Louis, and provision is usually made for that (off-days are often used to play exhibition games against farm clubs, or to make up games which had been postponed earlier, mostly due to rain or cold weather). When the White Sox take their first "eastern swing," it's to play a series each in Washington, Philadelphia, New York and Boston, the AL's eastern cities, though some of their games are rained out and postponed till later in the year. Cleveland, Detroit, St. Louis and Chicago comprise the AL's western half.

Generally, when the American League West is visiting its eastern cities, the National League East plays in the NL West. New York, Brooklyn, Boston and Philadelphia are the eastern bloc; Chicago, St. Louis, Cincinnati and Pittsburgh the western. St. Louis is as far "west" as major league baseball extends.

The top four teams in each league, dictated by won-lost percentage on a given day, are said to be in the "first division." The bottom four are the "second division" (when there's a tie for fourth and fifth places, you must judge for yourself; it happens often, early in a season). The eighth-place team is said to be "in the cellar," or "in the basement" of its league. They are "cellar dwellers."

Today, the Dodgers sell outfielder Goody Rosen and first baseman Jack Graham to the Giants, for an estimated $25,000. The veteran Rosen, third in National League batting with .325 last season, only played three games for Brooklyn this year. The rookie Graham played twice with the Dodgers. Each will appear in exactly 100 games for New York, Rosen hitting .281 to end his six seasons in the majors. Graham will bat just .218, not much to recommend him and, indeed, he won't return to the big leagues till 1949, with the Browns.

Further, Brooklyn options outfielder Johnny Rizzo to St. Paul, pitchers Chet Kehn and Cy Buker and catcher Homer (Dixie) Howell, to Montreal. None appear in the big leagues in 1946. Howell's career, such as it is, is ahead of him; the others', such as they were, are over. Rizzo hit .301 as a rookie with the Pirates in 1938 but was unable to fill Brooklyn's need for a righthanded-hitting outfielder these eight years later.

Outfielder Gil Coan, much-heralded rookie who hit a minor league record 28 triples last season, debuts for the Senators. *The Sporting News*' "Minor League Player of the Year" in 1945, he'll bat a disappointing .209 in 59 games in 1946. Coan won't come into his own till 1950–51, when he has back-to-back .303 seasons. He'll remain around for 11 years in the big leagues. Some critics say freshman teammate Ray Goolsby is a better hitter, but he's two years older than Coan (24), not as highly publicized, and destined for Chattanooga.

Pittsburgh catcher Vinnie Smith, back after four seasons in the Navy, hurts his right knee getting back to first against the Reds and is lost for the remainder of the season. He'll have an operation on May 10. Initially expected to miss perhaps six weeks, with his seven games so far this season, he's through as a major league ball player. Vin was Bob Feller's favorite catcher early in the war, when they played together at the Norfolk Naval Training Station. He was looked on as a coming star for the Pirates, which is not the way his story ends.

Taking on another life, Smith returns to the majors from 1957 to 1965, as a National League umpire. He'll be behind the plate on May 26, 1959, as Pittsburgh's Harvey Haddix pitches a 12-inning perfect game, lost in the 13th.

The Pirates assign shortstop Alf Anderson and pitcher Bill Brandt to Hollywood. Anderson played a bit before the war and got into his final two big league games early this season. In Hollywood, *The Sporting News* says, he "step(s) off the plane and into the lineup at third base, May 4." It will be a rewarding year out on the Coast for Anderson, who plays 142 games at short, doesn't bat much (.264), but he's voted the Stars' Most Valuable Player.

Brandt's only major league years were 1941–43. After mulling his future prospects, he reports to Hollywood on May 8 and makes his first appearance, in relief, on May 26. However, most of his season will be spent pitching for Columbus (AA) with a poor 0–3 record, and Chattanooga, 4–3.

The Indians option outfielder Ted Sepkowski to Oklahoma City. He hasn't played yet for Cleveland but will be recalled in time for a couple of games in mid–September (his name is variously spelled Sczepkowski, Scepkowski or Szepkowski; "Mac I" will say he was born Sczepkowski; he'll be Scepkowski in the 1947 *Official Baseball Guide*).

April 28

Outfielder Del Ennis debuts for the Phillies. Ennis just left the Navy April 5 and is thrust into the lineup only after Philadelphia can't secure waivers on him to send him to the minors for seasoning, the rest of the league blocking the move. A native Philadelphian and lifetime Phillies fan, the player isn't a stranger to the organization. He hit .346 for the Phillies' farm in Trenton, down in Class B, in 1943. But, as he tells Danny Peary in *We Played the Game*, the team has no clue as to his ability. Other major league players who competed with him in the Pacific do, and they urge their own clubs to claim Ennis, should he appear on the waiver list. Kit Crissey writes that an 18-year-old Ennis in 1944 was offered a $25,000 signing bonus by the Yankees, right then and there, but he already was a farmhand of his hometown team, which had secured his future services for $50 (illustrating how confusing all this can be, Peary quotes Ennis saying the Yankee bonus offer was $2,500, ten times less than Crissey's figure).

Unswayed by Ennis' reputation, Phillies manager Ben Chapman has agreed to keep him around only for 30 days, on trial. But once given the chance, the 21-year-old responds by becoming baseball's first *official* Rookie of the Year. He bats .313 with 17 homers, which doesn't appear to be a high power output, but Pittsburgh rookie Ralph Kiner will lead the NL with only 23.

Today is Dodger pitcher Curt Davis' only major league game this season, the last he ever pitches. On May 1, Davis will be released, closing out a memorable 13-year National League career. Once the ace of the Dodger staff, he's thought now to be headed for a scouting job. But he'll pitch the rest of the season for Montreal, 20 games with a 5–3 record, 3.00 ERA. Ol' Coonskin Curt, 42, will shut out the Louisville Colonels, to win Game 7 of the Junior World Series for the Royals this fall.

Released by the Dodgers yesterday was third baseman Lew Riggs, who played only on Opening Day for Brooklyn. Like Davis, the 10-year major league veteran will sign, as a free agent, with the Dodgers' farm club up in Montreal, playing his first game for the Royals on May 19. In part-time work (90 games) for Montreal, Riggs will hit .303, but at 36 he'll never make it back to the big leagues.

Coincidentally, Brooklyn pitcher Glen Moulder makes his debut today, his only big league game this season. Then he, too, will be sent down to Montreal, where he pitches 28 times, for a 10–6 record. His next big league appearance will be with the Browns, for a while, next year.

White Sox pitcher Ralph Hamner pitches his first big league game today. Hamner, 2–7 this year, will spend the next three seasons with the crosstown Cubs. Outfielder George Washington Bradley of the Browns debuts, too. He'll play in three more games between now and May 13, then find his way down to Toledo, closing out his only season in the majors.

Giants righthander "Prince Hal" Schumacher, 35, a Navy veteran beloved in New York for his 154–116 record in a dozen seasons before going off to war. (Hal Newhouser of the Tigers is now the reigning "Prince Hal" in most other big league cities). Schumacher wins the first game of a doubleheader against the Dodgers today, in his first appearance since 1942. New York's Bob Joyce, 31, goes the route in the second game, winning too.

Mickey Witek, Giants second baseman making his return after two seasons in the Coast Guard, crashes into the concrete wall of the Polo Grounds grandstand and is knocked out, injuring his elbow in the process. Thus hampered, he's limited to 82 games all season and is through as a front-liner. He's hitting .370, but will end up at .264. Next time on the field will be June 6, as a pinch-hitter. His first name, by the way, is Nicholas, though he's not called "Nicky," as one might expect. Due to childhood pronunciation problems, he wound up as "Mickey," instead.

Fellow war vet Buddy Blattner, who came up for a very short time with the Cardinals before entering the Navy, takes Witek's place. Blattner, well-known as a world-class ping-pong champion, will play 114 games at second, Witek 42.

It will be disclosed that Witek's elbow is fractured, but he doesn't get that news till June 19. He thinks it's simply a torn ligament.

Shortstop Marty Marion of the Cardinals is hit in the foot by a pitch from Claude Passeau of the Cubs. It's the first game of a twin bill today, and Marion will sit out the nightcap.

Emmett O'Neill, purchased from the Cubs after pitching one game for them on April 17, makes his first of two appearances for the White Sox. O'Neill was a wartime Red Sox starter, 6–11 in 1944, 8–11 in '45.

Sign of the times: after he runs into an overflow crowd in Minneapolis, St. Paul left fielder Eric Tipton's catch of a fly ball is ruled "no catch" by umpire Robert Hicks. Tipton and Saints manager Ray Blades argue the call so vehemently, they're not only thumbed out, but fined $10 each, for abusive language and delay of the game.

April 29

The Yankees release outfielder Tuck Stainback, who hasn't yet played this year. He will get into 91 games for the Athletics, his seventh big league employer.

The Giants option outfielders Morrie Arnovich and Jim (Buster) Maynard to Jersey City. Maynard, a sort of regular in 1943 before he went into the service, played seven games for New York in 1946, now will end his career down in the minors. Arnovich, who made one final appearance in the big leagues on April 21, was around a lot with the Phillies in the 1930s. He got into the 1940 World Series with the Reds, spent the whole war in the military and was trying a comeback at 35. He's soon to be transferred to the Giants' Minneapolis farm, then will be given his unconditional release around June 15.

The American Baseball Guild, a union with no members, files suit today against the Washington Nationals for unfair labor practices. The action by Boston "labor relations counselor" (*his* phrase; he adds he isn't a real lawyer) Robert Murphy is submitted to the National Labor Relations Board. Murphy charges club owner Clark Griffith "attempted to dissuade the Washington players from joining the Guild." "That's ridiculous!" Griffith tells Washington writer Shirley Povich, "baseball can't exist without the reserve clause and when a union wants to tear that from our game, I'll continue to speak." The whole thing, Griffith concludes, "is silly."

The Phillies release pitcher Si Johnson. He pitched on the 24th, his only regular-season game for the Phils this year. Signing immediately with the Braves, "Old Silas," now 40 and recently out of the Navy after three years away, will get full-time work at Boston, beginning the 13th of May. His big league career began in 1928. When he retires after next season, he'll have a lifetime won-lost record of 101–165.

April 30

Bob Feller of the Indians no-hits the Yankees, 1–0, the second no-hitter of his career. His first was on Opening Day 1940, against the White Sox; his next will come in 1951, against the Tigers. Until Sandy Koufax pitches four in the 1960s, Feller's three no-hitters will be the major league record (in the 1970s, 1980s and 1990s, Nolan Ryan will pitch seven, but "Noley" won't even be born till January of next year). The Cleveland catcher today is Frankie Hayes, who, later in the season, playing for the White Sox, will break up a Feller no-hitter.

Ellis Kinder of the Browns, newly arrived from a year's military service, debuts on the mound today. Turning 32 this summer, the aging rookie will come into his own with the Red Sox from 1948 to 1955, part of his dozen years in the majors, becoming known as "Old Folks."

Veteran first baseman Buddy Hassett, regular for the Yankee pennant winners in 1942, is let go without playing a game, at 35 never again to perform in the majors. His career was cut off by the war (he went through the invasions of Iwo Jima and Okinawa as an officer aboard the aircraft carrier *Bennington*), the lost years unrecoverable. Hassett is well-remembered as one of the great Irish tenors of baseball lore, his songs gracing many a clubhouse and banquet hall. (Kit Crissey writes that Hassett once went ashore on the island of Mog Mog, to sing at a touring ballplayers' party.)

Ace Adams, who jumped to the Mexican League the other day, has arrived in Mexico City, where he says he'll get $10,000. The Giants wouldn't have dreamed of paying him that much.

May 1

Third baseman Billy Johnson of the Yankees is reported in the separation center at Fort McPherson, Georgia, awaiting discharge from the Army. He played 155 games for New York's 1943 World Champions; he'll play 85 this year, becoming a staple of the immediate postwar-era Yanks. He'll rejoin them on May 5 and play his first game three weeks later. (In 18 games for the Infantry School at Fort Benning, Georgia, he batted .454.)

The Giants trade catcher Clyde Kluttz to the Phillies for outfielder Vince DiMaggio. Within four hours, Kluttz is traded again, to the Cardinals, for second baseman Emil Verban. The oldest ball playing DiMaggio played six games with the Phils, gets into 15 for the

Giants, then reluctantly returns to San Francisco for 43 with the Seals, his big league career over.

Kluttz played five games for New York, will catch in 49 more for the Cards. Verban, St. Louis' regular second sacker the last two years, has lost his first-string job and only appeared once so far this season. He'll play 138 times for Philadelphia, enjoying a sort of metamorphosis, being named to the NL All-Star team in July.

Pittsburgh pitcher Edson "Ed" Bahr debuts. He'll have an 8–6 year, yet spend only two seasons in the majors. In 1945, he was 12–9 at Kansas City in the Yankee farm system. New York actually traded him to Pittsburgh, for cash and a "player to be named later." The Bucs' Frankie Zak, reserve shortstop, is the "player," who'll be released to Kansas City in mid–June.

Phillies catcher Rollie Hemsley breaks his wrist in a collision with Pittsburgh's Elbie Fletcher. Andy Seminick comes in for Hemsley today, but Rollie is still catching on the 4th, as the injury isn't first diagnosed as a break. X-rays taken soon reveal a fracture and a bone chip, however. Hemsley stays home when the Phillies take to the road, May 7. The injury limits him to 49 games this season, fewest since he broke in, back in 1928. He'll pinch-run once, May 15, but not catch again till June 16.

In his first home game for Montreal, Jackie Robinson is a modest 1-for-4, with a run scored, in a 12–9 win over Jersey City. The crowd of 15,745 is second largest in Montreal history.

May 2

The American Baseball Guild has outlined its demands, through Robert Murphy, whose brainchild it is:

- ♦ $7,500 a year minimum salary (the average salary is now $4,500).
- ♦ 50 percent of the sale price should revert to a player purchased by a major league team, with arbitration if parties can't agree.
- ♦ A provision for performance bonuses, presently taboo.
- ♦ All Guild officers are to be present or past professional players.

Some of that's a lot for club owners to swallow.

The Red Sox assigned outfielder Sam Mele and first baseman Al Flair to Louisville, at the end of April. Mele's first game for the Colonels is played today, 4-for-5. His ten-year regular season big league career won't begin till 1947. "Broadway" Al Flair's one year in the majors covered 10 games for the Bosox in 1941. He'll spend the rest of his playing days in the minors.

On April 26, the Braves optioned infielder Bob Detweiler to Indianapolis, for whom he plays his first game today. He gets two hits and scores the winning run in a 10-inning, 3–1 victory over St. Paul. "Ducky" Detweiler will be recalled to play one game for Boston this season, the 1st of June, then will be sent back to Indy again. He was in 12 Braves games in 1942, his only other trip to the majors. The war caught up with him.

"Deals of the Week" in today's *Sporting News*

The White Sox option infielder Floyd Baker and pitcher Al (Pard) Epperly to Milwaukee. A second-stringer for the 1944 Browns and 1945 Chisox, Baker will come back for full-time substitute status in mid–September. He'll hang around through 1955, with the Chisox, Nats, Red Sox and Phillies. Epperly, momentary prewar Cub who saw no action for the White Sox this season, will reappear with the Dodgers a very short while in 1950.

The Reds assign pitcher Millard (Dixie) Howell, pitcher Arnold Carter and outfielder Hank Sauer to Syracuse.

Carter pitched for the Reds last year and the year before, with an 11–7 record in 1944. Those two seasons comprise the extent of his big league career. Sauer played a few times for the Reds in 1941-42, and most of last September, after returning from military duty, picking up a couple of home runs. He's played no games for Cincinnati this season and won't, till 1948. In the interim, he'll belt 21 round-trippers in 1946 for Syracuse, 50 next year. When he finally comes up to stay, he'll enjoy a long career in the majors, belting 286 more home runs between 1948 and 1959.

Regarding Millard Fillmore Howell, he's the *other* Dixie Howell, not the catcher just sent to Montreal by Brooklyn. They were born within a few months of each other, but no evidence revealed that they're related. Could be cousins, or uncle/nephew. It's possible, as they're both Kentuckians—Millard from Bowman, Homer from Louisville. Millard is slightly older, or slightly younger, than Homer (sources disagree on Homer's birthday). They'll briefly be teammates on the Reds in 1949.

The pitcher, Millard (Dixie) Howell, started his pro baseball career in 1937. The catcher, Homer (Dixie) Howell, started his in 1938. Homer won't play in the major leagues till next year; Millard's already had a three-game trial, with the Indians in 1940. He hasn't yet pitched for Cincinnati and won't till 1949. He'll do well in the mid–1950s for the White Sox, then suffer an untimely death at age 40 in 1960, of a heart attack during spring training with Indianapolis, down in Florida, following a workout that gives him chest pains. Homer will live 30 years more, till 1990.

The Yankees option pitchers Karl Drews and Al Lyons to Kansas City today, and assign pitcher Herb Karpel to Newark, where he'll lead the International League in ERA (2.41, 14–8). The pitching-rich Yankees will never give him another chance: he's done in the majors, after just two games.

Drews' big league career is just starting. A Staten Islander signed out of a Yankee tryout school, he was 19-9 at Newark in 1945. He pitches three times for New York this year, but hasn't done so, yet, and will not until September. Like Drews, Lyons hasn't pitched, so far, for the Yanks, but will, later this season.

The Red Sox option catcher Howard Doyle to Louisville today. "Danny" Doyle's only big league games were in 1943.

The Braves sell pitcher Johnny Hutchings to Indianapolis today, after his one appearance for Boston in 1946. It ends Hutchings' six years in the majors. Pitcher Don Hendrickson is sold to Kansas City, following two games with the Braves. Last year, in his only other big league season, Hendrickson appeared on the mound 37 times for Boston.

The Tigers assign pitcher Les Mueller to Buffalo. A war vet, Mueller was 6–8 last year, an early-season sensation. Now, having not appeared at all in 1946, his big league career is finished (Mueller initially refuses to go, declaring he'll quit and enter the business world; but he relents, has a 10–8 mark at Buffalo).

White Sox manager Jimmie Dykes personally pilots his club for the first time this year. Chicago loses to Washington (*The New York Times* says he took over his team back on April 27, but that was just the date he first saw this year's Chisox).

May 3

On April 29, the Browns sold infielder George Archie to Los Angeles of the Pacific Coast League. He plays first base today for the Angels, but he'll become their regular third baseman this season. Having been in four games for St. Louis, Archie, who spent 1942–45 away at war, has completed his three terms in the major leagues. Archie was third baseman for the Senators in 1941, before moving to St. Louis in a late-season trade for outfielder Roberto Estalella.

The Yankees sell pitcher Emerson (Steve) Roser to the Braves. His last of four games (1–1) for New York was April 25; his first for Boston will be May 7, where he'll also have a 1–1 record, in 14 appearances.

Yesterday, second baseman Danny Murtaugh was sold by the Phillies to Rochester, for whom he plays his first game tomorrow. Murtaugh played six games for Philadelphia. His swell Opening Day was the high point of his 1946 big league tour. He'll be up for three games next year with the Braves, then finally have four decent full seasons with the Pirates.

Also in his first game for Rochester tomorrow will be outfielder Clyde Vollmer, optioned there by the Reds. Vollmer, a Cincinnati native who broke in prior to going off to war, pinch-hit on April 24 and will be back in September.

May 4

Cincinnati infielder Bobby Adams is carried from the field on a stretcher, after pulling ligaments in his right knee during batting practice before the Reds' game with the Phillies. He'll be lost till the 28th. Adams will play only 94 times this season, batting .244, but his future seems reasonably assured. Chicago sports writer John P. Carmichael's always-effusive photo-filled annual, *Who's Who in the Major Leagues* (15th edition, 1947, 35 cents), will say of Adams next spring, he "may be the regular mid-station guardian this year. He will see plenty of action whether he wins the infield berth or not."

Detroit left fielder Dick Wakefield is hit by a pitch today in the Tigers' game against the Yankees, resulting in bone chips in his wrist. Wakefield will pinch-hit once and pinch-run once in coming days, but otherwise is out of action till the 19th. It's the first, but not the last, of his physical problems this summer.

The New York Times says today that Brooklyn infielder Stan Rojek may be headed for the Mexican League. Situated behind Pee Wee Reese in the Dodger pecking order, thereby playing seldom for the Dodgers, Rojek makes $4,500 a year. The Pasquels have offered him a $10,000 bonus and an annual salary of $8,000. Rojek won't go: he rides the bench for Brooklyn this year and next, then becomes a regular with the 1948 Pirates, playing every game, hitting .290.

May 5

Dodger pitcher Jean-Pierre Roy makes his major league debut. See below, his problems with the Mexican League.

Cubs pitcher Charles (Red) Adams debuts today.

Detroit infielder Billy Hitchcock fractures a finger playing against the Red Sox today, in his third and final game for the Tigers. On the 16th, apparently while still recovering, he'll be sold to Washington.

Pittsburgh pitcher Rip Sewell becomes ill in the ninth inning of the opener of today's doubleheader against the Dodgers at Forbes Field. Complaining of a "funny feeling" in his pitching arm, he leaves the game and goes to the clubhouse. Somewhat better after a rest, Sewell is able to dress and return to the dugout, to watch the second game. Another wave of sickness overcomes him, though, and, going to the dressing room again, he collapses. Rushed to the hospital, it's first assumed he's had a slight stroke. When that's ruled out, Sewell is diagnosed with meningitis. After release from the hospital, the pitcher goes home to Plant City, Florida, to recuperate. He'll return to Pirates on the 26th and make his next mound appearance on June 2.

Ray Sanders, first baseman of the Braves, is hit by a Max Lanier pitch in the first game of today's Boston-Cardinals doubleheader. Some blood vessels in Sanders' hand are damaged, and he'll be out till the 10th, missing four games. It's not a good omen. It won't be Sanders' year.

"Grandma" Johnny Murphy, from 1934 through 1943 one of the game's early generation of relief specialists, pitches a regular-season game for the first time since 1943 (in relief, of course), against Detroit. He left the Yankees three years ago to enter civilian war work.

The A's sell pitcher Jonas Berry to Toronto. "Jittery Joe," 41, toiled in the minors from 1927 till he got a chance with Cubs late in 1942. He surfaced again at Philadelphia in 1944 as a star reliever. Berry, who led the AL in games pitched last year, will work 16 times for Toronto, first of which is May 12 against Buffalo (after arriving from Philadelphia only an hour before the game). He'll return for 21 appearances with the Indians, the 1st of July. He pitched five times for the 1946 A's, most recently two days ago against the Browns.

Third baseman Whitey Kurowski of the Cardinals says he's spurned a $100,000 contract from the Mexican League.

May 6

Shortstop Vern Stephens of the Browns injures his shoulder and, except for a try at pinch-hitting on the 28th, is shelved till he returns to the field on June 5, a month from now.

Pitcher Phil Marchildon of the Athletics makes his first 1946 appearance, starting against the Tigers. Tail gunner on a Handley Page Halifax bomber in the Royal Canadian Air Force, Flying Officer Marchildon's plane was shot down over Kiel Harbour, Germany, August 16, 1944, his 26th bombing mission. He baled out, spent nine months in a German prisoner-of-war camp, *Stalag Luft III*, where "The Great Escape," the *real* one, had been made earlier.

Marchildon's experience took a heavy toll on him, physically and emotionally. He returned to baseball last summer, only a month after becoming a civilian again. Way out of shape, he pulled a groin muscle, from which he still hasn't entirely recovered.

In retrospect, Marchildon knew he should have spent the remainder of the 1945 season at home, recovering his strength, rather than trying to play ball. He came back in deference to pressure from kindly old Connie Mack, who was never adverse to making a dollar, even off a somewhat shaky war hero, scarce as dollars have been for him for so long. Not only was Mister Mack kindly, by the way, he was also tight-fisted and the very devil from whom to wrest a pay increase.

Marchildon's slow return to form in 1946 training camp almost prematurely concluded for good, when he was accidentally struck in the index finger of his pitching hand by a knife, thrown during locker room merriment by outfielder Ford Garrison, who fancied himself something of an expert. Garrison, as noted earlier, now resides with the Newark Bears of the International League, perhaps a victim of cause and effect.

May 7

Detroit outfielder Hoot Evers, still recovering from a broken ankle and thumb on March 17th, suits up for the first time, today in Philadelphia. He won't be able to play for two more weeks, pinch-hitting on the 21st.

The Dodgers option pitchers Ray Hathaway and Glen Moulder to Montreal. Hathaway pitched four games for Brooklyn last year, his only regular-season play in the big leagues (the first *Mac* said it was 49 games, not 4, subsequently corrected). Moulder pitched his only Dodger game this season when he debuted on April 28th. His first Montreal game is tomorrow, May 8th. He'll work 32 times for the Browns next year and 33 for the White Sox in 1948.

May 8

The Pirates release pitcher Bob Klinger, without his having pitched a game this year. He spent six seasons prewar with Pittsburgh, losing an NL-high 17 times in 1939. Tomorrow, the Navy vet will sign with the Red Sox. At Boston, Klinger will work primarily in relief. About to turn 36, he's got another big league season in him after 1946 and, up from the National League depths, he'll get a World Series check this fall. *The Baseball Register* dates Klinger's release tomorrow, signing with Boston May 10, although *Who's Who in Baseball* says he signs May 9. The "Official Commissioner's Bulletin" No. 8 says Pittsburgh released him yesterday.

To give you an idea of the time lapse between some transactions and their being carried in *The Sporting News*, Klinger's release and signing are reported in the "Deals of the Week" column in its May 16 issue, eight days late. It doesn't always happen that far after the fact, but it's not without precedent.

The Red Sox option pitchers Mel Deutsch and Jim Wilson, along with outfielder Andy Gilbert, to Louisville. This was Deutsch's lone tour of the big leagues, with three games for Boston, last of which was against the Browns yesterday. Wilson will pitch in a dozen big league seasons, highlighted by a no-hitter for the Milwaukee Braves in 1954 and a 15–8 record for the White Sox in 1957. This year, he worked just once for the Bosox, on April 23.

Gilbert played twice this year for Boston, his second and last part-season with the Red Sox (neither of which extends past a half-dozen games). His most lasting contribution comes later, starting in 1950, when he's named manager at Springfield (Ohio) in the Ohio-Indiana League. He'll manage 25 years in the minors, a quarter-century, with a record of 2,009–1,899, finishing first in such diverse places as Springfield (Mass.), Shreveport, Muskogee and Amarillo.

Cookie Lavagetto, Dodgers third baseman, plays his first game since 1941. He's been on the shelf, following surgery on his right elbow. He was in the Navy Air Force from 1942 through 1945. Cookie pinch runs against the Reds today, takes over his old third base spot on the 15th.

Pitcher Earl Reid makes his big league debut for the Braves today. He'll only pitch twice for Boston (1–0), then never be seen again on a major league diamond.

With rookie first baseman Dick Sisler slightly injured, outfielder Stan Musial of the

Cardinals moves in, to a new position. It isn't seen as permanent, by either the team or Stan, as he's never played first before. The move, for now, will only last one game. The Cards don't play again till the 12th, when Sisler and Musial resume their regular positions. Things will stay that way a month, till Musial plays first base on June 7 and remains there.

Outfielder Goody Rosen of the Giants hurts his left shoulder diving for a ball and will be sidelined till May 30.

Outfielder Vern Benson, who on May 5 was a pinch-runner in his final game with the Athletics this year, plays his first game for Toronto, where he's been optioned. He'll end up at Savannah, then be recalled to ride the bench in the closing days of the season.

May 9

This week on the 11th, the Cubs option infielder Alban Glossop to Los Angeles and pitcher Ed Hanyzewski to Nashville. Al Glossop, back from the Service, played his last four big league games this spring. He'll report to the Angels on the 17th, delayed by the illness of his son. Earlier in his career, he was with the Giants, Braves, Phillies and Dodgers.

Eddie Hanyzewski, often injured, pitched some for the Cubs during the war. He will have a 1–0 record in three Cubs games this season but has only appeared once so far. After moving from Nashville to Tulsa, Chicago's other Double-A farm club, Hanyzewski will be recalled by the Cubs in September, his final chance.

In July, while still with Nashville, Hanyzewski falls for the Old Hidden Ball Trick, but not in your usual way. He's on the mound, when his shortstop, Hal Quick, is about to nail Lew Flick, baserunner for Little Rock. Quick isn't quite quick enough, it appears. Before he can pull it off, Hanyzewski, himself losing track of the ball's location, asks the umpire for another, thereby nullifying the play. Yes, that's your Old Hidden Ball Trick, backfiring.

"Deals of the Week" in this edition of *The Sporting News*

Still cleaning house, the Phillies release former star outfielder Joe Marty, without his playing a game. Marty finished his major league career in 1941. He owns, or will own, a restaurant in Sacramento. He was born and will die in the California capitol.

Optioned to Utica are Phillies pitchers Don Grate, George Eyrich and Eli Hodkey, shortstop Bitsy Mott and third baseman Nick Picciuto. Otherwise assigned to Utica are pitchers Andy Lapihuska (last active in 1943 and never more to play in the big leagues) and Dale Jones and catcher Bill Peterman. Eyrich, who survived kamikaze attacks in the Battle of Leyte Gulf, only has nine games in 1943 for his entry in major league records. Mott and Picciuto were 1945 Phillies, that year only. Jones pitched twice in 1941, like innumerable others losing his career to the war. Peterman played once in 1942, then also became just a name in the books. Hodkey hasn't appeared yet; he'll be back in September; ditto Grate.

The Pirates option infielder Vic Barnhart to Albany. Son of 1920s Pittsburgh sometime-star Clyde Barnhart, Vic played just two games with the Pirates this year, ending his three partial seasons in the majors, all with Pittsburgh.

The Reds option outfielder Frankie Baumholtz to Columbia. Baumholtz, who'll spend a decade with the Reds, Cubs and Phillies, is a year away. Down in Class A, he'll finish right behind teammate Ted Kluszewski in this year's Sally League batting race. Next season, he will play pretty good center field for Cincinnati. Once an All-America basketball player at Ohio U., Baumholtz was a Naval gunnery officer, seeing considerable action in the war. His baseball record carries a footnote shared by only a select few other big leaguers: he has a brief but successful tenure in pro basketball (catcher Del Rice of the Cardinals and Dodger farmhand Chuck Connors are others who play both sports). At war's end, Baumholtz starred for the Youngstown Bears of the National Basketball League. After this baseball season, in the Basketball Association of America, forerunner of the N.B.A., he'll make Second-Team All-League for Cleveland, behind such stalwarts as mid-century pro pioneers Joe Fulks and Max Zaslofsky. At a little less than 5'11," Baumholtz plays very good basketball, in a relatively *short* man's league.

The Tigers assign outfielder Ned Harris to Portland (PCL) and catcher Joe Erautt to Buffalo. Harris, called "Bob" in at least one encyclopedia (his first name is Robert), pinch-hit once, on April 28, for Detroit this year and plays no more in the majors. Erautt, whose younger brother Eddie will pitch for the Reds and Cardinals six seasons starting next year, won't get into a big league game himself till 1950, with the White Sox.

The Cardinals option pitcher Max Surkont to Rochester. Rookie Surkont, sent to the Braves and sent back because he arrived hurt, will come up three years from now with the White Sox. He'll spend nine summers with the Chisox, Braves, Pirates, Cardinals and Giants. He'll pitch for the Red Wings this season (9–17), next season (15–10) and the season after (15–11).

Cardinals pitcher Johnny Grodzicki, badly wounded in Germany and still wearing a leg brace, is put on the disabled list today, having been unable to play at all. He'll be reactivated in July, finally making his first appearance since 1941 on the 11th, roughly two months from now. Grodzicki will pitch only three times this year.

May 10

Ted Gray, 21-year-old southpaw, is discharged from the Navy and signed for a guaranteed 15-day trial with the Tigers. He'll only pitch once, before being farmed out to Buffalo, but it's a beginning. One day, Gray will have moderate success in the big leagues, making the All-Star Game in 1950, but over the course of a relatively short career he'll lose more than win.

After he starts for the Tigers in an exhibition game at Buffalo today, Detroit leaves pitcher Ruffus Gentry behind, on option with their Triple-A farm team. With the Bisons, he'll work in 25 games, posting a 10–8 record. His only full season in the majors was 1944, when he won 12, lost 14. In 1945, the record books say he was a holdout. In 1946, he pitched just twice for Detroit, earlier this month.

(Unfortunately for Rufe, in August he volunteers to help rid Buffalo's Offerman Park of a surfeit of pigeons. With .22 caliber repeating rifle, he begins the hunt. Finding his front sight set too high the first day, August 23rd, the next day he places what he thinks is his unloaded rifle in a vise, to file the sight down a bit. The firearm, though, isn't empty; it goes off into, or near, his hands. He suffers severe injuries to the digits of both hands, fracturing his right index finger, losing part of his left index finger and running the risk of tetanus and gangrene. It's feared he may have seen the end of his baseball days, but penicillin and other drugs save his hands and he'll make brief appearances for the Tigers in 1947-48.)

The Yankees send catcher Gus Niarhos down, to Kansas City, having not played yet. He'll be back in June and see action in 37 games for New York. This is his first of nine seasons in the majors, though in only a couple does he appear with much frequency.

To get Niarhos, on May 12 Kansas City prospect Lawrence Berra is sent to Newark, in a swap of catchers between Class Triple-A Yankee farms. Berra is just out of the Navy, didn't appear for the Blues. He'll play 70 games behind the bat and 10 in the outfield for the Bears, before getting a late-season call-up from New York. In a gang of Yankee backstops, Gus Niarhos is regarded much the better candidate. *Street & Smith's Baseball Year Book* says Niarhos "probably would have Bill Dickey's job right now" if he hadn't been in military service (completely ignoring Aaron Robinson, who, since leaving the Coast Guard last summer, is the incumbent). While you're at it, "keep an eye on Mel Serafini, who hit .335 last year" for Kansas City, the magazine says. Everyone is a better catching candidate than Lawrence Berra: the Yankees employ six men at the position this season.

The Sporting News says Yankee president Larry MacPhail has a policy against sending any player to Newark or Kansas City who might be recalled later in the season and deplete his top minor league clubs in the heat of their own pennant races. This in mind, righthander Frank (Spec) Shea is optioned to Oakland, where he'll post a 15–5 record, with a marvelous 1.66 ERA in a hitter's league, setting him up for an outstanding rookie season with the Yankees next year. But, if needed earlier, his assignment to Oakland absolves MacPhail of any commitment to keeping him there. Shea, by the way, is just recovering from an appendectomy.

Neither Newark nor Kansas City will make their league's playoffs. Oakland, on the other hand, gets to the PCL finals against San Francisco.

Red Sox outfielder Leon Culberson has played the last four games at third base, an unfamiliar position. It has its consequences today, as he fields a Joe DiMaggio line drive with the end of a finger, splitting the digit and perhaps fracturing it. He will be out of action, except for a pinch-run and two pinch-hit appearances, till the 8th of June. He won't return to third base till 1947.

May 11

The Yankees beat the Red Sox 2–0, to end Boston's 15-game winning streak, fourth longest in American League history. This may be an appropriate time to acknowledge the core of the Bosox' incipient juggernaut consists of ex-servicemen back from the war, reassembled at last after as many as four years away. Outfielders Ted Williams and Dominic DiMaggio, shortstop Johnny Pesky and second baseman Bobby Doerr, all ex-servicemen, are the heart of the offense. All three catchers—Roy Partee, Hal Wagner and Eddie McGah—are war vets, too. So are ace pitchers David (Boo) Ferriss, Cecil (Tex) Hughson, Maurice (Mickey) Harris, Joe Dobson and Earl Johnson, a much-decorated hero of the Battle of the Bulge. For this one season, they make up much of one of the great ball clubs ever assembled.

Attendance is booming in this first full postwar season. The Red Sox' visit to Yankee Stadium draws huge crowds. Yesterday, there were 55,889 paid. Today, 52,011. Tomorrow, Sunday, there will be 68,193. It adds up to 177,093, the largest total for a three-game series in the history of baseball.

A final note on the day's activities in New York: Yanks catcher Aaron Robinson sustains a split finger and will be out till pinch-hitting on the 28th. He won't go behind the plate till May 30.

Athletics' pitcher Orge (Pat) Cooper appears in his first big league game, his only one till next year.

Detroit second baseman Jimmy Bloodworth rejoins the Tigers after his Army discharge. Last active in 1943, he'll play 76 games this year and bat .245.

Cliff Fannin, righthander of the Browns, makes his first appearance of the season, still nursing a sore arm, hurt in the spring. Fannin will appear 27 times, with a 5–2 record. He'll see duty with the Browns through 1952.

Brooklyn righthander Rex Barney is discharged from the Army and will quickly rejoin the team. The wild but hard-throwing Barney advanced from Durham to Montreal to Brooklyn in his only previous season, 1943, then went where most able-bodied 19 year olds did, into military uniform. He'll make his first 1946 appearance on May 30, but, as he reports considerably out of condition for baseball, will be used sparingly. He'll begin to hit his stride next year, though always notoriously unacquainted with the strike zone. In 1948, putting everything together at last, Barney will blossom, with a 15–13 record and a no-hitter against the Giants. But his erratic arm will fail him completely by 1950, and he'll turn to other pursuits. Becoming a long-time fan favorite in Baltimore, Barney will work as public address announcer for the Orioles from 1970 until his death in 1997.

May 12

In his only game played this season, Phillies manager Ben Chapman pitches in relief against the Dodgers, winding up 15 years as a major leaguer (mostly in the outfield, prewar).

May 13

The Giants sign John Carden, once a Texas Aggie, on his discharge from the U.S. Marines. Carden, lacking any professional experience, will pitch once for New York, then disappear to the lower minor leagues.

The Cardinals sell sore-armed pitcher Ernie White to the Braves. White, 17–7 in 1941, was discharged from the Army in January, after two years away. He'll throw a dozen times for Boston in 1946. Next year, his arm troubles rendering him unable to pitch, he'll be a coach right up until the season's final game. The current transaction date is today, reported as a sale in this year's *Baseball Register*. *The New York Times* says White is unconditionally released, signed by Boston on the 15th. In any case, he goes to the Braves without appearing for St. Louis at all.

May 14

Righthander Hal Gregg, Brooklyn's top pitcher last year, pulls a muscle in his throwing arm and won't return till June 22nd. He'll still pitch 26 times (6–4), but in 1945 was in 42 games (18–13).

The Giants sign pitcher Gene (Junior) Thompson, released a month ago by Cincinnati. He worked out for the Giants when New York went to play the Cubs and the Reds. Signing was contingent upon examination of his knees, in which there's cartilage damage. Surgery is prescribed, after the season's over. He pitches his first game for New York tomorrow, losing to the Reds.

Lefthander Frank Biscan of the Browns is expected to rejoin the club today, following military service and an arm operation. However, it will still be over a month before he can pitch, on June 23. Briefly with the Browns in 1942, he'll appear 16 times for St. Louis this season.

The Montreal Royals send pitcher John Wright to Three Rivers in the Canadian-American League. Wright was at Montreal primarily to keep Jackie Robinson company in a potentially hostile environment. Feeling the precaution still necessary, Roy Partlow, southpaw from the Philadelphia Stars and formerly of the Homestead Grays, is signed, thus keeping Montreal's black players at two.

May 15

The Indians sell pitcher Johnny Podgajny to Baltimore, where he was a 20-game winner last year. Known as "Specs," he pitched in six games this spring for Cleveland, last time the 13th. It was the end of his five seasons in the majors.

Detroit's Ted Gray makes his major league debut on the pitcher's mound.

Cubs first baseman Eddie Waitkus bruises an elbow and is out till June 1.

The Tigers' Billy Hitchcock, less than two weeks after fracturing a finger, sprains his right thumb. It did not occur in a regulation ball game, as he's been out of action since the 5th; it probably happened in practice. Tomorrow, he'll move on, to the Senators.

Pittsburgh pitcher Hank Gornicki, who began the season with the Pirates' farm in Hollywood, is returned to the parent club about now, sore-armed, in which condition he started in the spring. He worked twice for the Stars, most recently on the 5th, shutting out the Oakland Oaks in his only start on the Coast. With his sore wing, he doesn't work for the Pirates till the 17th of June. In 1943, before entering military service, Gornicki was 9–13 in 42 games for Pittsburgh. He'll pitch seven times this summer, closing out four seasons in the majors.

May 16

Re the Mexican League, it's indicative of a certain national attitude to quote a headline in this week's *Sporting News*: "13 Jumping Beans Placed on O.B. Restricted List." Dodger farmhand Roland Gladu a Canadian-born infielder who played 21 games for the 1944 Braves and hit .338 for Montreal last season, has joined the Mexican League.

This is the day the Tigers sell infielder Billy Hitchcock to Washington for the $7,500 waiver price. He played three games for Detroit, breaking a finger and spraining a thumb (though not necessarily at the same time). This is early in his big league career, which lasts through 1953 (he was Detroit's semiregular shortstop in 1942, before military service). But after Eddie Lake beat him out for the first-string job and Jimmy Bloodworth returned from the Army yesterday, Hitchcock was excess baggage. Washington needs him as insurance for shortstop Cecil Travis, trying to come back on feet frozen during the Battle of the Bulge. Hitchcock plays 98 games for the Senators this year. He'll later manage the Tigers, Orioles and Braves.

The Giants option pitcher Bill Emmerich to Jersey City. "Slim" Emmerich appeared twice this year for New York, April 23 and 26, the last of his two terms in the big leagues. He'll be recalled toward the end of the season, but get no further work with the parent club. In 1945, he was 4–4 in 31 games.

The Braves option outfielder Chet Ross to Indianapolis and pitcher Ray Martin to Evansville. Neither plays in the big leagues this year. Ross was with Boston from 1939 through 1944 but won't be back. He'll finish 1946 with Montreal and spend next year at Milwaukee and

Baltimore. Martin hasn't played in the majors since 1943. Next season, he'll win his only game for Boston.

"Deals of the Week," *The Sporting News* dated May 16

Having played his allotted two games for Pittsburgh this year, on May 7 outfielder Ben Guintini is optioned by the Pirates to Hollywood. He'll be sent back to Pittsburgh in June moved to San Diego, till ends his season.

The Braves option catcher Hugh Poland, who appeared in four games for Boston this year (last of which was May 8), to Seattle. Poland was active in 1943–44 with the Giants and Boston, will return to the big leagues in 1947–48, with the Phillies and Reds. Pitcher Bob (Ace) Williams, after a solitary game for the Braves this season, is also optioned to Seattle, pitching his first game for the Rainiers May 26. Just out of the service, he won't appear again in the majors, though he does get called back — from Hartford — later this year. He had five prewar games for the Braves in 1940, thus accounting for both his seasons in the majors.

The Cardinals option catcher Del Wilber to Columbus (American Association). Babe Wilber, a rookie and former Army officer, only played four times for the Cards this season, the last on April 28. He'll catch, sparingly, for St. Louis, the Phillies and Red Sox between 1947–54, nevertheless leaving a lasting impression on front office people looking for coaches, managers and friends — of which he collects legions.

The Phillies release second baseman Glen Crawford to Portland (PCL). He played one game, adding it to his previous big league total of 86, with the Cardinals and Phillies last year. Philadelphia also releases former defensive standout third baseman Merrill (Pinky) May, who hasn't played since 1943. His son, Milt, will catch in the big leagues from 1970 to 1984, then coach for many years afterward.

Dario Lodigiani of the White Sox, having a great spring at the bat, finally has to go into the hospital today. Having fought off the pain as long as possible, Lodigiani will undergo surgery on his fractured right elbow tomorrow. It'll be over two months, July 26, before he returns to the lineup.

The White Sox sell catcher Vince Castino to Toledo. He spent the last three years with Chicago, but his big league tour is over, without having played a game for these White Sox.

May 18

The A's trade third baseman George Kell to Detroit for outfielder Barney McCosky. McCosky was a prewar star for the Tigers, and his loss is loudly bemoaned by fans in the Motor City, his home town. He will hit .318 this season, but Detroit has enough outfielders, presumably, and no satisfactory third baseman. Kell, not yet 24, is en route to the Hall of Fame, though neither McCosky fans nor anyone else can predict the future. Still, this season Kell will bat .322, at least easing the anguish of naysayers. His acquisition lets the Tigers send Pinky Higgins to Boston tomorrow, without worrying they'll miss him much. Kell, a nonentity in the mind of most, is described in *The New York Times* as "an Arkansas schoolteacher."

The Athletics are busy. Pitcher Norm Brown is sold to Toronto. Brown pitched four times for the A's this year, his second of two brief stays in the majors. Also today, the A's release pitcher Jack Knott, a righthander returned from four years in the Army. He's a decorated hero who received a battlefield commission in the Battle of the Bulge. With an 0–1 record in three games this year, he's wound up his 11 seasons in the major leagues.

John Carden of the Giants makes his debut today in relief against the Cubs, turning in the kind of performance every ball player dreads. In two innings, he surrenders four hits, seven runs (five earned), walk four and hit a batter. His own fielding error results in the pair of unearned runs. He'll never pitch another game in the big leagues.

The Giants send pitcher Jack (Buddy) Brewer to Minneapolis. Brewer was a mound mainstay in 1945 (28 games, 8–6), but only appeared once this year, a month ago. The Giants also option outfielder Jesse Pike, to Jersey City. This was his one year in the big leagues, in which he's appeared 16 times.

Brooklyn pitcher Rube Melton is discharged from the Army. Last active in 1944, he'll appear 23 times this season, going 6–3. Beforehand, he'll go home to his farm in Virginia to get in a little relaxation. (A regular feature in the annual *Baseball Register* of the time is a facsimile of each players' autograph. Melton, whose full name is Reuben Frank Melton, signs as "Frank Melton," which I've never seen used anywhere else. *Macmillan*, to take this a step further, says his name is Reuben Franklin Melton. His first game of the year is June 5th, in relief against the Pirates at Forbes Field. More on *Register* highlights in a moment.)

May 19

Pinky Higgins, aging longtime standout third baseman, is sold to the Red Sox by the Tigers. Discharged from the Navy in February, he played steadily for Detroit (.217 in 18 games) till he came down with the flu early this month and lost his job to Jimmy Outlaw (who, in turn, will be ousted by George Kell). Higgins will share the hot corner for Boston's AL champs (.275, 64 games) with Rip Russell (.208, 80 games) and a couple others. It's Higgins' 14th and last year as a big league player and, while an improvement over Russell, he's no longer physically up to playing every day.

Southpaw pitcher Ray Prim of the Cubs pulls an arm muscle and is out for three months. He'll return to the mound on August 29.

It is on ominous day for the Dodgers, who are suffering already from a flurry of minor injuries. Pete Reiser bounces off the center field wall of Ebbets Field, hurries his throw to the infield and further damages his already-separated shoulder. Pitcher Ed Head's sore arm forces him out in the first inning of the game (against the Reds). Cookie Lavagetto's arm needs rest, so Billy Herman is put in his place at third base and Eddie Stanky, despite a bad thumb, goes back to second base. The Bums are shut out by Ed Heusser, 4–0. Neither Reiser nor Head is out long for the moment, but the hurts contribute to the gradual physical deterioration of each. Lavagetto won't return to the regular lineup for a month, till Herman is traded away.

May 20

Rookie Joe Garagiola, discharged from the Army at Jefferson Barracks, Missouri, reports to the Cardinals in Philadelphia. *The Sporting News* describes him as having "dark, wavy hair." Garagiola has been keenly anticipated as the man who will fill Walker Cooper's shoes. His imminent arrival made it less worrisome to sell Cooper to the Giants in January. Joe will become far more famous, but he'll never be the player Cooper is.

Pitcher Alejandro (Alex) Carrasquel, a Mexican League jumper who pitched with the Senators from 1939 through 1945 and is now White Sox property, wants to come back to the big leagues. Chicago road secretary Frank McMahon says, "Nobody around our club is bothering with him." Carrasquel was released by the Mexican League and has no place to play.

Today is White Sox outfielder Taft Wright's last game till he returns from having his tonsils removed on June 6. Altogether, he'll miss a month.

May 22

The Yankees beat the Tigers, 5–3, at Briggs Stadium. In the 8th inning, a Detroit rally is throttled by an unusual triple play. Eddie Mayo of the Tigers starts the potential comeback by drawing a walk. Jimmy Outlaw singles, sending Mayo to third.

Dick Wakefield then grounds to New York first baseman Nick Etten, who throws to catch Mayo off third. Mayo, trapped between third and home, is tagged out by third sacker Snuffy Stirnweiss. Outlaw, meanwhile, has advanced to second, overruns the base and tries to return. But Wakefield has also gone to second base, arriving at precisely the moment Outlaw gets there.

Trying to make things right, Outlaw breaks toward third, but is tagged out by Yankee second baseman Joe Gordon.

Meanwhile, the New York outfielders, Charlie Keller, Joe DiMaggio and Tommy Henrich, have come in to back up the play, should a ball go astray.

Wakefield, unsure of where he should be, decides to retreat to first base, but is run down by shortstop Phil Rizzuto.

Henrich, the right fielder, virtually an innocent bystander, is somehow stepped on by Wakefield. Henrich isn't even aware of Wakefield spiking him, until his shoe feels wet. It's his blood, flowing out. He's hospitalized, out of action till May 28th, missing almost a week.

Alva (Bear Tracks) Javery, 17-game winner for the Braves in 1943, is released to Toronto by Boston, putting an end to his major league career. His final game was pitched on the 16th. Part of this season, according to *Mac I*, Javery is said to be sidelined by "illness."

Along with that transaction, the Braves option pitcher Earl Reid to Indianapolis, for whom he was 10–7 in 1942, before spending three years in military service. His 1946 two-game major league career ended May 13th.

Cubs catcher Mickey Livingston sprains an ankle. He'll miss a month and a half of the season, but will still play 66 games (.256). Livingston's next appearance will be July 7.

Over the next two days, the Cubs and Dodgers engage in some interesting and exciting byplay in Brooklyn. The festivities begin today, as the Bums' rookie center fielder, Carl Furillo, injures a shoulder, sliding hard into Chicago's Don Johnson at second base. Perhaps not in retaliation, soon Cubs lefthander Johnny Schmitz steps on Pee Wee Reese's foot, spiking the Dodger shortstop. In the tenth inning, Chicago shortstop Lennie Merullo, sliding into second, becomes entangled with second baseman Eddie Stanky of Brooklyn. Both players throw punches, though they mostly roll around on the ground, Stanky's legs briefly holding Merullo's neck in a hammerlock.

Both benches empty onto the field. Merullo gets popped in the eye, he thinks by Reese. Merullo and Stanky are ejected.

Tomorrow during batting practice, Merullo allegedly tells Reese, "Next time you take a sock at me, hit me when I'm looking and I'll break your neck." Standing nearby, Brooklyn outfielder Dixie Walker overhears this and unexpectedly takes a swing at Merullo (according to Merullo). Walker then heads for the Dodger dugout, whereupon Merullo leaps upon him from behind (according to Walker). In moments they're on the ground, fighting. The

Chicago bench empties again, led by first baseman–captain Phil Cavarretta and coach Red Smith (that, of course, may be a one-sided view: Walker says Cavarretta was on his back when he hit Merullo; Merullo tells author Peter Golenbock that Walker slugs him behind the ear while Merullo and Reese are still trading words).

The umpires aren't yet on the field, so Chicago police must intervene to separate the teams. The Dodgers' batboy tries to get all the bats put away, out of reach, a wise and prudent move.

By the time it's all over, Walker, Merullo and Smith are fined $150 each, Reese and Cavarretta $100. Merullo is suspended for eight days; Walker and Smith are hit for five apiece. Walker has also lost 1.5 teeth.

May 23

In a shocking development, Cardinal star southpaw Max Lanier defects to the Mexican League, along with teammates Freddie Martin, a rookie righthander, and regular second baseman Lou Klein, who's reclaimed the position he held on the team's 1943 NL champs, prior to his joining the Coast Guard.

Klein's departure does open the position for young utilityman Red Schoendienst, who fashions the opportunity into a Hall of Fame career. Martin, 30 years old, was on the brink of the big leagues when the war came along. Cardinal property from way back, he's been 2–1 in six games as a rookie and is still well-thought of, but he hasn't really been able to crack the well-stocked St. Louis pitching rotation.

Lanier, on the other hand, was off to a spectacular start, with a 6–0 record (two shutouts, 1.93 ERA, indicating he's currently the best pitcher in the National League). However, he has long feuded with St. Louis owner Sam Breadon over salary. Breadon's final, take-it-or-leave-it offer was a $500 raise over Lanier's previous salary, a raise to $10,500 a year. Given few options at the time, Lanier took it. But when Jorge Pasquel offered him a $25,000 signing bonus and $20,000 a year for five years, Lanier jumped.

A postscript appears in *the New York Times*, quoting a note from Lanier to Schoendienst, his roommate on the team's road trips. "Keep hitting those line drives, kid," Lanier wrote, "I guess this is good-bye for now, but I'll see you next winter and we'll do some hunting together."

On the subject of hunting, in the 1940s, such publications as *The Baseball Register* contain, under each player's name, not only his career records but such information as his ancestry (a violation of countless federal, state and other unspecified laws in decades ahead). Other intrusive tidbits, for instance his spouse's maiden name, and their wedding date, are also to be found. The blanks are filled in by players answering a questionnaire, which they return to the publisher.

Hobbies are a vital part of this information. Overwhelmingly, "hunting and fishing" is the number one hobby of players, managers and coaches. "Golf" and "movies" are also high on the list. As this is a day when most players must take second or third jobs in the off-season to make ends meet, their hobbies somehow get shoehorned into otherwise-busy lives. It's often managed by committee, several players taking a hunting trip together in the fall, before dispersing to tend gas stations, toil in oil fields, or work as salesmen and the like. Ball players, notoriously, make little use of the winter months to seriously prepare themselves for life after baseball. Nor do many prepare for the next season: weight training, for instance, is widely frowned upon as injurious to a baseball player's conditioning.

Phillies third baseman Jim Tabor is out with an injured arm, and won't be back in the lineup till June 16.

Today's *Sporting News* headlines a burgeoning dilemma, in part created by a nationwide rail strike that doesn't last long but scares everyone not ready to take newer, postwar alternatives. Before the crisis ends, the Office of Defense Transportation suggests train schedules may be stretched to the crippling point. ODT declares teams should look into bus schedules, or plan car-pooling on the shortest trips (as a for-instance, in Detroit, the Tigers hire eight cars to transport players to Chicago for a series against the White Sox).

Some teams, notably the Yankees, decide they'll fly from city to city. Many players love it, or at least say they do. Some players say no, thanks, no way. Players Red Ruffing, Frankie Crosetti and Bill Wight refuse to fly for the moment, and are allowed to travel by train. After a particularly bad excursion, Phil Rizzuto momentarily swears off airliners. However, later in the season, only Crosetti will remain a holdout. Next year, he'll still be on the "not for me, thanks," list.

Says Boston writer John Drohan in *The Sporting News*, "The Red Sox' first flight of the season — from Chicago to St. Louis, May 15 — was a howling success! That is, most of the boys are howling they don't want to fly again." In fact, the Bosox return to train travel almost immediately. In the late 1950s and early 1960s, the migration of the majors to California and the South will make it impractical to continue riding the rails.

The American Baseball Guild says it now has 90 percent membership on the Pittsburgh Pirates, and insists on meeting with team president Bill Benswanger to talk about money and working conditions.

"Deals of the Week," Sporting News issue of May 23

The Reds sell outfielder Howie Moss, discharged this spring from the Navy, to Baltimore. Moss played seven games with Cincinnati between April 21st and May 7th. He'll later play eight games for Cleveland. In between, he'll lead the International League with 38 home runs and next year, again, with 53. Yet, in 22 career big league games dating back to 1942 with the Giants, he'll hit no homers. Such is the way of many a minor league slugger.

Outfielder Earl Naylor is sent by Brooklyn to Montreal, after his final three games in the majors (concluding May 14th). Naylor came to the Dodgers from the Cardinals, for whom he didn't play at all, early in the season.

The Senators send first baseman Jack Sanford and outfielder Ray Goolsby to Chattanooga. Sanford, back from four years in the Army, played ten games with Washington this season, ending his last of three trips to the majors. (This is John *Howard* Sanford, not John *Stanley* Sanford, no visible relation, who at the moment has just turned 17; *that* Jack Sanford will be a pitcher, with a pretty good big league career, but it won't begin for another decade; neither of these are *Fred* Sanford, also a pitcher, recently sent to Toledo by the Browns.)

Here's a good story about *this* Jack Sanford. While a student at the University of Richmond in 1939, he was given a workout at Griffith Stadium, with Clark Griffith himself on hand. An "around the horn" throw eluded Sanford and conked Griffith on the head, knocking him out. Old Griff, the Silver Fox, somehow was so impressed, upon waking up, the boy was signed on the spot.

Goolsby played his only three big league games in April. He remains a prospect — this year he'll hit .306 down in the Southern Association — but he never makes it back.

The Athletics option outfielder Bruce Konopka to San Diego. Konopka, in his third and last big league season, has been in 14 games so far for Philadelphia. He'll play 25 times out on the Coast for the Padres, hitting .202. In late June, he comes back, is demoted again, to Toronto in July, where he bats .282 in 61 games, then comes back to the A's again.

May 24

Pitcher Ted Lyons of the White Sox is named Chicago's manager, replacing Jimmie Dykes, who had run the team on the field since 1934. Dykes was ill and unable to manage this year till late April (in the record books, he's credited with a won-lost record of 10–20). According to reports, yesterday he demanded a two-year extension to his contract, resigning when he was refused (it's possible he was encouraged by the Chisox front office). On August 8, he'll become manager of the Hollywood Stars, out in the Coast League.

Lyons will lead the Sox through 1948. It's the end of his 21-year big league pitching career, though. His first official announcement as manager is that he's retired as a player, having pitched his last five games this year. A 20-game winner three times, he was also a 20-game loser twice, lifetime 260–230, all for the White Sox. Lyons will receive a plaque at Cooperstown in 1955.

Knocking the Dykes/Lyons story off the headlines, "Marse Joe" McCarthy, manager of the Yankees, reportedly resigns after holding the job since 1931. Long rumored to have a considerable drinking problem, McCarthy cites ill health. He and team president Larry MacPhail, at best, have not been close, the effect of which may have resulted in McCarthy getting dumped at the first opportunity.

The catalyst for the change, wherever its impetus, was a loud tongue-lashing McCarthy gave carousing pitcher Joe Page, in front of the whole team, while on an airliner flight. McCarthy couldn't abide Page's off-the-field behavior, which constantly provoked sparks between them. After the trip, McCarthy went home to his farm near Buffalo, his health somewhat the worse for wear, and didn't return.

The fact remains, however, McCarthy led the Yanks to eight pennants and seven World Championships between 1932 and 1943. He'll be remembered as one of the game's great managers, perhaps the greatest.

He's replaced by popular catcher Bill Dickey, who says he'll continue as the regular backstop for New York. Rumor is, Dickey was offered the managerial reins of the Yanks' Newark farm team when he returned from the Navy last year, but he declined. Pundit Dan Daniel writes in *The Sporting News* that the New York job has been long coveted by Dickey. But Bill grows to hate it, apparently (and MacPhail, possibly), quitting before the end of the season.

McCarthy goes on to pilot Red Sox powerhouses of 1948–50. Dickey, after he leaves, returns in 1949 to teach Yogi Berra to be a proficient catcher. Berra, down at Newark most of this season, will learn his lessons well.

Marty Marion, shortstop of the Cardinals, refuses to fly with the team to Cincinnati from New York. Taking the train, he misses a three-game series against the Reds, then picks up the club in Chicago. Marion gives his chronic bad back as the reason he won't fly.

May 25

Cleveland outfielder George Case is sidelined with *his* back problems; he's been out since the 19th. Still under study by team doctors, Case doesn't accompany the Indians on their trip to visit the Browns today. He will be back in the lineup when the Tribe returns home to play the Tigers on the 28th.

Maybe guys are just getting tired. On the 20th, after a month of spring training and more than a month of the regular season, Joe DiMaggio missed starting a game for the first time this year, due to a groin injury. He later pinch-hit and played center field, but this is just the first of his physical woes this season.

On the 21st, pinch-hitter Roy (Stormy) Weatherly of the Yanks, ex–Cleveland Indian just out of the Army, got his first hit of 1946, tried to stretch it to a double, caught his spikes on the bag, was carried off the field with a severe sprain of his right ankle. It was his only hit of the year, the only one he gets in the big leagues till 1950, for the Giants. Cubs third baseman Stan Hack, getting old as ballplayers go, was sidelined with a thigh injury on the 19th and won't return till the 28th.

On the 22nd, pitcher Mel Harder of the Indians was hit on the hand by a Glenn Russell line drive and had to leave the Tribe's game against the Red Sox. He'll be out of action till July 1st. Today against the Browns, Kenny Keltner of the Indians takes a Bob Dillinger grounder in the jaw and is carted off to the hospital (just a bad but painful bruise). White Sox coach Bing Miller has smallpox (later reports say it's chicken pox, which also fells trainer Packy Schwartz). American League umpire Art Pasarella, who suffered a broken jaw in Philadelphia, just returned to duty on the 23rd.

Looking on the bright side, catcher Al Lopez of Pittsburgh made his first start of the season on the 19th of May. He broke his hand on April 20th.

In Bill Dickey's first game as a manager, Yankee pitcher Frank Hiller makes his major league debut, first of his three mound appearances in 1946 (no wins, two losses). He had arm and knee surgery earlier this year, apparently while still in the Army. First baseman Steve Souchock debuts, too, pinch-hitting, after three years in the Army, where he was a hero in the Battle of the Bulge. He bats .302 in 47 games. Not a bad start, but he doesn't become the player many expect him to. Slow to round into shape, he won't play a game in the field until mid–July.

May 26

White Sox first baseman Murrell (Jake) Jones, World War II Navy flying ace, breaks his arm in a collision with Detroit's Eddie Lake, in game two of a twin bill. Jones is limited to the 24 games he's already played; the season, for him, is over.

In the first half of the doubleheader, Chicago pitcher John Rigney reinjures the shoulder he originally hurt in a game on the island of Guam, last July 4th. He'll make one start on June 6, otherwise be inactive till July 18. He'll only pitch 15 times in 1946, 11 more in 1947, then hang up his glove. In his case, the future, regardless, is somewhat secure: five years ago, he married Dorothy Comiskey, one of the White Sox heirs; Rigney will assume a role in the front office when his playing days are over.

Cardinals catcher Joe Garagiola makes his major league debut today. This is the only season Garagiola doesn't play in the shadow of his lifelong pal from the old neighborhood in St. Louis, Larry (Yogi) Berra. As Berra comes up to stay and turns into a major star, Garagiola will fade out as a player, spend the rest of his life telling funny Berra stories, to bring him far more attention than playing ever does.

Giants manager Mel Ott benches himself for the second time this season, complaining he can't see the ball clearly. He has but two hits in 41 at-bats, for an .049 batting average. He'll finish at .074, in his 21st year with the team.

The Montreal Royals complete their first homestand, with questions about Jackie Robinson's ability and potential for stardom somewhat put to rest. Having played each of the Royals' first 36 games, he's hitting .347, playing the unfamiliar position of second base almost flawlessly.

Third baseman Billy Johnson of the Yankees, just back from the Army, plays his first game since 1943, as a pinch-hitter against the Red Sox. It'll be June 9 before he can reclaim the hot corner: Snuffy Stirnweiss, last year's American League batting champ and New York's starting second baseman during the war, has been playing third so well it's been hard to dislodge him. The same day Johnson takes over third, Stirnweiss will begin to dislodge the Yanks' prewar second sacker, Joe Gordon.

After starting the opener of today's doubleheader against the Dodgers, Phillies' pitcher Al Jurisich is sidelined with arthritis in his arm, according to manager Ben Chapman. The pitcher isn't out for long. His next game will be on June 2, when he starts the nightcap of a doubleheader in Pittsburgh.

May 27

Former Milwaukee Brewer owner Bill Veeck adamantly denies he's trying to buy the Cleveland Indians. "Where would I get that kind of money?" he asks, according to a blurb in *The Sporting News*.

Outfielder Danny Litwhiler of the Cardinals, just out of the Army, appears for the first time this season, as a pinch-hitter. He went into the Army in March 1945, after holding down right field for the 1944 World Champs. As previously illustrated, the Cards don't need everyone they own. Litwhiler is just passing through, on his way to the Braves early next month.

Infielder Billy Burich of the Phillies is discharged from military service. He'll appear in a couple of games next month, then find himself shuttled down to Houston.

Prewar Dodger-Cardinal-Red-Phillie outfielder Ernie Koy, who hit .301 in 1940, is released by the Phillies, after recently becoming a civilian again. "Chief" Koy, half–Native American and once a star fullback for the Texas Longhorns, is through in baseball, without playing a game in 1946. Already 32 when he exchanged his Philadelphia uniform for military dress three years ago, he lost his career to the war. It's an epitaph of great, sad redundancy throughout the game this year. Back in 1938, he hit a home run in his first major league at-bat.

The Cubs sell first baseman Heinz Becker to Nashville, going to the minors at his own request, in order to play regularly somewhere (with Eddie Waitkus and Phil Cavarretta ahead of him in Chicago, playing time was scarce). Becker was born in Berlin, Germany, a certain distinction (though he now lives in Dallas and considers himself a Texan). He played only nine games for Chicago but will bat a torrid .379 during 51 games in the Southern Association, breaking in with a home run two days from now. It's the longest hit in Nashville since Red Ruffing belted one to dead center field, ten years ago. Becker will return to the big leagues to play 50 games more with the Cleveland Indians, batting .299 later this year for them. That's an interesting tale, which you'll read shortly. But it's practically the end, not the beginning, of his four years in the majors. Next year, he'll play only twice for Cleveland, his final two games, then limp back to the minors on extremely bad feet (bunions).

May 28

Those innovative Yankees have done it again, adding "hit" and "error" lights to the scoreboard at the Stadium. Two decades ago, numbers on uniforms created controversy. Clark Griffith has lately been urged to put more than a "W" on his team's home uniform shirts. "W" stands for "Washington," the Old Fox says: our nation's capital needs no further identification. The team's flannels bore WASHINGTON in 1901 and 1908, NATIONALS in 1905, so it wouldn't be without precedent, but it won't be.

May 29

Cincinnati outfielder Garland (Butch) Lawing debuts. He'll play only two games, then quickly find himself on the Giants.

Brooklyn's Pete Reiser, having run into yet another center field wall, has to take himself out of action, a week after his last accident. His arm hurts, he says, from his shoulder to his elbow and on down to his fingertips, which are numb. Though Reiser will pinch hit some, he won't return to the outfield till June 10, almost two weeks from now. Over the course of the season, he only plays 122 games; his .277 batting average far down from his .343 batting title in 1941. He will, despite it all, again lead the National League in stolen bases (34, his most ever) and set a record stealing home (seven times).

Catcher Ken Silvestri of the Yankees, working today's game with pitcher Red Ruffing, suffers a fracture of his right index finger. He'll be lost a little over three weeks, till June 21. Silvestri plays only 13 games for New York all season.

The Browns sell outfielder Lou Finney and pitcher Al Milnar to the Phillies. It isn't much of a deal. Milnar, about to wind up an eight-year major league career, was 1–1 in four games for the Browns, though he did pitch a shutout against Cleveland for his only win. He won't receive a decision in one game for Philadelphia—can't get out of the first inning in his lone attempt. Finney, in his 14th year in the majors, has played in 16 games for St. Louis, batting .300, but the Phillies will return him to the Browns unused, and send Milnar packing with him, on June 12. They'll both be given outright releases upon returning to St. Louis. Finney ends his big league career next year, back with the Phils, pinch-hitting a few times. Having found him useless this year, it begs a question about why they acquire him for 1947.

The Browns unconditionally release pitcher Steve Sundra. Sundra has returned from the war with two bad knees. One and eleven for the 1939 Yankees, he went 15–11 for the 1943 Browns and was briefly sensational (2–0, 1.42) in three games before entering the Army in 1944. But Sundra was able to work only twice this season, his last in the big leagues.

The Giants option first baseman Mike Schemer to Jersey City and pitcher John Carden to Richmond today.

Schemer played 31 games for New York in 1945, just one in 1946, pinch-batting in late April. Carden's sole appearance in the majors was May 18, described earlier. Sent down to Class B, the pitcher will slowly work his way up the ladder of the Giants' farm system. In February of 1949, preparing to report for spring training with the Giants' top farm team at Minneapolis, Carden is killed in a freak accident at his rural home in Mexia, Texas, about a hundred miles northeast of Killeen, where he was born. Mexia is a tiny community where, if you want something fixed, you do it yourself. Carden's phone gives him continual trouble and, for the umpteenth time, he climbs the service pole outside to try repairing the line, so his wife won't have to cope with the problem while he's away at training camp. By some horrible mistake, he brushes against a power line, which shoots 2300 volts through his body, electrocuting him.

May 30

The Sporting News is not issued this date. Because of a change in publication procedures, its next issue will be dated June 5.

Cincinnati's Bob Malloy, out of the Navy and pitching for the first time since 1944, makes his initial appearance of the season. This year, at 2–5 with a 2.75 ERA, will be the best of his five in the big leagues, which cover the period beginning in 1943 and ending with 1949.

Backup catcher Eddie McGah of the Red Sox, catching Tex Hughson in warmups, gets a finger in the way and it's split by Tex's pitch. McGah is out only a few days, returning on June 3. Hughson, on the other hand, tears tendons in his wrist today and won't return till June 16.

Senators infielder George Myatt makes his first start since breaking his ankle on Opening Day, taking the field against the Red Sox at Fenway Park (he did pinch-run on the 19th, pinch-hit the 25th). He soon reinjures his leg and may face surgery to repair the damage.

May 31

Phillies southpaw Dick Mulligan enters Temple University Hospital to have his tonsils out. He won't return to the mound till July 2, missing a month.

Red Sox manager Joe Cronin makes his retirement as a player official, removing himself from the active list. He hasn't played at all this year, only three times in 1945 before he broke his ankle early in the season. A decade from now, he'll be elected to the Hall of Fame as a shortstop, where he last played in 1942. In the meantime, he'll become vice-president of the team in 1948, replacing himself in the dugout with Joe McCarthy. Cronin, who at 26 was known as "The Boy Manager" when he led the Senators to their last pennant, will serve as American League president from 1959 to 1973.

June 1

Cubs outfielder Andy Pafko steps on a ball and slips, sustaining a fractured ankle. He'll be out till July 18, when he pinch-hits. He'll return to his regular center field spot the 19th, after which he'll fracture his right arm August 27, after which he won't play again till next year. For Pafko and the Cubs, it's a cruddy season. He'll hit .283 and play only 65 games; Chicago will finish a poor third. It ain't all Andy's fault: at times, it seems *everybody's* injured. The Cubs, last year's champs, will end up 11 games above .500, but 14½ games out. They won't see the light of day again for two decades. Pafko's ankle doesn't appear to set up right, so a new cast is put on, next week. "Handy Andy Pafko," they call him.

Cleveland sold infielder Blas Monaco to Seattle at the end of May. His only other big league season was 1937, when he played a handful of games for Cleveland. Monaco played a dozen times for the 1946 Indians. His final big league game was May 22; his first for Seattle will be on the 5th of June.

Today, infielder Ducky Detweiler of the Braves, recalled from Indianapolis on May 25, pinch-hits for his only big league appearance of 1946. He made it into 12 Boston games in 1942; that's his whole major league career.

You may wonder who the stout, matronly lady is, over there in the Griffith Stadium box seats today, as the Nationals begin a homestand against the Tigers. Well, it's none other than the First Lady of the Land, Bess Truman, a baseball fan in her own right, taking in a ball game with her daughter, Margaret. It's the first time in anyone's memory that the president's family has attended — without the president.

June 2

Cincinnati pitcher Howie Fox rejoins the Reds, after more than a month recovering from his appendectomy.

With Brooklyn batting in the fifth frame of the nightcap in today's twin bill at Cincinnati, Dodger pitcher Art (Sandy) Herring, riding a potential no-hitter, asks Leo Durocher to let someone bat for him. Pete Reiser draws the assignment and the pitching is placed in the capable hands of Hugh Casey. Durocher is booed by the Crosley Field crowd for abandoning a no-hit bid, but Herring insists his arm began to tighten and he could pitch no more. The Bums get a 1–0 shutout and sweep the doubleheader. It's one of only two starting assignments for Herring, the other to come in late September, after 23 turns in relief. He'll gather another victory over the Reds, inching Brooklyn closer to St. Louis, during the closing days of the pennant race. Herring, a journeyman, has been around since 1929, when he broke in with the Tigers. He's pitching the best of his major league career and will compile a 7–2 record with a 3.35 ERA. Next year, though, he'll be at Pittsburgh, end up at 1–3 and hang 'em up, at age 40.

June 3

The Reds sell outfielder Mike McCormick to the Braves. After batting .216 in 23 games for Cincinnati, the 1940 World Series star will play 59 times at Boston (.262). McCormick's season will end at the end of August, with torn ligaments in a leg, but he'll return for two solid seasons in Boston, including .303 for the Braves' 1948 pennant winners. The Dodgers trade Pete Reiser for McCormick, when they finally gave up on him, in December of 1948. McCormick will complete a decade in the majors in 1951, playing with the Senators.

A's pitcher Bobo Newsom (Louis Norman Newsom is his real name; many folks refer to him as "Buck," though his more lasting nickname is "Bobo," which he calls everybody else) is granted his unconditional release. He's been after Connie Mack for more money, which Mr. Mack says he doesn't have, certainly not the $12,500 Newsom required. Since the pitcher wants out, Mr. Mack appears happy to discard the aging Bobo, who lost 20 games last year and is only 3–5 now, ridding himself of an expensive 3-and-5 in the bargain. Then, maybe, he can sign a younger, less-demanding replacement. Ability isn't a major sticking point, it appears, as the Athletics aren't going anywhere in 1946.

In two days, Newsom will sign with the Senators, for whom he'll accomplish an 11–8 record. It'll be his fourth fling in Washington. Hold on: he'll leave for the Yankees next season, then pitch for the Giants and (again) the Athletics and, in 1952, toil for Washington a fifth time, before being dealt back to the Athletics, before he finally leaves the game in 1953, at 46.

Going after a Dutch Leonard pop fly today, Detroit center fielder Hoot Evers, just recovered from a broken ankle, suffers a broken jaw in a collision with teammate Eddie Mayo. Second baseman Mayo is also hurt: charley horse and bruised chest. Pitcher Stubby Overmire is hurt, too, sliding into second base, spraining his pitching hand. He'll be out of action till June 22, his only game between now and July 4. Evers will be out till June 21. Mayo, not believed as seriously injured, won't return to the lineup till July 13.

Infielder Ben Steiner, who played his last of three 1946 games for the Red Sox on the 21st of last month, appears with the Toronto Maple Leafs for the first time today, against the Jersey City Little Giants. He shared second base for Boston last year, playing in 77 games, but that was before Bobby Doerr returned from the Army in the off-season.

Overloaded with catchers and potential catchers, the Yankees give Mike Garbark his outright release. Garbark played 89 games for the 1944 Yanks, another 50 last year, but hasn't played at all in 1946, and won't again in the big leagues, even though he'll play pro ball into the 1950s. Garbark's older brother, Bob, played seven seasons in the majors, finishing in 1945 with the Red Sox.

Over in Newark, Garbark runs into another bevy of backstops. Charley Fallon, Larry Berra and Bill Deininger are already there. The light-hitting Deininger (.188) is odd man out, followed in mid-month by Fallon, who opts to enter the carpentry business run by his dad and brother in Quincy, Massachusetts. Later, after a Berra broken wrist, Fallon will unretire and return to the Bears.

Marty Marion, shortstop of the Cardinals, hurts his arm in today's game against the Giants in New York. He'll miss the next three games in Boston and be limited to pinch-hitting on the 7th, opening a four-game set against the Phillies.

June 4

Giants pitcher Bob Carpenter hurts his pitching elbow, while ahead of the Cubs, one to nothing. He suffers ligament damage and can pitch just one more time in June, in relief against the Phillies on the 29th.

Pittsburgh shortstop Billy Cox is benched in the second game of today's twin bill against Brooklyn, his play suffering due to a recurrence of the malaria he contracted in Europe, with the Army. Cox, away from 1942 to 1945, will hit .290 this season, but he's pretty weak right now. He's played 35 of the Pirates' first 37 games and the pace is telling on him. He'll see limited duty until the 23rd, when he gets five straight hits against the Braves. Yes, this is the same Billy Cox who becomes a great Brooklyn third baseman.

The Pirates option pitcher Jim Hopper to Columbus, Ohio (American Association). After two early-season games with Pittsburgh—the only ones he ever pitches in the big leagues—Hopper at Columbus works 15 times with a 1–4 record. On July 8, he'll move further down, to Birmingham (4 games, 1–1).

June 5

Red Sox pitchers Bill Butland (today) and Charley Wagner (tomorrow) finally get to start for the high-flying Bosox, who're hip deep in mound talent. For "Broadway Charley" (perhaps excepting Leo Durocher, Wagner is baseball's snazziest, classiest dresser, thus his nickname), it's his first game since 1942, prior to his entering the Navy that November. He's been suffering aftereffects of dysentery, the illness that first laid him low in the Philippines and will limit him to his final eight games as a professional ball player. Next season, he'll become Boston's assistant farm director.

Butland, who was in the Army roughly the same length of time, has also been slow getting into shape.

White Sox catcher Tom Jordan breaks into the lineup with a triple and two doubles, 3-for-4 against the Yankees in New York today. Jordan played briefly in 1944, then joined the "voluntary retired" list, apparently working in civilian or defense activities. He was injured in spring training.

The Yankees option catcher Bill Drescher to Kansas City, in exchange for Gus Niarhos, promoted after 17 games for the Blues. Niarhos' catching skills are needed. First-stringer Aaron Robinson has had to fight off injuries; backup Ken Silvestri is on the shelf till the 21st, and, though no one realizes it, in a week new manager Bill Dickey will catch his last game. As for Drescher, he caught 33 games for the Yankees in 1945, plus five more this year (in an eight-day stretch in late May), closing out his brief stay in the big leagues.

The Yanks also sell pitcher Charley Stanceau to the Phillies today, for whom he starts his first game on the 16th, the bottom half of a twin bill against Pittsburgh. Stanceau, 3–3 with New York's great World Series champions in 1941, has pitched only three times in 1946. It's been almost a month since his last game. He'll work 14 times with the Phils (2–4), ending his major league career.

Cleveland farmhand Dale Mitchell makes his pro debut for Oklahoma City. Pride of the Oklahoma Sooners before and after the war (batting .507 this spring), he's a veteran of 37 months with the Air Force in Europe. Mitchell will lead the Texas League with .337 at Ok City. In September, he'll be called up to Cleveland. Mitchell's 11 seasons in the big leagues (.312 career) will end, ignobly, with his taking a called strike three to end Don Larsen's perfect game in the 1956 World Series. Unfortunately, that's what we will remember most about Mitchell, despite his being a good outfielder and fine hitter.

The Indians sell ex–Cub infielder Charlie Brewster to Milwaukee, after the last three games of a three-year big league career. He says he's going to look into the Mexican League unless he gets a third of the purchase price. "Here I am, 30 years old," he says, "and still kicking around for peanuts." It's not disclosed whether he gets his percentage *or* peanuts, but he begins play for the Brewers tomorrow, appears in 104 games, bats an even .300, and runs off a 15-game hit streak in late June–early July.

"Deals of the Week," *The Sporting News* issue of June 5

The Red Sox send outfielder Sam Mele to Scranton. Mele, who'll manage the Minnesota Twins to a pennant in 1965, won't play his first regular-season big league game till next spring.

Infielder Danny Reynolds, who played his lone season in the majors last year, is sold by the White Sox to Shreveport. Also sent to Shreveport is Phillies infielder Fred Daniels, who, like Reynolds, saw big league service just in 1945.

TSN's announcements this week include a transaction of May 23. The A's optioned pitcher Herman Besse to Toronto. Up and down with Philadelphia before he went to war, he pitched his final seven big league games this year, most recently against the White Sox on May 21. He pitched his first game with the Maple Leafs the First of June.

It's noted in a column adjacent to "Deals" that pitcher Johnny Gee, who's been on the voluntary retired list, has applied to rejoin the Giants. Gee missed last season with a sore left arm, which has plagued him throughout his career. The 6'8" hurler says it's all better now and he wants to return. Badly in need of pitching help, the Giants welcome Gee back. Beginning mid–July, he pitches the last 13 games of his six-year big league career, going 2 and 4 for New York, with a 3.99 earned run average.

Red Sox catcher Frankie Pytlak, sidelined with an arm injury, has left the club to see his family physician in Buffalo. He's been placed on the voluntary retired list and will play no more in the major leagues. Soon, he'll have surgery, performed by the noted orthopedist, Dr. Robert F. Hyland, in St. Louis. Pytlak, by the way, at 5'6" is the shortest big league catcher since Cracker Schalk, honest backstop of the Black Sox.

Minor league note: Billy Goodman, 1944 sensation with the Atlanta Crackers who hit .336 at age 18, rejoins the team after being discharged from the Navy. *The Sporting News* says he carries "a $30,000 price tag." He won't be really ready for the major leagues till 1948, when he hits .310 in his first full year with the Red Sox. In 1946, in 86 games for the Crackers, he'll hit .389. Ahead of him are 16 seasons in the big leagues and a 1950 AL batting title. With so many "can't miss" youngsters emerging from the war, Goodman is one of a relatively small group who really can't miss.

June 6

White Sox outfielder Taft Wright, out of the lineup since May 20, goes into Chicago's Mercy Hospital to have his tonsils removed. He'll be back in the lineup on June 21, just over two weeks from now.

Chisox pitcher John Rigney, who started today's game in New York, has been sent back to Chicago for treatment of adhesions in his right shoulder.

June 7

Garland Lawing is bought by the Giants from the Reds to fill the hole that will be created with the release of Vince DiMaggio tomorrow. Lawing, who hit .000 with Cincinnati, will raise his average to .167 in eight games for New York. In his only big league season, he is headed for history's back closet. Presently, he's got an upset stomach and won't be able to play till the 10th, when he pinch-hits against his old teammates, the Reds.

Pittsburgh players, voting as members of the American Baseball Guild, decide not to strike their game against the Giants tonight. Pitcher Rip Sewell, infielder Jimmy Brown and a few others were dead-set against the strike, but infielder Lee Handley says the vote failed because of respect the players have for team president Bill Benswanger.

Max Butcher, 10-year big league vet, mainstay of Pittsburgh pitching staffs during the war but cut loose this spring, has signed with the semipro Dormont club of the Greater Pittsburgh League. He'll spend part of this season down in Class C, with Raleigh in the Carolina League (5 games, 2–2) and in Class D, with Welch of the Appalachian League (7 games, 4–3). Max was 10–8 for last year's Pirates but won't pitch professionally again after this year.

The Dodgers come into Chicago not knowing what to expect, given their brawl with the Cubs last month in Brooklyn. Nothing untoward happens, though there are a few confrontations, such as another between Lennie Merullo and Pee Wee Reese. Dixie Walker challenges the whole Cubs bench, but nothing comes of it. Chicago wins all three games and the Dodgers are happy to get out of town, heading down to St. Louis. There, pennant race aside, Pete Reiser and Ed Head seek medical advice about their shoulder problems, from the same

Dr. Hyland mentioned a couple of days ago. Reiser is told he should consider surgery after the season, to have his separated shoulder wired together. Head, who last pitched on June 4, is incapacitated by scar tissue in his shoulder, and about the best he can do for it is rest. He'll miss a month this time, won't pitch till the 4th of July.

Pitcher Johnny Beazley of the Cardinals, 21-game winner in 1942 before he entered the Air Force, hurts his arm today against the Phillies. He won't rejoin the team until the 21st, meanwhile working out with the crosstown Browns after a short rest.

Stan Musial of the Cards takes over first base for good, playing the unfamiliar position throughout the rest of the season. Next year, Stan will be a first baseman exclusively, then return to the outfield, almost full-time, into 1950. In the 1950s, he'll split time between first and outfield.

The Giants sell Vince DiMaggio to San Francisco, land of his birth. In 15 games since coming over from the Phillies, he hasn't got a base hit. He says New York didn't give him a fair chance, but statistics is statistics. After a slow drive across the country with his pregnant wife, loudly declaring he might just go to Mexico, DiMaggio finally agrees to terms with the Seals on the 22nd.

Pitcher Al (Boots) Hollingsworth has been sold by the Browns to the White Sox. Hollingsworth, a very nice man who'll later (1951–53) manage the Houston Buffs of the Texas League, is in the last of his 11 years pitching in the big leagues. He worked five times for St. Louis and will appear in 21 games for Chicago, beginning the 9th.

June 8

Catcher Frank Mancuso of the Browns reinjures his back, first hurt in a wartime paratroop training jump. St. Louis' other catchers, Joe Schultz and Hank Helf, are also hurt, but they'll have to play that way, as they're all the team's got.

Detroit third baseman George Kell pulls a charley horse and is out of the lineup till June 12. He'll be shelved again when his calf muscle resnaps on the 22nd and he will be laid up, once more, till July 4.

June 9

Vernal (Nippy) Jones, infielder of the Cardinals, recently out of the Army, makes his major league debut, as a pinch-hitter and replacement for second baseman Red Schoendienst in the opener of a doubleheader against the Phillies. Some sources place his debut yesterday, but he isn't in a box score till today.

The Cardinals sell outfielder Danny Litwhiler to the Braves. Litwhiler, recently discharged from the Army, played for the Cards in two World Series. He'll hit an overall .286 this season. With the Phillies in 1942, he set the record for fielding average in 150-plus games by an outfielder, 1.000. His place on the St. Louis roster is taken by Nippy Jones.

Cincinnati pitcher George Burpo debuts. Also playing his first major league game is Yankee catcher Gus Niarhos, back from Kansas City.

Outfielder Max West of the Reds is sidelined with an infection in his back, from now through the 15th and again from the 22nd through July 7. He'll return to limited action after the All-Star break, pinch-hitting on the 12th of next month, but won't resume full-time duty till the end of July.

Detroit catcher Paul Richards collides with first baseman Hank Greenberg, tears ligaments in his knee and is out till July 3. Pitcher Johnny Gorsica of the Tigers makes his first appearance of the season in the nightcap of today's doubleheader against the Red Sox. Discharged from the Navy in March after a year away, he's apparently been injured or out of shape.

Athletics pitcher Everett Fagan makes his first appearance of the year, in relief against the Browns. Returning after military service since 1943, he's in his last of two seasons in the majors: he'll pitch 20 times, all in relief.

Having been optioned to Buffalo by the Red Sox (for whom he last played on May 16) May 29, third baseman Ernie Andres goes 1-for-3 today, then is returned to Boston, after playing that one game. The Bosox will move him on to Minneapolis, where he'll get into the lineup on the 15th.

After pitching in relief today, Yankees righthander Frank Hiller will be sent to Johns Hopkins Hospital in Baltimore on the 11th, for an examination of his still-ailing arm. After that, he'll proceed to join the Newark Bears, where he's been optioned, on the 14th. He won't be back in the big leagues till he pitches for the Yanks, again, in 1948.

The Phillies will sell catcher Hal Spindel to Los Angeles on the 18th, after playing his one 1946 game for Philadelphia today. However, he doesn't go all that willingly and will initially be suspended for refusing the assignment. This marks the end of a brief big league career which began in 1939 and didn't pick up again till 1945, when he appeared in three dozen games for the Phils.

June 10

Wartime Yankee pitcher Mel Queen is discharged from a year and a half in the Army today and will rejoin the team tomorrow. Having pitched some games in Hawaii, he declares he's in good shape and ready to play. But when he returns to action June 29 against the Athletics, he won't fare well, nor will he on July 5 against Washington. In 14 games, he'll post a 1–1 record.

June 11

Ex-Reds pitcher Gene Thompson starts for the Giants against Cincinnati and develops a sore arm to go along with his bad knee. He'll be sidelined till pitching relief on the 29th.

The Reds sell pitcher Frankie Dasso to Hollywood, where his first start comes the 15th, a one-hitter against San Diego. Dasso pitched 16 games for Cincinnati last season, two games in 1946, most recently on June 6, completing his stay in the majors. He returns to the league where he racked up a 20–19 record at San Diego in 1944. Back in 1941, he was 15–15 for Hollywood.

June 12

The Pirates trade outfielder Johnny ("Jack") Barrett to the Braves for third baseman–outfielder Chuck Workman. Barrett's in his last of his five seasons in the big leagues, which will be short-circuited by injury. He led the NL in stolen bases in 1944. Workman's six years in the majors also end this season. He hit 25 homers for Boston in 1945.

Randy Heflin, Red Sox lefthander, pitches his last of five big league games this season, winding up a two-year career in the majors. Heflin will be sent to Louisville, June 18, but pitches only three times there. Having checked every league down through Class B and finding no other evidence of him, it's assumed he's hurt and can't pitch; he also may balk at going, and prefers sitting it out. The Red Sox will recall him in late summer, but he's worked all the big league games he ever will.

First baseman Joe Kuhel of Washington, having lost his job to imminent AL bat champ Mickey Vernon, requests his release and signs with the White Sox. Known as a superb fielder, Kuhel's in his 17th big league season and will hit a combined .264, not far off his lifetime .277. In 1948-49, he'll return to the Nats as their manager.

Branch Rickey is reelected president of the Dodgers by the team's board of directors. His power is still on the ascendancy, though Walter O'Malley, vice president and team secretary who disagrees with Rickey's financial policies, is gathering his forces. It'll take him four more years, but O'Malley will have his way.

The Phillies option shortstop Bill Burich to Houston after the final two games in a pair of big league seasons (he played briefly in 1942, before going into the military).

Veteran catcher Don Padgett is sold by the Dodgers to the Braves. Padgett's been around since 1937, with time out for the Navy. He batted .167 in 19 games with Brooklyn this year and will hit .255 in 44 more games for Boston.

"Deals of the Week" in today's issue of *The Sporting News*

The Pirates sold infielder Pete Coscarart to San Diego on June 1st. Coscarart, who's finished the last three games of a nine-year big league career, balked at returning to the Coast League and said he'd join the Mexican League instead. He was, after all, on the All-Star team as a prewar Dodger, regular second baseman for the wartime Pirates. Instead of Mexico, though, he'll enter the Padres' lineup on the 14th and hit .215 in 76 games.

June 13

The Pirates option pitcher Aldon "Lefty" Wilkie to Hollywood, at the end of his three seasons in the big leagues. He's from Zealandia, Saskatchewan, Canada, hotbed of baseball talent. Lefty will post a 9–7 record for the Stars.

June 14

Bill Zuber, Yankee pitcher, finds himself victim of the numbers game. To trim their roster in order to make room for Mel Queen, the Yanks release Zuber. "Goober" Zuber has been around since 1936 with the Indians and Yankees, mostly without distinction. For New York, he was 0–1 in three games this year. At loose ends back home in Cedar Rapids, Zuber gets a call from his wife, saying he's been picked up by the Red Sox. "Bill, Kris Kringle has come early this year," she says. "She never said a truer thing in her life," he says. At Boston, he'll appear 15 times, with a 5–1 record, and collect a World Series check. His first game for the Bosox will be June 23rd, when he starts against Cleveland.

The Yankees sell third baseman Hank Majeski to the Athletics. "Heeney" Majeski didn't do much for the pre-war Braves or this year's Yanks, but he'll become somewhat more successful with the A's. After batting .250 this season, he'll go up to .280 and .310 in the next two years.

June 15

Manager Ben Chapman of the Phillies removes his name from the active list, putting an end, as noted, to his playing days.

This is not only Cut-Down Day but it's Trading Deadline Day, too. The Dodgers trade infielder Billy Herman to the Braves for catcher Stew Hofferth. Herman, once the best all-around second baseman in the NL, is obtained to play third base for Boston. He's not the player he was before he went into the Navy and, at $16,000, is paid far too much for Branch Rickey's taste. After opening the season in place of wartime second baseman Eddie Stanky, Herman had been Brooklyn's third baseman, mostly, since early May. The trade is supposedly enabled by the upcoming availability of young Dodger infielder Eddie Miksis, due back any day from the military. Miksis, however, who broke in at 17 in 1944, will hit only .146 in 23 games this season.

To make room for Herman on the roster, Boston sends Al "Skippy" Roberge, regular third baseman in Boston's first 47 games, to Indianapolis. It's his last year in the major leagues. He was also around in 1941-42.

Hofferth, wartime substitute backstop, has now completed his third and final year in the big leagues. He played 20 games for the Braves with a swell .218 batting average but doesn't appear at all for the Dodgers. Actually, they got him to ship to their farm club at Mobile, in order to call up their rising star catcher, Bruce Edwards. But Hofferth, who disappears for a few days, apparently refuses to go to the minors, so Edwards' ascension is put on hold. Next we hear of Hofferth will be 1948, his last season in pro ball, down in the minors.

As throw-in compensation from the Braves for Herman, Brooklyn gets pitcher Armond (Big Ben) Cardoni, now with Milwaukee, who is transferred to Montreal. He pitched for the Braves during the war, but will never get up to the major leagues again. So, all told, what the June 15th Brooklyn-Boston deal amounts to, is the Dodgers get rid of Herman's salary, or just Herman himself.

In addition to this trade, Boston pitcher Jim Konstanty is sent down to Toronto.

The Senators, who acquired outfielder Jeff Heath from Cleveland in the off-season, trade him to the Browns today for outfielder Joe Grace and pitcher Al LaMacchia. According to *The Sporting News*, Heath is "hefty" and carries a questionable reputation. Browns manager Luke Sewell, however, is quoted as saying, "I'm not concerned with what Heath used to do, or the things they said he did. If he can hit that ball for me, I'm sure we'll get along." Heath, .283 at Washington, will bat .275 for St. Louis. Grace, .230 at St. Louis, will hit .302 in 77 games for the Nats. LaMacchia, nothing-and- nothing for the Browns, was once an American Legion star as a kid in St. Louis. He'll go 0–1 in two games with Washington. It's his third try in the big leagues: three times and out.

The Phillies buy outfielder Charlie Gilbert from the Cubs. Charlie hit .077 for Chicago. He'll do some better for Philadelphia, .234 in 88 games.

The Phillies release outfielder–first baseman Jimmy Wasdell, who hit .300 in 1945. This is his 10th big league season; he'll close out the year with 32 games for the Cleveland Indians, but his career is in its next-to-last round.

Detroit outfielder Anse Moore splits a finger which, except for pinch-hitting, will keep him out of the lineup till the 26th.

The Dodgers option pitcher Jean-Pierre Roy to Montreal. This is an odd notice. Roy, whose only big league appearances were three Brooklyn games in May, has cropped up several times in stories about the Mexican League. First, he rejected Brooklyn's original contract offer, tendered on the heels of his 25 wins for Montreal in 1945. He's said to have gone South of the Border during the spring, then not, then did so, and was away *somewhere* for two weeks. He left again and came back yesterday. He complains the Pasquels lied to him about the money he'd been promised, and it's not clear whether he actually played ball in the Mexican League. He says all former big league players in Mexico are unhappy, except Danny Gardella.

There's a wonderful line in *The Sporting News* story about Roy, another native of Montreal. It says he probably crossed back, North of the Border, "disguised as a French-Canadian."

The White Sox released pitcher Emmett O'Neill to San Francisco a couple of days ago and optioned pitcher Lem Perme to Milwaukee the same day. Both are through in the major leagues. Perme pitched his last four big league games this year for Chicago, matching his other four, in 1942, before he entered the military.

The Cubs decide to place injured pitcher Ray Prim on the voluntary retired list on the 20th. "Pop" Prim, 39, spent many years in the Pacific Coast League. He'll pitch again for the Los Angeles Angels next season. After helping the Cubs win the pennant in 1945 with a 13–8 record, this year he's 2–3 in 14 games, five of which he's pitched so far. It'll be almost September before he's ready to play again.

June 16

The Sporting News indicates the Giants purchase pitcher Nate Andrews from Cincinnati on waivers. According to *The New York Times*, the Reds made him a free agent on the 11th, and the Giants sign him today. In this, the finale to his six seasons in the major leagues, Andrews was 2–4 in seven games for the Reds (last of them on the 10th) and will pitch only three times for New York (0–1, first appearance tomorrow, just hours after joining his new team) for a ten-day trial that doesn't work.

Shortly after A's outfielder Hal Peck plays in the nightcap of today's doubleheader against Detroit, he's sold to the Yankees. He played 48 games with Philadelphia, but does not see action for New York. Sidelined with effects of a nervous breakdown and then an injured elbow which requires surgery, he'll next appear in the majors with Cleveland, in 1947. He will join the Yankees, though, at least momentarily, suited up and sitting on their bench, June 21st.

Frankie Zak, shortstop late of the Pirates, plays for the first time with the Kansas City Blues, in the second half of today's doubleheader at Indianapolis. His arrival completes the spring deal that sent Ed Bahr to Pittsburgh from the Blues. Zak is just 24, but after the 21 games he just played for Pittsburgh, won't appear again in the major leagues. He'll bat only .221 in 68 contests for the Blues.

Against the Pirates today, with a teammate on base, Ron Northey of the Phillies sends a Rip Sewell blooper ball to the top of the right field wall in Shibe Park. Sewell long claims no one ever hit a homer off his special pitch, whose identifying characteristic is that its flight from the pitching mound to home plate resembles the arc you might see in a slow-pitch softball game. Popular legend will attest that Ted Williams is the first to homer off the blooper, next month in the All-Star game. But Northey did it today.

June 17

The Phillies sell outfielder Lou Novikoff and pitcher Ike Pearson to Seattle. This was Lou's last dance in the majors. He hit .304 in 17 games at Philadelphia, but it wasn't good enough to carry his weak glove and carefree attitude. The celebrated minor league hitter will extend his reputation, batting .301, .325 and .327 in the Coast League. Pearson was a fair prewar pitcher, but only appeared five times this season for the Phils. He'll resurface, with the White Sox, in 1948.

First baseman Frank McCormick of the Phillies breaks a rib today and will be out till July 2. Philadelphia scurries to recall farmhand Vance Dinges from Utica, to take over the position in the interim. Only one game passes, seldom-used Dee Moore playing first tomorrow, before Dinges arrives and takes over, temporarily, on the 21st. Moore, who caught briefly for the Reds in the late 1930s, then split 74 games between the 1943 Dodgers and Phils, was written up in a *Sporting News* story a year ago, telling of a shutout he had pitched for the U.S. Fleet Marine Force against a Navy all-star congregation, "somewhere in the Pacific" (military censorship was harsh, particularly if a story was datelined close to a current or impending military action). Moore did pitch twice for the Reds in 1936, but his pitching days are mostly over: this year, he plays first base twice and catches six times, not much action for a returning Marine veteran. He'll pitch a few games in the future, down in the minor leagues. This year, he appears for the Phillies sporadically, playing first, catching and pinch-hitting.

Standings in the Mexican League show Monterrey in first place. Vera Cruz, whose roster is jammed with ex–big leaguers, is last. On the Blues are manager Mickey Owen, Max Lanier, Lou Klein, Harry Feldman, Ace Adams, Roberto Estalella, Chile Gomez (prewar Phillies and Nats) and Danny Gardella. Owen will soon be deposed as manager.

Ernie White of the Braves makes his first start on the mound since he pitched for the Cardinals in 1943. Among the four pitchers who follow him in this first game of two against the Cardinals is young, hawknosed southpaw Warren Spahn. Spahn made a handful of appearances toward the end of the 1942 season after coming up from Hartford. He takes the mound today for the first time since then, only six days after his discharge from the Army. Next month, while Spahn is beating the Cardinals in Boston, Browns radio announcer Dizzy Dean, reading the Western Union tickertape, on which scores come into press boxes everywhere, will pose a question. "Who in the world," scoffs Diz, "is Spahn?" That about sums it up.

The unheralded moundsman was a combat engineer, veteran of the Bulge, wounded at the taking of Remagen Bridge on the River Rhine, late in the war. With his season just beginning and after three and a half years away, he'll go only 8–5 in 1946. Before he's done, he'll win 20 games 13 times, 363 major league victories in all, most of any lefthander who ever lived. In time, the bronze plaque honoring Ol' Diz will be joined by another, bearing the name and likeness of Ol' Spahnie, on the walls of the Baseball Hall of Fame.

The Pirates release outfielder Frank Colman to Newark, for whom he plays a doubleheader in Montreal on the 21st. It is rumored to be the first of two steps that will see Colman with Newark's parent club, the Yankees. A wartime semi-regular in Pittsburgh, his final game there was June 15. He batted .170 in 26 games for the Pirates. He will, indeed, end up in New York, but just to play five games. First, Colman will hit .304 in 84 games for the Bears.

June 18

As noted in April, substitute catcher Bennie Warren of the Giants pinch-hits today in his only appearance for their Jersey City farm team. He'll be back playing for New York at the end of the month.

June 19

St. Louis Cardinals owner Sam Breadon makes an unannounced visit to Mexico, to meet with Jorge Pasquel to discuss the current situation, in which he's lost several players to Pasquel's "outlaw" league. Breadon says he'll report to major league owners at the All-Star Game next month, but seems to have many impressive stories to tell about the Pasquels and their resolve. His trip was a "lone wolf" kind of thing, unauthorized by anyone else in the game.

Sure enough, Happy Chandler will fine Breadon $5,000 for usurping the commissioner's own efforts to create a solution to the Mexican League situation. A protracted series of "misunderstandings" follows, capped by Breadon's payment and a meeting with Chandler at the major league offices in Cincinnati. Through intercession of Ford Frick, Breadon's check is torn up and all is forgiven, sort of. It won't be long before Breadon, disgusted with the way everything's going, and in declining health, sells his Cardinals, having seen them win nine pennants and six World Series.

Pitcher Hal Manders, sent by the Tigers to Buffalo, arrives during the first game of tonight's doubleheader against Jersey City, pitches in the nightcap, goes the distance and wins 5–4. He only pitched twice for the Tigers, last time on the 8th. He'll post a 10–4 record in 20 games for the Bisons.

Outfielder Johnny Barrett, just obtained by the Braves, injures his right knee running the bases. Two days from now, he'll have an operation, to remove a blood clot which results. He'll be out of action till August 11 and will play only 24 games for Boston, batting .233. They're the last 24 he'll ever play in the big leagues.

"Deals of the Week" in *The Sporting News* dated today
(made in advance of Cut-Down Day)

The Cubs option pitcher Hal Kleine to Nashville. Kleine pitched 17 games for the Indians in 1944-45, but that's the extent of his big league career.

The Phillies sell second baseman Ken Richardson to Hollywood after the final six of his 12 games in the big leagues. Philadelphia also options third baseman Ralph (Putsy) Caballero to Utica, though he spends most of the season's remainder at Terre Haute. Putsy, not yet 20, saw action for the Phillies in 1944-45. He won't appear for them this season, but will return for a half dozen more years, starting in 1947.

June 21

A federal judge in Seattle has ruled the Selective Service Act protects every ex-serviceman who returns to his old ball club. The player's salary, the judge says, must be paid a year in full, if he's sent down or released. Organized baseball, he indicates, can't alter federal law to suit its own needs.

The decision comes in the case of Al Niemec, former Naval officer who was let go by the Seattle Rainiers, then played a short time for Providence. Judge Lloyd L. Black rules Niemec must be paid by Seattle for the whole season, per his contract with the club, minus the salary he made playing for Providence. Judge Black emphasizes the Rainiers don't have to play him, just give him his money. Niemec, now 36 and no longer good enough for the Coast League, in the opinion of the Rainiers, nevertheless shouldn't be penalized by the advent of younger players, the Judge says. "Youth must be served," he concludes, "but not at the expense of men who have worn the uniform, and contrary to law." If his ruling holds up, some 140 big league players previously sent to the minors or released would be affected (as well as hundreds of minor leaguers), but it doesn't mean each automatically is due a year's salary paid in full. Lawsuits, if pursued by individual players, will have to be taken to court, one at a time.

Former Phillies first baseman Tony Lupien has also sued for his old job back, after his release by Philadelphia to the Hollywood Stars. Lupien and the Phillies reportedly settle the matter and Lupien plays 170 games in the Coast League this year, hitting .305 for Hollywood. In 1948, the Harvard graduate will return to the majors for a final season, playing 154 times for the White Sox.

The Yankees sell outfielder Roy Weatherly to Indianapolis today, mostly to make room for Hal Peck, just acquired from the Athletics. Weatherly appeals the assignment, saying he's a ten-year man in the big leagues and thus a free agent, according to his contract. American League president Will Harridge looks into it, concludes the player is nine days short of ten full years, thus is subject to assignment. Stormy unhappily agrees to go to Indianapolis and plays his first game there on July 5.

The New York Times reports a denial by Mrs. Barney Dreyfuss, widow of the late owner of the Pirates, that the team is for sale. The paper quotes a *Pittsburgh Post-Gazette* statement that efforts "definitely are being made" to get rid of the team. Mrs. Dreyfuss, chairman of the board of the club, says, "I don't know why they are trying to sell the ball club. The newspapers seem to know more than me." (See August 8, when her husband's estate sells the team.)

June 22

At 12:46 P.M., Bill Veeck, 32, buys the Cleveland Indians at the head of an investment group which includes radio-movie star Bob Hope. Veeck takes over the club presidency from Alva Bradley, incumbent since 1927. Even such a conservative organ as *The Sporting News* cheers the purchase, decrying the team's outgoing ownership of "bankers and others whose interest was always business." Veeck, who recently sold his Triple-A Milwaukee franchise in the American Association, is a Marine veteran who lost part of a leg in consequence of an artillery accident in the South Pacific (he'll lose a little more at a time in surgeries for years ahead). His father ran the Cubs from 1917 till his death in 1933. As a young man, Bill Jr. was in charge of planting the ivy on Wrigley Field's outfield walls.

He's antiestablishment, a maverick, wearing open-collared sports shirts when other owners wear coats and ties, mixing with fans in the stands when others bask in private boxes, bringing zany promotions and unheard-of ideas to major league baseball when his peers wish he'd just go away. In slightly over two years, his Indians will win a world championship. In 1991, long, long overdue, he'll be voted, posthumously, into the Baseball Hall of Fame, literally over the dead bodies of his fellow magnates.

It's worth noting, among the first questions the working press asks is, how long will you keep Lou Boudreau as manager of the Indians? It's rumored Veeck thinks very little of Boudreau's managing skills, but the shortstop-skipper is very popular in Cleveland and such a move might result in cataclysmic local reaction. For the moment, Veeck says Lou is his manager through 1946.

Today, the Browns option infielder Len Schulte to Toledo, in exchange for outfielder George Washington Bradley, who made his big league debut in April. Schulte played the final game of his short big league career at mid-month; Bradley played the only four games of his *very* short career back in late April and early May.

June 23

Bruce Edwards, just promoted from Mobile (where he hit .332 in 62 games), makes his major league debut with the Dodgers. Rookie Ferrell Anderson has been doing the bulk of the catching for Brooklyn, but he's found wanting. Edwards immediately takes over the first string job, plays 92 games, hits .267 and soon makes everyone forget the long-departed Mickey Owen, as well as Anderson, who becomes the Dodgers' backup catcher. Not quite 23, Edwards has a bright future before him — till injuries and Roy Campanella come along. But, for now, he's the catcher the Dodgers have been looking for.

Frank Biscan, Browns pitcher, makes his first appearance of the season. An arm operation in the spring, to remove bone chips, has kept him out till now. He'll see limited duty in 16 games, all in relief, with a win and loss to show for it. Next year, his third and last in the major leagues, he'll appear 47 times for St. Louis, winning six, losing seven.

Newly-acquired outfielder Joe Grace makes his first appearance for Washington, after manager Ossie Bluege benches rookie gardener Gil Coan. Coan, who's spent most of the season on the bench, yesterday blew a catch in the field, was picked off base and later was ruled out for leaving third before a fly ball was caught. As mentioned, it isn't a real satisfying rookie season for Coan.

Southpaw Marius Russo, twice a 14-game winner for the prewar Yankees (and winner of a game in two consecutive World Series), leaves the team to have his pitching arm examined at Johns Hopkins Hospital in Baltimore. He'll be back on the 28th, after finding there's calcification in his left shoulder. It should respond, his doctors tell him, to heat and exercise. This is nothing new. A little more than a year ago, while serving as an athletic director with the Signal Corps in Hawaii, Russo's arm was in a cast, following discovery of bone chips inside. This year, in early August, the Yanks will bid a last farewell to Russo and ship him to Kansas City, after closing out his big league career.

June 24

A bus carrying the Spokane Indians team of the Class B Western International League plunges 300 feet off a narrow road over the Snoqualmie Pass in the Cascade Mountains of Washington State. Eight players are killed, seven injured in the rainstorm accident (another will die, several days from now).

Among the survivors is Ben Geraghty, who played parts of three seasons with the Dodgers and Braves. Geraghty is thrown out of a window, along with the frame. His knee is broken, his head so badly cut the wound requires 28 stitches to close. His playing days ended, Geraghty will soon be named Spokane's manager, replacing Mel Cole, who was among the fatalities. During the 17-year managing career he begins with this tragedy, Geraghty will be twice named *Sporting News* Minor League Manager of the Year.

Spared from the disaster is infielder Jack Lohrke, who had six hits last night. He was pulled off the bus at its final stop before the Pass and told he's to report, instead, to the San Diego Padres, to whom he's just been promoted. "Lucky Lohrke" will be third baseman of the New York Giants in 1947, going from B ball to the major leagues in less than a year.

It's not his first encounter with fate. He survived the Normandy Invasion and the Battle of the Bulge; he was in a train wreck that killed and injured several others; last September, he missed a military transport flight in Jersey City that crashed in Kansas, killing all 23 passengers.

Later this summer the Boston Braves make a deal with San Diego for Lucky Lohrke's services next year. Boston is to give the Padres one player (or $7,500) and three players on option by February 1, 1947. If Lohrke is still with the Braves 30 days into the season, San Diego will receive $25,000 and another player (or $7,500). But Boston has to exercise the option by October 1st this year, and by mistake doesn't do it. Lohrke becomes eligible for sale to other clubs, at the annual major league draft. The Giants step in and obtain him, at the $10,000 draft price. There's a huge row over this, with Braves president Lou Perini begging other clubs not to select Lohrke and screw up his deal. Sorry, say the Giants, for these purposes the sport of baseball is a business. Boston will have to make do with Bob Elliott at third, who'll be obtained this fall from Pittsburgh.

Cleveland releases pitcher Tom Ferrick to the St. Louis Browns. Ferrick has only pitched nine games for the Indians, last of them on June 9th, with no won-lost record. He'll appear 25 times for the Browns (4–1), beginning the end of the month.

Accordingly, the Browns option pitcher Johnny Miller to Toledo, to make room for Ferrick. "Ox" Miller plays parts of four seasons in the majors; this is his third. Previously with the Senators, he'll return to the majors next year with the Cubs. Ox pitched 11 games for St. Louis, his big league high, the last of them on June 16 (1–3).

At the end of June, catcher Boris (Babe) Martin is recalled by the Browns from Oakland. His stay will be brief, as he'll soon be sent on to Toledo, without yet playing for St. Louis this year (that comes later).

June 25

A's pitcher Lee Griffeth, a 21-year-old lefty out of Duke University, makes his first of ten appearances for Philadelphia, three innings of shutout ball in relief against the Red Sox.

The Senators release pitcher John Niggeling. Only 3–2 in eight games for the Nats, he'll finish out his nine years in the big leagues in eight games for the Braves, when he signs with Boston on July 1. Niggeling was one of the Senators' memorable quartet of knuckleballers during the war: he, Dutch Leonard, Roger Wolff and Mickey Haefner.

White Sox pitcher Bill Dietrich sustains a double fracture of the middle finger on his pitching hand, trying to field a line drive off the bat of Washington's Cecil Travis. It ends Dietrich's season, after 11 mound appearances.

Joe Medwick, released by the Browns on April 5, signs with Brooklyn, for whom he played, 1940–43. Medwick, inactive since spring, will be used mostly as a pinch-hitter, appearing in 41 games (same old Ducky at the plate, .312).

Yankee southpaw Tommy Byrne, making his first start of the season, is belted from the mound by the Indians, with only two out in the first inning. Byrne, who has a million-dollar arm and fifty-cent control, will three times win 15 or more games for New York, and three times lead the American League in walks allowed. He won't blossom till 1948-49, a long wait for a kid signed in 1943. Joe McCarthy is said to have tried to make an outfielder of Byrne, who resisted the effort. Indeed, this season the Army vet will work as a pinch-hitter or pinch-runner 10 times and pitch only four times.

June 26

A's outfielder–first baseman Bruce Konopka pinch-hits against the Browns tonight, his first appearance since being recalled from San Diego on June 21.

The Indians purchase first baseman Heinz Becker from Nashville. Bill Veeck says Becker's bunions have been operated on and he's all better. Heinz played for Bill at Milwaukee earlier in the 1940s, and is a Veeck favorite. The Becker deal involves Cleveland sending first baseman Mickey Rocco and cash to Nashville, and optioning pitcher Eddie Klieman to Indianapolis.

But Rocco says he won't go down to Nashville. Becker, consequently, can't come up to the Indians till Rocco changes his mind, as the Vols have no other first baseman. Cleveland suspends Rocco, sort of to help him rethink his decision. Finally, on July 16, it all works out and Becker gets into the lineup for the Indians, playing his first Cleveland game that day. He'll be chosen as first baseman for the Southern Association All-Stars, who play league-leading Atlanta on July 24. Becker can't take part, under the circumstances, but probably couldn't care less. Rocco will play 37 games for the Vols and not appear again in the major leagues.

Klieman-to-Indianapolis is related to the deal because Indy pitcher Al Treichel is then sent to Nashville, where pitching help is needed. Five-and-three in Triple A, Treichel is no better than two-two in Double A. It appears his chief claim to fame is that he's 6'5" and is one of at least two contemporary pitchers nicknamed "Li'l Abner" for his height (righthander Paul Erickson of the Cubs, not quite as tall but with a 9–7 big league record this year, is the other). The bespectacled Klieman, wartime starter for Cleveland, had no record in nine games with the AL club in 1946. At Indianapolis, he'll post a record of 8–5 in 18 games, giving a boost to his sagging career. In the next two seasons, he'll return to Cleveland as a reliever, pitching a total of 102 games without a start.

The Giants release pitcher Nate Andrews today, his ten-day trial having gone bad. Andrews is done in the big leagues and supposedly done in baseball. But, later in the summer, he tells the press in North Carolina he had planned to retire after this year, anyway, and declares he wasn't released but left the Giants of his own accord. Signing with the Wilmington Pirates of the Class D Tobacco State League, Nate finishes out the season there. (In the closed community of baseball, old acquaintances continually reappear in players' lives. Van Lingle Mungo pitches 17 games for the rival Clinton Blues and replaces the Blues' original manager in mid-season. In August, the hot-tempered Mungo will be suspended the remainder of the season for his involvement in near-riot conditions in a game at, of all places, Wilmington.)

"Deals of the Week" in today's *Sporting News* (assuming most of these were made at, or just before, Cut-Down Day)

On June 10, the Pirates sent outfielder Ben Guintini, returned by Hollywood, to San Diego. His combined PCL batting average will be .257. When a knee injury lays him low in late summer, he'll be returned to Pittsburgh but won't see any more action for the Pirates (nor any more in the big leagues at all, till 1950 with the Athletics).

Washington options pitcher Maxie Wilson to Chattanooga. He'll go 4–10 in 20 games there. Maxie, who spent 1942 through 1945 in the Navy, pitched briefly for the Nats in 1940, his only other big league season. He saw a lot of mound duty in the Navy, writer Kit Crissey noting Wilson once was traded by Norfolk Naval Training Station to Bainbridge NTS, either for a basketball player or (depends on the source) for Johnny Rigney. This was Wilson's last big league term, with a final nine major league games (he pitched three times for the 1940 Nats). In early September, he'll be recalled, but his games are all pitched up.

The Braves sell pitcher Al Javery, returned by Toronto after two games (lost one) to Little Rock.

The unfortunate baseball fate of Frank "Creepy" Crespi, second baseman of the 1941-42 Cardinals, is mentioned in this week's *Sporting News*. He broke a leg while playing ball for the Fort Riley (Kansas) Centaurs, after entering the Army (though at least two sources say it was in a tank accident). In a "wheelchair race" along hospital corridors, Crespi was dumped to the floor, breaking the leg in another place. It was initially feared he might never walk again. He never fully recovers, and despite hopes Creepy might be ready to play again next year in the big leagues, he won't, ever.

June 27

The Braves purchase pitcher Francis (Frank) Barrett from Indianapolis, right after he pitches 8⅔ innings of relief to beat Columbus, 14–6, tonight. At the same time, Boston options pitcher Jim (Lefty) Wallace to Indianapolis. Lefty's 27 games for Boston this summer are his last in the majors, but he's only appeared 15 times so far. Due to a waiver rule technicality, he'll be back pitching for the Braves on July 13, after working one solitary game for Indy, June 30 (which he wins). Commissioner Chandler will decide proper waivers weren't obtained on the pitcher, and he must be with Boston by the 6th of July.

Barrett, with the Red Sox last season, will pitch in 23 games for the Braves. Like Charley Barrett of the Cardinals—a once and future Brave—Frank Barrett is also known as "Red."

June 28

After his final big league appearance today, the Phillies option pitcher Charley Ripple to Memphis. This was the third of his brief three big league seasons, 1–0 with a 10.50 ERA. He'll first pitch for the Chicks in the second game of a July 4th doubleheader. ("Chicks" is a regionalism based upon the Chickasaw Bluffs, above the Mississippi River, where Memphis was founded in 1819. It was the site of a Chickasaw Indian village and a 1797 U.S. fort. The nickname is, formally, Chickasaws, not Chicks.)

June 29

Working against Philadelphia, Red Ruffing, veteran Yankee pitcher, takes a Hank Majeski line drive off his kneecap, breaking it. Ruffing, in the majors since 1924, served three years in the Air Force, returning late last season to post a 7–3 record. This year, he's pitched only eight times, going 5–1 with a 1.77 ERA. He's placed on the 60-day disabled list July 19 and is through for 1946. Ruffing, one of the best-hitting pitchers ever to play in the big leagues (.269 over 22 years), will return to complete his Hall of Fame career in 1947, one last season, with the White Sox.

Dick Culler, shortstop of the Braves, is believed to have fractured a bone in his left leg, when hit by Brooklyn's Bruce Edwards, coming into second base standing, attempting to foil a double play. Culler is made of stern stuff: it's only a sprain and he'll be back at it on July 4.

On the 28th, Cleveland optioned pitcher Vic Johnson to Baltimore, for whom he pitches today against Montreal. With nine games on the hill for the Indians (last of which was on the 11th), he's completed his three seasons in the big leagues. He'll work a trio of games for the Orioles, be found further wanting and sent on to Nashville, making his first appearance for the Vols on July 22. He pitches twice there, then is sold, on option, to the rival New Orleans Pelicans.

Pitcher Bob Carpenter of the Giants, who hurt his elbow on June 4, makes his next appearance today, in relief against the Phillies. Elbow pain not eased by his layoff, bone chip surgery at Johns Hopkins Hospital will follow, sidelining him another two months, till August 28. Carpenter was 11–10 in 1942, before the war interrupted his career. His injury limits him to 12 games in 1946.

June 30

Jorge Pasquel himself takes over as manager of the Vera Cruz Blues, piloting his charges to two losses. When, decades from now, Ted Turner tries that with his Atlanta Braves, Turner will be dissuaded from it by baseball officials after one game. But Pasquel owns the Mexican League and can do what he wants, since he makes the rules. One supposes he can manage forever, should he choose. But he quickly hands the reins to infielder Chile Gomez, the team's fourth manager of the season. Mickey Owen remains down in the ranks.

The White Sox have signed shortstop Frank Whitman, a bright Illinois Wesleyan prospect, whom manager Ted Lyons says is the best collegian he's seen in 20 years. Whitman makes his big league debut today, in the second half of a twin bill. In 17 games, Whitman bats .063. In 1948, playing three more times, he'll go hitless in six at-bats.

Tom Ferrick, recently acquired from the Indians, makes his first appearance for the Browns, pitching in relief during the second half of today's doubleheader against Detroit.

Cubs captain Phil Cavarretta injures a hand in the opener of today's twin bill in Cincinnati. He'll pinch-hit in the second game and again tomorrow and again on the 6th of July, but otherwise won't be back in action till the All-Star Game, where he shares first base time with Johnny Mize and Frank McCormick.

The Pirates option reserve catcher Hank Camelli to Toronto. Injuries to other Pittsburgh backstops will require him back with the Pirates in September. But that's a couple months from now: at the moment, he refuses to go down to Triple-A, asking to make a deal for himself at the major league level. Management stands fast, as usual. Camelli will relent, playing his first game for the Maple Leafs on July 6. Next year, with the Braves, he'll end five years in the big leagues, with a .193 batting average.

July 1

The Indians purchase pitcher Joe Berry from Toronto. He was dispatched there by the A's in May. "Jittery Joe" makes it to Cleveland in time to enter a tie game tonight, singling in the winning run against the Browns.

The Tribe also obtains pitchers Charlie Gassaway from Oakland and Les Webber from Brooklyn. Gassaway, who had brief stints with the Athletics and Cubs during the war, will pitch 13 times for Cleveland. It's his third and last year in the majors. Webber, 3–3 for the Dodgers in 11 games, will pitch four contests (1–1) for the Indians. His spot on Brooklyn's roster was taken by the arrival of Ducky Medwick a few days ago.

Bill Veeck's been a busy man, as this flurry of deals indicates, since taking over the Indians. He also signs Jimmy Wasdell, outfielder–first baseman, released two weeks ago by the Phillies. Wasdell pinch-hits against the Browns today, getting a single.

Art Lopatka, Phillies southpaw obtained from the Cardinals this spring, makes his first (and only) start today, after three early-season relief jobs. The Dodgers drive him from the mound. Incidentally, Lopatka appeared in four games last year, too, for St. Louis, getting his only major league win, ironically over the Dodgers.

July 3

Free agent Russ Bauers, twice a 13-game winner for Pittsburgh in the late 1930s, now back from four years in the military, signs today with the Cubs. He pitches his first postwar game July 18. He'll work 15 times for Chicago (2–1), then fade from the major league scene till 1950, with the Browns, for one last game. The Cubs purchase pitcher Doyle Lade from Shreveport for fall delivery, but in time to pitch three games for Chicago. At the same time, Chicago options pitcher Red Adams back to Los Angeles, where last year he had a 21–15 record. He pitched eight games for Chicago, the only eight of his half-season big league career. More than fifty years from now, this forgotten ballplayer's name will be prominently mentioned during induction ceremonies at the Hall of Fame. Pitcher Don Sutton, winner of 324 games in the big leagues, in his acceptance speech will gratefully credit Adams, his old pitching coach, with teaching him the skills that carry him to Cooperstown.

"Deals of the Week," from today's issue of *The Sporting News*

The unforgettable Calvin Coolidge Julius Caesar Tuskahoma McLish of the Dodgers, 3–10 in his rookie season of 1944, is reported en route home from Army duty in Czechoslovakia. Cal, only 20, will pitch just a third of an inning in pro ball this year, in the second half of a doubleheader against the Cardinals on August 25. Talk about being thrown to the lions: McLish emerges with a 54.00 ERA for 1946. He has many seasons ahead, achieving a 92–92 record over 15 years with seven major league clubs.

Another sign of the times: *The Sporting News*, in its weekly coverage of the International League, includes the following Montreal blurb: "Roy Partlow, Negro pitcher, has developed into one of the club's best relief chuckers." In less than two weeks, Partlow will be sent to the Canadian-American League.

Two blurbs later, the item begins, "Jackie Robinson, Negro keystoner…" At some indeterminate time in the future, African Americans in baseball will be known as just "Jackie Robinson," or "Roy Campanella," or "Willie Mays," period.

Further sign of the times: same publication, same issue, notes on the Pacific Coast League: "SAN DIEGO — Debs Garms, veteran outfielder, was out of uniform a week after suffering a slight heart attack following the June 16 twin bill. Although a checkup revealed nothing seriously wrong with his ticker, Garms was advised to give up smoking."

July 4

Early Wynn, righthander of the Senators who's been in the Army since the 1944 season, is discharged at Camp Meade, Maryland, and will rejoin the team as quickly as he can. Wynn, who led the American League in losses two years ago but won 18 the year before that, will pitch 17 games and post an 8–5 won-lost record this year. His first game back won't be till July 16, in relief against the Browns. He'll win 300 before he's finished, though he's won only 39 so far and is already 26 years old.

Cleveland outfielder–pinch hitter Colonel Buster Mills, 37, is removed from the active list and made a coach for the Indians. Returned from three years in military service, he's wrapped up all or parts of nine seasons in the major leagues, mostly with the Cardinals but also with the Dodgers, Red Sox, Browns, Yankees and Indians.

Alvin (Blackie) Dark, gridiron luminary just out of the Army, signs his first professional baseball contract, with the Boston Braves. Dark inked the pact in Detroit, under the nose of the Tigers, for whom he'd been working out. A former college football star, Dark, 23, played two years on the gridiron at Louisiana State, then two in an Army training program at Southwestern Louisiana Institute. In the Oil Bowl at Houston on New Year's Day, 1944, he led SLI to victory over the Arkansas Aggies (the college crop was slim at the time, with many university football programs closed till war's end). More on Dark on July 14, when he makes his debut.

This is the traditional date on which the teams in first place are supposed to win the major league pennants. The Red Sox and the Dodgers, who met in the World Series exactly 30 years ago, are in first place today.

The Indians purchase catcher Tom Jordan from the White Sox. The sale is reported as July 9 in the *"New York Times,"* but Jordan is behind the plate for Cleveland today. It's easy enough to miscalculate: the teams are finishing a two-game series in Cleveland and all Jordan has to do is move from one locker room to the other, then go into the All-Star break. He played his last game for Chicago yesterday, as a pinch-hitter. Jordan began the season on the injured list, sore-armed and unable to play at all till a month ago. He hit .267 in 10 games for Chicago and will bat .200 in 14 for Cleveland. Another of Bill Veeck's Milwaukee Brewer alumni, it might be assumed he's Cleveland's catcher of the future, but he doesn't appear again, after this year, until 1948, by which time Jim Hegan, out of the Coast Guard and having already pushed Frankie Hayes aside, has made the catchership of the Indians his own, a job he'll keep through 1957.

July 6

The Braves option pitcher Steve Roser to Indianapolis. Pitching for the first time there on the 13th, Roser will go 7–3 in 13 games for the American Association club. His transfer makes up for Indianapolis' loss of Lefty Wallace, ordered by the commissioner's office to return to Boston by today. Roser will be recalled by Boston one last time in September, but on June 29, Steve's last big league game was pitched.

July 7

Brooklyn shortstop Pee Wee Reese irritates an old neck injury while turning a double play against the Braves today. Reese continues in the game, in which he hits two doubles, drives in a run and takes nine chances in the field with no problem, but can't sleep tonight. X-rays disclose a chipped vertebra. He'll be out till the 15th, watching the All-Star Game from the stands, his neck in a leather collar. Reese, hitting .319 at the moment (he'll finish the year at .284), explains he first hurt his neck while carrying his wife on his shoulders, back in his younger days.

Another Brooklyn shortstop (*well, maybe*), Tommy Brown, still in the Army at Fort Monmouth, New Jersey, plays for the semipro Brooklyn Bushwicks when he's not on duty. Today, the Bushwicks are 4–0 victors over the Asheville, North Carolina, Blues, of the Negro Southern League. The story in the "*Times*" says the win was "paced by the hitting of Tom Brown, ex-Dodger shortstop."

Joe DiMaggio suffers cartilage damage to his left knee, sliding into a base in the first game of today's doubleheader against the Athletics at Yankee Stadium. It's the same knee DiMaggio injured while with the San Francisco Seals in 1934. He's sprained his left ankle, too, but it doesn't get the headlines enjoyed by his knee. He'll miss the All-Star Game and won't return to the field till pinch-hitting on the 2nd of August.

Catcher Mickey Livingston of the Cubs, out since May 22 with a sprained ankle, pinch-bats against the Reds today, his first game since being hurt.

LeRoy Jarvis, kid catcher drafted by Pittsburgh from Brooklyn's farm club at Montreal, has been discharged from the Navy after being away since 1944. Roy just turned 20, but has only one more season in the major leagues, seeing limited duty next year. He makes his first of only two appearances this year, pinch-hitting against the Cardinals, in the second half of today's doubleheader.

The Browns option catcher Boris (Babe) Martin to Toledo.

July 8

The Dodgers sign Penn State football star Joe Tepsic, attracting him with a $17,000 bonus, most ever paid a free agent by Brooklyn. In less than a week, his name will crop up in the box scores, but his time in the big leagues is not a happy one, for neither the player nor the club.

July 9

The Cardinals sell catcher Ken O'Dea to the Braves in a waiver deal. O'Dea, now in his 12th and final big league season, was St. Louis' regular backstop last year, when Walker Cooper was in the Navy. Most of his career, though, he's been a backup backstop, with the Cubs, Giants and Cards. There have been saving graces: he made it to the World Series in 1935, 1938, 1942, 1943 and 1944.

While Sam Breadon is in a dealing mode, the Cardinals sell pitcher Sylvester "Blix" Donnelly to the Phillies. Blix last pitched for St. Louis on July 2 and won't make his first appearance for Philadelphia till the 25th, when he goes the route to beat the Pirates, 9–2. Donnelly pitched some relief for St. Louis in 1944-45, but 8–10 last year was his best record. This season, he's pitched 13 times (1–2). With Philadelphia in 12 games, he'll garner a 3–4 record.

The Dodgers option catcher Mike Sandlock to Mobile (his last game for Brooklyn was July 5). He's to replace Stew Hofferth, who wouldn't report as the replacement for Bruce Edwards. Sandlock does report, but is billed as the Bears' next third baseman, not catcher. In any event, he's almost immediately promoted to Triple-A Montreal, due to pressing needs there. Just as quickly, he's shuffled to the Brooklyn farm at Triple-A St. Paul, in exchange for two players sent to Mobile. A wartime fill-in at short, third, second and behind the bat for the Braves and Dodgers, Sandlock was in 19 games this year for Brooklyn (.197), before all this touring began. He'll be recalled late summer, but he's used up his time in the majors until 1953, when he plays for the Pirates.

Baseball's 13th annual All-Star Game is played at Fenway Park in Boston. Well, *almost* annual: last year, the contest was called off in deference to government travel restrictions. It's Ted Williams's day, with two home runs, two singles and a walk. In all, Williams sets six All-Star Game records and ties two more. The American League wins, 12–0, its ninth victory in the series that began in 1933. Williams, incidentally, is just three home runs off the pace of Babe Ruth in 1927, when the Babe hit 60, but Ted will finish way behind Ruth's mark, with 38.

The squads were chosen by the 16 major league managers, and there is a healthy round of criticism from the public and press regarding their choices. In the American League, for instance, among the omissions are Lou Boudreau of the Indians, Hank Greenberg of the Tigers, Tex Hughson of the Red Sox and Johnny Berardino of the Browns, all having banner years (Berardino is hitting some 80 points higher than Joe Gordon of New York, chosen on reputation, rather than his subpar 1946 performance).

Joining the press in its objections to squad selection, owners Bill Veeck of Cleveland and Bill DeWitt of the Browns complain loudly at snubs of their players. American League president Will Harridge neatly ducks the issue by saying his office has "no say in it." One problem is that ballots had to be in by June 18, with the game not until today. That's a lot of lead time, and a lot of games still to go before the second week of July.

Incidentally, there isn't much demand for a return to fan voting. Old Judge Landis openly suspected newspaper shenanigans when public ballots were solicited — could lead to ballot box stuffing and the like. Plus, the job of counting thousands of public votes is considered too burdensome a task.

There are many places to read about (and see, on film or video tape) Ted Williams' epic second homer, off Rip Sewell's blooper pitch. You can see Williams happily loping around the bases, almost laughing all the way, at having come through against the blooper. But what of minutia such as the All-Star rosters? They aren't available in most texts any more, so here they are:

American League

Pitchers: Spud Chandler, New York; Bob Feller, Cleveland; Hal Newhouser, Detroit; Mickey Harris and Boo Ferriss, Boston; Jack Kramer, St. Louis. *Catchers*: Bill Dickey, New York; Hal Wagner, Boston; Frank Hayes, Cleveland; Buddy Rosar, Philadelphia. *Infielders*: Mickey Vernon, Washington; Rudy York, Boston; Bobby Doerr, Boston; Joe Gordon, New York; Vern Stephens, St. Louis; Luke Appling, Chicago; Johnny Pesky, Boston; Snuffy Stirnweiss, New York; Ken Keltner, Cleveland. *Outfielders*: Joe DiMaggio and Charlie Keller, New

York; Ted Williams and Dom DiMaggio, Boston; Sam Chapman, Philadelphia; Stan Spence, Washington.

Joe D., as noted, can't play, but isn't replaced on the AL roster. Given the outcome, it doesn't much matter.

National League

Pitchers: Claude Passeau and Johnny Schmitz, Chicago; Howie Pollet, St. Louis; Rip Sewell, Pittsburgh; Kirby Higbe, Brooklyn; Ewell Blackwell, Cincinnati; Mort Cooper, Boston. *Catchers*: Walker Cooper, New York; Phil Masi, Boston; Ray Lamanno, Cincinnati. *Infielders*: Frank McCormick, Philadelphia; Johnny Mize, New York; Emil Verban, Philadelphia; Red Schoendienst, St. Louis; Marty Marion, St. Louis; Pee Wee Reese, Brooklyn; Frankie Gustine, Pittsburgh; Whitey Kurowski, St. Louis. *Outfielders*: Stan Musial and Enos Slaughter, St. Louis; Phil Cavarretta and Peanuts Lowrey, Chicago; Dixie Walker and Pete Reiser, Brooklyn; Johnny Hopp, Braves; Del Ennis, Phillies.

In addition to the injury which has shelved Reese, teammate Reiser has to sit out the game, too (although he stole two bases this weekend). He's replaced on the squad by Phillies first baseman Frank McCormick. Shortstop Eddie Miller of the Reds, selected to the team, says he isn't feeling well and, besides, his arm hurts, so he's replaced by Emil Verban. It's the second straight time Miller has ducked out of the game. In 1944, when it was played in Pittsburgh, Miller also declined and was to be replaced by Pete Coscarart of the Pirates. But the selection came so late that Coscarart was out of touch, on a fishing trip, taking advantage of the three-day break in the schedule. That's when substitute Pittsburgh shortstop Frankie Zak was pressed into service, since he happened to be in town and had nothing else to do.

Reserve infielder Dick Bartell of the Giants is the only remaining active player among the 30 men who saw action in the first All-Star Game, in 1933. Bill Dickey is on his 11th American League squad, the senior participant in that respect. He was chosen in 1933 but didn't play: in fact, he's only been in seven of the games. Giants manager Mel Ott, not chosen this year, played in 11 straight games, dating from 1934.

At their joint meeting in Los Angeles next December, owners and officials will decide to give the All-Star vote back to the fans, except for pitchers. The game continues as a grand baseball tradition (with a few stumbles along the way, such as two contests a year from 1959–62), but a method of selecting the squads will never quite satisfy everyone or, perhaps, anyone.

Former big league infielder Don Gutteridge, till now managing the Browns' farm team, the Toledo Mud Hens of the American Association, is purchased from St. Louis today by the Red Sox, as insurance for second baseman Bobby Doerr, who's had an injured hand. Gutteridge, a Cardinal and Brown between 1936 and 1945, will only play 22 times for Boston, but he'll appear in his second World Series this fall. To obtain him, the Red Sox transfer outfielder Andy Gilbert from Louisville to Toledo. Press speculation is, if Gutteridge hadn't been brought up by Boston, he'd probably have been fired by Toledo, where the team isn't doing well. If this is true, he's twice a beneficiary.

To make room on the roster for Gutteridge, Bill Butland, so-so righthander early in the war with the Red Sox, is optioned to Louisville after five so-so appearances postwar. His record is 1–0, but with an ERA of 11.02.

Gordon Maltzberger, former White Sox relief standby now in the Army, is said to be coming home after being away since the 1944 season. Maltzberger, from Utopia, Texas, will pitch 19 times, beginning July 26 against the Yankees. An early practitioner of the craft of relief work as a specialty, all Maltzberger's appearances will be in relief, as customary (2–0, 1.59).

July 10

Cleveland first baseman Les Fleming is hit in the temple by a thrown ball during an exhibition game against Wilkes-Barre. He's replaced by Jim Wasdell and won't play again till the 21st. Fleming, by the way, batted .414 for Nashville in 1941. That wasn't as high as the .418 by Lew Flick at Class D Elizabethton, but a mite higher than the .406 by Austin Knickerbocker at Class C Oneonta. Of the three, only Fleming would make much of an impression in the big leagues. Don Smith of Class D Huntington also hit .406 that season, but made no impression at all in the big leagues. It is interesting that Ted Williams led the majors with .406 in 1941, the same mark as two of the four bush leaguers named in this paragraph. Williams, of course, made a *forever* impression.

"Deals of the Week," *Sporting News* issue dated today

The A's option pitcher Pat Cooper to Savannah.

Tomorrow, following the All-Star Break, the Cardinals option infielder Nippy Jones to Rochester. He plays his first game there on the 14th. Nippy never fulfils his high pre-war promise, but he'll be up and down through 1957. Despite his long range shortcomings, he has a heck of a half-season at Rochester, batting .344.

The Browns have optioned catcher Ken (Ziggy) Sears to San Antonio. Sears was with the Yankees in 1943, and hit .278 in 60 games as a backup to Bill Dickey. Coming back from wartime military duty, he was obtained last off-season, for outfielder Milt Byrnes, now at Kansas City. Sears apparently reported to St. Louis with a sore arm and was subject of a dispute between the Browns and Yankees. After five sporadic appearances for the Browns, he was held out of further action from May 9 till a decision on St. Louis' appeal came down from Commissioner Chandler. On June 19, Sears was declared property of the Browns, sore arm or not. Sears then played two additional games, the last on July 3, putting a lid on his big league career. The player's father, the *real* Ziggy Sears, ended a long National League umpiring career last fall and is presently officiating out in the Coast League.

July 11

Infielder Oscar Grimes is sold by the Yankees to the A's. This makes room on New York's 30-man roster for rookie lefthander Bill Wight. The Yanks tried to farm Wight out, but were blocked by waiver claims from other teams. Staying with the Yanks, he posts a 2–2 record in 14 games. Grimes, who batted .205 in 14 appearances for New York, will hit .262 in 59 games for Philadelphia, beginning the 14th of the month. This season marks the end of his nine-year big league career.

Pitcher Johnny Grodzicki, a vastly-regarded prewar prospect, makes his first postwar appearance for the Cardinals today, in relief against the Giants. He last played professional ball in 1941, when he was 19–5 for Columbus (AA) and 2–1 in a handful of games for St. Louis. His return has been long-delayed, due to slow recovery from serious hip and leg wounds received late in the war. He's been coming along, very deliberately, as a batting practice pitcher.

He'll only pitch three games in the regular season, 16 next, his great potential left just on the other side of the River Rhine.

Dick Wakefield, Detroit left fielder, injures an elbow. He doesn't play again till a pinch-hit assignment against the A's, on the 28th. It's said to be a fracture, but apparently the problem is bone chips, floating below his left elbow.

Big things were envisioned for Wakefield this year. He was a marvel in 1943-44, but illness and his arm injuries limit him to 111 games in 1946, and he will never be the player most expect him to be (.268 this year; he'll get back into the regular lineup July 29). Like Ted Williams, Wakefield will be castigated by the press throughout his career, but without benefit of Williams' great performance. The press, he'll say, is "brutal." He seems, to his critics, to be lackadaisical in the outfield and unconcerned that his team doesn't do better.

Bob Feller announces he'll front a nationwide postseason exhibition series between his major league all-stars (whom he will choose, and pay) against a squad of "the finest Negro players." Famed pitcher Satchel Paige will lead the Negro all-stars, who are to include Jackie Robinson and the great catcher Josh Gibson, whom the *New York Times* tells us, is "a catcher noted for his great arm." Arm aside, Gibson is best known as "the Black Babe Ruth," and there are calculations that he totals as many as 823 home runs before he's through. Tragically, that's to be very soon. Despite many cries by black observers that he, or other long-time Negro League stars, deserved to be signed first by Branch Rickey, by the time it might have happened, in Gibson's case it would have been doomed to failure. Playing despite long-failing health, he will die of a stroke next January, at only 35. In 1972, a Special Committee on the Negro Leagues will vote Gibson into the Baseball Hall of Fame, recognition far too late, but recognition still.

July 12

Brooklyn outfielder Joe Tepsic pops up in his first big league appearance. He's a veteran of the battle for Guadalcanal which, combined with his huge bonus and college grid star credentials, should make him the All-American Boy. Instead, he'll play 15 games this year, his only year in the majors, and leave a bad taste in everyone's mouth.

With the Dodgers in a tight pennant race, Tepsic refuses to accept assignment to the minor leagues, to make way for a *real* major leaguer (or, at least, one with a little more experience). And there's nothing Branch Rickey or anyone else can do about it: Tepsic's contract, tendered by Mr. Rickey, allows him to refuse a demotion to the minors. He takes advantage of the agreement, saying he hasn't been given a chance to play. He demands to know why he should be sent down without getting a fair shot at a job. In a team meeting, he declares he's a better ballplayer than the majority of the Dodgers anyway, an unfortunate thing to say, under the circumstances.

The majority of the Dodgers, for their part, see a valuable roster spot taken up by someone who is out of his element and belligerent to boot. When it comes time, the players, in retaliation, vote him only a one-twelfth share of any postseason money they'll receive. It's increased to an eighth-share because Mr. Rickey worries Tepsic might bring legal action against the team for a bigger share (putting this rebuff of Tepsic in sharper perspective, Tommy Brown, in the Army all season, is voted a half-share by Brooklyn players; Mike Sandlock, who spends half the season in the minors, gets a half share; Jean-Pierre Roy, who pitched three times in early May, gets a quarter-share).

July 14

The fabled Williams Shift, also called the "Boudreau Shift," is born today, out of Cleveland's desperation to find a way to thwart pull-hitting left-handed batter Ted Williams. After Ted belts three homers and a single in Game 1 of today's doubleheader, and a double in Game 2, Indians manager Lou Boudreau changes his defensive strategy against Williams. Boudreau brings virtually the entire Cleveland defense over to the right of second base, erecting a sort of human wall against him. Only left fielder George Case stays to the left of second. Third baseman Ken Keltner plays on the first base side of second, second baseman Jack Conway is back in short right field, center fielder Pat Seerey is up against the fence, and so forth. "Teddy Ballgame" laughs at the strategy, it's said, but The Shift endures as part of Williams' legend. The slugger, his critics declare (particularly Boston writers, many of them well-resented adversaries throughout his career), is stubborn and selfish. They say he hurts his team by refusing to hit to left field, which would negate the odd defense. On the other hand, Williams hits .342 this year, .343 next, .369 and .343 the years after that, winning the fourth and fifth of his seven batting titles, with various permutations of The Shift employed against him, well into the future.

Alvin Dark of the Braves makes his major league debut, as a pinch-runner in the second game of today's doubleheader against the Pirates. Dark will stay with Boston the remainder of this season, playing 15 games, hitting .231. He needs regular work in the minor leagues, it's obvious. But after one year at Milwaukee, he'll return to the big leagues in 1948, a .322 batter, as Boston's shortstop. In later days, he'll manage 13 years in the majors.

Dark's future keystone partner with the Braves and Giants, Eddie Stanky of the Dodgers, hurts his back in the nightcap of today's doubleheader against the Cardinals and has to be carried from the field on a stretcher. He'll miss the rest of the St. Louis series, not returning until the 17th.

Enos Slaughter of St. Louis, coming in from first, dumped the bantam rooster second baseman, cutting his legs out from under him. Stanky, "The Brat," who'd do the same if given the opportunity, is detested by most of the Cardinals (and every other team in the National League; he isn't too popular with all his own teammates). The other side is generally delighted at the sight of the stretcher.

Rookie utility man Bob Ramazzotti fills in well for Stanky, getting nine hits in 16 at bats, for a .563 average during the Cardinal series. But the Cards sweep the Bums four straight and the Dodgers limp out of town to Cincinnati, where they'll lose again.

Joining the Dodgers today is infielder Eddie Miksis, out of the military at last. He's a pinch-runner in the opener of the twin bill at Sportsman's Park.

July 15

Cleveland sells catcher Frankie Hayes to the White Sox on waivers. Connie Mack says he was going to claim him for the Athletics (because of their position in the standings, the A's had first shot at him), but decided not to, for what that's worth. Hayes was starting backstop for the American League in the All-Star Game, but he's gone from being, literally, an everyday catcher, to over-the-hill-and-out. In 51 games for the Indians, he hit .256; in 53 games for the Chisox, he'll bat .212. Next season, only 32 and in his 14th year in the majors, Hayes will play five early-season games for the Red Sox and never again appear in big league ball.

This turn of events has been building. Hayes, in a long batting slump before the All-Star Game, was benched by manager Lou Boudreau. He heard about it, not from the manager, but from rookie catcher Sherman Lollar. Hayes and Boudreau then had words, the end result being today's sale. Ironically, young Lollar is optioned today to Baltimore, where he was International League MVP in 1945. Having come up short in his first trial in the big leagues, he'll get plenty of opportunity in the future. Lollar will be around for 17 more years, through 1963, appearing in the World Series for 1947's Yankees and 1959's White Sox.

Phillies manager Ben Chapman, who pitched one game this season (on May 12), takes himself off the active list. A lifetime .302-hitting outfielder who turned to the mound during the war, Chapman closes out his 15 years as a big league player.

Shoulder still hurting, Brooklyn's Pete Reiser benches himself during today's St. Louis game, with a bad back. Dick Whitman substitutes. "The Pistol" will return to the lineup tomorrow; he appears not to know the meaning of the word "quit." Because of his condition, however, he's been placed in left field, as he can no longer throw hard enough, or far enough, to play center.

For the first (and last) time this season, Leo Durocher puts Ducky Medwick in the Brooklyn lineup at first base, in St. Louis, to get more righthanded power in the batting order. Medwick played the position a few times in 1943 and 1945, but hardly with less success. He makes two errors; the experiment is declared over.

Ralph (Red) Kress, 40-year-old Giants coach and one-time shortstop, is activated to fill in as a pitcher. On the 17th, he'll work 3⅔ innings against the Pirates, his last of 1,391 games in the big leagues, the first (and last) he ever pitches in the majors. Many years ago a .300 hitter for the Browns, he began a second career as a manager and coach, mostly in the minors, in 1940. With a growing universal shortage of pitchers, Kress put himself in for a little work on the mound in 1941, at St. Paul (it was at Toronto, in 1943, that he began pitching with any regularity). This year, one of his duties with the Giants has been to pitch batting practice. Due to widespread sore arms on the New York pitching staff, Kress signs an active player contract, just in case. "Just in case" happens two days from now. It's not a very good idea, as Kress gets hit hard and quickly goes back to the coaching ranks. Much later, in 1962, he'll be a coach for the Mets in their first year, scant months before a heart attack kills him.

July 16

Walker Cooper, Giants catcher, breaks his right middle finger, his second broken finger of the season. He'll pinch-hit on the 29th, don the "tools of ignorance" (as catching gear is called at mid-century), on August 2.

Broken arm still healing, White Sox first baseman Jake Jones has returned from his Louisiana home to begin light workouts at Comiskey Park. Workouts won't help. His next game, still, isn't till next season.

Roy Partlow, teammate of Jackie Robinson at Montreal, is optioned to Three Rivers, after a reasonably successful couple of months with the Royals. Pitcher John Wright, Robinson's first "Negro companion" player, was sent to Three Rivers in May, partly to make room at Montreal for Partlow, though chiefly because of Wright's difficulty reacting to the pressure of being a pioneer. Wright pitches 31 games at Three Rivers this summer, with a 12–8 record, so it doesn't appear he's incapable. Partlow, 2–0 in the International League, is too old, white baseball wisdom dictates (born in 1912, contemporary accounts say he's "30," six years younger), to waste any time planning to promote him to the major leagues. But he's far too good a pitcher for the Canadian-American League, and will post a 10–1 mark in 14 games. Next year, Wright and Partlow both will be back in the Negro National League.

Ex-Negro Leaguers Don Newcombe and Roy Campanella, at Nashua, New Hampshire, of the New England League, are Mister Rickey's hopes for the next wave of black trailblazers, not Partlow and Wright. Partlow, by the way, is not replaced in his unique capacity at Montreal. By now, it's felt, Robinson can withstand the pressure of organized baseball without the crutch of another member of his race to lean on.

July 17

Yankee shortstop Phil Rizzuto is hit in the face by a Nelson Potter fastball in the second game of today's twin bill against the Browns. He's carried off the field and replaced by his predecessor at the position, player-coach Frankie Crosetti. Rizzuto won't return to the lineup till July 29. In the aftermath of the incident, team president Larry MacPhail decrees that henceforth all Yankees will wear protective liners inside their caps while batting. It's becoming increasingly common. The *New York Times* of the 21st says an order has been placed with a helmet maker by the Yankees. The paper notes the use of such gear used to be commonplace, but player apathy has gradually taken hold.

The Indians option pitcher Don Black to Milwaukee, where he works seven times, to earn an 0–5 record. That's not any improvement on the 1–2 mark he's posted in 18 games with Cleveland. His private demons continue to pursue him: late August in Toledo, he'll disappear from sight, missing a Brewers' trip to Columbus, for which the team will suspend him.

Pitcher Claude Passeau of the Cubs goes out with a recurrence of back troubles. He'll be shelved, this time, till the 31st.

Johnny Gee, mentioned earlier, was reinstated from the voluntary retired list yesterday, pitches his first of 13 games for the Giants today, following Red Kress to the mound.

The Phillies try to sell pitcher Art Lopatka to Louisville, but he has a sore arm and the Colonels call off the deal. He's already seen his four games on the mound for Philadelphia and now disappears from the major league scene forever.

President W.C. Bramham of the minor league National Association suspends Louisville manager Nemo Leibold for the rest of the season, in consequence of Leibold's verbal and physical attack on umpire Forrest (Frosty) Peters, during a June 16 doubleheader with Milwaukee. On July 31, the suspension will be abbreviated to 45 days, retroactive to today. Leibold, till now a highly-respected minor league manager, 13-year big league outfielder and one of the honest Black Sox, violently protested a play that ended the first game, then refused to leave the field for the second game. American Association president Roy Hamey originally fined Leibold $100 and suspended him till June 22. Umpires Peters and Milt Steengrafe, who also worked the twin bill on the 16th, both resigned in protest of what they felt was Hamey's light penalty for Leibold taking a swing at Peters.

Figuring they're paying him, anyway, the Red Sox, who own the Louisville club, use Leibold as a scout during his suspension.

The Phillies sign pitcher Dick Koecher, 6'4" southpaw from King of Prussia, Pennsylvania, and Temple University. "Highpockets" Koecher becomes a three-year major leaguer, but only for brief terms each season, 1946–48. In 1946, he appears just once for Philadelphia, late this September. First, he's sent to Terre Haute, hopefully to begin learning his craft.

July 18

Meeting in Chicago, a joint committee of representatives from both major leagues votes to give players a voice in drafting a uniform player contract. It may be the first time in history players have been invited to participate in the process (not counting the ill-fated Players' League of 1890, ostensibly run by the athletes themselves).

Over the past several days, the Athletics optioned first baseman Bruce Konopka and shortstop Jack Wallaesa to Toronto, infielder Irv Hall to Kansas City and catcher George "Dodo" Armstrong to Savannah. Konopka's already been sent to the Pacific Coast League, brought back, now farmed out again. He's going to play 38 games altogether for the A's this year, but, including his most recent appearance on the 14th, has only been in 21 to date.

Wallaesa most recently played for the A's on the 13th.. He and Konopka make their initial Toronto appearances today.

Hall, in his final major league season, has appeared 59 times for the Athletics so far. The A's regular second baseman earlier in the year, he was in Connie Mack's lineup yesterday and will play his first game for the Blues on the 20th. Like Konopka and Wallaesa, Hall will return to the A's in September. Armstrong, one of many single-season big leaguers to appear in 1946, got into eight early games for the A's and won't be back.

July 19

The White Sox absorb a series sweep by the Red Sox, losing today 9–2, giving Chicago a record of oh-and-seven in Boston's Fenway Park this season. What makes the game memorable is umpire Red Jones' ejecting 14 White Sox, leaving only four men on the bench (manager Ted Lyons, coach Mule Haas, trainer Packy Schwartz and bat boy Donald Fitzpatrick). Trouble starts in the third inning, when Jones cautions Chicago pitcher Joe Haynes, after Ted Williams has to hit the dirt on a close pitch. Jones is heckled loudly from the Chisox bench, at which point he gives the thumb to coach Bing Miller and players Ralph Hodgin, Eddie Smith and Dario Lodigiani. Later, infielder Leo Wells is ejected. Next inning the clamor continues, and Jones thumbs another nine men from the dugout: Mike Tresh, John Rigney, Eddie Lopat, Earl Caldwell, Hal Trosky, Frank Whitman, Guy Curtright, Whitey Platt and Wally Moses.

The Chisox protest that Haynes wouldn't have deliberately thrown at Williams and, besides, he is, after all, the brother-in-law of Boston manager Joe Cronin.

July 21

In the second game of today's doubleheader against Washington, Bob Feller pitches relief for the first time since before the war. He went the route against the Nats yesterday and will do the same against the A's three days from now.

In the first game of today's doubleheader down in the Texas League, *The Sporting News* reports, "Ed Snider, 19-year-old flychaser recently released from service, crashed a pair of home runs in leading Fort Worth to a 13 to 1 rout of Houston." That would be *Duke* Snider.

July 23

Giants outfielder Garland Lawing, obtained June 7 from Cincinnati, is optioned to Jersey City. His big league career, which covered ten games and two teams this season, is over. It's thought by some observers that Lawing's arrival on the Little Giants will make it possible to send outfielder Don Mueller to a lower classification league, where he can work on his shoddy fielding. Mueller, whose dad played big league ball in the twenties, is just out of the armed forces. He'll go down to Jacksonville in the Sally League next year, but the 19-year-old's hitting .389 right now, making it difficult to send him out.

On the 22nd, over the weekend, Washington pitcher Vern Curtis was optioned to Buffalo. He'll return to pitch once more, on September 13, to conclude an abbreviated three-year big league career.

The White Sox sell outfielder Wally Moses, lifetime .291 hitter, to the Red Sox. Though some publications date this tomorrow, official commissioner's bulletins say it's today. The Chisox and Bosox are playing each other in the Windy City and Moses doesn't play the Bosox till his Boston bow on the 26th, in St. Louis. Moses will make it to his only World Series this year, prompting him to exult, in going from lowly Chicago to pennant-bound Boston, "words couldn't express my happiness. I am glad to get my nose out of the mud."

To keep the roster at the 30-man limit (which includes five returning servicemen, of which Boston has plenty), Red Sox coach-infielder Tom Carey, who in June and early July played his last three major league games, is assigned full-time to his coaching duties. "Scoops" Carey spent years in the Cardinal farm system, came up with the Browns in 1935 at second base, a position he'd never played. Later in the decade, 1938, Carey was optioned to Hollywood, the just-relocated Mission franchise of San Francisco. For the Stars, Carey was the Pacific Coast League's top shortstop, earning another trip to the majors, with the Boston Americans in 1939. Three years away in the Navy ate up the rest of his playing days.

July 24

Banner headline in this week's issue of *The Sporting News* says New York papers predict Larry MacPhail is going to "break up the Yankees," a cry often heard in the 1930s, when they dominated baseball. This is for the opposite reason: the Yankees are a major disappointment. There appear to be a million opinions of what to do about it. First to go, the stories say, will be second baseman Joe Gordon, supposedly headed for the Indians.

MacPhail is incensed about the stories, claiming they're all wrong. Gordon is incensed, too. He's not having a good year (.210), but he was MVP in 1942. He spent two years in the Army, and his supporters argue he's still only 31 and going to come around. Look at the great DiMaggio: he's having an off-year after the war, but does anyone doubt he'll rebound? Peace between MacPhail and Gordon will be restored and things will settle down, though something's simmering beneath the top of the pot.

During the World Series, Gordon will be traded to the Indians.

White Sox second baseman Don Kolloway dislocates his shoulder today. Other than pinch-running on July 31, he won't play again for almost a month, returning as the Chisox' third baseman on August 22.

First baseman Eddie Waitkus of the Cubs fractures his right little finger. He'll be out till the 6th of August. A *Sporting News* game story will report Waitkus has returned to the lineup after being out a month. That's not exactly right, as he does appear twice at first base between now and the 6th and pinch-hits or -runs on several other occasions, but he is far less than par during the period.

Waitkus will be best-known as the Philadelphia Phillie who gets shot and almost killed, by a lovelorn, deranged fan, in her Chicago hotel room, in 1949. Looking backward rather than forward, the thin, wiry Waitkus batted .336 at Los Angeles in 1942, then spent three years in the Army, mostly as a machine gunner with amphibious engineers, taking part in several Pacific island landings. He pays his dues, you might say.

"Deals of the Week," undated as usual

On the 22nd, the Reds optioned pitcher George Burpo to Syracuse, to get more experience than he's able to with the Reds. He's another of 1946's one-season major leaguers. The same thing happened to him in 1942, before he got the chance to pitch at all for Cincinnati. After these many years, at least in part due to the war, the two games he pitched in 1946 are the only ones in his entire big league career. Burpo's arrival at Syracuse gives the Chiefs six lefthanded pitchers. However, he won't be any more successful in Triple-A than he was in the majors: three games pitched, two losses.

Back on the 15th, Washington sent pitcher Al LaMacchia to Chattanooga. LaMacchia, who came over in the Jeff Heath deal, June 15, at first refuses to report to the Lookouts, then changes his mind. His three years in the big leagues, covering 16 games since 1943, are now over. In a few weeks, he'll be sold to San Antonio, property of the Browns again, as he was till traded to Washington in June. For San Antonio, he'll split two decisions in eight games.

July 25

Oft-injured Hoot Evers, rookie Detroit outfielder, pulls a tendon in his wrist today and will be out, once more, till the 31st.

Bill Voiselle of the Giants was a 21-game winner as a rookie on a lousy New York team two years ago. In June of 1945, he stood at 9 and 0, when, apparently ignoring Mel Ott's standing order to "waste" an 0-2 pitch, Voiselle blew a lead against the Cardinals by giving up successive hits to Johnny Hopp, Ray Sanders and Whitey Kurowski. It cost him the ball game. It also cost him $500, five times the standing fine which Ott had threatened for violating his "waste the 0-and-2 pitch" order.

The pitcher feels he's been in Ott's doghouse ever since, losing more than he's won, finishing 1945 at 14–14 after his 9–0 beginning. Today, pitching against this year's Cardinals, Voiselle injures a knee and will be out till the 11th of August. He's on his way to 9–15. Fed up with him, the Giants will send him packing to the Braves next June. By coincidence, he'll pitch in the 1948 World Series (losing the final game, to the Indians), about three months after Mel Ott loses his managing job in New York.

Meanwhile, today the Giants call up pitcher Woody Abernathy from Minneapolis. He'll make his big league debut on the 28th and pitch 15 times for New York. To obtain Abernathy, New York options pitcher Bob Joyce to Minneapolis. This was Joyce's last of two seasons in the big leagues, dating back to a brief stay with the Athletics in 1939. He was 3-4 in 14 games this year for New York. A wartime pitcher out in the Coast League, he won 22, 20, 21 and 31 games for San Francisco from 1942 to 1945. It's difficult to give up on a 30-game winner, war season or not. Next year, peace season, he'll return to the Seals and post a 15–15 record.

With Joyce, the Giants also release pitcher Reuben Fischer to Minneapolis, ending his five seasons in the big leagues. A wartime moundsman for New York, Rube only pitched 15 times for this year's Giants, compiling a 1–2 record and 6.31 ERA. With the Millers, he'll win five and lose three in 10 games.

July 27

Rudy York of the Red Sox hits two grand slam home runs tonight off Tex Shirley of the Browns. It's only the third time in major league history anyone's accomplished the feat: Tony Lazzeri of the Yankees in 1936 and Jim Tabor of the Red Sox in 1939 did it earlier. York also belts a double, driving in ten runs for the game, one shy of Lazzeri's American League record, set the day of his two grand slams (the major league mark of 12 RBI in a game was set by Sunny Jim Bottomley of the Cardinals, in 1924).

After winning his 20th game today, Detroit's Hal Newhouser is diagnosed with a nerve injury in his pitching arm. He won't return till August 4, when the Red Sox score seven runs off him and he loses his fourth game of the year. They were talking about 30 wins, but he'll finish with a 26–9 record though his 26 wins will lead the American League, as his 25 did last year and his 29 the year before.

Today in Game One of a doubleheader against the Phillies, Hank Borowy of the Cubs is knocked out of the box after 2⅔ innings. He's the losing pitcher. Tomorrow, manager Charlie Grimm starts Hank again, in Game One of another twin bill against the Phils. He'll go the distance, beating Philadelphia 11–3. That's not unheard of in the 1940s, but it's increasingly rare for any pitcher to start two days in a row.

July 29

Preliminary meetings are held today in New York (National League) and Chicago (American), between players chosen to represent their teams, owners and league presidents, to discuss proposals for a new formal player contract, as well as several unprecedented benefits. Marty Marion, shortstop of the Cardinals, has drafted a pension proposal to discuss.

The players evidently want experienced and or college-educated teammates to take up their side. Those chosen as representatives, first of their kind, are: *American League:* Pinky Higgins, Boston; Joe Kuhel, Chicago; Mel Harder, Cleveland; Hank Greenberg, Detroit; Johnny Murphy and Tommy Henrich, New York; Gene Desautels, Philadelphia; Babe Dahlgren, St. Louis; alternate, Johnny Berardino; and Bobo Newsom, Washington. From the National League are: Billy Herman and Bill Lee, Boston; Dixie Walker and Augie Galan, Brooklyn; Billy Jurges and Phil Cavarretta, Chicago; Joe Beggs and Bucky Walters, Cincinnati; Hal Schumacher and Buddy Blattner, New York; Roy Hughes and Rollie Hemsley, Philadelphia; Rip Sewell and Lee Handley, Pittsburgh; and Marty Marion and Terry Moore, St. Louis.

National League president Ford Frick says the average National League player already makes $9,500 a year. Only 29 of 250 NL players, he claims, get less than the $5,000 annual salary the players are rumored to be seeking.

Not much gets done, other than the enormous achievement of the hired help to be included. Further talks are defrayed until August 5, in the offices of Yankee president Larry MacPhail. Those talks mainly will result in setting up another meeting, August 27, in Chicago.

MacPhail says nothing will be disclosed till then, and the players seem to go along with his dictates. There appear to be 15 proposals. According to the *New York Times*, it's almost with relief that MacPhail proclaims, "not more than one percent of players want any change to the Reserve Clause." The story says players "realize its importance in the game." It's easy to assume most of them yet have little idea what "Reserve Clause" means.

White Sox ace Thornton (Lefty) Lee, limited to only seven starts this year (2-4), is placed on the voluntary retired list, which shelves him for the rest of the season. He's trying to recover from elbow surgery to remove a bone splinter, having last pitched on June 16 against Boston. He'll return next year, but with only a 3–7 record in 21 games, then move on to the Giants in 1948, ending 16 years in the major leagues.

July 30

The Cubs have sent pitcher Bill Fleming to Los Angeles, for whom he makes his first appearance today. He goes 9–5 in 15 games for the Angels, after completion of his six seasons in the majors. He was with the Cubs in 1944 (winning 9, losing 10, 3.13), then went into the Army for a year. (This is Leslie *Fletchard* Fleming, as opposed to Leslie *Harvey* Fleming, Cleveland first baseman. The Cubs' Fleming is called Bill, perhaps to tell him from the guy in Cleveland, whose nickname is "Moe." They aren't known to be related.

July 31

Ken O'Dea, Braves catcher, suffers a fracture of his right hand when hit by a foul bunt off the bat of Pittsburgh's Al Gionfriddo. At first it's thought to be only a bruise, and O'Dea shrugs it off, working more games. August 4 and 6, before X-rays reveal the break. Though later restored to the Boston roster, O'Dea is finished for the year. In fact, at 33, he's finished in the major leagues.

Another former Cardinal, pitcher George "Red" Munger, is due back from duty with the Army of Occupation in Germany. He'll make his first appearance in the second game of an August 25 doubleheader, against the Dodgers. Before he was inducted in 1944, Munger had an 11–3 record for St. Louis. In the remaining days of 1946, he'll appear ten times and go 2–2.

Cincinnati shortstop Eddie Miller is sidelined with an arm injury, a recurring problem that has haunted him since mid-1944. In this case, he'll be out a month, returning to pinch-hit on September 2, Labor Day. Earlier this month, he was out for six days. Last season, Miller broke a kneecap. Injuries plague the defensive star throughout the mid-1940s, but they won't wear him down. He'll play full-time the next two seasons and last through 1950.

Cleveland's Bob Feller pitches a one-hit, 4–1 victory over the Red Sox, to win his twentieth game of the season. Bobby Doerr gets the only Boston hit. The Indians have to play without their third baseman, Ken Keltner, whose father-in-law has passed away in Milwaukee. Keltner won't be back till the sixth of August. Like others, Kenny lost something in the war, in his case only a year of Navy service, but in 1944 he batted .295; in 1946, .241. He'll do better in 1947, great in 1948. Then chronic back problems will begin to do him in.

Returning from the Navy is young Washington infielder Eddie Yost, after two years away. Yost, not yet 20, was signed off the crack Brooklyn Bushwicks semipro team in 1944, playing seven games for the Senators. This season, he'll only get into eight, beginning with a pinch-hit appearance in the opener of an August 8 doubleheader. Yost has 16 more years ahead of him in the big leagues, most of them at third base. Between 1949 and 1955, he'll play 838 consecutive games (which still ranks among the top ten such streaks, more than five decades later).

Today is the final day for most minor league clubs to acquire player help from higher classifications, including the majors. It's to keep clubs from stocking up at the last minute, while driving for their league pennant or a shot at the playoffs, which most loops have. The Pacific Coast League, with its longer schedule, does not share this deadline date.

August 1

In a memorable interview with author Donald Honig, Pete Reiser will one day admit to a single, overriding thought as he played the outfield: "hit it to me, hit it to me." Reiser again runs into the Ebbets Field wall today, but other than staying in another hospital another couple of days for tests, he isn't badly hurt — if you don't count multiple lacerations and a near-concussion. He'll be back on the field August 8th. His return is complicated by the explosion of his kitchen stove, which Reiser ill-advisedly volunteers to light for his wife. Fortunately, his few burns are superficial. Typically, Reiser, in his first game back, homers and triples, to lead the Bums to a ten-inning, 3–1 victory over the Giants.

The Cubs have optioned pitcher Russ Meers to Nashville for whom he pitches tomorrow. With the Cubs for one game prewar, Meers spent three years in the Navy. One-and-two for Chicago this season, he'll pitch a final 35 big league games next year. (Meers' assignment to Nashville is listed as August 12, by the commissioner's bulletin.)

Most observers regard Joe DiMaggio as the very essence of grace on a ball field. You know, never throws to the wrong base, never makes a mistake on the basepaths, wants never to look bad in front of fans who've come out just to see him play. Well, in batting practice today, the graceful, aristocratic DiMag, returning from a month's layoff with knee problems, bonks himself in the knee with his bat. He'll wait till tomorrow to play again.

August 3

Second baseman Johnny Berardino and right fielder Al Zarilla of the Browns collide in the field against the A's. Zarilla leaves the game, but Berardino continues. Tomorrow, however, he's diagnosed with a torn right calf muscle and joins Zarilla on the bench.

Pinky Higgins, veteran third baseman of the Red Sox, is spiked today by the young third baseman who replaced him in Detroit, George Kell. Higgins, slashed just above his left knee, will be out till the 11th.

August 4

Stan Hack, veteran third baseman of the Cubs, fractures his left thumb trying to stop a line drive hit by the Braves' Don Padgett. Hack returns to his home in Sacramento to recuperate and will return late in the season to play another dozen times.

Phillies pitcher Schoolboy Rowe pulls a groin tendon while trying to field a line drive hit by Erv Dusak of the Cardinals. He's out till the 10th of September, when he returns, one time, as a pinch-hitter. Rowe won't pitch again until 1947, though. He comes out of this season at 11–4; he'll make it 14–10, next.

The Dodgers beat Cincinnati, 5–4, in 14 innings, while the Cardinals split with Philadelphia. It gives Brooklyn a two-game lead in the National League pennant race.

Before what's described as "the largest crowd in baseball history," 74,529, the Indians lose to the Yankees, 2–0. It's the first game of a doubleheader, but rain washes out the second. Also washed out is Bob Feller, Cleveland starter in the opener, who has to leave with a pulled back muscle. Not to worry—next start he's destined to pitch a one-hitter against the White Sox.

Yankee president MacPhail will soon challenge the accuracy of "largest crowd," citing a Boston–New York doubleheader at Yankee Stadium in 1938, which he says was attended by 81,481. Actually, it was 81,841, but either way, MacPhail is right. For all his brag and bluster, he usually is.

August 5

Johnny Mize suffers a broken hand when hit by a Joe Page pitch at New York Mayor William O'Dwyer's charity exhibition game between the Giants and Yankees. Mize will play only one more game. Big Jawn's already hit 22 home runs, just one shy of Ralph Kiner's eventual league-leading 23. Mize would likely take the honors, were it not for injuries. The two future Hall of Famers will tie for the National League title with 51 each in 1947 and 40 each in 1948.

The Yankees sell pitcher Jake Wade to Washington. "Whistlin' Jake," formerly a Tiger, a Red Sock, Brown and White Sock, is going to his last big league stop, but first he holds out for more money, saying the Senators or somebody owes him for World Series cash he's going to miss, being dealt to a second division team (there's no published evidence that he wins his case). After 13 games and a 2–1 mark for the Yanks, he'll only pitch six more times, with no decisions for the Nats, beginning tomorrow, against his recent teammates from New York. In relief, he strikes out four but walks four, too, as his new ball club loses.

The Red Sox release catcher Frankie Pytlak, who's been on the 60-day D.L. Paid off for the year though having played only four games with Boston, the 12-year American League vet is through in the majors.

The Phillies option pitcher Johnny Humphries to Kansas City, his nine seasons in the major leagues at an end. His final game for Philadelphia was July 28. However, Humphries will not appear for the Blues, possible explanations being he's injured or he's refused the assignment, which would likely result in a long suspension by the parent club.

The prospect of better help for KC comes from the Yankees, optioning out veteran pitcher Marius Russo, who made his final big league appearance, as a pinch-runner, yesterday. Unfortunately, he isn't any more help to the Blues than Humphries, mustering an 0–1 record in three games.

August 6

Tonight in Cincinnati, Peanuts Lowrey of the Cubs, on his way to score a run, is struck behind the left ear by a throw from center fielder Lonny Frey, and knocked out as he crosses the plate. Lowrey finishes the game in Christ Hospital. It's a definitive weird play. With Ewell

Blackwell pitching for the Reds, catcher Mickey Livingston doubles to lead off the top of the second for Chicago. Shortstop Lennie Merullo then singles into a double play, as Reds' right fielder Al Libke throws out Livingston at home and catcher Ray Mueller throws out Merullo trying for second. Cubs pitcher Claude Passeau singles and third baseman Lowrey does, too. A wild pitch moves them up a base. Chicago second baseman Don Johnson gets the fifth Bruin hit in a row, scoring Passeau and Lowrey, at which moment, as described, Lowrey is cold-cocked crossing the plate.

Peanuts, by the way, signs his autograph *Harry "P-nuts" Lowrey* (his nickname is spelled that way, apparently, only by him).

Adding insult to injury, Cubs pitcher Paul Erickson, leaving the park after today's game, steps on the tail of a stray cat he doesn't see. The cat, offended, bites him on the legs. Between guffaws, teammates ask if the cat survives.

After making his final big league appearance of the season today, pitcher Les Webber of the Indians will be optioned to Baltimore on the 20th. His first game for the Orioles will be on the 21st. Webber, purchased from Brooklyn at the start of July, will be back with Cleveland for one appearance in 1948, his last in the majors.

The Athletics' Lee Griffeth makes the 10th and last appearance of his sole season in the majors today. On the 13th, he'll be optioned to Philadelphia's last place Lancaster farm in the Inter-State League, where he pitches five games (two complete), for a 2–3 record. The Inter-State League playoffs, which don't include the Red Roses, start on September 10th. Griffeth's five appearances have to be run off within a month, before the regular season ends on the 8th of September.

Mickey Owen is back in the States, saying again, in Brownsville, Texas, that he wants to rejoin the Dodgers. "I figure I've given all I can to the Mexican League," he's quoted as telling the *New York Times*. But, unlike him, others who jumped to the Outlaw league aren't so eager to come north. Max Lanier, commenting in Florida, where he's undergoing treatment for an ailing pitching elbow, says he's happy in Mexico. "They have treated me just as well, even a little better, than they promised." True to his word, he'll return to Mexico on August 16.

Owen's desire to play big league ball again is not universally supported by other players in the majors. Marty Marion is quoted as saying, "Owen jumped his team to go down there for that big money, now let him stay there." The Phillies report "unanimous" agreement against Owen.

Upon reaching Houston, Owen claims the Pasquels broke their agreement with him. He says he was signed to be catcher-manager of Torreon, then reneged, sending him to the Vera Cruz Blues. Owen insists, "I signed for the Torreon outfit and I wanted to play with Torreon." Assigned to play first base, he complains he'd never played the position before. Happy Chandler's assistant, former catcher Herold (Muddy) Ruel, cites a convenient clause in baseball law, which declares Owen can't be reinstated this year, no matter what.

August 7

Detroit second baseman Eddie Mayo undergoes back surgery for what's described as "arthritis of the spine." He won't return to action this season.

Approximately this date—after pinch-hitting yesterday, he won't play again till the 17th—first baseman Les Fleming of the Indians returns home to Beaumont, Texas, to be at the side of his seriously ill 19-month-old son.

"Deals of the Week" in this issue of *The Sporting News*

The Phillies optioned shortstop Don Hasenmayer to Utica on July 23. He hadn't played for the Phillies yet, being fresh out of the Army. He'll respond with a .184 batting average in 56 games with Philadelphia's Eastern League farm team. He'll only play six more times for the parent club, toward the end of the season, his second of two brief big league stints. His first cup of coffee was in 1945, when he played five games for the Phils.

The Red Sox buy pitcher Bill Kennedy from Rocky Mount of the Class D Coastal Plain League, for fall delivery, though he won't make his big league debut till 1948, with Cleveland. This is William *Aulton* Kennedy, en route to a 28–3 record in 1946, with a minor league high 456 strikeouts, an unprecedented number. He'll pitch parts of eight seasons in the big leagues, when he finally makes it. William *Gorman* Kennedy, also called Bill, also a lefty, is already in the American League, at Washington. But he'll be gone before the Rocky Mount Bill gets here.

August 8

The Pittsburgh Pirates are sold by the estate of Barney Dreyfuss, ending a 47-year family ownership. The new owner is a syndicate, fronted by Frank E. McKinney, heretofore part-owner of the Braves. Also involved are singer–movie star Bing Crosby, Pittsburgh attorney Thomas P. Johnson, and Columbus, Ohio, realtor John W. Galbreath, who will become the power behind the throne. Crosby's share provides him endless publicity in an ongoing, good-natured one-upmanship mock feud with Hollywood pal and motion picture co-star Bob Hope, new minority stockholder of the Indians. They'll mug for countless photos, each wearing his team's cap and or jersey, a pointless but pleasant public relations diversion, furthering their popularity.

Pittsburgh's sale price is estimated around $2 million. McKinney says the group are roughly equal partners. He, himself, is also part-owner of the Indianapolis Indians of the American Association and says he'll hold onto that stock. The Braves are in the process of selling their shares in the minor league club to McKinney, too, apparently as part of the deal to divest of his Boston investment. It will make Indianapolis a Pittsburgh farm team.

Bob Feller of the Indians pitches his second one-hitter in three starts, beating the White Sox, 5–0. Ex-teammate Frank Hayes gets the only Chicago hit. This sets a major league record for career low-hit games (10), breaking a tie Feller held with Addie Joss.

August 9

As they begin a series against the Reds in Cincinnati, there isn't much bench strength remaining in the Cardinals' outfield. Captain and center fielder Terry Moore, hampered all season by injuries, hasn't played outfield since the 16th of July. He'll be limited almost exclusively to pinch-hitting duties the rest of the season, due to torn cartilage in his right knee. He faces surgery in the off-season. Harry Walker, who often replaces Moore, is called to come home when his son is struck by a car. Little Terry Walker, not quite four, suffered a hip fracture and skull wounds, but it's not as serious as feared, and Harry returns to the lineup on the 12th. Outfielder Buster Adams hurries home today, to attend to his wife, who's just given birth to a daughter, their first child. He'll be back on the 11th, taking Walker's place in a doubleheader against the Reds.

Moore says his ailing left knee might keep him out of center field the rest of the season, as he's playing in constant pain. That's a bit pessimistic: he'll be in his old, familiar center field post in 22 of the Cards' final 54 games, including the playoffs.

Tonight is the first time in history that the full slate of major league games is played under the lights. The largest crowd is in Yankee Stadium, where tonight's game with the Red Sox draws 63,040. The smallest is in Sportsman's Park, where the Browns, hosting the Indians, can only pull in 7,378 fans. All together, the eight games attract 205,980.

August 10

Bob Feller pitches relief again, coming in today and tomorrow against the Browns. The idea, which manager Lou Boudreau says is his, not Feller's, is to give the pitcher an increased chance to break Rube Waddell's major league strikeout record for a single season. As of now, that's supposed to be 343, but toward the end of the year, statisticians will reveal 347 as the mark. That, too, will prove erroneous. More to come.

Johnny Groth, 20-year-old outfielder just discharged by the Navy and signed by the Tigers, makes his first appearance in an exhibition game today. He'll get his first regular-season chance on September 5. Groth played with Feller's Great Lakes NTS team last year. This season, he'll only play four games for Detroit (his 1946 appearances won't even be listed in the *Who's Who* of 1950, first time he shows up in that annual publication, but he *does* play for the Tigers in 1946, venerable booklet to the contrary). Groth will spend most of the next two years at Buffalo. All told, he'll see action in 15 big league seasons.

August 11

Hooper Triplett, Army vet leading his Sally League Columbus (Ga.) Cardinals with a .314 batting average, is fined $500 and suspended indefinitely by the loop's directors for making a $20 bet on the Columbia Reds, his team's opponent in their game on August 3. He'd walked and struck out, fielded well enough that day, until lifted on orders of business manager Bing Devine, who, moments earlier, had learned of the bet. Batting champion of the Sally League in 1940, brother of ex–big leaguer Coaker Triplett (now with Buffalo), on the 21st the outfielder will be expelled from baseball for life, by National Association president W.G. Bramham.

Lonnie Goldstein, just out of the Army, pinch-hits for the Reds today in Pittsburgh, one of six appearances he'll make this year. A first baseman, he got into five games in 1943, the first of two short stays in the major leagues. Goldstein reported on the 9th, after driving 3,300 miles from Fort Lewis, Washington. Next season, and every season till 1954, he'll play minor league ball, and manage some, down in the Class B Big State League.

In the second game of the Reds doubleheader, Pittsburgh second baseman Frank Gustine is spiked in the foot by center fielder Jim Russell, as they chase a Texas Leaguer blooped between them. Gustine is so badly gashed he has to be carried off the field before stitches can be taken. He won't return to the lineup until August 28.

Two days ago, Cincinnati optioned pitcher Howie Fox to Syracuse, for whom he makes his first appearance today. He pitched four times for the Reds, hampered by his appendectomy. Fox, 8–12 in 45 games last year, will be recalled for later this season, but, in the International League Playoffs, sustains an incomplete fracture of his pitching arm. He won't pitch again in a big league game till 1948. In 1949, he'll lead the National League with 19 losses, but in 1950, he'll turn it around and post an 11–8 record for Cincinnati.

The Giants have announced purchase of pitcher Larry Jansen, now 23–3 at San Francisco, for later delivery — which will be next spring. Ending the year with 30 wins for the Seals, it's hoped he won't struggle the way ex–Seal Bob Joyce did this season for New York, despite *his* 30 wins for San Francisco a year ago. Jansen will have considerably more success as a big league freshman, posting a 21–5 record in 1947. The last pitcher to win 30 in the minors before Joyce was 1937, when Ash Hillin of Oklahoma City in the Texas League (in 62 games) and Red Lynn of Jacksonville, East Texas League (56 appearances) did it. A pitcher named Bill Thomas will win 35 this season for Houma, but way down in the Evangeline League. It'll happen to four other guys in the 1950s, also in the low minors, and that's it for modern 30-game winners below the big leagues. (Thomas, who never pitches once in the majors, wins more lifetime games in the minors, 383, and loses more, 346, than anyone else in history.)

August 12

Cubs pitcher Claude Passeau's back goes out again. This time he'll be sidelined till the 24th. When it flares up again that day, he'll take himself home for the rest of the season.

The Cubs sell outfielder Frank Secory to Kansas City, for whom he plays his first game the 14th (he pinch-hit for Chicago on the 10th, his last game in the majors). Secory was in portions of five seasons with the Tigers, Reds and Cubs, not much of which has been distinguished (other than two-for-five as a pinch-hitter in last fall's World Series). Six years from now, he'll return to the National League as an umpire.

August 13

Cubs catcher Clyde McCullough, hospitalized briefly yesterday for a sinus condition, fractures a little finger. He'll be out of action till September 10.

Boo Ferriss of the Red Sox beats the Athletics 7–5 to become the first pitcher to win 20 games in each of his first two seasons since Wes Ferrell of Cleveland, in 1929-30. It's Ferriss' eighth straight win. A phenomenon in 1945 when, as a rookie, he went 21–10, he'll finish at 25–6 this year. Only 24 now, arm problems and asthma will limit him to 12 wins next season, one the next, and none ever after. It was his asthma that forced Ferriss out of the Air Corps in early 1945. Virtually unbeatable at the moment, his big league career will end with a single appearance in 1950.

Tonight in Pittsburgh, outfielder Eddie Lukon of the Reds is honored by his hometown fans from Burgettstown, Pennsylvania. Lukon, veteran of the Battle of the Bulge, is serenaded by his high school marching band, given a shotgun, portable radio, handbag (as described in *The Sporting News*) and a diamond-studded American Legion pin. Lukon goes hitless, playing left field against the Pirates.

Vern Stephens, shortstop of the Browns, plays his last game in the field until August 31, due to recurring shoulder problems. He'll pinch-hit in a couple of days, otherwise be out of action till month's end.

The Braves option pitcher Elmer Singleton to Indianapolis today. He'll be recalled next month, but has already made all his 16 Boston appearances for this year. His first trip to the mound for Indy will be on the 18th of this month. Next season, he'll pitch 36 games for Pittsburgh.

August 14

Braves pitcher Mort Cooper, working against the Phillies, sprains his pitching elbow, gives way to Johnny Sain and Si Johnson. Cooper won't take the hill again till the nightcap of a doubleheader two weeks from now.

August 15

Baltimore outfielder Howie Moss is selected for promotion to the Indians, per the working agreement which allows Cleveland its choice of two Orioles players for $10,000 each. With 38 home runs and 112 RBI, Moss, formerly with the Giants and Reds, might be a bonanza for Cleveland. Except, as it develops, he'll hit .063 in eight games and his short big league career will be over. Moss won't report till Baltimore's season ends a month from now, making his first appearance for the Indians on September 19.

White Sox pitcher Bill Dietrich, sidelined since June 25th with a broken finger, is suspended by manager Ted Lyons today, supposedly for refusing to report to the team in Detroit. It appears a moot point, since Bullfrog Bill (for his deep voice) is done for the year, anyway. He tells reporters, "I acted in good faith when I left Chicago after the team physician told me I would have to wait several weeks for additional X-rays." Next year, he'll pitch for the Athletics.

August 16

Aaron Robinson, Yankee catcher, breaks a knuckle on his throwing hand. The injury isn't as bad as first thought: Robinson returns to the lineup on the 22nd.

In this same game at Boston's Fenway Park, Joe DiMaggio strains his right shoulder in making a throw to third base. He leaves the game, replaced by Johnny Lindell. Tomorrow, Joe D. will move to left field, with Charlie Keller going to right and Lindell remaining in center. Joltin' Joe will also play left in both halves of a Boston doubleheader, the day after tomorrow.

August 17

Today, Boo Ferriss beats the Yankees, 7–4, for his 21st win, his ninth in a row and 14th straight complete game. The Red Sox extend their American League lead to 14 games.

August 18

Jackie Price, purchased from Oakland, makes his big league debut at shortstop for the Indians. He'll play seven games for Cleveland this year, his only season as a major league player. At 33, he's no threat to Lou Boudreau's job security, but he's not really with Cleveland to play ball. When Bill Veeck still ran the Milwaukee Brewers just after his return from the war, he saw Price doing incredible acrobatic comedy baseball routines, all the while employed as an infielder. According to Veeck, Price can hang upside down from a trapeze at home plate and hit pitched balls. He can throw two balls, one a fastball and the other a curve, to two different players at the same time. Price shoots a ball from a cannon mounted on a jeep, drives the jeep from the outfield to the grandstands and catches the ball backhanded, on the fly.

Veeck promised Price he'd get him into the major leagues and let him perform at the World Series, both of which promises he keeps.

Five days ago, Price teamed for the first time with Max Patkin, a sort of "coach" (described in *The Sporting News* as "a double-jointed comedian, from Wilkes-Barre") whose funnyman routines will be seen at all levels of the game for five decades. Their hijinks are so well-received that Veeck quickly gets inquiries from other clubs about the act's availability. Price's life as a ball player virtually over, his career as an *artiste* has begun.

Price and Patkin quickly gain fame as baseball crowd-pleasers, much to the displeasure of baseball's stuffy "Old Guard," whose collective nose Bill Veeck loves to tweak. On the 25th, as Patkin goofily imitates Joe Cronin when the Boston manager walks to his third base coaching box, Cronin turns and snaps at the Cleveland bench, "So this is big league baseball, is it?"

Joe Medwick of the Dodgers is beaned by a pitch from Frank Hoerst of the Phillies, more Hoerst's wildness than intent. Medwick, who was almost killed by a Bob Bowman pitch back in 1940 against the Cardinals, is carried off the field on a stretcher, but tests in the hospital reveal he has only a concussion.

White Sox first baseman Joe Kuhel rounds first in the 11th inning of today's game against Cleveland and pulls a leg muscle. He'll be out till the second game of Chicago's August 25 doubleheader against Philadelphia. Tomorrow, Hal Trosky replaces Kuhel. Trosky, once-feared slugger, missed three of the last four seasons with chronic migraine headaches. He'll bow out after 1946.

August 20

In a second union ballot, players of the Pirates vote "no" to the American Baseball Guild's attempt to become their bargaining agent. As earlier this season, pitcher Rip Sewell leads the opposition, which prevails by a 15–3 vote. Many players abstain from taking part. This ends the 1946 move toward a union, but it certainly isn't the end of the story.

Second baseman Don Johnson of the Cubs suffers a broken hand and is out the remainder of the 1946 season. The chronicle of Chicago injuries rendered in these pages is a good place to start when trying to answer the question that rings down through the ages: "*What happened to the Cubs? Why did they fade so quickly after their pennant of '45?*"

Army 1st Lt. George Munger is discharged at Camp Dix, New Jersey. Within 24 hours, he'll sign to rejoin the Cardinals.

There's a story in today's *Sporting News* that former White Sox pitcher Monty Stratton, who lost a leg in a 1938 hunting accident, may have a movie made about his life. Twice a 15-game winner for the Chisox but forgotten for years, Stratton, pitching on a wooden leg, achieves a remarkable 18–8 record this year for the Sherman Twins in the Class C East Texas League. Nobody knows, yet, that 1949's "*The Stratton Story*" will be one of James Stewart's most memorable movies.

This is the night Bob Feller's fastball is clocked at 98.6 miles per hour, fastest speed yet recorded, by an Army machine called the Lumiline, or Sky Screen, Chronograph. It's supposed to be accurate to one ten-thousandth of a second.

Atley Donald of the Yankees was clocked in the mid-nineties before the war; this was faster than that previously-calculated high. For lack of other proof, Bob Feller is looked upon by many as the fastest of all, though there were no such meters in the days of Walter Johnson, Smoky Joe Wood, Addie Joss and Rube Waddell.

August 21

Braves first baseman Ray Sanders suffers a broken left arm in a collision with Erv Dusak of the Cardinals, finishing his season. With earlier ailments, it holds Sanders to 80 games in 1946. He'll play no games in 1947, 14 in 1948 to 1949. The injury basically ends the career of a fine wartime player who helped the St. Louis Cardinals win three consecutive pennants.

Pittsburgh shortstop Billy Cox injures a hand playing against Brooklyn and is shelved till the 28th (excluding a couple of games as a pinch-runner).

August 22

Dewey Williams, called up after catching his last game for Los Angeles on the 18th, pinch-hits for the Cubs today against the Braves. "Dee" Williams caught a game for Chicago in last year's World Series. This year, he played 98 times for the Angels, but hit only .200 and was expendable when Los Angeles acquired Hal Spindel from the Phillies. Spindel's .210 is but little improvement over Williams, whose most productive years in the majors were his first two, 1944–45. Williams will play four games for Chicago in 1946, three next year for the Reds and 48 for the 1948 Cincy's.

Today and tomorrow are black-and-blue letter days for the Pirates, hosting the Giants at Forbes Field. Sidelined are third baseman Bob Elliott (plays in the field one time, between the 16th and 25th); shortstop Billy Cox (see above, the 21st); sore-armed pitcher Fritz Ostermueller; second baseman Frankie Gustine (still nursing a spike wound) and, within a few days, utility outfielder Al Gionfriddo (about to undergo an appendectomy).

Under terms of a 1938 agreement with the Sacramento Solons of the Coast League, the Cardinals say they will buy pitcher Gerry Staley, at a prearranged price of $5,000 (the Cards had the right to purchase one returning serviceman). Staley won't report till next year, after a 13–12 record for the Solons in 1946. The transaction formally concludes the association between St. Louis and Sacramento, which otherwise ended in 1944.

August 23

Dom Dallessandro, diminutive Cubs outfielder, fractures an ankle. His .368 for San Diego won the Pacific Coast League batting title in 1939, ahead of Dom DiMaggio's .360 for San Francisco. During the war, "Dim Dom" was a solid contributor to the Cubs, hitting .304 in his best season, 1944. He returned in 1946 from a year in the Army; he'll be back in two weeks (!) to pinch-hit.

Giants third baseman Bill Rigney is out with a cold and will miss three games.

August 24

Braves catcher Bob Brady, brought up from Indianapolis to help fill the void left by the injured Ken O'Dea, makes his major league debut, one of three games he'll play this year for Boston. In the American Association, he hit .233 in 67 games.

Claude Passeau, Chicago pitcher starting against the Braves, hurts his back yet again (*see* August 12) and leaves the mound after two innings. Though he hits a home run off Bill Lee before departing, Passeau's through for the year.

Third baseman Grady Hatton of the Reds, candidate for Rookie of the Year, suffers a season-ending accident under the stands before the start of today's Dodgers game in Crosley Field. Hatton is running on the concrete walkway in sneakers, carrying his spikes. He swerves to avoid a child in the crowd and runs into Harold Parrott, Brooklyn road secretary. Hatton slips, lands hard on the concrete, hurting his right knee. Limping, he still plays the game, but overnight the knee stiffens. X-rays on the 26th show he's fractured his kneecap, chipped the bone, and ended his season.

August 25

Charlie Letchas, who played 116 games as a Philadelphia Blue Jays utilityman in 1944, makes his first appearance for the now–Phillies after his discharge from military service August 14. He fills in at second base for Emil Verban, during the first half of a doubleheader against the Reds. Prewar, Letchas played 14 games with the 1939 Phils and 1941 Nats. This will be his last term in the big leagues.

In the doubleheader's second game, Lou Possehl makes his debut, one of four games he'll pitch for Philadelphia this season. A week ago, the 20-year-old ex–G.I. was pitching semipro ball in Chicago. Today, he beats the Reds, 4–1. He'll pitch parts of five seasons in the big leagues, but never much and never with more than one win in a year.

Two other former big league pitchers, each just arrived from the Army, find themselves in the second game of today's double-dip between the Dodgers and Cardinals. Cal McLish pitches a bad one-third inning for Brooklyn, while Red Munger throws a better one-third inning for St. Louis.

Brooklyn's Ed Head pitches in relief for his final appearance in the big leagues, closing out a year which began so brilliantly with his April no-hitter. Lost to shoulder and arm trouble, his career in the majors is at an end. The Cards win, 14–8, after having dropped the twin bill's opener, 3–2.

Washington pitcher Milo Candini, back from a season and a half in the Army, makes his first appearance today, in relief against the Browns, getting the win in the 12th inning. The *Baseball Register* says Candini was discharged in February, but the commissioner's office says it was August 14th. An ex–Yankee farmhand, he was 11–7 for Washington in 1943, 6–7 in 1944. Arriving so late, he'll still make nine appearances this season (0–2).

The Browns hold an intramural one-punch boxing match in this game, down in the dugout at Griffith Stadium. In the 10th inning of their overtime 5–4 loss to Washington, St. Louis center fielder Walt Judnich, normally a very mild-mannered man, nails a left uppercut to the nose of pitcher Tex Shirley, breaking it in several places. Shirley had just blown a 4–1 lead, helped no little by a bad Judnich throw, which escaped third baseman Bob Dillinger. "That was the dumbest play I ever saw," Shirley observed. "Why weren't you backing up the play, as you should have been?" inquired Judnich. One thing led to another, which led to Shirley's busted beak.

It's been that kind of year for the Browns, who are destined to finish seventh after winning the pennant just two seasons ago. Shirley was Rudy York's victim when the Red Sox slugger hit his two grand slams in their July 27 game. The team's best player, Vern Stephens, is still out with a shoulder injury and will miss over 40 games this season. Among recent distractions, Pitcher Frank Biscan declined to depart on the current road trip, after being assigned an upper berth on the train, resulting in his brief suspension; pitcher Jack Kramer got so angry on the mound in Boston that he chucked a ball out of Fenway Park and pushed umpire Hal Weafer, resulting in his five-day suspension and $200 fine; Shirley earlier was fined for flinging a ball into the left field bleachers.

August 27

The injury-plagued Cubs are struck again. Center fielder Andy Pafko, just recovered from a fractured ankle, breaks an arm and is lost for the rest of the season. Next year, he'll have the kind of year he should have had *this* year.

August 28

Pirates outfielder Al Gionfriddo, who's spent much of the season on the bench, has his appendectomy today and is lost for the remainder of 1946.

"Deals of the Week" in *The Sporting News* issue of this date

The Athletics bring up a bunch of guys, including Hank Biasetti, first baseman, purchased from Toronto, who doesn't appear in big league box scores this season. Born in Beano, Italy, he won't play in the majors till 1949.

From Savannah, the Athletics recall outfielder Vern Benson, though he's already been in his total of seven major league games this year. He was sent to Toronto in the spring, then demoted to the Sally League. Benson will next surface in a big league box score with the Cardinals, in 1951. He'll contribute a great deal more as a coach for the Cards, Yankees, Reds, Braves and Giants, between 1961 and 1980.

August 29

Ray Prim of the Cubs, injured all summer, pitches in relief of Hank Borowy against the Dodgers, the first time he's worked since mid–May. If the stat category of "Save" were kept yet, he'd get one: Cubs win, 3–2.

The Browns announce promotions from the minors, once the players' seasons end on September 8, for catcher Ken Sears of San Antonio and infielder Len Schulte, outfielder-catcher Babe Martin and pitchers Chet Johnson and Fred Sanford of Toledo. Sears and Schulte have already played their big league games this year, but they'll come up anyway. Sears won't last very long.

The Cards beat the Giants, while the Cubs win over the Dodgers. St. Louis leads the NL by 2½ games.

In a deal announced today, the Boston Braves buy the Milwaukee Brewers franchise and will operate the American Association team in their farm system, beginning next season. It's not discussed at the moment, but it opens up the territory for a move there by the Boston franchise, in 1953. Whether this figures in the deal is idle speculation, but when the move comes, there will be no "territorial rights" fee to pay, since the territory now belongs to the Braves. The sale becomes effective October 1. Oscar Salenger bought the Brewers from Bill Veeck last fall, for a reported $200,000. The Braves are paying him around $270,000, giving Salenger a tidy profit.

August 30

Trying to improve the team for next year, the Braves purchase southpaw Glenn Elliott from Seattle, for delivery in the spring. Elliott will get three seasons in the majors, pitching best in his 1949 swan song at Boston.

A Jackie Robinson note in *The Sporting News* reports that, by the second game of Montreal's doubleheader at Toronto today, injuries had depleted the Royals' third base corps. "Jackie Robinson, Negro infield star, was shifted to the hot corner," the blurb says, "a station he is said to be ticketed to play for Brooklyn next season." Robinson will play more there than at any position but second base in the big leagues, though in 1947 he'll work only at first base.

August 31

Luke Sewell, manager of the Browns, "resigns" after a fateful meeting with club president Richard C. Muckerman, local ice house magnate (who bought the team last year from another ice house magnate, Don Barnes). Having led the Browns to the 1944 pennant, Sewell's departure doesn't sit well with his players, which doesn't bother Muckerman in the least. Sewell's contract reportedly was to run through 1947, but little is said about that. Longtime coach James (Zack) Taylor, once a big league catcher, is appointed interim manager.

In turn, three weeks from now it will be disclosed that next year's manager is going to be another former catcher, Herold (Muddy) Ruel, presently with the commissioner's office. Ruel, it's said, signs a two-year contract. Regardless, in 1948 the revolving door will find him out and Taylor back in. Two-year contracts appear to be the stuff dreams are made of.

The Braves make a trade with Seattle to get first baseman Earl Torgeson, a .285 hitter with potential power, for 1947 delivery. Along with a rumored $50,000, Boston sends the PCL club four minor league players. They're taking a chance, as Torgeson was sidelined for the remainder of the season after dislocating his right shoulder on August 7. But he's young (22), hit .312 for Seattle in 1942 at 18, and his future is ahead, not behind him, as in the case of Ray Sanders.

Meanwhile, the Braves suffer more injuries. Left fielder Danny Litwhiler is hit by a Dick Mauney pitch in the first game of a twin bill today against the Phils, breaking his cheekbone. Litwhiler will miss nine games and return to the lineup on September 8. He's replaced this afternoon by Mike McCormick, who then tears leg ligaments in the nightcap, sliding into a base. His cast comes off on the 8th and he's said to be "day-to-day," but his next day will be next year.

The Pirates announce the dissolving of Pittsburgh's farm team relationships with Hollywood of the Coast League and Birmingham of the Southern Association. Each had working agreements this year.

September 1

Louisville manager Nemo Leibold returns to his job, having served a long suspension for attacking an umpire (*see* June 16, above), though not till the end of the season, as previously dictated. While he was away, catcher Fred Walters managed the Colonels into first place, with a 33–13 record. Louisville president Bruce Dudley, loyal to his manager of record, announces Leibold will also pilot the club next year. Walters will be rewarded for his work with the manager's job at the Red Sox' Southern Association farm club in New Orleans, in 1947.

September 2

Utility infielder Rusty Peters, away in the Army since April 1945, has returned from Germany. Freed from duty at the end of July, he plays shortstop for the Indians in the nightcap of this evening's doubleheader against the Browns (a 2–2 tie in 13 innings, called by darkness). Peters will make it into nine games, then be sold to St. Louis for next season. (The 1947 "Baseball Register" says his discharge is effective September 8, almost a week from now; it could be correct, as many servicemen, with "terminal leave" owed them, put their uniforms away and begin civilian life a little early.)

Two of Pittsburgh's three catchers are rendered *hors de combat* today. In the first of two games against the Cubs, Bill Salkeld is hit by a foul tip and carried off the field. He only misses a couple of games, but in the nightcap, Al Lopez is struck by another foul tip, injuring a finger on his right hand, putting him out for the rest of the season. Bill Baker, reserve backstop, is brought forward to replace the wounded in both games. Lopez, injuries aside, has extended his major league record for lifetime games caught to 1,861. Gabby Hartnett had the old mark, which Lopez broke in 1945. Next year with the Cleveland Indians, catching a final 57 times, Lopez will extend his big league record to 1,918 games behind the plate.

The Red Sox, cannonballing toward the pennant, sweep New York in today's Labor Day doubleheader at Yankee Stadium. It's the first time Boston has won both halves of a twin bill against the Yanks since 1939. The wins propel the Bosox into a 15½ game American League lead, their largest of the season to date. For the Yankees, there's the consolation that their 73,551 head count is the biggest Stadium crowd of the year.

The Yanks announce they'll recall infielder Bobby Brown and pitchers Marius Russo and Frank Hiller from Newark, but the players will remain with the Bears until their team is eliminated from the International League playoffs, September 18. Catcher Larry Berra is also due from Newark. He and Brown will make their big league debuts on the 22nd. Russo and Hiller already have pitched their 1946 Yankee games, but they'll be around, just in case. Kansas City pitcher Al Lyons and infielder Eddie Bockman are also called up by New York. Lyons will work twice for the Yanks, beginning on the 11th.

From their offices across the Harlem River at the Polo Grounds, the Giants announce the purchase of pitcher Sheldon (Available) Jones from Jersey City. Yesterday, the Little Giants recalled Jones from Jacksonville, Florida (19–9 down there). He debuts September 9 with the

Big Giants, against the Phillies (New York will lose, Junior Thompson absorbing the loss). In Jones' case, he's one player who feels three years spent in the Air Force helped his game, rather than hurt. He's overcome a poor record prewar (11–25 at Salina, Oklahoma City, Jersey City and Fort Smith), by improving his fastball and curve, while pitching in service games down in Florida. He won't be well established till working 55 games for the Giants in 1948, but he's on his way. He'll split next season between New York and Jersey City (his nickname derives from a character in cartoonist Al Capp's popular comic strip, "Li'l Abner").

September 4

Cecil Garriott, left-handed pinch-hitter just out of the Army, debuts for the Cubs today. He'll play in six games, bat five times in this solitary chance at the big leagues. Batting .000, his chance will be wasted. Next year, he'll be in the outfield of the Los Angeles Angels.

September 5

Tigers outfielder Johnny Groth, signed out of the Navy last month, debuts today. He was with Bob Feller's Great Lakes Naval Station team in the latter stages of the war. He'll play in the majors through 1960, his most consistent performances coming in the late 1940s and early 1950s.

Third Baseman Grady Hatton, star rookie of the Reds, goes home to Texas for the remainder of the season to rest his damaged knee. Doctors project a full recovery (he'll play 11 more years and improve from .271 to .281 in 1947).

The Braves release pitcher Johnny Niggeling, at his request. He's been unable to sleep, due to a stomach ulcer. He hopes to come back next year, but won't.

September 7

The Braves purchase the Southern Association's MVP, outfielder Tommy Neill of Birmingham. Neill, whose .374 led the league for a seventh-place ball club, was originally to report to Boston later. Injuries to Braves outfielders Mike McCormick and Danny Litwhiler have left the team sort of frantic for help right now. Neill debuts on the 10th.

Three members of the Toronto Maple Leafs—infielder Bruce Konopka, pitchers Joe Coleman and Bill McCahan—are excused from tomorrow's season-ending doubleheader against the Montreal Royals, to join the Philadelphia A's, who have promoted each of them.

September 8

Yankee pitcher Karl Drews, just up from Kansas City, debuts after a 14–9 record with the Blues. He'll pitch three times this month, be invited back in 1947, and see duty with a trio of big league teams through 1954.

The regular season ends in the American Association, International League, Southern Association and Texas League today, freeing a number of players who aren't on playoff clubs to report to their major league parent team (if recalled). With its 183-ish game schedule, the

Pacific Coast League doesn't wind up its regular season till the 22nd, four of its eight clubs remaining active for the playoffs which follow.

Clyde Vollmer, outfielder with seventh-place Rochester, farm team of the Cardinals, rejoins the Reds once he's able to make connections. Vollmer pinch-hit once for Cincinnati in April and will play eight more games for the Reds in the next 20 days, beginning the 12th.

Catcher Del Wilber of Columbus (American Association) who debuted in April, returns to the Cardinals, though he won't play again for them this season.

St. Louis also recalls infielder Nippy Jones from Rochester, where he tied for second with Newark's Allie Clark in International League batting (.344 over the last half of the season). He was sent down July 24, after playing eight games for St. Louis. He makes his return on the 10th, pinch-hitting on the 11th, altogether batting .333 during his 16 games with the Cardinals.

Jones still needs work in the minors and when he's about seasoned, suffers a back injury in 1950 that dulls his promise. (Jones' final at-bat in the big leagues comes in the 1957 World Series, when he proves he's hit in the foot by a Tommy Byrne pitch by pointing out a smudge of shoe polish on the ball.)

September 9

Jim Gladd, new catcher for the Giants, makes his big league debut after coming up from Jersey City (.269 in 50 games). He plays four games with New York this month, the only ones he'll ever play in the majors, batting .091. Gladd's Jersey City teammate, third baseman and occasional outfielder Bobby Thomson (.280, 26 homers there) also breaks in today.

Thomson, native of Scotland, will be remembered as "The Staten Island Scot," but, only 22 at the moment, he's dubbed "the Staten Island *youngster*" in the press. He's up to stay, playing 18 games for the Giants this month, batting .315.

Also up from Jersey City are catcher Mickey Grasso, pitcher Marv Grissom and infielder Dick Lajeskie. The latter two will debut tomorrow. It'll be the first of Grissom's four games for New York (already 28, younger brother of ex–big leaguer Lee Grissom, Marv will be a grizzled old gent in his forties, before retiring as a ten-year big league vet). Second baseman Lajeskie, who pocketed $20,000 to sign with New York a couple of years ago, plays six games for the Giants this month. Just 20, after this year he'll never again appear in a big league box score.

Grasso won't make his first big league game till the 18th. A prisoner-of-war of the Germans in North Africa, he's spent a long time getting here, counting four years in military service. Already 25, he'll spend all or parts of seven seasons in the majors, though his next trip upward won't be taken till 1950, with Washington.

Art Houtteman, 19, who pitched for the International League's fifth-place Buffalo Bisons (16–13), has been called up to Detroit, for whom he pitched last year.

The Oklahoma City Indians send two outfielders up to the Cleveland Indians: Dale Mitchell and Ted Sepkowski. They'll both play on the 15th. Pitcher Ralph McCabe is also elevated, to pitch his only big league game, on the 18th.

Also from the Texas League come four Cubs—Tulsa's Clarence Maddern, Henry Schenz and Eddie Hanyzewski, and Shreveport's Doyle Lade. To the Cubs from Nashville come catcher Ted Pawelek, pitcher Russ Meyer, and infielder Cy Block.

The Yankees' Larry MacPhail announces long-time big league manager Bucky Harris, currently general manager in Buffalo, has been hired to an unspecified "advisory" position in the front office. MacPhail says Harris will serve as his eyes and ears, scouting and evaluating other major league teams as well as players in the New York farm system, because he's too busy to do it himself.

September 10

Ben Chapman is awarded a one-year contract extension to continue managing the Phillies. He has an attendance clause in the pact. As the Phils have drawn nearly 900,000, reports are that he's collecting bonus money already. His team will finish fifth, not real good unless you consider the past. From 1933 through 1945, the Phils finished last or next-to-last.

The Red Sox, losing their sixth straight, are in a slight swoon, but it's negligible in the scheme of things. Today's loss is to Detroit, 7–3, allowing the Tigers to move into second place ahead of the Yankees.

Infielder Damon Phillips, released from military service after occupation duty in Tokyo, rejoins the Braves. He was a regular at third and short in 1944, but plays only twice this late in the season, getting a hit in two times up, with no appearances in the field, concluding his three seasons as a big leaguer. Phillips' first game will be on the 21st, as a pinch-hitter.

Three rookies from Toledo, called up to the Browns, also debut: outfielder Paul Lehner, catcher Les Moss and first baseman Jerry Witte. Lehner gets into 16 games this month, hitting .222. He'll play regularly with the Browns and the A's through 1950, then take a couple more years to fade out. Moss, in 12 Brownie games this season, hits .371. For a dozen years ahead, he'll be one of the American League's more reliable backstops.

Witte, American Association MVP, belted 46 home runs for Toledo. In 1949, he'll hit 50 at Dallas but is not destined for a future in the big leagues. In 18 games with the Browns this month, he hits .192 with two homers. His total big league career will consume only 52 games, most of them in 1947, his second of two seasons in the majors. Already 30, he may have lost the edge one needs to rise above Triple-A in his key production years, which he spent in the Service.

Dave Philley, fresh from a .329 season at Milwaukee, plays his first postwar game for the White Sox today (he performed seven times with Chicago in 1941). At Milwaukee on option, the Sox thought about taking him from the Brewers at midseason, but were prevailed upon to let him stay and help the minor league club (didn't help; Brews finished fifth). Philley will hit .363 in 17 games for the Sox, beginning a long stay in the majors.

Third baseman Don Richmond, .292 hitter at Toronto, plays his first game for the Athletics this year, his first since a handful of games for the A's in 1941. He spent the next four seasons in military uniform.

First baseman–outfielder Bruce Konopka, sent to Toronto in July and recalled three days ago, is again in the A's lineup, his third and final session with Philadelphia this season (in his third and final big league season). He replaces George McQuinn for the last 17 games of the season. Also recalled from Toronto is shortstop Jack Wallaesa (sent down in July, the bulk of his 63 games for the A's are behind him, but he does have a couple of weeks to go).

September 11

The Reds and Dodgers play a 19-inning, 0–0 tie in Ebbets Field today, called by darkness. It's the longest scoreless tie in major league history. The game lasts 4 hours, 40 minutes, and will be replayed in its entirety on the 20th.

Bill Dickey says he's asked Larry MacPhail not to consider him as manager next year. MacPhail says he told Dickey the team's relatively poor showing was not the great catcher's fault.

Yankee infielder Eddie Bockman, slugging third baseman from Kansas City, debuts in the first of his four games for New York. Bockman, 25, is destined to be a spear carrier during four seasons in the majors, unable to capitalize on his 1946 performance with the Blues. After three years away at war, out in KC he hit .303, smacked 12 homers and drove in 95 runs, figures he'll never match till he bats in the thin air at Albuquerque, in 1955. Excess baggage with the Yankees, who have Billy Johnson settling back in and Bobby Brown about to arrive, Bockman will go to the Indians this fall, part of the Allie Reynolds deal.

Coming from the Blues with Bockman is pitcher Al Lyons, who had a mediocre season with Kansas City. Lyons pitched half a year for New York in 1944, before donning a military uniform. He'll throw once more in 1946, starting against the Red Sox in Boston.

Hank Camelli, reserve Pittsburgh catcher sent to Toronto at the end of June, has returned and pinch-hits today against the Giants. Pirates catchers are having the devil of a time staying healthy: Bill Baker, third-stringer, has been sharing duty with second-stringer Bill Salkeld, who's at less than full speed (as noted, first-stringer Al Lopez' season ended at the start of the month). Camelli is a warm body: he's been around for years, comes back to the majors off a .226 batting average with the Maple Leafs.

Date uncertain, Pirates pitcher Preacher Roe, hampered all season by injuries from a winter basketball game and who last pitched in early August, is sent home to rest until next spring. He pitched just 21 games, compiling a 3–8 record. He won't have much better fortune next year, but in 1948, traded to the Dodgers, he'll have six significant seasons with the Boys of Summer.

It's announced in this issue of *The Sporting News* that Roy Campanella, catcher of Nashua, has been named the backstop on the New England League's all-star team. Campanella, one day in the Hall of Fame, will catch for Montreal next year, St. Paul and Brooklyn the next. He and Don Newcombe formed organized ball's first all-black battery this season. Newcombe, 14–4 at Nashua, will return next year, winning 19 and losing 6.

There's speculation the Dodgers are about to sign outfielder Monte Irvin, star of the champion Newark Eagles in the Negro National League. Branch Rickey feels it prudent, though, to step back and let other teams pick from the Negro League crop. It'll be 1949 before the New York Giants are able to purchase the future Hall of Famer's contract from Eagles owner Effa Manley, for $5,000.

September 12

Bill Dickey resigns as manager of the Yankees, retiring as a major league player as well (in 1947, he'll play eight final professional games down home in Little Rock, as player-manager of the Travelers). His accomplishments: seventeen years behind the bat, 202 home runs, lifetime .313 in the American League, and .362 in 1936, the major league season record for a catcher.

New York coach Johnny Neun has taken over for the rest of the year. He, too, will leave the Yankees, at season's end, to replace Bill McKechnie as manager of the Reds. There are the inevitable stories that, after a mere two weeks on the job, Neun has all he cares for of working for Leland S. MacPhail (it's possible he finds no encouragement from MacPhail to stay, anyway). The Yankee president keeps denying Bucky Harris will be next year's manager.

Speculation grows, one thing and another, past the end of the season, as the New York press becomes convinced MacPhail wants Leo Durocher or, at the very least, his top coach, Chuck Dressen, for the job. Harris will get it.

The Cardinals beat the Dodgers, 10–2, in Brooklyn, to open a crucial series in the National League pennant race. St. Louis' lead increases to 2½ games.

Pitcher Paul Minner of the Dodgers, purchased from Mobile, debuts today. He was 16–11 for the Bears of the Southern Association and will go 0–1 for Brooklyn in three games. Minner will work again at Mobile in 1947, begin 1948 at Montreal, and finish with the Dodgers. Moving to the Cubs in 1950, he'll have some good seasons for Chicago, but lead the National League with 17 losses in 1951. He'll be a ten year man stopped by back problems in 1956.

Third baseman Seymour (Cy) Block plays his first game for the Cubs this year, after batting a torrid .354 in half a season at Nashville. Block, who began 1946 at Los Angeles, is on his third (and last) trip to the majors. Injured third baseman Stan Hack, who broke a thumb early in August, makes his first appearance since then, as a pinch-hitter today against the Phillies.

Phillies pitcher Aloysius (Eli) Hodkey, in relief, debuts today in game two. Hodkey, who toiled in the minors from 1938 to 1942 and spent three seasons at war, was promoted after 13–7 this year at Utica. All that for half a month in the majors, which is what he gets.

For the St. Louis Browns, pitcher Chet Johnson debuts. Catcher Babe Martin plays in the first of his three games for St. Louis, pinch-hitting today.

September 13

After six straight losses, the Red Sox beat Cleveland to capture their first American League pennant since 1918. By the end of the season, the Bosox will finish 12 games ahead of the second-place Tigers, 17 over the once-mighty Yankees.

As many of Boston's players are tired, owner Tom Yawkey allows some to return to the Hub City for a rest, rather than play against the Browns in a meaningless series beginning the 18th. Ted Williams goes, as do Johnny Pesky, Bobby Doerr, Hal Wagner, Dom DiMaggio, Boo Ferriss, Tex Hughson and Mickey Harris. Rudy York and Wally Moses remain, along with the team's reserves. York says he's a 154-game player and doesn't need a vacation (besides, he's had two days off already). In St. Louis, the Browns refund about $500 to fans who are angry because Boston's stars aren't there to play the 18th. Even using subs, Boston wins, 6 to 2. When the Bosox move to Washington, the vacationing stars, having been on a five-day sabbatical, are back in the lineup.

Big Jawn Mize, Giants first baseman who suffered a broken hand in August, returns to action today against the Reds and breaks what is described as "his right toe" (probably the big one, taking for granted he likely has four others on his right foot). Mize is known as "The Big Cat," four decades before Andres Galarraga comes along.

The Dodgers score four runs in the first inning, then hold on for a 4–3 win over the Cardinals at Ebbets Field today. The win brings Brooklyn up to 1½ games behind St. Louis.

Running against the Cardinals today, Pete Reiser of Brooklyn pulls up lame, with an injured thigh muscle. Unable to throw because of his bad shoulder, Reiser is now unable to run. Dodgers manager Leo Durocher, never one to let up, will put Reiser back in to pinch-hit within a few days, on the 16th. Between now and the 25th, Pete will do that twice, and play left field once. Reiser also missed Brooklyn's first seven games in September, starting with the Labor Day doubleheader, because of pleurisy. With the pennant hanging in the balance, he'll be limited to three more games in the field (left, not center, now a distant memory).

Pitcher Hal Manders of the Cubs, ex–Tiger up from Buffalo, makes his first National League appearance today, giving up six hits and three runs in two innings against the Phillies. Manders, Bob Feller's cousin from Waukee, Iowa (Feller's from Van Meter), was 10–4 after being sent down to the Bisons by Detroit. Things won't go well at Chicago. He'll pitch just two games, winding up three part-seasons in the majors.

Two other Cubs, up from Nashville, debut: catcher Ted Pawelek (.335 for the Vols, four games for the Cubs, a solitary stint behind the bat in his only trial in the majors) and pitcher Russ Meyer (13–8 in his third season with the Vols, four games this season for Chicago, no decisions, a long major league career ahead).

A's catcher Joe Astroth, up from Lancaster, sees duty behind the plate in the first game of today's doubleheader against the White Sox in Chicago. Astroth began the season on option to Toronto, played once there before being sent farther down, to the Class B Inter-State League. He'll play four times this month for Philadelphia, not seeing consistent duty in the big leagues until 1950. His is not a common name, not well-known: last season, making his brief pro debut with the A's, he was first listed in box scores as "Schroft" and then "Stroth." Today, he's "Ostroth."

Senators pitcher Vern Curtis, recalled from Buffalo, makes his final big league mound appearance today. He was recalled right after the end of the International League season, on September 9.

September 14

The Dodgers narrow the Cardinals' NL lead to a half game, with Ralph Branca shutting out St. Louis, 5–0.

Gerry Priddy, Washington second baseman, goes home to Los Angeles to rest his injured left knee, hurt while sliding into a base against the White Sox on the 11th. Priddy has torn cartilage and wants to avoid surgery if possible. He has five full-time seasons ahead of him, so his decision to rest the knee must be successful.

Infielder Don Hasenmayer pinch-hits for the Phillies, starting a brief return to the major leagues. He played five games last year and will play six now. Up from Utica, September 1946 marks the last we'll see of him in the big leagues.

Pitcher Jim "Junior" Walsh makes his big league debut in relief for the Pirates against the Braves. Brought up from York with his pitching mate Lee Howard (*see* Sept. 22), he's also spent time at Birmingham, following World War II military service. After this season, Walsh won't appear here again till 1948.

With Fort Worth sweeping Tulsa in the first round of the Texas League playoffs last night, selected Oiler players are free to answer recalls to the parent Cubs. Ed Hanyzewski, who started the second game of the playoffs, is among those who leave, with outfielder Clarence Maddern and third baseman Henry Schenz.

September 15

The Cardinals sweep the Giants today, while the Dodgers and Cubs split. Brooklyn again is a game and a half behind St. Louis.

New Indians center fielder Dale Mitchell debuts in the big leagues. The Texas League bat champ, he'll hit .432 in 11 games for Cleveland. Ted Sepkowski, also up from Oklahoma City (.300), makes his first appearance for the Indians since a brief trial in 1942, at third base (he played left and center in the Texas League). They both play both ends of today's doubleheader against the A's.

Recalled from Toronto a week ago, A's pitchers Joe Coleman (14–10 there) and Bill McCahan (11–7) start the first and second games, respectively, of the Indians' twin bill. Coleman loses; McCahan beats Bob Feller with a 2–0 shutout.

McCahan, Philly hometown guy whom Connie Mack put through Duke University to secure his services, makes his major league debut. He'll pitch in four games for the A's this month. In 1947, he'll toss a no-hitter against the Nationals, one of only five rookies to accomplish it in American League history. Arm trouble, however, will cut short his career at 27.

Joseph Patrick Coleman will be a ten-year man. His prior big league experience was a single game in 1942, before he went into the service. As does McCahan, he works four games for the Athletics in 1946 (and fathers a son in 1947, Joseph Howard Coleman, who'll pitch 14 seasons in the big leagues, twice win 20 games and spend many years as a pitching coach).

Catcher Walker Cooper of the Giants enters the hospital today, with blood poisoning in his left leg. Beset all season by physical ailments and injury, Cooper could hardly throw during the last half of the year, his broken fingers unable to properly grip a baseball. He's done for 1946.

Fred Sanford, Browns' rookie righthander, shuts out the Yankees, 1–0, in the opener of today's doubleheader. Sanford had a three-game trial in 1943, before going off to war. With the Toledo Mud Hens, he was 15–10 this season. Three years from now, after losing an American League–high 21 games for the Browns, he'll be sent to New York for $100,000 and three players. It'll be one of the Yankees' worst deals ever: 12–10 in two and a half years as a part-time starter for two World Championship teams, Sanford will never himself make it into the Series. By then, the Yankees will be able to easily afford a mistake or two in player acquisition.

Floyd Baker, infielder sent to Milwaukee by the White Sox early this season, pinch-hits for Chicago against the Red Sox in his first game after being recalled.

Tenure seems not to be important. Up from Wilkes-Barre, Cleveland purchases farmhand pitcher Bob Kuzava today. His fans and friends waste no time. Bob Kuzava Day is due in Detroit on the 27th, his debut day in the majors. Kuzava will get a watch from his friends in Wyandotte, Michigan, where he went to high school, though he doesn't get a car like White Sox third baseman Don Kolloway did today in Chicago.

September 16

The Dodgers lose to the Cubs on a grand slam by fading slugger Bill Nicholson, to fall another half game behind the idle Cardinals. St. Louis leads by two.

Pitcher Tommy Bridges is released by the Tigers, only big league team he's ever played for (from 1930 through 1946, with all of 1944 and most of 1945 in the Army). The righthander worked in nine games this summer. Looking back, he had a good ride, 194–138 in 16 seasons. Born in Tennessee, Thomas Jefferson Davis Bridges possessed the wickedest curve in the game, until Bobby Feller came along. Six times on the American League All-Star Game squad, Bridges led the AL in strikeouts twice and was a 20-game winner three straight years in the mid 1930s. He pitched in four World Series, compiling a record of four-and-one. A victim of timing, Bridges will be mostly forgotten in the years to come, though he does pitch another 33 games in a Coast League swan song that keeps him active till 1950.

September 17

Howard Pollet becomes the first lefty to win 20 games in the National League since Carl Hubbell in 1937, beating the Giants 10 to 2. Pollet will finish the season at 21–10. Other 20-game winners this year include Johnny Sain of Boston (20–14) in the NL and, in the AL, Hal Newhouser (26–9), Bob Feller (26–15), Dave Ferriss (25–6), and Tex Hughson (20–11) of the Red Sox and Spud Chandler of New York (20–8).

While St. Louis beats New York, Brooklyn is beating Chicago, 4–2. No change in the NL pennant race — the Cards are still two up.

For the Cubs, rookie Clarence Maddern debuts as a pinch-hitter. He'll play three games for Chicago this season but won't be back here again till 1948.

September 18

Brooklyn splits a doubleheader with Pittsburgh while St. Louis loses a single game to Boston. The Cardinals' lead is cut to one and a half games again.

The debuts of Cubs third baseman Henry Schenz and pitcher Doyle Lade are made today against the Giants. Schenz was Texas League MVP for a fourth-place team eliminated in the first round of the playoffs. Lade, today's other newcomer, will have a record of 11–10 for the Cubs in 1947.

As mentioned earlier, catcher Mickey Grasso of the Giants debuts today.

Catcher Ralph Weigel and pitcher Dick McCabe of Cleveland debut today. Weigel, who'll play six games in the remaining 10 days of the season, is up from Wilkes-Barre, where he hit .288. After three years in military service, this is the first of his three brief visits to the major leagues. McCabe, 10–7 at Oklahoma City, was discovered by old Yankee pitcher-manager Bob Shawkey, who at the time was prospecting in the gold fields of Canada, with a little scouting-for-fun on the side. McCabe, a native of Napanee, Ontario, starts against the Senators and lasts four innings in his one big league ball game.

Right fielder Joe Smaza of the White Sox, .257 and 28 stolen bases at Shreveport, debuts today in the second game of Chicago's doubleheader against the Yankees. It's his first season of professional ball and his single season in the major leagues, where he plays twice.

Making his first appearance of the season is Phillies pitcher Don Grate, recalled from Utica. "Buckeye" Grate, so-called because he once played for the Ohio State University Buckeyes, works three games this year, after four last year with Philadelphia, thus completing his entire big league career.

The Phillies are said to have signed "Edward Jones," whose name never comes up in major league box scores. It could, however, be *Willie* Edward Jones, "Puddin' Head Jones," who's discharged from the Army about now, and whose professional career doesn't begin till next season, at Terre Haute. Puddin' Head spends 15 years in the big leagues.

The Braves recall pitcher Elmer Singleton from Indianapolis, where he was optioned last month. In his second season with Boston, the righthander has already pitched his total of 15 games for the Braves, six for Indy, and doesn't see further action. At the end of the month, he'll find himself in the Billy Herman trade, going to Pittsburgh. He'll be with the Pirates, Senators and Cubs, off and on, through 1959.

September 19

The Dodgers and Cardinals each win today, Brooklyn blanking Pittsburgh 7–0 and St. Louis stopping Boston's six-game winning streak, 5–4, at Braves Field. Cards still lead the National League by a game and a half. Red Sox manager Joe Cronin and several of his players are on hand, scouting the Cardinals, en route to the Bosox-Washington series which starts the day after tomorrow.

Indians first baseman Eddie Robinson plays his first 1946 Cleveland game. A .318 hitter with 34 home runs at Baltimore, he bats .407 in 27 times up during the next ten days, despite a sore leg. Howie Moss, up from Baltimore, too, plays with Cleveland for the first time, at third base. Like Robinson, he gets into eight games, but hits just .063, perhaps sealing his fate. Robinson plays 13 years in the majors and has a long career as an executive in the game. Moss will not return after this year.

Andy Seminick, catcher of the Phillies, breaks a right toe (the big toe, assumedly) when he meets with a wall chasing a foul ball. He's sent home for the rest of the season. *The Sporting News* reports this happens on the 22nd, but he doesn't play that day and the Phils are off between now and then.

September 20

Called up from Baltimore under the same working agreement that saw Howie Moss purchased from the Orioles, Cleveland pitcher Ray Flanigan debuts, in relief. It's Flanigan's first of three games in his only major league season, and is a disastrous introduction: starter Allie Reynolds, pretty awful himself today, yields four runs in an inning and a third, then gives way to Flanigan, who surrenders five tallies in two-thirds of an inning.

Compared to where he's been, that's nothing. During the Allied drive across Europe, Flanigan was decorated for bravery in combat, recommended for a Silver Star after action in Belgium, and received a Purple Heart for arm wounds. At the time, Flanigan, a sergeant, had learned a solitary phrase of German, which served him well. After killing two enemy soldiers and helping wipe out a machine gun nest, he shouted to the survivors, in German, "Come out with your hands up!" A prisoner even complimented him on his excellent command of the language. (The Orioles once valued him at a lordly $40,000, just out of high school, but real life doesn't always have Hollywood endings: Flanigan posted a 13–14 record at Baltimore, and that's the best he'll ever do in baseball.)

Pitching in relief against Cleveland, Teddy Gray makes the second appearance of his rookie season for the Tigers. Gray was 7–11 at Buffalo after his big league debut May 15.

The idle Cardinals have their National League lead sliced to one game, as the Dodgers beat the Reds, 5–3. This is the replay of their 0–0 19-inning marathon staged on September 11. As the Dodgers are at home, their departure for tomorrow's game with Boston is held up, so the Cincinnati tie can be completely cleared off the books.

September 21

Rookie Bob Kuzava makes his major league debut for the Indians today, against the Tigers. He pitches twice for Cleveland in the closing days of the year (0–1) and will be back for a long stay (49–44 in 10 seasons) with eight different teams, primarily in relief. As a Yankee, he'll pitch in three World Series.

Pitcher Ray Shore, 12–12 for Springfield (Ill.) in the Three-I League, makes his debut with the Browns, against the White Sox. Not much as a pitcher, he'll appear in parts of three seasons at St. Louis, but later make his mark evaluating others as an advance scout for Cincinnati's fabled Big Red Machine. His uncle, John (Dots) Miller, was a big leaguer in the early 1900s.

Other Brownies, Ken Sears and George Bradley, are released outright to San Antonio. Sears just got back from there, late last month.

Dick Mulligan, new pitcher for the Braves, makes his first appearance since being purchased from the Phillies on the 18th. Mulligan, 2–2 in 19 games at Philadelphia, will have a 1–0 record in four games with Boston.

Phillies first baseman Vance Dinges, badly shaken up in a collision during a game against the Cardinals, goes home for the rest of the season.

The Dodgers and Cardinals both win today (Brooklyn's 15th victory in 18 games). St. Louis maintains its one-game NL lead.

September 22

The Dodgers, splitting their doubleheader with the Braves while the Cardinals lose a single game to the Cubs, climb to within a half game of the NL lead.

Brooklyn pitcher Harry Taylor, 27, purchased from St. Paul a couple weeks ago, debuts today, one of four games he'll pitch with this year's Dodgers. Next year, he'll ring up a 10–5 record for Brooklyn and start Game 4 of the World Series but, with a sore arm, he'll be lifted after facing four batters and walking in a run. Taylor will be out of the big leagues by 1953.

Lefty Al Gerheauser, marginal Pirates wartime pitcher, plays his first and only major league game as an outfielder. Two-and-two on the mound this season, Gerheauser bats .333 this year and it's worth giving him a shot. That's all he gets, however. He'll spend 1947 at Montreal.

Pittsburgh's Lee Howard, 9–7 with the York White Roses of the Inter-State League, debuts. He's destined for an 0–1 record in three big league games this month. In 1947, he'll make a brief stopover, then disappear from view. Howard starts game one of today's twin bill against the Reds; former York teammate Junior Walsh starts game two. Cincinnati wins both, after which Reds manager Bill McKechnie announces his resignation.

"Deacon Bill" says he'll depart at the end of the season, after nine years at the helm, during which he guided the Reds to two pennants and a World Championship. His tenure is fourth-longest in the history of the National League, though Leo Durocher will press him, with eight straight years at Brooklyn, if he doesn't take the Yankee job next season. McKechnie-led teams won NL pennants in 1925 at Pittsburgh, 1928 at St. Louis, and 1939–40 at Cincinnati. This unique record will earn the quiet, unassuming, unheralded McKechnie induction into the Hall of Fame, in 1962.

Yankee rookies Yogi Berra and Bobby Brown make their big league debuts in the opener of today's doubleheader against the A's. Each will play seven games, Berra hitting .364, Brown .333. Brown, who played at shortstop for Newark, will begin a transition to third base in the next few days. That's where he'll spend most of his big league career.

Yogi, who will catch 1,626 games for the Yankees and play outfield 260 times in the years ahead, will become subject to slight forgetfulness as the years elapse. In 1999, interviewed by

James Brady in *Parade Magazine*, he'll recall, "Aaron Robinson was catcher, and I mostly played outfield" in 1946. In fact, he pinch-hits once this month, catches six games, plays no outfield at all.

In the second game of today's twin bill, outfielder Frank Colman, former Pirate also recalled from Newark by the Yanks, plays right field.

A's' wartime infielder Irv Hall, back from Kansas City, pinch-hits in the first game of the doubleheader. He'll pinch-hit five times between now and the end of the season, his last hurrah.

After the two games against Detroit, the Indians excuse Don Ross, Dutch Meyer, Les Fleming, Ken Keltner, Mel Harder, Rusty Peters, Joe Berry, Tom Jordan, Joe Krakauskas, George Case, Red Embree and Heinz Becker from taking part in the final week of the season. The idea, ostensibly, is to let rookies and young guys play, but a third of the above will not return to the major leagues (Ross, Meyer, Berry, Krakauskas). The Indians aren't alone in this respect: the Yankees send Ernie Bonham, Nick Etten, Ken Silvestri, Johnny Murphy and Frankie Crosetti home. With nothing left of the season, it's time to look at the subs and rooks.

The Phillies declare their 1946 aggregate home attendance total is 1,045,245, called "unprecedented" in the *New York Times*. It almost doubles the previous club record, set in 1916. Next spring's *1947 Official Baseball Guide* will show the figure at 1,045,247.

Clamoring for recognition as a third major league, the Pacific Coast League ends its regular season with a record attendance of 3,718,716 paid. The San Francisco Seals led the entire minor leagues, with 670,563. Across the Bay, Oakland's Oaks are runners-up, drawing 634,311, a franchise record. Overall, the minor leagues drew 32,704,315, highest total ever.

September 23

Brooklyn beats the Phillies 6–1, while Harry Brecheen of the Cardinals shuts out the Cubs, 1–0. No change: St. Louis still leads by a half-game.

Yankees pitcher Red Ruffing is released unconditionally, after a 5–1 season garnered in only eight games, before two months recovering from a fractured knee. In December, he'll sign with the White Sox and complete his 22-year major league career in Chicago.

Bill Dickey is also released as a player, but the last time he played was on the 8th of the month, a few days before he quit as New York's manager. He's reported to already be down in Little Rock, far from Yankee Stadium.

Unlike Ruffing and Dickey, at the front end of his career is rookie Yankee pitcher Vic Raschi, who debuts today. He'll win twice this week, two complete game victories. He's up from a brief stint with Newark, after a 10–10 season at Binghamton. Raschi almost didn't make it in time: somebody neglected to inform Raschi he'd been promoted to the Yankees, so he'd already returned home to Canisius, New York, where the team had to ask the town sheriff to find him and give him the news and ask if he'd please drop by.

The Browns depart for their final road trip of the season, going to Detroit and Chicago. Left behind, in order to let newcomers play, are Nelson Potter, Tex Shirley, Frank Mancuso, Babe Martin and Babe Dahlgren. Chet Laabs goes to the Detroit series but no farther, as the Motor City is his hometown and he's allowed to stay.

September 24

Erv Dusak's tenth-inning home run for the Cardinals beats the Reds, 2–1. The idle Dodgers fall a full game behind St. Louis, with five days left in the regular season.

Pittsburgh pitcher Ken Heintzelman leaves the Pirates for St. Louis, near his hometown at Peruque, Missouri, to have a sinus operation.

Eddie Hanyzewski, banished by the Cubs to Nashville early this season, is back from Tulsa, pitching today in relief for Chicago in the bottom half of today's twin bill against Pittsburgh. Hanyzewski had been transferred from the Southern Association to the Texas League in time to pitch eight games with the Oilers, and another in the playoffs.

September 25

Bucky Walters of the Reds shuts out the Cardinals, 6–0, in a night game, after the Dodgers lose an 11–9 battle with the Phillies in the afternoon. Brooklyn sets a National League record (matching the American League mark) as manager Leo Durocher employs eight pitchers in the loss. Ralph Branca, Hal Gregg, Hugh Casey, Hank Behrman, Harry Taylor, Vic Lombardi, Art Herring and Kirby Higbe all pitch for the Bums, Lombardi taking the loss in a five-run Phillies rally, top of the ninth. The Cardinals still lead the League by one game, with three to play.

Young righthander Art Houtteman, up from Buffalo, starts for Detroit against the Browns. He lasts eight innings, gives up all 15 St. Louis hits and is tagged for the loss. Art's still a year away. By 1950, he'll win 19 for the Tigers; then, after a year in military service, he will lose 20, in 1952. Ruffus Gentry, mangled hands and all, has been recalled from Buffalo, too, but won't pitch any more in 1946. He had no decisions for Detroit in two games.

September 26

Hampered by his hamstring pull, Brooklyn's Pete Reiser tells manager Leo Durocher, "I can play, but I can't run." First inning against the Phillies, Reiser is on first base. Durocher, he says, flashes the "steal" sign. Trapped off base, trying to get back to first and avoid a pickoff throw, Reiser catches his spikes in the dirt, falls and fractures his leg. Durocher, who has continually prodded Reiser through this injury-plagued season, screams, "Get up! Get up! You're not hurt!" Reiser, in agony, reportedly points to his fibula, protruding through the skin. There's no more getting up for Pistol Pete, not in 1946.

Despite his many hurts, Reiser leads the majors with a record seven steals of home this year and in total stolen bases, with 34. But the season robs him, at the end, of his last remaining matchless skill, his speed. He'll have shoulder surgery in the off-season, but now he's not much more than an ordinary ball player. Ahead of him, next year, he has a .309 season, but again will be hurt. After that, he never plays more than 84 games in a year and never hits .300 again.

With their 8–2 victory over the Phillies, the Dodgers again pull to within a half-game of the Cards, idle today. Despite having lost Reiser much of the season and again in this critical week, the Bums make an unprecedented race of it.

Twenty-five year old Lou Kretlow makes his big league debut for the Tigers, beating the Browns and getting himself two hits. The righthander will spend all or parts of 10 years in the majors, but not win more than six games in a season.

Detroit's Hank Greenberg, in his final week as a Tiger, hits his major league–high 44th home run and lifts his RBI total to 125 (he'll lead his league with 127).

Though it's been one of his greatest seasons, Ted Williams wins none of the Triple Crown titles (Mickey Vernon of the Senators wins the AL batting title, with .353), yet later takes the Most Valuable Player vote by a resounding margin, 227 points to Hal Newhouser's 187 and Bobby Doerr's 158.

September 27

Today the Dodgers, who are idle, find themselves tied for the National League lead with the Cardinals, who lose, 7–2, to the Cubs. St. Louis had been alone in first place since August 26, a month ago.

Late-season debut: Pittsburgh pitcher Al Tate. He came to the Pirates from Class B Selma, where he went 5–9 in the Southeastern League (he'd been 0–3 at Baltimore, earlier this season). Someone must have seen something in Tate, though in truth the Pirates are desperate to find any pitcher who can find the general vicinity of home plate. Pushing 30, the war vet will start against the Reds, day after tomorrow, long enough to lose, putting an unhappy end to his short big league career.

Late-season exodus: Cubs second baseman Bob Sturgeon suffered a lacerated finger on his left hand yesterday. He'll be replaced by Lou Stringer for the final weekend of the season.

September 28

First place remains deadlocked in the National League. This afternoon, Brooklyn tops Boston 7–4; tonight, St. Louis beats Chicago 4–1. The Dodgers and Cards go into the season's final day, still all tied up.

Shortstop Granville (Granny) Hamner, 19 and already a two-year big leaguer (of sorts), makes his first appearance for the Phillies this season, following military service. Pitcher Don Grate makes his last appearance for Philadelphia.

Giants coach-infielder Dick (Rowdy Richard) Bartell, after 18 seasons in the big leagues, is released by New York. His five games in 1946 were his last. It's rumored he's going to get the managing job in Pittsburgh, or one out in San Diego. He won't. Through the mid–1950s, he'll be on coaching staffs at Detroit and Cincinnati.

Pirates manager Frankie Frisch, one of the game's most colorful characters, resigns in the wake of a seventh-place finish. Frisch isn't through trying, as he will run the Cubs, 1949–51, albeit with similar success. There's a long and much-honored tradition in baseball to resuscitate failed managers with new teams, the logic being he would not have got earlier jobs if he weren't Real Good. Frankie was, with the Gas House Gang, but that's a dozen years ago, unfortunately, and he isn't any more. Coach Spud Davis, former catcher and a teammate of Frisch's from the Cardinals, is appointed interim manager, but it's just for three games.

September 29

Phillies pitcher Dick Koecher, 9–3 at Terre Haute, makes his major league debut, starting and losing his only game of the year. Rookie Sheldon Jones, making his first start for the Giants, beats Koecher, to end the regular season.

Reds regular right fielder "Big Al" Libke is starting pitcher in the nightcap of Cincinnati's doubleheader against the Pirates. His only seasons in the majors are 1945 and 1946; last year, he pitched four times. He lasts five innings today, holding a two-nothing lead when he departs, but reliever Johnny Hetki is handed the 3–2 season-ending loss. Libke was a pitcher in leagues out on the West Coast at the start of his baseball career, back in 1941-42. In 1944, with Seattle, he added outfield and first base to his repertoire.

St. Louis and Brooklyn tie for the National League pennant, each with identical 98–57 records. Both teams lose today, the Cubs beating the Cardinals 8–3, the Dodgers being shut out 4–0 by Boston's Mort Cooper.

Technically, it's called the first pennant tie in big league history, though back in 1908 the Cubs and Giants met after the season ended, to replay their 1–1 tie game of September 23, result of "The Merkle Boner"—in which New York rookie first baseman Fred Merkle, with joyous fans overflowing onto the field, neglected to touch second at the end of what would have been his RBI double to win the game. The run, it was ruled, didn't count, and the game was declared a tie. It was replayed October 8, the Cubs winning the NL flag, 4–2.

In the American League, the Red Sox have won the pennant in a breeze, 12 games ahead of the Tigers and 17 ahead of the Yankees. Now, they'll have to wait and see who their opponent will be in the World Series.

Major league attendance for the season is 18,612,704 paid, 80 percent ahead of the previous record of 10,951,502, set just last year. Twelve of the sixteen major league clubs—six in each league—broke old marks, some dating as far back as 1916. These include the Yankees, who drew 2,309,029, over a million more than their previous high, in 1920. The Dodgers were next best, drawing 1,796,155 paid, half a million more than their previous best, in 1941.

With 348 strikeouts, Cleveland's Bob Feller momentarily goes into the record books. The American League's official statistician says, upon deep research, the old mark for one season in the 20th century belonged to Rube Waddell, zany, mercurial southpaw of the A's, in 1904. Earl J. Hilligan, AL Service Bureau chief, declares without reservation that Waddell's total was 343 in 1904.

Others disagree. Ernest J. Lanigan, highly-respected baseball historian and now director of the National Baseball Museum and Hall of Fame, says his research shows Waddell struck out 349 that year. Still another total is 352, arrived at by "figure filbert" Leonard Gettelson, who compiled the 1942 *Sporting News Dope Book*, though there seems to be some disparity with catcher putout totals in that case. In due time, everyone seems to settle on 349 for Rube Waddell in 1904, one better than Bob Feller in 1946. Nineteen years from now, Sandy Koufax of the Dodgers will put an end to the discussion, striking out 382 in 1965, laying to rest the Feller-Waddell argument. Nolan Ryan of the Angels, not born till next January, will top Koufax's mark, with 383 strikeouts in 1973. That is not the all-time record, by the way. Old Hoss Radbourne of the National League Providence Grays is credited with 411 strikeouts in 72 games, 1884; Matt Kilroy of the American Association's Baltimore Orioles went into the record books with 505 K's in 65 games, 1886. Different rules (it took six balls to get a walk in 1884, seven in 1886), different circumstances (iron-man pitchers; the distance from the mound to home plate was 50 feet from 1881 until 1893), but those are the all-time highs.

September 30

The Braves trade infielders Billy Herman and Whitey Wietelmann, pitcher Elmer Singleton and outfielder Stan Wentzel to the Pirates for third baseman-outfielder Bob Elliott and catcher Hank Camelli. Herman is named Pittsburgh's manager. It's one of the worst trades ever made, as next year's Pirates finish tied for seventh and Herman, at the end of a long,

Hall of Fame playing career, gets into just 15 games. He'll be dismissed as manager with a game left in the season. Surprisingly unprepared, Herman is one of those "natural" leaders who turns out to be a flop in the job. He won't get another chance in the big leagues till 1965 with the Red Sox, whom he pilots dismally before he's fired in late 1966. Perhaps it's an example of the "Peter Principle," which says some people are inevitably promoted to a position just one step above their capabilities. The 1947 Pittsburgh club will be one of the worst-run, least disciplined in years.

The newly-acquired Bob Elliott, on the other hand, is going to be National League MVP in Boston next year.

October 1

In the first pennant playoff in major league history, the Cardinals and Dodgers begin a best-two-of-three series to determine the National League championship. Today's game is in St. Louis, where the Cards win, 4 to 2. Howie Pollet is the winning pitcher, Ralph Branca the loser. The players, by the way, get an extra six days' pay for the playoff, as the rules forbid awarding of bonuses.

Individual playoff batting, fielding and pitching records will count in 1946 final stats. NL president Ford Frick declares playoff team won-lost records will also be counted, with an asterisk noting they were additional games.

Johnny Neun, quickly gone from the Yankees, is announced as manager of the Reds today. Cincinnati's ex-skipper, Bill McKechnie, will become a coach on next year's staff at Cleveland, where he'll be given a great deal of credit helping Lou Boudreau guide the 1948 Indians to a World Championship.

Because the American League race was finished many days ago, the American League has gathered a group of All-Star "volunteers" to play three games against the Red Sox, to help get them back in shape. The "Stars" will be paid by dividing up the gate receipts; Red Sox salaries will be extended on a pro-rated basis. It's rumored Tom Yawkey, Boston owner, will make up any cash shortage out of his very deep pockets (so deep, it should be added, that the unofficial nickname for the team is "The Millionaires").

The weather is cold, the crowds small, and the results disastrous. Among the opposition are Snuffy Stirnweiss, Joe DiMaggio, Hank Greenberg, Luke Appling, Stan Spence, Mickey Haefner, Ed Lopat, Hal Newhouser, Dizzy Trout, Phil Marchildon and Birdie Tebbetts. Lopat, 13-game winner of the White Sox, is pressed into duty at first base for Game One. Greenberg is late arriving, due to a business conflict.

The first game is a combined 2–0 shutout for Boston, by Tex Hughson, Joe Dobson and Bill Zuber. Not much is made of a pitch thrown by Washington's Mickey Haefner in the fifth inning, which hits Ted Williams in the elbow. Williams leaves the game with a "bruise," but it's key to his miserable performance in the World Series coming up. He refuses to blame it, but goes into the Fall Classic with a badly swollen and painful elbow, and a cold.

Everybody makes mistakes when trying to piece history together. The much-respected Ed Linn, a Williams biographer, says in his book, *Hitter*, that the rest of the makeshift series is canceled. It isn't.

October 2

Sporting News item in this week's edition, blithely elaborating on the point that the Yankees drew well this year: "Winding up the 1946 season with a total paid attendance of 2,309,029, the New York Yankees set a record that probably will stand for all time."

Today the American League beats the Boston Red Sox, 4–2, to even their series at a game apiece. Williams doesn't play.

October 3

Moving their National League Playoff to Brooklyn (St. Louis won the toss: Game 1 at home, Games 2 and — if necessary — 3 away), the Cardinals and Dodgers meet for the second time in their best-of-three series. The Cards make it a sweep, winning the pennant with an 8–4 victory. Murry Dickson is the winning pitcher, with help from Harry (The Cat) Breecheen — long before the term "save" is coined, The Cat gets the save. Joe Hatten is the losing pitcher.

The Red Sox win the rubber game of their series against the American League volunteers, 4–1, Jim Bagby beating Hal Newhouser. Again, Ted Williams is out.

October 4

Eligible lists for the World Series:

BOSTON — *Pitchers* Jim Bagby Jr., Mace Brown, Joe Dobson, Clem Dreisewerd, Boo Ferriss, Mickey Harris, Tex Hughson, Earl Johnson, Bob Klinger, Mike Ryba, Charley Wagner, Bill Zuber; *Catchers* Eddie McGah, Roy Partee, Hal Wagner; *Infielders* Paul Campbell, Bobby Doerr, Don Gutteridge, Pinky Higgins, Eddie Pellagrini, Johnny Pesky, Glen Russell, Rudy York; *Outfielders* Leon Culberson, Dom DiMaggio, Johnny Lazor, Tom McBride, George Metkovich, Wally Moses, Ted Williams.

ST. LOUIS — *Pitchers* Red Barrett, Johnny Beazley, Alpha Brazle, Harry Brecheen, Ken Burkhart, Murry Dickson, Johnny Grodzicki, Howie Krist, Red Munger, Howie Pollet, Freddie Schmidt, Ted Wilks; *Catchers* Joe Garagiola, Clyde Kluttz, Del Rice; *Infielders* Joffre Cross, Nippy Jones, Whitey Kurowski, Marty Marion, Stan Musial, Red Schoendienst; *Outfielders* Buster Adams, Erv Dusak, Bill Endicott; Terry Moore, Walter Sessi, Dick Sisler, Enos Slaughter, Harry Walker.

Montreal beats Louisville, 4–2 today, to win the Junior World Series, the annual contest between champions of the American Association and International League, which dates back to 1904. The Royals breezed through the last half of the season, winning the pennant by 18½ games, then breezed through the IL playoffs, turning back Newark and then Syracuse (Louisville, which also won its regular-season pennant, defeated St. Paul and Indianapolis, to advance in the AA playoffs). Star of the Series is Jackie Robinson, batting .333, with seven hits in the final three games. He, manager Clay Hopper and pitcher Curt Davis are paraded around the home field on the shoulders of cheering fans.

October 6

World Series, Game 1, at St. Louis. Rudy York of Boston wins it in the tenth inning with a home run, breaking a 2–2 tie. Tex Hughson starts for the Red Sox, but the winning pitcher is Earl Johnson, who comes on in the ninth. As he does, manager Joe Cronin asks him, "What was that battle you took part in while you were in Europe?" "You mean the Battle of the Bulge?" asks Johnson, twice decorated there for heroism. "Yeah," Cronin replies, "well, this ain't it. Relax." Howie Pollet goes the route for the Cardinals and is the losing pitcher.

Creepy Crespi, still in the Army and still trying to recover from his injuries, is one of the 36,218 in the crowd. A variation of the Williams Shift is utilized by St. Louis manager Eddie Dyer. Slightly different than Lou Boudreau's defense, Dyer's has left fielder Harry Walker and shortstop Marty Marion on the left side of the field, everyone else on the right. Ted Williams is 1-for-3, a single, with two walks. Stan Musial, by comparison, is 1-for-5, with a double.

October 7

World Series, Game 2, at St. Louis. Harry Brecheen shuts out Boston, 3–0. The Cards aren't overpowering, but the Bosox are underpowered today. Williams and Musial go hitless, while "The Cat" drives in St. Louis' first run with a single, later scores their third. Mickey Harris is the losing pitcher.

October 9

World Series, Game 3, at Boston. Big Rudy York hits his second home run of the Series, good for three runs in the first inning, to put Boston ahead early. Dave Ferriss shuts out the Cardinals, 4–0. Murry Dickson is the losing pitcher. Musial and Williams are both 1-for-3: Stan's is a triple, but it leads nowhere. Ted's hit is another single. He's also walked intentionally in the first, scoring moments later, with Johnny Pesky, on York's four-bagger.

October 10

World Series, Game 4, at Boston. The Cardinals suddenly burst out of their low-hit mode, battering the Red Sox, 12–3, with 20 hits. Red Munger is the winning pitcher, going the distance; Tex Hughson and five others pitch for Boston. York has a double and Bobby Doerr a homer for the Red Sox, but the 4-5-6 hitters for the Cardinals—Slaughter, Whitey Kurowski and Joe Garagiola—have four hits each. Included in St. Louis' totals are a pair of doubles for Kurowski, and a double and homer by Enos Slaughter. Williams is 1-for-3 with a walk, Musial 1-for-5.

October 11

World Series, Game 5, at Boston. Joe Dobson stops the Cardinals and Pollet, 6–3, enabling Boston to move ahead, again, in the Series, three games to two. Pollet, who's pitched twice in the Series with an injured back taped up, can't make it out of the first inning and is done for the fall. He's replaced by Al Brazle (who takes the loss) and, in the eighth, Johnny Beazley. The Cards, 20 hits yesterday, get four today. Slaughter, batting star for St. Louis thus far, is hit by a Dobson pitch to his right elbow in the fourth inning. He plays two more frames but has to be replaced when his elbow swells. Erv Dusak takes his place in the order. Don Gutteridge and Leon Culberson each get two hits today for Boston, including a homer by Culberson. Ted Williams singles once in five trips up, Stan Musial once in three. The aging vet, Gutteridge, has replaced Bobby Doerr for a second straight game, since the regular second baseman left action yesterday with a migraine and was ordered by his doctor to stay home today.

The story is, sitting in the stands, Larry MacPhail says to Joe DiMaggio that New York second baseman Joe Gordon is, after all, going to the Indians in a trade. We have two choices, MacPhail continues: they've offered us Red Embree or Allie Reynolds. MacPhail, story goes, tends toward Embree (8–12, 3.47) over Reynolds (11–15, 3.88).

Take Reynolds, DiMaggio replies. Thus Allie Reynolds joins the Yankees. Gordon will be a major factor in 1948's World Championship in Cleveland, certainly accomplishing Bill Veeck's goal in obtaining him. Reynolds will help pitch the Yankees to six World Titles. Eddie Bockman is a throw-in, going to Cleveland with Gordon.

October 13

The Series returns to St. Louis for Game 6. *The Sporting News* says Harry Brecheen isn't as effective today as he was in Game 2, but The Cat wins again, 4 to 1. Boston gets four of its seven hits off Brecheen in the first inning, but the little lefthander emerges without giving up a run. He holds off the Bosox till the seventh, having blanked Boston for 15 straight innings. By the time the Red Sox score on a York triple and Doerr fly ball, St. Louis has already picked up three runs. Kurowski, Slaughter (in action after two days' rest), Marty Marion and Terry Moore each drive in runs for the Cards. Williams has a single in three trips up, Musial one in four. York, by the way, somewhat offsets his pair of homers earlier and triple today, by grounding into two double plays. The first ends the Bosox rally in the first inning, the second ends the game.

October 15

In one of the more memorable World Series contests, the Cardinals win Game Seven, 4 to 3. It's the third game Harry (The Cat) Brecheen wins in the Series, pitching the Cards out of trouble in the 8th, in relief of starter Murry Dickson.

This is the day of Country Slaughter's legendary run from first to the plate, score tied 3–3, bottom of the eighth. In the top of the inning, when Boston gets two runs to tie it, center fielder Dom DiMaggio hurts an ankle turning a base and must be replaced by Leon Culberson, first as pinch-runner and then out in center field. With the Cardinals at bat and Bosox reliever Bob Klinger on the mound, Slaughter singles to center.

The next two St. Louis batters are retired. Harry Walker, "Little Dixie," belts a line drive, over shortstop Johnny Pesky's head.

Critics through the decades will say what follows wouldn't have followed if Dominic DiMaggio were still in center. But he isn't. Culberson's there. Slower to react than Dom might have been, Culberson retrieves the ball, throws it in to Pesky, the cutoff man.

All the while, with Pesky's back turned to him, Slaughter just keeps running, Pesky unaware. Does Pesky hesitate? Does he hold the ball a split-second longer than he should? Is he confused? Can he hear his teammates' warning shouts, or are they lost in the roar of the crowd?

There are many theories, but Pesky's throw home is late, Slaughter scores from first base, his breakneck sprint one of the steadfast legends of the game, one with its own name: "*Country Slaughter's Mad Dash Home.*" Walker is credited with a double. Pesky will be reminded for the rest of his days how it all hinged on his holding the ball. The Cardinals win the World Series when Brecheen proceeds to shut down the Red Sox in the ninth, his third win of St. Louis' four.

Ted Williams and Stan Musial are soon to be announced as their leagues' Most Valuable Players, and surely they are the greatest batters in the game for two decades. But Ted Williams is hitless today. Stan Musial goes one-for-three, a double. Williams ends the Series batting .200; Musial .222. All Ted's hits are singles, including one bunt hit, with a lone RBI. Stan has four doubles, a triple and four RBI. It is not the defining moment for either player, but it's the last World Series for each of them.

In hindsight, that, itself, is one of the more surprising developments to arise from this season. At this moment, it's unthinkable neither will ever again play in the Series.

Epilogue

In its November 6 issue, *The Sporting News* names its All-Rookie team for 1946: at first base is Eddie Waitkus of the Cubs; second base, Buddy Blattner, Giants; shortstop, Billy Cox, Pirates; third base, Grady Hatton, Reds; left field, Del Ennis, Phillies; center field, Hoot Evers, Tigers; right field, Ralph Kiner, Pirates; catcher, Bruce Edwards, Dodgers; pitchers, Joe Hatten Dodgers; Ewell Blackwell, Reds; Warren Spahn, Braves. The paper takes pains to point out that every man on the team is a war veteran. All but one are National Leaguers. It doesn't mean much, but it's mentioned, anyway. It's a fine rookie crop, with two future Hall of Famers and some of the game's great character studies. It's not every year such a crop is harvested.

It was a remarkable season. But it wasn't what it might have been: too many players were rusty from years away, or were not yet ready. Too many had lost the best ballplaying years of their lives to the war and couldn't hang on much longer. Too many more were all washed up; too few wartime big leaguers were able to compete in peacetime. Too much was unrealized, even granted the thrills of the National League pennant race, the awesome power and pitching of the Red Sox, the artistry of the Cardinals.

Though record crowds flocked to ball parks, the marks were there to be broken, before television started eating into the game's days of glory. New stars were growing in the minors, soon to reach full bloom. An American social revolution was dawning; everything in baseball was changing: the best was yet to come.

The Grids

The following section graphically outlines daily player use of every member of every big league roster during the 1946 regular season, all 633 of them. Such use is displayed in a straightforward manner, including notation of what position(s) each man played on a given day for each team, or whether he was on the bench, injured, in the minor leagues, or in the Armed Forces. Many players were still in the Service as the season began, joining their team weeks or months into the pennant races. A very few players, such as young Tommy Brown of the Dodgers, spent the whole season in military service. (Brown, incidentally, was valued highly enough by his civilian teammates to be voted a share of the team's World Series money.)

Positions played are mostly stated in traditional scorekeeper shorthand, a common standard for anyone keeping score since the 1800s. The standard number for nonpitching positions are:

2 = catcher; 3 = first base; 4 = second base; 5 = third base; 6 = shortstop;
7 = left field; 8 = center field; 9 = right field

Number "1" traditionally is a pitcher, in keeping score. However, to avoid confusion, for this account I've substituted "**SP**" for a game's starting pitcher, "**RP**" for a relief pitcher. Pinch-hitter is indicated by "**ph**"; pinch-runner by "**pr**." If a player pinch-bats, then takes the field as a position player, his entry might be "**h9**" (pinch-hitter, then right fielder), or "**r5**" (pinch-runner, then played third base). A player at more than one position in a game might be listed as "**46**" (second baseman, then moved to shortstop); or "**75**" (left fielder–third baseman).

In this study of Major League Baseball transactions in 1946, an attempt has been made to chronologically include every roster move — trades, sales, options or releases to the minor leagues, recalls and purchases from there, outright releases, discharges from military service, suspensions, injury and illness absences. Some deals were well-publicized at the time and still can be read about, in an array of record books. Others were hardly noted at all. Most of these events and their exact dates have generally been lost to baseball historians. Many of the players involved were in and out of the spotlight in the blink of an eye, becoming no more than hazy figures in the foggy past of the National Pastime.

My source material, listed after the text, is extensive and was most helpful, particularly as second or third references in confirming events. But through most of two years, it was almost impossible to follow every trace of every last man who appeared in 1946.

Then, almost too late to be of value to this work, a chance discovery by a respected fellow researcher at the National Baseball Library in the Baseball Hall of Fame and Museum in Cooperstown, New York, seems to have broken the seal hiding original source material believed to be lost — or never to have existed at all.

Official Commissioner's Bulletins, begun as far back as the 1920s, consist of various numbers of pages per issue and are distributed periodically by the Commissioner's Office to various baseball authorities such as the Hall of Fame and contemporary big league organizations. Issued every week or so in-season, every several weeks off-season, they "officially" document every transaction in a given year.

Yet their existence has been neglected as a historical resource, perhaps because serious study of seasonal transactions has previously received little attention.

So I thank my friend Kerry Leibowitz of Chicago for discovering this mother lode of transaction information, and sharing it. Roughly six weeks apart in Summer 2000, he and I were given inestimable help by personnel of the National Baseball Library—Tim Wiles, director of research and Tom Heitz, former librarian of the Hall. Particularly helpful were Ann McFarland, director of technical services; Helen Stiles, library technical assistant/accessions (my patient, always helpful primary contact at the Hall, over a period of many months, who, by the way, provided white gloves to handle the fragile documents); Dylis Burdt, library technical assistant; Bill Francis, senior researcher; Bill Burdick, senior photo research assistant; and Eric Enders and David Jones, research assistants.

It wasn't until after completion of this manuscript that we were able to revisit the Library, just a few weeks after Kerry's trip there. I hoped to tie together several loose ends and, thanks to Kerry's discovery, study the Commissioner's Bulletins for 1946.

After months talking to library officials, others at Major League Baseball and its official statisticians, Elias Sports Bureau, I'd begun to doubt there was any "official" source of these annual records. Many told me as much. Original paper game score sheets, which I wrongly imagined to be the prime source of this information, were long since destroyed, due to the lack of storage space and absence of interest. With their loss went, it seemed, the absolute final authority on players joining or leaving a team's roster (surprisingly, when I bemoaned the loss while in Cooperstown, Helen Stiles confirmed the original paper score sheets do exist, but are stored off-site in cartons, unavailable for research, awaiting the budgetary means to copy them onto microfilm). The Hall has copies of Commissioner's Bulletins from the late 1920s into, at least, the 1970s, though not all years are complete. For instance, only issue #16 for the year 1927 is there. There are none, in the Hall's archives, for 1930–32. Of 1946's Bulletins, Nos. 2 and 3 are missing, covering most of January and February. The run then proceeds through #21, issued in December.

To incorporate so many changes in the text itself was impractical, given publishing timetables and manuscript adjustments required. On the other hand, the graphic portion of this book, the following "Grids," were completely revised to utilize this newfound information (the original text, which still covers every transaction of the period, does note the date of most and gives a narrow span of time for the remainder).

It was possible to completely revise the Grids—the basic, elemental research reference I create (from contemporary newspaper box scores) when tracing season transactions, and building the database which becomes my central reference. They visually outline the placement of every player on every team, every day of the season, while leaving the original text mostly untouched. The adjusted Grids now represent my prior research, updated to include my findings in the 1946 Commissioner's Bulletins. If there are further printings, incorporation of all transactions in the text body will be a matter of highest priority.

Robert J. Levy
Portland, Oregon
February 2001

DAILY PLAYER USE, 1946

Wide-lined box denotes a player's big league Debut.

Wide vertical lines between dates separate Sunday & Monday.

BOS AL	Games	APRIL 16 @Ws	17 @Ws	18 @Ws	20 Ph	[1] 21 Ph	[2] 21 Ph	22 Wsh	23 Wsh	24 NY	25 NY	26 @Ph	[1] 28 @Ph	[2] 28 @Ph	30 Det
DiMAGGIO, Dom	142	8	8	8	8	8	8		8	8					8
PESKY, Johnny	153	6	6	6	6	6	6	6		6	6	6	6	6	6
WILLIAMS, Ted	150	7	7	7	7	7	7	7	7	7	7	7	7	7	7
DOERR, Bobby	151	4	4	4	4	4	4	4	4	4	4	4	4	4	4
YORK, Rudy	154	3	3	3	3	3	3	3	3	3	3	3	3	3	3
METKOVICH, George	86	9	9	9	9	9	9	9		9	9	9	9	9	
ANDRES, Ernie	15	5	5	5	5	5	5	5	5						
WAGNER, Hal	117	2	2		2	2	2		2	2		2			2
HUGHSON, Cecil (Tex)	39	SP			SP					SP		SP			
FERRISS, Dave (Boo)	45		SP			SP						SP			
JOHNSON, Earl	29		RP						SP						
PYTLAK, Frankie	4			2		2		2			ph	INJURED ARM.			
HARRIS, Maurice (Mickey)	34			SP				SP						SP	
DUETSCH, Mel	3					RP			RP						
CAMPBELL, Paul	28					ph	ph								
RYBA, Dominic (Mike)	9					RP			RP	RP					
RUSSELL, Glen (Rip)	80					ph			ph	ph					
BROWN, Mace	18					RP			RP						
DOBSON, Joe	32					RP					SP				SP
BAGBY, Jim, Jr.	21						SP		RP						
HEFLIN, Randy	5						RP								
CULBERSON, Leon	59							8	9		8	8	8	8	9
PELLAGRINI, Eddie	22							6	6	5	5	5	5	5	5
STEINER, Ben	3								5						
DREISEWERD, Clem	20								RP						
WILSON, Jim	1								RP						
McBRIDE, Tom	61								ph						
PARTEE, Roy	40								2						
BUTLAND, Bill	5								RP						
GILBERT, Andy	2								ph						
McGAH, Eddie	15											2		2	
LAZOR, Johnny	23														
KLINGER, Bob	28	RELEASED BY PIRATES MAY 7, SIGNED BY BOSTON MAY 9 (DIDN'T PLAY FOR PTS.)													
HIGGINS, Mike (Pinky)	64	PURCHASED FROM DETROIT, MAY 19th.													
WAGNER, Charley	8	STILL RECOVERING FROM ILLNESS CONTRACTED IN THE PHILIPPINES.													
ZUBER, Bill	15	RELEASED BY YANKEES, JUNE 14th. SIGNS JUNE 18th W/ BOSTON, AS FREE AGENT.													
CAREY, Tom	3														
GUTTERIDGE, Don	22	RELEASED AS TOLEDO MANAGER & PURCHASED BY BOSTON, JULY 9th.													
MOSES, Wally	48	FROM WHITE SOX ON WAIVERS, JULY 23rd.													

BOS AL

	MAY 1 Det	2 Det	3 Cle	4 Cle	SUN MAY 5, RAIN [1] 6 StL	[2] 6 StL	7 StL	8 Chi	9 Chi	10 @NY	*11 @NY	12 @NY	14 @Chi	15 @Chi	16 @StL
DiMAGGIO, Dom	8	8	8	8	8	8	8	8	8	8	8	8	8	8	8
PESKY, Johnny	6	6	6	6	6	6	6	6	6	6	6	6	6	6	6
WILLIAMS, Ted	7	7	7	7	7	7	7	7	7	7	7	7	7	7	7
DOERR, Bobby	4	4	4	4	4	4	4	4	4	4	4	4	4	4	4
YORK, Rudy	3	3	3	3	3	3	3	3	3	3	3	3	3	3	3
METKOVICH, George	9	9	9	9	9	9	9	9		9	9	9	9	9	9
ANDRES, Ernie			5							5	5	5	5	5	5
WAGNER, Hal	2	2	2	2		2	2	2		2	2	2	2	2	2
HUGHSON, Cecil (Tex)		SP					SP				SP			SP	
FERRISS, Dave (Boo)	SP				SP			RP			RP		SP	ph	
JOHNSON, Earl										RP					
PYTLAK, Frankie	VOLUNTARY RETIRED LIST MAY 28th, HAS ARM SURGERY IN JUNE.														
HARRIS, Maurice (Mickey)		SP					SP				SP				
DUETSCH, Mel							RP						TO LOUISVILLE.		
CAMPBELL, Paul								ph				ph			
RYBA, Dominic (Mike)															
RUSSELL, Glen (Rip)								ph						pr	
BROWN, Mace									RP						
DOBSON, Joe							SP			SP					SP
BAGBY, Jim, Jr.				SP					SP						
HEFLIN, Randy							RP								
CULBERSON, Leon	7		7				5	5	5	5	SPLITS A FINGER, FIELDING.				
PELLAGRINI, Eddie	5	5	56	5	5	5	5								
STEINER, Ben														pr	
DREISEWERD, Clem		RP					RP								RP
WILSON, Jim										OPTIONED TO LOUISVILLE, MAY 9th.					
McBRIDE, Tom									9					ph	
PARTEE, Roy														ph	
BUTLAND, Bill															
GILBERT, Andy							pr		OPTIONED TO LOUISVILLE, MAY 9th.						
McGAH, Eddie				2					2						
LAZOR, Johnny															ph
KLINGER, Bob															
HIGGINS, Mike (Pinky)															
WAGNER, Charley															
ZUBER, Bill	("OFFICIALLY", ZUBER TO BOSTON IS CATEGORIZED AS A WAIVER DEAL)														
CAREY, Tom															
GUTTERIDGE, Don															
MOSES, Wally															

* Red Sox' 15-game win streak ends May 11th, as the Yankees beat Boston 2-0.

BOS AL

	MAY	[1]	[2]					[1]	[2]		[1]	[2]	[1]	[2]	
	18	19	19	21	22	23	25	26	26	29	30	30	3	3	4
	@StL	@Det	@Det	@Det	@Cle	@Cle	NY	NY	NY	Phl	Wsh	Wsh	Chi	Chi	StL
DiMAGGIO, Dom	8	8	8	8			8	8	8	8	8	8	8	8	8
PESKY, Johnny	6	6	6	6	6	6	6	6	6	6	6	6	6	6	6
WILLIAMS, Ted	7	7	7	7	7	7	7	7	7	7	7	7	7	7	7
DOERR, Bobby	4	4	4	4	4	4	4	4	4	4	4	4	4	4	4
YORK, Rudy	3	3	3	3	3	3	3	3	3	3	3	3	3	3	3
METKOVICH, George	9	9	9	9	8	8	9	9		9	9	9			9
ANDRES, Ernie										TO BUFFALO, MAY 29th.					
WAGNER, Hal	2	2	2	2	2	2	2	2		2	2	2			2
HUGHSON, Cecil (Tex)			SP		RP			SP			RP		WRIST INJURY.		
FERRISS, Dave (Boo)		SP		ph	RP		SP			SP			SP		
JOHNSON, Earl			RP	RP			RP				RP				RP
PYTLAK, Frankie															
HARRIS, Maurice (Mickey)	SP				SP			SP			SP				
DUETSCH, Mel		(DATE OF OPTION IS MAY 13th.)													
CAMPBELL, Paul											3				
RYBA, Dominic (Mike)															
RUSSELL, Glen (Rip)	5	5	5	5	5	5	5	5	5	5	5	5	5	5	
BROWN, Mace															
DOBSON, Joe				SP					RP		SP			SP	
BAGBY, Jim, Jr.				RP											
HEFLIN, Randy						RP									SP
CULBERSON, Leon				pr	FINGER INJURY LINGERS.			ph		ph		FINGER INJURY.			
PELLAGRINI, Eddie															
STEINER, Ben				pr									TO TORONTO.		
DREISEWERD, Clem					RP						RP				
WILSON, Jim															
McBRIDE, Tom	7		ph	8				9			ph		9	9	
PARTEE, Roy											h2			2	
BUTLAND, Bill															
GILBERT, Andy		(OPTION TRANSFERRED TO TOLEDO, JULY 9th.)													
McGAH, Eddie									2				2		
LAZOR, Johnny				*9	9						9				
KLINGER, Bob					SP										RP
HIGGINS, Mike (Pinky)				ph							ph			5	5
WAGNER, Charley															
ZUBER, Bill															
CAREY, Tom															
GUTTERIDGE, Don															
MOSES, Wally															

SUN JUNE 2, RAIN

* Lazor in box scores as relief pitcher May 21st, but was right fielder instead.

American League — BOS AL

Tie 6/5, replay 8/20(2)

JUNE	5	6	8	9 [1]	9 [2]	10	11	12	14	15	16 [1]	16 [2]	17	18	20
BOS AL	StL	StL	Det	Det	Det	Cle	Cle	Cle	@Chi	@Chi	@Chi	@Chi	@StL	@StL	@StL
DiMAGGIO, Dom	8	8	8	8	8	8	8	8	8	8	8	8			
PESKY, Johnny	6	6	6	6	6	6	6	6	6	6	6	6	6	6	6
WILLIAMS, Ted	7	7	7	7	7	7	7	7	7	7	7	7	7	7	7
DOERR, Bobby	4	4	4	4	4	4	4	4	4	4	4	4	4	4	4
YORK, Rudy	3	3	3	3	3	3	3	3	3	3	3	3	3	3	3
METKOVICH, George	9	9	9	9	9	9	9	9	9		9		9		
ANDRES, Ernie		ANDRES RETURNED TO BOSTON JUNE 18th, SENT TO MINNEAPOLIS JUNE 24th..													
WAGNER, Hal	2	2	2	2		2	2	2	2	2	2		2	2	2
HUGHSON, Cecil (Tex)		HUGHSON SIDELINED WITH TORN WRIST TENDONS.								SP					
FERRISS, Dave (Boo)	ph	RP			SP				SP				SP		
JOHNSON, Earl	RP					RP			RP			RP			
PYTLAK, Frankie															
HARRIS, Maurice (Mickey)	RP		SP					SP				SP			
DUETSCH, Mel															
CAMPBELL, Paul	ph						ph	ph	ph						pr
RYBA, Dominic (Mike)							RP	RP				RP			
RUSSELL, Glen (Rip)			5		5		ph					5			ph
BROWN, Mace	RP	RP					RP	RP				RP			
DOBSON, Joe			SP						SP		RP				SP
BAGBY, Jim, Jr.	RP							SP				RP			
HEFLIN, Randy							RP								
CULBERSON, Leon			7							9		8	8	8	8
PELLAGRINI, Eddie															
STEINER, Ben		OPTION TO TORONTO DATED MAY 30th.													
DREISEWERD, Clem	RP						RP		RP						
WILSON, Jim															
McBRIDE, Tom	9										97	9			9
PARTEE, Roy	2											2			ph
BUTLAND, Bill	SP				SP										
GILBERT, Andy															
McGAH, Eddie					2							2			2
LAZOR, Johnny		ph					ph		ph					9	
KLINGER, Bob			RP			RP		RP	RP						
HIGGINS, Mike (Pinky)	5	5	5	5		5	5	5	5	5			5	5	5
WAGNER, Charley		SP					SP					SP			
ZUBER, Bill															
CAREY, Tom															
GUTTERIDGE, Don															
MOSES, Wally															

NOTE: Manager Joe Cronin, who hasn't played since April of 1945, is released as a player and given new, two-year contract to continue managing Boston, on June 6th.

* Metkovich (probably) listed as "Mierkowicz" in June 25th box score. Ed Mierkowicz, ex-Tiger, plays for Buffalo this year (see Cleveland, June 9th).

BOS AL

Tie 6/24, No replay

	JUNE		[1]	[2]			[1]	[2]			[1]	[2]	JULY		[1]
	21	22	23	23	24	25	26	26	28	29	30	30	2	3	4
	@Cle	@Cle	@Cle	@Cle	@Det	@Det	@Det	@Det	Wsh	Wsh	Wsh	Wsh	@NY	@NY	@Phl
DiMAGGIO, Dom		8	8	8	8	8	8	8	8	8	8	8	8	8	8
PESKY, Johnny	6	6	6	6	6	6	6	6	6	6	6	6	6	6	6
WILLIAMS, Ted	7	7	7	7	7	7	7	7	7	7	7	7	7	7	7
DOERR, Bobby	4	4	4	4	4	4	4	4	4	4	4	4	4	4	4
YORK, Rudy	3	3	3	3	3	3	3	3	3	3	3	3	3	3	3
METKOVICH, George	9	9	9	9	9	*9	9	9					9	9	9
ANDRES, Ernie															
WAGNER, Hal	2	2		2	2	2		2	2	2	2		2	2	2
HUGHSON, Cecil (Tex)	SP					SP				SP				SP	
FERRISS, Dave (Boo)		SP					SP				SP		ph		SP
JOHNSON, Earl					RP							SP			
PYTLAK, Frankie															
HARRIS, Maurice (Mickey)			SP					SP					SP		
DUETSCH, Mel															
CAMPBELL, Paul		pr			ph		3						pr		pr
RYBA, Dominic (Mike)															
RUSSELL, Glen (Rip)		ph		5			5					54			
BROWN, Mace												RP			
DOBSON, Joe					SP		SP					RP			
BAGBY, Jim, Jr.							RP								
HEFLIN, Randy	HEFLIN OPTIONED TO LOUISVILLE, JUNE 18th.														
CULBERSON, Leon	8			8			8		9	9	98	9	9		9
PELLAGRINI, Eddie							6								
STEINER, Ben															
DREISEWERD, Clem															
WILSON, Jim															
McBRIDE, Tom		ph			ph		9				9	ph			
PARTEE, Roy			2				2					2			2
BUTLAND, Bill					RP		RP								
GILBERT, Andy															
McGAH, Eddie												2	ph		
LAZOR, Johnny					ph		7					7			
KLINGER, Bob					RP		RP			RP					
HIGGINS, Mike (Pinky)	5	5	5		5	5	5	5	5	5	5	5	5	5	5
WAGNER, Charley					RP							RP			
ZUBER, Bill			SP												
CAREY, Tom							4								
GUTTERIDGE, Don															
MOSES, Wally															

American League — BOS AL

	JULY	[2]			[1]	[2]	ALL-STAR BREAK			[1]	[2]		[1]	[2]		
		4	5	6	7	7	11	12	13	14	14	16	17	17	18	19
BOS AL		@Phl	@Phl	@Ws	@Ws	@Ws	Det	Det	Det	Cle	Cle	Cle	Chi	Chi	Chi	Chi
DiMAGGIO, Dom		8	8	8	8	8	8	8	8	8	8	8	8	8	8	8
PESKY, Johnny		6	6	6	6	6	6	6	6	6	6	6	6	6	6	6
WILLIAMS, Ted		7	7	7	7	7	7	7	7	7	7	7	7	7	7	7
DOERR, Bobby		4			4	4	4	4	4	4	4	4	4	4	4	4
YORK, Rudy		3	3	3	3	3		3	3	3	3	3	3	3	3	3
METKOVICH, George					9	9						9		9		
ANDRES, Ernie																
WAGNER, Hal		2	2		2	2	2	2	2	2	2	2		2	2	2
HUGHSON, Cecil (Tex)			RP		SP		SP			RP		SP				
FERRISS, Dave (Boo)								SP			RP			SP		
JOHNSON, Earl		RP														
PYTLAK, Frankie																
HARRIS, Maurice (Mickey)				SP					SP						SP	
DUETSCH, Mel																
CAMPBELL, Paul			ph				3					ph				
RYBA, Dominic (Mike)		RP														
RUSSELL, Glen (Rip)		5	54	4	5	5	5	5	5	5	5	5	5	5	5	5
BROWN, Mace		RP										RP				
DOBSON, Joe			SP							SP			SP			
BAGBY, Jim, Jr.				RP						RP						
HEFLIN, Randy																
CULBERSON, Leon		9	9	9	7	9	9	9	9	9	9					
PELLAGRINI, Eddie																
STEINER, Ben																
DREISEWERD, Clem		RP				SP				RP						
WILSON, Jim																
McBRIDE, Tom		ph		ph							9		9		9	9
PARTEE, Roy			2							2			2			
BUTLAND, Bill							TO LOUISVILLE JULY 10th, TO MAKE ROOM FOR GUTTERIDGE.									
GILBERT, Andy																
McGAH, Eddie																
LAZOR, Johnny		ph	ph							ph		ph				
KLINGER, Bob		RP			RP			RP							RP	
HIGGINS, Mike (Pinky)			5	5												
WAGNER, Charley																
ZUBER, Bill		SP									SP					SP
CAREY, Tom			4		4											
GUTTERIDGE, Don																
MOSES, Wally																

BOS AL

	JULY	[1]	[2]						[1]	[2]			AUG		
	20	21	21	23	24	25	26	27	28	28	30	31	1	2	3
	StL	StL	StL	@Chi	@Chi	@Chi	@StL	@StL	@StL	@StL	@Cle	@Cle	@Cle	@Det	@Det
DiMAGGIO, Dom	8	8	8	8	8	8	8	8	8	8	8	8	8		8
PESKY, Johnny	6	6	6	6	6	6	6	6	6	6	6	6	6	6	6
WILLIAMS, Ted	7	7	7	7	7	7	7	7	7	7	7	7	*7	7	7
DOERR, Bobby	4	4	4	4	4	4	4	4	4	4	4	4	4	4	4
YORK, Rudy	3	3	3	3	3	3	3	3	3	3	3	3	3	3	3
METKOVICH, George		9	9	9		pr		7		7				ph	
ANDRES, Ernie															
WAGNER, Hal	2	2		2	2	2	2	2	2		2	2	ph	2	2
HUGHSON, Cecil (Tex)	SP				SP			SP					SP		
FERRISS, Dave (Boo)		SP					SP				SP				SP
JOHNSON, Earl	RP							RP			RP				
PYTLAK, Frankie	REINSTATED FROM VOLUNTARY RETIRED LIST JULY 30th, PYTLAK RELEASED AUGUST 5th.														
HARRIS, Maurice (Mickey)												SP			
DUETSCH, Mel															
CAMPBELL, Paul	ph			ph		pr							pr		
RYBA, Dominic (Mike)															
RUSSELL, Glen (Rip)	5		5	5		ph	5	5		5	5		5	5	
BROWN, Mace															
DOBSON, Joe			SP		SP							SP			
BAGBY, Jim, Jr.									SP					RP	
HEFLIN, Randy															
CULBERSON, Leon															
PELLAGRINI, Eddie															
STEINER, Ben															
DREISEWERD, Clem				RP								RP			
WILSON, Jim															
McBRIDE, Tom	9				9	9								9	9
PARTEE, Roy			2			2				2			2		
BUTLAND, Bill															
GILBERT, Andy															
McGAH, Eddie															
LAZOR, Johnny												ph			
KLINGER, Bob			RP		RP							RP			
HIGGINS, Mike (Pinky)	ph	5			5	5			5			5	ph		5
WAGNER, Charley				RP				SP							
ZUBER, Bill				SP											
CAREY, Tom				BECOMES FULL-TIME COACH, JULY 23rd.											
GUTTERIDGE, Don						ph							ph	pr	5
MOSES, Wally						9	9	9	9		9	9	9	8	89

* On August 1st, Williams bats leadoff vs. Cleveland.

American League — BOS AL

	AUG		[1]	[2]			[1]	[2]						[1]	[2]
	4	6	8	8	9	10	11	11	13	14	15	16	17	18	18
BOS AL	@Det	Phl	Phl	Phl	@NY	@NY	@NY	@NY	@Phl	@Phl	@Phl	NY	NY	NY	NY
DiMAGGIO, Dom	8	8	8	8	8	8	8	8	8	8	8	8	8	8	8
PESKY, Johnny	6	6	6	6	6	6	6	6	6	6	6	6	6	6	6
WILLIAMS, Ted			7		7	7	7	7	7	7	7	7	7	7	7
DOERR, Bobby	4	4	4	4	4	4	4	4	4	4	4	4	4	4	4
YORK, Rudy	3	3	3	3	3	3	3	3	3	3	3	3	3	3	3
METKOVICH, George						9		8		9					
ANDRES, Ernie															
WAGNER, Hal		2			2	2	2		2	2		2	2	2	
HUGHSON, Cecil (Tex)		SP				SP				SP		SP		SP	
FERRISS, Dave (Boo)				SP					SP		SP				
JOHNSON, Earl						RP	RP								SP
PYTLAK, Frankie															
HARRIS, Maurice (Mickey)	SP						SP	RP				SP			
DUETSCH, Mel															
CAMPBELL, Paul														ph	
RYBA, Dominic (Mike)														RP	
RUSSELL, Glen (Rip)			5	5	5	5	5		5	5	5	5	5	5	
BROWN, Mace						RP									RP
DOBSON, Joe			SP				RP				SP				
BAGBY, Jim, Jr.								SP							
HEFLIN, Randy															
CULBERSON, Leon															
PELLAGRINI, Eddie		6						6							
STEINER, Ben															
DREISEWERD, Clem						RP								RP	
WILSON, Jim															
McBRIDE, Tom	7	7		7		ph	9	9	9	9	9			ph	9
PARTEE, Roy	2		2	2				2			2				2
BUTLAND, Bill															
GILBERT, Andy															
McGAH, Eddie															
LAZOR, Johnny								7							
KLINGER, Bob				RP			RP				RP				RP
HIGGINS, Mike (Pinky)	INJURED, SPIKED BY KELL.							5						ph	5
WAGNER, Charley				RP											
ZUBER, Bill				SP				RP							
CAREY, Tom															
GUTTERIDGE, Don	5	5						54							
MOSES, Wally	9	9	9	9	9	9						9	9	9	9

The Grids — American League

BOS AL

	AUG [1] 20 StL	REPLAY of 6/5 TIE [2] 20 StL	21 StL	22 Chi	[1] 24 Chi	[2] 24 Chi	[1] 25 Cle	[2] 25 Cle	26 Cle	28 Det	29 Det	[1] 30 Phl	[2] 30 Phl	31 Phl	SEP 1 Phl
DiMAGGIO, Dom	8	8	8	8	8	8	8	8	8	8	8	8	8	8	8
PESKY, Johnny	6	6	6	6	6	6	6	6	6	6	6	6	6	6	6
WILLIAMS, Ted	7	7	7	7	7	7	7	7	7	7	7	7	7	7	7
DOERR, Bobby	4	4	4	4	4	4	4	4	4	4	4	4	4	4	4
YORK, Rudy	3	3	3	3	3	3	3	3	3	3	3	3	3	3	3
METKOVICH, George		ph	9												
ANDRES, Ernie	RECALL ANNOUNCED AUG. 27th, BUT MINNEAPOLIS IS IN PLAYOFFS THROUGH SEP.17th.														
WAGNER, Hal		2	2	2	2	2	2		2	2	2	2		2	2
HUGHSON, Cecil (Tex)			SP					SP			SP				RP
FERRISS, Dave (Boo)	*ph		SP			SP			SP						
JOHNSON, Earl				RP			RP		RP						
PYTLAK, Frankie															
HARRIS, Maurice (Mickey)		**SP			SP				SP						
DUETSCH, Mel	RECALL FROM LOUISVILLE ANNOUNCED ON AUGUST 27th.														
CAMPBELL, Paul		pr													
RYBA, Dominic (Mike)											RP				
RUSSELL, Glen (Rip)					5							5			
BROWN, Mace				RP	RP						RP				RP
DOBSON, Joe								SP							SP
BAGBY, Jim, Jr.	SP					SP						SP			
HEFLIN, Randy	RECALL FROM LOUISVILLE ANNOUNCED AUG. 27th, BUT HIS BIG LEAGUE CAREER IS OVER.														
CULBERSON, Leon					ph		9	9	9	9	9			9	9
PELLAGRINI, Eddie															
STEINER, Ben	RECALL FROM TORONTO ANNOUNCED AUG. 27th, EFFECTIVE SEPTEMBER 8th.														
DREISEWERD, Clem				RP					RP	RP					
WILSON, Jim	RECALLED FROM LOUISVILLE AUGUST 27th, BUT WON'T PITCH AGAIN IN MAJORS TILL 1948.														
McBRIDE, Tom			ph	9	ph	9		7			ph				ph
PARTEE, Roy	2					2		2					2		2
BUTLAND, Bill	RECALL FROM LOUISVILLE ANNOUNCED AUG.27th, BUT NEXT BIG LEAGUE GAME IS IN 1947.														
GILBERT, Andy	RECALL FROM TOLEDO ANNOUNCED 8/27, BUT RELEASED BACK TO LOUISVILLE, SEP. 25th.														
McGAH, Eddie															
LAZOR, Johnny				ph	ph						ph				
KLINGER, Bob			RP						RP	RP				RP	
HIGGINS, Mike (Pinky)	5	5	5	5	5		5	5	5	5	5		5	5	
WAGNER, Charley															
ZUBER, Bill		RP			RP									SP	
CAREY, Tom															
GUTTERIDGE, Don		pr				pr									pr
MOSES, Wally	9	9	9	9	9		9			ph	ph		9		ph

* On August 20th, Official records credit Ferriss with ph, Game 1 or 2 (not specified), but doesn't appear in TSN boxes for either game.

** *The Sporting News* box score for Aug 20th (2) lists Harris as pinch-hitter for Zuber. As Harris is the starting pitcher, who is the ph?

American League — The Grids

RED SOX WIN AL PENNANT, ON FRIDAY THE 13th

BOS AL	SEP	[1] 2 @NY	[2] 2 @NY	4 @Ws	5 @Ws	6 @Ws	7 @Phl	8 @Phl	10 @Det	11 @Det	12 @Cle	13 @Cle	[1] 15 @Chi	[2] 15 @Chi	18 @StL	19 @StL
DiMAGGIO, Dom		8	8	8	8	8	8	8	8	8	8	8	8	8	*	*
PESKY, Johnny		6	6	6	6	6	6	6	6	6	6	6	6	6	*	*
WILLIAMS, Ted		7	7	7	7	7	7	7	7	7	7	7	7		*	*
DOERR, Bobby		4	4	4	4	4	4	4	4	4	4	4	4	4	*	*
YORK, Rudy		3	3	3	3	3	3	3	3	3	3	3	3		3	3
METKOVICH, George						7			ph					8	7	7
ANDRES, Ernie		(ANDRES RELEASED OUTRIGHT TO LOUISVILLE, SEPTEMBER 25th)														
WAGNER, Hal		2		2			2	2		2	2	2			*	*
HUGHSON, Cecil (Tex)			SP				SP			SP		SP			*	*
FERRISS, Dave (Boo)		SP				SP			SP			SP			*	*
JOHNSON, Earl					RP			RP					SP			SP
PYTLAK, Frankie																
HARRIS, Maurice (Mickey)			SP			SP			SP						*	*
DUETSCH, Mel		(DEUTSCH RELEASED OUTRIGHT TO LOUISVILLE, SEPTEMBER 25th.)														
CAMPBELL, Paul														3		ph
RYBA, Dominic (Mike)																
RUSSELL, Glen (Rip)				5	5	5		5	5	5		5	5	5	5	5
BROWN, Mace										RP						
DOBSON, Joe									RP		RP				SP	
BAGBY, Jim, Jr.				SP							SP					RP
HEFLIN, Randy																
CULBERSON, Leon							9	ph		ph				7		8
PELLAGRINI, Eddie															6	6
STEINER, Ben		(STEINER RELEASED OUTRIGHT TO LOUISVILLE, SEPTEMBER 25th.)														
DREISEWERD, Clem									RP							
WILSON, Jim																
McBRIDE, Tom			9					ph	ph	9	ph	9	9		9	
PARTEE, Roy			2		2	2		2					2			
BUTLAND, Bill																
GILBERT, Andy																
McGAH, Eddie														2	2	2
LAZOR, Johnny									ph							ph
KLINGER, Bob						RP		RP		RP						RP
HIGGINS, Mike (Pinky)		5	5					5								
WAGNER, Charley																
ZUBER, Bill											RP			RP		RP
CAREY, Tom																
GUTTERIDGE, Don								pr		5	5	5		54	4	4
MOSES, Wally		9	9	9	9	9		9	9	ph	9			9	9	9

* After winning AL Pennant, owner Tom Yawkey offers time off to key players. Eight take advantage of it, resting for five days, actually missing only two games.

	SEP							
	21	22	24	25	27	28	29	
BOS AL	@Ws	@Ws	NY	NY	Wsh	Wsh	Wsh	156g
DiMAGGIO, Dom	8	8	8	8	8	8	8	WS
PESKY, Johnny	6	6	6	6	6	6	6	WS
WILLIAMS, Ted	7	7	7	7	7	7	7	WS
DOERR, Bobby	4		4	4	4	4	4	WS
YORK, Rudy	3	3	3	3	3	3	3	WS
METKOVICH, George	ph		9	9		9	7	WS
ANDRES, Ernie								
WAGNER, Hal	2		2			2	2	WS
HUGHSON, Cecil (Tex)		SP			SP			WS
FERRISS, Dave (Boo)	SP					SP		WS
JOHNSON, Earl							RP	WS
PYTLAK, Frankie								
HARRIS, Maurice (Mickey)	RP		SP			RP		WS
DUETSCH, Mel								
CAMPBELL, Paul	pr			3				WS
RYBA, Dominic (Mike)								WS
RUSSELL, Glen (Rip)	5	5				5	5	WS
BROWN, Mace								WS
DOBSON, Joe				SP			SP	WS
BAGBY, Jim, Jr.							RP	WS
HEFLIN, Randy								
CULBERSON, Leon	7			8	8	8	9	WS
PELLAGRINI, Eddie			5	6				WS
STEINER, Ben								
DREISEWERD, Clem								WS
WILSON, Jim								
McBRIDE, Tom			7	7	7	7	8	WS
PARTEE, Roy	2	2		2	2	2	2	WS
BUTLAND, Bill								
GILBERT, Andy								
McGAH, Eddie							2	WS
LAZOR, Johnny							ph	WS
KLINGER, Bob								WS
HIGGINS, Mike (Pinky)				5	5	5	5	WS
WAGNER, Charley								WS
ZUBER, Bill	RP					RP		WS
CAREY, Tom								
GUTTERIDGE, Don	4	4		4		4	4	WS
MOSES, Wally	9	9	9	9	9	9	9	WS

WS = eligible for World Series.

American League — CHI AL

	Games	APRIL 16	17	20	21	[1] 21	[2] 21	22	23	25	26	27	[1] 28	[2] 28	30	MAY 3
		Cle	Cle	@StL	@StL	@StL	@StL	Det	Det	@Cle	@Cle	StL	StL	StL	@Ws	@Phl
MOSES, Wally	56	9	9	9	9	9		ph	ph					ph	ph	8
BAKER, Floyd	9	5	5										TO MILWAUKEE.			
JONES, Murrell (Jake)	24	ph	ph									ph		ph	3	3
WRIGHT, Taft	115	7	7	7	7	7		9	9	9	9	9	9	9	9	9
APPLING, Luke	149	6	6	6	6	6		6	6	6	6	6	6	6	6	6
TROSKY, Hal	88	3	3	3	3	3		3	3	3	3	3	3	3		
KOLLOWAY, Don	123	4	4	4	4	4		4	4	4	4	4	4	4	4	4
TUCKER, Thurman	121	8	8	8	8	8		8	8	8	8	8	8	8		
TRESH, Mike	80	2	2	2	2			2	2			2	2			2
HODGIN, Ralph	87	ph				ph		7	7	7	7	7	7	7	7	7
DICKEY, George (Skeets)	37	2				ph							ph			
DIETRICH, Bill	11	SP						SP								SP
KENNEDY, Bob	113	ph										ph		ph		
RIGNEY, John	15		SP													
GROVE, Orval	33		RP					RP				SP		RP		
LODIGIANI, Dario	44			5	5	5		5	5	5	5	5	5	5	5	5
LOPAT, Ed	30			SP						SP				SP		
HAYNES, Joe	32			RP					RP		SP					
LYONS, Ted	5				SP								SP			
FERNANDES, Ed	14					2			2	2			2	2		
LEE, Thornton (Lefty)	7					SP										
PAPISH, Frank	31					RP						RP		RP		
MICHAELS, Cass	91					pr										6
SMITH, Eddie	24							SP						SP		RP
PLATT, Mizell (Whitey)	84	* FROM THE CUBS.										8	8	8		
CALDWELL, Earl	39											RP		RP		
O'NEILL, Emmett	2	** FROM THE CUBS, APRIL 23rd.												RP		
HAMNER, Ralph	25													RP		
PERME, Len	4													RP		
WELLS, Leo	45													pr		
CURTRIGHT, Guy	23													ph		
JORDAN, Tom	10	ARM INJURY KEEPS JORDAN OUT UNTIL JUNE 4th.														
HOLLINGSWORTH, Al	21	PURCHASED ON WAIVERS FROM THE BROWNS, JUNE 6th.														
KUHEL, Joe	64	EX-CHICAGO 1B ASKS RELEASE FROM SENATORS, REJOINS CHISOX JUNE 13th.														
WHITMAN, Frank	17	SIGNED OUT OF ILLINOIS WESLEYAN, JUNE 27th.														
HAYES, Frankie	53	PURCHASED FROM CLEVELAND, JULY 15th.														
MALTZBERGER, Gordon	19	IN U.S. ARMY, REINSTATED FROM NATIONAL DEFENSE SERVICE LIST ON JULY 18th.														
PHILLEY, Dave	17															
SMAZA, Joe	2	SENT TO SHREVEPORT JUNE 18th. RECALLED AUG. 30, DEBUTS SEPTEMBER 18th.														

*Platt obtained on waivers April 20th from Chicago NL. He didn't play for the Cubs. **O'Neill bought from Cubs April 23rd, after pitching one game for Chicago NL.

NOTE: Alejandro (Alex) Carrasquel, Washington pitcher 1939-45 and now White Sox property, suspended for five years May 15th, for joining the Mexican League.

CHI AL

	MAY											[1]	[2]		
	5	6	8	9	11	12	13	14	15	17	18	19	19	20	22
	@NY	@NY	@Bos	@Bos	@Det	@Det	@Det	Bos	Bos	NY	NY	Wsh	Wsh	Wsh	Phl
MOSES, Wally	9	89	9	8	8	8	9	9		ph		ph		ph	9
BAKER, Floyd	\multicolumn{15}{l}{BAKER'S OPTION TO MILWAUKEE DATED APRIL 28th.}
JONES, Murrell (Jake)	3	3	3	3	3	3	3	3	3	3	3	3	3	3	3
WRIGHT, Taft	ph	9	ph	9	9	9	ph	7	9	9	9	9	9	9	
APPLING, Luke	6	6	6	6	6	6	6	6	6	6	6	6	6	6	6
TROSKY, Hal	3			ph	ph		ph			ph					ph
KOLLOWAY, Don	4	4	4	4	4	4	4	4	4	4	4	4	4	4	4
TUCKER, Thurman	8	8			ph			ph	8	8					
TRESH, Mike	2	2	2	2	2	2	2	2		2		2			
HODGIN, Ralph	7	7	7	7	7	7	ph	ph		7	7	7	7	7	7
DICKEY, George (Skeets)				ph	2			2	2	ph	2	ph	2	2	2
DIETRICH, Bill					SP					SP					
KENNEDY, Bob	pr		ph					5	5	5	5	5	5	5	5
RIGNEY, John				RP					SP						
GROVE, Orval			RP		RP		RP				SP				
LODIGIANI, Dario	5	5	5	5	5	5	5			\multicolumn{7}{l}{ELBOW SURGERY, MAY 22nd.}
LOPAT, Ed				SP									SP		
HAYNES, Joe			SP				SP								SP
LYONS, Ted	SP					SP						SP			
FERNANDES, Ed			2				2								
LEE, Thornton (Lefty)		SP				SP									
PAPISH, Frank			RP							RP				RP	
MICHAELS, Cass															
SMITH, Eddie				RP					RP					SP	
PLATT, Mizell (Whitey)			8				8	8	7	78	8	8	8	8	8
CALDWELL, Earl			RP				RP	RP		RP					RP
O'NEILL, Emmett															
HAMNER, Ralph														RP	
PERME, Len															
WELLS, Leo			ph									pr			
CURTRIGHT, Guy			ph				7			ph				ph	ph
JORDAN, Tom															
HOLLINGSWORTH, Al															
KUHEL, Joe															
WHITMAN, Frank															
HAYES, Frankie															
MALTZBERGER, Gordon															
PHILLEY, Dave	\multicolumn{15}{l}{OPTIONED TO MILWAUKEE, MAY 3rd.}
SMAZA, Joe															

CHI AL

	5/25, Lyons new manager					SUN JUNE 2, RAIN									
		[1]	[2]			[1]	[2]	[1]	[2]					[1]	[2]
	MAY 24	26	26	27	28	30	30	3	3	4	5	6	7	8	8
	Det	Det	Det	@StL	@StL	@Cle	@Cle	@Bos	@Bos	@NY	@NY	@NY	@Ws	@Ws	@Ws
MOSES, Wally	9	9	9	9		8	8	8	8		ph	8	8	8	89
BAKER, Floyd															
JONES, Murrell (Jake)	3	3	3	BREAKS ARM IN BASEPATH COLLISION, OUT REST OF SEASON.											
WRIGHT, Taft	ILL; OUT OF LINEUP WITH TONSILLITIS. TONSILLECTOMY, JUNE 6th.														
APPLING, Luke	6	6	6	6	6	6	6	6	6	6	6	6	6	6	6
TROSKY, Hal			3	3	3	3	3	3	3	3	3	3	3	3	3
KOLLOWAY, Don	4	4	4	4	4	4	4	4	4	4	4	4	4	4	4
TUCKER, Thurman			ph		8	ph	ph	ph				ph			8
TRESH, Mike	2	2									ph		2	2	2
HODGIN, Ralph	7	7	7	7	7	7	7	7	7	7	7	7	7	7	ph
DICKEY, George (Skeets)		2	2	2	2	2	2	2	2	2	ph			2	
DIETRICH, Bill							SP				RP				
KENNEDY, Bob	5	5	5	5	5	5	5	5	5	5	5	5	5		5
RIGNEY, John		SP		SHOULDER INJURY LIMITS DUTY.							SP		INJURED.		
GROVE, Orval	SP				SP						SP				SP
LODIGIANI, Dario	LODIGIANI WON'T RETURN UNTIL JULY 26th.														
LOPAT, Ed				SP					SP						
HAYNES, Joe						SP				SP					
LYONS, Ted	* LYONS NAMED MANAGER, RETIRES AS PLAYER ("OFFICIALLY", JUNE 14th).														
FERNANDES, Ed															2
LEE, Thornton (Lefty)		SP							SP					SP	
PAPISH, Frank												RP			RP
MICHAELS, Cass									ph						ph
SMITH, Eddie													SP		
PLATT, Mizell (Whitey)	8	8	8	8						8	8			ph	7
CALDWELL, Earl	RP		RP					RP							RP
O'NEILL, Emmett											RP				
HAMNER, Ralph							RP				RP			RP	
PERME, Len										RP	RP				
WELLS, Leo															ph
CURTRIGHT, Guy	ph				9	9	9	9	9	9	9	9	9	9	9
JORDAN, Tom											2	2			
HOLLINGSWORTH, Al															
KUHEL, Joe															
WHITMAN, Frank															
HAYES, Frankie															
MALTZBERGER, Gordon															
PHILLEY, Dave															
SMAZA, Joe															

* NOTE: Jimmie Dykes, manager since May 1934, is fired and released on May 25th. He's replaced by longtime White Sox star pitcher Ted Lyons, who retires as a player, after 21 years on the mound (and 3 in the Marine Corps during World War II).

CHI AL

	JUNE [1]	[2]					[1]	[2]	[1]	[2]			[1]	[2]	
	9	9	10	11	14	15	16	16	20	20	21	22	23	23	24
	@Ws	@Ws	@Phl	@Phl	Bos	Bos	Bos	Bos	NY	NY	Phl	Phl	Phl	Phl	Wsh
MOSES, Wally	9	9	9	9	9		ph	ph		ph	ph				
BAKER, Floyd															
JONES, Murrell (Jake)															
WRIGHT, Taft											ph	ph	9		9
APPLING, Luke	6		6	6	6	6	6		6		6	6	6	6	6
TROSKY, Hal	3	3	3	3	3	3	3	3	3		3	3	3		3
KOLLOWAY, Don	4	4	4	4	4	4	4	4	4	4	4	4	4	4	4
TUCKER, Thurman	8	8	8	8	8	8	8	8	8	8	8	8	8	8	8
TRESH, Mike	2		2	2	2	2	2		2		2	2	2		2
HODGIN, Ralph				ph	9	9	9	9	9	9	9	9		9	
DICKEY, George (Skeets)		2					2	2		2	2				
DIETRICH, Bill			SP			RP			SP						
KENNEDY, Bob	ph				5			5		5	ph			5	
RIGNEY, John	OUT WITH SHOULDER INJURY TILL JULY 18th.														
GROVE, Orval					SP					RP			SP		
LODIGIANI, Dario															
LOPAT, Ed		SP						SP				SP			
HAYNES, Joe	SP					SP					SP	RP			
LYONS, Ted															
FERNANDES, Ed	2											2		2	
LEE, Thornton (Lefty)							SP		INJURED ELBOW ENDS LEE'S SEASON.						
PAPISH, Frank										RP				SP	
MICHAELS, Cass	ph	6						6		6					6
SMITH, Eddie				SP						SP					SP
PLATT, Mizell (Whitey)	7	7	7	7	7	7	7	7	7	7	7	7	7	7	7
CALDWELL, Earl					RP			RP			RP				
O'NEILL, Emmett					SOLD OUTRIGHT TO SAN FRANCISCO, JUNE 14th.										
HAMNER, Ralph					RP	RP					RP			RP	
PERME, Len	RP				OPTIONED TO MILWAUKEE, JUNE 14th.										
WELLS, Leo	5	5	5	5	5	5	5	5	5		5	5	5		5
CURTRIGHT, Guy															
JORDAN, Tom	ph			ph		ph						ph		ph	
HOLLINGSWORTH, Al	RP			RP			RP				RP				RP
KUHEL, Joe								3		3		ph		3	
WHITMAN, Frank															
HAYES, Frankie															
MALTZBERGER, Gordon															
PHILLEY, Dave															
SMAZA, Joe															

CHI AL

	JUNE				[1]	[2] TIE 6/30(2). No replay	JULY			[1]	[2]			[1] ALL-STAR BREAK	[2]
	25	26	28	29	30	30	1	2	3	4	4	5	6	7	7
	Wsh	Wsh	Cle	Cle	Cle	Cle	@Det	@Det	@Det	StL	StL	StL	@Cle	@Cle	@Cle
MOSES, Wally		ph	ph			9	9	9		ph	ph			ph	9
BAKER, Floyd															
JONES, Murrell (Jake)															
WRIGHT, Taft	9	9	9	9	9	ph	7	7		9	9	9	9	9	
APPLING, Luke	6	6	6	6	6	6	6	6	6	6	6	6	6	6	
TROSKY, Hal	3	3	3	3	3	3	3	3	3	3		3	3	3	
KOLLOWAY, Don	4	4	4	4	4	4	4	4	4	4	4	4	4	4	4
TUCKER, Thurman	8	8	8	8	8	8	8	8		8	8	8	8	8	8
TRESH, Mike	2	2	2	2	2	2	2	2	2	2		2	2		2
HODGIN, Ralph	ph			ph											
DICKEY, George (Skeets)											2			2	
DIETRICH, Bill	SP	LINE DRIVE BROKE FINGER JUNE 25th. TO DISABLED LIST 6/26 & OUT REST OF SEASON.													
KENNEDY, Bob	5	5				ph			9	7	7	7	7	7	7
RIGNEY, John															
GROVE, Orval				SP				SP						SP	
LODIGIANI, Dario															
LOPAT, Ed						SP		SP							SP
HAYNES, Joe		SP	RP				SP			RP			SP		
LYONS, Ted															
FERNANDES, Ed						2	ph							ph	
LEE, Thornton (Lefty)															
PAPISH, Frank		RP				RP				SP					
MICHAELS, Cass						5			pr		5			pr	6
SMITH, Eddie				SP						SP					
PLATT, Mizell (Whitey)	7	7	7	7	7	7			8		ph			ph	
CALDWELL, Earl	RP			RP		RP		RP							
O'NEILL, Emmett															
HAMNER, Ralph	RP		SP			RP					SP				
PERME, Len															
WELLS, Leo		5	5	5	ph	5	5	5	5		5	5	5	5	
CURTRIGHT, Guy						ph			7						
JORDAN, Tom		ph				ph				ph		TO CLEVELAND.			
HOLLINGSWORTH, Al				RP						RP					
KUHEL, Joe						3		3	3		3				3
WHITMAN, Frank						pr									
HAYES, Frankie															
MALTZBERGER, Gordon															
PHILLEY, Dave															
SMAZA, Joe															

CHI AL	JULY 11 @Ws	[1] 13 @Ws	[2] 13 @Ws	[1] 14 @Phl	[2] 14 @Phl	15 @Phl	16 @Phl	[1] 17 @Bos	[2] 17 @Bos	18 @Bos	19 @Bos	20 @NY	[1] 21 @NY	[2] 21 @NY	23 Bos
MOSES, Wally				ph				ph				ph			
BAKER, Floyd															
JONES, Murrell (Jake)															
WRIGHT, Taft		9		9	9	9	9	9	9	ph	9	9	9	9	9
APPLING, Luke	6	6	6	6	6	6	6	6	6	6	6	6	6	6	6
TROSKY, Hal	3	3		3		3	3	3							
KOLLOWAY, Don	4	4	4	4	4	4	4	4	4	4	4	4	4	4	4
TUCKER, Thurman		8	8	8	8	8	8	8	8	8	8	8	8	8	8
TRESH, Mike	2	2			2	2	2	2					2		2
HODGIN, Ralph		ph		ph		ph			ph						
DICKEY, George (Skeets)			2	2		2					ph		2		
DIETRICH, Bill															
KENNEDY, Bob	7	7	7	7	7	7	7	7	7	7	7	7	7	7	7
RIGNEY, John										RP					SP
GROVE, Orval				SP				SP							
LODIGIANI, Dario															
LOPAT, Ed		SP						SP					SP		
HAYNES, Joe					SP						SP				
LYONS, Ted															
FERNANDES, Ed															
LEE, Thornton (Lefty)	(AFTER ELBOW SURGERY, GOES ON VOLUNTARY RETIRED LIST, JULY 29th.)														
PAPISH, Frank			SP		RP				SP		RP				
MICHAELS, Cass		5	5	pr	5	4			5	5	5	5	5	5	5
SMITH, Eddie	SP					SP					SP				
PLATT, Mizell (Whitey)	9		9	ph		8		ph	ph	9			ph	9	
CALDWELL, Earl	RP	RP												RP	
O'NEILL, Emmett															
HAMNER, Ralph						SP			RP		RP			SP	
PERME, Len															
WELLS, Leo	5	5		5		5	5	5							
CURTRIGHT, Guy	8					ph				8					
JORDAN, Tom	(DATE OF JORDAN'S SALE IS JULY 4th.)														
HOLLINGSWORTH, Al				RP	RP						RP				
KUHEL, Joe			3		3				3	3	3	3	3	3	3
WHITMAN, Frank						6					6				
HAYES, Frankie									2	2	2	2		2	
MALTZBERGER, Gordon															
PHILLEY, Dave															
SMAZA, Joe															

CHI AL

	24 Bos	25 Bos	26 NY	27 NY	[1] 28 NY	[2] 28 NY	29 NY	30 Phl	31 Phl	AUG 1 Phl	2 Wsh	3 Wsh	[1] 4 Wsh	[2] 4 Wsh	6 Cle
MOSES, Wally	WAIVED TO BOSTON, JULY 23rd.														
BAKER, Floyd															
JONES, Murrell (Jake)	GOES ON VOLUNTARY RETIRED LIST, JULY 29th.														
WRIGHT, Taft	9	9	9	9	9	9	9	9	9	9	9	9	9		9
APPLING, Luke	6	6	6	6	6	6	6	6	6	6	6	6	6	6	6
TROSKY, Hal						3									
KOLLOWAY, Don	4	SUSTAINS SHOULDER INJURY.							pr	OUT TILL AUGUST 22nd.					
TUCKER, Thurman	8	8	8	8	8	8	8	8	8	8	8	8		8	8
TRESH, Mike				2										2	
HODGIN, Ralph	ph		ph			ph	ph		ph	ph	ph				
DICKEY, George (Skeets)				2											
DIETRICH, Bill	DIETRICH SUSPENDED AUGUST 15th, REINSTATED SEPT. 10th, RELEASED SEPTEMBER 18th.														
KENNEDY, Bob	7	7	7	7	7	7	7	7	7	7	7	7	7	7	7
RIGNEY, John				SP							SP				
GROVE, Orval	SP						SP					SP			
LODIGIANI, Dario		5	5	5	5	5	5	5	5	5	5	5	5	5	5
LOPAT, Ed		SP						SP							SP
HAYNES, Joe	RP		SP							SP					
LYONS, Ted															
FERNANDES, Ed															
LEE, Thornton (Lefty)															
PAPISH, Frank			RP	RP				SP					SP		
MICHAELS, Cass	54	4	4		4	4	4	4	4	4	4	4	4	4	4
SMITH, Eddie		SP										SP			
PLATT, Mizell (Whitey)				ph		ph	9	ph		ph			8	9	
CALDWELL, Earl		RP				RP	RP			RP			RP		
O'NEILL, Emmett															
HAMNER, Ralph						SP		RP			RP				
PERME, Len	TRANSFERRED TO SHREVEPORT, JULY 25th.														
WELLS, Leo	5	5		6											
CURTRIGHT, Guy															
JORDAN, Tom															
HOLLINGSWORTH, Al				RP					RP	RP					
KUHEL, Joe	3	3	3	3	3		3	3	3	3	3	3	3		3
WHITMAN, Frank				4			pr							3	
HAYES, Frankie	2	2	2	2		2	2	2	2	2	2	2	2		2
MALTZBERGER, Gordon			RP			RP				RP					
PHILLEY, Dave															
SMAZA, Joe															

CHI AL

	AUG	[1]	[2]		[1]	[2]	[1]	[2]				[1]	[2]		[1]
	7	8	8	9	11	11	13	13	15	16	17	18	18	20	21
	Cle	Cle	Cle	Det	Det	Det	@StL	@StL	@Det	@Det	@Cle	@Cle	@Cle	@NY	@NY
MOSES, Wally															
BAKER, Floyd															
JONES, Murrell (Jake)															
WRIGHT, Taft	9	9	ph	9		9		9	9	9	9	9	9	9	9
APPLING, Luke	6			6	6	6	6	6	6	6	6	6	6	6	6
TROSKY, Hal											3	3	3	3	3
KOLLOWAY, Don															
TUCKER, Thurman	8	8	8	8	8	8	8	8				ph			
TRESH, Mike			2			2		2					2		
HODGIN, Ralph	ph	ph	ph	ph						7	7	7	7	7	7
DICKEY, George (Skeets)													ph		
DIETRICH, Bill															
KENNEDY, Bob	7	7	7	7	7	7	7	7	7	8	8	8	8	8	8
RIGNEY, John	SP											RP			SP
GROVE, Orval		SP						SP				SP			
LODIGIANI, Dario	5	5	5	5	5	5	5	5	5	5	5	5			
LOPAT, Ed					SP			SP						SP	
HAYNES, Joe	RP			RP							SP				
LYONS, Ted															
FERNANDES, Ed															
LEE, Thornton (Lefty)															
PAPISH, Frank			SP									RP			
MICHAELS, Cass	4	4	4	4	4	4	4	4	4	4	4	4	4	4	4
SMITH, Eddie				SP		SP									
PLATT, Mizell (Whitey)	ph		9	ph	9	ph	9		8				ph		ph
CALDWELL, Earl	RP		RP	RP		RP	RP					RP			
O'NEILL, Emmett															
HAMNER, Ralph		RP	RP										SP		
PERME, Len															
WELLS, Leo			6									5	5	5	5
CURTRIGHT, Guy															
JORDAN, Tom															
HOLLINGSWORTH, Al	RP	RP				SP				SP					RP
KUHEL, Joe	3	3	3	3	3	3	3	3	3	3	3	3	MUSCLE INJURY.		
WHITMAN, Frank		6	6									pr	6		
HAYES, Frankie	2	2	ph	2	2		2		2	2	2	2		2	2
MALTZBERGER, Gordon			RP								RP				RP
PHILLEY, Dave															
SMAZA, Joe															

American League — CHI AL

	AUG [2]		[1]	[2]	[1]	[2]					SEP	[1]	[2]		
	21	22	24	24	25	25	26	27	28	31	1	2	2	3	4
CHI AL	@NY	@Bos	@Bos	@Bos	@Phl	@Phl	@Phl	@Phl	@Ws	Cle	Cle	Det	Det	Det	StL
MOSES, Wally															
BAKER, Floyd	RECALL ANNOUNCED 8/30. BAKER TO JOIN SOX AT END OF A.A. SEASON, SEPTEMBER 8th.														
JONES, Murrell (Jake)															
WRIGHT, Taft	9	9	9	9	9	*9	9	9	9	9	9	9	9	9	9
APPLING, Luke	6	6	6	6	6	6	6	6	6	6	6	6	6	6	6
TROSKY, Hal	3	3	3	3	3	3	3	3	3						
KOLLOWAY, Don		r5	5	5	5	5	5	5	5	5	5	5	5	5	5
TUCKER, Thurman		8		8	8	8	8	8	8	8		ph			
TRESH, Mike	2	2		2		2							2		
HODGIN, Ralph	7	ph			ph	ph					7	7	7	7	7
DICKEY, George (Skeets)															
DIETRICH, Bill															
KENNEDY, Bob	8	7	7	7	7	7	7	7	7	8	8	8	8	8	8
RIGNEY, John															
GROVE, Orval			SP					SP			SP				
LODIGIANI, Dario															
LOPAT, Ed		ph			SP				SP						SP
HAYNES, Joe	RP					SP				SP					
LYONS, Ted															
FERNANDES, Ed															
LEE, Thornton (Lefty)															
PAPISH, Frank	SP		SP									SP			
MICHAELS, Cass	4	4	4	4	4	4	4	4	4	4	4	4	4	4	4
SMITH, Eddie		SP					SP						SP		
PLATT, Mizell (Whitey)	ph	ph	8			ph	ph	ph		8				ph	
CALDWELL, Earl	RP	RP	RP											RP	
O'NEILL, Emmett															
HAMNER, Ralph							SP								
PERME, Len	RECALL FROM SHREVEPORT ANNOUNCED 8/30, BUT HIS BIG LEAGUE CAREER IS OVER.														
WELLS, Leo	5	5													
CURTRIGHT, Guy															
JORDAN, Tom															
HOLLINGSWORTH, Al						RP									
KUHEL, Joe						3				3	3	3	3	3	3
WHITMAN, Frank	6	pr						pr			pr				
HAYES, Frankie		2	2		2		2	2	2	2	2	2		2	2
MALTZBERGER, Gordon	RP	RP					RP	RP							
PHILLEY, Dave	RECALL ANNOUNCED 8/30. PHILLEY TO JOIN SOX AT END OF A.A. SEASON, SEPT. 8th.														
SMAZA, Joe															

* Aug 25th (2), Wright and Kennedy are both in *TSN* box as left fielder. Assume Wright played right field, his usual position.

CHI AL

	SEP		[1]	[2]			[1]	[2]		[1]	[2]	[1]	[2]	[1]	[2]
	5	7	8	8	10	11	13	13	14	15	15	18	18	21	21
	StL	@Det	@Det	@Det	Wsh	Wsh	Phl	Phl	Phl	Bos	Bos	NY	NY	@StL	@StL
MOSES, Wally															
BAKER, Floyd										ph		ph			5
JONES, Murrell (Jake)															
WRIGHT, Taft	9	9			9	9	9	9	9	9		9			9
APPLING, Luke	6	6	6	6	6	6	6	6	6	6	6	6	6	6	6
TROSKY, Hal	3	ph		3				3		ph	3		3	ph	3
KOLLOWAY, Don	5	5	5	5	5	5	5	5	5	5	5	5	5	5	
TUCKER, Thurman	ph	ph	8	8	8	8	8	8	8	8		8	8	8	8
TRESH, Mike				2				2	2		2	2	2	2	2
HODGIN, Ralph	7	7			7					ph		ph	ph		
DICKEY, George (Skeets)															
DIETRICH, Bill															
KENNEDY, Bob	8	8	7	7							7			ph	
RIGNEY, John											SP				
GROVE, Orval		SP					SP							SP	
LODIGIANI, Dario															
LOPAT, Ed			SP					SP							SP
HAYNES, Joe	SP					SP						SP			
LYONS, Ted															
FERNANDES, Ed															
LEE, Thornton (Lefty)															
PAPISH, Frank				SP				SP					SP		
MICHAELS, Cass	4	4	4	4	4	4	4	4	4	4	4	4	4	4	4
SMITH, Eddie					SP				SP						
PLATT, Mizell (Whitey)	ph		9	9							9		9		
CALDWELL, Earl			RP									RP	RP		
O'NEILL, Emmett															
HAMNER, Ralph													RP		
PERME, Len															
WELLS, Leo															
CURTRIGHT, Guy															
JORDAN, Tom															
HOLLINGSWORTH, Al		RP													
KUHEL, Joe	3	3	3		3	3	3		3	3		3		3	
WHITMAN, Frank	pr							pr						pr	
HAYES, Frankie	2	2	2		2	2	2		2	2		2		2	
MALTZBERGER, Gordon	RP	RP			RP					RP		RP		RP	
PHILLEY, Dave					7	7	7	7	7	7	8	7	7	7	7
SMAZA, Joe													9	pr	

American League — CHI AL

	SEP	[1] 22 @StL	[2] 22 @StL	25 @Cle	[1] 27 StL	[2] 27 StL	29 StL	155g
MOSES, Wally								
BAKER, Floyd		ph	5	5		5		
JONES, Murrell (Jake)								
WRIGHT, Taft		9	9	9	9	9		
APPLING, Luke		6	6	6	6	6	6	
TROSKY, Hal			3			3		
KOLLOWAY, Don		5			5	ph	5	
TUCKER, Thurman		8	8	8	8	8	8	
TRESH, Mike			2		2	2	2	
HODGIN, Ralph								
DICKEY, George (Skeets)								
DIETRICH, Bill								
KENNEDY, Bob			9			9	9	
RIGNEY, John			SP			RP		
GROVE, Orval							SP	
LODIGIANI, Dario								
LOPAT, Ed				SP				
HAYNES, Joe				SP				
LYONS, Ted								
FERNANDES, Ed								
LEE, Thornton (Lefty)								
PAPISH, Frank		SP				SP		
MICHAELS, Cass		4	4	4	4	4	4	
SMITH, Eddie								
PLATT, Mizell (Whitey)							7	
CALDWELL, Earl								
O'NEILL, Emmett								
HAMNER, Ralph								
PERME, Len								
WELLS, Leo								
CURTRIGHT, Guy								
JORDAN, Tom								
HOLLINGSWORTH, Al		RP						
KUHEL, Joe		3		3	3		3	
WHITMAN, Frank								
HAYES, Frankie		2		2				
MALTZBERGER, Gordon			RP			RP	RP	
PHILLEY, Dave		7	7	7	7	7	7	
SMAZA, Joe								

American League

CLE AL

	Games	APRIL 16 @Chi	17 @Chi	20 Det	21 Det	24 @StL	25 Chi	26 Chi	27 @Det	28 @Det	MAY 30 @NY	1 @NY	2 @NY	3 @Bos	4 @Bos
CASE, George	118	7	7	7	7	7	7	7	7	7	7	7	7	7	7
LEMON, Bob	55	8	8	8	8	8		8	8		8	8	8		ph
EDWARDS, Hank	124	9	9			9		9	9		9	9	9		8
FLEMING, Les	99	3	3	3	3	3	3	3	3	3	3	3	3	3	3
KELTNER, Ken	116	5	5	5	5	5	5	5	5	5	5	5	5	5	5
BOUDREAU, Lou	140	6	6	6	6	6	6	6	6	6	6	6	6		
HAYES, Frankie	51	2	2	2	2	*		2	2	2	2	2	2	2	2
MACK, Ray	61	4	4	4	4	4	4	4	4	4	4	4	4		
FELLER, Bob	48	SP			SP		SP				**SP				SP
WOODLING, Gene	61		9		ph		ph					ph	ph		ph
REYNOLDS, Allie	35		SP				SP				SP				
SEEREY, Pat	117			9	9		9			9			7	9	9
LOLLAR, Sherman	28			2	2	2	2			2				ph	
GROMEK, Steve	37			SP					SP						
BLACK, Don	18			RP					RP			RP			
CENTER, Pete	21			RP			RP							RP	RP
MONACO, Blas	12			ph	pr		ph			pr		ph			
EMBREE, Chas. (Red)	28				SP				SP					SP	
MACKIEWICZ, Felix	78						8			8				8	
HEGAN, Jim	88						2			2					
JOHNSON, Vic	9						RP					SP			
PODGAJNY, Johnny	6						RP					RP		RP	
MEYER, L.D. (Dutch)	72						ph			4			4	4	4
BREWSTER, Charley	3						ph								
ROSS, Don	55									ph			5	ph	
ROCCO, Michael (Mickey)	34	OUT WITH BROKEN BONE IN FOOT.								3					
MILLS, Buster	9									ph					
KLIEMAN, Eddie	9											RP	RP		
CONWAY, Jack	68												6	6	6
FERRICK, Tom	9												RP	RP	RP
KRAKAUSKAS, Joe	29														
HARDER, Mel	13														
BERRY, Jonas (Jittery Joe)	21	WITH A's TILL EARLY MAY, BOUGHT FROM TORONTO ON JULY 1st.													
WASDELL, Jimmy	32	RELEASED BY THE PHILLIES, SIGNED AS FREE AGENT ON JULY 1st.													
WEBBER, Les	4	PURCHASED ON WAIVERS FROM BROOKLYN, JULY 2nd.													
GASSAWAY, Charlie	13	PURCHASED OUTRIGHT FROM OAKLAND, JULY 1st.													
JORDAN, Tom	14	PURCHASED ON WAIVERS FROM CHICAGO, JULY 4th.													
BECKER, Heinz	50	SENT BY CUBS TO NASHVILLE MAY 27th; TO CLEVELAND FOR ROCCO, JULY 16th.													
PRICE, John (Jackie)	7	BOUGHT OUTRIGHT FROM OAKLAND JULY 23rd, TO REPORT AUGUST 13th.													
PETERS, Russell (Rusty)	9	IN ARMY, DISCHARGED JULY 31st, RELEASED FROM NDSL ON AUGUST 8th.													
SEPKOWSKI, Ted	2										OPTIONED TO OKLAHOMA CITY APRIL 27th.				
MITCHELL, Dale	11	WILL REPORT FROM OKLAHOMA CITY AT END OF TEXAS LEAGUE SEASON, SEPT. 8th.													
WEIGEL, Ralph	6	TO WILKES-BARRE APRIL 10th, RECALLED AFTER EASTERN LEAGUE PLAYOFFS.													
McCABE, Ralph	1	OPTIONED TO BALTIMORE APRIL 9th, SENT TO OKLAHOMA CITY APRIL 19th.													
MOSS, Howie	8	REDS TO BALTIMORE IN MAY, "CONDITIONALLY" OBTAINED BY INDIANS AUGUST 30th.													
ROBINSON, Eddie	8	TO BALTIMORE APRIL 22nd, RECALLED WHEN PLAYOFFS END, SEPTEMBER 16th.													
FLANIGAN, Ray	3	BOUGHT FROM BALTIMORE 8/30, REPORTS WHEN ORIOLES LOSE IN I.L. PLAYOFFS.													
KUZAVA, Bob	2	PURCHASED FROM WILKES-BARRE FARM TEAM, SEPTEMBER 18th.													

* Hayes' string of 312 straight games caught ends April 24th, still the big league record at the Millennium.

** Feller no-hits Yankees 1-0 on April 30th, the third no-hitter of his big league career.

CLE AL

	MAY 5 @Ws	6 @Ws	7 @Ws	8 @Ph	9 @Ph	[1] 12 StL	[2] 12 StL	[1] 13 StL	[2] 13 StL	[1] 15 Phl	[2] 15 Phl	[1] 17 Wsh	[2] 17 Wsh	[1] 19 NY	[2] 19 NY
CASE, George	7	7	7	7	7	7	7	7	7	7	7	7	RP	7	ph
LEMON, Bob	ph	ph	pr	8	8		RP						RP		ph
EDWARDS, Hank	9	9	9	9	9	9	9			9	9		9	9	9
FLEMING, Les	3	ph	3		3								ph		
KELTNER, Ken	5	5	5	5				5	5	5	5	5	5	5	5
BOUDREAU, Lou		6	6	6	6	6	6	6	6	6	6	6	6	6	6
HAYES, Frankie	2	2				2		2	2	2		2		2	2
MACK, Ray		4	4	4	4	4	4								
FELLER, Bob				SP		SP						SP			
WOODLING, Gene	8	8			ph	8	8			8	8		8	8	8
REYNOLDS, Allie	SP						SP							SP	
SEEREY, Pat	ph		9					9	9			9			7
LOLLAR, Sherman	2		2	2	2		2		ph		2		2		
GROMEK, Steve		SP			RP						SP		ph		
BLACK, Don		RP			SP		RP						RP		
CENTER, Pete													RP		
MONACO, Blas	pr	ph	pr		ph		ph								ph
EMBREE, Chas. (Red)		SP						SP							SP
MACKIEWICZ, Felix	ph		8			ph		8	8			8			
HEGAN, Jim			2										2		
JOHNSON, Vic		RP							RP						RP
PODGAJNY, Johnny	RP			RP					RP	SOLD TO BALTIMORE, MAY 15th.					
MEYER, L.D. (Dutch)	4		h4		4	ph		4	4	4	4	4	4	4	4
BREWSTER, Charley	6														
ROSS, Don			ph	5	5	5	5								
ROCCO, Michael (Mickey)	ph	3	3	3	3	3	3	3	3	3	3	3	3	3	3
MILLS, Buster			ph										7		
KLIEMAN, Eddie	RP						RP								RP
CONWAY, Jack	6								ph						
FERRICK, Tom		RP			RP				RP						RP
KRAKAUSKAS, Joe	RP								SP			SP		RP	
HARDER, Mel			RP							SP					
BERRY, Jonas (Jittery Joe)															
WASDELL, Jimmy															
WEBBER, Les															
GASSAWAY, Charlie															
JORDAN, Tom															
BECKER, Heinz															
PRICE, John (Jackie)															
PETERS, Russell (Rusty)															
SEPKOWSKI, Ted															
MITCHELL, Dale															
WEIGEL, Ralph															
McCABE, Ralph															
MOSS, Howie															
ROBINSON, Eddie															
FLANIGAN, Ray															
KUZAVA, Bob															

CLE AL

	MAY				[1]	[2]			[1]	[2]	JUNE	[1] SUN 6/2, RAIN	[2]	
	20	21	22	23	25	26	26	28	29	30	30	1	3	3	4
	NY	NY	Bos	Bos	@StL	@StL	@StL	Det	Det	Chi	Chi	@Phl	@Phl	@Phl	@Ws
CASE, George	INJURED BACK.							7	7	7	7	7	7	7	7
LEMON, Bob			ph						RP		ph			SP	
EDWARDS, Hank	h9	9	h9	9		9	9	9				9	9	9	
FLEMING, Les			ph	ph			ph	ph				ph	3	3	3
KELTNER, Ken	5	5	5	5	5			5	5	5	5	5	5	5	5
BOUDREAU, Lou	6	6	6	6	6	6	6	6	6	6	6	6	6	6	6
HAYES, Frankie	2	2	2	2	2	2		2	2	2	2	2		2	2
MACK, Ray															
FELLER, Bob		SP			SP				SP						SP
WOODLING, Gene	8	8	ph	8		8	8	8		8	8	8	8	8	
REYNOLDS, Allie				SP				SP							
SEEREY, Pat	9		9	7	9	7	7		9	9	9	9		ph	9
LOLLAR, Sherman							2		ph			2			
GROMEK, Steve	SP					SP				SP			RP		
BLACK, Don											RP			RP	
CENTER, Pete			RP								RP				
MONACO, Blas			pr							SOLD TO SEATTLE, 5/31.					
EMBREE, Chas. (Red)				SP				SP					SP		
MACKIEWICZ, Felix	8		8		8				8						8
HEGAN, Jim	2						2								
JOHNSON, Vic			RP										RP		
PODGAJNY, Johnny															
MEYER, L.D. (Dutch)	4	4	4	4	4	4	4	4	4	4	4	4	4	4	4
BREWSTER, Charley									ph						
ROSS, Don					5	5	5								
ROCCO, Michael (Mickey)	3	3	3	3	3	3	3	3	3	3	3	3		ph	
MILLS, Buster	7	7	7	7	7							ph			
KLIEMAN, Eddie								RP						RP	
CONWAY, Jack															
FERRICK, Tom												RP			
KRAKAUSKAS, Joe									RP			SP			
HARDER, Mel			SP	SIDELINED WITH INJURED HAND UNTIL JULY 1st.											
BERRY, Jonas (Jittery Joe)															
WASDELL, Jimmy															
WEBBER, Les															
GASSAWAY, Charlie															
JORDAN, Tom															
BECKER, Heinz															
PRICE, John (Jackie)															
PETERS, Russell (Rusty)															
SEPKOWSKI, Ted															
MITCHELL, Dale															
WEIGEL, Ralph															
McCABE, Ralph															
MOSS, Howie															
ROBINSON, Eddie															
FLANIGAN, Ray															
KUZAVA, Bob															

CLE AL

	JUNE				[1]	[2]						[1]	[2]		
	5	6	7	8	9	9	10	11	12	14	15	16	16	20	21
CLE AL	@Ws	@Ws	@NY	@NY	@NY	@NY	@Bos	@Bos	@Bos	Phl	Phl	Phl	Phl	Wsh	Bos
CASE, George	7	7			7		7	7	7	7	7	7	7	7	7
LEMON, Bob		SP			RP			RP		** ph/pr?					
EDWARDS, Hank	9	9	9	9		9	9	9		9	9	9	9	9	9
FLEMING, Les	3	3	3	3	3	3	3	3	3	3	3	3	3	3	3
KELTNER, Ken	5	5	5		5		5	5	5	5	5	5	5	5	5
BOUDREAU, Lou	6	6	6	6	6	6	6	6	6	6	6	6	6	6	6
HAYES, Frankie		2	2	2					2	2	2	2		2	2
MACK, Ray			4	4	4	4					4				4
FELLER, Bob				SP					SP		SP				SP
WOODLING, Gene	8	8	8	8		8				8	8	8		ph	ph
REYNOLDS, Allie					SP					SP				SP	
SEEREY, Pat			7	7	9	7	79	79	9				2	8	8
LOLLAR, Sherman	2				2		2	2		2			2	2	
GROMEK, Steve	SP		pr				SP								
BLACK, Don		RP			SP						SP			RP	
CENTER, Pete	RP		RP				RP						RP		
MONACO, Blas															
EMBREE, Chas. (Red)			SP					SP				SP			
MACKIEWICZ, Felix				*8			8	8	8			pr	8		
HEGAN, Jim						2									
JOHNSON, Vic			RP					RP							
PODGAJNY, Johnny															
MEYER, L.D. (Dutch)	4	4	ph			4	4	4	4	4	4	4	4	4	4
BREWSTER, Charley		SOLD TO MILWAUKEE JUNE 5th, FIRST GAME THERE IS JUNE 6th.													
ROSS, Don		ph	5	5		5	ph								
ROCCO, Michael (Mickey)						ph						ph		ph	
MILLS, Buster															
KLIEMAN, Eddie							RP								
CONWAY, Jack							ph								
FERRICK, Tom				RP											
KRAKAUSKAS, Joe		RP	RP			RP				RP	RP			RP	
HARDER, Mel															
BERRY, Jonas (Jittery Joe)															
WASDELL, Jimmy															
WEBBER, Les															
GASSAWAY, Charlie															
JORDAN, Tom															
BECKER, Heinz															
PRICE, John (Jackie)															
PETERS, Russell (Rusty)															
SEPKOWSKI, Ted															
MITCHELL, Dale															
WEIGEL, Ralph															
McCABE, Ralph															
MOSS, Howie															
ROBINSON, Eddie															
FLANIGAN, Ray															
KUZAVA, Bob															

* In June 9th (Game 1) box score, Mackiewicz is mistaken for Ed Mierkowicz, who played for Detroit in 1945 but spends 1946 at Buffalo and Milwaukee.

** On June 14th, box scores don't indicate whether Lemon is ph or pr, but he does it for Hayes.

THE GRIDS — American League

	JUNE	[1]	[2]						[1]	[2]	JULY			[1]	[2]
	*22	23	23	24	25	26	28	29	30	30	1	2	3	4	4
CLE AL	Bos	Bos	Bos	NY	NY	NY	@Chi	@Chi	@Chi	@Chi	StL	StL	StL	@Det	@Det
CASE, George	7	7	7	7	7	7	7	7	7	7	7	7	7	7	7
LEMON, Bob		RP	RP	pr		ph			RP		RP				RP
EDWARDS, Hank	9	9					9	9				9	9	9	9
FLEMING, Les	3	3	3	3	3	3	3	3	3	3	3	3	3	3	3
KELTNER, Ken	5	5	5	5	5	5			ph			5			5
BOUDREAU, Lou	6	6	6	6	6	6	6	6	6	6	6	6	6	6	6
HAYES, Frankie	2	2	2						ph						2
MACK, Ray				4											
FELLER, Bob					SP			SP					SP		
WOODLING, Gene			8					ph				ph			ph
REYNOLDS, Allie		pr		SP				SP							SP
SEEREY, Pat	8	8	9	9	9	9	89	8	9	**9	9	8	8	8	98
LOLLAR, Sherman		2		2				ph							
GROMEK, Steve		SP		pr			SP			RP		pr		SP	
BLACK, Don			SP						RP					RP	
CENTER, Pete				RP		RP			RP					RP	
MONACO, Blas															
EMBREE, Chas. (Red)	SP					SP			SP						
MACKIEWICZ, Felix				8	8	8	8	8	8	**8	8				8
HEGAN, Jim				2	2	2	2	2	2	2	2	2	2	2	
JOHNSON, Vic							TO BALTIMORE ON OPTION, JUNE 28th.							
PODGAJNY, Johnny															
MEYER, L.D. (Dutch)	4	4	4	4	4	4		ph			4				
BREWSTER, Charley															
ROSS, Don		ph				ph	5	5	5	5	5	5	5	5	5
ROCCO, Michael (Mickey)	ph			ph		TO NASHVILLE FOR BECKER 6/26. WON'T GO, SUSPENDED 7/5.								
MILLS, Buster														COACH, 7/3.	
KLIEMAN, Eddie		RP				TO INDIANAPOLIS JUNE 27th, AS PART OF BECKER DEAL.								
CONWAY, Jack		ph					4	4	4	4	4	4	4	4	4
FERRICK, Tom				RELEASED ON WAIVERS TO THE BROWNS, JUNE 24th.											
KRAKAUSKAS, Joe	RP					RP			RP	RP		SP		RP	RP
HARDER, Mel											SP				
BERRY, Jonas (Jittery Joe)		BERRY HAS WINNING RBI IN FIRST INDIANS GAME.								RP			RP	RP
WASDELL, Jimmy												ph		ph	
WEBBER, Les															
GASSAWAY, Charlie															
JORDAN, Tom															
BECKER, Heinz															
PRICE, John (Jackie)															
PETERS, Russell (Rusty)															
SEPKOWSKI, Ted															
MITCHELL, Dale															
WEIGEL, Ralph															
McCABE, Ralph															
MOSS, Howie															
ROBINSON, Eddie															
FLANIGAN, Ray															
KUZAVA, Bob															

TIE 6/30(2). No replay

* On June 22nd, Bill Veeck-led group buys the Indians.

** Mackiewicz and Seerey both listed as right fielder in box score of June 30th (2). Assume Mackiewicz plays center field.

CLE AL

	JULY		[1]	[2]	ALL-STAR BREAK		[1]	[2]						[1]	[2]
	5	6	7	7	11	13	14	14	16	17	18	19	20	21	21
	@Det	Chi	Chi	Chi	@NY	@NY	@Bos	@Bos	@Bos	@Phl	@Phl	@Phl	@Ws	@Ws	@Ws
CASE, George	7	7	7	7	7	7	7	7	7	7	7	7	7	7	7
LEMON, Bob		RP					RP							RP	
EDWARDS, Hank	9	9	9		9	9	9	9	9	9	9	9	9	9	9
FLEMING, Les	3	3	3	3	HIT ON HEAD BY THROWN BALL.										3
KELTNER, Ken		5	5	5	5	5	5	5	5	5	5	5	5	5	5
BOUDREAU, Lou	6	6	6	6	6	6	6	6	6	6	6	6			
HAYES, Frankie	2	2	2						WAIVED TO THE WHITE SOX, JULY 15th.						
MACK, Ray														4	4
FELLER, Bob			SP		SP			SP				SP			*RP
WOODLING, Gene	ph	ph		7	ph		ph							pr	
REYNOLDS, Allie						SP			SP						
SEEREY, Pat	8	8	8	9	8	8	8	8	8	8	8	8	8	8	8
LOLLAR, Sherman								2	OPTIONED TO BALTIMORE, JULY 15th.						
GROMEK, Steve		pr				SP				RP					
BLACK, Don	RP					RP					TO MILWAUKEE.				
CENTER, Pete															
MONACO, Blas															
EMBREE, Chas. (Red)	SP					SP									SP
MACKIEWICZ, Felix	ph		8		ph									*ph	
HEGAN, Jim	2	2		2	2	2	2		2	2	2	2	2	2	2
JOHNSON, Vic	(PITCHES 3 GAMES FOR BALTIMORE, OPTIONED TO NASHVILLE ON JULY 8th.)														
PODGAJNY, Johnny															
MEYER, L.D. (Dutch)				ph			ph								4
BREWSTER, Charley															
ROSS, Don	5	ph			ph									pr	5
ROCCO, Michael (Mickey)	REINSTATED FROM SUSPENSION JULY 13th, ROCCO REPORTS TO NASHVILLE JULY 15th.														
MILLS, Buster	(WITH RELEASE AS PLAYER, MILLS' BIG LEAGUE PLAYING CAREER IS NOW ENDED.)														
KLIEMAN, Eddie	(KLIEMAN TO INDY COMPLETES THE BECKER ACQUISITION.)														
CONWAY, Jack	4	4	4	4	4	4	4	4	4	4	4	4	4	6	6
FERRICK, Tom															
KRAKAUSKAS, Joe				RP	RP										RP
HARDER, Mel		SP										SP			
BERRY, Jonas (Jittery Joe)					RP		RP								
WASDELL, Jimmy	ph	ph			3	3	3	3							ph
WEBBER, Les			SP								SP				
GASSAWAY, Charlie			RP				RP							SP	
JORDAN, Tom			ph					2						2	
BECKER, Heinz									3	3	3	3	3	3	ph
PRICE, John (Jackie)															
PETERS, Russell (Rusty)															
SEPKOWSKI, Ted															
MITCHELL, Dale															
WEIGEL, Ralph															
McCABE, Ralph															
MOSS, Howie															
ROBINSON, Eddie															
FLANIGAN, Ray															
KUZAVA, Bob															

* July 21(2), Feller pitches relief for first time since before the war. Also this game, Mackiewicz pinch-hits in Official records (0-for-1, strikes out), not shown in TSN box s

NOTE: July 31st (next page), Feller pitches one-hitter against Boston. Only safety is single by Doerr.

CLE AL

	JULY					[1]	[2]	[1]	[2]			AUG			
	23	24	25	26	27	28	28	29	29	30	31	1	2	4	6
	Phl	Phl	Phl	Wsh	Wsh	Wsh	Wsh	Wsh	Wsh	Bos	Bos	Bos	NY	NY	@Chi
CASE, George	7	7	7	7	7	7	7	7	7	7	7	7	7	7	7
LEMON, Bob			RP					ph	RP					RP	
EDWARDS, Hank	9	9	9	9	9	9	9	9	8	9			9	9	9
FLEMING, Les			ph		ph			ph	9					ph	3
KELTNER, Ken	5	5	5	5	5	5	5	5	5	5		*			5
BOUDREAU, Lou	6	6	6	6	6	6	6	6	6	6	6	6	6	6	6
HAYES, Frankie															
MACK, Ray															4
FELLER, Bob		SP				SP					SP			SP	
WOODLING, Gene					pr			ph							7
REYNOLDS, Allie	SP			pr			SP	pr					SP		
SEEREY, Pat	8	8	8	8	8	8	8	8		8	9	8	8	8	98
LOLLAR, Sherman															
GROMEK, Steve				SP					SP						SP
BLACK, Don	(BLACK WAS OPTIONED TO MILWAUKEE ON JULY 17th.)														
CENTER, Pete										RP					RP
MONACO, Blas															
EMBREE, Chas. (Red)				SP											
MACKIEWICZ, Felix								8			8			8	8
HEGAN, Jim	2	2	2	2	2	2	2	2	2	2	2	2	2	2	2
JOHNSON, Vic	RETURNED TO INDIANS BY NASHVILLE 7/31; OPTIONED TO NEW ORLEANS AUGUST 7th.														
PODGAJNY, Johnny															
MEYER, L.D. (Dutch)			4					4							
BREWSTER, Charley															
ROSS, Don											5	5	5	5	5
ROCCO, Michael (Mickey)															
MILLS, Buster															
KLIEMAN, Eddie															
CONWAY, Jack	4	4	4	4	4	4	4	4	4	4	4	4	4	4	4
FERRICK, Tom															
KRAKAUSKAS, Joe					RP				SP						
HARDER, Mel			SP									SP			
BERRY, Jonas (Jittery Joe)			RP	RP				RP		RP		RP		RP	
WASDELL, Jimmy			ph		ph			ph	ph	ph					9
WEBBER, Les										RP					RP
GASSAWAY, Charlie			RP					SP							
JORDAN, Tom										2					2
BECKER, Heinz	3	3	3	3	3	3	3	3	3	3	3	3	3	3	3
PRICE, John (Jackie)															
PETERS, Russell (Rusty)															
SEPKOWSKI, Ted															
MITCHELL, Dale															
WEIGEL, Ralph															
McCABE, Ralph															
MOSS, Howie															
ROBINSON, Eddie															
FLANIGAN, Ray															
KUZAVA, Bob															

* Due to the death of Keltner's father-in-law, the third baseman misses four games, July 31-August 4, while attending the funeral in Milwaukee.

CLE AL

	AUG	[1]	[2]			[1]	[2]						[1]	[2]	
	7	8	8	9	10	11	11	12	13	14	15	17	18	18	20
	@Chi	@Chi	@Chi	@StL	@StL	@StL	@StL	Det	Det	Det	StL	Chi	Chi	Chi	@Ws
CASE, George	7	7	7	7	7	7	7	7	7	7		7	7	7	7
LEMON, Bob			RP						RP				RP		
EDWARDS, Hank	9	9	9	9	9	9	9	9	9	9	9		ph		
FLEMING, Les	ph	HOME WITH SICK SON.									ph	ph	ph	3	3
KELTNER, Ken	5	5	5	5	5	5	5	5	5	5	5	5	5		ph
BOUDREAU, Lou	6	6	6	6	6	6	6	6	6	6	6	6	6	6	6
HAYES, Frankie															
MACK, Ray	4		4												
FELLER, Bob		**SP			RP		RP		SP			SP			SP
WOODLING, Gene	7							ph					8	7	ph
REYNOLDS, Allie	SP		RP			SP					SP		RP		pr
SEEREY, Pat	8	8	8								78	9	9	9	9
LOLLAR, Sherman															
GROMEK, Steve				RP				SP			RP		RP		pr
BLACK, Don															
CENTER, Pete															
MONACO, Blas															
EMBREE, Chas. (Red)			SP		SP				RP				SP		
MACKIEWICZ, Felix	8		8	8	8	8	8	8	8	8	8	8	8	8	8
HEGAN, Jim	2	2	2	2	2	2	2	2	2	2	2	2	2	2	2
JOHNSON, Vic															
PODGAJNY, Johnny															
MEYER, L.D. (Dutch)													4	4	4
BREWSTER, Charley															
ROSS, Don										ph				5	5
ROCCO, Michael (Mickey)															
MILLS, Buster															
KLIEMAN, Eddie															
CONWAY, Jack	4	4	46	4	4	4	4	4	4	4	4	4	46		
FERRICK, Tom															
KRAKAUSKAS, Joe										RP					
HARDER, Mel					SP								SP		
BERRY, Jonas (Jittery Joe)			RP				RP						RP		
WASDELL, Jimmy	ph		ph					ph	ph		7		ph		
WEBBER, Les															
GASSAWAY, Charlie					SP						SP				
JORDAN, Tom													2		
BECKER, Heinz	3	3	3	3	3	3	3	3	3	3	3	3	3		ph
PRICE, John (Jackie)													ph		
PETERS, Russell (Rusty)															
SEPKOWSKI, Ted															
MITCHELL, Dale															
WEIGEL, Ralph															
McCABE, Ralph															
MOSS, Howie															
ROBINSON, Eddie															
FLANIGAN, Ray															
KUZAVA, Bob															

* Feller has 1-hitter vs. Chi Aug.8th (1st game), wins 5-0. Only hit by Hayes, ex-teammate. It's Feller's second 1-hitter in 3 games, gaining him a record 10 no-or-1 hitters.

CLE AL

	AUG				[1]	[2]					SEP	[1] TIE 9/2(2), replay 9/3(2)	[2]	[1]	[2]
	21	22	23	24	25	25	26	28	29	31	1	2	2	3	3
	@Ws	@Phl	@Phl	@Phl	@Bos	@Bos	@Bos	@NY	@NY	@Chi	@Chi	@StL	@StL	@StL	@StL
CASE, George	7							7	7	7	7				
LEMON, Bob	RP					SP		RP				RP		SP	
EDWARDS, Hank	9	9	9	9	9	9	9	9	9	9	9	9	9		9
FLEMING, Les	3	3	3	3	3	3	3		ph				3	3	3
KELTNER, Ken	ph	5	5	5	5	5	5	5	5	5	5	5	ph		
BOUDREAU, Lou	6	6	6	6	6	6	6	6	6	6	6	6	6		
HAYES, Frankie															
MACK, Ray		4	4	4	4	4	4	4	4	4	4	4	4		
FELLER, Bob		RP		SP				SP			SP			RP	
WOODLING, Gene	ph														
REYNOLDS, Allie		SP				SP						SP			
SEEREY, Pat		7	7	7	7	7	7					7	7	7	7
LOLLAR, Sherman	RECALL ANNOUNCED 9/6, WON'T REPORT TILL ORIOLES ELIMINATED IN I.L. PLAYOFFS 9/16.														
GROMEK, Steve	pr							SP				RP			
BLACK, Don															
CENTER, Pete												RP			
MONACO, Blas															
EMBREE, Chas. (Red)					SP							SP			
MACKIEWICZ, Felix	8	8	8	8	8	8	8	8	8	8	8	8	8	8	8
HEGAN, Jim	2	2	2	2		2	2	2	2	2	2	2		2	
JOHNSON, Vic	JOHNSON RECALLED FROM PELICANS 9/6, SOLD OUTRIGHT TO OKLAHOMA CITY 9/19.														
PODGAJNY, Johnny															
MEYER, L.D. (Dutch)	4												4	4	4
BREWSTER, Charley															
ROSS, Don	5												9	9	
ROCCO, Michael (Mickey)															
MILLS, Buster															
KLIEMAN, Eddie															
CONWAY, Jack													5	5	5
FERRICK, Tom															
KRAKAUSKAS, Joe		RP					RP					RP			
HARDER, Mel			SP						SP						
BERRY, Jonas (Jittery Joe)		RP				RP		RP							RP
WASDELL, Jimmy	ph	ph					ph	ph	ph			ph			
WEBBER, Les	OPTIONED TO BALTIMORE AUGUST 20th, PITCHES FOR THE ORIOLES NEXT DAY.														
GASSAWAY, Charlie	SP					RP									SP
JORDAN, Tom				2									2		2
BECKER, Heinz	ph							3	3	3	3	3	3		
PRICE, John (Jackie)									6						
PETERS, Russell (Rusty)													6	6	6
SEPKOWSKI, Ted	RECALLED SEP. 6th, REPORTS AT END OF TEXAS LEAGUE SEASON, SEPTEMBER 8th.														
MITCHELL, Dale	RECALLED SEP. 6th, REPORTS AT END OF TEXAS LEAGUE SEASON, SEPTEMBER 8th.														
WEIGEL, Ralph	RECALLED 9/6, PENDING WILKES-BARRE ELIMINATION FROM EASTERN LG. PLAYOFFS (9/13).														
McCABE, Ralph	RECALLED SEP. 6th, REPORTS AT END OF TEXAS LEAGUE SEASON, SEPTEMBER 8th.														
MOSS, Howie	RECALLED SEP 6, REPORTS WHEN ORIOLES ELIMINATED FROM I.L. PLAYOFFS, SEP. 16.														
ROBINSON, Eddie	RECALLED SEP. 6, REPORTS WHEN ORIOLES ELIMINATED FROM I.L. PLAYOFFS, SEP. 16.														
FLANIGAN, Ray															
KUZAVA, Bob															

CLE AL	SEP 4 @Det	5 @Det	6 @Det	7 StL	[1] 8 StL	[2] 8 StL	10 NY	11 NY	12 Bos	13 Bos	[1] 15 Phl	[2] 15 Phl	18 Wsh	19 Wsh	20 Det
CASE, George	7	7									7	7	7		
LEMON, Bob		RP									SP				RP
EDWARDS, Hank		9	9	9	9	9	9	9	9	9	9		9	9	9
FLEMING, Les	3	3		3	3	3	3	3	3	3	3	3	3	ph	
KELTNER, Ken			5	5											
BOUDREAU, Lou	ph		6	6	6	6	6	6	6	6	6	6			
HAYES, Frankie															
MACK, Ray			4	4	4	4	4	4	4	4	4	4	4	4	4
FELLER, Bob		SP				SP			SP			SP		SP	
WOODLING, Gene				8	ph										
REYNOLDS, Allie	RP			SP				SP							SP
SEEREY, Pat	9		7	7	7	7	7	7	7	7	79	9	7	7	7
LOLLAR, Sherman	LOLLAR DOESN'T PLAY AGAIN IN THE BIG LEAGUES TILL 1947, WITH THE YANKEES.													
GROMEK, Steve	SP						SP								
BLACK, Don	RECALLED SEPTEMBER 6th, WON'T PITCH AGAIN FOR INDIANS TILL 1947.													
CENTER, Pete			RP	RP	RP										
MONACO, Blas															
EMBREE, Chas. (Red)					SP				SP						RP
MACKIEWICZ, Felix	8	8	8	8	8	8	8	8	8	8					
HEGAN, Jim		2	2	2		2	2	2	2	2		2	2	2	
JOHNSON, Vic															
PODGAJNY, Johnny															
MEYER, L.D. (Dutch)	4	4		ph								4			ph
BREWSTER, Charley															
ROSS, Don	5	5			5	5	5	5	5	5		5	5		
ROCCO, Michael (Mickey)															
MILLS, Buster															
KLIEMAN, Eddie	RECALLED SEPTEMBER 6th, WON'T PITCH AGAIN FOR INDIANS TILL 1947.													
CONWAY, Jack															
FERRICK, Tom															
KRAKAUSKAS, Joe													RP		
HARDER, Mel			SP												
BERRY, Jonas (Jittery Joe)			RP	RP											
WASDELL, Jimmy				ph								ph			
WEBBER, Les	RECALLED SEPT. 6th, BUT WON'T PITCH AGAIN IN MAJORS TILL 1948.													
GASSAWAY, Charlie			RP										RP		RP
JORDAN, Tom	2				2						2				2
BECKER, Heinz			3	3									ph	ph	
PRICE, John (Jackie)			ph										6	6	6
PETERS, Russell (Rusty)	6	6		ph									ph	6	
SEPKOWSKI, Ted											5	5			
MITCHELL, Dale											8	8	8	8	8
WEIGEL, Ralph													2		2
McCABE, Ralph													SP		
MOSS, Howie														5	5
ROBINSON, Eddie														3	3
FLANIGAN, Ray															RP
KUZAVA, Bob															

CLE AL

	SEP 21 Det	[1] 22 Det	[2] 22 Det	25 Chi	27 @Det	28 @Det	29 @Det	156g
CASE, George		7		* EXCUSED.				
LEMON, Bob	RP		RP			RP		
EDWARDS, Hank	9		9	9	9	9	9	
FLEMING, Les	ph		ph	* EXCUSED.				
KELTNER, Ken		5		* EXCUSED.				
BOUDREAU, Lou		6						
HAYES, Frankie								
MACK, Ray	4		4	4	4	4	4	
FELLER, Bob		SP		SP	RP		SP	
WOODLING, Gene	ph					ph		
REYNOLDS, Allie								
SEEREY, Pat	7	9	7	7	7	7	7	
LOLLAR, Sherman								
GROMEK, Steve	pr		SP					
BLACK, Don								
CENTER, Pete								
MONACO, Blas								
EMBREE, Chas. (Red)				* EXCUSED.				
MACKIEWICZ, Felix		8					9	
HEGAN, Jim		2		2	2	2	2	
JOHNSON, Vic								
PODGAJNY, Johnny								
MEYER, L.D. (Dutch)	4	4		* EXCUSED.				
BREWSTER, Charley								
ROSS, Don		ph	5	* EXCUSED.				
ROCCO, Michael (Mickey)								
MILLS, Buster								
KLIEMAN, Eddie								
CONWAY, Jack	6		6	6	6	6	6	
FERRICK, Tom								
KRAKAUSKAS, Joe				* EXCUSED.				
HARDER, Mel				* EXCUSED.				
BERRY, Jonas (Jittery Joe)	RP			* EXCUSED.				
WASDELL, Jimmy	ph		ph			9		
WEBBER, Les								
GASSAWAY, Charlie								
JORDAN, Tom	2			* EXCUSED.				
BECKER, Heinz	ph	3	ph	* EXCUSED.				
PRICE, John (Jackie)								
PETERS, Russell (Rusty)			6	* EXCUSED.				
SEPKOWSKI, Ted								
MITCHELL, Dale	8		8	8	8	8	8	
WEIGEL, Ralph	2		2		2	2		
McCABE, Ralph	RETURNED OUTRIGHT TO OK. CITY, 9/19							
MOSS, Howie	5		5	5	5	5	5	
ROBINSON, Eddie	3		3	3	3	3	3	
FLANIGAN, Ray			RP			SP		
KUZAVA, Bob	SP				SP			

* A dozen players are allowed to go home early, enabling rookies and others to get more playing time.

DET AL

	G	APRIL 16 StL	17 StL	18 StL	20 @Cle	21 @Cle	22 @Chi	23 @Chi	25 @StL	26 @StL	27 Cle	28 Cle	MAY 30 @Bos	1 @Bos	2 @Bos
	155														
LAKE, Eddie	155	6	6	6	6	6	6	6	6	6	6	6	6	6	6
MAYO, Eddie	51	4	4	4	4	4	4	4	4	4	4	4	4	4	4
McCOSKY, Barney	25	8	8	8	8	8	8	8	8	8	8	8	8	8	8
GREENBERG, Hank	142	3	3	3	3	3	3	3	3	3	3	3	3	3	3
WAKEFIELD, Dick	111	7	7	7	7	7	7	7	7	7	7	7	7	7	7
MULLIN, Pat	93	9	9	9	9	9	INJURED.				ph	9	9	98	9
HIGGINS, Mike (Pinky)	18	5	5	5	5	5	5	5	5	5	5	5	5	5	5
RICHARDS, Paul	57	2		2							2	2	2		2
NEWHOUSER, Hal	37	SP			SP				SP				SP		
OUTLAW, Jimmy	92		pr								pr	pr		5	ph
TEBBETTS, George (Birdie)	87		2		2	2	2	2	2	2	2	2		2	2
CULLENBINE, Roy	113		ph				9	9	9	9	9	9		3	ph
TRUCKS, Virgil	32		SP			RP				SP					SP
OVERMIRE, Frank (Stubby)	24		RP			SP						SP			
CASTER, George	26		RP								RP				
MOORE, Anselm (Anse)	51		ph					ph			ph	ph		9	ph
BENTON, Alton (Al)	28			SP				SP						SP	
TROUT, Paul (Dizzy)	40						SP				SP				
CRAMER, Roger (Doc)	68							ph			ph	ph			ph
WEBB, James (Skeeter)	64								6		6	6			
HARRIS, Bob (Ned)	1											ph	TO PORTLAND.		
SWIFT, Bob	42	OUT WITH PULLED LEFT ANKLE TENDON.												2	2
WHITE, Hal	11													RP	
HUTCHINSON, Fred	40													ph	
GENTRY, Ruffus (Rufe)	2													RP	
HITCHCOCK, Billy	3													ph	
BRIDGES, Tommy	9														RP
BLOODWORTH, Jimmy	76	REINSTATED FROM NDSL (ARMY) MAY 6th, REPORTS MAY 11th.													
MANDERS, Hal	2														
GRAY, Ted	3	REINSTATED FROM NDSL (NAVY) May 6th, GIVEN 15-DAY TRIAL, ENDING MAY 26th.													
KELL, George	105	TRADED FROM ATHLETICS FOR McCOSKY, MAY 18th.													
EVERS, Walter (Hoot)	81	SUSTAINED BROKEN ANKLE & THUMB, MARCH 17th; SIDELINED TILL MAY 21st.													
LIPON, Johnny	14														
GORSICA, Johnny	14														
GROTH, Johnny	4	SIGNED OUT OF USN, PLAYS IN AUGUST 10th EXHIBITION, DEBUTS SEPTEMBER 5th.													
HOUTTEMAN, Art	1	16-13 AT BUFFALO, PITCHES ONCE FOR DETROIT, LATE SEPTEMBER.													
KRETLOW, Lou	1	TO BUFFALO APRIL 14th, RETURNED JUNE 24th & OPTIONED TO WILLIAMSPORT.													

May 2nd, Pre-War Detroit infielder Murray Franklin joins Mexican League and is suspended for five years along with other "jumpers". After Franklin had refused earlier assignments to Buffalo, the Tigers voided his contract on March 21st.

American League

	MAY		[1]	[2]											
	3	4	5	5	6	7	8	9	11	12	13	14	15	17	18
DET AL	@NY	@NY	@Ph	@Ph	@Ph	@Ph	@Ws	@Ws	Chi	Chi	Chi	Wsh	Wsh	Phl	Phl
LAKE, Eddie	6	6	6	6	6	6	6	6	6	6	6	6	6	6	6
MAYO, Eddie	4	4	4	4	4	4	4	4	4	4	4	4	4	4	4
McCOSKY, Barney	ph		8	8	8	8	8	8	8	8	8	8			
GREENBERG, Hank	3	3	3	3	3	3	3	3	3	3	3	3			
WAKEFIELD, Dick	7	7		pr	INJURED.			ph	WAKEFIELD HAS BONE CHIP IN WRIST.						
MULLIN, Pat	9	ph	9	9	9	9	9	9	9	9	9	9	9	9	9
HIGGINS, Mike (Pinky)	5	5	OUT WITH FLU.					ph					h5		
RICHARDS, Paul		2		2	2		2		2		2	INJURED ELBOW.			
NEWHOUSER, Hal							SP				SP				
OUTLAW, Jimmy	pr	87	5	5	5	5	5	5	5	5	5	5	58	5	5
TEBBETTS, George (Birdie)	2			2		2		2		2	2	2	2		2
CULLENBINE, Roy		9	3	ph	9			9					3	3	3
TRUCKS, Virgil					SP				SP					SP	
OVERMIRE, Frank (Stubby)		SP					SP				SP				
CASTER, George		RP					RP				RP				
MOORE, Anselm (Anse)	ph		7	7	7	7	7	7	7	7	7	7	7	7	7
BENTON, Alton (Al)			SP					RP							
TROUT, Paul (Dizzy)	SP	ph				SP		RP		SP			ph		
CRAMER, Roger (Doc)	8	8	ph									8	8	8	8
WEBB, James (Skeeter)			pr	6									pr		
HARRIS, Bob (Ned)		DATE OF ASSIGNMENT TO PORTLAND (PCL) WAS APRIL 29th.													
SWIFT, Bob	2	2	2										2	2	
WHITE, Hal			RP				RP						RP		
HUTCHINSON, Fred				RP							RP				SP
GENTRY, Ruffus (Rufe)			RP						OPTIONED TO BUFFALO, MAY 11th.						
HITCHCOCK, Billy			ph	4	HURT FINGER & THUMB, MAY 5th, SOLD TO WASHINGTON MAY 16th.										
BRIDGES, Tommy				SP							RP				
BLOODWORTH, Jimmy											ph				
MANDERS, Hal											RP				
GRAY, Ted											SP				
KELL, George															
EVERS, Walter (Hoot)															
LIPON, Johnny															
GORSICA, Johnny															
GROTH, Johnny															
HOUTTEMAN, Art															
KRETLOW, Lou															

DET AL	MAY 19 Bos	[1] 19 Bos	[2] 21 Bos	22 NY	23 NY	24 @Chi	[1] 26 @Chi	[2] 26 @Chi	28 @Cle	29 @Cle	[1] 30 @StL	[2] 30 @StL	JUNE 1 @Ws	2 @Ws	3 @Ws
LAKE, Eddie	6	6	6	6	6	6	6	6	6	6	6	6	6	6	6
MAYO, Eddie	4	4	4	4	4	4	4	4	4	4	4	4	4	4	4
McCOSKY, Barney	TRADED TO A'S FOR KELL, MAY 18th.														
GREENBERG, Hank	3	3	3	3	3	3	3	3	3	3	3	3	3		3
WAKEFIELD, Dick	7	7	7	7	7	7	7	7	7	7		7	7	7	7
MULLIN, Pat	9	9	9	9	9						ph	ph			
HIGGINS, Mike (Pinky)	SOLD TO THE RED SOX, MAY 19th.														
RICHARDS, Paul	2	2	2	2		2		2		2		2		2	
NEWHOUSER, Hal		SP				SP				SP				SP	
OUTLAW, Jimmy		8	8	8	8		9	pr			7		pr		8
TEBBETTS, George (Birdie)	2			2			2		2		2		2		2
CULLENBINE, Roy	ph		ph	9			ph				9	ph	ph	3	ph
TRUCKS, Virgil			SP		RP		SP				SP				
OVERMIRE, Frank (Stubby)					SP										SP
CASTER, George	RP				RP										RP
MOORE, Anselm (Anse)	ph		9	ph	9		9	9	9		9	9	9	9	9
BENTON, Alton (Al)	RP	RP													
TROUT, Paul (Dizzy)	SP			RP			SP				SP				
CRAMER, Roger (Doc)	8												ph		
WEBB, James (Skeeter)				pr			6								
HARRIS, Bob (Ned)															
SWIFT, Bob					2							2	2		
WHITE, Hal					RP										RP
HUTCHINSON, Fred			SP						SP			ph	SP		
GENTRY, Ruffus (Rufe)															
HITCHCOCK, Billy															
BRIDGES, Tommy					RP						RP				
BLOODWORTH, Jimmy			ph												4
MANDERS, Hal															
GRAY, Ted					OPTIONED TO BUFFALO, MAY 24.										
KELL, George	5	5	5	5	5	5	5	5	5	5	5	5	5	5	5
EVERS, Walter (Hoot)			ph			8	8	8	8	8	8	8	8	8	8
LIPON, Johnny				pr											
GORSICA, Johnny															
GROTH, Johnny															
HOUTTEMAN, Art															
KRETLOW, Lou															

DET AL

	JUNE			[1]	[2]										
	4	5	8	9	9	10	11	12	14	15	16	19	20	21	22
	@Phl	@Phl	@Bos	@Bos	@Bos	@NY	@NY	@NY	Wsh	Wsh	Wsh	Phl	Phl	NY	NY
LAKE, Eddie	6	6	6	6	6	6	6	6	6	6	6	6	6	6	6
MAYO, Eddie	INJURED IN COLLISION WITH EVERS JUNE 3rd, OUT TILL JULY 13th.														
McCOSKY, Barney															
GREENBERG, Hank	3	*3	3	3	3	3	3	3	3	3	3	3	3	3	3
WAKEFIELD, Dick	7	7	7	7	7	7	7	7	7	7	7	7	7	7	7
MULLIN, Pat	9	9	9		9	9	9	9		9	9	9	9		9
HIGGINS, Mike (Pinky)															
RICHARDS, Paul		2	2	2	TEARS KNEE LIGAMENTS IN COLLISION WITH GREENBERG.										
NEWHOUSER, Hal			SP				SP			SP				SP	
OUTLAW, Jimmy	8	85	8	5	5	5	5	5	8					9	
TEBBETTS, George (Birdie)				2	2	2	2		2	2	2	2		2	2
CULLENBINE, Roy				9	ph			9		ph					ph
TRUCKS, Virgil		SP				SP			SP			SP			
OVERMIRE, Frank (Stubby)	FELL ON (LEFT) PITCHING HAND JUNE 3rd, SPRAINED IT.														RP
CASTER, George			RP								RP				RP
MOORE, Anselm (Anse)			ph		ph										
BENTON, Alton (Al)		RP			RP						RP				
TROUT, Paul (Dizzy)	SP			SP				SP					SP		
CRAMER, Roger (Doc)		8		8	8	8	8	8		8	8	8	8		
WEBB, James (Skeeter)				4											
HARRIS, Bob (Ned)															
SWIFT, Bob	2			2				2					2		
WHITE, Hal			RP												
HUTCHINSON, Fred				SP							SP				SP
GENTRY, Ruffus (Rufe)															
HITCHCOCK, Billy															
BRIDGES, Tommy				RP											
BLOODWORTH, Jimmy	4	4	4	ph	4	4	4	4	4	4	4	4	4	4	4
MANDERS, Hal		RP										TO BUFFALO 6/20.			
GRAY, Ted															
KELL, George	5	5	5	HAS CHARLEY HORSE.					5	5	5	5	5	5	5
EVERS, Walter (Hoot)	COLLIDES WITH MAYO, BREAKS JAW, OUT TILL JUNE 21st.													8	8
LIPON, Johnny				ph											
GORSICA, Johnny					RP										
GROTH, Johnny															
HOUTTEMAN, Art															
KRETLOW, Lou															

* Greenberg's name is spelled "Greenhalgh" in *Sporting News* box score of June 5th.

American League — DET AL

	JUNE			[1]	[2]		[1]	[2]	JULY			[1]	[2]		
	23	24	25	26	26	28	30	30	1	2	3	4	4	5	6
DET AL	NY	Bos	Bos	Bos	Bos	@StL	@StL	@StL	Chi	Chi	Chi	Cle	Cle	Cle	StL
LAKE, Eddie	6	6	6	6	6	6	6	6	6	6	6	6	6	6	6
MAYO, Eddie															
McCOSKY, Barney															
GREENBERG, Hank	3	3	3	3	3	3	3		3	3	3	3	3	3	3
WAKEFIELD, Dick	7	7	7			ph		7		ph			ph		
MULLIN, Pat	9	9	9	9		9			9	9	9	9	9	9	9
HIGGINS, Mike (Pinky)															
RICHARDS, Paul											2		2		
NEWHOUSER, Hal	RP			SP			SP				SP				
OUTLAW, Jimmy	5	5	5	5	5	5	5	5	5	5	5	5	57		
TEBBETTS, George (Birdie)	2		2	2			2		2	2	2	2		2	
CULLENBINE, Roy	ph		ph	73	7	7	7	3	7	7	7	7	73	7	7
TRUCKS, Virgil	SP				SP				SP				SP		
OVERMIRE, Frank (Stubby)													SP		
CASTER, George	RP				RP	RP				RP			RP		
MOORE, Anselm (Anse)	ph			9	9	ph	9	9	9		ph		ph		
BENTON, Alton (Al)	RP				RP	RP							RP		
TROUT, Paul (Dizzy)		SP				SP				SP			RP		SP
CRAMER, Roger (Doc)	ph			8	ph			8	8		ph		8		
WEBB, James (Skeeter)			pr	6		6					pr				
HARRIS, Bob (Ned)															
SWIFT, Bob	2	2			2	2		2		2					2
WHITE, Hal													RP		
HUTCHINSON, Fred	ph		SP				SP					SP	ph		
GENTRY, Ruffus (Rufe)															
HITCHCOCK, Billy															
BRIDGES, Tommy		RP								RP					
BLOODWORTH, Jimmy	4	4	4	4	4	4	4	4	4	4	4	4	4	4	4
MANDERS, Hal															
GRAY, Ted															
KELL, George		OUT WITH CHARLEY HORSE (AGAIN).										5	5	5	
EVERS, Walter (Hoot)	8	8	8	87	8	8	8		8	8	8	ph	8	8	
LIPON, Johnny			5												
GORSICA, Johnny	RP								RP			RP			
GROTH, Johnny															
HOUTTEMAN, Art															
KRETLOW, Lou															

Note: TIE 6/24, no replay

DET AL

	JULY 7	ALL-STAR BREAK 11	12	13	[1] 14	[2] 14	15	17	18	19	20	[1] 21	[2] 21	23	24
	StL	@Bos	@Bos	@Bos	@NY	@NY	@NY	@Ws	@Ws	@Ws	@Phl	@Phl	@Phl	Wsh	Wsh
LAKE, Eddie	6	6	6	6	6	6	6	6	6	6	6	6	6	6	6
MAYO, Eddie				ph	4		4	4	4	4					
McCOSKY, Barney															
GREENBERG, Hank	3		3	3	3	3	3	3	3	3	3	3		3	3
WAKEFIELD, Dick		7		HAS BONE CHIPS BENEATH LEFT ELBOW.											
MULLIN, Pat	9	9	9	9	9	9	9	9	9	9			9		ph
HIGGINS, Mike (Pinky)															
RICHARDS, Paul						2							2		
NEWHOUSER, Hal	SP			SP					SP					SP	
OUTLAW, Jimmy		75	7	7	7	7	7	7	7	7	7	7	7	7	7
TEBBETTS, George (Birdie)	2	2	2		2		2	2		2	2	2		2	
CULLENBINE, Roy	7	3						ph			9	9	3	9	9
TRUCKS, Virgil			SP					SP				SP			
OVERMIRE, Frank (Stubby)						SP							SP		
CASTER, George															
MOORE, Anselm (Anse)															ph
BENTON, Alton (Al)								RP				RP			
TROUT, Paul (Dizzy)				SP					SP				RP		SP
CRAMER, Roger (Doc)		8		ph	ph	8					8	8		8	8
WEBB, James (Skeeter)		4		pr				4		4		4	4		4
HARRIS, Bob (Ned)															
SWIFT, Bob		2		2					2						2
WHITE, Hal															
HUTCHINSON, Fred		SP					SP				SP				ph
GENTRY, Ruffus (Rufe)															
HITCHCOCK, Billy															
BRIDGES, Tommy											RP				
BLOODWORTH, Jimmy	4	4	4	4		4					4	4	4	4	4
MANDERS, Hal															
GRAY, Ted															
KELL, George	5	53	5	5	5	5	5	5	5	5	5	5	5	5	5
EVERS, Walter (Hoot)	8	87	8	8		8	8	8	8	8			8		ph
LIPON, Johnny		pr													
GORSICA, Johnny													RP		
GROTH, Johnny															
HOUTTEMAN, Art															
KRETLOW, Lou															

American League — DET AL

	JULY			[1]	[2]				AUG						
	25	26	27	28	28	29	30	31	1	2	3	4	6	7	9
DET AL	Wsh	Phl	Phl	Phl	Phl	Phl	NY	NY	NY	Bos	Bos	Bos	@StL	@StL	@Chi
LAKE, Eddie	6	6	6	6	6	6	6	6	6	6	6	6	6	6	6
MAYO, Eddie	ph														
McCOSKY, Barney															
GREENBERG, Hank	3	3	3	3	3		3	3	3	3	3	3	3	3	3
WAKEFIELD, Dick				ph		7	7	7	7	7	7	7	7	7	7
MULLIN, Pat				9	9				ph		ph			ph	
HIGGINS, Mike (Pinky)															
RICHARDS, Paul		2		2	2		2		2		2		2		
NEWHOUSER, Hal			SP								SP				RP
OUTLAW, Jimmy	7	7	7	7	7	9					ph		pr		
TEBBETTS, George (Birdie)	2		2	2		2		2		2	2	2		2	2
CULLENBINE, Roy	9	9	9	9		3	9	9	9	9	9	9	9	9	9
TRUCKS, Virgil		SP					SP								
OVERMIRE, Frank (Stubby)	RP				SP				SP						
CASTER, George	RP											RP			
MOORE, Anselm (Anse)				pr											
BENTON, Alton (Al)								SP					SP		RP
TROUT, Paul (Dizzy)			SP							SP			SP		
CRAMER, Roger (Doc)	ph	8	8	8	8	8	8		8		ph			ph	
WEBB, James (Skeeter)				4	4	4	4	4	4	4	4	4	4		4
HARRIS, Bob (Ned)															
SWIFT, Bob															
WHITE, Hal	RP														
HUTCHINSON, Fred	SP					SP			ph		SP			ph	SP
GENTRY, Ruffus (Rufe)															
HITCHCOCK, Billy															
BRIDGES, Tommy															
BLOODWORTH, Jimmy	4	4	4	4						4			4		
MANDERS, Hal															//
GRAY, Ted															
KELL, George	5	5	5	5	5	5	5	5	5	5	5	5	5	5	5
EVERS, Walter (Hoot)	8	WRIST INJURY.					8		8	8	8	8	8	8	8
LIPON, Johnny				pr											
GORSICA, Johnny	RP							RP			RP				
GROTH, Johnny															
HOUTTEMAN, Art															
KRETLOW, Lou															

DET AL

		[1]	[2]							[1]	[2]			[1]	[2]	
	AUG	11	11	12	13	14	15	16	17	18	18	20	21	23	23	24
		@Chi	@Chi	@Cle	@Cle	@Cle	Chi	Chi	StL	StL	StL	@Phl	@Phl	@Ws	@Ws	@Ws
LAKE, Eddie		6	6	6	6	6	6	6	6	6	6	6	6	6	6	6
MAYO, Eddie		BACK SURGERY ENDS MAYO'S SEASON.														
McCOSKY, Barney																
GREENBERG, Hank		3	3	3	3	3	3	3	3	3		3	3	ph		3
WAKEFIELD, Dick		7	7	7	7	7		7	7	7	7	7	7	7	7	7
MULLIN, Pat						9				ph	9		ph	ph		
HIGGINS, Mike (Pinky)																
RICHARDS, Paul			2	2		2	2	2	2	2		2				
NEWHOUSER, Hal		SP					SP					SP		RP		
OUTLAW, Jimmy		ph	9			ph	7	5	ph		pr			9	9	
TEBBETTS, George (Birdie)		2			2						2		2	2		2
CULLENBINE, Roy		9		9	9	9	9	9	9	9	3	9	9	3	3	9
TRUCKS, Virgil			SP					SP					SP			
OVERMIRE, Frank (Stubby)			RP										RP			
CASTER, George				RP					RP	RP			RP			
MOORE, Anselm (Anse)																
BENTON, Alton (Al)				SP					SP							SP
TROUT, Paul (Dizzy)					SP					SP					SP	
CRAMER, Roger (Doc)					ph					8		ph	ph	8		8
WEBB, James (Skeeter)		4	4	4	4	4	4	4	4	4	4	4	4	4	4	
HARRIS, Bob (Ned)																
SWIFT, Bob			2		2	2									2	
WHITE, Hal																
HUTCHINSON, Fred				ph	SP					SP	ph		SP			
GENTRY, Ruffus (Rufe)																
HITCHCOCK, Billy																
BRIDGES, Tommy																
BLOODWORTH, Jimmy			ph			4				4			4	4		4
MANDERS, Hal		MANDERS DEALT TO THE CUBS, AUGUST 9th.														
GRAY, Ted																
KELL, George		5	5	5	5	5	5		5	5	5	5	5	5	5	5
EVERS, Walter (Hoot)		8	8	8	8	8	8	8	8		8	8	8		8	
LIPON, Johnny			pr													
GORSICA, Johnny		RP							RP							
GROTH, Johnny																
HOUTTEMAN, Art																
KRETLOW, Lou																

American League — DET AL

	AUG						SUN SEP 1, RAIN [1]	[2]						[1]	[2]
	25	26	27	28	29	31	2	2	3	4	5	6	7	8	8
	@NY	@NY	@NY	@Bos	@Bos	@StL	@Chi	@Chi	@Chi	Cle	Cle	Cle	Chi	Chi	Chi
LAKE, Eddie	6	6	6	6	6	6	6	6	6	6	6	6	6	6	6
MAYO, Eddie															
McCOSKY, Barney															
GREENBERG, Hank	3	3	3	3	3	3	3	3	ph	3	3	3	3	3	
WAKEFIELD, Dick	7	7	7		7	7	7		7	7	7	7	7	7	7
MULLIN, Pat		ph	ph											ph	
HIGGINS, Mike (Pinky)															
RICHARDS, Paul	2		2		2	2	ph	2	2					2	
NEWHOUSER, Hal	SP				SP			SP					SP		
OUTLAW, Jimmy			9	7			7	9						pr	9
TEBBETTS, George (Birdie)		2		2	2			2			2		2		
CULLENBINE, Roy	9	9	9	9	9	9	9	9	3	9	9	9	9	9	3
TRUCKS, Virgil		SP			RP			SP							SP
OVERMIRE, Frank (Stubby)		RP	RP					RP							RP
CASTER, George		RP											RP		
MOORE, Anselm (Anse)														ph	
BENTON, Alton (Al)					SP		SP					SP			
TROUT, Paul (Dizzy)			SP		RP	SP						SP			
CRAMER, Roger (Doc)	8	8	8		8	8	8						8	ph	
WEBB, James (Skeeter)	4	4	4	4	4	4	4		4	4	4	4	4	4	
HARRIS, Bob (Ned)															
SWIFT, Bob			2				2		2			2			2
WHITE, Hal															
HUTCHINSON, Fred	ph		ph	SP							SP				
GENTRY, Ruffus (Rufe)	RECALL ANNOUNCED AUG. 30th, BUT WON'T PITCH AGAIN FOR THE TIGERS THIS YEAR.														
HITCHCOCK, Billy															
BRIDGES, Tommy															
BLOODWORTH, Jimmy	4		4	ph			4								4
MANDERS, Hal															
GRAY, Ted	RECALLED AUGUST 30th, REPORTS AT THE END OF BUFFALO'S SEASON, SEPTEMBER 8th.														
KELL, George	5	5	5	5	5	5	5	5	5	5	5	5	5	5	5
EVERS, Walter (Hoot)				8	pr			8	8	8	8	8		8	8
LIPON, Johnny											6				
GORSICA, Johnny				RP										RP	
GROTH, Johnny											8				
HOUTTEMAN, Art	RECALLED AUGUST 30th, REPORTS AT END OF BUFFALO'S SEASON, SEPTEMBER 8th.														
KRETLOW, Lou	RECALLED AUGUST 30th, FOR END OF EASTERN LEAGUE SEASON.														

DET AL

	SEP 10	11	12	13	14	15	16	17	18	19	20	21	[1] 22	[2] 22	[1] 24
	Bos	Bos	NY	NY	NY	Wsh	Wsh	Wsh	Phl	Phl	@Cle	@Cle	@Cle	@Cle	StL
LAKE, Eddie	6	6	6	6	6	6	6	6	6	6	6	6	6	6	6
MAYO, Eddie															
McCOSKY, Barney															
GREENBERG, Hank	3	3	3	3	3	3		3	3	3	3	3	3		3
WAKEFIELD, Dick	7	7	7	7	7	7	7	7	7	7	7	7	7	7	7
MULLIN, Pat			pr	ph		9	9	ph	9	9				9	
HIGGINS, Mike (Pinky)															
RICHARDS, Paul			2	2			2	2	2				2		
NEWHOUSER, Hal				SP				SP					SP		
OUTLAW, Jimmy															
TEBBETTS, George (Birdie)	2	2	2		2	2		2		2	2	2			2
CULLENBINE, Roy	9	9	9	9	9	9	3	9	93	93	9	9	9	3	9
TRUCKS, Virgil										SP					
OVERMIRE, Frank (Stubby)							SP							RP	
CASTER, George			RP				RP								
MOORE, Anselm (Anse)					ph										
BENTON, Alton (Al)			SP					SP						SP	
TROUT, Paul (Dizzy)		SP			SP			RP				SP			
CRAMER, Roger (Doc)		8	*8	8										8	
WEBB, James (Skeeter)	4								4					4	
HARRIS, Bob (Ned)															
SWIFT, Bob						2								2	
WHITE, Hal						RP									
HUTCHINSON, Fred	SP				SP				ph		SP				SP
GENTRY, Ruffus (Rufe)															
HITCHCOCK, Billy															
BRIDGES, Tommy					RELEASED SEPTEMBER 14th, ENDING HIS BIG LEAGUE CAREER.									
BLOODWORTH, Jimmy		4	4	4	4	4	4	4	4	4	4	4	4		4
MANDERS, Hal															
GRAY, Ted											RP				
KELL, George	5	5	5	5	5	5	5	5	5	5	5	5	5	5	5
EVERS, Walter (Hoot)	8			8	8	8	8	8	8	8	8	8			8
LIPON, Johnny					6					6					
GORSICA, Johnny					RP										
GROTH, Johnny										8					
HOUTTEMAN, Art															
KRETLOW, Lou															

* On September 12th, *TSN* box lists Cramer as pitcher. He only pitched once his in career, in 1938. Assume he plays center field this date.

American League — DET AL

	SEP [2] 24 StL	25 StL	26 StL	27 Cle	28 Cle	29 Cle	155g
LAKE, Eddie	6	6	6	6	6	6	
MAYO, Eddie							
McCOSKY, Barney							
GREENBERG, Hank	3	3	3	3	3	3	
WAKEFIELD, Dick	7			ph		7	
MULLIN, Pat		9	9	9	9	ph	
HIGGINS, Mike (Pinky)							
RICHARDS, Paul							
NEWHOUSER, Hal						SP	
OUTLAW, Jimmy		5	5	5			
TEBBETTS, George (Birdie)							
CULLENBINE, Roy	9					9	
TRUCKS, Virgil							
OVERMIRE, Frank (Stubby)				RP			
CASTER, George							
MOORE, Anselm (Anse)		7	7	7	7	ph	
BENTON, Alton (Al)							
TROUT, Paul (Dizzy)	SP						
CRAMER, Roger (Doc)	8					8	
WEBB, James (Skeeter)	4		4	4			
HARRIS, Bob (Ned)							
SWIFT, Bob	2	2	2	2	2	2	
WHITE, Hal					SP		
HUTCHINSON, Fred							
GENTRY, Ruffus (Rufe)							
HITCHCOCK, Billy							
BRIDGES, Tommy							
BLOODWORTH, Jimmy		4			4	4	
MANDERS, Hal							
GRAY, Ted				SP			
KELL, George	5				5	5	
EVERS, Walter (Hoot)		ph		8	8	8	
LIPON, Johnny		6	6	6	6	6	
GORSICA, Johnny		RP					
GROTH, Johnny		8	8				
HOUTTEMAN, Art		SP					
KRETLOW, Lou			SP				

American League

NY AL

	G	APRIL 16	17	18	19	20	21	22	23	24	25	26	27	28	30
	154	@Ph	@Ph	@Ph	Wsh	Wsh	Wsh	Phl	Phl	@Bos	@Bos	@Ws	@Ws	@Ws	Cle
CROSETTI, Frank	28	6	PULLS CALF MUSCLE ON OPENING DAY, DOESN'T PLAY AGAIN TILL JUNE.												
STIRNWEISS, George(Snuffy)	129	5	5	5	5	5	5	5	5	5	5	5	5	5	5
HENRICH, Tom	150	9	9	9	9	9	9	9	9	9	9	9	9	9	9
DiMAGGIO, Joe	132	8	8	8	8	8	8	8	8	8	8	8	8	8	8
ETTEN, Nick	108	3	3	3	3	3	3	3	3	3	3	3	3	3	3
LINDELL, Johnny	102	7	7	7	7	7								ph	
DICKEY, Bill	54	2			2	2	2	2	2			2		2	2
GRIMES, Oscar	14	4	6	6	6	6	6	6	6						
CHANDLER, Spurgeon(Spud)	34	SP					SP					SP			
GORDON, Joe	112		4	4	4	4	4	4	4	4	4	4	4	4	4
ROBINSON, Aaron	100		2	2						2	2		2		
GUMPERT, Randy	33		SP							SP					
WIGHT, Bill	14		RP			SP					RP				
ROSER, Emerson (Steve)	4		RP		RP	RP					SP				
GETTEL, Al	26			SP					SP					SP	
PAGE, Joe	32				SP							SP			
KARPEL, Herb	2				RP	RP				TO NEWARK, APRIL 24th					
KELLER, Charlie	150				ph		7	7	7	7	7	7	7	7	7
STANCEAU, Charlie	3					RP					RP				
METHENY, Arthur (Bud)	3					ph					ph				
BEVENS, Floyd (Bill)	31							SP							SP
RIZZUTO, Phil	126	OUT WITH PULLED LEFT CALF MUSCLE.								6	6	6	6	6	6
MARSHALL, Clarence (Cuddles)	23									RP					
WADE, Jacob (Whistlin' Jake)	13									RP		RP			
SILVESTRI, Ken	13										2				
ZUBER, Bill	3										RP				
MAJESKI, Hank	8										ph				
RUFFING, Charles (Red)	8														
MURPHY, Johnny	27														
BONHAM, Ernie (Tiny)	18														
RUSSO, Marius (Lefty)	10														
DRESCHER, Bill	5														
WEATHERLY, Roy (Stormy)	2	FROM NATIONAL DEFENSE SERVICE LIST ON APRIL 23rd, AFTER ARMY DISCHARGE.													
SOUCHOCK, Steve	47	IN ARMY, DISCHARGED IN MAY, DEBUTS MAY 25th.													
HILLER, Frank	3	IN ARMY TILL MAY, NOW RECOVERING FROM SURGERY IN SPRING.													
JOHNSON, Billy	85	RELEASED FROM NDSL (ARMY) MAY 6th, AFTER JOINING TEAM MAY 5th.													
NIARHOS, Constantine (Gus)	37														
BYRNE, Tommy	14														
QUEEN, Mel	14	OUT OF ARMY JUNE 10th, JOINS TEAM JUNE 11th, RELEASED FROM NDSL JUNE 13th.													
DREWS, Karl	3									OPTIONED TO KANSAS CITY, APRIL 24.					
BOCKMAN, Eddie	4	OPTIONED TO KC APR.13, RECALLED AUG.16, TO REPORT AT END OF AA SEASON.													
LYONS, Al	2									OPTIONED TO KANSAS CITY, APRIL 24.					
BROWN, Bobby	7	OPTIONED TO NEWARK APRIL 13th, DEBUTS WITH YANKEES SEPT. 22nd (1).													
BERRA, Larry (Yogi)	7	LATE OUT OF NAVY, REPORTS TO KANSAS CITY. MAY 12th, MOVED TO NEWARK.													
COLMAN, Frank	5	FROM PIRATES TO KANSAS CITY, THEN YANKEES OUTRIGHT ON SEPTEMBER 20th.													
RASCHI, Vic	2	FARMHAND AT BINGHAMTON & NEWARK, CALLED UP BY NEW YORK SEPT. 20th.													

Note: Outfielder Tuck Stainback, who doesn't play for New York this season, is released April 26th. He's signed by the Athletics on May 3rd.

American League — NY AL

	MAY														
	1	2	3	4	5	6	8	9	10	11	12	14	15	17	18
NY AL	Cle	Cle	Det	Det	Chi	Chi	StL	StL	Bos	Bos	Bos	@StL	@StL	@Chi	@Chi
CROSETTI, Frank															
STIRNWEISS, George (Snuffy)	5	5	5	5	5	5	5	5	5	4	4	5	5	5	5
HENRICH, Tom	9	9	9	9	9	9	9	9	9	9	9	9	9	9	9
DiMAGGIO, Joe	8	8	8	8	8	8	8	8	8	8	8	8	8	8	8
ETTEN, Nick	3	3	3	3	3	3	3	3	3	3	3	3	3	3	3
LINDELL, Johnny						9			ph		ph				ph
DICKEY, Bill	2	2	2	2	2	2	2	2	2	2	2	2	2	2	2
GRIMES, Oscar							4	4	4						
CHANDLER, Spurgeon (Spud)		SP					SP				SP				
GORDON, Joe	4	4	4	4	4	4						4	4	4	4
ROBINSON, Aaron										2	SPLIT FINGER, OUT TILL 5/28.				
GUMPERT, Randy												RP	RP		
WIGHT, Bill															
ROSER, Emerson (Steve)			SOLD TO THE BRAVES, MAY 3rd.												
GETTEL, Al		SP					SP					SP			
PAGE, Joe			SP						RP				SP		
KARPEL, Herb		KARPEL, RELEASED OUTRIGHT APRIL 24th, LEADS INTERNATIONAL LEAGUE WITH 2.41 ERA.													
KELLER, Charlie	7	7	7	7	7	7	7	7	7	7	7	7	7	7	7
STANCEAU, Charlie															
METHENY, Arthur (Bud)								ph				TO K.C.			
BEVENS, Floyd (Bill)						SP					SP				
RIZZUTO, Phil	6	6	6	6	6	6	6	6	6	6	6	6	6	6	6
MARSHALL, Clarence (Cuddles)															RP
WADE, Jacob (Whistlin' Jake)								RP							
SILVESTRI, Ken													2		
ZUBER, Bill								RP							
MAJESKI, Hank						ph				5	5				
RUFFING, Charles (Red)	SP							SP							
MURPHY, Johnny			RP								RP				
BONHAM, Ernie (Tiny)				SP						SP					SP
RUSSO, Marius (Lefty)									RP		RP	RP			
DRESCHER, Bill															
WEATHERLY, Roy (Stormy)															
SOUCHOCK, Steve															
HILLER, Frank															
JOHNSON, Billy															
NIARHOS, Constantine (Gus)											OPTIONED TO KANSAS CITY, MAY 10th.				
BYRNE, Tommy															
QUEEN, Mel															
DREWS, Karl															
BOCKMAN, Eddie															
LYONS, Al															
BROWN, Bobby															
BERRA, Larry (Yogi)															
COLMAN, Frank															
RASCHI, Vic															

American League

Dickey replaces Joe McCarthy as mgr, May 24th.   SUN 6/2, RAIN

NY AL

	MAY [1]	[2]					[1]	[2]			[1]	[2]		JUNE
	19	19	20	21	22	23	25	26	26	28	29	30	30	31	1
	@Cle	@Cle	@Cle	@Cle	@Det	@Det	@Bos	@Bos	@Bos	Wsh	Wsh	Phl	Phl	Phl	StL
CROSETTI, Frank															
STIRNWEISS, George (Snuffy)	5	5	5	5	5	5	5	5	5	5	5	5	5	5	5
HENRICH, Tom	9	9	9	9	9		SPIKED.			9	9	9	9	9	9
DiMAGGIO, Joe	8	8	8	8	8	8	8	8	8	8	8	8	8	8	8
ETTEN, Nick	3	3	3	3	3	3	3	3	3	3	3	3	3	3	3
LINDELL, Johnny			8		9	9	9	9	9						
DICKEY, Bill	2		2	2	2	2	2	2		2			2		
GRIMES, Oscar				pr	4										
CHANDLER, Spurgeon (Spud)	SP						SP					SP			
GORDON, Joe	4	4	4	4	4	4	4	4	4	4	4	4	4	4	4
ROBINSON, Aaron										ph	2		2	2	
GUMPERT, Randy				SP		RP						RP			
WIGHT, Bill				RP											
ROSER, Emerson (Steve)															
GETTEL, Al			RP			SP		RP							
PAGE, Joe									SP					SP	
KARPEL, Herb															
KELLER, Charlie	7	7	7	7	7	7	7	7	7	7	7	7	7	7	7
STANCEAU, Charlie				RP											
METHENY, Arthur (Bud)		SOLD OUTRIGHT, ON MAY 16th.													
BEVENS, Floyd (Bill)				SP			SP					SP			
RIZZUTO, Phil	6	6	6	6	6	6	6	6	6	6	6	6	6	6	6
MARSHALL, Clarence (Cuddles)			RP		RP					SP					
WADE, Jacob (Whistlin' Jake)			RP	RP						RP					RP
SILVESTRI, Ken							2		2	2	INJURED. SEE NXT PAGE.				
ZUBER, Bill			RP												
MAJESKI, Hank							ph								
RUFFING, Charles (Red)		SP								SP					
MURPHY, Johnny													RP		
BONHAM, Ernie (Tiny)															
RUSSO, Marius (Lefty)			SP												
DRESCHER, Bill		2			ph		2	2		ph					
WEATHERLY, Roy (Stormy)			ph	ph	ANKLE INJURY; HE WON'T PLAY AGAIN IN MAJORS TILL 1950.										
SOUCHOCK, Steve							ph	pr		pr					
HILLER, Frank							RP								SP
JOHNSON, Billy								ph							
NIARHOS, Constantine (Gus)						NIARHOS RECALLED FROM KANSAS CITY, JUNE 9th.									
BYRNE, Tommy															
QUEEN, Mel															
DREWS, Karl															
BOCKMAN, Eddie															
LYONS, Al															
BROWN, Bobby															
BERRA, Larry (Yogi)															
COLMAN, Frank															
RASCHI, Vic															

American League — NY AL

	JUNE						[1]	[2]						[1]	[2]
	3	4	5	6	7	8	9	9	10	11	12	14	15	16	16
NY AL	StL	Chi	Chi	Chi	Cle	Cle	Cle	Cle	Det	Det	Det	@StL	@StL	@StL	@StL
CROSETTI, Frank	6							6	6	6	6			6	
STIRNWEISS, George (Snuffy)	5	5	5	5	5	5	56	4	4	4	4	4	4	4	4
HENRICH, Tom	9	9	9	9	9	9	9	9	9	9	9	9	9	9	9
DiMAGGIO, Joe	8	8	8	8	8	8	8	8	8	8	8	8	8	8	8
ETTEN, Nick	3	3	3	3	3	3	3	3	3			3	3	3	ph
LINDELL, Johnny					ph	ph	ph	ph	ph	3	3			38	3
DICKEY, Bill	2	2		2		2		2			2				
GRIMES, Oscar															
CHANDLER, Spurgeon (Spud)		SP					SP					SP			
GORDON, Joe	4	4	4	4	4	4	4								ph
ROBINSON, Aaron			2		2	2	2	ph	2		ph	2	2		2
GUMPERT, Randy					RP	RP			RP						RP
WIGHT, Bill									RP						
ROSER, Emerson (Steve)															
GETTEL, Al			RP						SP						
PAGE, Joe			SP				SP				RP				SP
KARPEL, Herb															
KELLER, Charlie	7	7	7	7	7	7	7	7	7	7	7	7	7	7	7
STANCEAU, Charlie			SOLD TO THE PHILLIES, JUNE 5th.												
METHENY, Arthur (Bud)															
BEVENS, Floyd (Bill)					SP				SP				SP		
RIZZUTO, Phil	6	6	6	6	6	6	6					6	6	6	6
MARSHALL, Clarence (Cuddles)	SP					SP					SP				
WADE, Jacob (Whistlin' Jake)					RP	RP			RP						
SILVESTRI, Ken			SILVESTRI FRACTURED HIS RIGHT INDEX FINGER ON MAY 29th, IS OUT 3 WEEKS.												
ZUBER, Bill												RELEASED, JUNE 14th.			
MAJESKI, Hank							ph	ph	ph			TO THE A's, JUNE 14th.			
RUFFING, Charles (Red)			SP										SP		
MURPHY, Johnny		RP		RP							RP		RP		
BONHAM, Ernie (Tiny)															
RUSSO, Marius (Lefty)					RP										
DRESCHER, Bill		OPTIONED TO KANSAS CITY, JUNE 2nd.													
WEATHERLY, Roy (Stormy)															
SOUCHOCK, Steve					pr	pr		pr	ph	ph					
HILLER, Frank							RP					TO NEWARK, JUNE 14th.			
JOHNSON, Billy						ph	5	5	5	5		5	5	5	5
NIARHOS, Constantine (Gus)							2	2		2			2	2	2
BYRNE, Tommy							RP		RP						pr
QUEEN, Mel															
DREWS, Karl															
BOCKMAN, Eddie															
LYONS, Al															
BROWN, Bobby															
BERRA, Larry (Yogi)															
COLMAN, Frank															
RASCHI, Vic															

American League

NY AL

	JUNE	[1]	[2]										JULY		[1]	[2]
		20	20	21	22	23	24	25	26	28	29	30	2	3	4	4
		@Chi	@Chi	@Det	@Det	@Det	@Cle	@Cle	@Cle	Phl	Phl	Phl	Bos	Bos	@Ws	@Ws
CROSETTI, Frank																
STIRNWEISS, George(Snuffy)		4	4	ph							6	*6	5	5	5	5
HENRICH, Tom		9	9	9	9	9	9	9	9	9	9	9	9	9	9	9
DiMAGGIO, Joe		8	8	8	8	8	8	8	8	8	8	8	8	8	8	8
ETTEN, Nick							ph	ph		ph	3	3	3	3	3	3
LINDELL, Johnny		3	3	3	3	3	3	3	3	3	3	ph			ph	
DICKEY, Bill								ph		ph	ph					
GRIMES, Oscar											ph					
CHANDLER, Spurgeon(Spud)		SP			RP			SP					SP			
GORDON, Joe		ph	4	4	4	4	4	4	4	4	4	*4	4	4	4	4
ROBINSON, Aaron		2			2	2	2	2		2	2	2		2	2	2
GUMPERT, Randy			RP		RP		RP			SP						
WIGHT, Bill							RP									
ROSER, Emerson (Steve)																
GETTEL, Al			RP				RP				RP					
PAGE, Joe				SP										RP		SP
KARPEL, Herb																
KELLER, Charlie		7	7	7	7	7	7	7	7	7	7	7	7	7	7	7
STANCEAU, Charlie																
METHENY, Arthur (Bud)																
BEVENS, Floyd (Bill)			SP			SP			SP					SP		
RIZZUTO, Phil		6	6	6	6	6	6	6	6	6	6		6	6	6	6
MARSHALL, Clarence (Cuddles)					SP							RP				
WADE, Jacob (Whistlin' Jake)														SP		
SILVESTRI, Ken				2				2	2							
ZUBER, Bill		("OFFICIALLY" ON WAIVERS FROM NEW YORK, ZUBER SIGNS WITH THE RED SOX, JUNE 18th.)														
MAJESKI, Hank																
RUFFING, Charles (Red)				SP						SP			LINE DRIVE BREAKS KNEECAP.			
MURPHY, Johnny				RP	RP					RP					RP	
BONHAM, Ernie (Tiny)											SP					
RUSSO, Marius (Lefty)						SORE ARM EXAM.										
DRESCHER, Bill																
WEATHERLY, Roy (Stormy)			\\			SOLD TO INDIANAPOLIS JUNE 20th, TO MAKE ROOM FOR PECK.										
SOUCHOCK, Steve				ph							pr	pr				
HILLER, Frank																
JOHNSON, Billy		5	5	5	5	5	5	5	5	5	5	*5		5		
NIARHOS, Constantine (Gus)			2	2		2			2		pr		2			
BYRNE, Tommy								SP								
QUEEN, Mel											RP					
DREWS, Karl																
BOCKMAN, Eddie																
LYONS, Al																
BROWN, Bobby																
BERRA, Larry (Yogi)																
COLMAN, Frank																
RASCHI, Vic																

NOTE: June 20th, Yanks buy Hal Peck from A's, but he's ill, doesn't play for New York. In consequence, Yankees suspend him on July 6th. He'll be with the Indians in 19

* June 30th, Stirnweiss & Johnson in box score at 2B, Gordon at SS. Johnson played only 3B in 1946, Gordon only at 2B. Assume Stirnweiss SS, Johnson 3B, Gordon 2

NY AL

	JULY		[1]	[2]	ALL-STAR BREAK			[1]	[2]		[1]	[2]			[1]	[2]
	5	6	7	7	11	13	14	14	15	17	17	18	20	21	21
	@Ws	@Phl	@Phl	@Phl	Cle	Cle	Det	Det	Det	StL	StL	StL	Chi	Chi	Chi
CROSETTI, Frank						ph				6	6	6	6		
STIRNWEISS, George (Snuffy)	5	5	56	56	5	5	5	5	5	5	5	5	5	5	6
HENRICH, Tom	9	9	9	9	9	9	9	9	9	9	9	9	9	9	9
DiMAGGIO, Joe	8	8	8	SUSTAINS KNEE INJURY JULY 7th; WILL BE OUT ALMOST A MONTH.											
ETTEN, Nick	3	3	3	3	3	3	3	ph	3	3	3	3			
LINDELL, Johnny	ph		8	8	8	8	8	8	8	8	8	8	8	8	8
DICKEY, Bill			ph	ph		ph									
GRIMES, Oscar					SOLD ON WAIVERS TO PHILADELPHIA AL, JULY 11th.										
CHANDLER, Spurgeon (Spud)			SP	SP			SP				SP				
GORDON, Joe	4	4	4	4	4	4	4	4	4	4	4	4	4	4	4
ROBINSON, Aaron	2	2	2	2	2	2	ph	2	2	2	2	2	2	2	2
GUMPERT, Randy		RP						RP							
WIGHT, Bill	RP														
ROSER, Emerson (Steve)															
GETTEL, Al	RP					SP									SP
PAGE, Joe			RP				SP								RP
KARPEL, Herb															
KELLER, Charlie	7	7	7	7	7	7	7	7	7	7	7	7	7	7	7
STANCEAU, Charlie															
METHENY, Arthur (Bud)															
BEVENS, Floyd (Bill)			SP			SP			SP			SP		SP	
RIZZUTO, Phil	6	6	6	6	6	6	6	6	6	6	6	HIT IN FACE BY PITCH.			
MARSHALL, Clarence (Cuddles)		SP													
WADE, Jacob (Whistlin' Jake)						RP									RP
SILVESTRI, Ken															2
ZUBER, Bill															
MAJESKI, Hank															
RUFFING, Charles (Red)			(PLACED ON VOLUNTARY RETIRED LIST JUNE 30th. RUFFING'S SEASON IS ENDED.)												
MURPHY, Johnny			RP				RP	RP							
BONHAM, Ernie (Tiny)	RP									SP					
RUSSO, Marius (Lefty)						RP									
DRESCHER, Bill															
WEATHERLY, Roy (Stormy)															
SOUCHOCK, Steve						ph	3					3	3	3	
HILLER, Frank															
JOHNSON, Billy	ph		h5	5		ph	ph	ph							5
NIARHOS, Constantine (Gus)			2		pr	2	ph								
BYRNE, Tommy											pr				RP
QUEEN, Mel	SP					RP				SP					
DREWS, Karl															
BOCKMAN, Eddie															
LYONS, Al															
BROWN, Bobby															
BERRA, Larry (Yogi)															
COLMAN, Frank															
RASCHI, Vic															

47.

B.

American League

NY AL	JULY 23 @StL	24 @StL	26 @Chi	27 @Chi	28 @Chi	[1] 28 @Chi	[2] 29 @Chi	30 @Det	31 @Det	AUG 1 @Det	2 @Cle	4 @Cle	7 @Ws	[1] 8 @Ws	[2] 8 @Ws
CROSETTI, Frank	6	6	6	6	6	6	6	6	6		6	6			6
STIRNWEISS, George (Snuffy)	5	5	5	5	5	5	54	5	4	4	4	4	4	4	4
HENRICH, Tom	9	9	9	9	9	9	9	9	9	9	9	9	9	3	3
DiMAGGIO, Joe										ph	8	8	8	8	8
ETTEN, Nick	ph			ph	ph	ph	ph	ph	ph			ph			
LINDELL, Johnny	8	8	8	8	8	8	8	8	8	8	8	8		9	9
DICKEY, Bill							ph	ph		ph	ph				
GRIMES, Oscar															
CHANDLER, Spurgeon (Spud)		SP					SP			RP			SP		
GORDON, Joe	4	4	4	4	4	4	4	4							
ROBINSON, Aaron	2	2	2	2	2	2	2	2	2	2	2	2	2	2	2
GUMPERT, Randy	RP				SP				SP						SP
WIGHT, Bill														SP	
ROSER, Emerson (Steve)															
GETTEL, Al				RP			RP				RP				
PAGE, Joe		RP					RP	RP							
KARPEL, Herb															
KELLER, Charlie	7	7	7	7	7	7	7	7	7	7	7	7	7	7	7
STANCEAU, Charlie															
METHENY, Arthur (Bud)															
BEVENS, Floyd (Bill)			SP					SP			SP				
RIZZUTO, Phil							6	pr	6	6	6	6	6	6	6
MARSHALL, Clarence (Cuddles)									RP						
WADE, Jacob (Whistlin' Jake)												SOLD TO WASH.			
SILVESTRI, Ken				2			ph								
ZUBER, Bill															
MAJESKI, Hank															
RUFFING, Charles (Red)															
MURPHY, Johnny							RP				RP	RP			
BONHAM, Ernie (Tiny)				SP						SP					
RUSSO, Marius (Lefty)	SP			ph					SP			pr	TO KANSAS CITY.		
DRESCHER, Bill															
WEATHERLY, Roy (Stormy)															
SOUCHOCK, Steve	3	3	3	3	3	3	3	3	3	3	3	3	3		
HILLER, Frank															
JOHNSON, Billy	ph		ph				h5	ph	5	5	5	5	5	5	5
NIARHOS, Constantine (Gus)				2			pr				2			2	2
BYRNE, Tommy	ph						pr		ph						
QUEEN, Mel				SP					RP						
DREWS, Karl															
BOCKMAN, Eddie															
LYONS, Al															
BROWN, Bobby															
BERRA, Larry (Yogi)															
COLMAN, Frank															
RASCHI, Vic															

NOTE: on August 6th, Hal Peck is placed on baseball's Ineligible List for not playing after purchase from the Athletics.

NY AL

	AUG		[1]	[2]		[1]	[2]		[1]	[2]		[1]	[2]	[1]
	9	10	11	11	14	15	15	16	17	18	18	20	21	21	22
	Bos	Bos	Bos	Bos	Wsh	Wsh	Wsh	@Bos	@Bos	@Bos	@Bos	Chi	Chi	Chi	StL
CROSETTI, Frank															
STIRNWEISS, George (Snuffy)	4	4	4	4	4	4	4	4	4		5	ph		4	
HENRICH, Tom	3	3	3	3	3	3	3	39	3	3	3	3	3	3	3
DiMAGGIO, Joe	8	8	8	8	8	8	8	8	*7	*7	*7	8	8	8	8
ETTEN, Nick	ph		ph											ph	
LINDELL, Johnny	9	9	9	9	9	9	9	98	8	8	8	9	9	9	9
DICKEY, Bill		ph	ph												
GRIMES, Oscar															
CHANDLER, Spurgeon (Spud)			SP				SP					SP			
GORDON, Joe									ph	ph	4	4	4	4	4
ROBINSON, Aaron	2	2	2	2	2	2	2	2	INJURED.			2	2	2	
GUMPERT, Randy			RP				SP				SP				
WIGHT, Bill			RP			SP									
ROSER, Emerson (Steve)															
GETTEL, Al												RP			
PAGE, Joe	RP			SP		RP				SP					
KARPEL, Herb															
KELLER, Charlie	7	7	7	7	7	7	7	7	*9	*9	*9	7	7	7	7
STANCEAU, Charlie															
METHENY, Arthur (Bud)															
BEVENS, Floyd (Bill)	SP				SP				SP						SP
RIZZUTO, Phil	6	6	6	6	6	6	6	6	6	6	6	6	6	6	6
MARSHALL, Clarence (Cuddles)			RP					RP						SP	
WADE, Jacob (Whistlin' Jake)	(SOLD ON WAIVERS, AUGUST 5th.)														
SILVESTRI, Ken										2					
ZUBER, Bill															
MAJESKI, Hank															
RUFFING, Charles (Red)															
MURPHY, Johnny		RP												RP	
BONHAM, Ernie (Tiny)		SP							SP						
RUSSO, Marius (Lefty)	(OPTIONED TO KANSAS CITY AUGUST 5th; RECALL ANNOUNCED ON AUGUST 16th.)														
DRESCHER, Bill	RECALL FROM KANSAS CITY ANNOUNCED ON AUGUST 16th.														
WEATHERLY, Roy (Stormy)															
SOUCHOCK, Steve						ph		3		ph	ph				
HILLER, Frank	RECALL ANNOUNCED ON AUGUST 16th.														
JOHNSON, Billy	5	5	5	5	5	5	5	5	5	5	5	5	5	5	5
NIARHOS, Constantine (Gus)			pr	2		2			pr	2		2	2	2	
BYRNE, Tommy			ph						ph						
QUEEN, Mel			RP						RP			RP		RP	
DREWS, Karl	RECALL ANNOUNCED ON AUGUST 16th.														
BOCKMAN, Eddie	RECALL ANNOUNCED ON AUGUST 16th.														
LYONS, Al	RECALL ANNOUNCED ON AUGUST 16th.														
BROWN, Bobby	RECALL ANNOUNCED ON AUGUST 16th.														
BERRA, Larry (Yogi)															
COLMAN, Frank															
RASCHI, Vic															

* August 17-18-18, DiMaggio is in left field, due to a sore arm. Keller shifts to right.

American League

NY AL

	AUG [2]									SEP [1]	[2]			
	22	23	24	25	26	27	28	29	31	1	2	2	4	5	6
	StL	StL	StL	Det	Det	Det	Cle	Cle	@Ws	@Ws	Bos	Bos	@Phl	@Phl	@Phl
CROSETTI, Frank				ph		ph									
STIRNWEISS, George (Snuffy)						5				4	4	4			pr
HENRICH, Tom	3	3	3	39	9	9	9	9	9	9	9	9	9	9	9
DiMAGGIO, Joe	8	8	8	8	8	8	8	8	8	8	8	8	8	8	8
ETTEN, Nick			ph		3	3	3	3	3	3	3	3	3	3	3
LINDELL, Johnny	9	9	9	9							ph	ph			ph
DICKEY, Bill				ph											ph
GRIMES, Oscar															
CHANDLER, Spurgeon (Spud)					SP					SP					
GORDON, Joe	4	4	4	4	4	4	4	4	4				4	4	4
ROBINSON, Aaron		2	2	2	2	2	2	2	2		2	2	2	2	2
GUMPERT, Randy				SP				SP				RP		SP	
WIGHT, Bill			SP								RP				
ROSER, Emerson (Steve)															
GETTEL, Al				RP											
PAGE, Joe	SP				RP	RP						SP			
KARPEL, Herb															
KELLER, Charlie	7	7	7	7	7	7	7	7	7	7	7	7	7	7	7
STANCEAU, Charlie															
METHENY, Arthur (Bud)															
BEVENS, Floyd (Bill)						SP		SP				SP			
RIZZUTO, Phil	6	6	6	6	6	6	6	6	6	6	6	6	6	6	6
MARSHALL, Clarence (Cuddles)			RP		RP						RP				SP
WADE, Jacob (Whistlin' Jake)															
SILVESTRI, Ken															
ZUBER, Bill															
MAJESKI, Hank															
RUFFING, Charles (Red)	REINSTATED FROM THE DISABLED LIST, SEPTEMBER 11th.														
MURPHY, Johnny			RP		RP							RP		RP	RP
BONHAM, Ernie (Tiny)		SP				SP				SP					
RUSSO, Marius (Lefty)	(STAYS WITH KC TILL AMERICAN ASSOCIATION SEASON ENDS 9/8, BUT DNP AGAIN FOR NY.)														
DRESCHER, Bill	(STAYS WITH KC TILL AMERICAN ASSOCIATION SEASON ENDS 9/8, BUT DNP AGAIN FOR NY.)														
WEATHERLY, Roy (Stormy)															
SOUCHOCK, Steve			ph	3	ph	3					ph	ph			ph
HILLER, Frank	(HILLER STAYS WITH NEWARK TILL BEARS ELIMINATED FROM PLAYOFFS; DNP FOR NY.)														
JOHNSON, Billy	5	5	5	5	5	5	5	5	5	5	5	5	5	5	5
NIARHOS, Constantine (Gus)	2		2	ph					2		2				
BYRNE, Tommy			ph								pr				
QUEEN, Mel				RP											
DREWS, Karl	(DREWS REPORTS FROM KC IN TIME TO DEBUT FOR NY, SEPTEMBER 8th.)														
BOCKMAN, Eddie	(BOCKMAN STAYS WITH KANSAS CITY TILL AMERICAN ASSOCIATION SEASON ENDS.)														
LYONS, Al	(LYONS REMAINS WITH KANSAS CITY TILL AMERICAN ASSOCIATION SEASON ENDS)														
BROWN, Bobby	(BROWN STAYS WITH NEWARK TILL BEARS ELIMINATED FROM PLAYOFFS, SEPTEMBER 18th.)														
BERRA, Larry (Yogi)	(BERRA STAYS WITH NEWARK TILL BEARS ELIMINATED FROM PLAYOFFS, SEPTEMBER 18th.)														
COLMAN, Frank															
RASCHI, Vic															

American League

SEP. 12, DICKEY OUT, NEUN IN

NY AL

	SEP 7 Wsh	[1] 8 Wsh	[2] 8 Wsh	10 @Cle	11 @Cle	12 @Det	13 @Det	14 @Det	[1] 15 @StL	[2] 15 @StL	16 @StL	[1] 18 @Chi	[2] 18 @Chi	[1] 22 Phl	[2] 22 Phl
CROSETTI, Frank			6							pr					
STIRNWEISS, George (Snuffy)	4	4	4	4	4					5			ph	4	4
HENRICH, Tom	3	3	3	3	3	3	3	3	3	9	3	3	3	3	3
DiMAGGIO, Joe	8	8	8	8	8	8	8	8	8	8	8	8	8	8	8
ETTEN, Nick			ph	ph	ph	ph		ph	ph	3			ph		ph
LINDELL, Johnny	9	9	9	9	9	9	9	9	9		9	9	9	9	
DICKEY, Bill			ph				DICKEY RETIRES AFTER QUITTING AS MANAGER.								
GRIMES, Oscar															
CHANDLER, Spurgeon (Spud)			SP			SP		SP			SP		SP		
GORDON, Joe			4		4	4	4	4	4	4	4	4	4		
ROBINSON, Aaron	2	2	2	2	2	2	2	2	2	2	2	2	2		2
GUMPERT, Randy				RP		SP				RP					RP
WIGHT, Bill			RP										RP		
ROSER, Emerson (Steve)															
GETTEL, Al			RP						SP				RP		RP
PAGE, Joe	SP		pr				RP			RP					
KARPEL, Herb															
KELLER, Charlie	7	7	7	7	7	7	7	7	7	7	7	7	7	7	7
STANCEAU, Charlie															
METHENY, Arthur (Bud)															
BEVENS, Floyd (Bill)		SP			SP			SP							
RIZZUTO, Phil	6	6	6	6	6	6	6	6	6	6	6	6	6		
MARSHALL, Clarence (Cuddles)					RP						SP				SP
WADE, Jacob (Whistlin' Jake)															
SILVESTRI, Ken										2					
ZUBER, Bill															
MAJESKI, Hank															
RUFFING, Charles (Red)	REINSTATED FROM DISABLED LIST SEPT. 11th; RELEASED UNCONDITIONALLY, SEPT. 20th.														
MURPHY, Johnny		RP			RP		RP	RP							
BONHAM, Ernie (Tiny)	RP			SP		RP							SP		RP
RUSSO, Marius (Lefty)															
DRESCHER, Bill															
WEATHERLY, Roy (Stormy)															
SOUCHOCK, Steve			ph	ph		ph		ph	ph				ph		
HILLER, Frank															
JOHNSON, Billy	5	5	5	5	5	5	5	5	5		5	5	5	5	5
NIARHOS, Constantine (Gus)			2										pr		
BYRNE, Tommy			ph												
QUEEN, Mel			RP		RP										
DREWS, Karl			SP										RP		
BOCKMAN, Eddie					5										
LYONS, Al					RP										
BROWN, Bobby														6	6
BERRA, Larry (Yogi)														2	ph
COLMAN, Frank															9
RASCHI, Vic															

NY AL

	SEP 23 Phl	24 @Bos	25 @Bos	[1] 29 @Phl	[2] 29 @Phl	154g
CROSETTI, Frank	* EXCUSED.					
STIRNWEISS, George(Snuffy)	4	4	4	4	4	
HENRICH, Tom	3	3	3	3	3	
DiMAGGIO, Joe	8	8	8	8	8	
ETTEN, Nick	* EXCUSED.					
LINDELL, Johnny		9			9	
DICKEY, Bill						
GRIMES, Oscar						
CHANDLER, Spurgeon(Spud)				SP		
GORDON, Joe						
ROBINSON, Aaron			ph			
GUMPERT, Randy		RP				
WIGHT, Bill						
ROSER, Emerson (Steve)						
GETTEL, Al						
PAGE, Joe						
KARPEL, Herb						
KELLER, Charlie	7	7	7	7	7	
STANCEAU, Charlie						
METHENY, Arthur (Bud)						
BEVENS, Floyd (Bill)						
RIZZUTO, Phil				6	6	
MARSHALL, Clarence (Cuddles)			SP			
WADE, Jacob (Whistlin' Jake)						
SILVESTRI, Ken	* EXCUSED.					
ZUBER, Bill						
MAJESKI, Hank						
RUFFING, Charles (Red)						
MURPHY, Johnny	* EXCUSED.					
BONHAM, Ernie (Tiny)	* EXCUSED.					
RUSSO, Marius (Lefty)						
DRESCHER, Bill						
WEATHERLY, Roy (Stormy)						
SOUCHOCK, Steve			pr			
HILLER, Frank						
JOHNSON, Billy						
NIARHOS, Constantine (Gus)						
BYRNE, Tommy						
QUEEN, Mel			RP			
DREWS, Karl			RP			
BOCKMAN, Eddie	5	5	5			
LYONS, Al		SP				
BROWN, Bobby	6	6	6	5	5	
BERRA, Larry (Yogi)	2	2	2	2	2	
COLMAN, Frank	9		9	9	9	
RASCHI, Vic	SP				SP	

* Bonham, Crosetti, Etten, Murphy and Silvestri are all excused for the last week of the season.

NOTE: September 23rd, Ruffing and Dickey both declared free agents by Yankee management.

PHL AL	Games	APRIL 16 NY	17 NY	18 NY	20 @Bos	21 [1] @Bos	21 [2] @Bos	22 @NY	23 @NY	24 @Ws	26 Bos	28 [1] Bos	28 [2] Bos	30 StL	MAY 1 StL
GARRISON, Ford	9	7	7	7	7	7			ph	7	7		7		
PECK, Hal	48	9	9	9	9	9	9	9	9	9	9	9	9	9	9
WALLAESA, John (Jack)	63	6	6	6	6	6	6	6	6	6	6	6	6	6	6
CHAPMAN, Sam	146	8	8	8	8	8	8	8	8	8	8	8	8	8	8
McQUINN, George	136	3	3	3	3	3	3	3	3	3	3	3	3	3	3
ROSAR, Warren (Buddy)	121	2	2	2	2	2	2				2	2	2	2	2
KELL, George	26	5	5	5	5	5	5	5	5	5	5			5	5
HANDLEY, Gene	89	4	4	4	4	4	4	4	4	4	4		ph		
CHRISTOPHER, Russ	30	SP			SP				RP				SP		
FOWLER, Dick	32	RP		SP						SP					SP
KONOPKA, Bruce	38	ph		ph	ph		ph	ph		ph					ph
HARRIS, Luman (Lum)	34	RP			RP				SP				RP		
NEWSOM, Louis (Bobo or Buck)	10		SP			SP					SP				
FLORES, Jesse	29		SP												RP
SAVAGE, Bob	40		RP							RP					
BESSE, Herman (Herm)	7		RP						SP				RP		
VALO, Elmer	108			ph		7	7	7		ph			7		
KNERR, Luther (Lou)	30		RP				SP				SP				
BERRY, Jonas (Jittery Joe)	5		RP	RP				RP					RP		
VAUGHAN, Porter	1			RP											
BENSON, Vern	7					pr		ph	pr	h7	7				ph
DESAUTELS, Gene	52					2	2	2	2	2					
HALL, Irv	63							4	ph		4	4	4	4	
SUDER, Pete	128							h5	ph		5	5			
CAULFIELD, John (Jake)	44								ph			ph			
BROWN, Norm	4									RP					
ARMSTRONG, George	8								ph						
DERRY, Russ	69	* FROM YANKEES APRIL 30th, FOR GARRISON & VAUGHAN.													7
STAINBACK, Tuck	91	RELEASED BY YANKEES APRIL 29th, SIGNED BY A'S MAY 3rd.													
MARCHILDON, Phil	36	STILL HAMPERED BY 1945 GROIN INJURY, PLUS ACCIDENTAL STABBING OF HAND.													
KNOTT, Jack	3														
COOPER, Orge (Pat)	1														
McCOSKY, Barney	92	FROM DETROIT FOR KELL, MAY 18th.													
FAGAN, Everett	20	ON NDSL TILL APRIL 26th.													
MAJESKI, Hank	78	PURCHASED FROM THE YANKEES, JUNE 14th.													
GRIFFETH, Leon (Lee)	10	SIGNED OUT OF DUKE UNIVERSITY, DEBUTS JUNE 25th.													
GRIMES, Oscar	59	PURCHASED FROM THE YANKEES, JULY 11th.													
RICHMOND, Don	16	FROM TORONTO, AT END OF INTERNATIONAL LEAGUE SEASON, SEPT. 8th.													
ASTROTH, Joe	4	FROM LANCASTER, FIRST GAME FOR PHILADELPHIA IS SEPTEMBER 13th.													
COLEMAN, Joe	4	WAS OPTIONED TO TORONTO APRIL 5th; FIRST A's GAME SEPTEMBER 15th (1).													
McCAHAN, Bill	4	WAS OPTIONED TO TORONTO APRIL 5th; BIG LEAGUE DEBUT SEPT. 15th (2).													

NOTE: on April 18th, former A's outfielder Roberto Estalella placed on Ineligible List for 5 years, in consequence of his playing in the Mexican League this season.

* Derry obtained from the Yankees for Garrison & Vaughan, April 30th. Did not play for New York, was released outright to Newark Apr. 17th, but refused to report.

American League

PHL AL

	MAY		[1]	[2]				MAY 10 TIE, replay Aug 17	[1]	[2]	[1]	[2]	
	2	3	5	5	6	7	8	9	10	11	12	12	15	15	17
	StL	Chi	Det	Det	Det	Det	Cle	Cle	Wsh	Wsh	Wsh	Wsh	@Cle	@Cle	@Det
GARRISON, Ford		SOLD TO NEWARK MAY 3rd, AS PART PAYMENT FOR DERRY..													
PECK, Hal	9		9	9	9	9	*9	9	9	9	9	9	9	ph	ph
WALLAESA, John (Jack)	6	6	6	6	6	6	6						6	6	6
CHAPMAN, Sam	8	8	8	8	8	8							8	8	8
McQUINN, George	3	3	3	3	3	3	3	3	3	3	3	3	3	3	3
ROSAR, Warren (Buddy)	2	2	2	2	2	2	2	2	2	2	2	2	2	2	2
KELL, George	5	5	5	5	5	5	5	5	5	5	5		5	5	5
HANDLEY, Gene		ph			pr	pr	pr		pr			5		4	
CHRISTOPHER, Russ				SP				RP				SP			
FOWLER, Dick						SP					SP				
KONOPKA, Bruce	ph			ph	ph	ph	ph		ph	ph			TO SAN DIEGO.		
HARRIS, Luman (Lum)		RP									RP	RP			
NEWSOM, Louis (Bobo or Buck)			SP				SP	RP						SP	
FLORES, Jesse						RP									
SAVAGE, Bob	RP						RP		RP			SP		RP	
BESSE, Herman (Herm)	SP							SP					RP		
VALO, Elmer		9	9		pr	ph	ph		ph	ph		ph	ph	9	9
KNERR, Luther (Lou)		SP		RP			SP								
BERRY, Jonas (Jittery Joe)	RP				SOLD TO TORONTO, MAY 6th.										
VAUGHAN, Porter		SOLD TO KANSAS CITY MAY 2nd, AS PART PAYMENT FOR DERRY.													
BENSON, Vern				pr	OPTIONED TO TORONTO MAY 7th, TO SAVANNAH JUNE 24th.										
DESAUTELS, Gene				2			2							2	
HALL, Irv	4	4	4	4	4	4	4	4	4	4	4	4	4		4
SUDER, Pete		ph					ph		6	6	6	6	ph		ph
CAULFIELD, John (Jake)							6	6	6						
BROWN, Norm		RP					RP			RP			ph		ph
ARMSTRONG, George		ph					ph								
DERRY, Russ		7	7	7	7	7	7	7	7	7	7	7	7	7	7
STAINBACK, Tuck		7					*8	8	8	8	8			ph	ph
MARCHILDON, Phil				SP					SP						SP
KNOTT, Jack				RP			RP						SP		
COOPER, Orge (Pat)										RP					
McCOSKY, Barney															
FAGAN, Everett															
MAJESKI, Hank															
GRIFFETH, Leon (Lee)															
GRIMES, Oscar															
RICHMOND, Don															
ASTROTH, Joe															
COLEMAN, Joe															
McCAHAN, Bill															

NOTE: Fagan released from National Defense Service List April 26th, but doesn't pitch for A's till June 9th.

* May 8th, Peck & Stainback are both in *TSN* box score as center fielder, with no right fielder listed. Likely Peck is in RF, his regular spot.

PHL AL

	MAY	[1]	[2]			[1]	[2]			[1]	[2]	SUN 6/2, RAIN JUNE	[1]	[2]
	18 @Det	19 @StL	19 @StL	21 @StL	22 @Chi	25 @Ws	25 @Ws	26 @Ws	29 @Bos	30 @NY	30 @NY	31 @NY	1 Cle	3 Cle	3 Cle
GARRISON, Ford															
PECK, Hal	ph	9	9	9	9	ph	9	9	9	9	ph			ph	
WALLAESA, John (Jack)	6					6	6	6	6	6	6	6			
CHAPMAN, Sam	8	8	8	8	7	7	7	7	7	7	78	8	7	7	7
McQUINN, George	3	3	3	3	3	3	3	3	3	3	3	3	3	3	3
ROSAR, Warren (Buddy)		2	2	2	2	2	2		2	2	2	2	2	2	
KELL, George	TO DETROIT FOR McCOSKY, MAY 18th.														
HANDLEY, Gene							pr			ph			SP	pr	
CHRISTOPHER, Russ	RP			RP			RP						SP		
FOWLER, Dick		SP					SP					SP			SP
KONOPKA, Bruce	DATE OF KONOPKA'S OPTION IS MAY 12th.														
HARRIS, Luman (Lum)					RP			SP		RP				RP	
NEWSOM, Louis (Bobo or Buck)	SP					SP					SP			NEXT PAGE.	
FLORES, Jesse						RP				RP					
SAVAGE, Bob			SP								RP	RP			
BESSE, Herman (Herm)					RP	TO TORONTO, MAY 23rd.									
VALO, Elmer	9	9		ph			ph			ph	ph	9	9	9	9
KNERR, Luther (Lou)			SP							SP					
BERRY, Jonas (Jittery Joe)															
VAUGHAN, Porter															
BENSON, Vern															
DESAUTELS, Gene	2							2						2	2
HALL, Irv	4	4	4	4	4	4	4	4	4	4	4	4	4	4	4
SUDER, Pete	5	5	5	5	5	5	5	5	5	5	5	5	5	5	5
CAULFIELD, John (Jake)	6	6	6	6	6	6					6	6	6	6	6
BROWN, Norm					SOLD TO TORONTO, MAY 19th.										
ARMSTRONG, George															
DERRY, Russ				ph			ph				7		ph		ph
STAINBACK, Tuck	7	7	7	7		9	9	ph			9	7		ph	
MARCHILDON, Phil					SP				SP					SP	
KNOTT, Jack					GIVEN UNCONDITIONAL RELEASE, MAY 18th.										
COOPER, Orge (Pat)															
McCOSKY, Barney					8	8	8	8	8	8	8		8	8	8
FAGAN, Everett															
MAJESKI, Hank															
GRIFFETH, Leon (Lee)															
GRIMES, Oscar															
RICHMOND, Don															
ASTROTH, Joe															
COLEMAN, Joe															
McCAHAN, Bill															

PHL AL

	JUNE				[1]	[2]					[1]	[2]			
	4	5	7	8	9	9	10	11	14	15	16	16	19	20	21
	Det	Det	StL	StL	StL	StL	Chi	Chi	@Cle	@Cle	@Cle	@Cle	@Det	@Det	@Chi
GARRISON, Ford															
PECK, Hal	ph	ph	ph		ph		ph		ph	ph		9		TO NY, 6/20.	
WALLAESA, John (Jack)		6			6		ph	6	6	6	6	6	6	*6	6
CHAPMAN, Sam	7	7	7	7	7	7	7	7	78	8	8	8	8	8	7
McQUINN, George	3	3	3	3	3	3		ph	3	3	3	3	3	3	3
ROSAR, Warren (Buddy)	2	2	2	2	2	2			2	2	2		2	2	2
KELL, George															
HANDLEY, Gene		pr	4	4	4	4	5	5	46	4	4	4	4	4	4
CHRISTOPHER, Russ			SP					SP					SP		
FOWLER, Dick				SP					SP				RP		
KONOPKA, Bruce					RETURNED BY SAN DIEGO, JUNE 21st.										
HARRIS, Luman (Lum)			RP		RP			RP	RP					RP	
NEWSOM, Louis (Bobo or Buck)			UNHAPPY WITH SALARY, GIVEN RELEASE JUNE 3rd, SIGNS WITH SENATORS JUNE 5th.												
FLORES, Jesse		SP					SP							RP	
SAVAGE, Bob	RP				SP		RP				SP		RP		
BESSE, Herman (Herm)															
VALO, Elmer	9	9	9	9	9	9	9	9	9	9	9		9	9	9
KNERR, Luther (Lou)	SP											SP		SP	
BERRY, Jonas (Jittery Joe)															
VAUGHAN, Porter															
BENSON, Vern															
DESAUTELS, Gene			2		2		2	2	2			2			2
HALL, Irv	4	4			ph		4	4	4	ph			ph	ph	ph
SUDER, Pete	5	5	5	5	5	5	3	3	5	5	5	5	ph	ph	
CAULFIELD, John (Jake)	6	6	6	6	6	6	6	6						6	6
BROWN, Norm															
ARMSTRONG, George							2	2							
DERRY, Russ		ph	ph		ph		ph		7	7	7	7	7	7	9
STAINBACK, Tuck	ph		ph		ph			ph	pr		9				
MARCHILDON, Phil		RP	RP			SP				SP					SP
KNOTT, Jack															
COOPER, Orge (Pat)															
McCOSKY, Barney	8	8	8	8	8	8	8	8	8	ph					8
FAGAN, Everett				RP			RP				RP				
MAJESKI, Hank													5	5	5
GRIFFETH, Leon (Lee)															
GRIMES, Oscar															
RICHMOND, Don															
ASTROTH, Joe															
COLEMAN, Joe															
McCAHAN, Bill															

* June 20th, Wallaesa is in *Sporting News* and *NY Times* boxes at 2B, but he never played there as a major leaguer. Assume he's at SS.

American League — PHL AL

	JUNE	[1]	[2]						JULY	[1]	[2]			ALL-STAR BREAK [1]	[2]
	22	23	23	25	26	28	29	30	3	4	4	5	6	7	7
PHL AL	@Chi	@Chi	@Chi	@StL	@StL	@NY	@NY	@NY	Wsh	Bos	Bos	Bos	NY	NY	NY
GARRISON, Ford															
PECK, Hal			PECK IS ILL, WON'T PLAY FOR YANKEES, WHO SUSPEND HIM JULY 6th.												
WALLAESA, John (Jack)		6			ph						ph	6	6	6	
CHAPMAN, Sam	78	78	8	8	8	8	8	8	7	7	7	7	7	7	7
McQUINN, George	3	3	3	3	3	3	3	3	3	3	ph	3	3	3	
ROSAR, Warren (Buddy)	2	2		2	2	2	2	2	2	2		2	2	2	
KELL, George															
HANDLEY, Gene	4	4	4	4	4						4		4	ph	4
CHRISTOPHER, Russ					RP		SP				SP			RP	
FOWLER, Dick	SP			SP								SP			
KONOPKA, Bruce					ph				ph		3		ph		3
HARRIS, Luman (Lum)			SP						SP						
NEWSOM, Louis (Bobo or Buck)															
FLORES, Jesse		RP		RP			RP						SP		
SAVAGE, Bob		SP			RP	RP		RP	RP		RP				SP
BESSE, Herman (Herm)															
VALO, Elmer					ph				9	9	9	9	9	9	9
KNERR, Luther (Lou)				SP			SP				RP			SP	
BERRY, Jonas (Jittery Joe)															
VAUGHAN, Porter															
BENSON, Vern															
DESAUTELS, Gene			2						2		2				2
HALL, Irv		4		ph	6	6	6	6	6	6	ph			ph	
SUDER, Pete		3			ph	4	4	4	4	4	4	4	4	4	6
CAULFIELD, John (Jake)	6	6	6	6	6						6				
BROWN, Norm															
ARMSTRONG, George		2													
DERRY, Russ	7	97	7	7	7	7	7	7			ph	ph	ph		
STAINBACK, Tuck	9	9	9	9	9	9	9	9			ph		ph		
MARCHILDON, Phil					SP				SP		RP				
KNOTT, Jack															
COOPER, Orge (Pat)															
McCOSKY, Barney	8	8		ph					8	8	8	8	8	8	8
FAGAN, Everett		RP									RP		RP		
MAJESKI, Hank	5	5	5	5	5	5	5	5	5	5	5	5	5	5	5
GRIFFETH, Leon (Lee)				RP	RP									RP	
GRIMES, Oscar															
RICHMOND, Don															
ASTROTH, Joe															
COLEMAN, Joe															
McCAHAN, Bill															

American League

PHL AL	JULY 11 StL	12 StL	13 StL	[1] 14 Chi	[2] 14 Chi	15 Chi	16 Chi	17 Cle	18 Cle	19 Cle	20 Cle	[1] 21 Det	[2] 21 Det	23 @Cle	24 @Cle
GARRISON, Ford															
PECK, Hal															
WALLAESA, John (Jack)			pr			OPTIONED TO TORONTO, JULY 16th.									
CHAPMAN, Sam	7	7	7	8	8	8	8	8	8	8	8	8	8	7	7
McQUINN, George	3	3	3	3	3	3	3	3	3	3	3	3	3	3	3
ROSAR, Warren (Buddy)	2	2	2	2		2	2	2	2	2	2	2		2	2
KELL, George															
HANDLEY, Gene	4	4	4	4	4	4	4	4		4	4	4	4	4	4
CHRISTOPHER, Russ				SP			RP		SP						
FOWLER, Dick		SP					SP					SP			RP
KONOPKA, Bruce			ph		37	OPTIONED TO TORONTO, JULY 16th.									
HARRIS, Luman (Lum)												SP			
NEWSOM, Louis (Bobo or Buck)															
FLORES, Jesse			RP				RP		RP						
SAVAGE, Bob	RP				SP					SP			RP		SP
BESSE, Herman (Herm)															
VALO, Elmer	9	9	9	9				9	9	9	9	9	9	9	9
KNERR, Luther (Lou)			SP					SP			RP			RP	
BERRY, Jonas (Jittery Joe)															
VAUGHAN, Porter															
BENSON, Vern															
DESAUTELS, Gene			2		2								2		
HALL, Irv				ph		ph	ph	OPTIONED TO KANSAS CITY, JULY 17th.							
SUDER, Pete	6	6	6	6	6	6	6	6	5	5	5	5	5	6	6
CAULFIELD, John (Jake)			5	pr		pr	pr	6	pr	pr	pr	pr			
BROWN, Norm															
ARMSTRONG, George				ARMSTRONG OPTIONED TO SAVANNAH, JULY 13th.											
DERRY, Russ	ph		9	*7	79	7	7	7	ph			7			
STAINBACK, Tuck			8		9	9	9	ph	7	7	7	ph	7	ph	ph
MARCHILDON, Phil	SP			RP		SP					SP			SP	
KNOTT, Jack															
COOPER, Orge (Pat)		JULY 11th, COOPER SENT TO SAVANNAH ON OPTION.													
McCOSKY, Barney	8	8	8					ph	ph	ph	ph	ph		8	8
FAGAN, Everett				RP			RP			RP			RP		
MAJESKI, Hank	5	5	5		ph		ph		ph					5	5
GRIFFETH, Leon (Lee)			RP					RP		RP					
GRIMES, Oscar				5	5	5	5	5	4	6	6	6	6		
RICHMOND, Don															
ASTROTH, Joe															
COLEMAN, Joe															
McCAHAN, Bill															

* Left fielder for Philadelhia July 14th (2) is listed as Doerr (the Boston 2B) in *Sporting News* box score. Assume a typo: Derry should be LF.

American League — PHL AL

	JULY			[1]	[2]				AUG			[1]	[2]		[1]
	25	26	27	28	28	29	30	31	1	2	3	4	4	6	8
PHL AL	@Cle	@Det	@Det	@Det	@Det	@Det	@Chi	@Chi	@Chi	@StL	@StL	@StL	@StL	@Bos	@Bos
GARRISON, Ford															
PECK, Hal															
WALLAESA, John (Jack)															
CHAPMAN, Sam	7	7	7	7	7	ph	7	7	7	7	7	7	7	7	7
McQUINN, George	3	3	3	3	3	3	3	3	3	3	3	3	3	3	3
ROSAR, Warren (Buddy)	2	2			2	2				2	2	2		2	2
KELL, George															
HANDLEY, Gene	4	4	4	4		4	4	4	4	4	4	4	4	*h4	5
CHRISTOPHER, Russ															
FOWLER, Dick		SP					SP			RP				SP	
KONOPKA, Bruce															
HARRIS, Luman (Lum)	RP		SP					SP				RP			
NEWSOM, Louis (Bobo or Buck)															
FLORES, Jesse	RP			SP				RP				SP			
SAVAGE, Bob						SP				SP					
BESSE, Herman (Herm)															
VALO, Elmer	9	9											ph	*ph	ph
KNERR, Luther (Lou)	SP				SP						SP				
BERRY, Jonas (Jittery Joe)															
VAUGHAN, Porter															
BENSON, Vern															
DESAUTELS, Gene	2		2	2			2	2	2				2		
HALL, Irv	("OFFICIAL" NOTIFICATION SAYS OPTION DATE WAS JULY 16th.)														
SUDER, Pete	6	6	6	6	6	6	6	6	6	6	6	6	6	6	6
CAULFIELD, John (Jake)														pr	pr
BROWN, Norm															
ARMSTRONG, George															
DERRY, Russ		7				7						ph	ph	8	ph
STAINBACK, Tuck	ph		9	9	9	9	9	9	9	9	9	9	9	9	9
MARCHILDON, Phil				SP		RP			SP						SP
KNOTT, Jack															
COOPER, Orge (Pat)															
McCOSKY, Barney	8	8	8	8	8	8	8	8	8	8	8	8	8	8	8
FAGAN, Everett	RP			RP								RP			
MAJESKI, Hank	5	5	5	5	5	5	5	5	5	5	5	5	5	5	5
GRIFFETH, Leon (Lee)			RP			RP						RP		RP	
GRIMES, Oscar			ph	4	4	ph							4	*4	4
RICHMOND, Don															
ASTROTH, Joe															
COLEMAN, Joe															
McCAHAN, Bill															

* Aug. 6th, Grimes starts at 2B. In box score, Valo ph for him in 8th, with no second base replacement listed. Handley also pinch hits in 8th, must have then gone to 2B.

REPLAY of 5/10 TIE

PHL AL	AUG 8 @Bos [2]	9 @Ws	10 @Ws [1]	10 @Ws [2]	11 @Ws [1]	11 @Ws [2]	13 Bos	14 Bos	15 Bos	17 Wsh [1]	17 Wsh [2]	18 Wsh [1]	18 Wsh [2]	20 Det	21 Det
GARRISON, Ford															
PECK, Hal															
WALLAESA, John (Jack)							RECALL ANNOUNCED, AUGUST 15th.								
CHAPMAN, Sam	7	7	7	7	7	7	7	7	7	7	7	7	7	7	7
McQUINN, George	3	3	3	3	3	3	3	3	3	3	3	3	3	3	3
ROSAR, Warren (Buddy)		ph	2		ph	2	2	2	2	ph	2		2		
KELL, George															
HANDLEY, Gene	4	4	4	4						pr					
CHRISTOPHER, Russ										RP					
FOWLER, Dick			SP					SP					SP		
KONOPKA, Bruce							RECALL ANNOUNCED, AUGUST 15th.								
HARRIS, Luman (Lum)		SP								SP			RP		
NEWSOM, Louis (Bobo or Buck)															
FLORES, Jesse	RP			SP								SP			
SAVAGE, Bob	SP					SP				RP	RP			SP	
BESSE, Herman (Herm)															
VALO, Elmer	ph		9	9	9	9	9	9	9	9	9	9	9	9	9
KNERR, Luther (Lou)	RP			SP					SP						
BERRY, Jonas (Jittery Joe)															
VAUGHAN, Porter															
BENSON, Vern							RECALL ANNOUNCED, AUGUST 15th.								
DESAUTELS, Gene	2	2		2	2					2		2		2	2
HALL, Irv							RECALL ANNOUNCED, AUGUST 15th.								
SUDER, Pete	6	6	6	6	6	6	6	6	6	6	6	6	6	6	6
CAULFIELD, John (Jake)															
BROWN, Norm															
ARMSTRONG, George	RECALLED AUGUST 9th, BUT DOESN'T PLAY AGAIN FOR THE A's.														
DERRY, Russ		pr								8					
STAINBACK, Tuck	9	9		8			ph			ph	ph		ph		
MARCHILDON, Phil					SP						SP		RP		SP
KNOTT, Jack															
COOPER, Orge (Pat)							RECALL ANNOUNCED, AUGUST 15th.								
McCOSKY, Barney	8	8	8		8	8	8	8	8	8	8	8	8	8	8
FAGAN, Everett	RP									RP					
MAJESKI, Hank	5	5	5		5	5	5	5	5	5	5	5	5	5	5
GRIFFETH, Leon (Lee)							OPTIONED TO LANCASTER, AUGUST 13th.								
GRIMES, Oscar		ph	ph	5	4	4	4	4	4	4	4	4	4	4	4
RICHMOND, Don															
ASTROTH, Joe							RECALL ANNOUNCED, AUGUST 15th.								
COLEMAN, Joe							RECALL ANNOUNCED, AUGUST 15th.								
McCAHAN, Bill							RECALL ANNOUNCED, AUGUST 15th.								

PHL AL

	AUG			[1]	[2]				[1]	[2]		SEP	[1]	[2]	
	22	23	24	25	25	26	27	28	30	30	31	1	2	2	4
	Cle	Cle	Cle	Chi	Chi	Chi	Chi	StL	@Bos	@Bos	@Bos	@Bos	@Ws	@Ws	NY
GARRISON, Ford															
PECK, Hal															
WALLAESA, John (Jack)	(WALLAESA WILL REPORT AT THE END OF TORONTO'S SEASON, SEPTEMBER 8th.)														
CHAPMAN, Sam	7	7	7	7	7	7	7	7	7	7	7	7	7	7	7
McQUINN, George	3	3	3	3	3	3	3	3	3	3	3	3	3	3	3
ROSAR, Warren (Buddy)			2		2			2		2	2	2	2	2	2
KELL, George															
HANDLEY, Gene			ph	ph							pr		ph		
CHRISTOPHER, Russ			RP				SP				SP				
FOWLER, Dick	SP				SP						SP				
KONOPKA, Bruce	FROM TORONTO, SEPTEMBER 7th (excused a day before IL season ends).														
HARRIS, Luman (Lum)	RP		SP										SP		
NEWSOM, Louis (Bobo or Buck)															
FLORES, Jesse		SP				SP							SP		
SAVAGE, Bob			SP				RP				SP				
BESSE, Herman (Herm)															
VALO, Elmer	9	9	9	9	9	9	9	9	9	9	9	9	9	9	9
KNERR, Luther (Lou)			RP				RP	SP							
BERRY, Jonas (Jittery Joe)															
VAUGHAN, Porter															
BENSON, Vern	(REPORTS AT END OF SALLY LEAGUE SEASON SEPTEMBER 4th, DNP FOR THE ATHLETICS.)														
DESAUTELS, Gene	2	2	2		2		2		2				2		
HALL, Irv	(REMAINS WITH KANSAS CITY TILL AMERICAN ASSOCIATION SEASON ENDS, SEPT. 8th.)														
SUDER, Pete	6	6	6	6	*6	6	6	6	6	6	6	6	6	6	6
CAULFIELD, John (Jake)				ph											
BROWN, Norm															
ARMSTRONG, George															
DERRY, Russ	ph														
STAINBACK, Tuck	8	8	8	8	8	8	8	ph			ph		ph		
MARCHILDON, Phil				SP						SP					SP
KNOTT, Jack															
COOPER, Orge (Pat)	(REPORTS AT END OF SALLY LEAGUE SEASON, SEPTEMBER 4th, DNP AGAIN FOR A's.)														
McCOSKY, Barney	8						8	8	8	8	8	8	8	8	8
FAGAN, Everett								RP					RP		
MAJESKI, Hank	5	5	5	5	5	5	5	5	5	5	5	5	5	5	5
GRIFFETH, Leon (Lee)	RECALL ANNOUNCED AUGUST 15th, BUT GRIFFETH'S BIG LEAGUE CAREER IS OVER.														
GRIMES, Oscar	4	4	4	4	*4	4	4	4	4	4	4	4	4	4	4
RICHMOND, Don															
ASTROTH, Joe	(REPORTS AT END OF INTER-STATE LEAGUE SEASON, SEPTEMBER 8th).														
COLEMAN, Joe	FROM TORONTO, SEPTEMBER 7th (excused a day before the International League season ends).														
McCAHAN, Bill	FROM TORONTO, SEPTEMBER 7th (also excused a day early).														

* On Aug 25(2), Suder is listed in *TSN* box at 2B. As Grimes is also at 2B, assume Suder plays shortstop, his regular position.

PHL AL

	SEP 5 NY	6 NY	7 Bos	8 Bos	10 @StL	11 @StL	[1] 13 @Chi	[2] 13 @Chi	14 @Chi	[1] 15 @Cle	[2] 15 @Cle	18 @Det	19 @Det	[1] 22 @NY	[2] 22 @NY
GARRISON, Ford															
PECK, Hal															
WALLAESA, John (Jack)					6	6	6		6	6		6	6	6	6
CHAPMAN, Sam	7	7	7	7	7	7	8	8	8	8	8	8	8	8	8
McQUINN, George	3	3	3	3											
ROSAR, Warren (Buddy)	2	2	2	2	2	2		2	2	2		2	2	2	2
KELL, George															
HANDLEY, Gene					4	4	4	ph	4	4		4	4		
CHRISTOPHER, Russ	RP				RP		RP						RP		
FOWLER, Dick	SP				SP										
KONOPKA, Bruce					3	3	3	3	3	3	3	3	3	3	3
HARRIS, Luman (Lum)	RP						RP						RP		RP
NEWSOM, Louis (Bobo or Buck)															
FLORES, Jesse			SP					SP						SP	
SAVAGE, Bob		SP					SP								
BESSE, Herman (Herm)															
VALO, Elmer	9	9	9	9	9	9	9	9	9	9					
KNERR, Luther (Lou)						SP									
BERRY, Jonas (Jittery Joe)															
VAUGHAN, Porter															
BENSON, Vern															
DESAUTELS, Gene						2				2			2		2
HALL, Irv														ph	
SUDER, Pete	6	6	6	6			ph	6			6			9	9
CAULFIELD, John (Jake)															
BROWN, Norm															
ARMSTRONG, George					(SOLD OUTRIGHT TO LANCASTER ON SEPTEMBER 28th)										
DERRY, Russ					pr						9				
STAINBACK, Tuck	ph					ph				9		9	9	7	7
MARCHILDON, Phil				SP			SP			RP		SP			SP
KNOTT, Jack															
COOPER, Orge (Pat)															
McCOSKY, Barney	8	8	8	8	8	8	7	7	7	7		7	7		
FAGAN, Everett								RP		RP					
MAJESKI, Hank	5	5	5	5			ph	5						ph	ph
GRIFFETH, Leon (Lee)															
GRIMES, Oscar	4	4	4	4			ph	4			4		ph	4	4
RICHMOND, Don					5	5	5		5	5		5	5	5	5
ASTROTH, Joe							*2			2					
COLEMAN, Joe										SP			SP		
McCAHAN, Bill											SP				RP

* Sept 13th (1), Astroth is called "Ostroth" in *TSN* box score.

American League — PHL AL

	AUG			[1]	[2]				[1]	[2]		SEP	[1]	[2]	
	22	23	24	25	25	26	27	28	30	30	31	1	2	2	2	4
PHL AL	Cle	Cle	Cle	Chi	Chi	Chi	Chi	StL	@Bos	@Bos	@Bos	@Bos	@Ws	@Ws		NY
GARRISON, Ford																
PECK, Hal																
WALLAESA, John (Jack)	(WALLAESA WILL REPORT AT THE END OF TORONTO'S SEASON, SEPTEMBER 8th.)															
CHAPMAN, Sam	7	7	7	7	7	7	7	7	7	7	7	7	7	7		7
McQUINN, George	3	3	3	3	3	3	3	3	3	3	3	3	3	3		3
ROSAR, Warren (Buddy)				2		2		2		2	2	2	2	2		2
KELL, George																
HANDLEY, Gene			ph	ph							pr		ph			
CHRISTOPHER, Russ				RP				SP								
FOWLER, Dick	SP					SP					SP					
KONOPKA, Bruce		FROM TORONTO, SEPTEMBER 7th (excused a day before IL season ends).														
HARRIS, Luman (Lum)	RP		SP										SP			
NEWSOM, Louis (Bobo or Buck)																
FLORES, Jesse		SP					SP							SP		
SAVAGE, Bob			SP					RP			SP					
BESSE, Herman (Herm)																
VALO, Elmer	9	9	9	9	9	9	9	9	9	9	9	9	9	9		9
KNERR, Luther (Lou)				RP				RP	SP							
BERRY, Jonas (Jittery Joe)																
VAUGHAN, Porter																
BENSON, Vern		(REPORTS AT END OF SALLY LEAGUE SEASON SETEMBER 4th, DNP FOR THE ATHLETICS.)														
DESAUTELS, Gene	2	2	2		2		2		2				2			
HALL, Irv		(REMAINS WITH KANSAS CITY TILL AMERICAN ASSOCIATION SEASON ENDS, SEPT. 8th.)														
SUDER, Pete	6	6	6	6	*6	6	6	6	6	6	6	6	6	6		6
CAULFIELD, John (Jake)				ph												
BROWN, Norm																
ARMSTRONG, George																
DERRY, Russ	ph															
STAINBACK, Tuck	8	8	8	8	8	8	8	ph			ph		ph			
MARCHILDON, Phil				SP					SP							SP
KNOTT, Jack																
COOPER, Orge (Pat)		(REPORTS AT END OF SALLY LEAGUE SEASON, SEPTEMBER 4th, DNP AGAIN FOR A's.)														
McCOSKY, Barney	8						8	8	8	8	8	8	8	8		8
FAGAN, Everett								RP					RP			
MAJESKI, Hank	5	5	5	5	5	5	5	5	5	5	5	5	5	5		5
GRIFFETH, Leon (Lee)		RECALL ANNOUNCED AUGUST 15th, BUT GRIFFETH'S BIG LEAGUE CAREER IS OVER.														
GRIMES, Oscar	4	4	4	4	*4	4	4	4	4	4	4	4	4	4		4
RICHMOND, Don																
ASTROTH, Joe		(REPORTS AT END OF INTER-STATE LEAGUE SEASON, SEPTEMBER 8th).														
COLEMAN, Joe		FROM TORONTO, SEPTEMBER 7th (excused a day before the International League season ends).														
McCAHAN, Bill		FROM TORONTO, SEPTEMBER 7th (also excused a day early).														

* On Aug 25(2), Suder is listed in *TSN* box at 2B. As Grimes is also at 2B, assume Suder plays shortstop, his regular position.

PHL AL	SEP 23 @NY	[1] 25 Wsh	[2] 25 Wsh	26 Wsh	[1] 29 NY	[2] 29 NY	155g
GARRISON, Ford							
PECK, Hal							
WALLAESA, John (Jack)	6	6		6	6	6	
CHAPMAN, Sam	8				8	8	
McQUINN, George							
ROSAR, Warren (Buddy)	2	ph	2	2	2		
KELL, George							
HANDLEY, Gene							
CHRISTOPHER, Russ	RP		RP	RP			
FOWLER, Dick							
KONOPKA, Bruce	3	3	3	3	3	3	
HARRIS, Luman (Lum)		SP					
NEWSOM, Louis (Bobo or Buck)							
FLORES, Jesse				SP			
SAVAGE, Bob	SP						
BESSE, Herman (Herm)							
VALO, Elmer		9	9	9			
KNERR, Luther (Lou)			SP				
BERRY, Jonas (Jittery Joe)							
VAUGHAN, Porter							
BENSON, Vern							
DESAUTELS, Gene							
HALL, Irv	ph	ph	ph	ph			
SUDER, Pete	ph	ph	6	4	4	4	
CAULFIELD, John (Jake)							
BROWN, Norm							
ARMSTRONG, George							
DERRY, Russ	7	7	7	7	7	7	
STAINBACK, Tuck	9	8	8	8	9	9	
MARCHILDON, Phil					SP		
KNOTT, Jack							
COOPER, Orge (Pat)							
McCOSKY, Barney							
FAGAN, Everrett	RP						
MAJESKI, Hank							
GRIFFETH, Leon (Lee)							
GRIMES, Oscar	4	4	4				
RICHMOND, Don	5	5	5	5	5	5	
ASTROTH, Joe		2				2	
COLEMAN, Joe		RP			RP		
McCAHAN, Bill			RP			SP	

American League — STL AL

	Games	APRIL 16 @Det	17 @Det	18 @Det	20 Chi	[1] 21 Chi	[2] 21 Chi	24 Cle	25 Det	26 Det	27 @Chi	[1] 28 @Chi	[2] 28 @Chi	30 @Ph	MAY 1 @Ph
STL AL	156														
DILLINGER, Bob	83	5	5		ph	pr						pr		ph	
GRACE, Joe	48	9	ph	ph		9	9	9		9	9	9	9	9	9
McQUILLEN, Glenn	59	7	h7		7		7		7	7		ph	7	7	
JUDNICH, Walt (Wally)	142	8	8	8	8	8	8	8	8	8	8	8		8	8
BERARDINO, John	144	4	4	4	4	4	4	4	4	4	4	4	4	4	4
CHRISTMAN, Mark	128	6	6	6	5	5	5	5	5	5	5	5	5	5	
MANCUSO, Frank	87	2	2	2	2	2	2	2	2	2	2		2	2	
ARCHIE, George	4	3	pr		3		3							TO L.A.	
POTTER, Nelson (Nels)	23	SP				SP			SP						SP
LUCADELLO, Johnny	87		5	5		ph		ph	ph			ph		5	5
ZARILLA, Al (Zeke)	125		7	7	ph	7	7	7			7	78	7	7	7
STEPHENS, Vern (Junior)	115		ph		6	6	6	6	6	6	6	6	6	6	6
MILLER, John (Ox)	11		RP		SP				SP				RP		
FINNEY, Lou	16		9	9							9		7	ph	
HELF, Hank	71		2												
STEVENS, Chuck	122		3	3		3					3	3	3	3	3
SHIRLEY, Alvis (Tex)	35		SP			SP								SP	
ZOLDAK, Sam	35		RP						RP	SP					
GALEHOUSE, Denny	30			SP				SP			SP				
FERENS, Stan	34			RP	RP			RP	RP				RP		
HOLLINGSWORTH, Al	5			RP									RP	RP	
SEARS, Ken	7			ph								2		2	2
LaMACCHIA, Al	8			RP	RP									RP	
LAABS, Chet	80				9				9						
SCHULTE, Len	4				ph				ph						
DAHLGREN, Ellsworth (Babe)	28	* FROM PITTSBURGH, APRIL 23rd.						3	3	3	3				
KRAMER, John (Jack)	31							RP	RP				SP		
MILNAR, Al	4											RP			
BRADLEY, George	4													8	8
KINDER, Ellis	33													RP	
SCHULTZ, Joe	42													ph	
SUNDRA, Steve	2													RP	
FANNIN, Cliff	27	SORE ARM IN SPRING TRAINING SIDELINES FANNIN TILL MID-MAY.													
MUNCRIEF, Bob	29	RECOVERING FROM BROKEN TOE IN SPRING TRAINING.													
HEATH, Jeff	86	TRADED TO BROWNS FROM WASHINGTON FOR GRACE & LaMACCHIA, JUNE 15th.													
BISCAN, Frank	16	ARM OPERATION IN MAY, REINSTATED FROM VOLUNTARY RETIRED LIST JUNE 19th.													
FERRICK, Tom	25	PURCHASED ON WAIVERS FROM CLEVELAND, JUNE 24th.													
MARTIN, Boris (Babe)	3	OPTIONED TO OAKLAND APRIL 12th, WILL BE RECALLED AT THE END OF JUNE.													
LEHNER, Paul	16	PURCHASED OUTRIGHT FROM TOLEDO, SEPTEMBER 9th.													
WITTE, Jerry	18	PURCHASED OUTRIGHT FROM TOLEDO, SEPTEMBER 7th.													
MOSS, Les	12	PURCHASED OUTRIGHT FROM TOLEDO SEPTEMBER 9th.													
JOHNSON, Chet	5	OPTIONED TO TOLEDO APRIL 14th, RECALLED SEPTEMBER 8th.													
SANFORD, Fred	3	OPTIONED TO TOLEDO APRIL 14th, RECALLED SEPTEMBER 8th.													
SHORE, Ray	1	OUTRIGHT FROM SPRINGFIELD (Ill.) AT END OF 3-I *LEAGUE* SEASON, SEPT. 2nd.													

* Dahlgren bought from the Pirates April 23rd, without playing for Pittsburgh this season.

STL AL

	MAY		SUN MAY 5, RAIN [1]	[2]				[1]	[2]	[1]	[2]				
	2	3	6	6	7	8	9	12	12	13	13	14	15	16	18
	@Ph	@Ws	@Bos	@Bos	@Bos	@NY	@NY	@Cle	@Cle	@Cle	@Cle	NY	NY	Bos	Bos
DILLINGER, Bob				ph	ph			pr							
GRACE, Joe	9	9	9	9	9	9	9	9	9	9		ph	9	9	
McQUILLEN, Glenn	7	7	7	7	7		7	ph	7	h7	7	7	7	7	7
JUDNICH, Walt (Wally)	8	8	8	8	8	8	8	8	8	8		8	8	8	8
BERARDINO, John	4	4	4	4	4	4	4	4	4	4	4	4	4	4	4
CHRISTMAN, Mark	5	5	5	56	6	6	6	6	6	6	6	6	6	6	6
MANCUSO, Frank	2	2	2	2	2	2	2	2			2	2			
ARCHIE, George	ARCHIE SOLD TO LOS ANGELES, APRIL 29th.														
POTTER, Nelson (Nels)							SP				SP				
LUCADELLO, Johnny			5	5	5	5	5	5	5	5	5	5	5	5	5
ZARILLA, Al (Zeke)	7	7	ph	7		7	7	7	79	7			7	7	
STEPHENS, Vern (Junior)	6	6	6	6	INJURED SHOULDER, MISSES 25 GAMES IN STARTING LINEUP.										
MILLER, John (Ox)				SP											
FINNEY, Lou			ph			ph		ph							
HELF, Hank			pr					2	2	2			2	2	2
STEVENS, Chuck	3	3	3	3	3	3	3	3	3	3	3	3	3	3	3
SHIRLEY, Alvis (Tex)			RP		RP	RP			SP						SP
ZOLDAK, Sam		SP			SP		RP					SP			
GALEHOUSE, Denny			SP							RP					RP
FERENS, Stan				RP					SP						RP
HOLLINGSWORTH, Al															
SEARS, Ken			ph				(PURCHASED FROM NY APRIL 2nd; SEE NEXT PAGE)								
LaMACCHIA, Al										RP					RP
LAABS, Chet										ph	9	9	9	9	9
SCHULTE, Len															
DAHLGREN, Ellsworth (Babe)															ph
KRAMER, John (Jack)	SP				SP		SP						SP		
MILNAR, Al			RP							SP					
BRADLEY, George							pr			8					
KINDER, Ellis										RP					RP
SCHULTZ, Joe							ph								
SUNDRA, Steve															
FANNIN, Cliff								RP				RP			RP
MUNCRIEF, Bob															
HEATH, Jeff															
BISCAN, Frank															
FERRICK, Tom															
MARTIN, Boris (Babe)															
LEHNER, Paul															
WITTE, Jerry															
MOSS, Les															
JOHNSON, Chet															
SANFORD, Fred															
SHORE, Ray															

NOTE: first baseman Dick Siebert, obtained in off-season from A's in trade for first baseman George McQuinn, refused to report after salary disagreement. The Browns place him on *Ineligible List* May 8th, grant him *Voluntary Retirement* May 15th. He ends his playing career by announcing his retirement.

American League — STL AL

	MAY	[1]	[2]				[1]	[2]			[1]	[2]	SUN JUNE 2, RAIN		TIE JUNE 5, Replay 8/20(2)
		19	19	21	22	25	26	26	27	28	30	30	1	3	4	5
STL AL		Phl	Phl	Phl	Wsh	Cle	Cle	Cle	Cle	Chi	Det	Det	@NY	@NY	@Bos	@Bos
DILLINGER, Bob				5	5	5	5	5	5	5	5	5	5	5	5	5
GRACE, Joe	ph	9	9	9	9	9	9		9	9	9		ph	9	9
McQUILLEN, Glenn	7		7	7			7					ph		ph
JUDNICH, Walt (Wally)	8	8	8	8	8	8	8	8	8	8	8	8	8	8	8
BERARDINO, John	4	4			ph	4	4	4	4	4	4	4	4	4	4
CHRISTMAN, Mark	6	6	6	6	6	6	6	6	6	6	6	6	6	6	
MANCUSO, Frank		2			2		2	ph	2	2	2	2	2	2	2
ARCHIE, George															
POTTER, Nelson (Nels)						SP							SP		RP
LUCADELLO, Johnny	5	5	4	4	4	4	ph						ph	h5	4
ZARILLA, Al (Zeke)	7	ph	7	r7	h7	7	ph		7	7	7	9	9	97	7
STEPHENS, Vern (Junior)		INJURED SHOULDER.						ph		INJURED.					6
MILLER, John (Ox)		RP						RP				RP			
FINNEY, Lou	ph	ph	ph	ph	7	7	7		ph		SOLD TO PHILA. NL, MAY 29th.				
HELF, Hank	2		2	2	2	2	2	2	2						
STEVENS, Chuck	3	3	3	3	3	3	3	3	3	3					
SHIRLEY, Alvis (Tex)			pr	SP	pr		SP							RP	
ZOLDAK, Sam	SP				SP				SP						SP
GALEHOUSE, Denny		RP						RP		SP			SP		
FERENS, Stan		RP					RP		SP				RP		
HOLLINGSWORTH, Al		RP						RP							
SEARS, Ken		(DOESN'T PLAY DURING ST.L-NY CONTRACT DISPUTE; AWARDED TO BROWNS JUNE 19th.)													
LaMACCHIA, Al								RP	RP						
LAABS, Chet	9	7					9		ph	9	7	7	7	7	7
SCHULTE, Len															4
DAHLGREN, Ellsworth (Babe)							ph		3	3	3	3	3	3
KRAMER, John (Jack)			SP			SP				SP				
MILNAR, Al		SP							SOLD TO THE PHILLIES MAY 29th.						
BRADLEY, George									OPTIONED TO TOLEDO MAY 30th.						
KINDER, Ellis						RP								RP
SCHULTZ, Joe									ph		2		2
SUNDRA, Steve							RP		RELEASED, MAY 29th.						
FANNIN, Cliff	RP								RP			RP		
MUNCRIEF, Bob					RP							RP		RP
HEATH, Jeff														
BISCAN, Frank														
FERRICK, Tom														
MARTIN, Boris (Babe)														
LEHNER, Paul														
WITTE, Jerry														
MOSS, Les														
JOHNSON, Chet														
SANFORD, Fred														
SHORE, Ray														

	JUNE			[1]	[2]						[1]	[2]			
	6	7	8	9	9	10	11	12	14	15	16	16	17	18	20
STL AL	@Bos	@Phl	@Phl	@Phl	@Phl	@Ws	@Ws	@Ws	NY	NY	NY	NY	Bos	Bos	Bos
DILLINGER, Bob	5	5	5	5	5	5	5	5	5	5	5				
GRACE, Joe	9	9	9	9	9	9	9	9	9	9	TO WASHINGTON FOR HEATH.				
McQUILLEN, Glenn											ph	7			
JUDNICH, Walt (Wally)	8	8	8	8	8	8	8	8	8	8	8	8	8	8	8
BERARDINO, John	4	4	4	4	4	4	4	4	4	4	4	4	4	4	4
CHRISTMAN, Mark											6	5	5	5	5
MANCUSO, Frank	2	2	2	OUT WITH BACK INJURY FROM WW2 PARATROOP TRAINING.											
ARCHIE, George															
POTTER, Nelson (Nels)				SP											
LUCADELLO, Johnny			h5		h5				ph	ph	4				
ZARILLA, Al (Zeke)	7	7	7	7	7	7	7	7	7	7	9	ph			
STEPHENS, Vern (Junior)	6	6	6	6	6	6	6	6	6	6	6	6	6	6	6
MILLER, John (Ox)	RP				RP						RP				
FINNEY, Lou		RETURNED BY PHILS, JUNE 10th.													
HELF, Hank			2	2	2	2	2	2	2	2		2	2	2	
STEVENS, Chuck		3							3	3	3	3	3	3	3
SHIRLEY, Alvis (Tex)							SP					SP			
ZOLDAK, Sam						SP					SP				SP
GALEHOUSE, Denny				SP						SP					
FERENS, Stan	RP		RP									RP			
HOLLINGSWORTH, Al	SOLD TO THE WHITE SOX ON WAIVERS, JUNE 6th.														
SEARS, Ken															
LaMACCHIA, Al			RP								TO WASHINGTON FOR HEATH.				
LAABS, Chet	ph								ph	ph	7	9	9	9	9
SCHULTE, Len											h5				
DAHLGREN, Ellsworth (Babe)	3		3	3	3	3	3	3	3	3					
KRAMER, John (Jack)	SP							SP			RP		SP		
MILNAR, Al	RETURNED BY PHILLIES & RELEASED, JUNE 13th.														
BRADLEY, George	RETURNED JUNE 15th, SUSPENDED JUNE 18th.														
KINDER, Ellis			SP		RP			RP			RP				
SCHULTZ, Joe									2	2	2				2
SUNDRA, Steve															
FANNIN, Cliff					RP										
MUNCRIEF, Bob		SP							SP					SP	
HEATH, Jeff													7	7	7
BISCAN, Frank															
FERRICK, Tom															
MARTIN, Boris (Babe)															
LEHNER, Paul															
WITTE, Jerry															
MOSS, Les															
JOHNSON, Chet															
SANFORD, Fred															
SHORE, Ray															

American League — STL AL

	JUNE		[1]	[2]				[1]	[2]	JULY			[1]	[2]	
	21	22	23	23	25	26	28	30	30	1	2	3	4	4	5
STL AL	Wsh	Wsh	Wsh	Wsh	Phl	Phl	Det	Det	Det	@Cle	@Cle	@Cle	@Chi	@Chi	@Chi
DILLINGER, Bob	pr		ph							pr					
GRACE, Joe	DATE OF HEATH TRADE IS JUNE 15th.														
McQUILLEN, Glenn			ph												
JUDNICH, Walt (Wally)	8	8	8	8	8	8	8	8	8	8	8	8	8	8	8
BERARDINO, John	4	4	4	4	4	4	4	4	4	4	4	4	4	4	4
CHRISTMAN, Mark	5	5	5	5	5	5	5	5	5	5	5	5			
MANCUSO, Frank													2		
ARCHIE, George															
POTTER, Nelson (Nels)														SP	
LUCADELLO, Johnny										ph	ph	5	5	5	5
ZARILLA, Al (Zeke)	ph									ph	ph	ph		7	7
STEPHENS, Vern (Junior)	6	6	6	6	6	6	6	6	6	6	6	6	6	6	6
MILLER, John (Ox)										OPTIONED TO TOLEDO JUNE 30th.					
FINNEY, Lou										RELEASED, JUNE 29th.					
HELF, Hank	2	2	2	2	2	2	2	2	2	2	2		2	2	2
STEVENS, Chuck	3	3	3	3	3	3	3	3	3	3	3	3	3	3	3
SHIRLEY, Alvis (Tex)		SP				SP					SP				
ZOLDAK, Sam			RP	SP						SP					
GALEHOUSE, Denny	SP						SP					SP			
FERENS, Stan		RP										RP			
HOLLINGSWORTH, Al															
SEARS, Ken				2								ph			
LaMACCHIA, Al	DATE OF HEATH TRADE IS JUNE 15th.														
LAABS, Chet	9	9	9	9	9	9	9	9	9	9	9	9	9	9	9
SCHULTE, Len		OPTIONED TO TOLEDO, JUNE 22nd.													
DAHLGREN, Ellsworth (Babe)															
KRAMER, John (Jack)			SP				SP					SP			
MILNAR, Al															
BRADLEY, George															
KINDER, Ellis			RP									RP			
SCHULTZ, Joe	ph				2		2			2	ph	ph	2	ph	
SUNDRA, Steve															
FANNIN, Cliff			RP			RP				RP					SP
MUNCRIEF, Bob				SP				SP							
HEATH, Jeff	7	7	7	7	7	7	7	7	7	7	7	7	7	7	7
BISCAN, Frank			RP									RP			
FERRICK, Tom									RP						
MARTIN, Boris (Babe)	RECALLED FROM OAKLAND, JUNE 30th.														
LEHNER, Paul															
WITTE, Jerry															
MOSS, Les															
JOHNSON, Chet															
SANFORD, Fred															
SHORE, Ray															

American League

STL AL

	JULY	6	7	ALL-STAR BREAK 11	12	13	[1] 14	[2] 14	15	16	[1] 17	[2] 17	18	20	[1] 21	[2] 21
		@Det	@Det	@Phl	@Phl	@Phl	@Ws	@Ws	@Ws	@Ws	@NY	@NY	@NY	@Bos	@Bos	@Bos
DILLINGER, Bob			ph					ph				ph				ph
GRACE, Joe																
McQUILLEN, Glenn			ph				9	7	7				ph			
JUDNICH, Walt (Wally)		8	8	8	8		8					8	8	8	8	8
BERARDINO, John		4	4		4	4	4	4	4	4	4	4	4	4	4	4
CHRISTMAN, Mark			ph	5					ph					5	5	5
MANCUSO, Frank			2	2	2	2	2	2	2	2	2	2	2	2	2	2
ARCHIE, George																
POTTER, Nelson (Nels)				SP								SP				RP
LUCADELLO, Johnny		5	5	4	5	5	5	5	5	5	5	5	5		ph	ph
ZARILLA, Al (Zeke)				7	ph	8	9	8	8	8	8	9	9	9	9	9
STEPHENS, Vern (Junior)		6	6	6	6	6	6	6	6	6	6	6	6	6	6	6
MILLER, John (Ox)		OPTION DISALLOWED: MILLER OUT OF OPTIONS, SO TRANSACTION CHANGED TO A SALE.														
FINNEY, Lou																
HELF, Hank		2	2	2	2			2				2				
STEVENS, Chuck		3	3	3	3	3	3	3	3	3	3	3	3	3	3	3
SHIRLEY, Alvis (Tex)			SP						SP				RP		SP	
ZOLDAK, Sam						SP						RP				RP
GALEHOUSE, Denny											SP					
FERENS, Stan				RP		RP							SP		RP	
HOLLINGSWORTH, Al																
SEARS, Ken				SEARS OPTIONED TO SAN ANTONIO, JULY 11th.												
LaMACCHIA, Al																
LAABS, Chet		9	9	9	9	9		ph	9	9	9				ph	
SCHULTE, Len																
DAHLGREN, Ellsworth (Babe)																
KRAMER, John (Jack)				SP					SP				SP			
MILNAR, Al																
BRADLEY, George																
KINDER, Ellis		RP	RP		RP		RP				RP				RP	
SCHULTZ, Joe			ph		ph		ph	ph					ph			
SUNDRA, Steve																
FANNIN, Cliff					SP											SP
MUNCRIEF, Bob		SP						SP								
HEATH, Jeff		7	7	7	7	7	7	7			7	7	7	7	7	7
BISCAN, Frank															RP	
FERRICK, Tom							RP						RP			
MARTIN, Boris (Babe)				OPTIONED TO TOLEDO, JULY 8th.												
LEHNER, Paul																
WITTE, Jerry																
MOSS, Les																
JOHNSON, Chet																
SANFORD, Fred																
SHORE, Ray																

STL AL

	JULY				[1]	[2]		AUG				[1]	[2]		
	23	24	26	27	28	28	30	31	1	2	3	4	4	6	7
STL AL	NY	NY	Bos	Bos	Bos	Bos	Wsh	Wsh	Wsh	Phl	Phl	Phl	Phl	Det	Det
DILLINGER, Bob		pr	ph	5		ph	pr			ph				5	
GRACE, Joe															
McQUILLEN, Glenn		ph		ph											
JUDNICH, Walt (Wally)		ph	8	8	8	8	ph	8	8	8	8	8	8	8	8
BERARDINO, John	4	4	4	4	4	4	4	4	4	4	4				
CHRISTMAN, Mark	5	5	5	56	5	5	5	5	5	5	5	5	5	5	5
MANCUSO, Frank	2	2	2	2	2	2	2	2	2	2	2	2			
ARCHIE, George															
POTTER, Nelson (Nels)			SP					SP							
LUCADELLO, Johnny		ph	5	4			ph	ph			ph		4	4	4	4
ZARILLA, Al (Zeke)	8	8	89	9	9	9	8	9	9	9	9			ph	
STEPHENS, Vern (Junior)	6	6	6	6	6	6	6	6	6	6	6	6	6	6	6
MILLER, John (Ox)															
FINNEY, Lou															
HELF, Hank				2									2	2	2
STEVENS, Chuck	3	3	3	3	3	3	3	3	3	3	3	3	3	3	3
SHIRLEY, Alvis (Tex)		pr	RP									SP			
ZOLDAK, Sam		RP	RP			RP				RP					
GALEHOUSE, Denny	SP				SP					SP			RP		
FERENS, Stan				RP			SP				SP				
HOLLINGSWORTH, Al															
SEARS, Ken															
LaMACCHIA, Al															
LAABS, Chet	9	9	9				9			ph	9	9	9	9	9
SCHULTE, Len															
DAHLGREN, Ellsworth (Babe)				ph											
KRAMER, John (Jack)		SP			SP			SP					SP		
MILNAR, Al															
BRADLEY, George															
KINDER, Ellis				RP		RP					RP				
SCHULTZ, Joe		ph	ph												
SUNDRA, Steve															
FANNIN, Cliff			RP			RP				RP		RP			
MUNCRIEF, Bob			SP			RP					SP				SP
HEATH, Jeff	7	7	7	7	7	7	7	7	7	7	7	7	7	7	7
BISCAN, Frank			RP			RP									
FERRICK, Tom								RP		RP		RP	RP		
MARTIN, Boris (Babe)															
LEHNER, Paul															
WITTE, Jerry															
MOSS, Les															
JOHNSON, Chet															
SANFORD, Fred															
SHORE, Ray															

American League

		AUG	[1]	[2]	[1]	[2]		[1]	[2]	[1]	REPLAY of 6/5 TIE [2]		[1]	[2]
		9	10	11	11	13	13	15	17	18	18	20	20	21	22	22
STL AL		Cle	Cle	Cle	Cle	Chi	Chi	@Cle	@Det	@Det	@Det	@Bos	@Bos	@Bos	@NY	@NY
DILLINGER, Bob	ph	5	pr	5	ph	5	5	5	5	5	5	5	5	5	5
GRACE, Joe															
McQUILLEN, Glenn												7			7
JUDNICH, Walt (Wally)	8	8	8	8	8	8	8	8	8	8	8	8	8	8	8
BERARDINO, John				4	4	4	4	4	4	4	4	4	4	4	4
CHRISTMAN, Mark	5	5	5	5	5		6	6	6	6	6	6	6	6	6
MANCUSO, Frank	2	2	2	2	2	2	2	2	2	2	2	2	2	2	2
ARCHIE, George															
POTTER, Nelson (Nels)		SP						SP							
LUCADELLO, Johnny	4	4	4	ph	ph		ph	ph						ph	
ZARILLA, Al (Zeke)	ph	ph	ph	ph	ph	9	9	9	9	9	9		ph		
STEPHENS, Vern (Junior)	6	6	6	6	6	6		ph	SHOULDER RE-INJURED.						
MILLER, John (Ox)															
FINNEY, Lou															
HELF, Hank	2												2		
STEVENS, Chuck	3	3	3	3	3	3	3	3	3	3	3	3	3	3	3
SHIRLEY, Alvis (Tex)			RP								SP				
ZOLDAK, Sam	RP				SP		RP								SP
GALEHOUSE, Denny	SP									SP			SP		
FERENS, Stan							RP						RP		
HOLLINGSWORTH, Al															
SEARS, Ken	RECALL ANNOUNCED AUGUST 9th, BUT SEARS' BIG LEAGUE CAREER IS ENDED.														
LaMACCHIA, Al															
LAABS, Chet	9	9	9	9	9							9	9	9	9
SCHULTE, Len	RECALL ANNOUNCED AUGUST 9th, TO REPORT AT END OF A.A. SEASON.														
DAHLGREN, Ellsworth (Babe)															ph
KRAMER, John (Jack)			SP			SP									
MILNAR, Al															
BRADLEY, George															
KINDER, Ellis	RP	RP			SP		RP					SP			
SCHULTZ, Joe		ph	ph			ph							ph	ph	
SUNDRA, Steve															
FANNIN, Cliff	RP				RP										
MUNCRIEF, Bob			SP			SP			SP				SP		
HEATH, Jeff	7	7	7	7	7	7	7	7	7	7	7		7	7	
BISCAN, Frank													RP		
FERRICK, Tom	RP			RP		RP			RP		RP				RP
MARTIN, Boris (Babe)	RECALL ANNOUNCED AUGUST 9th, TO REPORT AT END OF TOLEDO'S SEASON.														
LEHNER, Paul															
WITTE, Jerry															
MOSS, Les															
JOHNSON, Chet	RECALL ANNOUNCED AUGUST 9th, TO REPORT AT END OF TOLEDO'S SEASON.														
SANFORD, Fred	RECALL ANNOUNCED AUGUST 9th, TO REPORT AT END OF TOLEDO'S SEASON.														
SHORE, Ray															

STL AL

8/31, Taylor interim manager

TIE 9/2(2), replay 9/3(2)

STL AL	AUG 23 @NY	24 @NY	25 @Ws	26 @Ws	27 @Ws	28 @Ws	SUN SEP 1, RAIN 31 @Phl Det	[1] 2 Cle	[2] 2 Cle	[1] 3 Cle	[2] 3 Cle	4 @Chi	5 @Chi	7 @Cle	[1] 8 @Cle
DILLINGER, Bob	5	5	5	5	5	5	5	5	5	5	ph				
GRACE, Joe															
McQUILLEN, Glenn		7	7						7		7	7		97	9
JUDNICH, Walt (Wally)	8	8	8	8	8	8	8	8	8	8	8	8	8		
BERARDINO, John	4	4	4	4	4	4	4	4	4	4	4	4	4	4	4
CHRISTMAN, Mark	6	6	6	6	6	6	ph		ph	ph	5	5	5	5	5
MANCUSO, Frank		2	2	2	2	2	2				2		2		
ARCHIE, George															
POTTER, Nelson (Nels)	SP					SP						SP			
LUCADELLO, Johnny			ph					ph	ph	ph	ph		ph		
ZARILLA, Al (Zeke)		9	79	9	9	9		9	9	9	9	7		9	9	9
STEPHENS, Vern (Junior)							6	6	6	6	6	6	6	6	6
MILLER, John (Ox)															
FINNEY, Lou															
HELF, Hank	2							2	2	2	ph	2	2		2
STEVENS, Chuck	3	3	3	3	3	3		3	3	3	3	3	3	3	3
SHIRLEY, Alvis (Tex)			SP				RP	pr	RP						
ZOLDAK, Sam				SP				SP					SP		
GALEHOUSE, Denny					SP			SP			RP				
FERENS, Stan			RP	RP							SP				
HOLLINGSWORTH, Al															
SEARS, Ken															
LaMACCHIA, Al															
LAABS, Chet	9	9	9				7				9	9		9	
SCHULTE, Len	(SCHULTE'S MAJOR LEAGUE CAREER IS ALREADY OVER)														
DAHLGREN, Ellsworth (Babe)					3	3	3	3	3	3					
KRAMER, John (Jack)															SP
MILNAR, Al															
BRADLEY, George	REINSTATED FROM SUSPENDED LIST, SEPT. 9th.														
KINDER, Ellis		SP								RP			RP		
SCHULTZ, Joe				ph				ph	ph	2	2		2		
SUNDRA, Steve															
FANNIN, Cliff						RP	RP					SP			
MUNCRIEF, Bob				SP				RP	RP	RP		RP			
HEATH, Jeff	7	7	7	7	7	7		7	7	7	ph		7	7	7
BISCAN, Frank				RP					RP	RP	RP		RP		
FERRICK, Tom		RP	RP						RP		SP				
MARTIN, Boris (Babe)															
LEHNER, Paul															
WITTE, Jerry															
MOSS, Les															
JOHNSON, Chet															
SANFORD, Fred															
SHORE, Ray															

STL AL

	SEP	[2]						[1]	[2]				[1]	[2]	[1]	[2]
		8	10	11	12	13	14	15	15	16	18	19	21	21	22	22
STL AL		@Cle	Phl	Phl	Wsh	Wsh	Wsh	NY	NY	NY	Bos	Bos	Chi	Chi	Chi	Chi
DILLINGER, Bob					ph				5	ph	ph	pr		5		6
GRACE, Joe																
McQUILLEN, Glenn		9			7					7		79		7	7	
JUDNICH, Walt (Wally)				7	7	7	7	87	8	8	ph	7	9			8
BERARDINO, John		4	4	4	4	4	4	4	4	4	4		4	4	4	4
CHRISTMAN, Mark		5	5	5	5	5	5	5		5	5	5	5	6	5	5
MANCUSO, Frank														ph		
ARCHIE, George																
POTTER, Nelson (Nels)										RP				RP		
LUCADELLO, Johnny										ph	4	4	ph	4		
ZARILLA, Al (Zeke)		9	9	9	9	9	9	9	pr	9	9	89		8	8	9
STEPHENS, Vern (Junior)		6	6	6	6	6	6	6	6	6	6	6	6	6	6	
MILLER, John (Ox)																
FINNEY, Lou																
HELF, Hank						2	2	2			2					2
STEVENS, Chuck		3														3
SHIRLEY, Alvis (Tex)					RP				pr			pr	pr			
ZOLDAK, Sam						SP						RP				
GALEHOUSE, Denny		SP							SP					SP		
FERENS, Stan										RP	RP		RP			
HOLLINGSWORTH, Al																
SEARS, Ken									TO SAN ANTONIO, SEPTEMBER 17th.							
LaMACCHIA, Al																
LAABS, Chet										9		9		9	9	
SCHULTE, Len																
DAHLGREN, Ellsworth (Babe)																
KRAMER, John (Jack)					SP					SP						SP
MILNAR, Al																
BRADLEY, George										TO SAN ANTONIO, SEPTEMBER 17th.						
KINDER, Ellis			SP			RP						SP				
SCHULTZ, Joe		2								ph	2	ph	2			2
SUNDRA, Steve																
FANNIN, Cliff			SP							SP		RP				
MUNCRIEF, Bob					RP					RP	RP		RP			
HEATH, Jeff		7	7					7	7	7	7	7	7			7
BISCAN, Frank				RP			RP									RP
FERRICK, Tom					RP					RP	RP			RP		RP
MARTIN, Boris (Babe)					ph							2	2			
LEHNER, Paul			8	8	8	8	8	8	9	ph	8	8	8			ph
WITTE, Jerry			3	3	3	3	3	3	3	3	3	3	3	3	3	3
MOSS, Les			2	2	2				2	2				2	2	
JOHNSON, Chet					SP		RP						SP			
SANFORD, Fred								SP							SP	
SHORE, Ray													RP			

STL AL	[1] 24 @Det	[2] 24 @Det	25 @Det	26 @Det	[1] 27 @Chi	[2] 27 @Chi	29 @Chi	156g
DILLINGER, Bob		5			ph	5		
GRACE, Joe								
McQUILLEN, Glenn	ph		7	7	7	7		
JUDNICH, Walt (Wally)	8	ph	8	8	8	ph	8	
BERARDINO, John	4		4	4	4	4	4	
CHRISTMAN, Mark	5		5	5	5	ph	5	
MANCUSO, Frank	* SENT HOME EARLY.							
ARCHIE, George								
POTTER, Nelson (Nels)	* SENT HOME EARLY.							
LUCADELLO, Johnny		4					ph	
ZARILLA, Al (Zeke)	9	9	9	9	9	9	9	
STEPHENS, Vern (Junior)	6	6	6	6	6	6	6	
MILLER, John (Ox)								
FINNEY, Lou								
HELF, Hank	2	2	2		2		2	
STEVENS, Chuck		3		ph	ph	3	3	
SHIRLEY, Alvis (Tex)	* SENT HOME EARLY.							
ZOLDAK, Sam	SP						RP	
GALEHOUSE, Denny				SP				
FERENS, Stan		RP		RP				
HOLLINGSWORTH, Al								
SEARS, Ken								
LaMACCHIA, Al								
LAABS, Chet					* HOME.			
SCHULTE, Len								
DAHLGREN, Ellsworth (Babe)	* SENT HOME EARLY.							
KRAMER, John (Jack)						SP		
MILNAR, Al								
BRADLEY, George								
KINDER, Ellis		SP				RP		
SCHULTZ, Joe						ph	ph	
SUNDRA, Steve								
FANNIN, Cliff			SP		RP			
MUNCRIEF, Bob		RP			RP		RP	
HEATH, Jeff	7	7	ph	ph			7	
BISCAN, Frank			RP				RP	
FERRICK, Tom			RP			RP	RP	
MARTIN, Boris (Babe)	* SENT HOME EARLY.							
LEHNER, Paul		8	ph			8	ph	
WITTE, Jerry	3		3	3	3			
MOSS, Les	2	2	2	2		2		
JOHNSON, Chet		RP					SP	
SANFORD, Fred					SP			
SHORE, Ray								

* Potter, Shirley, Mancuso, Martin, Dahlgren all allowed to go home early. Laabs allowed to miss the final series in Chicago. On September 28th, Dahlgren is released.

WSH AL

	Games	APRIL 16	17	18	19	20	21	22	23	24	26	27	28	30	MAY 3
		Bos	Bos	Bos	@NY	@NY	@NY	@Bs	@Bs	Phl	NY	NY	NY	Chi	StL
ROBERTSON, Sherry	74	5	5			5	5	5	5	5	5	5	5	5	5
LEWIS, John (Buddy)	150	9	9	9	9	9	9	9	9	9	9	9	9	9	9
SPENCE, Stan	152	8	8	8	8	8	8	8	8	8	8	8	8	8	8
TRAVIS, Cecil	137	6	6	6	6	6	6	6	6	6	6	6	6	6	6
HEATH, Jeff	48	7	7	7	7		ph		7	7	7				
VERNON, James (Mickey)	148	3	3			ph				3			3	3	3
PRIDDY, Gerry	138	*4	4	4	4	4	4	4	4	4	4	4	4	4	4
EVANS, Al	88	2	2	2	2	2		2	2	2	2			2	2
WOLFF, Roger	21	SP				SP			RP			SP			SP
HUDSON, Sid	31	*RP		RP				SP			SP				RP
KUHEL, Joe	14	ph	ph		3	ph	3		ph	3	3	3			
BINKS, George	65	ph				7	7			ph		7	7	7	7
MASTERSON, Walter	29		SP		RP				SP			SP			
CURTIS, Vern	11		RP	RP											
WILSON, Maxie	9		RP								RP				RP
PIERETTI, Marino	30		RP		RP				RP		RP	RP			
KENNEDY, Bill G.	21		RP								RP				
SANFORD, John H. (Jack)	10		ph	3	3	3		3	3	ph	ph				3
TORRES, Gilberto	63			5	5										
SCARBOROUGH, Rae	32			*SP		RP				SP			SP		
GOOLSBY, Ray	3			ph	ph			7							
GUERRA, Fermin (Mike)	41			ph	ph		ph	ph	ph		2				ph
HAEFNER, Milton (Mickey)	33				SP		RP			RP		RP			
NIGGELING, Johnny	8				RP										
EARLY, Jake	64					2	2					2	2		
LEONARD, Emil (Dutch)	26					SP									
COAN, Gil	59											ph			
MYATT, George	15	OPENING DAY, MYATT TRIPS IN DUGOUT, CHIPS ANKLE. HE WON'T PLAY TILL MAY 19th.													
HITCHCOCK, Billy	98	PURCHASED FROM DETROIT, MAY 16th.													
NEWSOM, Louis (Bobo or Buck)	24	RELEASED BY A'S JUNE 3rd, SIGNS WITH NATIONALS JUNE 5th.													
GRACE, Joe	77	OBTAINED IN TRADE WITH BROWNS FOR HEATH, JUNE 15th.													
LaMACCHIA, Al	2	OBTAINED IN TRADE WITH BROWNS FOR HEATH, JUNE 15th.													
WYNN, Early	25	DISCHARGED BY ARMY JULY 4, REJOINS TEAM THAT DAY (reinstated from NSDL July 5).													
WADE, Jacob (Whistlin' Jake)	6	PURCHASED ON WAIVERS FROM THE YANKEES, AUGUST 5th.													
YOST, Eddie	8	IN U.S. ARMY; YOST IS RELEASED FROM NATIONAL DEFENSE SERVICE LIST, JULY 25th.													
CANDINI, Milo	9	DISCHARGED FROM ARMY & REINSTATED FROM NDSL, AUGUST 14th.													

NOTE: *Neft & Cohen* shows Kuhel with 6 games at first base; but box scores and *Total Baseball* show 5 games.

* Hudson, Priddy & Scarborough all on National Defense Service List till April 26th, but are in Washington lineup before then, perhaps playing on military "terminal leave"..

WSH AL

	MAY					TIE 5/10, replay Aug 17		[1]	[2]			[1]	[2]	[1]	[2]
	5	6	7	8	9	10	11	12	12	14	15	17	17	19	19
	Cle	Cle	Cle	Det	Det	@Phl	@Phl	@Phl	@Phl	@Det	@Det	@Cle	@Cle	@Chi	@Chi
ROBERTSON, Sherry	5	5	5		5	5	5	5	5			5		5	
LEWIS, John (Buddy)	9	9	9	9	9	9	9	9	9	9	9	9	9	98	9
SPENCE, Stan	8	8	8	8	8	8	8	8	8	8	8	8	8	8	
TRAVIS, Cecil	6	6	6	6	6	6	6	6	6	6	6	6	6	6	6
HEATH, Jeff	7	7	7	7	7	7	7	7	7	7	7	7	7	7	7
VERNON, James (Mickey)	3	3	3	3	3	3	3	3	3	3	3	3	3	3	3
PRIDDY, Gerry	4	4	4	4	4	4	4	4	4	4	4	4	4	4	4
EVANS, Al	2	2	2	2	2	2	2	2		2	2	2	2	2	
WOLFF, Roger				SP		RP				SP				SP	
HUDSON, Sid					SP			RP						RP	
KUHEL, Joe						ph		ph							
BINKS, George						ph	ph	7						ph	8
MASTERSON, Walter		RP				RP	RP						SP		
CURTIS, Vern						RP									
WILSON, Maxie						RP									
PIERETTI, Marino	RP					RP									
KENNEDY, Bill G.	RP					RP	RP				RP				
SANFORD, John H. (Jack)						ph									
TORRES, Gilberto				5	5	5				5	5		5		5
SCARBOROUGH, Rae		SP						SP							
GOOLSBY, Ray															
GUERRA, Fermin (Mike)									2						2
HAEFNER, Milton (Mickey)			SP					SP				SP			
NIGGELING, Johnny				RP					SP						SP
EARLY, Jake	2														
LEONARD, Emil (Dutch)	SP					SP					SP				
COAN, Gil								ph						9	
MYATT, George														pr	
HITCHCOCK, Billy															
NEWSOM, Louis (Bobo or Buck)															
GRACE, Joe															
LaMACCHIA, Al															
WYNN, Early															
WADE, Jacob (Whistlin' Jake)															
YOST, Eddie															
CANDINI, Milo															

WSH AL

	MAY		[1]	[2]				[1]	[2]	JUNE					
	20	22	25	25	26	28	29	30	30	1	2	3	4	5	6
	@Chi	@StL	Phl	Phl	Phl	@NY	@NY	@Bos	@Bos	Det	Det	Det	Cle	Cle	Cle
ROBERTSON, Sherry		5	5	5	5	5	5								
LEWIS, John (Buddy)	9	9	9	9	9	9	9	9	9	9	9	9	9	9	
SPENCE, Stan	8	8	8	8	8	8	8	8	8	8	8	8	8	8	8
TRAVIS, Cecil	6	6	6	6	6	6	6	6	6	6	6	6	6	6	6
HEATH, Jeff	7	7	7	7	7	7	7	7	7	7	7	7	7	7	7
VERNON, James (Mickey)	3	3	3	3	3	3	3	3	3	3	3	3	3	3	3
PRIDDY, Gerry	4	4	4	4	4	4	4	4	4	4	4	4		4	4
EVANS, Al	2	2	2	2		2	2	2	ph	2	ph	2	2	2	
WOLFF, Roger				SP				*SP						SP	
HUDSON, Sid						RP	RP		RP						SP
KUHEL, Joe		ph		ph					ph						
BINKS, George		ph		ph									ph		9
MASTERSON, Walter		SP							SP						
CURTIS, Vern				RP				RP			RP				
WILSON, Maxie								RP			RP		RP		
PIERETTI, Marino									RP	RP			RP		
KENNEDY, Bill G.				RP				RP				RP			
SANFORD, John H. (Jack)		OPTIONED TO CHATTANOOGA, MAY 20th.													
TORRES, Gilberto	5														
SCARBOROUGH, Rae				RP					SP		RP				
GOOLSBY, Ray		OPTIONED TO CHATTANOOGA, MAY 20th.													
GUERRA, Fermin (Mike)				2	2				2	2	2				
HAEFNER, Milton (Mickey)			SP				SP						SP		
NIGGELING, Johnny					SP						SP				
EARLY, Jake															2
LEONARD, Emil (Dutch)	SP					SP						SP			
COAN, Gil							ph								
MYATT, George				ph				5		5		4	4	5	
HITCHCOCK, Billy									5		5	5	5		5
NEWSOM, Louis (Bobo or Buck)															
GRACE, Joe															
LaMACCHIA, Al															
WYNN, Early															
WADE, Jacob (Whistlin' Jake)															
YOST, Eddie															
CANDINI, Milo															

* Wolff, starting pitcher, bats 8th in the *Sporting News* box score May 30th (1), but that's probably a typographical error.

American League — WSH AL

	JUNE	[1]	[2]	[1]	[2]										[1]
	7	8	8	9	9	10	11	12	14	15	16	20	21	22	23
WSH AL	Chi	Chi	Chi	Chi	Chi	StL	StL	StL	@Det	@Det	@Det	@Cle	@StL	@StL	@StL
ROBERTSON, Sherry								ph	ph		ph				
LEWIS, John (Buddy)		ph		9	9	9	9	9	9	9	9	9	9	9	7
SPENCE, Stan	8	8	8	8	8	8	8	8	8	8	8	8	8	8	8
TRAVIS, Cecil	6	6	6	6	6	6	6	6	6	6	6	6	6	6	6
HEATH, Jeff	7	7	7	7	7	7	7	7	7	7	TRADED TO THE BROWNS.				
VERNON, James (Mickey)	3	3	3	3	3	3	3	3	3	3	3	3	3	3	3
PRIDDY, Gerry	4	4	4	4	4	4	4	4	4	4	4	4	4	4	4
EVANS, Al	2			2	ph	2		2	2			2	2	2	2
WOLFF, Roger						SP					SP				
HUDSON, Sid							SP				RP				
KUHEL, Joe									TO THE WHITE SOX, JUNE 13th.						
BINKS, George	9	9	9				ph	ph							
MASTERSON, Walter												RP			
CURTIS, Vern															
WILSON, Maxie			RP		RP				OPTIONED TO CHATTANOOGA, 6/13.						
PIERETTI, Marino			RP						RP					RP	
KENNEDY, Bill G.			SP												
SANFORD, John H. (Jack)															
TORRES, Gilberto			RP		ph									RP	
SCARBOROUGH, Rae		RP					RP		RP					RP	
GOOLSBY, Ray															
GUERRA, Fermin (Mike)		2			2					2	2				
HAEFNER, Milton (Mickey)				SP					SP						SP
NIGGELING, Johnny		SP												SP	
EARLY, Jake		2	2				2				2				
LEONARD, Emil (Dutch)				SP						SP			SP		
COAN, Gil		pr	9					ph			7	7	7	7	
MYATT, George											ph		5	5	
HITCHCOCK, Billy	5	5	5	5	5	5	5	5	5	5	5	5		5	5
NEWSOM, Louis (Bobo or Buck)	SP							SP			SP				
GRACE, Joe															9
LaMACCHIA, Al															
WYNN, Early															
WADE, Jacob (Whistlin' Jake)															
YOST, Eddie															
CANDINI, Milo															

		JUNE	[2]					[1]	[2]	JULY	[1]	[2]		[1]	[2]
		23	24	25	26	28	29	30	30	3	4	4	5	6	7	7
WSH AL		@StL	@Chi	@Chi	@Chi	@Bos	@Bos	@Bos	@Bos	@Phl	NY	NY	NY	Bos	Bos	Bos
ROBERTSON, Sherry							6									
LEWIS, John (Buddy)		7	7	7	7	7	7	7	9	9	9	9	9	9	9	9
SPENCE, Stan		8	8	8	8	8	8	8	8	8	8	8	8	8	8	8
TRAVIS, Cecil		6	6	6	6	6	*6	6	6	6	6	6	6		6	ph
HEATH, Jeff		TRADED FOR LAMACCHIA & GRACE, JUNE 15th.
VERNON, James (Mickey)		3	3	3	3	3	3	3	3	3	3	3	3	3	3	3
PRIDDY, Gerry		4	4	4	4	4	4	4	4	4	4	4	4	4	4	4
EVANS, Al		ph	2		2	ph		2				2		2		2
WOLFF, Roger			RP			SP						SP				
HUDSON, Sid		SP			RP					SP					SP	
KUHEL, Joe		(KUHEL REQUESTED HIS RELEASE, THEN SIGNED WITH CHICAGO).
BINKS, George				ph			ph	ph							ph	
MASTERSON, Walter			SP			SP	RP									SP
CURTIS, Vern							RP						RP		RP	
WILSON, Maxie																
PIERETTI, Marino						RP		RP								RP
KENNEDY, Bill G.		RP		RP								RP			RP	
SANFORD, John H. (Jack)																
TORRES, Gilberto		ph	ph		ph	6	RP					ph		6	6	6
SCARBOROUGH, Rae			RP			RP						RP			RP	
GOOLSBY, Ray																
GUERRA, Fermin (Mike)					ph	2			2		2				pr	
HAEFNER, Milton (Mickey)				RP				SP						SP		
NIGGELING, Johnny		RELEASED JUNE 25th. SIGNS WITH BRAVES JULY 1st.
EARLY, Jake		2		2			2	2		2			2		2	
LEONARD, Emil (Dutch)					SP						SP					RP
COAN, Gil		ph						7	7						ph	ph
MYATT, George		ph			5		*5									
HITCHCOCK, Billy		5	5	5	5	5	*56	5	5	5	5	5	5	5	5	5
NEWSOM, Louis (Bobo or Buck)			SP				SP					SP				RP
GRACE, Joe		9	9	9	9	9	9	9		7	7	7	7	7	7	7
LaMACCHIA, Al		RP					RP									
WYNN, Early																
WADE, Jacob (Whistlin' Jake)																
YOST, Eddie																
CANDINI, Milo																

* June 29th, in *TSN* box score, Hitchcock listed at 3b-SS, with no other 3b. Myatt replaces Travis but is listed at 2B: assume 3B instead.

WSH AL	JULY 11 Chi	13 Chi	13 Chi	[1] 14 StL	[2] 14 StL	15 StL	16 StL	17 Det	18 Det	19 Det	20 Cle	[1] 21 Cle	[2] 21 Cle	23 @Det	24 @Det
ROBERTSON, Sherry		ph						9			ph		6		56
LEWIS, John (Buddy)	9	9	9	9	9	9	9	9	9	9	9	9	9	9	9
SPENCE, Stan	8	8	8	8	8	8	8	8	8	8	8	8	8	8	8
TRAVIS, Cecil		6	ph	5	5	5	5	5	5		5	6			5
HEATH, Jeff															
VERNON, James (Mickey)	3	3	3	3	3	3	3	3	3	3	3	3	3	3	3
PRIDDY, Gerry	4	4	4	4	4	4	4	4	4	4	4	4	4	4	4
EVANS, Al	2	2	ph	2						2		2		2	
WOLFF, Roger										RP					
HUDSON, Sid				SP							SP				
KUHEL, Joe															
BINKS, George		87	7				ph	8			ph		ph		7
MASTERSON, Walter			RP							RP					
CURTIS, Vern											RP			TO BUFF.	
WILSON, Maxie															
PIERETTI, Marino			RP				RP			RP				RP	
KENNEDY, Bill G.							SP								
SANFORD, John H. (Jack)															
TORRES, Gilberto	6	6	6	6	6	6	6	6	6	6	6	6	6	6	6
SCARBOROUGH, Rae				SP						SP					
GOOLSBY, Ray															
GUERRA, Fermin (Mike)			2					pr			pr			ph	
HAEFNER, Milton (Mickey)	SP					SP					SP				
NIGGELING, Johnny															
EARLY, Jake					2	2	2	2	2		2		2		2
LEONARD, Emil (Dutch)			SP					SP					SP		
COAN, Gil	ph	ph		7	7	7	7	7	7	7	7	7	7	7	
MYATT, George		ph						ph							
HITCHCOCK, Billy	5	5	5	5						5		5	5	5	
NEWSOM, Louis (Bobo or Buck)		SP					SP						RP		SP
GRACE, Joe	7	7													
LaMACCHIA, Al						SOLD OUTRIGHT TO CHATTANOOGA, JULY 15th.									
WYNN, Early							RP			ph			SP		
WADE, Jacob (Whistlin' Jake)															
YOST, Eddie															
CANDINI, Milo															

American League

WSH AL

	JULY			[1]	[2]	[1]	[2]			AUG			[1]	[2]	
	25	26	27	28	28	29	29	30	31	1	2	3	4	4	7
	@Det	@Cle	@Cle	@Cle	@Cle	@Cle	@Cle	@StL	@StL	@StL	@Chi	@Chi	@Chi	@Chi	NY
ROBERTSON, Sherry	5	5	56	6	56			5	ph						
LEWIS, John (Buddy)	9	9	9	9	ph	9	9	9	9	9	9	9	9		ph
SPENCE, Stan	8	8	8	8	8	8	8	8	8	8	8	8	8	8	8
TRAVIS, Cecil		5	5	5	5	ph			ph	5	5	5	5		
HEATH, Jeff															
VERNON, James (Mickey)	3	3	3	3	3	3	3	3	3	3	3	3	3	3	3
PRIDDY, Gerry	4	4	4	4	4	4	4	4	4	4	4	4	4	4	4
EVANS, Al			2		2	2	2	2					2		2
WOLFF, Roger															
HUDSON, Sid			SP						SP						
KUHEL, Joe															
BINKS, George	7	7	7	7	7							ph			
MASTERSON, Walter			RP		RP			RP				RP			
CURTIS, Vern	(DATE OF OPTION TO BUFFALO, JULY 22nd.)														
WILSON, Maxie															
PIERETTI, Marino						RP									
KENNEDY, Bill G.									RP						
SANFORD, John H. (Jack)															
TORRES, Gilberto	6	6	6	4	64	6	6	6	6		4			5	5
SCARBOROUGH, Rae	SP				SP						SP				
GOOLSBY, Ray															
GUERRA, Fermin (Mike)						ph								2	
HAEFNER, Milton (Mickey)		SP				SP						SP			
NIGGELING, Johnny															
EARLY, Jake	2	2	2	2		2			2	2	2	2			2
LEONARD, Emil (Dutch)				SP					SP						
COAN, Gil				ph	pr		pr	pr			ph	ph	7	7	
MYATT, George															
HITCHCOCK, Billy					5	5	5	5	6	6	6	6	6	6	
NEWSOM, Louis (Bobo or Buck)		SP								SP				SP	
GRACE, Joe		ph	ph	9	7	7	7	7	7	7	7	7	7	9	9
LaMACCHIA, Al															
WYNN, Early						SP							SP		
WADE, Jacob (Whistlin' Jake)															
YOST, Eddie															
CANDINI, Milo															

WSH AL	[1] 8 NY	[2] 8 NY	9 Phl	[1] 10 Phl	[2] 10 Phl	[1] 11 Phl	[2] 11 Phl	14 @NY	[1] 15 @NY	[2] 15 @NY	[1] 17 @Phl	[2] 17 @Phl (REPLAY of 5/10 TIE)	[1] 18 @Phl	[2] 18 @Phl	20 Cle
ROBERTSON, Sherry							ph						ph		
LEWIS, John (Buddy)		9	9	9	9	9	ph	9	9	9	9	9	9	9	9
SPENCE, Stan	8	8	8	8	8	8	8	8	8	ph	8	8	8	8	
TRAVIS, Cecil			5	5	ph	5	5	5		5	5	5	5		5
HEATH, Jeff															
VERNON, James (Mickey)	3	3	3	3	3	3	3	3	3	3	3	3	3	3	3
PRIDDY, Gerry	4	4	4	4	4	4	4	4	4	4	4	4	4	4	4
EVANS, Al									2			2		2	
WOLFF, Roger														SP	
HUDSON, Sid					SP			RP				RP		RP	
KUHEL, Joe															
BINKS, George		8			ph		8		8	ph	ph	ph			
MASTERSON, Walter	RP					RP	RP				RP				
CURTIS, Vern	RECALL ANNOUNCED AUGUST 13th.														
WILSON, Maxie															
PIERETTI, Marino		RP					RP					RP			
KENNEDY, Bill G.					RP		RP					RP			
SANFORD, John H. (Jack)															
TORRES, Gilberto	5	5			5								5	5	
SCARBOROUGH, Rae		SP					SP					SP			
GOOLSBY, Ray															
GUERRA, Fermin (Mike)	2				2		2								
HAEFNER, Milton (Mickey)			SP						SP						SP
NIGGELING, Johnny															
EARLY, Jake		2	2	2		2	2	2		2	2		2		2
LEONARD, Emil (Dutch)	SP								SP				SP		
COAN, Gil	7		7	7		7	7	7	7						
MYATT, George															
HITCHCOCK, Billy	6	6	6	6	6	6	6	6	6	6	6	6	6	6	6
NEWSOM, Louis (Bobo or Buck)					SP					SP					
GRACE, Joe	9	7			7		9	ph	9	7	7		7	7	7
LaMACCHIA, Al															
WYNN, Early		RP		SP			ph			SP					
WADE, Jacob (Whistlin' Jake)	RP						RP					RP			
YOST, Eddie	ph								5						
CANDINI, Milo															

American League

WSH AL	AUG 21 Cle	[1] 23 Det	[2] 23 Det	24 Det	25 StL	26 StL	27 StL	28 Chi	31 NY	SEP 1 NY	[1] 2 Phl	[2] 2 Phl	4 Bos	5 Bos	6 Bos
ROBERTSON, Sherry				ph	5			ph	6	6	5	5	6	6	6
LEWIS, John (Buddy)	9	9	9	9	9	9	9	9	9	9	9	9	9	9	9
SPENCE, Stan	8	8	8	8	8			ph	8	8	8	8	8	8	8
TRAVIS, Cecil	5	5	5	5	5	5	5	5	5	5		ph	5	5	
HEATH, Jeff															
VERNON, James (Mickey)	3	3	3	3	3	3	3	3	3	3	3	3	3	3	3
PRIDDY, Gerry	4	4	4	4	4	4	4	4	4	4	4	4	4	4	4
EVANS, Al	2	2			2		ph		2	2					2
WOLFF, Roger															
HUDSON, Sid			SP				SP						SP		
KUHEL, Joe															
BINKS, George				ph	ph	ph	8	8	8	ph	ph		ph	ph	
MASTERSON, Walter				RP						RP					
CURTIS, Vern		CURTIS WILL REPORT AT END OF BUFFALO'S SEASON, SEPTEMBER 8th.													
WILSON, Maxie		RECALL ANNOUNCED AUG. 19th, THEN SOLD OUTRIGHT TO CHATTANOOGA SEPT. 6th.													
PIERETTI, Marino					RP				RP			RP			
KENNEDY, Bill G.				RP						RP					
SANFORD, John H. (Jack)		RECALL ANNOUNCED AUG. 19th, BUT SANFORD IS THROUGH IN BIG LEAGUES.													
TORRES, Gilberto					6		5			6	6				6
SCARBOROUGH, Rae			SP						SP				SP		
GOOLSBY, Ray		RECALL ANNOUNCED AUG. 19th, BUT BRIEF BIG LEAGUE CAREER IS OVER.													
GUERRA, Fermin (Mike)					2	2	2	2	2	2		2		pr	
HAEFNER, Milton (Mickey)					SP					SP					
NIGGELING, Johnny															
EARLY, Jake		2	2	2							2		2	2	
LEONARD, Emil (Dutch)				SP								RP			
COAN, Gil		ph	ph	ph	ph		pr	ph	ph		ph		ph		
MYATT, George															
HITCHCOCK, Billy	6	6	6	6	6	6	6	6	6	6					
NEWSOM, Louis (Bobo or Buck)		SP					SP			SP					SP
GRACE, Joe	7	7	7	7	7	7	7	7	7	7	7	7	7	7	7
LaMACCHIA, Al															
WYNN, Early	SP			ph	ph	SP		ph			SP		RP		
WADE, Jacob (Whistlin' Jake)				RP											
YOST, Eddie															5
CANDINI, Milo					RP				RP						

WSH AL

	SEP 7 @NY	[1] 8 @NY	[2] 8 @NY	10 @Chi	11 @Chi	12 @StL	13 @StL	14 @StL	15 @Det	16 @Det	17 @Det	18 @Cle	19 @Cle	21 Bos	22 Bos
ROBERTSON, Sherry	ph	5	ph		ph			4	4	4	4	4	4	4	4
LEWIS, John (Buddy)	9	9	9	9	9	9	9	9	9	9	9	9	9	9	9
SPENCE, Stan	8	8	8	8	8	8	8	8	8	8	8	8	8	8	8
TRAVIS, Cecil	6		5		5	5	5	5	5	5	5	5	5	5	5
HEATH, Jeff															
VERNON, James (Mickey)	3	3	3	3	3	3	3	3	3	3	3	3	3	3	3
PRIDDY, Gerry	4	4	4	4	4	OUT WITH TORN KNEE CARTILAGE, SENT HOME.									
EVANS, Al	2		2	2		2		2		2					
WOLFF, Roger									SP						
HUDSON, Sid			RP												
KUHEL, Joe															
BINKS, George	ph	ph					ph			ph	ph	9		ph	
MASTERSON, Walter							RP			RP					
CURTIS, Vern							RP								
WILSON, Maxie															
PIERETTI, Marino				SP							SP				
KENNEDY, Bill G.															
SANFORD, John H. (Jack)															
TORRES, Gilberto			4			4	4	4							
SCARBOROUGH, Rae			RP				SP						SP		
GOOLSBY, Ray															
GUERRA, Fermin (Mike)	ph														
HAEFNER, Milton (Mickey)	SP		RP			SP						SP		RP	
NIGGELING, Johnny															
EARLY, Jake	2	2			2		2		2		2	2	2	2	2
LEONARD, Emil (Dutch)			SP								RP				
COAN, Gil	ph						ph			ph	ph				
MYATT, George															
HITCHCOCK, Billy	6	6	6	6	6	6	6	6	6	6	6	6	6	6	6
NEWSOM, Louis (Bobo or Buck)					SP					SP			SP		
GRACE, Joe	7	7	7	7	7	7	7	7	7	7	7	7	7	7	7
LaMACCHIA, Al															
WYNN, Early		SP					SP	ph	RP	ph	SP				SP
WADE, Jacob (Whistlin' Jake)	RP						RP								
YOST, Eddie	5	5		5		5		5							
CANDINI, Milo	RP				RP		RP		RP	RP				RP	

WSH AL	SEP [1] 25 @Phl	[2] 25 @Phl	26 @Phl	27 @Bos	28 @Bos	29 @Bos	155g
ROBERTSON, Sherry	4	4	4	4	4	4	
LEWIS, John (Buddy)	9	9	9	9	9	9	
SPENCE, Stan	8	8	8	8	8	8	
TRAVIS, Cecil	5	5	5	5	5	5	
HEATH, Jeff							
VERNON, James (Mickey)	3	3	3	3	3	3	
PRIDDY, Gerry							
EVANS, Al		2			2	2	
WOLFF, Roger	SP						
HUDSON, Sid				RP			
KUHEL, Joe							
BINKS, George				ph			
MASTERSON, Walter							
CURTIS, Vern							
WILSON, Maxie							
PIERETTI, Marino				RP			
KENNEDY, Bill G.							
SANFORD, John H. (Jack)							
TORRES, Gilberto							
SCARBOROUGH, Rae						SP	
GOOLSBY, Ray							
GUERRA, Fermin (Mike)							
HAEFNER, Milton (Mickey)			SP				
NIGGELING, Johnny							
EARLY, Jake	2		2	2			
LEONARD, Emil (Dutch)		SP					
COAN, Gil				ph			
MYATT, George							
HITCHCOCK, Billy	6	6	6	6	6	6	
NEWSOM, Louis (Bobo or Buck)				SP			
GRACE, Joe	7	7	7	7	7	7	
LaMACCHIA, Al							
WYNN, Early				ph	SP		
WADE, Jacob (Whistlin' Jake)							
YOST, Eddie							
CANDINI, Milo		RP		RP			

National League — The Grids

Wide vertical lines between dates separate Sunday & Monday.

		APRIL			[1]	[2]					[1]	[2]	MAY	[1]	[2]
	G	16	17	20	21	21	22	23	24	25	28	28	3	5	5
BOS NL	154	Brk	Brk	@Phl	@Phl	@Phl	@Brk	@Brk	@NY	@NY	Phl	Phl	@Pts	@StL	@StL
RYAN, Connie	143	4	4	4	4	4	4	4	4	4	4	4	4	4	4
HOPP, Johnny	129	8	8	8	8	ph		8	8	8	8	8	3	83	3
HOLMES, Tommy	149	9	9	9	9	9	9	9	9	9	9	9	9	9	9
ROWELL, Carvel ('Bama)	95	7	7	7	7	7	7	7	7	7	7	7			7
McCARTHY, Johnny	2	3	3	SOLD OUTRIGHT TO MINNEAPOLIS, APRIL 19th.											
MASI, Phil	133	2	2	2	2	2	2	2	2	2		2	2	2	
ROBERGE, Al (Skippy)	48	5	5	5	5	5	5	5	5	5	5	5	5	5	5
CULLER, Dick	134	6	6	6	6								ph	ph	
SAIN, Johnny	40	SP			SP						SP	SP			
SISTI, Sebastian (Sibby)	1		pr	OPTIONED TO INDIANAPOLIS, APRIL 18th.											
WEST, Max	1		h3	TO CINCINNATI FOR KONSTANTY & CASH, APRIL 19th.											
WORKMAN, Chuck	25		ph	8	8	8	ph								
WIETELMANN, Wm. (Whitey)	44		6		5	6	6	6	6	6	6	6	6	6	6
WRIGHT, Ed	36		SP		RP			SP							
WALLACE, Jim (Lefty)	27		RP				SP							RP	
POLAND, Hugh	4		ph			2									
SANDERS, Ray	80	*		3	3	3	3	3	3	3	3	3		3	HBP.
LEE, Bill	25		SP						SP				SP		
GILLENWATER, Carden	99			8	pr							9	8	8	8
FERNANDEZ, Froilan (Nanny)	115					5			7	7	7	7	7	7	7
HUTCHINGS, Johnny	1				SP								TO INDY, MAY 2nd.		
SINGLETON, Elmer	16				RP								RP		
POSEDEL, Bill	19						RP		RP						
WILLIAMS, Bob (Ace)	1						RP								
HENDRICKSON, Don	2						RP		RP				TO K.C., MAY 3rd.		
COOPER, Mort	28							SP		SP					SP
HOFFERTH, Stew	20											2	ph	ph	2
JAVERY, Alva (Al)	2												RP		
KONSTANTY, Jim	10	**													RP
ROSER, Emerson (Steve)	14	PURCHASED FROM THE YANKEES, MAY 3rd.													
REID, Earl	2														
JOHNSON, Silas (Si)	28	RELEASED BY PHILLIES & SIGNED BY BRAVES, APRIL 29th.													
WHITE, Ernie	14	RELEASED BY THE CARDINALS MAY 13th, SIGNED BY THE BRAVES MAY 15th.													
DETWEILER, Bob (Ducky)	1										TO INDIANAPOLIS, APRIL 26th.				
McCORMICK, Mike	59	PURCHASED FROM CINCINNATI, JUNE 3rd.													
LITWHILER, Danny	79	PURCHASED FROM ST. LOUIS, JUNE 9th.													
BARRETT, Johnny	24	FROM PITTSBURGH, IN TRADE FOR WORKMAN, JUNE 12th.													
HERMAN, Billy	75	FROM THE DODGERS, IN TRADE FOR HOFFERTH, JUNE 15th.													
PADGETT, Don	44	PURCHASED FROM BROOKLYN ON WAIVERS, JUNE 12th.													
SPAHN, Warren	24	DISCHARGED FROM ARMY JUNE 11th (REINSTATED FROM NDSL MAY 29th).													
BARRETT, Frank	23	PURCHASED OUTRIGHT FROM LOUISVILLE, JUNE 28th.													
NIGGELING, Johnny	8	RELEASED BY THE SENATORS, SIGNED AS A FREE AGENT JULY 1st.													
O'DEA, Ken	12	PURCHASED FROM THE CARDINALS ON WAIVERS, JULY 8th.													
DARK, Alvin	15	EX-LSU GRID STAR, DISCHARGED FROM THE ARMY, SIGNED BY THE BRAVES JULY 4th.													
BRADY, Bob	3	PROMOTED FROM INDIANAPOLIS, AUGUST 19th.													
NEILL, Tommy	13	SOUTHERN ASSOCIATION MVP AT BIRMINGHAM, PURCHASED SEPTEMBER 7th.													
MULLIGAN, Dick	4	OBTAINED ON WAIVERS FROM THE PHILLIES, SEPTEMBER 18th.													
PHILLIPS, Damon	2	FROM THE ARMY SEPTEMBER 10th, REINSTATED FROM NDSL SEPTEMBER 21st.													

* April 16, Sanders from Cards w/ pitcher Matt (Max) Surkont for INF Tommy Nelson & est. $40,000. Nelson sent to Columbus (AA), sore-armed Surkont returned to St.L.

** Konstanty obtained (with cash) from Cincinnati April 19th, for outfielder-first baseman Max West. Konstanty didn't play for the Reds.

BOS NL

	MAY				[1]	[2]					[1]	[2]		
	7	8	9	10	11	12	12	13	14	16	17	19	19	20	22
	@StL	@Chi	@Chi	@Brk	NY	NY	NY	NY	Pts	StL	StL	Chi	Chi	Chi	Cin
RYAN, Connie	4	4	4	4	4	4	4	4	4	4	4	4	4	4	4
HOPP, Johnny	3	3	3	8	8	8	8	ph						ph	8
HOLMES, Tommy	9	8	9	9	9	9	9	9	9	9	9	9	9	9	9
ROWELL, Carvel ('Bama)	7	7	7	7		7	7	7	7	7	7	7	7	7	
McCARTHY, Johnny															
MASI, Phil	2	2	ph		ph	2	2	2		ph	2		2	ph	2
ROBERGE, Al (Skippy)	5	5	5	5	5	5	5	5	5	5	5	5	5	5	5
CULLER, Dick			6		6	6	6	6	6	6	6	6	6	6	6
SAIN, Johnny	SP				SP					pr	SP				SP
SISTI, Sebastian (Sibby)															
WEST, Max															
WORKMAN, Chuck	8	9		7		ph	ph	8		ph		ph	ph	ph	
WIETELMANN, Wm. (Whitey)	6	h4		ph	6	ph		5		ph		6		h4	
WRIGHT, Ed	RP	RP					SP							RP	
WALLACE, Jim (Lefty)			SP						SP		SP				
POLAND, Hugh	ph	2	OPTIONED TO SEATTLE, MAY 8th.												
SANDERS, Ray		INJURED HAND.		3	3	3	3	3	3	3	3	3	3	3	3
LEE, Bill						SP							SP		
GILLENWATER, Carden	ph	ph	8		ph				8	8	8	8	8	8	8
FERNANDEZ, Froilan (Nanny)	ph	6	67	6	7		75	6		h6			5	ph	7
HUTCHINGS, Johnny		(HUTCHINGS WAS RELEASED OUTRIGHT TO INDIANAPOLIS.)													
SINGLETON, Elmer		RP								RP				pr	
POSEDEL, Bill													RP	RP	
WILLIAMS, Bob (Ace)				OPTIONED TO SEATTLE, MAY 8th.											
HENDRICKSON, Don			(HENDRICKSON WAS SOLD OUTRIGHT TO KANSAS CITY.)												
COOPER, Mort			SP						SP				SP		
HOFFERTH, Stew		ph	2	2	2		2	ph	2	2		2		2	
JAVERY, Alva (Al)		SP													
KONSTANTY, Jim	RP							SP		RP					
ROSER, Emerson (Steve)	RP				RP			RP							
REID, Earl		RP						RP							
JOHNSON, Silas (Si)								RP		RP		RP			
WHITE, Ernie														pr	
DETWEILER, Bob (Ducky)					(WILL BE RECALLED FROM INDIANAPOLIS, MAY 25th.)										
McCORMICK, Mike															
LITWHILER, Danny															
BARRETT, Johnny															
HERMAN, Billy															
PADGETT, Don															
SPAHN, Warren															
BARRETT, Frank															
NIGGELING, Johnny															
O'DEA, Ken															
DARK, Alvin															
BRADY, Bob															
NEILL, Tommy															
MULLIGAN, Dick															
PHILLIPS, Damon															

BOS NL

	MAY		[1]	[2]			[1]	[2]	JUNE	[1]	[2]					
	24	25	26	26	29	30	30	1	2	2	4	5	6	7	8
BOS NL	@NY	@NY	@NY	@NY	@Phl	@Brk	@Brk	@Chi	@Chi	@Chi	@StL	@StL	@StL	@Cin	@Cin
RYAN, Connie	4	ph	4	4	4	4	4	4	4	4	4	4	4	4	4
HOPP, Johnny	8	8			8	8	8	8	8	8		8	3	3	3
HOLMES, Tommy	9	9	9	9	9	9	9	9	9	9	9	9	9	9	9
ROWELL, Carvel ('Bama)					7	7	7							7	7
McCARTHY, Johnny															
MASI, Phil	2	ph	2	2	2		2	2	2		2	2	2	2	2
ROBERGE, Al (Skippy)	5	5	5	5	5	5	5		5	5	5	5	5	5	5
CULLER, Dick	6	6	6	6	6		6		6	6	6	6	6	6	6
SAIN, Johnny					SP						SP				
SISTI, Sebastian (Sibby)															
WEST, Max															
WORKMAN, Chuck	7	ph	7	7	ph		ph			ph					ph
WIETELMANN, Wm. (Whitey)		4	ph	ph		ph		ph			ph				ph
WRIGHT, Ed	SP						SP					SP			
WALLACE, Jim (Lefty)		SP		RP		SP				RP	RP				RP
POLAND, Hugh															
SANDERS, Ray	3	3	3	3	3	3	3	3	3	3	3	3			
LEE, Bill			SP				SP								SP
GILLENWATER, Carden		8	8	8				7	87	7	7	7	7		
FERNANDEZ, Froilan (Nanny)		7		ph		6	6	6	7		ph		ph		
HUTCHINGS, Johnny															
SINGLETON, Elmer			SP				RP						SP		
POSEDEL, Bill			RP										RP		
WILLIAMS, Bob (Ace)															
HENDRICKSON, Don															
COOPER, Mort								SP						SP	
HOFFERTH, Stew		2			ph	2				2					
JAVERY, Alva (Al)	RELEASED TO TORONTO 5/22, RETURNED 6/11. OPTIONED TO LITTLE ROCK JUNE 15th..														
KONSTANTY, Jim			RP	RP	RP		RP				RP				RP
ROSER, Emerson (Steve)		RP		RP		RP		RP					RP		
REID, Earl			OPTIONED TO INDIANAPOLIS, MAY 25th.												
JOHNSON, Silas (Si)		RP				RP				SP					RP
WHITE, Ernie															RP
DETWEILER, Bob (Ducky)									ph						
McCORMICK, Mike											8		8	8	8
LITWHILER, Danny															
BARRETT, Johnny															
HERMAN, Billy															
PADGETT, Don															
SPAHN, Warren															
BARRETT, Frank															
NIGGELING, Johnny															
O'DEA, Ken															
DARK, Alvin															
BRADY, Bob															
NEILL, Tommy															
MULLIGAN, Dick															
PHILLIPS, Damon															

	JUNE	[1]	[2]					[1]	[2]	[1]	[2]					[1]
		9	9	10	11	14	15	16	16	17	17	19	20	21	22	23
BOS NL		@Cin	@Cin	@Pts	@Pts	Cin	Cin	Cin	Cin	StL	StL	StL	StL	Pts	Pts	Pts
RYAN, Connie		4	4	4	4	4	4	4	4	4	4			5	5	5
HOPP, Johnny		8	3		8	8	8	8	8	83	3	3	3	3	3	3
HOLMES, Tommy		9	9	9	9	9	9	9	9	9	9	9	9	9	9	9
ROWELL, Carvel ('Bama)		ph	7	7	7	7	7		7	7		7	7		8	7
McCARTHY, Johnny																
MASI, Phil		2		2	2	2		2	2	2	2	2	2	2	2	2
ROBERGE, Al (Skippy)		5	5	5			5	SOLD TO INDIANAPOLIS, JUNE 15th.								
CULLER, Dick		6	6	6	6	6	6	6	6	6	6	6	6	6	6	6
SAIN, Johnny		SP				SP						SP				
SISTI, Sebastian (Sibby)																
WEST, Max																
WORKMAN, Chuck		9	8			TO PITTSBURGH FOR JOHNNY BARRETT, JUNE 12th.										
WIETELMANN, Wm. (Whitey)		5	5		5	5	56									
WRIGHT, Ed			SP				SP					SP				
WALLACE, Jim (Lefty)												RP	RP			
POLAND, Hugh																
SANDERS, Ray		3	*3	3	3	3	3	3	3	3		INJURED ANKLE.			ph	
LEE, Bill											SP					SP
GILLENWATER, Carden		7		7	ph				ph	ph	ph					7
FERNANDEZ, Froilan (Nanny)		7			ph				ph							
HUTCHINGS, Johnny																
SINGLETON, Elmer					RP				RP			RP				
POSEDEL, Bill				RP			RP			RP						RP
WILLIAMS, Bob (Ace)																
HENDRICKSON, Don																
COOPER, Mort					SP				SP				SP			
HOFFERTH, Stew			2				2	TRADED TO BROOKLYN FOR HERMAN, JUNE 15th.								
JAVERY, Alva (Al)																
KONSTANTY, Jim							SOLD OUTRIGHT TO TORONTO, JUNE 14th.									
ROSER, Emerson (Steve)				RP					RP		RP			RP		
REID, Earl																
JOHNSON, Silas (Si)			SP			SP								SP		
WHITE, Ernie									SP							
DETWEILER, Bob (Ducky)							OPTIONED TO ROCHESTER, JUNE 14th.									
McCORMICK, Mike		87			8	ph		ph	87		8	8	8	8	pr	8
LITWHILER, Danny						ph	7		ph	7	5	5	7	7	7	7
BARRETT, Johnny						ph			ph	7	8	INJURED KNEE.				
HERMAN, Billy							5	5	5	5	4	4	4	4	4	4
PADGETT, Don										2		ph	ph		2	
SPAHN, Warren										RP		RP				
BARRETT, Frank																
NIGGELING, Johnny																
O'DEA, Ken																
DARK, Alvin																
BRADY, Bob																
NEILL, Tommy																
MULLIGAN, Dick																
PHILLIPS, Damon																

* June 9th (Game 2), Sanders is in box score as Catcher. He never caught during his big league career.

BOS NL	JUNE [2] 23 Pts	24 Chi	25 Chi	26 Chi	27 @Brk	28 @Brk	29 @Brk	30 @Brk	JULY 2 NY	3 Phl	[1] 4 Phl	[2] 4 Phl	6 Brk	[1] 7 Brk	[2] 7 Brk
RYAN, Connie	5	5	5	5	4	4	5	5	5	5	5	4	5	5	5
HOPP, Johnny	3	3	8	3	ph	ph	8	8		3	3	3	8	38	3
HOLMES, Tommy	9	9	9	9	9	9	9	9	9	9	9	9	9	9	9
ROWELL, Carvel ('Bama)			7	8	ph		7	7	ph			7	7	7	
McCARTHY, Johnny															
MASI, Phil	2	2	2	2	2	2	2	2	2	2	2	2	2	2	2
ROBERGE, Al (Skippy)															
CULLER, Dick	6	6	6	6	6	6	6	LEG INJURY.			6	6			
SAIN, Johnny	SP					SP	ph			SP					SP
SISTI, Sebastian (Sibby)															
WEST, Max															
WORKMAN, Chuck															
WIETELMANN, Wm. (Whitey)							4		5			ph			
WRIGHT, Ed		SP					SP				SP				
WALLACE, Jim (Lefty)			RP	** OPTIONED TO INDIANAPOLIS 6/27. "DISAPPROVED", RETURNS 7/13.											
POLAND, Hugh															
SANDERS, Ray			3				3	3	3				3	3	
LEE, Bill							RP							RP	
GILLENWATER, Carden	8	8	ph	8	8	8	8		ph			ph	ph	ph	ph
FERNANDEZ, Froilan (Nanny)			5		5	5	6	6	6	6	6	5	56	6	6
HUTCHINGS, Johnny															
SINGLETON, Elmer						RP	RP	RP							
POSEDEL, Bill							RP								
WILLIAMS, Bob (Ace)															
HENDRICKSON, Don															
COOPER, Mort				SP				SP			SP				
HOFFERTH, Stew															
JAVERY, Alva (Al)															
KONSTANTY, Jim															
ROSER, Emerson (Steve)			SP				RP								
REID, Earl															
JOHNSON, Silas (Si)					RP							RP	RP		
WHITE, Ernie						RP									
DETWEILER, Bob (Ducky)															
McCORMICK, Mike				*	8	7	7	ph	8	8	8	8	ph	8	8
LITWHILER, Danny	7	7	ph	7	7	7	ph	ph	7	7	7	7	ph	7	7
BARRETT, Johnny	(BARRETT HAD BLOOD CLOT SURGERY ON HIS RIGHT KNEE, JUNE 21st.)														
HERMAN, Billy	4	4	4	4	3	3	4	4	4	4	4	4	4	4	4
PADGETT, Don			ph	2	ph	2	2	2				ph	ph	ph	
SPAHN, Warren			RP	SP					SP					SP	
BARRETT, Frank									RP	RP			RP	RP	
NIGGELING, Johnny													SP		
O'DEA, Ken															
DARK, Alvin															
BRADY, Bob															
NEILL, Tommy															
MULLIGAN, Dick															
PHILLIPS, Damon															

* June 26th, McCormick in *TSN* box score at first base. Doesn't play there in 1946. It appears he's confused with *Frank* McCormick, Phillies first baseman.

** Wallace's June 27th option to Indianapolis "disapproved" by Commissioner Chandler ("waivers not in effect"). He returns to Boston for remainder of season.

BOS NL	JULY 11 @Cin	12 @Cin	[1] 13 @Cin	[2] 13 @Cin	[1] 14 @Pts	[2] 14 @Pts	15 @Pts	16 @Pts	17 @Chi	18 @Chi	19 @Chi	20 @StL	[1] 21 @StL	[2] 21 @StL	24 Cin
RYAN, Connie	5	5	54	4	4	4	4	5	54	5	5	4	4	4	4
HOPP, Johnny	8	8	8	8		8	8	8	3	8	8	8	8		8
HOLMES, Tommy	9	9	9	9		9		9	9	9	9	9		ph	9
ROWELL, Carvel ('Bama)	7	7	7	7		7		7		7	7	7			7
McCARTHY, Johnny															
MASI, Phil	2	2	2	2	2		2	2	2	2			2	2	
ROBERGE, Al (Skippy)															
CULLER, Dick	6	6	6	6	6	6	6	6	6	6	6	6	6	6	6
SAIN, Johnny		SP	RP						SP			SP		ph	
SISTI, Sebastian (Sibby)															
WEST, Max															
WORKMAN, Chuck															
WIETELMANN, Wm. (Whitey)					5									ph	
WRIGHT, Ed	RP					SP			RP					RP	
WALLACE, Jim (Lefty)				RP		RP								RP	
POLAND, Hugh	(TRANSFERRED TO INDIANAPOLIS ON OPTION, JULY 15th; RELEASED OUTRIGHT, JULY 30th)														
SANDERS, Ray	3	3	3	3	3	3	3	3		3	3	3	3	3	3
LEE, Bill		SP							SP						SP
GILLENWATER, Carden					8		87		ph	8			ph	8	
FERNANDEZ, Froilan (Nanny)			5	5	56	5	5		5			5	5	5	5
HUTCHINGS, Johnny															
SINGLETON, Elmer														RP	
POSEDEL, Bill			RP												
WILLIAMS, Bob (Ace)															
HENDRICKSON, Don															
COOPER, Mort	SP							SP						SP	
HOFFERTH, Stew															
JAVERY, Alva (Al)															
KONSTANTY, Jim															
ROSER, Emerson (Steve)			OPTIONED TO INDIANAPOLIS, JULY 11th.												
REID, Earl															
JOHNSON, Silas (Si)			SP						RP						RP
WHITE, Ernie									RP					RP	
DETWEILER, Bob (Ducky)															
McCORMICK, Mike	ph		7		9	ph	9	7	8	9			9	9	ph
LITWHILER, Danny					7	ph	7		7	7		ph	7	7	ph
BARRETT, Johnny															
HERMAN, Billy	4	4	4					4	4	4	4				
PADGETT, Don						ph									ph
SPAHN, Warren					SP						SP		RP		
BARRETT, Frank	RP	RP			RP								RP		
NIGGELING, Johnny							SP						SP		
O'DEA, Ken			2	2		2		2		2	2	2			2
DARK, Alvin						pr		6							
BRADY, Bob															
NEILL, Tommy															
MULLIGAN, Dick															
PHILLIPS, Damon															

BOS NL

	JULY					AUG	[1]	[2]			[1]	[2]		[1]	[2]
	25	27	28	29	31	3	4	4	5	6	8	8	9	11	11
BOS NL	Cin	StL	StL	StL	Pts	Chi	Chi	Chi	Brk	@Phl	@Phl	@Phl	NY	NY	NY
RYAN, Connie	4	4	5	4	4		ph		5				4	4	
HOPP, Johnny	3	3	3	3	3	3	ph	38	3	8	8	ph			
HOLMES, Tommy			ph	9	9	9	9	9	9	9	9	9	9	9	ph
ROWELL, Carvel ('Bama)		7	ph	7	7	7	7	ph	ph	8	ph	8	8		8
McCARTHY, Johnny															
MASI, Phil	2	2	2			2		2	2		2	2	2	2	2
ROBERGE, Al (Skippy)															
CULLER, Dick	6	6	6	6	6	6	6	6	6	6	6	6	6	6	6
SAIN, Johnny	SP			SP					SP				SP		
SISTI, Sebastian (Sibby)															
WEST, Max															
WORKMAN, Chuck															
WIETELMANN, Wm. (Whitey)							6								
WRIGHT, Ed							RP		RP			SP			RP
WALLACE, Jim (Lefty)							RP	RP							SP
POLAND, Hugh															
SANDERS, Ray							3	h3	ph	3	3	3	3	3	3
LEE, Bill							SP			SP					
GILLENWATER, Carden	8	8	8	8	8	8	8	8	8	8	8	ph	8	8	ph
FERNANDEZ, Froilan (Nanny)	5	5		5	5	5	5	5	5	65	5	5	5	5	5
HUTCHINGS, Johnny															
SINGLETON, Elmer											RP				
POSEDEL, Bill									RP		RP	RP			
WILLIAMS, Bob (Ace)	(OPTION WAS TRANSFERRED TO INDIANAPOLIS, JULY 24th)														
HENDRICKSON, Don															
COOPER, Mort				SP					SP						
HOFFERTH, Stew															
JAVERY, Alva (Al)															
KONSTANTY, Jim															
ROSER, Emerson (Steve)															
REID, Earl															
JOHNSON, Silas (Si)									RP		RP	RP			
WHITE, Ernie															RP
DETWEILER, Bob (Ducky)															
McCORMICK, Mike	9	9	9				pr				ph	8		9	ph
LITWHILER, Danny	7	7	7				ph	7	7	7	7	7	7	7	7
BARRETT, Johnny															9
HERMAN, Billy	ph		4			4	4	4	4	4	4	4	3	4	4
PADGETT, Don							ph	ph	ph		ph	2			2
SPAHN, Warren	RP	SP				SP								SP	RP
BARRETT, Frank			RP						RP		RP				
NIGGELING, Johnny			SP						SP						
O'DEA, Ken				2	2		2			2	BROKEN FINGER.				
DARK, Alvin									6		6			6	
BRADY, Bob															
NEILL, Tommy															
MULLIGAN, Dick															
PHILLIPS, Damon															

BOS NL	AUG 14 Phl	[1] 15 Phl	[2] 15 Phl	[1] 18 @NY	[2] 18 @NY	20 @StL	21 @StL	22 @Chi	23 @Chi	24 @Chi	[1] 25 @Pts	[2] 25 @Pts	26 @Pts	27 @Pts	[1] 28 @Cin
RYAN, Connie	4	4	4	4	4	4	4	4		4	4	4	4	4	4
HOPP, Johnny		ph		3		3	3	3	3	3	3	3	3	3	3
HOLMES, Tommy	9	9	9	9	9	9	9	9	9	9	9	9	9	9	9
ROWELL, Carvel ('Bama)	8	8		7				8	ph	ph	8	8		7	
McCARTHY, Johnny															
MASI, Phil	2	ph	2		2	2	2	2	2		2	2	2	2	2
ROBERGE, Al (Skippy)															
CULLER, Dick	6	6	6	6	6	6	6	6	6	6	6	6	6	6	6
SAIN, Johnny	RP	RP			SP				SP						SP
SISTI, Sebastian (Sibby)															
WEST, Max															
WORKMAN, Chuck															
WIETELMANN, Wm. (Whitey)		ph								RP					
WRIGHT, Ed		SP									SP				
WALLACE, Jim (Lefty)		RP								RP					
POLAND, Hugh															
SANDERS, Ray	3	3	3	3	3	3	3	BROKEN ARM, OUT REST OF SEASON.							
LEE, Bill			SP	RP						SP					
GILLENWATER, Carden	8	ph	8					8							
FERNANDEZ, Froilan (Nanny)	5	5	5	5	5	5	5	5	5	5	5	5	5	5	5
HUTCHINGS, Johnny															
SINGLETON, Elmer	TO INDIANAPOLIS, AUGUST 14th.														
POSEDEL, Bill		RP													
WILLIAMS, Bob (Ace)															
HENDRICKSON, Don															
COOPER, Mort	SP														
HOFFERTH, Stew															
JAVERY, Alva (Al)															
KONSTANTY, Jim															
ROSER, Emerson (Steve)															
REID, Earl															
JOHNSON, Silas (Si)	RP	RP					SP					SP			
WHITE, Ernie		RP								RP					
DETWEILER, Bob (Ducky)															
McCORMICK, Mike		7			8	8	8	8		8	8		8	8	8
LITWHILER, Danny	7	7	7	ph	7	7	7	7	7	7	7	7	7	7	7
BARRETT, Johnny		9		ph					8	8					
HERMAN, Billy						ph		3	4	4	3	4	3	3	3
PADGETT, Don		2		2					ph	ph		2			
SPAHN, Warren			SP					SP				RP		SP	
BARRETT, Frank		RP		RP		RP					RP				
NIGGELING, Johnny						SP						SP			
O'DEA, Ken	(MISDIAGNOSIS ALLOWED HIM TO PLAY 2 MORE GAMES, THEN OUT FOR THE SEASON.)														
DARK, Alvin		6		6	6					6				6	
BRADY, Bob										2					
NEILL, Tommy															
MULLIGAN, Dick															
PHILLIPS, Damon															

BOS NL	AUG 28 @Cin	29 @Cin	[2] 31 @Phl	[1] 31 @Phl	[2] 1 @Phl	[1] 1 @Phl	[2] 2 NY	[1] 2 NY	3 NY	4 Brk	5 Brk	7 Phl	[1] 8 Phl	[2] 8 Phl	10 Chi
RYAN, Connie		4	4	4	4		54	4	4	4	4	4	4	4	4
HOPP, Johnny	3	3	3	3	3	3	3	3	3	3	3	8	8	3	8
HOLMES, Tommy	9	9	9	9	9	9	9	9	9	9	9	9	9	7	9
ROWELL, Carvel ('Bama)	8	8	78	7	7	7	7	7	7		7	7		8	
McCARTHY, Johnny															
MASI, Phil	2	2	ph	2	2	2	2	2	2	2	2		2	ph	2
ROBERGE, Al (Skippy)	(ROBERGE RECALLED FROM INDIANAPOLIS AUG. 27th, BUT BIG LEAGUE CAREER IS OVER.)														
CULLER, Dick	6	6	6	6	6	6	6	6	6	6	6	6	6	6	6
SAIN, Johnny				SP					SP						SP
SISTI, Sebastian (Sibby)	(SISTI RECALLED FROM INDIANAPOLIS AUG. 27th, BUT DOESN'T PLAY AGAIN TILL 1947.)														
WEST, Max															
WORKMAN, Chuck															
WIETELMANN, Wm. (Whitey)			RP						ph						
WRIGHT, Ed		SP					SP						RP	RP	
WALLACE, Jim (Lefty)							RP	RP							
POLAND, Hugh															
SANDERS, Ray	(SANDERS' INJURY SHELVES HIM THROUGH 1947; PLAYS BRIEFLY IN 1948-49.)														
LEE, Bill							SP						SP		
GILLENWATER, Carden			8	8	8	8	8	8	8	8	8		ph	8	8
FERNANDEZ, Froilan (Nanny)	5	5	5	5	5	5	75	5	5	7	5	5	5	5	5
HUTCHINGS, Johnny															
SINGLETON, Elmer	(SINGLETON RECALLED FROM INDY AUG. 27, BUT WON'T REAPPEAR WITH PIRATES TILL '47.)														
POSEDEL, Bill			RP												
WILLIAMS, Bob (Ace)	(RECALLED AUGUST 27th, BUT WILLIAMS' MAJOR LEAGUE CAREER IS OVER.)														
HENDRICKSON, Don															
COOPER, Mort	SP					SP		RP				SP			
HOFFERTH, Stew															
JAVERY, Alva (Al)	(JAVERY RECALLED FROM LITTLE ROCK AUG. 27th. SOLD TO MILWAUKEE ON SEP. 9th.)														
KONSTANTY, Jim															
ROSER, Emerson (Steve)	(ROSER RECALLED FROM INDIANAPOLIS AUG. 27th, BUT BIG LEAGUE CAREER IS OVER.)														
REID, Earl	(REID RECALLED FROM INDIANAPOLIS AUG. 27th, BUT MAJOR LEAGUE CAREER IS OVER.)														
JOHNSON, Silas (Si)			SP								SP				
WHITE, Ernie	RP						RP	pr							
DETWEILER, Bob (Ducky)	(RECALLED FROM ROCHESTER AUG. 27th; RELEASED OUTRIGHT TO HARTFORD SEPT. 11th)														
McCORMICK, Mike			8	8	TORN LEG LIGAMENTS; McCORMICK DOESN'T PLAY AGAIN IN 1946.										
LITWHILER, Danny	7	7	7		HIT BY PITCH; BREAKS CHEEKBONE.							7			
BARRETT, Johnny	ph		ph		8									9	
HERMAN, Billy	4	4	4	4		4	4		ph	5		3	3		3
PADGETT, Don	2	2	2		2			2				2		2	2
SPAHN, Warren			SP						SP						
BARRETT, Frank			RP					RP		RP				RP	
NIGGELING, Johnny						SP					RELEASED AT OWN REQUEST.				
O'DEA, Ken															
DARK, Alvin			6	6			7								6
BRADY, Bob														ph	
NEILL, Tommy															7
MULLIGAN, Dick															
PHILLIPS, Damon															

	SEP	9/11 TIE, NO REPLAY	[1]	[2]	[1]	[2]		[1]	[2]						[1]	[2]
BOS NL		11	12	12	13	13	14	15	15	16	17	18	19	21	22	22
		Chi	Pts	Pts	Pts	Pts	Pts	Cin	Cin	Cin	Cin	StL	StL	Brk	Brk	Brk
RYAN, Connie		4	4	4	4	4	4	4	4	4	4	4	4	4	4	4
HOPP, Johnny		3	pr				3	3	3	3	3	3	3	3	38	
HOLMES, Tommy		9	9	9	9	9	9	9	9	9	9	9	9	9	9	9
ROWELL, Carvel ('Bama)														ph		
McCARTHY, Johnny																
MASI, Phil		2	ph	2	2		2	2	2	2	2	2	2	2	2	2
ROBERGE, Al (Skippy)																
CULLER, Dick		6	6	6	6	6	6	6	6	6	6	6	6	6	6	6
SAIN, Johnny							SP					SP			SP	
SISTI, Sebastian (Sibby)																
WEST, Max																
WORKMAN, Chuck																
WIETELMANN, Wm. (Whitey)						RP										
WRIGHT, Ed				SP						SP				RP		RP
WALLACE, Jim (Lefty)		SP														SP
POLAND, Hugh																
SANDERS, Ray																
LEE, Bill						SP		SP						RP		
GILLENWATER, Carden		8		8	8		8	8	8	8	8	8	8	8	8	8
FERNANDEZ, Froilan (Nanny)		5	5	5	5	5	5	5	5	5	5	5	5	5	5	5
HUTCHINGS, Johnny																
SINGLETON, Elmer																
POSEDEL, Bill			RP			RP										
WILLIAMS, Bob (Ace)																
HENDRICKSON, Don																
COOPER, Mort					SP							SP				
HOFFERTH, Stew																
JAVERY, Alva (Al)																
KONSTANTY, Jim																
ROSER, Emerson (Steve)																
REID, Earl																
JOHNSON, Silas (Si)			SP								SP					
WHITE, Ernie		RP											RP			
DETWEILER, Bob (Ducky)																
McCORMICK, Mike																
LITWHILER, Danny		9	ph		7		7		7	7	7	7		7	7	7
BARRETT, Johnny		ph	8	8		8		8	8	8	8		h8		ph	
HERMAN, Billy		3	3	3	3	3								ph	3	3
PADGETT, Don		ph	2	2		2			2	2	2		ph	ph		
SPAHN, Warren		SP						SP					SP			
BARRETT, Frank		RP											RP			RP
NIGGELING, Johnny		(DATE OF RELEASE WAS SEPTEMBER 4th.)														
O'DEA, Ken		(O'DEA'S BIG LEAGUE CAREER IS FINISHED.)														
DARK, Alvin														pr		
BRADY, Bob					ph											
NEILL, Tommy		h7	7	7		7		7	7	7	7		7	ph	7	
MULLIGAN, Dick														RP		RP
PHILLIPS, Damon														ph		ph

	SEP	[1]	[2]			
BOS NL	25 @NY	26 @NY	26 @NY	28 @Brk	29 @Brk	154g
RYAN, Connie	4	4	4	4	4	
HOPP, Johnny	8		3	8	3	
HOLMES, Tommy	9	9	9	9	9	
ROWELL, Carvel ('Bama)						
McCARTHY, Johnny						
MASI, Phil	2	2	2	2	2	
ROBERGE, Al (Skippy)						
CULLER, Dick	6	6	6	6	6	
SAIN, Johnny				SP		
SISTI, Sebastian (Sibby)						
WEST, Max						
WORKMAN, Chuck						
WIETELMANN, Wm. (Whitey)						
WRIGHT, Ed			SP	RP		
WALLACE, Jim (Lefty)						
POLAND, Hugh						
SANDERS, Ray						
LEE, Bill						
GILLENWATER, Carden	8	8	8	ph	8	
FERNANDEZ, Froilan (Nanny)	5	5	5	5	5	
HUTCHINGS, Johnny						
SINGLETON, Elmer						
POSEDEL, Bill						
WILLIAMS, Bob (Ace)						
HENDRICKSON, Don						
COOPER, Mort		SP			SP	
HOFFERTH, Stew						
JAVERY, Alva (Al)						
KONSTANTY, Jim						
ROSER, Emerson (Steve)						
REID, Earl						
JOHNSON, Silas (Si)	SP			RP		
WHITE, Ernie						
DETWEILER, Bob (Ducky)						
McCORMICK, Mike						
LITWHILER, Danny	7	7		7	7	
BARRETT, Johnny			8			
HERMAN, Billy	3	3		3	3	
PADGETT, Don			2			
SPAHN, Warren			RP			
BARRETT, Frank			RP			
NIGGELING, Johnny						
O'DEA, Ken						
DARK, Alvin						
BRADY, Bob						
NEILL, Tommy			7			
MULLIGAN, Dick	RP			RP		
PHILLIPS, Damon						

National League

			APRIL								[1]	[2]	MAY		
	G	16	17	18	20	21	22	23	24	26	28	28	30	1	2
BRK NL	157	@Bos	@Bos	NY	NY	NY	Bos	Bos	@Phl	@Phl	@NY	@NY	@Chi	@Chi	@Chi
REESE, Pee Wee	152	6	6	6	6	6	6	6	6	6	6	6	6	6	6
WALKER, Fred (Dixie)	150	ph		9	9	9	9	9	9	9	9	9	9	9	9
HERMAN, Billy	47	4	4	4	4	4	4	4	4	4					ph
WHITMAN, Dick	104	7	7	7	7	7	7	7	7	7	7	7	7	8	7
REISER, Pete	122	ph	5	5	5	5	5	5	5	5	5	5	5	5	5
CASEY, Hugh	46	RP			RP		RP				RP		RP		
HERMANSKI, Gene	64	9	9	9	9						ph	ph		7	7
GRAHAM, Jack	2	3	3								SOLD TO THE GIANTS, APRIL 27.				
FURILLO, Carl	117	8	8	8	8	8	8	8	8	8	8	8	8		8
RIGGS, Lew	1	5									RELEASED, APRIL 27th.				
ANDERSON, Ferrell	79	2	2	2	2	2	2	2	2	2		2	2		2
ROSEN, Goodwin (Goody)	3	ph			ph		cf				SOLD TO THE GIANTS, APRIL 27.				
GREGG, Hal	26	SP							RP					SP	
GALAN, Augie	99	h7			93		7				ph	ph	7	3	3
SCHULTZ, Howie	90		3		3										
BEHRMAN, Hank	47		SP				RP					SP			
STEVENS, Ed	103	BAD TOOTH.	3	3	3	3	3	3	3	3	3	3	3		
LOMBARDI, Vic	43			SP							SP				pr
CORRIDEN, Johnny	1				pr		OPTIONED TO MOBILE, APRIL 22nd.								
STANKY, Eddie	144				4		ph			4	4	4	4	4	4
PADGETT, Don	19				ph		ph				2	ph	ph		
ROJEK, Stan	45				4										
RAMAZZOTTI, Bob	62	w/MONTREAL.			ph		ph			5		5			
HIGBE, Kirby	42				SP				SP		RP				SP
HATTEN, Joe	42					SP					SP				
BRANCA, Ralph	24						SP					RP			
DAVIS, Otis (Scat)	1	* FROM ST. LOUIS.					pr							NXT PAGE	
HEAD, Ed	13						**SP					SP			
NAYLOR, Earl	3	* FROM St. LOUIS.								pr					
HERRING, Art (Sandy)	35										RP				RP
DAVIS, Curt	1										RP			NXT PAGE	
MOULDER, Glen	1	(FROM NDSL, APRIL 15th.)									RP			NXT PAGE	
SANDLOCK, Mike	19											ph		2	
ROY, Jean-Pierre	3														
WEBBER, Les	11														
LAVAGETTO, Harry (Cookie)	88	SIDELINED AFTER ELBOW SURGERY DURING SPRING.													
BARNEY, Rex	16	DISCHARGED BY ARMY MAY 11th, REINSTATED FROM NDSL MAY 13th.													
MELTON, Rube	24	OUT OF ARMY MAY 18th, OFF NDSL MAY 20th, JOINS TEAM MAY 22nd.													
EDWARDS, Bruce	92	EARLY-SEASON STAR AT MOBILE, PROMOTED THROUGH MONTREAL, JUNE 21st.													
MEDWICK, Joe (Ducky)	41	FREE AGENT, SIGNS WITH BROOKLYN JUNE 25th.													
TEPSIC, Joe	15	FORMER PENN STATE GRID STAR & WAR VET, SIGNS JULY 8th.													
MIKSIS, Eddie	23	DISCHARGED BY ARMY, REINSTATED FROM NDSL JULY 12th.													
McLISH, Cal	1	DISCHARGED BY ARMY, REINSTATED FROM NDSL JULY 15th.													
MINNER, Paul	3	PURCHASED OUTRIGHT FROM MOBILE, SEPTEMBER 9th.													
TAYLOR, Harry	4	PURCHASED FROM ST. PAUL, SEPTEMBER 3rd.													

Ramazzotti promoted from Montreal, April 19th.   * Otis Davis bought from St. Louis April 19th, Naylor April 23rd. Neither played for St. Louis this year.

NOTE: On April 26th, former Brooklyn catcher Arnold (Mickey) Owen declared ineligible for signing with Mexican League.

National League — BRK NL

MAY	[1] 5 @Pts	[2] 5 @Pts	8 @Cin	9 @Cin	10 Bos	11 Phl	12 Phl	13 Phl	14 StL	15 StL	17 Pts	19 Cin	20 Cin	22 Chi	23 Chi
REESE, Pee Wee	6	6	6	6	6	6	6	6	6	6	6	6	6	6	6
WALKER, Fred (Dixie)	9	9	9	9	9	9	9	9	9	9	9	9	9	9	9
HERMAN, Billy	5	ph	5	5	5	5	5	4	4	4	4	5	5	54	5
WHITMAN, Dick	87	8		ph	ph	h7	7		pr		8	ph	8	7	8
REISER, Pete	58	5	8	8	8	8	8	8	8	8	8	8		ph	7
CASEY, Hugh		RP		RP		RP									RP
HERMANSKI, Gene	7	7		ph	ph	ph	9				9	7			ph
GRAHAM, Jack															
FURILLO, Carl			7			7	8		7	7	7			8	
RIGGS, Lew	(RIGGS SIGNS WITH MONTREAL, FIRST GAME FOR THE ROYALS IS MAY 19th.)														
ANDERSON, Ferrell	2	2	2	2	2	2	2	2	2	2	2	2	2	2	2
ROSEN, Goodwin (Goody)															
GREGG, Hal		SP			SP			SP	PULLED MUSCLE IN PITCHING ARM.						
GALAN, Augie	3	3	37	7	7	73	7	7	3	3	37	78	7	7	7
SCHULTZ, Howie					3	3								3	3
BEHRMAN, Hank		RP			RP			RP			RP				SP
STEVENS, Ed		ph	3	3	3	3	3	3			3	3	3		3
LOMBARDI, Vic	SP		RP	pr			SP		RP			SP			
CORRIDEN, Johnny															
STANKY, Eddie	4	4	4	4	4	4	4		ph		4	4	4		4
PADGETT, Don		ph	pr	h2	ph	ph			2		2	ph			ph
ROJEK, Stan	ph	pr	h4	pr		6			ph		6				
RAMAZZOTTI, Bob		pr	ph		5		5	5	5	ph	5		5		
HIGBE, Kirby			SP			RP						RP		RP	
HATTEN, Joe				RP	RP	RP			RP	RP				SP	
BRANCA, Ralph				RP		SP				SP					
DAVIS, Otis (Scat)	...RELEASED OUTRIGHT TO MONTREAL, MAY 1st.														
HEAD, Ed							SP			SP	SORE ARM.			
NAYLOR, Earl			ph				ph			TO MONTREAL, MAY 18.				
HERRING, Art (Sandy)			RP	RP			RP			RP					RP
DAVIS, Curt	...RELEASED OUTRIGHT, SIGNED WITH MONTREAL, MAY 1st.														
MOULDER, Glen	...RELEASED OUTRIGHT TO MONTREAL, MAY 1st.														
SANDLOCK, Mike	2	2			2	2			2						
ROY, Jean-Pierre		RP		SP		RP									
WEBBER, Les		RP	RP			RP					SP				
LAVAGETTO, Harry (Cookie)			pr		pr	ph			ph	5	5			ph	pr
BARNEY, Rex															
MELTON, Rube															
EDWARDS, Bruce															
MEDWICK, Joe (Ducky)															
TEPSIC, Joe															
MIKSIS, Eddie															
McLISH, Cal															
MINNER, Paul															
TAYLOR, Harry															

NOTE: On May 1st, ex-Dodger outfielder Luis Olmo and ex-farmhand infielder Roland Gladu (a wartime Boston Brave) were declared ineligible for five years, after thei defection to the Mexican League.

BRK NL

	MAY		[1]	[2]			[1]	[2]	JUNE	[1]	[2]	[1]	[2]		
	24	25	26	26	28	29	30	30	1	2	2	4	4	5	6
	@Phl	@Phl	@Phl	@Phl	NY	NY	Bos	Bos	@Cin	@Cin	@Cin	@Pts	@Pts	@Pts	@Pts
REESE, Pee Wee	6	6	6	6	6	6	6	6	6	6	6	6	6	6	6
WALKER, Fred (Dixie)	SUSPENDED FOR FIGHTING.				9	9	9	9	9	9	9	9	9	9	9
HERMAN, Billy	5	5	5	5	5	5	5	5	5	5	5	5	5	5	5
WHITMAN, Dick					8			ph	8	8	8		8	8	8
REISER, Pete	8	8	8	8	8	* INJURED.		ph	ph	ph		ph	ph	ph	
CASEY, Hugh			RP		RP			RP			RP	RP			
HERMANSKI, Gene	9	9	9					8		8			ph		
GRAHAM, Jack															
FURILLO, Carl	9		9	9	9	8	8			8	8	8	8	8	8
RIGGS, Lew															
ANDERSON, Ferrell	2	2	2	2	2	2	2		2	2		2	2	2	2
ROSEN, Goodwin (Goody)															
GREGG, Hal	(GREGG DOESN'T START ANOTHER GAME TILL JULY 25th).														
GALAN, Augie	7	7	7	7	7	7	7	7	7	7	7	7	7	7	7
SCHULTZ, Howie	3		3	3	3	3	3					3	3	3	3
BEHRMAN, Hank				RP				SP					RP		RP
STEVENS, Ed	3	3	3			3		3	3	3	3		3	3	3
LOMBARDI, Vic		SP				SP				RP		SP			
CORRIDEN, Johnny															
STANKY, Eddie	4	4	4	4	4	4	4	4	4	4	4	4	4	4	4
PADGETT, Don			2					2			2				
ROJEK, Stan					ph								ph		
RAMAZZOTTI, Bob					ph			ph					h5		5
HIGBE, Kirby	SP						SP						SP		
HATTEN, Joe				SP									SP		
BRANCA, Ralph													RP		SP
DAVIS, Otis (Scat)															
HEAD, Ed				SP				SP				RP		INJURED...	
NAYLOR, Earl	NAYLOR WAS RELEASED OUTRIGHT TO MONTREAL, CLOSING BRIEF BIG LEAGUE CAREER.														
HERRING, Art (Sandy)			RP					RP			SP				RP
DAVIS, Curt															
MOULDER, Glen															
SANDLOCK, Mike									2	2	2				
ROY, Jean-Pierre															
WEBBER, Les			SP					RP		SP		RP			
LAVAGETTO, Harry (Cookie)				ph	pr			ph		pr	pr	ph			5
BARNEY, Rex								RP					RP		
MELTON, Rube														RP	
EDWARDS, Bruce															
MEDWICK, Joe (Ducky)															
TEPSIC, Joe															
MIKSIS, Eddie															
McLISH, Cal															
MINNER, Paul															
TAYLOR, Harry															

* On May 29th, Reiser is hurt when he chases a fly ball into the Ebbets Field outfield wall, first of his many injuries this season..

BRK NL

	JUNE 7 @Chi	8 @Chi	9 @Chi	10 @StL	11 @StL	12 @StL	14 Chi	15 Chi	16 Chi	18 Pts	19 Pts	20 Pts	21 StL	22 StL	23 StL
REESE, Pee Wee	6	6	6	6	6	r6	6	6	6	6	6	6	6	6	6
WALKER, Fred (Dixie)	9	9	9	9	9	9	9	9	9	9	9	9	9	9	9
HERMAN, Billy	5	5	5	5	5	5	5	* TRADED TO BOSTON, JUNE 15th.							
WHITMAN, Dick	8		ph			ph	ph		7			8			8
REISER, Pete			ph	8	8	8	8	7		7	7	7	7	7	7
CASEY, Hugh				RP		RP		RP					RP		
HERMANSKI, Gene			8	7	7	7	7		7						
GRAHAM, Jack															
FURILLO, Carl		8						8	8	8	8		8	8	8
RIGGS, Lew															
ANDERSON, Ferrell	2	2	2	2	2	2	2	2	2	2				ph	
ROSEN, Goodwin (Goody)															
GREGG, Hal														RP	
GALAN, Augie	7	7	7	ph		ph									
SCHULTZ, Howie		3	3	3	3	3		3	3	3	3	3	3	3	3
BEHRMAN, Hank				RP		RP			RP				RP		
STEVENS, Ed	3		h3	3	3	h3	3					3			3
LOMBARDI, Vic			SP			RP	SP					SP			
CORRIDEN, Johnny															
STANKY, Eddie	4	4	4	4	4	4	4	4	4	4	4	4	4	4	4
PADGETT, Don			h2	h2			SOLD TO THE BRAVES, JUNE 12th.								
ROJEK, Stan		pr	6			6								ph	
RAMAZZOTTI, Bob		ph	5					ph	ph				ph		
HIGBE, Kirby				SP		RP		SP			SP				
HATTEN, Joe	SP		RP		SP			SP	RP		SP				SP
BRANCA, Ralph															
DAVIS, Otis (Scat)															
HEAD, Ed			(OUT AGAIN WITH SORE ARM.)												
NAYLOR, Earl															
HERRING, Art (Sandy)			RP	RP				RP		RP					
DAVIS, Curt															
MOULDER, Glen															
SANDLOCK, Mike		2				2	2				2	2	2	2	
ROY, Jean-Pierre							OPTIONED TO MONTREAL, JUNE 15th.								
WEBBER, Les			RP			RP									
LAVAGETTO, Harry (Cookie)		ph			ph	ph	ph	5	5	5	5	5	5	5	5
BARNEY, Rex		SP				SP				SP			SP		
MELTON, Rube		RP			RP		RP								
EDWARDS, Bruce															2
MEDWICK, Joe (Ducky)															
TEPSIC, Joe															
MIKSIS, Eddie															
McLISH, Cal															
MINNER, Paul															
TAYLOR, Harry															

* June 15th, Herman is traded to Boston for catcher Stew Hofferth. Hofferth doesn't report to Brooklyn, refuses June 21st assignment to Mobile. Mobile "returns" him on July 1st. Hofferth will be placed on the Voluntary Retired List, July 9th.

BRK NL

	JUNE							JULY		[1]	[2]		ALL-STAR BREAK [1]	[2]
	24	25	26	27	28	29	30	1	2	4	4	5	6	7	7
	Cin	Cin	Cin	Bos	Bos	Bos	Bos	Phl	Phl	@NY	@NY	@NY	@Bos	@Bos	@Bos
REESE, Pee Wee	6	6	6	6	6	6	6	6	6	6	6	6	6	6	6
WALKER, Fred (Dixie)	9	9	9	9	9	9	9	9	9	9	9	9	9	9	9
HERMAN, Billy															
WHITMAN, Dick	ph	8	8	8	8	87	8	8	78		8	8	8		8
REISER, Pete	7	7	7	7	7	7	7		7	7	7	7	7	7	7
CASEY, Hugh	RP							RP				RP		RP	
HERMANSKI, Gene	8	ph				9		7	ph	pr	ph				
GRAHAM, Jack															
FURILLO, Carl	8					8		8	8	8	8	8		8	
RIGGS, Lew															
ANDERSON, Ferrell									2		2				2
ROSEN, Goodwin (Goody)															
GREGG, Hal		RP													
GALAN, Augie									ph			3			
SCHULTZ, Howie		ph	3	3	3			3		3	3	ph		3	
BEHRMAN, Hank	RP			RP				SP					SP		
STEVENS, Ed	3	3	3		3	3	3	3	3		3	3	3		3
LOMBARDI, Vic	RP	RP		SP							SP				
CORRIDEN, Johnny															
STANKY, Eddie	4	4	4	4	4	4	4	4	4	4	4	4	4	4	4
PADGETT, Don															
ROJEK, Stan		4				6		6		ph		pr			pr
RAMAZZOTTI, Bob		ph				4		4		ph					
HIGBE, Kirby	SP	RP				SP			SP		SP		RP	RP	
HATTEN, Joe				SP						SP					SP
BRANCA, Ralph		RP												SP	
DAVIS, Otis (Scat)															
HEAD, Ed										RP					
NAYLOR, Earl															
HERRING, Art (Sandy)	RP		RP						RP			RP	RP		
DAVIS, Curt															
MOULDER, Glen															
SANDLOCK, Mike						5					2				
ROY, Jean-Pierre															
WEBBER, Les		SP						TO CLEVELAND ON WAIVERS, JULY 2nd.							
LAVAGETTO, Harry (Cookie)	5	5	5	5	5	5	5	5	5	5	5	5	5	5	5
BARNEY, Rex		SP				SP						SP			
MELTON, Rube										RP					
EDWARDS, Bruce	2	2	2	2	2	2	2	2	2	2		2	2	2	2
MEDWICK, Joe (Ducky)								7	ph	ph	ph	ph		ph	
TEPSIC, Joe															
MIKSIS, Eddie															
McLISH, Cal															
MINNER, Paul															
TAYLOR, Harry															

BRK NL	JULY 11 @Chi	12 @Chi	13 @Chi	[1] 14 @StL	[2] 14 @StL	15 @StL	16 @StL	17 @Cin	18 @Cin	19 @Cin	20 @Pts	[1] 21 @Pts	[2] 21 @Pts	24 Chi	25 Chi
REESE, Pee Wee	IRRITATED OLD NECK INJURY.					6	6	6	6	6	6	6	6	6	6
WALKER, Fred (Dixie)	9	9	9	9	9	9	9	9	9	9	9	9	9	9	9
HERMAN, Billy															
WHITMAN, Dick		8	8	8	8	7		ph	ph	8			8	8	
REISER, Pete	7	7	7	7	7	7	7	8	8	87	7	7	7	7	7
CASEY, Hugh			RP			SP		RP		RP					
HERMANSKI, Gene		9		ph	ph	9		ph	ph						
GRAHAM, Jack															
FURILLO, Carl	8	7	8			8	8			8	8	8	8		8
RIGGS, Lew															
ANDERSON, Ferrell	2	2			2	h2	2	2	2						
ROSEN, Goodwin (Goody)															
GREGG, Hal		RP				RP							RP		SP
GALAN, Augie				ph	ph	ph		7	7	7					
SCHULTZ, Howie	3				3	3	3			3	3	3	3		3
BEHRMAN, Hank			SP					SP					SP		
STEVENS, Ed			3	3	3	3	ph		3	3	3		3	3	
LOMBARDI, Vic						SP				RP		SP			
CORRIDEN, Johnny															
STANKY, Eddie	4	4	4	4		INJURED.		4	4	4	4	4	4	4	4
PADGETT, Don															
ROJEK, Stan	6	6	6	6	6										
RAMAZZOTTI, Bob				4	4	4	4	5	5	5	5	5	5	5	5
HIGBE, Kirby			SP					SP							
HATTEN, Joe	SP					SP					SP			SP	
BRANCA, Ralph						RP									
DAVIS, Otis (Scat)															
HEAD, Ed						RP									
NAYLOR, Earl															
HERRING, Art (Sandy)		RP						RP		RP					
DAVIS, Curt															
MOULDER, Glen															
SANDLOCK, Mike	OPTIONED TO MOBILE, JULY 10th. OPTION TRANSFERRED TO ST. PAUL, JULY 15th.														
ROY, Jean-Pierre															
WEBBER, Les															
LAVAGETTO, Harry (Cookie)	5	5	5	5	5	5	5	ph							
BARNEY, Rex		SP				RP									
MELTON, Rube			RP							SP					
EDWARDS, Bruce			2	2	2	2			2	2	2	2	2	2	2
MEDWICK, Joe (Ducky)			ph			3									
TEPSIC, Joe		ph				ph			ph						
MIKSIS, Eddie				ph		6									
McLISH, Cal	(McLISH, REINSTATED JULY 15th AFTER ARMY DUTY, PITCHES ONLY ON AUGUST 25th).														
MINNER, Paul															
TAYLOR, Harry															

BRK NL

	JULY	[1]	[2]					AUG							
	26	27	27	28	29	30	31	1	2	3	4	5	6	8	9
	Pts	Pts	Pts	Pts	Cin	StL	StL	StL	Cin	Cin	Cin	@Bos	@NY	@NY	@Phl
REESE, Pee Wee	6	6	p:	6	6	6	6	6	6	6	6	6	6	6	6
WALKER, Fred (Dixie)	9	9	9	9	9	9	9	9	9	9	9	9	9	9	9
HERMAN, Billy															
WHITMAN, Dick		ph	8	8	8		8		8	8	8	8		pr	
REISER, Pete	7	7	7	7	7	7	7	7	* INJURED (& BURNED).					8	7
CASEY, Hugh		RP	RP				RP				RP			RP	
HERMANSKI, Gene				ph	ph		ph			ph	ph	ph			
GRAHAM, Jack															
FURILLO, Carl	8	8				8	ph	8			8		8		8
RIGGS, Lew															
ANDERSON, Ferrell		2						ph					ph		
ROSEN, Goodwin (Goody)															
GREGG, Hal					SP			SP				SP			
GALAN, Augie				ph	3		ph		7	7	7	7		7	
SCHULTZ, Howie	3	3			3	3		3			3	3	3	3	3
BEHRMAN, Hank		SP			RP	RP		RP			RP	RP			
STEVENS, Ed			3	3			3		3	3	ph			3	
LOMBARDI, Vic	SP							SP						SP	
CORRIDEN, Johnny		OPTION TRANSFERRED TO FORT WORTH, AUGUST 6th.													
STANKY, Eddie	4	4	4	4	4	4	4	ph		4	4	4	4	4	4
PADGETT, Don															
ROJEK, Stan								ph		ph		5	5		
RAMAZZOTTI, Bob	5	5	5	5	5	5	54	4	4		4				
HIGBE, Kirby			SP							SP					SP
HATTEN, Joe				RP		SP						SP	RP		
BRANCA, Ralph	RP			RP				RP				RP		RP	
DAVIS, Otis (Scat)															
HEAD, Ed				RP											
NAYLOR, Earl															
HERRING, Art (Sandy)				RP		RP					RP				
DAVIS, Curt															
MOULDER, Glen															
SANDLOCK, Mike															
ROY, Jean-Pierre															
WEBBER, Les															
LAVAGETTO, Harry (Cookie)								5						5	5
BARNEY, Rex				SP											
MELTON, Rube	RP					SP						SP	RP		
EDWARDS, Bruce	2		2	2	2	2	2	2	2	2	2	2	2	2	2
MEDWICK, Joe (Ducky)		ph						7		ph	7		7	ph	
TEPSIC, Joe				pr				pr							
MIKSIS, Eddie	ph	pr		ph			5	54	5	5	5				
McLISH, Cal															
MINNER, Paul															
TAYLOR, Harry															

* August 1st, Reiser again runs into Ebbets Field fence chasing a ball. He's hospitalized & released, then suffers burns lighting kitchen stove for his wife.

BRK NL	AUG 10 @Phl	[1] 11 @Phl	[2] 11 @Phl	12 NY	[1] 14 NY	[2] 14 NY	15 NY	16 Phl	18 Phl	20 @Pts	21 @Pts	22 @Cin	23 @Cin	24 @Cin	[1] 25 @StL
REESE, Pee Wee	6	6	6	6	6	6	6	6	6	6	6	6	6	6	6
WALKER, Fred (Dixie)	9	9	9	9	9	9	9	9	9	9	9	9	9	9	9
HERMAN, Billy															
WHITMAN, Dick		ph	ph	ph	ph				ph	8			87	87	
REISER, Pete	7	8	8	8	8	7	7	7	8	8	7	7	7	7	7
CASEY, Hugh		RP			RP			RP						RP	
HERMANSKI, Gene		ph	ph	ph	ph				ph	9					
GRAHAM, Jack															
FURILLO, Carl	8	ph	ph	8	8	8	8	8	ph		8	8	8	8	8
RIGGS, Lew															
ANDERSON, Ferrell		2		2	2			2		2		2			
ROSEN, Goodwin (Goody)															
GREGG, Hal			SP					SP						SP	RP
GALAN, Augie		7	7	7	7				7	7			5	5	5
SCHULTZ, Howie	3			3		3	3	3	3		3	3			3
BEHRMAN, Hank		SP			RP			RP	RP	RP				RP	RP
STEVENS, Ed		3	3	3	3	3			3	3			3	3	
LOMBARDI, Vic			SP							SP		RP		RP	RP
CORRIDEN, Johnny															
STANKY, Eddie	4	4	4	4	4	4	4	4	4	4	4	4	4	4	4
PADGETT, Don															
ROJEK, Stan				4						6			5	5	
RAMAZZOTTI, Bob			4	4		5				4					
HIGBE, Kirby							SP					SP			
HATTEN, Joe						SP					SP				
BRANCA, Ralph				RP				RP							SP
DAVIS, Otis (Scat)															
HEAD, Ed				SP						RP					
NAYLOR, Earl															
HERRING, Art (Sandy)		RP	RP				RP								
DAVIS, Curt															
MOULDER, Glen															
SANDLOCK, Mike															
ROY, Jean-Pierre															
WEBBER, Les															
LAVAGETTO, Harry (Cookie)	5	5								5	5	5			h5
BARNEY, Rex			RP							RP					
MELTON, Rube	SP							SP	RP			SP			
EDWARDS, Bruce	2		2	2	2	2	2	2	2	2	2	2	2	2	2
MEDWICK, Joe (Ducky)		ph	ph	ph		ph		ph	ph						
TEPSIC, Joe			pr			pr		pr	pr	7					
MIKSIS, Eddie			5	5	5	5	5	5	5	ph					
McLISH, Cal															
MINNER, Paul															
TAYLOR, Harry															

BRK NL

	AUG [2]						SEP [1]	[2]	[1]	[2]					
	25	26	27	28	29	31	1	1	2	2	3	4	5	7	8
	@StL	@StL	@StL	@Chi	@Chi	@NY	@NY	@NY	@Phl	@Phl	Phl	@Bos	@Bos	NY	NY
REESE, Pee Wee	6	6	6	6	6	6	6	6	6	6	6	6	6	6	6
WALKER, Fred (Dixie)	9	9	9	9	9	9	9	9	9	9	9	9	9	9	9
HERMAN, Billy															
WHITMAN, Dick	8	8	8		8		87	87	7	7	7	7	7		9
REISER, Pete	7	7	7	7	7	7	SIDELINED DUE TO PLEURISY.							7	7
CASEY, Hugh	RP				RP	RP		RP							
HERMANSKI, Gene	8	ph			ph		7	7							
GRAHAM, Jack															
FURILLO, Carl	8		8	8	ph	8	8	8	8	8	8	8	8	8	8
RIGGS, Lew															
ANDERSON, Ferrell	2					ph		2		2					
ROSEN, Goodwin (Goody)															
GREGG, Hal				SP						SP					
GALAN, Augie	ph	5	5	5	5	7	5	5			5		5		5
SCHULTZ, Howie	3		3	3		3			3	3		3		3	3
BEHRMAN, Hank			RP				RP				RP				
STEVENS, Ed	3	3	3		3		3	3			3		3		3
LOMBARDI, Vic		RP			RP		SP						SP		
CORRIDEN, Johnny		(CORRIDEN RECALLED AUGUST 29th, BUT HIS 1-GAME BIG LEAGUE CAREER IS OVER)													
STANKY, Eddie	4	4	4	4	4	4	4	4	4	4	4	4	4	4	4
PADGETT, Don															
ROJEK, Stan				pr	4		5			ph					
RAMAZZOTTI, Bob					4					ph					
HIGBE, Kirby			SP			SP					SP		SP		
HATTEN, Joe	SP	RP						SP				SP			SP
BRANCA, Ralph															
DAVIS, Otis (Scat)															
HEAD, Ed	RP	(CHRONIC SHOULDER PROBLEMS FINISH HEAD'S SHORT BIG LEAGUE CAREER)													
NAYLOR, Earl															
HERRING, Art (Sandy)	RP									RP					
DAVIS, Curt															
MOULDER, Glen															
SANDLOCK, Mike		(SANDLOCK RECALLED AUG. 29th, RELEASED OUTRIGHT TO MONTREAL SEP. 7th)													
ROY, Jean-Pierre		(ROY RECALLED AUG. 29th, THOUGH HE WON'T PITCH AGAIN IN THE MAJOR LEAGUES)													
WEBBER, Les															
LAVAGETTO, Harry (Cookie)	5				ph	ph	ph		5	5		5		5	5
BARNEY, Rex	RP														
MELTON, Rube		SP			SP				SP						
EDWARDS, Bruce	2	2	2	2	2	2	2	2	2	ph	2	2	2	2	2
MEDWICK, Joe (Ducky)					ph	ph		ph	7	7		7			7
TEPSIC, Joe	ph							pr							
MIKSIS, Eddie						5		pr		pr					
McLISH, Cal	RP														
MINNER, Paul															
TAYLOR, Harry															

National League — BRK NL

	SEP						[1]	[2]			[1]	[2]		[1]
		9/11 TIE 0-0, 19 INN											9/11 TIE	
		Replay 9/20											REPLAY	
BRK NL	10	11	12	13	14	15	15	16	17	18	18	19	20	21	22
	Cin	Cin	StL	StL	StL	Chi	Chi	Chi	Chi	Pts	Pts	Pts	Cin	@Bos	@Bos
REESE, Pee Wee	6	6	6	6	6	6	6	6	6	6	6	6	6	6	6
WALKER, Fred (Dixie)	9	9	9	9	9	9	9	9	9	9	9	9	9	9	9
HERMAN, Billy															
WHITMAN, Dick	7	ph		7				8				7			h7
REISER, Pete	7	78	7	7		* INJURED.		ph		* INJURED.		7	* INJURED.		ph
CASEY, Hugh		RP				RP		RP					RP		RP
HERMANSKI, Gene	9							ph				9			
GRAHAM, Jack															
FURILLO, Carl	8	8	8	8	8	8	8	8	8	8	8	8	8	8	8
RIGGS, Lew															
ANDERSON, Ferrell	2		ph			ph				ph		2			
ROSEN, Goodwin (Goody)															
GREGG, Hal		SP				RP						SP			
GALAN, Augie	5	7		5	7	7	7	73	7		7	5	7	7	75
SCHULTZ, Howie	3	3	3		3	3				3	3		3	3	
BEHRMAN, Hank		RP	RP			RP				RP			RP		RP
STEVENS, Ed	3	3		3	3	3	3	3	3			3	3		3
LOMBARDI, Vic								SP	RP						
CORRIDEN, Johnny															
STANKY, Eddie	4	4	4	4	4	4	4	4	4	4	4	4	4	4	4
PADGETT, Don															
ROJEK, Stan	6		ph									6	ph		
RAMAZZOTTI, Bob	4					ph		ph		ph		4			
HIGBE, Kirby			SP	RP			SP			SP					SP
HATTEN, Joe			SP			RP			SP					SP	
BRANCA, Ralph			RP		SP						SP			RP	
DAVIS, Otis (Scat)															
HEAD, Ed															
NAYLOR, Earl															
HERRING, Art (Sandy)		RP						RP					SP		
DAVIS, Curt															
MOULDER, Glen															
SANDLOCK, Mike		(SANDLOCK'S NEXT BIG LEAGUE GAME IS IN 1953, WITH THE PIRATES)													
ROY, Jean-Pierre															
WEBBER, Les															
LAVAGETTO, Harry (Cookie)	5	5	5		5	5	5	5	5	5	5		5	5	5
BARNEY, Rex			RP												
MELTON, Rube	SP				SP			RP							
EDWARDS, Bruce	2	2	2	2	2	2	2	2	2	2	2	2	2	2	2
MEDWICK, Joe (Ducky)		ph			7			h7		7	7		7	7	
TEPSIC, Joe								pr							
MIKSIS, Eddie										pr					pr
McLISH, Cal															
MINNER, Paul			RP					RP							RP
TAYLOR, Harry															RP

* September 13th, Reiser injures a thigh muscle. Except for one game in left field and pinch-batting twice, he's out of action till September 25th.

BRK NL	SEP 22 @Bos	[2] 23 Phl	25 Phl	26 Phl	28 Bos	29 Bos	**PLAYOFFS OCT 1 @StL	3 StL	157g
REESE, Pee Wee	6	6	6	6	6	6	6	6	
WALKER, Fred (Dixie)	9	9	9	9	9	9	9	9	
HERMAN, Billy									
WHITMAN, Dick	7			7			7	7	
REISER, Pete	INJURED.		7	7	* FRACTURED ANKLE.				
CASEY, Hugh			RP			RP			
HERMANSKI, Gene	9							ph	
GRAHAM, Jack									
FURILLO, Carl	8	8	8	8	8	8	8	8	
RIGGS, Lew									
ANDERSON, Ferrell									
ROSEN, Goodwin (Goody)									
GREGG, Hal			RP				RP		
GALAN, Augie	5	7	h5	57	7	7		5	
SCHULTZ, Howie	3	3	3		3		3	ph	
BEHRMAN, Hank			RP					RP	
STEVENS, Ed			ph	3	3	3		3	
LOMBARDI, Vic	SP		RP			SP	RP	RP	
CORRIDEN, Johnny									
STANKY, Eddie	4	4	4	4	4	4	4	4	
PADGETT, Don									
ROJEK, Stan	6	ph				pr	ph		
RAMAZZOTTI, Bob	4			5			ph		
HIGBE, Kirby			RP	SP		RP	RP	RP	
HATTEN, Joe					SP	RP		SP	
BRANCA, Ralph			SP				SP		
DAVIS, Otis (Scat)									
HEAD, Ed									
NAYLOR, Earl									
HERRING, Art (Sandy)			RP						
DAVIS, Curt									
MOULDER, Glen									
SANDLOCK, Mike									
ROY, Jean-Pierre									
WEBBER, Les									
LAVAGETTO, Harry (Cookie)	5	5	5		5	5	5	ph	
BARNEY, Rex									
MELTON, Rube		SP					RP	RP	
EDWARDS, Bruce	2	2	2	2	2	2	2	2	
MEDWICK, Joe (Ducky)	7	7	ph	7		ph	7	ph	
TEPSIC, Joe				ph			pr		
MIKSIS, Eddie									
McLISH, Cal									
MINNER, Paul									
TAYLOR, Harry		RP	RP					RP	

* Sep 26, Reiser fractures ankle trying to avoid a pickoff throw at first base. His season is ended.
** Individual records in Playoff games are counted in each player's season statistics.

CHI NL	G	APRIL 16 @Cin	17 @Cin	18 @Cin	20 StL	21 StL	23 @Pts	24 @Pts	25 Cin	27 @StL	[1] 28 @StL	[2] 28 @StL	30 Brk	MAY 1 Brk	2 Brk
HACK, Stan	92	5	5	5	5	5	5	5	5	5	5	5	5	5	
JOHNSON, Don	83	4	4	4	4	4	4	4	4	4	4	4	4	4	4
LOWREY, Harry (Peanuts)	144	7	7	7	7	7	7	7	7	7	7	7	7	7	7
CAVARRETTA, Phil	139	3	3	3	3	3	3	3	9	9	9	9	9	9	9
PAFKO, Andy	65	8	8		8	8	8			8	8				8
RICKERT, Marv	111	9	9	8	9			8	8		8	8	8	8	
LIVINGSTON, Mickey	66	2	2	2	ph		2	2	2	2	2				
GILBERT, Charlie	15	ph					ph	ph	ph		8			ph	ph
McCULLOUGH, Clyde.	95	2	ph	2	2	2					ph	2	2	2	2
SCHEFFING, Bob	63	2	2		ph	ph			2	ph				2	
GLOSSOP, Alban (Al)	4	6						6							
MERULLO, Lennie	65	6	6	6	6	6	6			6	6	6	6	6	
BECKER, Heinz	9	ph		ph		ph		ph	ph				ph	ph	ph
STRINGER, Lou	80	pr						pr	pr				pr		
STURGEON, Bobby	100	6				6			6	6			6	r6	6
PASSEAU, Claude	21	SP				SP				SP					
WAITKUS, Eddie	113	ph					ph	3	3	3	3	3	3	3	3
CHIPMAN, Bob	34	RP					RP			SP					SP
NICHOLSON, Bill	105	ph	ph	9		9	9	9						ph	
ERICKSON, Paul	32	RP						RP	RP				RP		
FLEMING, Bill	14	RP											SP		
PRIM, Ray	14	RP				SP	PRIM HURTS HIS PITCHING ELBOW.								
WYSE, Hank	40		SP		RP					RP					RP
SCHMITZ, Johnny	42		RP		RP	RP		RP				SP			
KUSH, Emil	40		RP						RP		RP		RP		
O'NEILL, Emmett	1		RP				SOLD TO THE WHITE SOX, APRIL 23rd.								
BITHORN, Hiram (Hi)	26			SP				SP			RP		RP		
BOROWY, Hank	33			SP					SP		SP				
DALLESSANDRO, Dom	65								ph				ph	ph	ph
OSTROWSKI, John	64									5					5
SECORY, Frank	33								ph						
HANYZEWSKI, Eddie	3												RP		
JURGES, Billy	82	ILL, CAN'T MAKE FIRST PITTS. TRIP.													6
ADAMS, Charles (Red)	8	ILL, CAN'T MAKE FIRST PITTS. TRIP.													
MEERS, Russ	7	ILLNESS HAMPERS MEERS AT START OF SEASON.													
OLSEN, Vern	5	ILLNESS SIDELINES OLSEN AT START OF SEASON.													
BAUERS, Russ	15	CUT BY PITTSBURGH 3/22 AFTER FOUR YEARS IN MILITARY, SIGNS WITH CUBS JULY 3rd.													
WILLIAMS, Dewey	4	"OFFICIAL" RECALL FROM LOS ANGELES AUG. 21st. FIRST CUBS GAME AUGUST 22nd.													
GARRIOTT, Cecil	6	DISCHARGED FROM ARMY, REINSTATED FROM NDSL AUG. 21. DEBUT SEPT. 4.													
BLOCK, Seymour (Cy)	6	RECALLED FROM NASHVILLE AUGUST 26th, FIRST GAME IS SEPTEMBER 12th (1).													
PAWELEK, Ted	4	PURCHASED OUTRIGHT FROM NASHVILLE, SEPTEMBER 11th.													
MANDERS, Hal	2	EX-TIGER, BOUGHT CONDITIONALLY AUG. 9th FROM BUFFALO, "FOR 1947 DELIVERY".													
MEYER, Russ	4	FROM NASHVILLE, BIG LEAGUE DEBUT SEPTEMBER 13th.													
MADDERN, Clarence	3	HIT .322 AT TULSA, PURCHASED OUTRIGHT FROM LOS ANGELES, SEPTEMBER 16th.													
SCHENZ, Henry (Hank)	6	HIT .333 AT TULSA, PURCHASED OUTRIGHT ON SEPTEMBER 16th.													
LADE, Doyle	3	BOUGHT FROM SHREVEPORT JULY 3rd "FOR 1947 DELIVERY", BUT DEBUTS SEP. 18th.													

On April 21st, outfielder Mizell (Whitey) Platt is sold to the Chicago White Sox, on waivers. He did not play for the Cubs this season.

On May 2nd, player-coach Billy Jurges is released from coaching duties, becomes full-time player.

CHI NL

	MAY		[1]	[2]					[1]	[2]				
	3	4	5	5	8	9	12	15	18	19	19	20	22	23	24
	NY	NY	Phl	Phl	Bos	Bos	Pts	@Phl	@NY	@Bos	@Bos	@Bos	@Brk	@Brk	@Pts
HACK, Stan							5	5	5	5	5	THIGH INJURY.			
JOHNSON, Don	4	4							4	4	4	4	4		
LOWREY, Harry (Peanuts)	5	5	5	5	5	5	7	7	7	7	7	7	7	7	7
CAVARRETTA, Phil	7	7	7	7	7	7	9	93	3	3	3	3	3	3	3
PAFKO, Andy	8	8	8	8	8	8	8	8	8	8	8	8	8	8	8
RICKERT, Marv								ph			ph		ph		
LIVINGSTON, Mickey	2	2	2	2	2	2	2	2			2	2	2	INJURED...	
GILBERT, Charlie											ph				
McCULLOUGH, Clyde.			2			2		2	2	2			2	2	2
SCHEFFING, Bob													2	2	
GLOSSOP, Alban (Al)			4	4			OPTIONED TO LOS ANGELES, MAY 11th.								
MERULLO, Lennie						pr		6	6	ph	pr	6	6	6	
BECKER, Heinz			ph												
STRINGER, Lou		4	pr		4	4	4	4		4				4	4
STURGEON, Bobby			6										6		6
PASSEAU, Claude				SP			SP					SP			
WAITKUS, Eddie	3	3	3	3	3	3	3	3	OUT WITH A BRUISED ELBOW.						
CHIPMAN, Bob						RP		RP		RP		RP			
NICHOLSON, Bill	9	9	9	9	9	9		9	9	9	9	9	9	9	9
ERICKSON, Paul		RP								RP					RP
FLEMING, Bill						RP				RP					
PRIM, Ray		SP				RP					RP	ARM INJURY...			
WYSE, Hank					SP			RP			SP			SP	
SCHMITZ, Johnny	SP					SP			SP					SP	
KUSH, Emil				RP		RP		RP			RP				
O'NEILL, Emmett															
BITHORN, Hiram (Hi)	RP			RP											
BOROWY, Hank			SP					SP		SP					SP
DALLESSANDRO, Dom			ph		7			ph		ph	ph		ph	ph	
OSTROWSKI, John		ph		ph		ph			5	ph	5		5		ph
SECORY, Frank				ph						ph					ph
HANYZEWSKI, Eddie							TO NASHVILLE ON OPTION, MAY 11th.								
JURGES, Billy	6	6	6	6	6	6	6	6	6	6		5	5	5	5
ADAMS, Charles (Red)				RP						RP					RP
MEERS, Russ															
OLSEN, Vern															
BAUERS, Russ															
WILLIAMS, Dewey															
GARRIOTT, Cecil															
BLOCK, Seymour (Cy)															
PAWELEK, Ted															
MANDERS, Hal															
MEYER, Russ															
MADDERN, Clarence															
SCHENZ, Henry (Hank)															
LADE, Doyle															

CHI NL

	MAY 26 @Pts	27 StL	28 StL	29 StL	30 [1] Cin	30 [2] Cin	JUNE 1 Bos	2 [1] Bos	2 [2] Bos	4 NY	5 NY	6 NY	7 Brk	8 Brk	9 Brk
HACK, Stan			5	5	5	5	5	*5	5	5	5	5	5	5	5
JOHNSON, Don										4		4	4	4	4
LOWREY, Harry (Peanuts)	7	7	7	7	7	7	7	7	7	7	7	7	7	7	7
CAVARRETTA, Phil	3	3	3	3	3	3	9	9	9	9	9	9	9	9	9
PAFKO, Andy	8	8	8	8	8	8	SLIPS ON A LOOSE BALL JUNE 1st, FRACTURES ANKLE...								
RICKERT, Marv						ph	8	8	8	8	8	8	8	8	8
LIVINGSTON, Mickey	(LIVINGSTON OUT WITH BADLY-SPRAINED ANKLE.)														
GILBERT, Charlie			ph			ph		ph			ph	pr			8
McCULLOUGH, Clyde.	2	2	2	2	2		2	2		2	2	2	2	2	2
SCHEFFING, Bob			ph			2			2			ph			ph
GLOSSOP, Alban (Al)															
MERULLO, Lennie	SUSPENDED 8 DAYS FOR FIGHTING.						6	6	6	6	6				r6
BECKER, Heinz		SENT TO NASHVILLE AT HIS OWN REQUEST (TO GET MORE PLAYING TIME), MAY 27th.													
STRINGER, Lou	4	4	4	4	4	4	4	4	4	4	4				ph
STURGEON, Bobby	6	6	6	6	6	6				6	6	6	6	6	6
PASSEAU, Claude			SP					SP				SP			
WAITKUS, Eddie							3	3	3	3	3	3	3	3	3
CHIPMAN, Bob			RP			RP	SP				RP			SP	
NICHOLSON, Bill	9	9	9	9	9	9		ph		ph	ph				ph
ERICKSON, Paul	RP		RP					RP				RP			RP
FLEMING, Bill	RP														RP
PRIM, Ray		...PULLED ARM MUSCLE WILL SIDELINE PRIM FOR 3 MONTHS. DISABLED LIST JUNE 20th.													
WYSE, Hank				SP						SP		RP			RP
SCHMITZ, Johnny		SP					SP				SP	RP			SP
KUSH, Emil				RP			RP				RP				RP
O'NEILL, Emmett															
BITHORN, Hiram (Hi)	SP			RP			RP				RP	RP			
BOROWY, Hank					SP						SP				
DALLESSANDRO, Dom			ph			ph		ph		ph	ph				ph
OSTROWSKI, John	ph		5	ph								ph			ph
SECORY, Frank	ph			ph								ph			ph
HANYZEWSKI, Eddie															
JURGES, Billy	5	5													
ADAMS, Charles (Red)			RP			RP									
MEERS, Russ			SP							RP					
OLSEN, Vern															
BAUERS, Russ															
WILLIAMS, Dewey															
GARRIOTT, Cecil															
BLOCK, Seymour (Cy)															
PAWELEK, Ted															
MANDERS, Hal															
MEYER, Russ															
MADDERN, Clarence															
SCHENZ, Henry (Hank)															
LADE, Doyle															

* June 2nd (1), Hack listed at 2B in box score; but should be at third base. He never plays second base in his 16-year big league career.

CHI NL

	JUNE								[1] 22	[2] 22	[1] 23	[2] 23				
	10	11	14	15	16	18	21	22	22	23	23	24	25	26	27
	Phl	Phl	@Brk	@Brk	@Brk	@Phl	@NY	@NY	@NY	@NY	@NY	@Bos	@Bos	@Bos	@Pts
HACK, Stan	5	5	5	5	5	5	5	5	5	5	5	5	5	5	5
JOHNSON, Don	4	4	4	4	4	4	4								
LOWREY, Harry (Peanuts)			8	8	8	8	8	8	8	8	8	8	8	8	8
CAVARRETTA, Phil	9	9	9	9	9	9	9	9	9	9	9	9	9	9	9
PAFKO, Andy		...INJURY SIDELINES PAFKO TILL JULY 18th.													
RICKERT, Marv	8	8	7	7	7	7	7		7	7	7	7	7	7	7
LIVINGSTON, Mickey															
GILBERT, Charlie	ph		SOLD TO THE PHILLIES, JUNE 14th.												
McCULLOUGH, Clyde.	2	2	2	2	2	2	2	2	2	2	2	2	2	2	2
SCHEFFING, Bob	ph	ph			2				2	2					h2
GLOSSOP, Alban (Al)															
MERULLO, Lennie	pr														pr
BECKER, Heinz															
STRINGER, Lou				pr	pr		4	4	4	4	4	4	4	4	4
STURGEON, Bobby	6	6	6	6	6	6	6	6	6	6	6	64	6	6	6
PASSEAU, Claude			SP					SP					SP		
WAITKUS, Eddie	3	3	3	3	3	3	3	3	3	3	3	3	3	3	3
CHIPMAN, Bob				SP											
NICHOLSON, Bill	ph	ph		ph		ph			ph	ph	ph	ph		ph	ph
ERICKSON, Paul				RP			RP								RP
FLEMING, Bill		RP							RP	RP				RP	
PRIM, Ray															
WYSE, Hank		SP					SP						SP		
SCHMITZ, Johnny		RP			SP		SP					SP			RP
KUSH, Emil		RP			SP						RP				SP
O'NEILL, Emmett															
BITHORN, Hiram (Hi)	RP								RP	RP				RP	
BOROWY, Hank	SP			RP						SP					
DALLESSANDRO, Dom	ph	7		ph	ph					ph		ph		ph	ph
OSTROWSKI, John	ph	*ph/pr			ph										
SECORY, Frank	7	7	7	7			7	7		ph	ph				7
HANYZEWSKI, Eddie															
JURGES, Billy			6	6		6					6	6			4
ADAMS, Charles (Red)										RP				RP	
MEERS, Russ	RP									SP					
OLSEN, Vern										RP					
BAUERS, Russ															
WILLIAMS, Dewey															
GARRIOTT, Cecil															
BLOCK, Seymour (Cy)															
PAWELEK, Ted															
MANDERS, Hal															
MEYER, Russ															
MADDERN, Clarence															
SCHENZ, Henry (Hank)															
LADE, Doyle															

* June 11th, Ostrowski is listed at CF in *TSN* box score, but he's not credited with playing outfield in the majors this year. PH? PR? for Rickert, apparently---with no AB

CHI NL

	JUNE	[1]	[2]	JULY			[1]	[2]	[1]	[2]		[1]	[2]	ALL-STAR BREAK	
	28	30	30	1	2	3	3	4	4	5	6	6	7	11	12
	@Cin	@Cin	@Cin	Pts	Pts	Pts	Pts	@StL	@StL	@StL	Cin	Cin	Cin	Brk	Brk
HACK, Stan	5	5	5	5	5	5	5	5	5	5	5	5	5	5	5
JOHNSON, Don				4			4	4	4	4	4	4	4	4	4
LOWREY, Harry (Peanuts)	8	8		8			8	8	8	8	8	8	8	8	8
CAVARRETTA, Phil	9	9	ph	ph		INJURED HAND.					ph			9	9
PAFKO, Andy															
RICKERT, Marv		7	8	7	8	8	89	9	9	9	9	9	9	7	7
LIVINGSTON, Mickey												ph			
GILBERT, Charlie															
McCULLOUGH, Clyde.	2	2		2	2	2	2	2	ph		2		2	2	2
SCHEFFING, Bob			2	2				2	2	2		2	ph		
GLOSSOP, Alban (Al)															
MERULLO, Lennie			6	6	6			pr	pr	pr		pr			
BECKER, Heinz															
STRINGER, Lou	4	4	4	4	4	4	4				4		ph		
STURGEON, Bobby	6	6		6		ph		ph	ph						6
PASSEAU, Claude			SP						SP						
WAITKUS, Eddie	3	3	3	3	3	3	3	3	3	3	3	3	3	3	3
CHIPMAN, Bob					SP				RP			RP			
NICHOLSON, Bill		9	9	9	9	9	9		h9		9				9
ERICKSON, Paul						SP					SP				
FLEMING, Bill					RP							RP			
PRIM, Ray															
WYSE, Hank	RP			SP				RP				SP			SP
SCHMITZ, Johnny		SP						SP			RP		pr	SP	
KUSH, Emil				RP		RP							SP		
O'NEILL, Emmett															
BITHORN, Hiram (Hi)		RP							SP			RP			
BOROWY, Hank	SP					SP									
DALLESSANDRO, Dom			7	ph	7	7	7	7	7	7	7	7	7		
OSTROWSKI, John				ph	5			h5	5				5	5	5
SECORY, Frank	7										ph		ph	ph	
HANYZEWSKI, Eddie															
JURGES, Billy		6	6			6	6	6	6	6	6	6	6	6	6
ADAMS, Charles (Red)						RP		OPTIONED TO LOS ANGELES, JULY 3rd.							
MEERS, Russ															
OLSEN, Vern															
BAUERS, Russ															
WILLIAMS, Dewey															
GARRIOTT, Cecil															
BLOCK, Seymour (Cy)															
PAWELEK, Ted															
MANDERS, Hal															
MEYER, Russ															
MADDERN, Clarence															
SCHENZ, Henry (Hank)															
LADE, Doyle															

CHI NL

	JULY							[1]	[2]	[1]	[2]				[1]
	13	14	15	16	17	18	19	20	20	21	21	24	25	26	27
	Brk	NY	NY	NY	Bos	Bos	Bos	Phl	Phl	Phl	Phl	@Brk	@Brk	@Phl	@Phl
HACK, Stan	5	5	5	5	5	5	5	5	5				5	5	5
JOHNSON, Don	4	4	4	4	4	4	4	4	4	4	4	4	4	4	4
LOWREY, Harry (Peanuts)	8	8	8	8	8	8	7		7	5	5	5		7	7
CAVARRETTA, Phil	9	9	9	9	9	9	9	9	9	9	9	9	3	3	3
PAFKO, Andy						ph	8	8	8	8	8	8	8	8	8
RICKERT, Marv	7	7	7	7	7	7		7	7	7	7	7	7		
LIVINGSTON, Mickey											ph	ph			2
GILBERT, Charlie															
McCULLOUGH, Clyde.	2	2	2	2	2	2	2		2	2	ph	2	2	2	2
SCHEFFING, Bob	ph			2	2	ph	2	2		2	ph	ph			
GLOSSOP, Alban (Al)															
MERULLO, Lennie														pr	
BECKER, Heinz															
STRINGER, Lou	4				4							pr	pr		
STURGEON, Bobby				6	ph	6					ph				6
PASSEAU, Claude	SP				SP						SP	BACK PROBLEMS.			
WAITKUS, Eddie	3	3	3	3	3	3	3	3	3	3	3	3	INJURED.		
CHIPMAN, Bob	RP				SP										
NICHOLSON, Bill	ph					ph							9		
ERICKSON, Paul											RP			SP	
FLEMING, Bill					RP	RP						TO LOS ANGELES.			
PRIM, Ray															
WYSE, Hank			SP				SP					SP			
SCHMITZ, Johnny				SP					SP				SP		
KUSH, Emil	RP	RP					SP					RP	RP		
O'NEILL, Emmett															
BITHORN, Hiram (Hi)							RP								
BOROWY, Hank		SP							SP						*SP
DALLESSANDRO, Dom	ph					ph		ph					ph	9	9
OSTROWSKI, John					5										5
SECORY, Frank	ph					ph	ph		ph		7	7	ph	ph	
HANYZEWSKI, Eddie	(OPTION TRANSFERRED TO TULSA, JULY 17th)														
JURGES, Billy	6	6	6	6	6	6	6	6	6	6	6	6	6	6	6
ADAMS, Charles (Red)															
MEERS, Russ	RP				RP	RP									
OLSEN, Vern					RP										
BAUERS, Russ					RP								RP		RP
WILLIAMS, Dewey															
GARRIOTT, Cecil															
BLOCK, Seymour (Cy)															
PAWELEK, Ted															
MANDERS, Hal															
MEYER, Russ															
MADDERN, Clarence															
SCHENZ, Henry (Hank)															
LADE, Doyle															

* July 27th (1), Borowy starts, pitche+CY144s 2 2/3 innings, loses. Next day, July 28th Game 1, starts again, pitches Complete Game, wins.

8/11(2) TIE 4-4, replay 9/2(2)

CHI NL	JULY [2] 27 @Phl	[1] 28 @Phl	[2] 28 @Phl	29 @NY	30 @NY	31 @NY	AUG 3 @Bos	[1] 4 @Bos	[2] 4 @Bos	6 @Cin	8 @Cin	9 @Pts	10 @Pts	[1] 11 @Pts	[2] 11 @Pts
HACK, Stan	5	5	5	5	5			5	5	FRACTURED THUMB.					
JOHNSON, Don	4	4	4	4	4	4	4	4	4	4	4	4	4	4	4
LOWREY, Harry (Peanuts)	8		7	7	7	7	7	7	7	5	5	7		7	7
CAVARRETTA, Phil	3	3	3	3	3	3	3	3	3	3	3	3	3	3	3
PAFKO, Andy	8	8	8	8	8	8	8	8	8	8	8	8	8	8	8
RICKERT, Marv	7	7	7	ph	7				ph		7		7		
LIVINGSTON, Mickey		2				2	2		2	2	2	2	2	2	2
GILBERT, Charlie															
McCULLOUGH, Clyde.	2		2	2	2		2	2						2	
SCHEFFING, Bob						ph									
GLOSSOP, Alban (Al)															
MERULLO, Lennie					pr					6	6	6	6	6	6
BECKER, Heinz															
STRINGER, Lou							pr								
STURGEON, Bobby	6	6		6	6	6	6		6						
PASSEAU, Claude						SP				SP					
WAITKUS, Eddie		FRACTURED FINGER, OUT TILL AUG. 6th.								3					
CHIPMAN, Bob				RP	RP										SP
NICHOLSON, Bill	9	9	9	9	9	9	9	9	9	9	9	9	9	9	9
ERICKSON, Paul					SP			RP			SP				
FLEMING, Bill	(DATE OF OPTION TO LOS ANGELES WAS JULY 22nd.)														
PRIM, Ray															
WYSE, Hank			SP				SP							SP	
SCHMITZ, Johnny			SP				SP						SP		
KUSH, Emil			RP			RP		RP					RP		
O'NEILL, Emmett															
BITHORN, Hiram (Hi)	SP						RP							RP	
BOROWY, Hank		*SP					SP				SP			RP	
DALLESSANDRO, Dom				ph	ph			ph			ph				
OSTROWSKI, John						5	5		5	5		5	5	5	5
SECORY, Frank				ph	ph		ph						ph		
HANYZEWSKI, Eddie															
JURGES, Billy	6	6	6	6	6	6		6							
ADAMS, Charles (Red)															
MEERS, Russ							OPTIONED TO NASHVILLE...								
OLSEN, Vern															
BAUERS, Russ				RP	RP										
WILLIAMS, Dewey															
GARRIOTT, Cecil															
BLOCK, Seymour (Cy)															
PAWELEK, Ted															
MANDERS, Hal	PURCHASED FROM BUFFALO (DETROIT) AUG. 9 FOR 1947 DELIVERY, HE REPORTS SEP. 8th.														
MEYER, Russ															
MADDERN, Clarence															
SCHENZ, Henry (Hank)															
LADE, Doyle															

CHI NL

	AUG 12	13	14	15 [1]	15 [2]	16	17	18	20 [1]	20 [2]	21	22	23	24	25
	StL	StL	StL	Cin	Cin	Cin	Pts	Pts	Phl	Phl	Phl	Bos	Bos	Bos	NY
HACK, Stan															
JOHNSON, Don	4	4	4	4	4	4	4	4	4	4	BROKEN HAND.				
LOWREY, Harry (Peanuts)	7	7	7	8	8	8	8	8	7	7	7	7	7	9	7
CAVARRETTA, Phil	3	3	3	3	3	3	3	3	3	3	3	3	3	7	9
PAFKO, Andy	8	8	8						8	8	8	8	8		8
RICKERT, Marv			pr	7	7	7	7	9		7			8	8	
LIVINGSTON, Mickey	2	2	2	2		ph	2	2	2		2	2	2	2	2
GILBERT, Charlie															
McCULLOUGH, Clyde.		2	BROKEN FINGER SIDELINES McCULLOUGH TILL SEPTEMBER 10th.												
SCHEFFING, Bob		2	ph		2	2	2			2		ph			
GLOSSOP, Alban (Al)															
MERULLO, Lennie	6	6	6	6	6	6	pr								
BECKER, Heinz															
STRINGER, Lou	ph		ph			pr			4	4	4	4	4	*4	4
STURGEON, Bobby			ph	ph			6	6	6	6	6	6	6	*6	6
PASSEAU, Claude	SP													SP	
WAITKUS, Eddie		pr	3			ph	ph				ph		ph	3	3
CHIPMAN, Bob			RP									RP			
NICHOLSON, Bill	9	9	9	9	9	9	9				9	9	9		
ERICKSON, Paul				SP			SP					SP			
FLEMING, Bill															
PRIM, Ray		REINSTATED FROM DISABLED LIST, AUGUST 19th.													
WYSE, Hank				SP					SP						
SCHMITZ, Johnny		SP				SP						SP			
KUSH, Emil	RP			RP								RP		RP	
O'NEILL, Emmett															
BITHORN, Hiram (Hi)						SP				RP					
BOROWY, Hank			SP					SP							SP
DALLESSANDRO, Dom				ph		ph		7	9	9			7	INJURED.	
OSTROWSKI, John	5	5	5	5	5	5	5	5	5	5	5	5	5	5	5
SECORY, Frank		SOLD OUTRIGHT TO KANSAS CITY, AUGUST 12th.													
HANYZEWSKI, Eddie															
JURGES, Billy													4		
ADAMS, Charles (Red)															
MEERS, Russ		..."OFFICIALLY" SENT TO NASHVILLE AUG. 12th, BUT PITCHED FOR VOLS AUGUST 2nd.													
OLSEN, Vern				RP											
BAUERS, Russ			RP			RP					SP				
WILLIAMS, Dewey												ph			
GARRIOTT, Cecil															
BLOCK, Seymour (Cy)															
PAWELEK, Ted															
MANDERS, Hal															
MEYER, Russ															
MADDERN, Clarence															
SCHENZ, Henry (Hank)															
LADE, Doyle															

* Aug 24th, Stringer and Sturgeon both in *TSN* box score at 2B, with no SS. Assume Sturgeon played short, Stringer second base.

	AUG					SEP	REPLAY of 8/11 TIE								
								[1]	[2]	[1]	[2]				
	26	27	28	29	31	1	1	2	2	3	4	5	7	8	10
CHI NL	NY	NY	Brk	Brk	@Cin	@Cin	@Cin	@Pts	@Pts	@Pts	@StL	@StL	Cin	Cin	@Bos
HACK, Stan															
JOHNSON, Don	JOHNSON'S INJURY ENDS HIS SEASON.														
LOWREY, Harry (Peanuts)	7	7	8	8	8	8	8	5	5	8	8	8	8	8	5
CAVARRETTA, Phil	9	9	9	9	9	9	9	8	8	9	9	9	9	9	8
PAFKO, Andy	8	8	BROKEN ARM SHELVES PAFKO THE REST OF 1946.												
RICKERT, Marv			7	7	7	7	7	7	7	7	7	7	7	7	7
LIVINGSTON, Mickey	2	2	2	2	2	2	ph	2			2				
GILBERT, Charlie															
McCULLOUGH, Clyde.															ph
SCHEFFING, Bob	2	ph	2				2		2	2		2	2	2	2
GLOSSOP, Alban (Al)	RECALLED FROM LOS ANGELES AUGUST 26th, BUT DOESN'T PLAY AGAIN IN MAJORS.														
MERULLO, Lennie		pr	pr								ph	pr			
BECKER, Heinz															
STRINGER, Lou	4	4	4	4	4	4	4	4	4	4	4	4	4		
STURGEON, Bobby	6	6	6	6	6	6	6	6	6	6	6	6	6	4	4
PASSEAU, Claude	PASSEAU'S BAD BACK SIDELINES HIM UNTIL NEXT YEAR.														
WAITKUS, Eddie	3	3	3	3	3	3	3	3	3	3	3	3	3	3	3
CHIPMAN, Bob		SP							SP			RP			RP
NICHOLSON, Bill			ph		ph		ph	9	9			ph			9
ERICKSON, Paul			RP					SP				SP			
FLEMING, Bill	RECALLED FROM LOS ANGELES AUGUST 26th, BUT DOESN'T PLAY AGAIN IN MAJORS.														
PRIM, Ray				RP		RP				RP	RP				
WYSE, Hank	SP			SP		RP				RP	RP			SP	
SCHMITZ, Johnny			SP		SP						SP				
KUSH, Emil					RP	RP					RP				
O'NEILL, Emmett															
BITHORN, Hiram (Hi)						SP									RP
BOROWY, Hank				SP						SP					SP
DALLESSANDRO, Dom	ANKLE "FRACTURED" BUT HE'S PINCH-HITTING IN TWO WEEKS.											ph			ph
OSTROWSKI, John	5	5	5	5	5	5	5			5	5	5	5	5	
SECORY, Frank															
HANYZEWSKI, Eddie	RECALLED AUGUST 26th, REPORTS AFTER 1st ROUND OF TEXAS LEAGUE PLAYOFFS.														
JURGES, Billy						5		6						6	6
ADAMS, Charles (Red)	RECALLED FROM LOS ANGELES AUGUST 26th, BUT DOESN'T PLAY AGAIN IN MAJORS.														
MEERS, Russ	RECALLED AUGUST 26th, BUT DOESN'T PLAY AGAIN FOR THE CUBS THIS YEAR.														
OLSEN, Vern															RP
BAUERS, Russ		RP							SP		RP				RP
WILLIAMS, Dewey											ph				
GARRIOTT, Cecil											ph	ph			ph
BLOCK, Seymour (Cy)	RECALLED AUGUST 26th, REPORTS AT END OF NASHVILLE SEASON.														
PAWELEK, Ted															
MANDERS, Hal															
MEYER, Russ	RECALLED AUGUST 26th, REPORTS AT END OF NASHVILLE SEASON.														
MADDERN, Clarence	RECALLED 8/26, TO REPORT AFTER 1st ROUND OF TEXAS LEAGUE PLAYOFFS, SEP. 13th.														
SCHENZ, Henry (Hank)	RECALLED 8/26, TO REPORT AFTER 1st ROUND OF TEXAS LEAGUE PLAYOFFS, SEP. 13th.														
LADE, Doyle															

CHI NL

9/11 TIE, NO REPLAY

	11	12 [1]	12 [2]	13	14	15 [1]	15 [2]	16	17	18	19	21	22	23	24 [1]
	@Bos	@Phl	@Phl	@Phl	@Phl	@Brk	@Brk	@Brk	@Brk	@NY	@NY	StL	StL	StL	Pts
HACK, Stan		ph		ph								5	5	5	5
JOHNSON, Don															
LOWREY, Harry (Peanuts)	5	8	8	8	5	75	5	58	8	8	8	8	8	8	8
CAVARRETTA, Phil	8	9	9	9	8	8	8	8							
PAFKO, Andy															
RICKERT, Marv	7	7	7	7	7	7	7	7	7	7		7	7	7	7
LIVINGSTON, Mickey	ph	2			2		2		2		ph		2	ph	
GILBERT, Charlie															
McCULLOUGH, Clyde.			2	2	ph	2		2				2	2	2	2
SCHEFFING, Bob	2				ph	ph			ph	2	2			ph	ph
GLOSSOP, Alban (Al)															
MERULLO, Lennie		pr	pr	6	pr	pr				6	6			pr	6
BECKER, Heinz															
STRINGER, Lou				5					ph						4
STURGEON, Bobby	4	4	4	4	4	4	4	4	4	4	4	4	4	4	4
PASSEAU, Claude															
WAITKUS, Eddie	3	3	3	3	3	3	3	3	3	3	3	3	3	3	3
CHIPMAN, Bob				RP		RP		RP		RP					RP
NICHOLSON, Bill	9	ph		ph	9	9	9	9	9	9	9	9	9	9	9
ERICKSON, Paul			SP						SP						SP
FLEMING, Bill															
PRIM, Ray		RP							RP	RP					
WYSE, Hank		RP						SP	RP		SP			SP	
SCHMITZ, Johnny	SP				SP				RP		SP		SP	RP	
KUSH, Emil	RP				SP	SP									
O'NEILL, Emmett															
BITHORN, Hiram (Hi)															
BOROWY, Hank	RP							SP	RP				SP		
DALLESSANDRO, Dom	ph	ph	ph	ph	ph							ph	ph		ph
OSTROWSKI, John					5			5							
SECORY, Frank															
HANYZEWSKI, Eddie															
JURGES, Billy	6	6	6	6	6	6	6	6	6			6	6	6	6
ADAMS, Charles (Red)															
MEERS, Russ															
OLSEN, Vern				RP											
BAUERS, Russ			RP	RP											
WILLIAMS, Dewey											2				
GARRIOTT, Cecil				ph					ph						
BLOCK, Seymour (Cy)		5	5	5				5		ph				ph	
PAWELEK, Ted				ph	ph										
MANDERS, Hal				SP											
MEYER, Russ				RP					RP						
MADDERN, Clarence									ph		7			7	
SCHENZ, Henry (Hank)										5	5				5
LADE, Doyle									SP						

CHI NL

	SEP [2] 24 Pts	25 Pts	26 Pts	27 @StL	28 @StL	29 @StL	155g
HACK, Stan	5	5	5	5	5	5	
JOHNSON, Don							
LOWREY, Harry (Peanuts)		8		7	7	7	
CAVARRETTA, Phil		89	8	8	8	8	
PAFKO, Andy							
RICKERT, Marv	8	78	7			7	
LIVINGSTON, Mickey	2	ph					
GILBERT, Charlie							
McCULLOUGH, Clyde.		2	2	2	2	2	
SCHEFFING, Bob					ph		
GLOSSOP, Alban (Al)							
MERULLO, Lennie	6	6	6				
BECKER, Heinz							
STRINGER, Lou	4		4	4	4	4	
STURGEON, Bobby	4	4	4	* INJURED.			
PASSEAU, Claude							
WAITKUS, Eddie	3	3	3	3	3	3	
CHIPMAN, Bob	RP				RP		
NICHOLSON, Bill	9	9	9	9	9	9	
ERICKSON, Paul					SP		
FLEMING, Bill							
PRIM, Ray		RP			RP		
WYSE, Hank				RP			
SCHMITZ, Johnny						SP	
KUSH, Emil			SP		RP		
O'NEILL, Emmett							
BITHORN, Hiram (Hi)							
BOROWY, Hank			pr	SP			
DALLESSANDRO, Dom	7	7	ph				
OSTROWSKI, John							
SECORY, Frank							
HANYZEWSKI, Eddie	RP		RP				
JURGES, Billy	6	6	6	6	6	6	
ADAMS, Charles (Red)							
MEERS, Russ							
OLSEN, Vern							
BAUERS, Russ	RP						
WILLIAMS, Dewey	2						
GARRIOTT, Cecil	ph						
BLOCK, Seymour (Cy)							
PAWELEK, Ted	2		ph				
MANDERS, Hal	RP	RETURNED TO BUFFALO, 9/25.					
MEYER, Russ		SP	RP				
MADDERN, Clarence							
SCHENZ, Henry (Hank)	5	pr	5				
LADE, Doyle	SP	RP					

* September 26th, Sturgeon suffers a lacerated finger, sits out remainder of schedule.

CIN NL	G	APRIL 16 Chi	17 Chi	18 Chi	20 @Pts	[1] 21 @Pts	[2] 21 @Pts	22 StL	23 StL	24 StL	25 @Chi	27 Pts	28 Pts	MAY 3 Phl	4 Phl
CLAY, Dain	121	8	8	8	8	8	8	8	8	7			7		
FREY, Lonny	111	4	4	4	4	4			ph		4	4	4	4	4
LAMANNO, Ray	85	ph	2	ph		2				ph			2		
HATTON, Grady	116	5	5	5	5	5	5	5	5		5	5	5	5	5
MILLER, Eddie	91	6	6	6	6	6	6	6	6	6	6	6	6	6	6
HAAS, Bert	140	3	3	3	3	3		3	3	3	3	3	3	3	3
LIBKE, Al	125	9	9	9	9	9	9							9	9
USHER, Bob	92	9	9	9						r9	9			pr	
LUKON, Eddie	102	7	7	7										ph	
CORBITT, Claude	82	pr	pr												
MUELLER, Ray	114	2	2	2	2	2	2	2	2	2	2	2	2	2	2
ZIENTARA, Benny	78	pr								5					
BEGGS, Joe	28	SP				SP					SP				
HEUSSER, Ed	29	RP			SP								SP		
ADAMS, Bobby	94	ph					4	4	4	4					
VANDER MEER, Johnny	33		SP					SP							
GUMBERT, Harry	36		RP												
SHOUN, Clyde	27		RP												
BLACKWELL, Ewell	33		RP							SP				SP	
ANDREWS, Nate	7			SP					SP						SP
WEST, Max	72		*		7	7	7	7	7		7	7	7	7	7
WALTERS, Wm. (Bucky)	24				SP					SP					
SHOKES, Eddie	31						3								
MOSS, Howie	7	FROM NDSL APRIL 22.						9	9	9	9	9	9		
McCORMICK, Mike	23	SPRING TRAINING INJURY.						ph		8	8	8	8	8	8
LAMBERT, Clay	23							RP		RP	RP			RP	
VOLLMER, Clyde	9									ph				NXT PAGE...	
FOX, Howie	4									RP			APPENDIX TROUBLE...		
HETKI, Johnny	32									RP	RP				
LAKEMAN, Al	23									ph					
LAWING, Garland	2	ON NATIONAL DEFENSE SERVICE LIST TILL MAY 3rd.													
MALLOY, Bob	27	IN USN, REINSTATED FROM NDSL ON MAY 8th.													
DASSO, Frank	2														
BURPO, George	2														
GOLDSTEIN, Leslie (Lonnie)	6	WILL BE DISCHARGED BY ARMY, RELEASED FROM NDSL AUGUST 8th.													

* West obtained from the Braves April 19th, for pitcher Jim Konstanty & cash (Konstanty did not play for the Reds).

CIN NL

	MAY	[1] 5 NY	[2] 5 NY	7 NY	8 Brk	9 Brk	[1] 12 @StL	[2] 12 @StL	15 @NY	17 @Phl	19 @Brk	20 @Brk	22 @Bos	24 StL	[1] 26 StL	[2] 26 StL
CLAY, Dain				7		7						7		7		87
FREY, Lonny		4	4	4	4	4	4	4	4	4	4	4	4	4	4	
LAMANNO, Ray			2	2	2	2	2	2	2	2	2	2	2	2	2	ph
HATTON, Grady		5	5	5	5	5	5	5	5	5	5	5	5	5	5	5
MILLER, Eddie		6	6	6	6	6	6	6	6	6	6	6	6	6	6	6
HAAS, Bert		3	3	3	3	*3	3	3	3	3	3	3	3	3	3	3
LIBKE, Al		9	9	9	9	9	9	9	9	9	9	9	9	9	9	9
USHER, Bob		9			9		9	8				ph			9	9
LUKON, Eddie		ph							ph			ph				ph
CORBITT, Claude																
MUELLER, Ray		2	2				2									2
ZIENTARA, Benny																4
BEGGS, Joe				SP				SP								SP
HEUSSER, Ed			SP			RP					SP					
ADAMS, Bobby		INJURED KNEE IN BATTING PRACTICE, MAY 4th.														
VANDER MEER, Johnny		SP				pr			SP				RP			
GUMBERT, Harry													RP			RP
SHOUN, Clyde		RP			SP								SP			RP
BLACKWELL, Ewell								SP		RP				SP		
ANDREWS, Nate					SP									SP		
WEST, Max		7	7	7	7	7	7	7	7	7	7		7		7	7
WALTERS, Wm. (Bucky)							SP					SP				
SHOKES, Eddie													ph			
MOSS, Howie					ph				TO BALTIMORE, MAY 16th							
McCORMICK, Mike		8	8	8	8	*8	8		8	8	8	8	8	8	8	8
LAMBERT, Clay		RP			RP								RP			
VOLLMER, Clyde		TO ROCHESTER, APRIL 30th.														
FOX, Howie		...UNDERGOES APPENDECTOMY, APRIL 27th, THEN GOES HOME TO RECOVER.														
HETKI, Johnny				RP								RP		RP		
LAKEMAN, Al				ph					ph		ph	ph	ph			
LAWING, Garland																
MALLOY, Bob																
DASSO, Frank																
BURPO, George																
GOLDSTEIN, Leslie (Lonnie)																

* May 9th, Haas & McCormick both in box scores at 1B, with no CF. Assume McCormick CF, not 1B (apparently confused with 1B Frank McCormick of Phils).

CIN NL

	MAY		[1]	[2]	JUNE	[1]	[2]					[1]	[2]		
	28	29	30	30	1	2	2	4	6	7	8	9	9	10	11
	@Pts	@Pts	@Chi	@Chi	Brk	Brk	Brk	Phl	Phl	Bos	Bos	Bos	Bos	NY	NY
CLAY, Dain	8	78	8	87	8	8	8	8	8	8	8	8	8	8	8
FREY, Lonny				ph	ph		ph		ph						
LAMANNO, Ray	2	2	2	ph	2	2		2	2	2	2	2		2	2
HATTON, Grady			5	5	5	5	5	5	5	5	5	5	5	5	5
MILLER, Eddie	6	6	6	6	6	6	6	6	6	6	6	6	6	6	6
HAAS, Bert	3	3	*3	ph	3	3	3	3	3						
LIBKE, Al	9	9	9	9	9	9	9	9	9	9	9	9	9	9	9
USHER, Bob	pr			9	pr							ph			
LUKON, Eddie			ph	ph			ph			ph		7	7	7	7
CORBITT, Claude				6								6			
MUELLER, Ray				2		ph	2						2		
ZIENTARA, Benny	5	5										4			
BEGGS, Joe	RP				SP			SP							
HEUSSER, Ed	SP					SP					SP				
ADAMS, Bobby	4	4	4	4	4	4	4	4	4	4	4	4	4	4	4
VANDER MEER, Johnny				RP					RP						SP
GUMBERT, Harry	RP	RP							RP			RP			
SHOUN, Clyde	RP	RP				RP				RP		SP			
BLACKWELL, Ewell				SP				SP					SP		
ANDREWS, Nate			SP											SP	
WEST, Max	7	7	*7	7	7	7	7	7	7	7	7	BACK INFECTION.			
WALTERS, Wm. (Bucky)		SP													
SHOKES, Eddie				3					3	3	3	3	3	3	3
MOSS, Howie	(LATE-SEASON, HOWIE MOSS WILL APPEAR FOR CLEVELAND.)														
McCORMICK, Mike				8	pr			SOLD TO THE BRAVES, JUNE 3rd.							
LAMBERT, Clay		RP							RP			RP			
VOLLMER, Clyde															
FOX, Howie												RP			
HETKI, Johnny			RP	RP		SP			SP				ph		
LAKEMAN, Al			ph												
LAWING, Garland		8							ph			SOLD TO GIANTS, JUNE 8th.			
MALLOY, Bob			RP						RP				RP		
DASSO, Frank			RP						RP						
BURPO, George												RP			
GOLDSTEIN, Leslie (Lonnie)															

* May 30th (1), Haas & West are both in box score as left fielder. Assume Haas is 1B as usual, not LF, as he doesn't play outfield this year.

TIE 6/23(2), REPLAY 9/18(2)

CIN NL	JUNE 12 NY	14 @Bos	15 @Bos	[1] 16 @Bos	[2] 16 @Bos	18 @NY	19 @NY	21 @Phl	[1] 22 @Phl	[2] 22 @Phl	[1] 23 @Phl	[2] 23 @Phl	24 @Brk	25 @Brk	26 @Brk
CLAY, Dain	8	8	8	8	8	8	8	8	8	8	8	8	8	8	8
FREY, Lonny												7	ph		*4
LAMANNO, Ray	2	2	2	2	ph	2	2	2	ph	2	2	ph	2		ph
HATTON, Grady	5	5	5	5	5	5	5	5	5	5	5	5	5	5	5
MILLER, Eddie	6	6	6	6	6	6	6	6	6	6	6	ph	6	6	6
HAAS, Bert				3	3	3	3	3	3	3	3	ph		3	3
LIBKE, Al	9	9	9	9	9	9	9	9	9	9	9	9	9	9	9
USHER, Bob	7							7	7	7	7	9		7	pr
LUKON, Eddie		7	7		7			ph		ph		7	7	7	7
CORBITT, Claude									6		6				6
MUELLER, Ray					2				2		2		2	2	2
ZIENTARA, Benny											4	4	4	4	
BEGGS, Joe					SP						SP				
HEUSSER, Ed			SP				SP								SP
ADAMS, Bobby	4	4	4	4	4	4	4	4	4	4	4	4	ph		ph
VANDER MEER, Johnny				SP					SP			ph			
GUMBERT, Harry										SP					
SHOUN, Clyde												SP			RP
BLACKWELL, Ewell		SP					SP				RP	RP			
ANDREWS, Nate		RELEASED JUNE 11th, SIGNS WITH THE GIANTS JUNE 16th.													
WEST, Max				7		7	7	7	INFECTION PERSISTS, OUT TILL JULY 11th.						
WALTERS, Wm. (Bucky)	SP					SP							SP		
SHOKES, Eddie	3	3	3									3	3	3	
MOSS, Howie															
McCORMICK, Mike															
LAMBERT, Clay												RP	RP		
VOLLMER, Clyde															
FOX, Howie															
HETKI, Johnny							RP						RP	SP	
LAKEMAN, Al		ph					ph		ph						
LAWING, Garland															
MALLOY, Bob		RP								RP			RP		
DASSO, Frank		SOLD OUTRIGHT TO HOLLYWOOD, JUNE 11th.													
BURPO, George															
GOLDSTEIN, Leslie (Lonnie)															

* June 26th, Frey is in *TSN* box score at 3B. However, he has no games at third base this year. Assume he plays 2B today.

CIN NL

	JUNE	[1]	[2]	JULY			[1]	[2]		[1]	[2]	ALL-STAR BREAK			[1]
	28	30	30	1	2	3	4	4	5	6	6	7	11	12	13
	Chi	Chi	Chi	@StL	@StL	@StL	Pts	Pts	Pts	@Chi	@Chi	@Chi	Bos	Bos	Bos
CLAY, Dain	8	8	8	8	8	8	8	8	8	8	8	8	8	8	8
FREY, Lonny	4	4	4	4	4	4	4				ph			ph	ph
LAMANNO, Ray		2	ph	2		2	2	ph		2				2	2
HATTON, Grady	5	5	5	5	5	57	5	5	5	57	5	5	5	5	5
MILLER, Eddie	6	6	6	6	6	6	6	6	6	6	6	6	6	6	6
HAAS, Bert	3	3	3	3	3	3	3	3	3	3	3	3	3	3	3
LIBKE, Al	9	9	9	9	9	9	9	9	9	9	9	9	9	9	9
USHER, Bob	9	7	7	7	7			9	7	9	pr		7	8	
LUKON, Eddie	7		7	7		7	7	7	7	7	7	7	7	7	7
CORBITT, Claude	6			6		6									6
MUELLER, Ray	2	ph	2	2	2		ph	2	2	ph	2	2	2		ph
ZIENTARA, Benny		4		pr	4	5				5					pr
BEGGS, Joe		SP								SP					
HEUSSER, Ed				RP			SP								SP
ADAMS, Bobby	ph	ph	ph	ph			ph	4	4	4	4	4	4	4	4
VANDER MEER, Johnny	SP				SP							SP			
GUMBERT, Harry			RP	RP			RP				SP				
SHOUN, Clyde		RP		RP				RP							RP
BLACKWELL, Ewell			SP					SP						SP	
ANDREWS, Nate															
WEST, Max														ph	
WALTERS, Wm. (Bucky)				SP				SP					SP		
SHOKES, Eddie			3			3									
MOSS, Howie															
McCORMICK, Mike															
LAMBERT, Clay						SP									RP
VOLLMER, Clyde															
FOX, Howie						RP									
HETKI, Johnny				RP											
LAKEMAN, Al				ph	2	ph									
LAWING, Garland															
MALLOY, Bob		RP			RP	RP									
DASSO, Frank															
BURPO, George						RP									
GOLDSTEIN, Leslie (Lonnie)															

CIN NL	JULY	[2] 13 Bos	[1] 14 Phl	[2] 14 Phl	15 Phl	16 Phl	17 Brk	18 Brk	19 Brk	20 NY	[1] 21 NY	[2] 21 NY	24 @Bos	25 @Bos	26 @NY	[1] 27 @NY
CLAY, Dain		8	8	8	8	8	8	8	8	8	8	8	8	8	8	8
FREY, Lonny		4	4		4	4	4		ph	9	9	9	9	9	9	9
LAMANNO, Ray												2				ph
HATTON, Grady		5	5	5	5	5	5	5	5	5	5	5	5	5	5	5
MILLER, Eddie		6		6	6	6	6	6	6	ARM INJURY.						
HAAS, Bert		3	3	3	3	3	3	3	3	3	3	3	3	3	3	3
LIBKE, Al		9	9	9	9	9	9	9	9							ph
USHER, Bob			7	7	7	pr	9	7			7	7	7	7	7	pr
LUKON, Eddie		7	7		7	7	7	7	7	7	7	ph	7	7		7
CORBITT, Claude			6	ph					ph	6	6	6	6	6	6	6
MUELLER, Ray		2	2	ph	2	2	2	2	2	2	2	ph	2	2	2	2
ZIENTARA, Benny				5												
BEGGS, Joe				SP								SP				
HEUSSER, Ed								SP								SP
ADAMS, Bobby		ph		4		ph		4	4	4	4	4	4	4	4	4
VANDER MEER, Johnny			SP							SP		pr		SP		
GUMBERT, Harry		SP					RP		RP							
SHOUN, Clyde									RP							
BLACKWELL, Ewell							SP				SP				SP	
ANDREWS, Nate																
WEST, Max									ph							
WALTERS, Wm. (Bucky)							SP					ph	SP			
SHOKES, Eddie																
MOSS, Howie																
McCORMICK, Mike																
LAMBERT, Clay				RP												
VOLLMER, Clyde																
FOX, Howie																
HETKI, Johnny						SP			SP							
LAKEMAN, Al				2					2							
LAWING, Garland																
MALLOY, Bob				RP					RP			RP				RP
DASSO, Frank																
BURPO, George		OPTIONED TO SYRACUSE, JULY 12th.														
GOLDSTEIN, Leslie (Lonnie)																

CIN NL

	JULY	[2]	[1]	[2]			[1]	[2]	AUG						[1]	[2]
		27	28	28	29	30	31	31	2	3	4	6	8	9	11	11
		@NY	@NY	@NY	@Brk	@Phl	@Phl	@Phl	@Brk	@Brk	@Brk	Chi	Chi	StL	StL	StL
CLAY, Dain			8	8		8										8
FREY, Lonny		8	9		8	ph	8	8		ph	8	8	8	8	8	9
LAMANNO, Ray		2		2				2	ph				2	ph	ph	2
HATTON, Grady		5	5	5	5	5	5	5	5	5	5	5	5	5	5	5
MILLER, Eddie		6		6	6	6	6	6	ARM INJURY, OUT TILL LABOR DAY.							
HAAS, Bert		ph	3	3	3	3	3	3	3	3	3	3	3	3	3	
LIBKE, Al		9			9	9		9	9	9	9	9	9	9	9	
USHER, Bob			7	7			7			7	9			7		
LUKON, Eddie		7			7	7		7	7	7	7		ph	ph	ph	7
CORBITT, Claude			6						6	6	6	6	pr	6	6	6
MUELLER, Ray			2		2	2	2		2	2	2	2	2	2	2	ph
ZIENTARA, Benny		4		4			4	4	4	4	4	4	6	4		
BEGGS, Joe			SP						RP	RP						RP
HEUSSER, Ed									SP							
ADAMS, Bobby		ph	4	9	4	4	9		pr			ph	2	94	4	4
VANDER MEER, Johnny					SP					SP				SP		
GUMBERT, Harry				SP		RP	RP	RP					SP			
SHOUN, Clyde		SP													RP	
BLACKWELL, Ewell							SP					SP				SP
ANDREWS, Nate																
WEST, Max					ph				8	8	ph	7	7	9	7	ph
WALTERS, Wm. (Bucky)					SP					SP			SP			
SHOKES, Eddie		3														3
MOSS, Howie																
McCORMICK, Mike																
LAMBERT, Clay		RP														
VOLLMER, Clyde																
FOX, Howie		RP												TO SYRACUSE.		
HETKI, Johnny					RP	RP						RP	RP		RP	
LAKEMAN, Al						2							ph	ph		
LAWING, Garland																
MALLOY, Bob		RP					SP							RP		RP
DASSO, Frank																
BURPO, George			(RECALL FROM SYRACUSE ANNOUNCED AUG. 13, BUT BURPO FINISHED IN BIG LEAGUES.)													
GOLDSTEIN, Leslie (Lonnie)																ph

CIN NL

	AUG 12 @Pts	13 @Pts	14 @Pts	[1] 15 @Chi	[2] 15 @Chi	16 @Chi	17 @StL	[1] 18 @StL	[2] 18 @StL	19 @StL	20 NY	21 NY	22 Brk	23 Brk	24 Brk
CLAY, Dain	8	8	pr	8	8	8	8	8	8	8	8	8	8	8	
FREY, Lonny	9	9	9	9	ph	9	9	9	9	ph	9	9	79	7	7
LAMANNO, Ray	ph				2			ph	2		ph				
HATTON, Grady	5	5	5	5	5	5	5	5	5	5	5	5	5	5	5
MILLER, Eddie															
HAAS, Bert	3	3	3	3	3	3	3	3	3	3	3	3	3	3	3
LIBKE, Al			ph	9	9	9		ph		9				9	9	9
USHER, Bob			8	8		7	7	r9	7		7	7	7	pr	7
LUKON, Eddie	ph	7	ph		7	7		9		7				ph	
CORBITT, Claude	6	6	6	6	6	6	6	6	6	6	6	6	6	6	6
MUELLER, Ray	2	2	2	2	ph	2	2	2	ph	2	2	2	2	2	2
ZIENTARA, Benny		4	4	4	4	4	4	4	4	4	4	4	4	4	4
BEGGS, Joe				SP				RP							
HEUSSER, Ed	SP							SP							SP
ADAMS, Bobby	4	4						ph							
VANDER MEER, Johnny								SP					SP		
GUMBERT, Harry		SP				RP	RP			SP					
SHOUN, Clyde					RP				RP						
BLACKWELL, Ewell	RP				SP					SP					
ANDREWS, Nate															
WEST, Max	7	ph	7	7	ph			7							
WALTERS, Wm. (Bucky)							SP	pr						SP	
SHOKES, Eddie															
MOSS, Howie															
McCORMICK, Mike															
LAMBERT, Clay					RP			RP							
VOLLMER, Clyde	SEPTEMBER RECALL ANNOUNCED ON AUGUST 13th.														
FOX, Howie	OPTIONED TO SYRACUSE, AUGUST 9th. SEPTEMBER. RECALL ANNOUNCED AUGUST 13th.														
HETKI, Johnny					SP						SP				
LAKEMAN, Al															
LAWING, Garland															
MALLOY, Bob			SP							RP					
DASSO, Frank															
BURPO, George															
GOLDSTEIN, Leslie (Lonnie)	ph														

CIN NL

	AUG	[1]	[2]		[1]	[2]			[1]	[2]	[1]	[2]				
		25	25	26	28	28	29	31	1	1	2	2	4	5	7	8
		Phl	Phl	Phl	Bos	Bos	Bos	Chi	Chi	Chi	StL	StL	Pts	Pts	@Chi	@Chi
CLAY, Dain			8		8	8		7	7	7	8	7			8	8
FREY, Lonny		4	4	4	4	4	4	4	4			ph		ph	4	4
LAMANNO, Ray			2			2			ph	2	ph	2				
HATTON, Grady		PRE-GAME AUG. 24th, SLIPS ON CONCRETE WALK UNDER STANDS, FRACTURES RIGHT KNEE.															
MILLER, Eddie												ph			6	
HAAS, Bert		3	3	3	3	3	3	3	3	3	3	3	3	3	3	3
LIBKE, Al		9	9	9	9	9	9	9	9	9	9		9	9	9	9
USHER, Bob		8	89	8		87	8	8	8	8	89	8	8	8	7	
LUKON, Eddie			7	7	ph	7	7	7	9	7	7	9	7	7	7	7
CORBITT, Claude		6	6	6	6	6	6	6	6	6	6	6	6	6	6	6
MUELLER, Ray		2	ph	2	2		2	2	2		2	ph	2	2	*2	2
ZIENTARA, Benny		5	5	5	5	5	5	5	5	5	5	5	5	5	5	5
BEGGS, Joe		SP							SP				RP			
HEUSSER, Ed							RP					SP				
ADAMS, Bobby									ph	4	4	4	4	4	4	4
VANDER MEER, Johnny			pr	SP							SP			SP		
GUMBERT, Harry			SP							SP		RP		RP	RP	
SHOUN, Clyde																
BLACKWELL, Ewell			RP			SP				RP						
ANDREWS, Nate																
WEST, Max		7	ph		7		ph			ph		7		ph		ph
WALTERS, Wm. (Bucky)						SP							SP			
SHOKES, Eddie										pr						
MOSS, Howie																
McCORMICK, Mike																
LAMBERT, Clay				RP			SP								SP	
VOLLMER, Clyde		REPORTS AT END OF ROCHESTER'S SEASON, SEPTEMBER 8th.															
FOX, Howie		FRACTURES ARM IN INTERNATIONAL LEAGUE PLAYOFFS, CAN'T PITCH AGAIN IN 1946.															
HETKI, Johnny			SP					RP	RP	RP						SP
LAKEMAN, Al												ph				
LAWING, Garland																
MALLOY, Bob				RP			RP			RP		RP				
DASSO, Frank																
BURPO, George																
GOLDSTEIN, Leslie (Lonnie)				ph								ph				

* September 7th, "Merullo" listed as catcher in *TSN* box score. Assume it's Mueller (Lennie Merullo is shortstop for the Cubs, Cincinnati's opponent today).

CIN NL

	SEP	9/11, 0-0 TIE, 19 INN, REPLAY 9/20				[1]	[2]			6/23 TIE, REPLAY [1]	9/11 TIE, REPLAY [2]				[1]
	10	11	12	13	14	15	15	16	17	18	18	19	20	21	22
	@Brk	@Brk	@NY	@NY	@NY	@Bos	@Bos	@Bos	@Bos	@Phl	@Phl	@Phl	@Brk	@Pts	@Pts
CLAY, Dain	8	8	8				8	8		8	8	8	8	8	8
FREY, Lonny	4	4		8	8	8		84	8	4	4		ph	ph	
LAMANNO, Ray	2		2					ph	2		2		ph		
HATTON, Grady															
MILLER, Eddie						ph								6	
HAAS, Bert	3	3	3	3	3	3	3	3	3	3	3	5	5	5	5
LIBKE, Al	9					ph		ph	ph	9	9	9	9	ph	
USHER, Bob			9	8			9	pr			9	9	8	pr	9
LUKON, Eddie	7	9		9	9	9		9	9		7	7	7	9	9
CORBITT, Claude	6	6	6	6	6	6	6	6	6	6	6	6	6	6	6
MUELLER, Ray	2	2	ph	2	2	2	ph	2	2	2		2	2	2	2
ZIENTARA, Benny	5	5	5	5	5	5	5	5	5	5		4	4	4	4
BEGGS, Joe				SP				SP							SP
HEUSSER, Ed	SP		RP			SP				RP	RP			RP	
ADAMS, Bobby			4	4	4	4	4	45	4	4					
VANDER MEER, Johnny		SP						RP					SP		
GUMBERT, Harry		RP					SP	RP			RP		RP	RP	
SHOUN, Clyde	RP					RP	RP		RP						
BLACKWELL, Ewell	RP				SP					SP					
ANDREWS, Nate															
WEST, Max	ph	7		7	7	7		7	7				ph	7	
WALTERS, Wm. (Bucky)		SP													
SHOKES, Eddie												3	3	3	3
MOSS, Howie															
McCORMICK, Mike															
LAMBERT, Clay									RP			SP			
VOLLMER, Clyde			7				7		7	7	87		pr		7
FOX, Howie															
HETKI, Johnny							RP		SP				RP	SP	
LAKEMAN, Al							2								
LAWING, Garland															
MALLOY, Bob	RP		RP							SP					
DASSO, Frank															
BURPO, George															
GOLDSTEIN, Leslie (Lonnie)	ph							ph							

CIN NL

	SEP	[2]				[1]	[2]	
		22	24	25	27	28	29	29	
		@Pts	@StL	@StL	Pts	Pts	Pts	Pts	156g
CLAY, Dain		8	8	8	8	8	8	8	
FREY, Lonny		ph		9	9	9	9		
LAMANNO, Ray		2				ph			
HATTON, Grady									
MILLER, Eddie									
HAAS, Bert		5	5	3					
LIBKE, Al		9	9			ph		*SP	
USHER, Bob		9	9	7			7	5	
LUKON, Eddie		7	7	7	7	7		7	
CORBITT, Claude		6	6	6	6	6	6	6	
MUELLER, Ray			2	2	2	2	2		
ZIENTARA, Benny		4	4	5	5	5	5	5	
BEGGS, Joe					SP				
HEUSSER, Ed									
ADAMS, Bobby				4	4	4	4	4	
VANDER MEER, Johnny			SP				SP		
GUMBERT, Harry						RP			
SHOUN, Clyde		RP				RP			
BLACKWELL, Ewell		SP				SP			
ANDREWS, Nate									
WEST, Max									
WALTERS, Wm. (Bucky)				SP					
SHOKES, Eddie		3	3		3	3	3	3	
MOSS, Howie									
McCORMICK, Mike									
LAMBERT, Clay									
VOLLMER, Clyde								9	
FOX, Howie									
HETKI, Johnny								RP	
LAKEMAN, Al						ph		2	
LAWING, Garland									
MALLOY, Bob		RP							
DASSO, Frank									
BURPO, George									
GOLDSTEIN, Leslie (Lonnie)									

* September 29th (2), outfielder Al Libke is the starting pitcher. He had pitched four times last season, so no precedent is set.

National League — NY NL

		APRIL										[1]	[2]	MAY	
	G	16	17	18	20	21	22	23	24	25	26	28	28	2	3
NY NL	154	Phl	Phl	@Brk	@Brk	@Brk	@Ph	@Ph	Bos	Bos	Brk	Brk	Brk	@StL	@Chi
RIGNEY, Bill	110	6	6	6	6	6	6	6	6	6	6	6	6	6	6
WITEK, Nick (Mickey)	82	4	4	4	4	4	4	4	4	4	4	4	HIT WALL, HURT.		
OTT, Mel	31	9	9		9	9	9		ph	ph	9				
YOUNG, Norman (Babe)	104	3	8	8	8		8	8	8	8	8				ph
LOMBARDI, Ernie	88	2	2	2		ph		ph		2	2	2		2	2
MARSHALL, Willard	131	87	7	7	7		7	9	9	9			7	7	
GORDON, Sid	135	7	INJURED.			ph		7	7	7	7	7		7	ph
RUCKER, Johnny	95	8	8		8	pr	8		8	pr				pr	pr
KERR, Buddy	145	5	5	5	5	5	5	5	5	5	5	5	5	5	5
VOISELLE, Bill	36	SP			SP						SP				SP
ADAMS, Ace	3	RP		RP			RP				JUMPS TO MEXICAN LEAGUE.					
TRINKLE, Ken	48	RP		RP		RP		RP							
MAYNARD, Jim (Buster)	7		9		pr	8	9		pr	pr	ph			TO J.C....	
MIZE, Johnny	101		3	3	3	3	3	3	3	3	3	3	3	3	3
JOYCE, Bob	14		SP			SP					SP				
PIKE, Jesse	16			9	ph			ph	pr			9	9	9	7
FELDMAN, Harry	3		SP				SP			RP	JUMPS TO MEXICAN LEAGUE.					
BUDNICK, Mike	35		RP		RP	RP	RP		RP						
WARREN, Bennie	39		ph								ph			2	**ph
BREWER, Jack	1		RP												
COOPER, Walker	87		ph	2	2	2	2	2	2	2	FRACTURED FINGER APR. 25th.					
KENNEDY, Monte	38		RP							SP					
KLUTTZ, Clyde	5		ph			ph		2		ph		2	TO PHILS...		
KOSLO, Dave	41			SP			SP						SP		
ARNOVICH, Morrie	1				7									TO J.C....	
FISCHER, Rube	15						RP	RP		RP					
EMMERICH, Bill	2							RP		RP					
BARTELL, Dick	5								5						
CARPENTER, Bob	12								RP						
SCHEMER, Mike	1								ph						
ROSEN, Goodwin (Goody)	100	PURCHASED FROM BROOKLYN, APRIL 27th.									8	8	8	9	
BLATTNER, Bob (Buddy)	126										4	4	4	4	
SCHUMACHER, Hal	24										SP				
GRAHAM, Jack	100	PURCHASED FROM BROOKLYN, APRIL 27th.												pr	pr
DiMAGGIO, Vince	15	IN TRADE FROM PHILLIES FOR KLUTTZ, MAY 1st.													8
THOMPSON, Gene (Junior)	39	RELEASED BY REDS, APRIL 30th (didn't play for Cincy); SIGNS WITH GIANTS, MAY 14th.													
KRAUS, Jack (Tex)	17	FROM PHILLIES APRIL 23rd. *													
CARDEN, John	1	SIGNED MAY 13th, AFTER DISCHARGE FROM USMC.													
LAWING, Garland	8	PURCHASED OUTRIGHT FROM CINCINNATI, JUNE 8th.													
ANDREWS, Nate	3	RELEASED BY CINCINNATI JUNE 11th, SIGNED BY THE GIANTS JUNE 16th.													
KRESS, Ralph (Red)	1	GIANTS' COACH, PITCHES JULY 17th DUE TO STAFF INJURIES. RETURNS TO COACHING.													
GEE, Johnny	13	REINSTATED FROM THE VOLUNTARY RETIRED LIST, JUNE 27th.													
ABERNATHY, Woody	15	PURCHASED OUTRIGHT FROM MINNEAPOLIS JULY 25th.													
THOMSON, Bobby	18	PURCHASED OUTRIGHT FROM JERSEY CITY, SEPTEMBER 9th.													
GLADD, Jim	4	PURCHASED OUTRIGHT FROM JERSEY CITY, SEPTEMBER 9th.													
JONES, Sheldon	6	19-9 AT JACKSONVILLE, BOUGHT OUTRIGHT FROM JERSEY CITY, SEPTEMBER 4th.													
LAJESKIE, Dick	6	PURCHASED OUTRIGHT FROM JERSEY CITY, SEPTEMBER 9th.													
GRISSOM, Marv	4	OPTIONED TO JERSEY CITY APRIL 2nd, SEPT. RECALL ANNOUNCED AUGUST 24th.													
GRASSO, Newton (Mickey)	7	PURCHASED OUTRIGHT FROM JERSEY CITY, SEPTEMBER 9th.													

* Kraus, purchased from Phillies April 23, did not play for Philadelphia this season.

** May 3rd, Warren credited with ph appearance in Official day-by-day records, but not in *TSN* box score. Had 0 AB; perhaps announced but replaced by another batter.

NY NL

	MAY	[1]	[2]					[1]	[2]				[1]	[2]	
	4	5	5	7	8	9	11	12	12	13	15	18	19	19	22
	@Chi	@Cin	@Cin	@Cin	@Pts	@Pts	@Bos	@Bos	@Bos	@Bos	Cin	Chi	Pts	Pts	StL
RIGNEY, Bill	6	6	6	6	5	5	5	5	56	5	5	5	5	5	5
WITEK, Nick (Mickey)	(WITEK FRACTURED ELBOW APRIL 28th (2), HITTING POLO GROUNDS WALL. OUT TILL JUNE 6th.)														
OTT, Mel								ph		ph					9
YOUNG, Norman (Babe)			ph	ph				ph		ph	ph				
LOMBARDI, Ernie	2	2		2	2	2	2	2		2	2	2	2		2
MARSHALL, Willard			ph					7	7	7	8				
GORDON, Sid	7	7			7	7					5	7	7	7	7
RUCKER, Johnny		pr				8	8	8	8	8			8	8	8
KERR, Buddy	5	5	5	5	6	6	6	6	6	6	6	6	6	6	6
VOISELLE, Bill						SP						SP			
ADAMS, Ace	(LEFT TEAM APRIL 26th. ON MAY 2nd SUSPENDED FIVE YEARS FOR JUMPING CONTRACT.)														
TRINKLE, Ken		RP	RP				RP								RP
MAYNARD, Jim (Buster)	(DATE OF OPTION TO JERSEY CITY WAS APRIL 29th.)														
MIZE, Johnny	3	3	3	3	3	3	3	3	3	3	3	3	3	3	3
JOYCE, Bob			SP					SP				RP			
PIKE, Jesse		7	7	7			7	7		ph		ph	ph		
FELDMAN, Harry	(LEFT TEAM APRIL 26th. ON MAY 2nd SUSPENDED FIVE YEARS FOR JUMPING CONTRACT.)														
BUDNICK, Mike			RP					RP	RP			RP			
WARREN, Bennie		2	2			2			2			2		2	ph
BREWER, Jack													TO MINNEAPOLIS.		
COOPER, Walker													ph		ph
KENNEDY, Monte	SP						SP					SP			
KLUTTZ, Clyde	(TO PHILLIES FOR VINCE DiMAGGIO, MAY 1st, THEN IMMEDIATELY TRADED TO CARDINALS.)														
KOSLO, Dave				SP				SP						SP	
ARNOVICH, Morrie	(DATE OF OPTION TO JERSEY CITY WAS APRIL 29th.)														
FISCHER, Rube								RP							RP
EMMERICH, Bill													TO JERSEY CITY.		
BARTELL, Dick									5		4				
CARPENTER, Bob			SP								SP		RP		SP
SCHEMER, Mike															
ROSEN, Goodwin (Goody)	9	9	9	98	8	HURT LEFT SHOULDER DIVING FOR BALL MAY 8th, OUT 3 WKS.									
BLATTNER, Bob (Buddy)	4	4	4	4	4	4	4	4	4	4	4	4	4	4	4
SCHUMACHER, Hal		SP							SP						
GRAHAM, Jack			ph	9	9	9	9	9	9	9	9	9	9	9	
DiMAGGIO, Vince	8	8	8	8	8					8					
THOMPSON, Gene (Junior)										RP					RP
KRAUS, Jack (Tex)												RP			
CARDEN, John												RP			
LAWING, Garland															
ANDREWS, Nate															
KRESS, Ralph (Red)															
GEE, Johnny															
ABERNATHY, Woody															
THOMSON, Bobby															
GLADD, Jim															
JONES, Sheldon															
LAJESKIE, Dick															
GRISSOM, Marv															
GRASSO, Newton (Mickey)															

April 26---Declared ineligible for five years for defection to the Mexican League were: George Hausmann, Sal Maglie, Roy Zimmerman, Adrian Zabala, Napoleon Reyes, Danny Gardella. Adams and Feldmen will soon join them on the Ineligible list.

NY NL

	MAY			[1]	[2]			[1]	[2]	JUNE [1]	[2]				
	23	24	25	26	26	28	29	30	30	2	2	3	4	5	6
	StL	Bos	Bos	Bos	Bos	@Brk	@Brk	@Phl	@Phl	@StL	@StL	@StL	@Chi	@Chi	@Chi
RIGNEY, Bill	5	5	5	5	5	5	5	5	5		6				
WITEK, Nick (Mickey)															ph
OTT, Mel	9	9	9	OUT WITH VISION PROBLEMS.								ph			9
YOUNG, Norman (Babe)	8	8	8	8	8	8	8	8	8	9	9	9	9	9	9
LOMBARDI, Ernie	2	ph					ph						ph		2
MARSHALL, Willard	7	7	7	7	7	7	7	7	7	7	7	7	7	7	7
GORDON, Sid		5					ph		ph	5	5	5	5	5	5
RUCKER, Johnny	ph	ph					pr				pr		ph		ph
KERR, Buddy	6	6	6	6	6	6	6	6	6	6	6	6	6	6	6
VOISELLE, Bill				SP			RP			SP					
ADAMS, Ace															
TRINKLE, Ken		RP	RP				RP	RP			RP	RP		RP	
MAYNARD, Jim (Buster)	RETURNED BY J. CITY MAY 28th, RELEASED JUNE 10, PLAYS 104 GAMES W/ MINNEAPOLIS..														
MIZE, Johnny	3	3	3	3	3	3	3	3	3	3	3	3	3	3	3
JOYCE, Bob															RP
PIKE, Jesse	OPTIONED TO JERSEY CITY, MAY 22nd.														
FELDMAN, Harry															
BUDNICK, Mike							RP		RP		RP	RP		RP	RP
WARREN, Bennie		2	2	2	2	2	2	2			2				2
BREWER, Jack	(DATE OF OPTION WAS MAY 18th.)														
COOPER, Walker	ph	ph					ph		2	2	2	2	2	2	ph
KENNEDY, Monte			SP				SP				SP				
KLUTTZ, Clyde															
KOSLO, Dave	SP					SP					SP				RP
ARNOVICH, Morrie				RETURNED BY JERSEY CITY, JUNE 6th.											
FISCHER, Rube							RP							SP	
EMMERICH, Bill	(DATE OF OPTION WAS MAY 16th.)														
BARTELL, Dick	5	54													
CARPENTER, Bob				SP				SP				SP		INJURED.	
SCHEMER, Mike							TO JERSEY CITY, MAY 29th.								
ROSEN, Goodwin (Goody)							ph		8	89	89	8	89	87	
BLATTNER, Bob (Buddy)	4	4	4	4	4	4	4	4	4	4	4	4	4	4	4
SCHUMACHER, Hal		SP					SP								SP
GRAHAM, Jack	ph	ph	9	9	9	9	9	9							ph
DiMAGGIO, Vince	pr					8	ph	8			8	8		8	pr
THOMPSON, Gene (Junior)	RP						RP				RP		RP		
KRAUS, Jack (Tex)															
CARDEN, John															
LAWING, Garland															
ANDREWS, Nate															
KRESS, Ralph (Red)															
GEE, Johnny															
ABERNATHY, Woody															
THOMSON, Bobby															
GLADD, Jim															
JONES, Sheldon															
LAJESKIE, Dick															
GRISSOM, Marv															
GRASSO, Newton (Mickey)															

NY NL

	JUNE 7 @Pts	8 @Pts	9 [1] @Pts	9 [2] @Pts	10 @Cin	11 @Cin	12 @Cin	15 StL	16 [1] StL	16 [2] StL	18 Cin	19 Cin	21 Chi	22 [1] Chi	22 [2] Chi
RIGNEY, Bill						ph							pr		
WITEK, Nick (Mickey)	5	5	5	5	5	5	5								5
OTT, Mel					ph		ph	9	9				ph	9	
YOUNG, Norman (Babe)	9			ph	ph						ph			ph	
LOMBARDI, Ernie				2		ph			ph		ph			ph	2
MARSHALL, Willard	ph			ph			7	7		7	7	7	7		
GORDON, Sid	7	7	7	7	7	7		5	5	5	5	5	5	5	7
RUCKER, Johnny	ph	8	8	8	8	8			pr	8	8	8	8	ph	
KERR, Buddy	6	6	6	6	6	6	6	6	6	6	6	6	6	6	6
VOISELLE, Bill	SP									SP					SP
ADAMS, Ace															
TRINKLE, Ken	RP			RP	RP			RP	RP				RP		RP
MAYNARD, Jim (Buster)															
MIZE, Johnny	3	3	3	3	3	3	3	3	3	3	3	3	3	3	3
JOYCE, Bob				SP		RP					RP			RP	
PIKE, Jesse															
FELDMAN, Harry															
BUDNICK, Mike	RP										RP		RP		
WARREN, Bennie						ph			ph		ONE GAME at J.C., JUNE 18th...				
BREWER, Jack															
COOPER, Walker	2	2	2		2	2	2	2	2	2	2	2	2	2	ph
KENNEDY, Monte			SP			RP		SP					SP		RP
KLUTTZ, Clyde															
KOSLO, Dave		SP					SP		SP			RP		SP	
ARNOVICH, Morrie															
FISCHER, Rube	RP				RP						RP			RP	
EMMERICH, Bill															
BARTELL, Dick															
CARPENTER, Bob	HURT PITCHING ELBOW JUNE 4th; OUT TILL JUNE 29th.														
SCHEMER, Mike	RETURNED BY JERSEY CITY, JUNE 18th.														
ROSEN, Goodwin (Goody)	8	9	9	9	9	9	8	8	8	9	9	9	9	8	8
BLATTNER, Bob (Buddy)	4	4	4	4	4	4	4	4	4	4	4	4	4	4	4
SCHUMACHER, Hal					SP					SP					
GRAHAM, Jack	ph				ph		9				ph	ph	ph	7	9
DiMAGGIO, Vince	SOLD TO SAN FRANCISCO, MAY 7th.														
THOMPSON, Gene (Junior)	RP					SP		SORE ARM, OUT TILL JUNE 29th.							
KRAUS, Jack (Tex)	RP						RP				RP				
CARDEN, John								OPTIONED TO RICHMOND, JUNE 13th.							
LAWING, Garland						ph			8	7			7		
ANDREWS, Nate									RP			SP			
KRESS, Ralph (Red)															
GEE, Johnny															
ABERNATHY, Woody															
THOMSON, Bobby															
GLADD, Jim															
JONES, Sheldon															
LAJESKIE, Dick															
GRISSOM, Marv															
GRASSO, Newton (Mickey)															

National League — NY NL

	JUNE	[1]	[2]				[1]	[2]	JULY	[1]	[2]			[1]	[2] ALL-STAR BREAK
	23	23	25	26	28	29	30	30	2	4	4	5	6	7	7
NY NL	Chi	Chi	Pts	Pts	@Phl	@Phl	@Phl	@Phl	@Bos	Brk	Brk	Brk	Phl	Phl	Phl
RIGNEY, Bill				5	5	5	5	5	5	5	56	6	6		
WITEK, Nick (Mickey)	5	5	5		5						5	5	5	5	5
OTT, Mel															
YOUNG, Norman (Babe)		ph			ph	ph		ph	ph			ph			
LOMBARDI, Ernie				2	2	2	2			2	ph	2	2	2	
MARSHALL, Willard	ph	ph	ph	8	89	8	8	8	8	8	87	8	8	8	8
GORDON, Sid	7	7	7	7	7	7	7	7	7	7	7	7	7	7	7
RUCKER, Johnny					8			pr	pr		8				
KERR, Buddy	6	6	6	6	6	6	6	6	6	6	6		6	6	6
VOISELLE, Bill		RP	RP			SP		RP			SP				
ADAMS, Ace															
TRINKLE, Ken		RP			RP			RP			RP	RP			
MAYNARD, Jim (Buster)															
MIZE, Johnny	3	3	3	3	3	3	3	3	3	3	3	3	3	3	3
JOYCE, Bob												SP			
PIKE, Jesse															
FELDMAN, Harry															
BUDNICK, Mike		SP						SP				RP	RP		
WARREN, Bennie		...RETURNS JUNE 30th.						2			ph				
BREWER, Jack															
COOPER, Walker	2	2	2		*ph	ph		2	2		2		2		2
KENNEDY, Monte	RP				SP			RP	SP		RP				SP
KLUTTZ, Clyde															
KOSLO, Dave				SP		SP			SP				SP		
ARNOVICH, Morrie															
FISCHER, Rube	RP					RP			RP						
EMMERICH, Bill															
BARTELL, Dick															
CARPENTER, Bob						RP	HAS ELBOW SURGERY FOR BONE CHIPS.								
SCHEMER, Mike															
ROSEN, Goodwin (Goody)	8	8	8		ph			ph	8	9	9	9	9	9	9
BLATTNER, Bob (Buddy)	4	4	4	4	4	4	4	4	4	4	4	4	4	4	4
SCHUMACHER, Hal			SP			RP					SP				
GRAHAM, Jack	9	9	9	9	9	9	9	9	9		9	ph	ph		
DiMAGGIO, Vince															
THOMPSON, Gene (Junior)							RP								
KRAUS, Jack (Tex)	RP	RP			RP						RP	RP			
CARDEN, John															
LAWING, Garland	9				pr							pr			
ANDREWS, Nate	SP		RELEASED JUNE 25th. EVENTUALLY SIGNS WITH WILMINGTON (N.C.).												
KRESS, Ralph (Red)															
GEE, Johnny															
ABERNATHY, Woody															
THOMSON, Bobby															
GLADD, Jim															
JONES, Sheldon															
LAJESKIE, Dick															
GRISSOM, Marv															
GRASSO, Newton (Mickey)															

*June 28th, Cooper in TSN box as *PITCHER*. Brother Mort, the pitcher, is with Boston, however. Assume catcher *WALKER* Cooper is pinch hitter, NOT pitcher.

National League

NY NL	JULY 11	[1] 12	[2] 12	13	14	15	16	17	18	20	[1] 21	[2] 21	24	[1] 25	[2] 25
	@StL	@StL	@StL	@StL	@Chi	@Chi	@Chi	@Pts	@Pts	@Cin	@Cin	@Cin	StL	StL	StL
RIGNEY, Bill				5	5	5	5	5	5	5	5	5	5	5	5
WITEK, Nick (Mickey)	5	5	5	54	4	4				ph		4	45	4	4
OTT, Mel															
YOUNG, Norman (Babe)		ph		ph	ph	ph	3	ph	ph				ph		
LOMBARDI, Ernie		2	2		2		2	2	2	2	2		2		2
MARSHALL, Willard	8	8	8	87	8	8	8	8	8	8	8	8	8	8	8
GORDON, Sid	7	7	7	7	7	7	7	7	7	7	7	7	7	7	7
RUCKER, Johnny		8	pr		pr		pr		pr		ph		pr		
KERR, Buddy	6	6	6	6	6	6	6	6	6	6	6	6	6	6	6
VOISELLE, Bill		SP		RP			SP			SP				SP	
ADAMS, Ace															
TRINKLE, Ken			RP	RP		RP		SP		SP					
MAYNARD, Jim (Buster)															
MIZE, Johnny	3	3	3	3	3	3	3	3	3	3	3	3	3	3	3
JOYCE, Bob			RP		RP										
PIKE, Jesse															
FELDMAN, Harry															
BUDNICK, Mike				SP							RP			RP	
WARREN, Bennie									2	ph		2	2	2	
BREWER, Jack															
COOPER, Walker	2	2	ph	2		2	2	BREAKS FINGER JULY 16th.							
KENNEDY, Monte															SP
KLUTTZ, Clyde															
KOSLO, Dave	SP					SP			SP				SP		
ARNOVICH, Morrie															
FISCHER, Rube					RP										
EMMERICH, Bill															
BARTELL, Dick															
CARPENTER, Bob															
SCHEMER, Mike		TO RICHMOND, JULY 12th.													
ROSEN, Goodwin (Goody)	9	9	9	98	9	9	9	9	9	9	9				
BLATTNER, Bob (Buddy)	4	4	4	4			4	4	4	4	4		4		
SCHUMACHER, Hal				SP											
GRAHAM, Jack			ph	9	ph	ph		ph			ph	9	9	9	9
DiMAGGIO, Vince															
THOMPSON, Gene (Junior)			RP		RP			RP		RP		RP			
KRAUS, Jack (Tex)			SP		RP						RP				
CARDEN, John															
LAWING, Garland										ph			TO J.C...		
ANDREWS, Nate															
KRESS, Ralph (Red)								RP							
GEE, Johnny								RP				SP			
ABERNATHY, Woody															
THOMSON, Bobby															
GLADD, Jim															
JONES, Sheldon															
LAJESKIE, Dick															
GRISSOM, Marv															
GRASSO, Newton (Mickey)															

NY NL

	JULY	[1]	[2]	[1]	[2]				AUG [1]	[2]	[1]	[2]			
	26	27	27	28	28	29	30	31	2	2	4	4	6	8	9
NY NL	Cin	Cin	Cin	Cin	Cin	Chi	Chi	Chi	Pts	Pts	Pts	Pts	Brk	Brk	@Bos
RIGNEY, Bill	5	5	5	5	5	5	5	5	5	5	56	6	6	6	6
WITEK, Nick (Mickey)	4	4	4	4	4	4	ph		ph		5	5	5	5	5
OTT, Mel					ph										
YOUNG, Norman (Babe)	ph		ph	ph		ph	ph						3	3	3
LOMBARDI, Ernie	2	2		2	ph	2	2			2	2			2	ph
MARSHALL, Willard	8	8	8	8	8	8	8	8	8	8	8	8	87	8	8
GORDON, Sid	7	7	7	7	7	7	7	7	7	7	7	7	7	7	7
RUCKER, Johnny	pr			pr	pr	pr			pr	pr			8	pr	
KERR, Buddy	6	6	6	6	6	6	6	6	6	6	6				
VOISELLE, Bill	INJURED KNEE JULY 25th, IS OUT TILL AUGUST 11th.														
ADAMS, Ace															
TRINKLE, Ken			SP			RP				SP				SP	
MAYNARD, Jim (Buster)															
MIZE, Johnny	3	3	3	3	3	3	3	3	3	3	3	3	HIT BY PITCH.		
JOYCE, Bob	TO MINNEAPOLIS FOR ABERNATHY, JULY 25th.														
PIKE, Jesse															
FELDMAN, Harry															
BUDNICK, Mike						RP		SP			SP				
WARREN, Bennie			2		2			2							
BREWER, Jack															
COOPER, Walker						ph			2	2	2	2	2	2	2
KENNEDY, Monte						SP	RP				SP				SP
KLUTTZ, Clyde															
KOSLO, Dave				SP					SP				SP	RP	
ARNOVICH, Morrie															
FISCHER, Rube	TO MINNEAPOLIS FOR ABERNATHY, JULY 25th.														
EMMERICH, Bill															
BARTELL, Dick															
CARPENTER, Bob															
SCHEMER, Mike															
ROSEN, Goodwin (Goody)	ph		ph			pr			9	9	9	9	9	9	9
BLATTNER, Bob (Buddy)	pr					4	4	4	4	4	4	4	4	4	4
SCHUMACHER, Hal		SP													
GRAHAM, Jack	9	9	9	9	9	9	9	9	9					ph	
DiMAGGIO, Vince															
THOMPSON, Gene (Junior)		RP		RP			RP			RP					RP
KRAUS, Jack (Tex)								RP			RP				RP
CARDEN, John	RECALL FROM RICHMOND ANNOUNCED AUG. 24th, BUT NEVER AGAIN PLAYS IN MAJORS.														
LAWING, Garland	OPTIONED TO JERSEY CITY, JULY 22nd; REFUSES TO REPORT, SUSPENDED SAME DAY.														
ANDREWS, Nate															
KRESS, Ralph (Red)															
GEE, Johnny	SP						SP								
ABERNATHY, Woody						SP		RP							
THOMSON, Bobby															
GLADD, Jim															
JONES, Sheldon															
LAJESKIE, Dick															
GRISSOM, Marv															
GRASSO, Newton (Mickey)															

NY NL	AUG [1] 11 @Bos	[2] 11 @Bos	12 @Brk	[1] 14 @Brk	[2] 14 @Brk	15 @Brk	[1] 18 Bos	[2] 18 Bos	20 @Cin	21 @Cin	22 @Pts	23 @Pts	24 @Pts	25 @Chi	26 @Chi
RIGNEY, Bill	6	6	6	6	6	5	5	5	5	5	5	HAS BAD COLD.			5
WITEK, Nick (Mickey)	5	ph	4	4	4	4		5							
OTT, Mel			ph												
YOUNG, Norman (Babe)	3	3	3	3	3	3	3	3	3	3	3	3	3	3	3
LOMBARDI, Ernie			ph		ph			2		ph					ph
MARSHALL, Willard	8	7	*7	7	7	8	8	8	8	87	87	7	7	7	8
GORDON, Sid	7	5	5	5	5	7	7	7	7	75	***75	5	5	5	7
RUCKER, Johnny	ph	8	pr	ph	**8	ph		ph		ph	8	ph			
KERR, Buddy					ph	6	6	6	6	6	6	6	6	6	6
VOISELLE, Bill		SP		RP				RP		RP			SP		
ADAMS, Ace															
TRINKLE, Ken			SP				SP					SP			
MAYNARD, Jim (Buster)															
MIZE, Johnny	MIZE HIT BY JOE PAGE PITCH IN EXHIBITION AGAINST THE YANKEES, BREAKING HIS HAND.														
JOYCE, Bob	RECALL ANNOUNCED AUGUST 24th, BUT HIS TWO SEASONS IN THE MAJORS ARE OVER..														
PIKE, Jesse	RECALL FROM JERSEY CITY ANNOUNCED AUGUST 24th, BUT BIG LEAGUE CAREER IS OVER.														
FELDMAN, Harry															
BUDNICK, Mike				SP			RP								
WARREN, Bennie	2														
BREWER, Jack	RECALL FROM MINNEAPOLIS ANNOUNCED AUG. 24th, BUT BIG LEAGUE CAREER IS OVER.														
COOPER, Walker	2	2	2	2	2	2	2		2	2	2	2	2	2	2
KENNEDY, Monte					RP			SP			SP				SP
KLUTTZ, Clyde															
KOSLO, Dave	SP		RP			SP			SP					SP	
ARNOVICH, Morrie															
FISCHER, Rube															
EMMERICH, Bill															
BARTELL, Dick															
CARPENTER, Bob															
SCHEMER, Mike	(ON AUGUST 11th, SCHEMER IS APPOINTED MANAGER AT RICHMOND.)														
ROSEN, Goodwin (Goody)	9	89	*8	8	8	ph	9	9	9	98	9	8	8	8	9
BLATTNER, Bob (Buddy)	4	4	4	pr		4	4	4	4	4	4	4	4	4	4
SCHUMACHER, Hal				RP											
GRAHAM, Jack	ph	9	9	9	9	9	ph	ph		9	ph	9	9	9	
DiMAGGIO, Vince															
THOMPSON, Gene (Junior)		RP		RP		RP					RP				
KRAUS, Jack (Tex)	RP				RP										
CARDEN, John															
LAWING, Garland															
ANDREWS, Nate															
KRESS, Ralph (Red)															
GEE, Johnny				RP					SP						
ABERNATHY, Woody	RP				RP				RP						
THOMSON, Bobby															
GLADD, Jim															
JONES, Sheldon															
LAJESKIE, Dick															
GRISSOM, Marv	RECALL FROM JERSEY CITY ANNOUNCED AUGUST 24th.														
GRASSO, Newton (Mickey)															

* Aug 12th, Rosen & Marshall both in TSN box score playing left field, with no center fielder: Rosen is CF.
** Aug 14 (2), Official daily records show Rucker in center field for 9th inning, but he doesn't appear in TSN box score.

National League — NY NL

	AUG	[1]	[2]				SEP [1]	[2]	[1]	[2]					
	27	28	28	29	30	31	1	1	2	2	3	4	5	6	7
NY NL	@Chi	@StL	@StL	@StL	Phl	Brk	Brk	Brk	@Bos	@Bos	@Bos	Phl	Phl	Phl	@Brk
RIGNEY, Bill	5	5		5		5	5	5	5	5	5		pr	56	
WITEK, Nick (Mickey)			ph					5		54	5	4	4	45	4
OTT, Mel	ph	ph		ph			ph		9	9	ph				
YOUNG, Norman (Babe)	3	3	3	3	3	3	3	3				3	3	3	3
LOMBARDI, Ernie		ph	2		ph			2	ph	2	ph	2	2	2	2
MARSHALL, Willard	8	87	7	8	7	7	8	8	8	7	7	7	7	8	7
GORDON, Sid	7	75	5	7	5		7	7	7	ph	ph	5	5	7	5
RUCKER, Johnny		ph	pr		ph	8		ph		8	8	8	8		8
KERR, Buddy	6	6	6	6	6	6	6	6	6	6	6	6	6	6	6
VOISELLE, Bill			SP				SP						SP		
ADAMS, Ace															
TRINKLE, Ken		SP						SP			RP			SP	
MAYNARD, Jim (Buster)	(MAYNARD RECALLED AUGUST 30th, SOLD BACK TO MINNEAPOLIS ON SEPTEMBER 18th.)														
MIZE, Johnny															
JOYCE, Bob															
PIKE, Jesse															
FELDMAN, Harry															
BUDNICK, Mike		RP			SP				RP			RP			
WARREN, Bennie												2			
BREWER, Jack															
COOPER, Walker	2	2	2	2	2	2	2		2	2	2				
KENNEDY, Monte		RP				SP						SP			
KLUTTZ, Clyde															
KOSLO, Dave		pr		SP			RP				SP				SP
ARNOVICH, Morrie															
FISCHER, Rube															
EMMERICH, Bill	RECALL FROM JERSEY CITY ANNOUNCED AUG. 30th, BUT HE'S RELEASED SEPTEMBER 8th.														
BARTELL, Dick															
CARPENTER, Bob		RP							RP						
SCHEMER, Mike	RECALL FROM RICHMOND ANNOUNCED AUGUST 30th, BUT BIG LEAGUE CAREER IS OVER.														
ROSEN, Goodwin (Goody)	9	98	8	9	8	8	9	9	9	h9	ph	ph			ph
BLATTNER, Bob (Buddy)	4	4	4	4	4	4	4	4	4	4	4	ph		4	
SCHUMACHER, Hal		RP			RP					SP		RP			
GRAHAM, Jack	ph	9	9		9	9	ph	3	3	3	3	9	9	9	9
DiMAGGIO, Vince															
THOMPSON, Gene (Junior)	RP			RP			RP	RP			RP				RP
KRAUS, Jack (Tex)															
CARDEN, John															
LAWING, Garland															
ANDREWS, Nate															
KRESS, Ralph (Red)															
GEE, Johnny	SP							SP							
ABERNATHY, Woody		RP			RP				RP				RP		RP
THOMSON, Bobby															
GLADD, Jim															
JONES, Sheldon															
LAJESKIE, Dick															
GRISSOM, Marv	GRISSOM WILL REPORT AT END OF INTERNATIONAL LEAGUE SEASON, SEPTEMBER 8th.														
GRASSO, Newton (Mickey)															

NY NL

	SEP			[1]	[2]				[1]	[2]				[1]	[2]
	8	9	10	11	11	12	13	14	15	15	17	18	19	22	22
	@Brk	@Phl	Pts	Pts	Pts	Cin	Cin	Cin	StL	StL	StL	Chi	Bos	@Phl	@Phl
RIGNEY, Bill	5			pr	ph				5	5	5				ph
WITEK, Nick (Mickey)	4	4	ph	4	4	4	4	4	4	4	4				
OTT, Mel															
YOUNG, Norman (Babe)	3	3	3	3	3	3	ph	3	3	3	3	3	3	3	ph
LOMBARDI, Ernie	ph	ph		2	ph		ph	2	2	2	2	ph			
MARSHALL, Willard	8			9	9	9	9	9	9	9	9	9	9	9	9
GORDON, Sid	7	7	7	7	7	7	7	7	7	7	7	7	7	7	7
RUCKER, Johnny	ph	8	8	8	8	8	8	8	8	8	8	8	8	8	8
KERR, Buddy	6	6	6	6	6	6	6	6	6	6	6	6	6	6	6
VOISELLE, Bill	RP				SP					SP					RP
ADAMS, Ace															
TRINKLE, Ken			SP						RP	RP	RP			SP	
MAYNARD, Jim (Buster)															
MIZE, Johnny							3		MIZE BREAKS TOE, HIS SEASON ENDED.						
JOYCE, Bob			RETURNED OUTRIGHT TO SAN FRANCISCO, SEPTEMBER 18th.												
PIKE, Jesse															
FELDMAN, Harry															
BUDNICK, Mike	RP			RP											
WARREN, Bennie	2								2	2	ph				
BREWER, Jack															
COOPER, Walker	ph	h2		ph	2	2	2		BLOOD POISONING IN LEFT LEG.						
KENNEDY, Monte	SP		RP			SP		RP		RP	SP				
KLUTTZ, Clyde															
KOSLO, Dave				SP					SP			SP			
ARNOVICH, Morrie															
FISCHER, Rube															
EMMERICH, Bill															
BARTELL, Dick															
CARPENTER, Bob															
SCHEMER, Mike															
ROSEN, Goodwin (Goody)	9	ph	9	ph			ph		ph					ph	ph
BLATTNER, Bob (Buddy)	ph		ph	4	pr		3		ph	ph	ph	pr		pr	4
SCHUMACHER, Hal	RP		RP				RP					RP			RP
GRAHAM, Jack	9	9		ph			ph	ph	ph			ph		ph	3
DiMAGGIO, Vince															
THOMPSON, Gene (Junior)	RP	RP		RP				RP		RP	RP			RP	RP
KRAUS, Jack (Tex)					RP										
CARDEN, John															
LAWING, Garland			REINSTATED FROM SUSPENDED LIST, SEPTEMBER 20th.												
ANDREWS, Nate															
KRESS, Ralph (Red)			KRESS RELEASED AS A PLAYER, RETURNS FULL-TIME COACH DUTIES, SEPTEMBER 16th.												
GEE, Johnny	RP			RP		RP				RP					
ABERNATHY, Woody		RP	RP			RP			RP	RP					
THOMSON, Bobby		*5	5	5	5	5	5	5	5	ph	ph	5	5	5	5
GLADD, Jim		2	2												2
JONES, Sheldon		SP		RP	RP		SP								SP
LAJESKIE, Dick			4				pr			pr		4	4	4	
GRISSOM, Marv			RP				SP					SP			
GRASSO, Newton (Mickey)												2	2	2	2

* Sept 9th, Thomson debuts, shown in *TSN* box score as "Thompson", with a "p". Gene Thompson, pitcher, also appears today.

NY NL

	SEP 25 Bos	[1] 26 Bos	[2] 26 Bos	28 Phl	29 Phl	
						154g
RIGNEY, Bill	ph		6			
WITEK, Nick (Mickey)	ph		ph		5	
OTT, Mel						
YOUNG, Norman (Babe)	ph	ph	3	3	3	
LOMBARDI, Ernie						
MARSHALL, Willard	9	9	7	9	9	
GORDON, Sid	7	7	ph	7	7	
RUCKER, Johnny	8	8	8	8	8	
KERR, Buddy	6	6	6	6	6	
VOISELLE, Bill	RP			SP		
ADAMS, Ace						
TRINKLE, Ken						
MAYNARD, Jim (Buster)						
MIZE, Johnny						
JOYCE, Bob						
PIKE, Jesse						
FELDMAN, Harry						
BUDNICK, Mike						
WARREN, Bennie			2			
BREWER, Jack						
COOPER, Walker						
KENNEDY, Monte	SP					
KLUTTZ, Clyde						
KOSLO, Dave		SP				
ARNOVICH, Morrie						
FISCHER, Rube						
EMMERICH, Bill						
BARTELL, Dick						
CARPENTER, Bob		RP				
SCHEMER, Mike						
ROSEN, Goodwin (Goody)			9			
BLATTNER, Bob (Buddy)	4	4	4	4	4	
SCHUMACHER, Hal	RP					
GRAHAM, Jack	3	3	ph			
DiMAGGIO, Vince						
THOMPSON, Gene (Junior)	RP		RP			
KRAUS, Jack (Tex)						
CARDEN, John						
LAWING, Garland						
ANDREWS, Nate						
KRESS, Ralph (Red)						
GEE, Johnny		RP				
ABERNATHY, Woody						
THOMSON, Bobby	5	5	5	5		
GLADD, Jim					2	
JONES, Sheldon					SP	
LAJESKIE, Dick						
GRISSOM, Marv			SP			
GRASSO, Newton (Mickey)	2	2		2		

National League

	G	APRIL 16	17	20	[1] 21	[2] 21	22	23	24	[1] 28	[2] 28	30	MAY 1	2	3
PHL NL	155	@NY	@NY	@NY	Bos	Bos	NY	NY	Brk	@Bos	@Bos	@Pts	@Pts	@Pts	@Cin
MURTAUGH, Danny	6	4	4	4	4	4	4						NEXT PAGE.		
WYROSTEK, Johnny	145	7	7	7	7	8	8	8	8	8	7	87	8	8	8
TABOR, Jim	124	5	5	5	5	5	5	5	5	5	5	5	5	5	
NORTHEY, Ron	128	9	9	9	9		ph	9	9	9	9	9	9	9	9
McCORMICK, Frank	135	3	3	3	3	3	3	3	3	3	3	3	3	3	3
DiMAGGIO, Vince	6	8	8	8	8					8	8	TO NY NL...			
HEMSLEY, Rollie	49	2	2	2	2		2		2			2	2		2
NEWSOME, Lamar (Skeeter)	112	6	6	6	6	6	6	6	6	6	6	6	6	6	6
JUDD, Oscar	46	SP						SP						SP	
MULCAHY, Hugh	16	RP					RP							RP	
WASDELL, Jimmy	26	ph		ph	ph	9	9	7	7	7	7	ph			
LOPATKA, Art	4	RP						RP							
NOVIKOFF, Lou	17	ph	ph	ph	ph	7	7			ph				ph	
O'NEIL, John	46	pr													
HOERST, Frank	18		SP					SP							
JURISICH, Al	13		RP		SP						SP				SP
MULLIGAN, Dick	19		RP	RP							RP				
DINGES, Vance	50			ph		ph		ph		OPTIONED TO UTICA, APRIL 25.					
SEMINICK, Andy	124		2	h2	2		2	2	2	2	2		2	2	
RAFFENSBERGER, Ken	39		SP					SP							
KARL, Anton (Andy)	39		RP								RP				
HUGHES, Roy	89			4		4						4	4	5	
ROWE, Lynwood (Schoolboy)	30			SP		ph					ph				
HUGHES, Tommy	29					SP					SP				
CRAWFORD, Glenn	1					ph									
RICHARDSON, Ken	6						4	4	4	4	4		**5		
JOHNSON, Silas (Si)	1							RP				RELEASED TO BRAVES.			
PEARSON, Isaac (Ike)	5							RP				SP			
ENNIS, Del	141	(FROM NDSL, APRIL 15th.)								*ph		7	7	7	7
SCHANZ, Charley	32								RP						
VERBAN, Emil	138	FROM THE CARDINALS FOR KLUTTZ, MAY 1st.													4
MAUNEY, Dick	25														
HUMPHRIES, John	10														
CHAPMAN, Ben	1														
RIPPLE, Charlie	6														
SPINDEL, Hal	1														
BURICH, Bill	2	RELEASED FROM THE NATIONAL DEFENSE SERVICE LIST, MAY 13th.													
MILNAR, Al	1	BOUGHT CONDITIONALLY FROM BROWNS MAY 29th, WITH 1B-OF LOU FINNEY.													
STANCEAU, Charley	14	PURCHASED OUTRIGHT FROM THE YANKEES, JUNE 5th.													
MOORE, D.C. (Dee)	11	WILL BE RELEASED FROM THE NATIONAL DEFENSE SERVICE LIST, JUNE 10th.													
GILBERT, Charlie	88	PURCHASED OUTRIGHT FROM THE CUBS, JUNE 14th.													
DONNELLY, Sylvester (Blix)	12	PURCHASED FROM THE CARDINALS, JULY 8th.													
LETCHAS, Charlie	6	BEGINS SEASON IN MILITARY SERVICE. REINSTATED FROM NDSL, AUGUST 14th.													
POSSEHL, Lou	4	EX-G.I. SEMI-PRO, 20, SIGNED IN MID-AUGUST, DEBUTS AUGUST 25th.													
HODKEY, Aloysius (Eli)	2											OPTIONED TO UTICA...			
HASENMAYER, Don	6	FROM NATIONAL DEFENSE SERVICE LIST, JULY 12th.													
GRATE, Don	3											OPTIONED TO UTICA, APRIL 25th.			
HAMNER, Granville (Granny)	2	IN MILITARY SERVICE MOST OF SEASON, REINSTATED FROM NDSL SEPTEMBER 18th.													
KOECHER, Dick	1	SIGNED OFF TEMPLE UNIVERSITY CAMPUS, JUNE 17th.													

* April 28 (1), Ennis called "Enos" in first box score.

** In May 2 box score, Richardson & 3B Tabor each bat 6th w /2AB (Hughes, leadoff/2B, has 5 AB). Richardson plays only 2B, so assume Hughes 3B when Tabor exits.

National League — PHL NL

	MAY	[1]	[2]							[1]	[2]				
	4	5	5	8	11	12	13	15	17	19	19	21	22	23	24
PHL NL	@Cin	@Chi	@Chi	@StL	@Brk	@Brk	@Brk	Chi	Cin	StL	StL	StL	Pts	Pts	Brk
MURTAUGH, Danny	MURTAUGH WAS SOLD TO ROCHESTER ON MAY 2nd.														
WYROSTEK, Johnny	8	8	8	8	8	8	8	8	8	8	8	8	8	8	8
TABOR, Jim						5	5	5	5			5	5	INJURED...	
NORTHEY, Ron	9	SUSPENDED.		9	9	9	9	9	9	9	9	9	9	9	9
McCORMICK, Frank	3	3	3	3	3	3	3	3	3	3	3	3	3	3	3
DiMAGGIO, Vince	(TO THE GIANTS FOR KLUTTZ, MAY 1st. KLUTTZ TRADED TO StL FOR VERBAN, SAME DAY.)														
HEMSLEY, Rollie	2	BROKE WRIST MAY 1st...					pr	...WASN'T DIAGNOSED FOR TWO WEEKS.							
NEWSOME, Lamar (Skeeter)	6	6	6	6			6			ph	ph		6	6	6
JUDD, Oscar		ph	SP		ph		SP								
MULCAHY, Hugh					RP					RP					
WASDELL, Jimmy	ph	9	9	9			ph	ph						ph	ph
LOPATKA, Art		RP													
NOVIKOFF, Lou			ph			7		ph		ph					
O'NEIL, John				6	6	6	6	6	6	6	6	6	6		
HOERST, Frank														RP	
JURISICH, Al							SP	RP		SP					
MULLIGAN, Dick			SP		RP	RP				SP					SP
DINGES, Vance															
SEMINICK, Andy		2	2	2	2	2	2	2	2	2	2	2	2	2	2
RAFFENSBERGER, Ken		RP			RP		RP			RP					
KARL, Anton (Andy)	RP	RP			RP		RP	RP			RP	RP	RP		
HUGHES, Roy	5	5	5	5	5	5	56	ph		ph	5	ph	5	5	5
ROWE, Lynwood (Schoolboy)		SP						ph	SP			SP	ph		
HUGHES, Tommy	SP				RP						SP		SP		
CRAWFORD, Glenn				SOLD OUTRIGHT TO PORTLAND (PACIFIC COAST LEAGUE), MAY 7th.											
RICHARDSON, Ken															
JOHNSON, Silas (Si)	(DATE OF RELEASE TO BOSTON WAS APRIL 29th.)														
PEARSON, Isaac (Ike)				SP	RP									RP	
ENNIS, Del	7	7	7	7	7	79	7	7	7	7	7	7	7	7	7
SCHANZ, Charley			RP		SP					RP					RP
VERBAN, Emil	4	4	4	4	4	4	4	4	4	4	4	4	4	4	4
MAUNEY, Dick	RP						RP			*pr?				RP	
HUMPHRIES, John		RP				RP									RP
CHAPMAN, Ben						RP									
RIPPLE, Charlie															
SPINDEL, Hal															
BURICH, Bill															
MILNAR, Al															
STANCEAU, Charley															
MOORE, D.C. (Dee)															
GILBERT, Charlie															
DONNELLY, Sylvester (Blix)															
LETCHAS, Charlie															
POSSEHL, Lou															
HODKEY, Aloysius (Eli)	(DATE OF OPTION TO UTICA WAS APRIL 29th.)														
HASENMAYER, Don															
GRATE, Don															
HAMNER, Granville (Granny)															
KOECHER, Dick															

NOTE: April 29th, outfielder Rene Monteagudo was suspended for 5 years after defection to the Mexican League.

*? May 19th, Official day-by-day records credit Mauney with pr appearance, though it's not specified whether it's in Game 1 or 2. He's in neither *TSN* box score.

	MAY	[1]	[2]		[1]	[2]	[1]	[2]						[1]	[2]
						JUNE									
	25	26	26	29	30	30	2	2	3	4	6	7	8	9	9
PHL NL	Brk	Brk	Brk	Bos	NY	NY	@Pts	@Pts	@Pts	@Cin	@Cin	@StL	@StL	@StL	@StL
MURTAUGH, Danny															
WYROSTEK, Johnny	8	8	8	8	8	8	8	8	8	8	8	8	8	8	8
TABOR, Jim		...OUT WITH ARM INJURY.													
NORTHEY, Ron	9	9	9	9	9	9	9	9	9	9	9	9	9	9	9
McCORMICK, Frank	3	3	3	3	3	3	3	3	3	3	3	3	3	3	3
DiMAGGIO, Vince															
HEMSLEY, Rollie															
NEWSOME, Lamar (Skeeter)	6	6	6	6	6	6	6	6	6	6	6	6	6	6	6
JUDD, Oscar		RP	ph		SP						RP			SP	
MULCAHY, Hugh	RP			SP											
WASDELL, Jimmy		ph	ph		ph			3		ph			ph	3	
LOPATKA, Art															
NOVIKOFF, Lou	ph	ph	ph										ph		
O'NEIL, John		pr		6										6	
HOERST, Frank	RP												RP		
JURISICH, Al		SP		OUT WITH ARTHRITIS.			SP								
MULLIGAN, Dick							TONSILLECTOMY, MAY 31.								
DINGES, Vance							FROM UTICA JUNE 19th, WHEN McCORMICK HURT.								
SEMINICK, Andy	2	2	2	2	2	2	2	2	2	2	2	2	2	2	2
RAFFENSBERGER, Ken		SP									SP				RP
KARL, Anton (Andy)							RP	RP	RP						RP
HUGHES, Roy	5	5	5	5	5	5	5	5	5	5	5	5	5	5	5
ROWE, Lynwood (Schoolboy)	ph	ph	ph	SP						SP					SP
HUGHES, Tommy	SP						SP						SP		
CRAWFORD, Glenn															
RICHARDSON, Ken									SOLD OUTRIGHT TO HOLLYWOOD, JUNE 3rd.						
JOHNSON, Silas (Si)															
PEARSON, Isaac (Ike)															
ENNIS, Del	7	7	7	7	7	7	7	7	7	7	7	7	7	7	7
SCHANZ, Charley							SP					RP			
VERBAN, Emil	4	4	4	4	4	4	4	4	4	4	4	4	4	4	4
MAUNEY, Dick										SP					
HUMPHRIES, John														RP	
CHAPMAN, Ben															
RIPPLE, Charlie														RP	
SPINDEL, Hal														2	
BURICH, Bill														h5	
MILNAR, Al															
STANCEAU, Charley															
MOORE, D.C. (Dee)															
GILBERT, Charlie															
DONNELLY, Sylvester (Blix)															
LETCHAS, Charlie															
POSSEHL, Lou															
HODKEY, Aloysius (Eli)															
HASENMAYER, Don															
GRATE, Don															
HAMNER, Granville (Granny)															
KOECHER, Dick															

* May 29th, Milnar & 1B-OF Lou Finney bought, conditionally, from the Browns, but are quickly returned. Finney doesn't play at all for the Phillies; Milnar doesn't last an inning on the mound.

PHL NL

	JUNE 10	11	15	[1] 16	[2] 16	17	18	21	[1] 22	[2] 22	[1] 23	[2] 23 TIE 6/23(2), REPLAY 9/18(2)	25	26	28
	@Chi	@Chi	Pts	Pts	Pts	Pts	Chi	Cin	Cin	Cin	Cin	Cin	StL	StL	NY
MURTAUGH, Danny															
WYROSTEK, Johnny	8	8	8	8	8	8	8	8	8	8	8	8	8	8	8
TABOR, Jim			5	5	5	5	5	5	5	5	5	5	5	5	5
NORTHEY, Ron	9	9	9	9	9	9	9	9	9	9	9	ph		ph	
McCORMICK, Frank	3	3		3	3	3	BROKEN RIB JUNE 17th, CAN'T PLAY TILL JULY.								
DiMAGGIO, Vince															
HEMSLEY, Rollie					2				2		2				
NEWSOME, Lamar (Skeeter)	6	6	65	6	6	6	6	6	6	6	6	6	6	6	6
JUDD, Oscar	ph	RP	RP										ph	SP	ph	ph
MULCAHY, Hugh		SP													
WASDELL, Jimmy	h9						RELEASED, JUNE 18th...								
LOPATKA, Art															
NOVIKOFF, Lou	ph						SOLD OUTRIGHT TO SEATTLE, JUNE 17th.								
O'NEIL, John	pr		6									6			
HOERST, Frank															
JURISICH, Al						SP					SP				
MULLIGAN, Dick															
DINGES, Vance							3	3	3	3	3	3	3	3	3
SEMINICK, Andy	2	2	2	2		2	2	2	2		2	ph	2	2	2
RAFFENSBERGER, Ken	RP		SP						RP		RP	RP		SP	
KARL, Anton (Andy)	RP			RP	RP		RP								RP
HUGHES, Roy	5	5	5												
ROWE, Lynwood (Schoolboy)		SP			ph		SP				RP				
HUGHES, Tommy				RP	RP				RP			RP			
CRAWFORD, Glenn															
RICHARDSON, Ken															
JOHNSON, Silas (Si)															
PEARSON, Isaac (Ike)			SOLD OUTRIGHT TO SEATTLE, JUNE 14th.												
ENNIS, Del	7	7	7	7	7	7	7	7	7	7	7	7	7	7	7
SCHANZ, Charley	RP					SP					SP	RP			RP
VERBAN, Emil	4	4	4	4	4	4	4	4	4	4	4	4	4	4	4
MAUNEY, Dick	RP		RP			RP		SP							SP
HUMPHRIES, John				RP		RP								RP	
CHAPMAN, Ben		JUNE 11th, MANAGER CHAPMAN TAKES HIMSELF OFF ACTIVE LIST.													
RIPPLE, Charlie	RP			RP	RP	RP									RP
SPINDEL, Hal			SUSPENDED.	//		SOLD TO LOS ANGELES, JUNE 18th.									
BURICH, Bill	pr		OPTIONED TO HOUSTON, JUNE 11th, RETURNED JUNE 18th & SUSPENDED.												
MILNAR, Al	SP	* BACK TO THE BROWNS, AGAIN WITH LOU FINNEY, JUNE 10th.													
STANCEAU, Charley				SP					SP						
MOORE, D.C. (Dee)					ph	3									
GILBERT, Charlie						ph			9	9	9	9	9	9	9
DONNELLY, Sylvester (Blix)															
LETCHAS, Charlie															
POSSEHL, Lou															
HODKEY, Aloysius (Eli)															
HASENMAYER, Don															
GRATE, Don															
HAMNER, Granville (Granny)															
KOECHER, Dick															

PHL NL

	JUNE	[1]	[2]	JULY			[1]	[2]		[1]	[2]	ALL-STAR BREAK			[1]
	29	30	30	1	2	3	4	4	6	7	7	11	12	13	14
	NY	NY	NY	@Brk	@Brk	@Bos	@Bos	@Bos	@NY	@NY	@NY	@Pts	@Pts	@Pts	@Cin
MURTAUGH, Danny															
WYROSTEK, Johnny	8	8	8	8	8	8	8	8	8	8	8	8	8	8	8
TABOR, Jim	5	5	5	5	5	5	5	5	5	5	5	5	5	5	5
NORTHEY, Ron	ph	9	9	9	9	9	9	9	9	9	9		ph		
McCORMICK, Frank				3	3	3	3	3	3	3	3	3	3	3	3
DiMAGGIO, Vince															
HEMSLEY, Rollie	2		2	2	2			2			2				2
NEWSOME, Lamar (Skeeter)	6	6	6	6	6	6	6	6	6	6	6	6	6	6	6
JUDD, Oscar	ph	SP		ph			SP						SP		
MULCAHY, Hugh															
WASDELL, Jimmy	...WASDELL LATER (JULY 1st) SIGNS WITH CLEVELAND.														
LOPATKA, Art				SP											
NOVIKOFF, Lou															
O'NEIL, John	pr		pr	6						ph		pr			
HOERST, Frank				RP						RP					
JURISICH, Al									SP						
MULLIGAN, Dick					RP			SP						RP	RP
DINGES, Vance	3	3	3	3	3	ph		ph					ph	7	
SEMINICK, Andy	ph	2	ph	2		2	2		2	2		2	2	2	ph
RAFFENSBERGER, Ken	RP					SP				SP					
KARL, Anton (Andy)	RP				RP						RP			RP	RP
HUGHES, Roy		ph	4										ph	ph	ph
ROWE, Lynwood (Schoolboy)		ph	SP								SP	SP			ph
HUGHES, Tommy		RP		RP											
CRAWFORD, Glenn															
RICHARDSON, Ken															
JOHNSON, Silas (Si)															
PEARSON, Isaac (Ike)															
ENNIS, Del	7	7	7	7	7	7	7	7	7	7	7	7	7		7
SCHANZ, Charley	RP							RP						SP	
VERBAN, Emil	4	4	4	4	4	4	4	4	4	4	4	4	4	4	4
MAUNEY, Dick						RP									SP
HUMPHRIES, John	RP														
CHAPMAN, Ben															
RIPPLE, Charlie	OPTIONED TO MEMPHIS, JUNE 29th.														
SPINDEL, Hal															
BURICH, Bill	REINSTATED & OPTIONED TO COLUMBUS (American Association), JULY 5th.														
MILNAR, Al															
STANCEAU, Charley	SP			SP				RP							
MOORE, D.C. (Dee)		3													
GILBERT, Charlie	9		ph	8	ph	ph			ph			9	9	9	9
DONNELLY, Sylvester (Blix)															
LETCHAS, Charlie															
POSSEHL, Lou															
HODKEY, Aloysius (Eli)															
HASENMAYER, Don															
GRATE, Don															
HAMNER, Granville (Granny)															
KOECHER, Dick				OPTIONED TO TERRE HAUTE, JULY 1st.											

PHL NL

JULY	[2] 14 @Cin	15 @Cin	16 @Cin	17 @StL	18 @StL	[1] 20 @Chi	[2] 20 @Chi	[1] 21 @Chi	[2] 21 @Chi	24 Pts	[1] 25 Pts	[2] 25 Pts	26 Chi	[1] 27 Chi	[2] 27 Chi
MURTAUGH, Danny															
WYROSTEK, Johnny	8	8	8	8	8	ph					ph				
TABOR, Jim	5	5	5	5	5	5	5	5	5	5	5	5	5	5	5
NORTHEY, Ron	9	9	9	9	9	9	9	9	*9	9	9	9	9	9	9
McCORMICK, Frank	3	3	3	3	3	3	3	3	3	3	3	3	3	3	3
DiMAGGIO, Vince															
HEMSLEY, Rollie		2	2			2	ph		2			2			2
NEWSOME, Lamar (Skeeter)						6	ph								
JUDD, Oscar		ph		SP			SP				SP				ph
MULCAHY, Hugh		RP													
WASDELL, Jimmy															
LOPATKA, Art				SOLD TO LOUISVILLE JULY 17th, BUT A SORE ARM KILLS THE DEAL.											
NOVIKOFF, Lou															
O'NEIL, John						pr									6
HOERST, Frank				RP	RP								SP		
JURISICH, Al															
MULLIGAN, Dick			RP			SP									RP
DINGES, Vance		ph			ph	ph									
SEMINICK, Andy	2		2	2	2	2	2	2		2	2		2	2	
RAFFENSBERGER, Ken	SP			SP		RP		SP						SP	
KARL, Anton (Andy)															RP
HUGHES, Roy	6	6	6	6	6	64	6	6	6	6	6	6	6	6	6
ROWE, Lynwood (Schoolboy)		SP				ph		SP							
HUGHES, Tommy				RP	RP										SP
CRAWFORD, Glenn															
RICHARDSON, Ken															
JOHNSON, Silas (Si)															
PEARSON, Isaac (Ike)															
ENNIS, Del		ph			ph	7	7	7	7	7	7	7	7	7	7
SCHANZ, Charley			RP												RP
VERBAN, Emil	4	4	4	4	4	4	4	4	4	4	4	4	4	4	4
MAUNEY, Dick															
HUMPHRIES, John						SP									
CHAPMAN, Ben															
RIPPLE, Charlie															
SPINDEL, Hal															
BURICH, Bill															
MILNAR, Al															
STANCEAU, Charley		SP													
MOORE, D.C. (Dee)															
GILBERT, Charlie	7	7	7	7	7	8	8	8	8	8	8	8	8	8	8
DONNELLY, Sylvester (Blix)											SP				
LETCHAS, Charlie															
POSSEHL, Lou															
HODKEY, Aloysius (Eli)															
HASENMAYER, Don										OPTIONED TO UTICA, JULY 23rd.					
GRATE, Don															
HAMNER, Granville (Granny)															
KOECHER, Dick															

* July 21 (2), Northey listed as "Norbert" in *TSN* box score. Ted Norbert, PCL slugger, never played in the majors.

PHL NL

	JULY [1]	[2]		[1]	[2]	AUG		[1]	[2]		[1]	[2]			[1]
	28	28	30	31	31	2	3	4	4	6	8	8	9	10	11
	Chi	Chi	Cin	Cin	Cin	StL	StL	StL	StL	Bos	Bos	Bos	Brk	Brk	Brk
MURTAUGH, Danny															
WYROSTEK, Johnny	ph	8	8	8	8	8	8	8	8	8	8	8	8	8	8
TABOR, Jim	5	5	5	5	5	5	5	5	5	5	5	5	5	5	5
NORTHEY, Ron	9	ph	9	ph	ph				ph	9	9	9	9	9	9
McCORMICK, Frank	3	3	3	3	3	3	3	3	3	3	3	3	3	3	3
DiMAGGIO, Vince															
HEMSLEY, Rollie		2			2			2				2			
NEWSOME, Lamar (Skeeter)			6	6	6	6	6	6	6	6	6	6	6	6	
JUDD, Oscar						SP		ph	RP				SP		
MULCAHY, Hugh	SP										RP				
WASDELL, Jimmy															
LOPATKA, Art	(THOUGH RETURNED TO THE PHILLIES, LOPATKA'S BIG LEAGUE CAREER IS OVER.)														
NOVIKOFF, Lou															
O'NEIL, John	6	pr		pr		pr				6		pr			
HOERST, Frank							SP				SP				RP
JURISICH, Al								RP							
MULLIGAN, Dick	RP														
DINGES, Vance	ph	ph								ph					
SEMINICK, Andy	2		2	2		2	2		2	2	2		2	2	2
RAFFENSBERGER, Ken				SP			SP		RP			SP			
KARL, Anton (Andy)											RP				
HUGHES, Roy	6	6						ph	ph						6
ROWE, Lynwood (Schoolboy)			SP		ph			SP		PULLED GROIN TENDON...					
HUGHES, Tommy											RP				
CRAWFORD, Glenn															
RICHARDSON, Ken															
JOHNSON, Silas (Si)															
PEARSON, Isaac (Ike)															
ENNIS, Del	7	7	7	7	7	7	7	7	7	7	7	7	7	7	7
SCHANZ, Charley				RP	RP			RP	RP		SP				
VERBAN, Emil	4	4	4	4	4	4	4	4	4	4	4	4	4	4	4
MAUNEY, Dick		RP						RP	RP		RP				RP
HUMPHRIES, John	RP									OPTIONED TO K.C., AUGUST 5th...					
CHAPMAN, Ben															
RIPPLE, Charlie															
SPINDEL, Hal															
BURICH, Bill															
MILNAR, Al															
STANCEAU, Charley		SP								SP					SP
MOORE, D.C. (Dee)															
GILBERT, Charlie	8	9	9	9	9	9	9	9	9	9		ph			
DONNELLY, Sylvester (Blix)				SP							RP				
LETCHAS, Charlie															
POSSEHL, Lou															
HODKEY, Aloysius (Eli)															
HASENMAYER, Don															
GRATE, Don															
HAMNER, Granville (Granny)															
KOECHER, Dick															

PHL NL

AUG	[2] 11 Brk	14 @Bos	[1] 15 @Bos	[2] 15 @Bos	16 @Brk	18 @Brk	[1] 20 @Chi	[2] 20 @Chi	21 @Chi	[1] 22 @StL	[2] 22 @StL	23 @StL	24 @StL	[1] 25 @Cin	[2] 25 @Cin
MURTAUGH, Danny															
WYROSTEK, Johnny	8	8	8	8	8	8	8	8	8	8	8	8	8	8	8
TABOR, Jim	5	5	5	5	5	5	5	5	5	5	5	5	5	5	5
NORTHEY, Ron	9	9	9	9	9	9	9	9	9	9	9	9	9		ph
McCORMICK, Frank	3	3	3	3	3	3	3	3	3	3	3	3	3	3	3
DiMAGGIO, Vince															
HEMSLEY, Rollie	2			2			2								
NEWSOME, Lamar (Skeeter)														6	6
JUDD, Oscar				SP		ph						SP		ph	
MULCAHY, Hugh									SP						RP
WASDELL, Jimmy															
LOPATKA, Art															
NOVIKOFF, Lou															
O'NEIL, John															
HOERST, Frank		SP				RP				SP					
JURISICH, Al					SUSPENDED AUG. 16th, FOR LEAVING TEAM WITHOUT PERMISSION.										
MULLIGAN, Dick										RP					
DINGES, Vance					3	ph	ph	ph	ph	ph				3	
SEMINICK, Andy		2	2	ph	2	2	2		2	2	2	2	2	2	2
RAFFENSBERGER, Ken			SP							SP					RP
KARL, Anton (Andy)		RP	RP							RP			RP	RP	
HUGHES, Roy	6	6	6	6	6	6	6	6	6	6	6	6	6	5	pr
ROWE, Lynwood (Schoolboy)		AUG. 4th (2), ROWE HURT CHASING ERV DUSAK LINER. DOESN'T PITCH AGAIN THIS YEAR.													
HUGHES, Tommy							RP			RP				RP	
CRAWFORD, Glenn															
RICHARDSON, Ken															
JOHNSON, Silas (Si)															
PEARSON, Isaac (Ike)															
ENNIS, Del	7	7	7	7	7	7	7	7	7	7	7	7	7	7	7
SCHANZ, Charley			SP			RP		SP					SP		
VERBAN, Emil	4	4	4	4	4	4	4	4	4	4	4	4	4	4	4
MAUNEY, Dick			RP						RP						
HUMPHRIES, John		"RETURNED" BY KANSAS CITY AUG. 17th, AS HE WON'T REPORT. SUSPENDED, AUG. 18th.													
CHAPMAN, Ben															
RIPPLE, Charlie															
SPINDEL, Hal															
BURICH, Bill															
MILNAR, Al															
STANCEAU, Charley						RP					RP				
MOORE, D.C. (Dee)										ph	ph			2	
GILBERT, Charlie		ph	9	ph	9	ph	ph	ph		ph			ph	9	9
DONNELLY, Sylvester (Blix)	SP		RP				SP							SP	
LETCHAS, Charlie														4	
POSSEHL, Lou															SP
HODKEY, Aloysius (Eli)															
HASENMAYER, Don															
GRATE, Don															
HAMNER, Granville (Granny)															
KOECHER, Dick															

		AUG				[1]	SEP [2]	[1]	[2]	[1]	[2]					
		26	28	29	30	31	31	1	1	2	2	3	4	5	6	7
PHL NL		@Cin	@Pts	@Pts	@NY	Bos	Bos	Bos	Bos	Brk	Brk	@Brk	@NY	@NY	@NY	@Bos
MURTAUGH, Danny																
WYROSTEK, Johnny		8	8	8	8	8	8	8	8	8	8	8	8	8	8	8
TABOR, Jim		5	5	5	5	5	5	5	5	5	5	5	5	5	5	5
NORTHEY, Ron						ph	9	9	9	9	9	9	9	9	9	9
McCORMICK, Frank		3	3	3	3	3	3	3	3	3	3	3	3	3	3	3
DiMAGGIO, Vince																
HEMSLEY, Rollie						2		2		2					ph	
NEWSOME, Lamar (Skeeter)		6	6	6	6	6	6	6	6	6	6	6	6	65	65	
JUDD, Oscar			SP				ph			SP				SP		
MULCAHY, Hugh							SP									RP
WASDELL, Jimmy																
LOPATKA, Art																
NOVIKOFF, Lou																
O'NEIL, John												6		6	6	6
HOERST, Frank							RP							RP		
JURISICH, Al																
MULLIGAN, Dick						RP										
DINGES, Vance						3	ph	ph			ph	ph	ph	3		
SEMINICK, Andy		2	2	2	2		2	2	2		2	2	2	2	2	2
RAFFENSBERGER, Ken			SP					SP			RP					
KARL, Anton (Andy)						RP						RP	RP			RP
HUGHES, Roy						4	6			6						
ROWE, Lynwood (Schoolboy)																
HUGHES, Tommy												SP				
CRAWFORD, Glenn																
RICHARDSON, Ken																
JOHNSON, Silas (Si)																
PEARSON, Isaac (Ike)																
ENNIS, Del		7	7	7	7	7	7	7	7	7	7	7	7	7	7	7
SCHANZ, Charley				SP									SP			
VERBAN, Emil		4	4	4	4	4	4	4	4	4	4	4	4	4	4	4
MAUNEY, Dick		SP			SP								RP			
HUMPHRIES, John		AUGUST 28th, PLACED ON INELIGIBLE LIST.														
CHAPMAN, Ben																
RIPPLE, Charlie		RECALLED FROM MEMPHIS SEP. 4th, THOUGH BIG LEAGUE CAREER ENDED IN JUNE.														
SPINDEL, Hal																
BURICH, Bill		RECALLED FROM COLUMBUS SEP. 4th, BUT 2-SEASON MAJOR LEAGUE CAREER IS OVER.														
MILNAR, Al																
STANCEAU, Charley								SP								
MOORE, D.C. (Dee)							2								2	
GILBERT, Charlie		9	9	9	9	9	9			ph	ph	ph	ph	ph	8	ph
DONNELLY, Sylvester (Blix)			RP						RP				SP			
LETCHAS, Charlie							ph							4		
POSSEHL, Lou							SP									SP
HODKEY, Aloysius (Eli)		RECALLED FROM UTICA, SEPTEMBER 4th.														
HASENMAYER, Don		RECALLED FROM UTICA, SEPTEMBER 4th.														
GRATE, Don		RECALLED FROM UTICA, SEPTEMBER 4th.														
HAMNER, Granville (Granny)																
KOECHER, Dick		RECALLED FROM TERRE HAUTE, SEPTEMBER 4th.														

PHL NL

	SEP	[1] 8 @Bos	[2] 8 @Bos	9 NY	10 StL	11 StL	[1] 12 Chi	[2] 12 Chi	13 Chi	14 Chi	15 Pts	16 Pts	[1] 18 Cin	[2] 18 Cin	19 Cin	22 NY
MURTAUGH, Danny																
WYROSTEK, Johnny		8	8	8	8	8	8	8	8	8	8	8	8	8	8	8
TABOR, Jim		5	5	5	5	5	5	5	5	5	5	5	5	5	5	5
NORTHEY, Ron		ph		ph	9		9	ph			ph			ph		
McCORMICK, Frank		3		3				ph			3	3	3	3	3	3
DiMAGGIO, Vince																
HEMSLEY, Rollie			2					2						2	2	2
NEWSOME, Lamar (Skeeter)		4			6	6		6		4	6		6	6	6	6
JUDD, Oscar					SP						ph		SP			ph
MULCAHY, Hugh								RP								
WASDELL, Jimmy																
LOPATKA, Art																
NOVIKOFF, Lou																
O'NEIL, John		6	6	6			6	6	6	6	6	6				
HOERST, Frank																
JURISICH, Al							REINSTATED, SEPT. 18.									
MULLIGAN, Dick					RP											
DINGES, Vance		3	3	ph	3	3	3	3	3	3	3					
SEMINICK, Andy		2		2	2	2	2	2	2	2	2	2	2	h2	2	
RAFFENSBERGER, Ken		SP					SP			RP		SP				
KARL, Anton (Andy)							RP	RP			RP					
HUGHES, Roy				ph			ph	ph	ph			pr			ph	
ROWE, Lynwood (Schoolboy)					ph											
HUGHES, Tommy			SP							SP				SP		
CRAWFORD, Glenn																
RICHARDSON, Ken																
JOHNSON, Silas (Si)																
PEARSON, Isaac (Ike)																
ENNIS, Del		7	7	7	7	7	7	7	7	7	7	7	7	7	7	7
SCHANZ, Charley			SP					SP						RP		
VERBAN, Emil		4	4	4	4	4	4	4	4		4	4	4	4	4	4
MAUNEY, Dick															SP	
HUMPHRIES, John																
CHAPMAN, Ben																
RIPPLE, Charlie																
SPINDEL, Hal																
BURICH, Bill																
MILNAR, Al																
STANCEAU, Charley																SP
MOORE, D.C. (Dee)																
GILBERT, Charlie		9	9	9	9	9	9	9	9	9	9	9	9	9	9	9
DONNELLY, Sylvester (Blix)					SP						SP					
LETCHAS, Charlie											pr					
POSSEHL, Lou								SP								
HODKEY, Aloysius (Eli)								RP								
HASENMAYER, Don											ph	pr			pr	
GRATE, Don															RP	RP
HAMNER, Granville (Granny)																
KOECHER, Dick																

6/23 TIE, REPLAY 9/18(2)

PHL NL

	SEP [2] 22	23	25	26	28	29	
	NY	@Brk	@Brk	@Brk	@NY	@NY	155g
MURTAUGH, Danny							
WYROSTEK, Johnny	8	8	8	8			
TABOR, Jim		5	5	5			
NORTHEY, Ron	9	ph	9	9	9	9	
McCORMICK, Frank	3	3	3	3		3	
DiMAGGIO, Vince							
HEMSLEY, Rollie	2	2	2	2		ph	
NEWSOME, Lamar (Skeeter)		6	6	6			
JUDD, Oscar			SP	RP			
MULCAHY, Hugh							
WASDELL, Jimmy							
LOPATKA, Art							
NOVIKOFF, Lou							
O'NEIL, John	6		ph		ph	6	
HOERST, Frank							
JURISICH, Al							
MULLIGAN, Dick	WAIVED TO BOS NL, SEP. 18th.						
DINGES, Vance							
SEMINICK, Andy	BROKEN TOE ENDS HIS SEASON.						
RAFFENSBERGER, Ken		SP	RP				
KARL, Anton (Andy)				RP			
HUGHES, Roy	4		ph	ph	3		
ROWE, Lynwood (Schoolboy)							
HUGHES, Tommy	SP		RP			RP	
CRAWFORD, Glenn							
RICHARDSON, Ken							
JOHNSON, Silas (Si)							
PEARSON, Isaac (Ike)							
ENNIS, Del	7	7	7		7	7	
SCHANZ, Charley				SP			
VERBAN, Emil		4	4	4			
MAUNEY, Dick			RP		RP		
HUMPHRIES, John							
CHAPMAN, Ben							
RIPPLE, Charlie							
SPINDEL, Hal							
BURICH, Bill							
MILNAR, Al							
STANCEAU, Charley				RP			
MOORE, D.C. (Dee)			2		2	2	
GILBERT, Charlie	7	9	87	7	8	8	
DONNELLY, Sylvester (Blix)							
LETCHAS, Charlie					4	4	
POSSEHL, Lou							
HODKEY, Aloysius (Eli)					SP		
HASENMAYER, Don	5				5	5	
GRATE, Don					RP		
HAMNER, Granville (Granny)					6	6	
KOECHER, Dick						SP	

PTS NL	G	APRIL 16 @StL	17 @StL	18 @StL	20 Cin	[1] 21 Cin	[2] 21 Cin	23 Chi	24 Chi	25 StL	26 StL	27 @Cin	28 @Cin	30 Phl	MAY 1 Phl
BROWN, Jimmy	79	4	4	4	4	4	4								
BARRETT, Johnny	32	9	9	9	9	9	9	8	8	9	ph		ph	ph	9
KINER, Ralph	144	8	8	8	8	8	8			8	8	8	8	8	8
ELLIOTT, Bob	140	5	5	5	5	5	5	5	5	5	5	5	5	5	5
FLETCHER, Elbie	148	3	3	3	3	3	3	3	3	3	3	3			3
RUSSELL, Jim	146	7	7	7	7	7	7	7	7	7	7	7	7	7	7
COX, Billy	121	6	6	6	6	6	6	6	6	6	6	6	6	6	6
SMITH, Vinnie	7	2	2	2			2	2		2		2	KNEE INJURY...		
OSTERMUELLER, Fritz	28	SP								SP					
COLMAN, Frank	26	ph			ph	9	9	ph		9	9	3	3		
BARNHART, Vic	2	pr			ph							NXT PAGE..			
HEINTZELMAN, Ken	32	RP								SP					
GABLES, Ken	32		SP		RP								SP		
ANDERSON, Alf	2		ph		ph						TO HOLLYWOOD...				
LANNING, Johnny	27		RP									RP			
ALBOSTA, Ed	17			SP			SP								SP
GUSTINE, Frankie	131			ph		4	4	4	4	4	4	4	4	4	4
STRINCEVICH, Nick	32			RP		RP						SP			
GERHEAUSER, Al	37			RP			RP								RP
GIONFRIDDO, Al	64				8	ph	ph		8	8	ph	ph	9	9	97
CAMELLI, Hank	42				2	2			2	2	2		2	2	
SEWELL, Truett (Rip)	26				SP				SP			SP			
HOPPER, Jim	2					SP									
GUINTINI, Ben	2					ph				9					
CLEMENSEN, Bill	1					RP						TO COLUMBUS...			
ROE, Elwin (Preacher)	21					RP			RP						
SALKELD, Bill	69					ph					2			2	2
HALLETT, Jack	35					SP						RP	RP		
VAN ROBAYS, Maurice	59					ph		ph	7						
HANDLEY, Lee	116					pr									
ZAK, Frankie	21										ph			pr	
BAKER, Bill	53										2	2			
WILKIE, Aldon (Lefty)	7											RP			
COSCARART, Pete	3												ph		
WHITEHEAD, Burgess	55	* SUSPENDED 3/13-5/3, THOUGH PINCH-BATTING ON 5/1.													ph
BAHR, Edson (Ed)	29	FROM KANSAS CITY (ZAK WILL GO TO KC LATER).													RP
LOPEZ, Al	56	BREAKS HAND APRIL 20th, OUT TILL MAY 19th.													
WORKMAN, Chuck	58	FROM BRAVES FOR JOHNNY BARRETT, JUNE 12th.													
GORNICKI, Hank	7	RETURNED TO PIRATES BY HOLLYWOOD MAY 15th; BEGAN SEASON WITH SORE ARM.													
JARVIS, LeRoy (Roy)	2	DRAFTED FROM DODGERS LAST YEAR, IS IN NAVY TILL REINSTATED JUNE 20.													
WALSH, Jim (Junior)	4	FROM YORK, SEPTEMBER 8.													
HOWARD, Lee	3	OPTIONED TO HOLLYWOOD APRIL 6th, WILL BE TRANSFERRED TO YORK JUNE 11th.													
TATE, Al	2										TO BIRMINGHAM...				

* Whitehead suspended March 13th-May 3rd for violating training rules.

NOTE: April 23rd, Pirates sell first baseman Ellsworth (Babe) Dahlgren to Browns. Dahlgren didn't play for the 1946 Pirates.

National League

PTS NL	MAY 2 Phl	3 Bos	[1] 5 Brk	[2] 5 Brk	8 NY	9 NY	12 @Chi	14 @Bos	17 @Brk	[1] 19 @NY	[2] 19 @NY	22 @Phl	23 @Phl	24 Chi	26 Chi
BROWN, Jimmy			ph			6		5				ph			
BARRETT, Johnny	8	8	pr	8		8			9		ph	ph			
KINER, Ralph	8		8	7	8	7	ph	8	8	8	8	8	8	8	8
ELLIOTT, Bob	9	9	9	9	9	9	9	9	9	9	9	9		9	9
FLETCHER, Elbie	3	3	3	3	3	3	3	3	3	3	3	3	3	3	3
RUSSELL, Jim					pr	ph	8	ph	7	7		ph	7	7	7
COX, Billy	6	6	6	6		6	6	6	6	6	6	6	6	6	6
SMITH, Vinnie	...SMITH'S APRIL 27th KNEE INJURY & MAY 10th SURGERY FORCES AN END TO HIS CAREER.														
OSTERMUELLER, Fritz	SP				SP				SP						
COLMAN, Frank			ph		ph		7		ph	7	7	7			
BARNHART, Vic	...OPTIONED TO ALBANY, APRIL 30th.														
HEINTZELMAN, Ken		SP					SP			SP		RP			SP
GABLES, Ken				SP				SP				RP			
ANDERSON, Alf	...OPTION DATE WAS APRIL 27th.														
LANNING, Johnny										RP					
ALBOSTA, Ed															
GUSTINE, Frankie	4	4	4	4	4	4	4	4	4	4	4	4	4	4	4
STRINCEVICH, Nick				RP					RP						
GERHEAUSER, Al			RP			RP	RP	RP	RP		RP				
GIONFRIDDO, Al	7	7		ph			ph					ph	9		
CAMELLI, Hank	2	2	2		ph			2	2		2	2		2	
SEWELL, Truett (Rip)			SP		COLLAPSES; DIAGNOSED WITH MENINGITIS. RETURNS MAY 26th.										
HOPPER, Jim										RP					
GUINTINI, Ben	OPTIONED TO HOLLYWOOD, MAY 7th.														
CLEMENSEN, Bill	(RELEASED OUTRIGHT TO COLUMBUS (AMERICAN ASSOCIATION), APRIL 27th.)														
ROE, Elwin (Preacher)			RP	RP		SP			SP				SP		
SALKELD, Bill			2	2		2	2		2						2
HALLETT, Jack			RP							RP		SP			
VAN ROBAYS, Maurice	7	7	7		7			7	ph						
HANDLEY, Lee	5	5	5	5	5	5	5	5	ph	5	5	5	5	5	5
ZAK, Frankie			pr	pr	6	6	pr					6			
BAKER, Bill			2		2										
WILKIE, Aldon (Lefty)								RP	RP		RP				
COSCARART, Pete						ph			6						
WHITEHEAD, Burgess			ph						4		ph	5			
BAHR, Edson (Ed)						RP							SP		
LOPEZ, Al										2		2	2		
WORKMAN, Chuck															
GORNICKI, Hank															
JARVIS, LeRoy (Roy)															
WALSH, Jim (Junior)															
HOWARD, Lee															
TATE, Al	(DATE OF OPTION TO BIRMINGHAM WAS APRIL 27th.)														

On May 7th, pitcher Bob Klinger given unconditional release (he didn't play for the Pirates). Klinger signs with the Boston Red Sox on May 9th.

		MAY			JUNE										
				[1]	[2]	[1]	[2]		[1]	[2]					[1]	[2]
		28	29	30	30	2	2	3	4	4	5	6	7	8	9	9
PTS NL		Cin	Cin	StL	StL	Phl	Phl	Phl	Brk	Brk	Brk	Brk	NY	NY	NY	NY
BROWN, Jimmy			ph						6	ph	5	5	5	5	5	5
BARRETT, Johnny					ph	8	ph	ph		ph	ph		8		8	8
KINER, Ralph		8	8	8	8	8	8	8	8	8	8	8	8	8		
ELLIOTT, Bob		*9	9	9	9	9	9	9	9	9	9	9	9	9	9	9
FLETCHER, Elbie		3	3	3	3	3	3	3	3	3	3	3	3	3	3	3
RUSSELL, Jim		*7	7	7	7	7	7	7	ph	7	7	7	7		7	7
COX, Billy		6	6	6	6	6	6	6	6		6	6			6	
SMITH, Vinnie		(SMITH IS PLACED ON THE DISABLED LIST, JUNE 7th)														
OSTERMUELLER, Fritz				SP				SP							SP	
COLMAN, Frank		ph	ph	ph	ph			ph	ph	ph	ph					
BARNHART, Vic																
HEINTZELMAN, Ken			RP		SP				SP							SP
GABLES, Ken			RP				RP				RP		RP			
ANDERSON, Alf																
LANNING, Johnny								RP		RP						RP
ALBOSTA, Ed					RP			SP				RP				
GUSTINE, Frankie		4	4	4	4	4	4	4	4	4	4	4	4	4	4	4
STRINCEVICH, Nick		RP	RP				RP				RP			SP		
GERHEAUSER, Al			SP				RP					RP				
GIONFRIDDO, Al			pr	9	ph		ph	ph	8	8	ph	ph		7		
CAMELLI, Hank		2	2	2	2		2							2		
SEWELL, Truett (Rip)					SP				RP		SP	pr				
HOPPER, Jim													TO COLUMBUS...			
GUINTINI, Ben																
CLEMENSEN, Bill																
ROE, Elwin (Preacher)					SP				SP							
SALKELD, Bill		2	2		2						2	ph	2			2
HALLETT, Jack			RP		RP		RP				RP					
VAN ROBAYS, Maurice								7	7			ph		7	7	
HANDLEY, Lee		5	5	5	5	5	5	5	5	5	5					
ZAK, Frankie		ph	pr		pr		pr		pr	ph	6	6	6	6	6	6
BAKER, Bill								2		2	2	2		ph		
WILKIE, Aldon (Lefty)						RP	RP				RP					
COSCARART, Pete						SOLD TO SAN DIEGO, JUNE 1st.										
WHITEHEAD, Burgess											5				ph	
BAHR, Edson (Ed)		SP					SP						SP			
LOPEZ, Al			2		2		2	2	2	2		2			2	
WORKMAN, Chuck																
GORNICKI, Hank																
JARVIS, LeRoy (Roy)																
WALSH, Jim (Junior)																
HOWARD, Lee																
TATE, Al		RETURNED BY BIRMINGHAM, JUNE 4th.														

* May 28th, Russell & Elliott are both listed as left fielder in newspaper box scores. Likely a typo, with Elliott in right field, as usual.

	JUNE			[1]	[2]							[1]	[2]		
	10	11	15	16	16	17	18	19	20	21	22	23	23	25	26
PTS NL	Bos	Bos	@Phl	@Phl	@Phl	@Phl	@Brk	@Brk	@Brk	@Bos	@Bos	@Bos	@Bos	@NY	@NY
BROWN, Jimmy	*5	6	6	ph	6	ph	6	6	6	6	6	ph			ph
BARRETT, Johnny	8	8	TRADED TO THE BRAVES FOR WORKMAN, JUNE 12th.												
KINER, Ralph			8	8	8	8	8	8	8	8	8	8	8	8	8
ELLIOTT, Bob	9	9	9	9	9	9	9	9	9	9	9	9	9	9	9
FLETCHER, Elbie	3	3	3	3	3	3	3	3	3	3	3	3		3	3
RUSSELL, Jim	7	7	7	ph	7	7	7	7	7	7	7	7	3	7	7
COX, Billy	ph			6		6				pr		6	6	6	6
SMITH, Vinnie															
OSTERMUELLER, Fritz				SP						SP					
COLMAN, Frank	ph		ph			SOLD OUTRIGHT TO NEWARK, JUNE 17th.									
BARNHART, Vic															
HEINTZELMAN, Ken							SP					SP			
GABLES, Ken	RP					SP						RP	RP		
ANDERSON, Alf															
LANNING, Johnny			RP						RP						
ALBOSTA, Ed	RP							RP				RP			
GUSTINE, Frankie	*4	4	4	4	4	4	4	4	4	4	4	4	4	4	4
STRINCEVICH, Nick			SP					SP					SP		
GERHEAUSER, Al						RP		RP				RP			RP
GIONFRIDDO, Al	ph		ph	7		ph		ph				ph	7		
CAMELLI, Hank		2	2	2		2		2			2	2	2		2
SEWELL, Truett (Rip)		SP		SP							SP				
HOPPER, Jim		OPTIONED TO COLUMBUS (AMERICAN ASSOCIATION), JUNE 7th, RETURNED JULY 1st.													
GUINTINI, Ben		RETURNED BY HOLLYWOOD JUNE 10th, OPTIONED TO SAN DIEGO, JUNE 14th.													
CLEMENSEN, Bill															
ROE, Elwin (Preacher)	SP					SP						SP			
SALKELD, Bill	2		ph		2		ph		ph	ph	ph	ph			
HALLETT, Jack								RP							
VAN ROBAYS, Maurice				7								ph			ph
HANDLEY, Lee		5	5	5	5	5	5	5	5	5	5	5	5	5	5
ZAK, Frankie	6		RELEASED OUTRIGHT TO KANSAS CITY, JUNE 13 (see next page).												
BAKER, Bill	ph			ph			ph								
WILKIE, Aldon (Lefty)				OPTIONED TO HOLLYWOOD, JUNE 14th.											
COSCARART, Pete															
WHITEHEAD, Burgess	5		pr				ph					ph			pr
BAHR, Edson (Ed)						RP									SP
LOPEZ, Al				2		2		2		2	2	2	2	2	2
WORKMAN, Chuck			pr		pr		pr		pr						
GORNICKI, Hank						RP									
JARVIS, LeRoy (Roy)		REINSTATED FROM NDSL, JUNE 20th.													
WALSH, Jim (Junior)															
HOWARD, Lee															
TATE, Al			OPTIONED TO SELMA, JUNE 12th.												

* June 10th, Brown is listed in box scores at second base, but Gustine plays the full game there. Likely a typo---Brown should be at third base.

National League — PTS NL

	JUNE		[1]	[2]	JULY		[1]	[2]	[1]	[2]			ALL-STAR BREAK		
	27	28	30	30	1	2	3	3	4	4	5	6	[1] 7	[2] 7	11
PTS NL	Chi	StL	StL	StL	@Chi	@Chi	@Chi	@Chi	@Cin	@Cin	@Cin	@StL	@StL	@StL	Phl
BROWN, Jimmy		ph		6		6		ph			5	5		6	ph
BARRETT, Johnny															
KINER, Ralph	8	8	8	8	8	8	8	8	8	8	8	8	8	8	8
ELLIOTT, Bob	9	9	9	9		9	9	9	9	9	9		9	9	9
FLETCHER, Elbie	3	3	3	3	3	3	3	3	3	3	3	ph	3	3	
RUSSELL, Jim	7		7	9	7		7	7	7	7	7	7	7	ph	3
COX, Billy	6	6	6		6	6	6	6	6	6	6	6	6	ph	6
SMITH, Vinnie															
OSTERMUELLER, Fritz			SP					RP					SP		
COLMAN, Frank															
BARNHART, Vic															
HEINTZELMAN, Ken	SP					SP							SP		
GABLES, Ken								RP		RP	SP				
ANDERSON, Alf															
LANNING, Johnny										SP					
ALBOSTA, Ed		RP						RP							
GUSTINE, Frankie	4	4	4	4	4	4	4	4	4	4	4	4	4	4	5
STRINCEVICH, Nick			SP					SP							SP
GERHEAUSER, Al		RP					SP					RP			
GIONFRIDDO, Al	7			pr		8		ph			ph	ph	pr		
CAMELLI, Hank					OPTIONED TO TORONTO, JULY 1st.										
SEWELL, Truett (Rip)				SP							SP				
HOPPER, Jim			OPTIONED TO BIRMINGHAM, JULY 8th.												
GUINTINI, Ben															
CLEMENSEN, Bill															
ROE, Elwin (Preacher)		SP						SP						RP	RP
SALKELD, Bill	2					2		ph	2		2	2		RP	RP
HALLETT, Jack	RP								RP	RP				RP	RP
VAN ROBAYS, Maurice	ph	7	7	7		7		ph		ph		3		7	
HANDLEY, Lee	5	5	5	5	5	5	5	5	5	5			5	5	ph
ZAK, Frankie			(ZAK SENT TO KANSAS CITY TO COMPLETE ED BAHR DEAL, MADE IN APRIL.)												
BAKER, Bill				2		2	2		2					2	2
WILKIE, Aldon (Lefty)															
COSCARART, Pete			SIGNS WITH SAN DIEGO JUNE 13th, DESPITE THREATS TO JOIN THE MEXICAN LEAGUE.												
WHITEHEAD, Burgess	4					4		pr		ph				4	4
BAHR, Edson (Ed)												RP		RP	
LOPEZ, Al		2	2							2	2	2	2		
WORKMAN, Chuck	ph				9	9	ph	ph			ph	9	9		7
GORNICKI, Hank										RP					
JARVIS, LeRoy (Roy)														ph	
WALSH, Jim (Junior)															
HOWARD, Lee															
TATE, Al															

| | JULY | | [1] | [2] | | | | | | [1] | [2] | | [1] | [2] | |
| | 12 | 13 | 14 | 14 | 15 | 16 | 17 | 18 | 20 | 21 | 21 | 24 | 25 | 25 | 26 |
PTS NL	Phl	Phl	Bos	Bos	Bos	Bos	NY	NY	Brk	Brk	Brk	@Phl	@Phl	@Phl	@Brk
BROWN, Jimmy		4	4	4	4	4			ph					6	
BARRETT, Johnny															
KINER, Ralph	8	8	8	8	8	8	8	8	8	8	8	7	7	7	7
ELLIOTT, Bob	9	9	9	9	9	9	9			ph	ph	5	5	5	5
FLETCHER, Elbie				3	3	3	3	3	3	3	3	3	3	3	3
RUSSELL, Jim	3	3	3	7	7	7	7	7		7	7	8	8	8	8
COX, Billy	6	6	6	6	6	6	6	6	6	6	6	6	6		6
SMITH, Vinnie															
OSTERMUELLER, Fritz			SP							SP					SP
COLMAN, Frank															
BARNHART, Vic															
HEINTZELMAN, Ken					SP			SP							
GABLES, Ken											RP			RP	
ANDERSON, Alf															
LANNING, Johnny		SP					RP	RP	RP				SP		
ALBOSTA, Ed						SP									
GUSTINE, Frankie	5	5	5	5	5	5	4	4	4	4	4	4	4	4	4
STRINCEVICH, Nick							SP				SP				
GERHEAUSER, Al			RP		RP					RP					
GIONFRIDDO, Al		8			ph				7		ph	ph	9	h8	
CAMELLI, Hank															
SEWELL, Truett (Rip)				SP						SP			SP		
HOPPER, Jim															
GUINTINI, Ben															
CLEMENSEN, Bill															
ROE, Elwin (Preacher)	RP				RP			RP							
SALKELD, Bill					ph						2			2	
HALLETT, Jack												RP			
VAN ROBAYS, Maurice	7		7					9	7		ph		9		9
HANDLEY, Lee		5	ph		5		5	5	5	5	5				
ZAK, Frankie															
BAKER, Bill			ph	2	2	2		ph		2			2		
WILKIE, Aldon (Lefty)															
COSCARART, Pete															
WHITEHEAD, Burgess	4	4								pr	5			ph	
BAHR, Edson (Ed)	SP							SP						RP	
LOPEZ, Al	2	2	2		2		2	2	2	2		2			2
WORKMAN, Chuck		7			ph		9	9	9	9	9	9	9	9	9
GORNICKI, Hank															
JARVIS, LeRoy (Roy)															
WALSH, Jim (Junior)															
HOWARD, Lee															
TATE, Al															

PTS NL	JULY 27 @Brk	AUG [1] 27 @Brk	[2] 28 @Brk	31 @Bos	[1] 2 @NY	[2] 2 @NY	[1] 4 @NY	[2] 4 @NY	7 StL	9 Chi	10 Chi	[1] 11 Chi	8/11(2) TIE 4-4, REPLAY 9/2(2) [2] 11 Chi	12 Cin	13 Cin
BROWN, Jimmy		6	6			6		ph	ph	ph	6	6	ph	4	4
BARRETT, Johnny															
KINER, Ralph	7	7	7	7	7	ph	7	7	7	7	7	ph	7		
ELLIOTT, Bob	5	5	5	5	5	5	5	5	5	5	5	5	5	5	5
FLETCHER, Elbie	3	3	3	3	3	3	3	3	3	3	3	3	3	3	3
RUSSELL, Jim	8	8	8	8	8	8	8	8	8	8	8	8	8	7	7
COX, Billy	6	ph	6	6	6		6	6	6	6			6	6	6
SMITH, Vinnie															
OSTERMUELLER, Fritz					SP				SP				SP		
COLMAN, Frank															
BARNHART, Vic															
HEINTZELMAN, Ken	SP					SP				SP			RP		
GABLES, Ken		RP					RP						RP		
ANDERSON, Alf															
LANNING, Johnny				SP				SP		RP		RP			SP
ALBOSTA, Ed		SP													
GUSTINE, Frankie	4	4	4	4	4	4	4	4	4	4	4	4	4	SPIKED...	
STRINCEVICH, Nick			SP			SP					SP				
GERHEAUSER, Al									RP	RP			RP		
GIONFRIDDO, Al	ph	9	9	9		7	ph	ph		9	9	7	9	8	8
CAMELLI, Hank															
SEWELL, Truett (Rip)												SP			
HOPPER, Jim															
GUINTINI, Ben															
CLEMENSEN, Bill															
ROE, Elwin (Preacher)	RP								RP						
SALKELD, Bill		2				ph				2		2			ph
HALLETT, Jack		RP				RP			RP			RP	RP		RP
VAN ROBAYS, Maurice		ph			9		9	9	9	ph	9	ph	ph		
HANDLEY, Lee		ph							ph	pr		ph	pr		
ZAK, Frankie															
BAKER, Bill		2	2	2		2	2	2	2				2		
WILKIE, Aldon (Lefty)															
COSCARART, Pete															
WHITEHEAD, Burgess		ph				ph	pr	6				4			
BAHR, Edson (Ed)		RP					RP	RP					SP		
LOPEZ, Al	2			2		2			2	2	2		2	2	2
WORKMAN, Chuck	9	ph			9				ph		9			9	9
GORNICKI, Hank															
JARVIS, LeRoy (Roy)															
WALSH, Jim (Junior)															
HOWARD, Lee															
TATE, Al															

PTS NL	AUG 13 Cin	16 @StL	17 @Chi	18 @Chi	20 Brk	21 Brk	22 NY	23 NY	24 NY	[1] 25 Bos	[2] 25 Bos	26 Bos	27 Bos	28 Phl	29 Phl
BROWN, Jimmy	4	4	4	4	4	46	6	6	6	6	6	6	6	ph	ph
BARRETT, Johnny															
KINER, Ralph		7	7	7	7	7	7	7	7	7	7	7	7	7	7
ELLIOTT, Bob	5	5			5	ph				h5	ph	5	5	95	9
FLETCHER, Elbie	3	3	3	3	3	3	3	3	3	3	3	3	3	3	3
RUSSELL, Jim	7	78	8	8	8	8	8	8	8	8	8	8	8	8	8
COX, Billy	6	6	6	6	6	6				pr		pr		6	6
SMITH, Vinnie															
OSTERMUELLER, Fritz					RP					SP			SP		
COLMAN, Frank															
BARNHART, Vic										RECALLED AUGUST 26th…					
HEINTZELMAN, Ken		SP				SP		RP			SP				
GABLES, Ken			RP						RP				RP		
ANDERSON, Alf										RECALLED AUGUST 26th…					
LANNING, Johnny								SP							
ALBOSTA, Ed													RP		
GUSTINE, Frankie		…SPIKE WOUND KEEPS GUSTINE SIDELINED TILL AUGUST 28th.												4	4
STRINCEVICH, Nick	SP			SP						SP					
GERHEAUSER, Al			RP		pr				RP						
GIONFRIDDO, Al	8	8							ph	ph			SEE NEXT WK…		
CAMELLI, Hank										RECALLED AUGUST 26th…					
SEWELL, Truett (Rip)							SP			RP				SP	
HOPPER, Jim		HOPPER IS RETURNED BY BIRMINGHAM, AUGUST 23rd.													
GUINTINI, Ben		OUT WITH A BAD KNEE, RETURNED BY SAN DIEGO AUGUST 19th.													
CLEMENSEN, Bill															
ROE, Elwin (Preacher)															
SALKELD, Bill				2					2	ph		ph		ph	
HALLETT, Jack				SP		RP			RP		RP		RP		
VAN ROBAYS, Maurice			9	ph	9	9	9		ph						
HANDLEY, Lee			5	5	5	45	5	5	5	5	5	pr	ph	5	5
ZAK, Frankie															
BAKER, Bill	2			3		ph	2			2		ph	ph		
WILKIE, Aldon (Lefty)										RECALLED AUGUST 26th…					
COSCARART, Pete															
WHITEHEAD, Burgess				ph		ph	4	4	4	4	4	4	4	ph	
BAHR, Edson (Ed)			SP					SP							SP
LOPEZ, Al		2	2		2	2		2		2		2	2	2	2
WORKMAN, Chuck	9	9		9		5	9	9	9	9	9	9	9		
GORNICKI, Hank				RP									RP		
JARVIS, LeRoy (Roy)															
WALSH, Jim (Junior)										RECALLED AUGUST 26th…					
HOWARD, Lee										RECALLED AUGUST 26th…					
TATE, Al		RECALLED AUGUST 26th, REPORTS AT END OF SOUTHEASTERN LEAGUE SEASON…													

PTS NL	AUG 31 StL	SEP [1] 1 StL	SEP [2] 1 StL	[1] 2 Chi	[2] 2 Chi (REPLAY of 8/11 TIE)	3 Chi	4 @Cin	5 @Cin	6 @StL	7 @StL	[1] 8 @StL	[2] 8 @StL	10 @NY	[1] 11 @NY	[2] 11 @NY
BROWN, Jimmy	6	6	6									ph			
BARRETT, Johnny															
KINER, Ralph	7	7	7	7	7	7	7	ph		7	7	7	7	7	7
ELLIOTT, Bob	9	9	9	9	9	9	9	9	9	9	9	9	9	9	
FLETCHER, Elbie	3	3	3	3	3	3	3	3	3	3	3	3	3	3	3
RUSSELL, Jim	8	8	8	8	8	8	8	8	8	8	8	8	8	8	8
COX, Billy		pr	6	6	6	6	6	6	6	6	6	6	6		
SMITH, Vinnie															
OSTERMUELLER, Fritz			SP							SP					
COLMAN, Frank															
BARNHART, Vic	...BARNHART REPORTS, BUT HIS BIG LEAGUE CAREER IS OVER.														
HEINTZELMAN, Ken		SP							SP					SP	RP
GABLES, Ken		RP			RP							RP			SP
ANDERSON, Alf	...ANDERSON CAN'T REPORT BECAUSE HOLLYWOOD IN PCL PLAYOFFS TILL SEP. 30th.														
LANNING, Johnny		RP					SP					RP		RP	
ALBOSTA, Ed												RP			
GUSTINE, Frankie	4	4	4	4	4	4	4	4						6	6
STRINCEVICH, Nick	SP						SP				SP				
GERHEAUSER, Al							RP		RP			RP	RP		
GIONFRIDDO, Al	...APPENDECTOMY AUGUST 28th CLOSES DOWN GIONFRIDDO'S SEASON.														
CAMELLI, Hank	(TORONTO'S SEASON ENDS SEPTEMBER 8th)												2		
SEWELL, Truett (Rip)		RP			SP			RP					SP		
HOPPER, Jim															
GUINTINI, Ben															
CLEMENSEN, Bill															
ROE, Elwin (Preacher)	DATE UNCERTAIN, ROE SENT HOME TO REST KNEE HURT IN WINTER BASKETBALL GAME.														
SALKELD, Bill	2	2		2			2	2	2		2		2	2	2
HALLETT, Jack					SP					SP					
VAN ROBAYS, Maurice		ph				3		7	7			ph		9	
HANDLEY, Lee	5	5	5	5	5	5	5	5	5	5	5	5	5	5	5
ZAK, Frankie															
BAKER, Bill		pr		2	2	2		2		2		2		2	
WILKIE, Aldon (Lefty)	...WILKIE CAN'T RETURN AS HOLLYWOOD IS IN PLAYOFFS THROUGH SEPTEMBER 30th.														
COSCARART, Pete															
WHITEHEAD, Burgess							pr	4	4	4	4	4	4	4	4
BAHR, Edson (Ed)			SP								RP				
LOPEZ, Al		ph	2		2	FOUL TIP INJURES FINGER; OUT REMAINDER OF SEASON.									
WORKMAN, Chuck				ph		ph				ph					9
GORNICKI, Hank							RP					RP			
JARVIS, LeRoy (Roy)															
WALSH, Jim (Junior)	...REPORTS AT END OF INTER-STATE LEAGUE SEASON.														
HOWARD, Lee	...TO REPORT AT END OF INTER-STATE LEAGUE SEASON, BUT SUSPENDED 8/30-9/3.														
TATE, Al	...ON SEPT 2nd.														

PTS NL	SEP [1] 12 @Bos	[2] 12 @Bos	[1] 13 @Bos	[2] 13 @Bos	14 @Bos	15 @Phl	16 @Phl	[1] 18 @Brk	[2] 18 @Brk	19 @Brk	21 Cin	[1] 22 Cin	[2] 22 Cin	[1] 24 @Chi	[2] 24 @Chi
BROWN, Jimmy		ph			4	4									
BARRETT, Johnny															
KINER, Ralph	7	7	7	7	7	7	7	7	7	7	7	7	h7	7	7
ELLIOTT, Bob		ph			9	9	9	9	9	9		5	5	ph	9
FLETCHER, Elbie	3	3	3	3	3	3	3	3	3	3	3	3	3	3	3
RUSSELL, Jim	8	8	8	8	8	8	8	8	8	8	8	8	8	8	8
COX, Billy					6	6	6	6	6					6	6
SMITH, Vinnie	(REINSTATED FROM DISABLED LIST SEP. 23rd, BUT DOESN'T PLAY AGAIN)														
OSTERMUELLER, Fritz			SP			ph	SP							SP	
COLMAN, Frank															
BARNHART, Vic															
HEINTZELMAN, Ken					RP			SP						SURGERY...	
GABLES, Ken					RP						RP				
ANDERSON, Alf	(ANDERSON SOLD OUTRIGHT TO INDIANAPOLIS, SEPTEMBER 27th)														
LANNING, Johnny						SP				RP		RP	RP		
ALBOSTA, Ed												RP	RP		
GUSTINE, Frankie	6	6	6	6	6	64	4	4	4	4	6	6	6	4	46
STRINCEVICH, Nick		SP				RP			SP						
GERHEAUSER, Al					SP			RP					*9		
GIONFRIDDO, Al															
CAMELLI, Hank		2			h2	2	2		2			2	ph		2
SEWELL, Truett (Rip)						RP									SP
HOPPER, Jim															
GUINTINI, Ben	(SOLD OUTRIGHT TO INDIANAPOLIS, SEPTEMBER 27th.)														
CLEMENSEN, Bill															
ROE, Elwin (Preacher)															
SALKELD, Bill	2	ph	2		2	2		2	ph	2	2		ph	2	
HALLETT, Jack	SP						SP		RP		SP				
VAN ROBAYS, Maurice					ph	pr	ph			ph		7			
HANDLEY, Lee	5	5	5	5	5	5	5	5	5	5	5	5	4	5	5
ZAK, Frankie															
BAKER, Bill		2		2		2						ph	2		
WILKIE, Aldon (Lefty)	(SOLD OUTRIGHT TO INDIANAPOLIS, SEPTEMBER 27th)														
COSCARART, Pete															
WHITEHEAD, Burgess	4	4	4	4					ph	4					4
BAHR, Edson (Ed)			SP		pr	RP			RP		pr	RP			
LOPEZ, Al															
WORKMAN, Chuck	9	9	9	9	9				ph	9	9	79	9		
GORNICKI, Hank													RP		
JARVIS, LeRoy (Roy)															
WALSH, Jim (Junior)					RP				RP			SP			
HOWARD, Lee											SP		RP		
TATE, Al															

* On September 22nd, Gerheauser plays outfield for the only time in his big league career.

Frisch quits 9/28. Spud Davis interim mgr. 3 games.

PTS NL	SEP 25 @Chi	26 @Chi	27 @Cin	28 @Cin	[1] 29 @Cin	[2] 29 @Cin	
BROWN, Jimmy							
BARRETT, Johnny							
KINER, Ralph	7	7	7	7	7	7	
ELLIOTT, Bob	9	9	9	9	9	9	
FLETCHER, Elbie	3	3	3	3	3	3	
RUSSELL, Jim	8	8	8	8	8	8	
COX, Billy	6	6	6	6	6	6	
SMITH, Vinnie							
OSTERMUELLER, Fritz							
COLMAN, Frank							
BARNHART, Vic							
HEINTZELMAN, Ken	SINUS SURGERY THIS WEEK.						
GABLES, Ken	RP						
ANDERSON, Alf							
LANNING, Johnny							
ALBOSTA, Ed							
GUSTINE, Frankie	45	4	4	4	4	4	
STRINCEVICH, Nick	SP			RP			
GERHEAUSER, Al	RP	RP					
GIONFRIDDO, Al							
CAMELLI, Hank	2			2			
SEWELL, Truett (Rip)							
HOPPER, Jim							
GUINTINI, Ben							
CLEMENSEN, Bill							
ROE, Elwin (Preacher)							
SALKELD, Bill	ph	2	2	2		2	
HALLETT, Jack		SP					
VAN ROBAYS, Maurice							
HANDLEY, Lee	5	5	5	5	5	5	
ZAK, Frankie							
BAKER, Bill							
WILKIE, Aldon (Lefty)							
COSCARART, Pete							
WHITEHEAD, Burgess	4					4	
BAHR, Edson (Ed)			SP				
LOPEZ, Al							
WORKMAN, Chuck	ph	ph	ph				
GORNICKI, Hank							
JARVIS, LeRoy (Roy)					2		
WALSH, Jim (Junior)				SP			
HOWARD, Lee					SP		
TATE, Al			RP			SP	

155g

National League

		APRIL											[1]	[2]	MAY
	G	16	17	18	20	21	22	23	24	25	26	27	28	28	2
STL NL	156	Pts	Pts	Pts	@Chi	@Chi	@Cin	@Cin	@Cin	@Pts	@Pts	Chi	Chi	Chi	NY
KLEIN, Lou	23	4	4	4	4	4	4	4	4	4	4	4	4	4	4
MOORE, Terry	91	8			ph					ph	8	8	ph	ph	8
MUSIAL, Stan	156	7	7	7	7	7	7	7	7	7	7	7	7	7	7
SLAUGHTER, Enos (Country)	156	9	9	9	9	9	9	9	9	9	9	9	9	9	9
KUROWSKI, George (Whitey)	142	5			ph		ph		ph			5	5	5	ph
SISLER, Dick	83	3	3	3	3	3	3	3	3	3	3	3	3	3	3
MARION, Marty	146	6	6	6	6	6	6	6	6	6	6	6			6
RICE, Del	55	2	2	2	2	2	2	2	2	2	2	2	2	2	2
BEAZLEY, Johnny	19	SP													
DICKSON, Murry	47	RP				RP				RP			RP		RP
ADAMS, Elvin (Buster)	81	ph		8		8	8	ph		8			ph	8	ph
BRECHEEN, Harry (the Cat)	37	RP		SP						SP			RP		SP
DUSAK, Erv	100	ph								ph				ph	
BURKHART, Ken	25	RP						RP						SP	
SCHOENDIENST, Al (Red)	142	ph	5	5	5	5	5	5	5	5	5	5	56	6	5
DONNELLY, Sylvester (Blix)	13	RP				RP							RP		
WALKER, Harry (Little Dixie)	112		8	8	8	ph		8	8				8		
LANIER, Max	6		SP				SP					SP			
POLLET, Howie	40			SP		RP			SP				SP		
WILBER, Del	4					2		2		2				2	
O'DEA, Ken	22					2									
BARRETT, Charley (Red)	23					SP		RP					RP	RP	
MARTIN, Freddie	6					RP						SP			
ENDICOTT, Bill	20					ph							ph		
CROSS, Joffre (Jeff)	49					pr		pr		pr					
WILKS, Ted	40							SP							
KRIST, Howie	15									RP					
SESSI, Walter	15												ph		
VERBAN, Emil	1													ph	
KLUTTZ, Clyde	52	TRADED FROM GIANTS TO PHILLIES TO CARDINALS, ALL ON MAY 1st.													2
BRAZLE, Alpha (Al)	37	DISCHARGED BY ARMY APRIL 24th, PITCHES HIS FIRST GAME ON MAY 16th.													
GARAGIOLA, Joe	74	RELEASED BY ARMY TO COLUMBUS (A A), PURCHASED BY CARDINALS MAY 15th.													
LITWHILER, Danny	6	REINSTATED FROM NATIONAL DEFENSE SERVICE LIST, MAY 1st.													
SCHMIDT, Freddy	16														
JONES, Vernal (Nippy)	16	IN USMC, RELEASED FROM NDSL JUNE 10th, (BUT MAKES DEBUT JUNE 9th).													
GRODZICKI, Johnny	3	GRODZICKI, WOUNDED WAR VET, ON DISABLED LIST MAY 3rd to JULY 5th,													
MUNGER, George (Red)	10	BEGINS SEASON IN ARMY, REINSTATED FROM NDSL AUGUST. 27th (PITCHES AUG. 25th).													

11pm April 15th, 1B Ray Sanders traded to the Braves with P Max Surkont, for INF Tommy Nelson & reported $40,000. Nelson is farmed out to Columbus (Ohio).

Surkont, sent to Boston with a sore arm, is returned. Farmed out to Rochester on May 4th, he won't pitch in the big leagues till 1949.

National League — STL NL

	MAY	[1] 5 Bos	[2] 5 Bos	7 Bos	8 Phl	[1] 12 Cin	[2] 12 Cin	14 @Brk	15 @Brk	16 @Bos	17 @Bos	[1] 19 @Phl	[2] 19 @Phl	21 @Phl	22 @NY	23 @NY
KLEIN, Lou					4	4	4	4	4	4	4	4	4			
MOORE, Terry		8			8	8		8	8	8	8	8	8	8	8	8
MUSIAL, Stan		7	7	7	3	7	7	7	7	7	7	7	7	7	7	7
SLAUGHTER, Enos (Country)		9	9	9	9	9	9	9	9	9	9	9	9	9	9	9
KUROWSKI, George (Whitey)		5	5	5	5	5		5	5	5	5	5	5	5	5	5
SISLER, Dick		3	3	3		3	3	3	3	3	3	3	3	3	3	3
MARION, Marty		6	6	6	6	6	6	6	6	6	6	6	6	6	6	6
RICE, Del			2				2			2		2				
BEAZLEY, Johnny				SP						SP						SP
DICKSON, Murry			RP		RP		RP			RP						
ADAMS, Elvin (Buster)			ph	8	7		8	ph			ph					
BRECHEEN, Harry (the Cat)					SP								SP			
DUSAK, Erv			ph				5									
BURKHART, Ken										RP						
SCHOENDIENST, Al (Red)		4	4	4	4									4	4	4
DONNELLY, Sylvester (Blix)								RP		RP						
WALKER, Harry (Little Dixie)		8	8	83				ph	3		ph			ph		
LANIER, Max		SP						SP			SP					
POLLET, Howie			SP						SP					SP		
WILBER, Del						OPTIONED TO COLUMBUS (AMERICAN ASSOCIATION), MAY 10th.										
O'DEA, Ken		2		2		2		2	2	2			2	2	2	
BARRETT, Charley (Red)							SP				RP					
MARTIN, Freddie			SP		RP					SP				RP		
ENDICOTT, Bill			ph				ph				ph					
CROSS, Joffre (Jeff)										pr						
WILKS, Ted			RP											SP		
KRIST, Howie			RP				RP									
SESSI, Walter			ph				ph									
VERBAN, Emil		TRADED TO THE PHILLIES FOR KLUTTZ, MAY 1st.														
KLUTTZ, Clyde			2		2		2				2					2
BRAZLE, Alpha (Al)									RP							
GARAGIOLA, Joe																
LITWHILER, Danny																
SCHMIDT, Freddy																
JONES, Vernal (Nippy)																
GRODZICKI, Johnny																
MUNGER, George (Red)																

May 13th, pre-war star pitcher Ernie White is released with a sore arm, having not appeared in a game for St. Louis. He signs with the Braves, May 15th.

STL NL	MAY 24 @Cin	[1] 26 @Cin	[2] 26 @Cin	27 @Chi	28 @Chi	29 @Chi	JUNE [1] 30 @Pts	[2] 30 @Pts	[1] 2 NY	[2] 2 NY	3 NY	4 Bos	5 Bos	6 Bos	7 Phl
KLEIN, Lou	JUMPED TO THE MEXICAN LEAGUE, MAY 23rd.														
MOORE, Terry	8	8	8	8	8	8	8	8	8	8	8	8	8	8	8
MUSIAL, Stan	7	7	7	7	7	7	7	7	7	7	7	7	7	7	3
SLAUGHTER, Enos (Country)	9	9	9	9	9	9	9	9	9	9	9	9	9	9	9
KUROWSKI, George (Whitey)	5	5	5	5	5	5	5	5	5	5	5	5	5	5	5
SISLER, Dick	3	3	3	3	3	3	3	3	3					ph	
MARION, Marty	* WON'T FLY.			6	6	6	6	6	6	6	6	SORE ARM.			ph
RICE, Del						2	2			2					
BEAZLEY, Johnny					SP										SP
DICKSON, Murry				RP			RP	RP	RP	RP	RP			RP	RP
ADAMS, Elvin (Buster)	ph			ph	8		ph			ph	ph		ph	ph	7
BRECHEEN, Harry (the Cat)	SP					SP						SP			
DUSAK, Erv				ph	5					pr				4	ph
BURKHART, Ken		SP					SP						SP		
SCHOENDIENST, Al (Red)	4	4	4	4	4	4	4	4	4	4	4	4	4	46	4
DONNELLY, Sylvester (Blix)			RP					RP		RP					RP
WALKER, Harry (Little Dixie)	ph		ph	3				ph	ph	3	3	3	3	3	
LANIER, Max	JUMPED TO THE MEXICAN LEAGUE, MAY 23rd (HAD 6-0 RECORD FOR THE CARDS).														
POLLET, Howie				SP			RP		SP					SP	
WILBER, Del															
O'DEA, Ken	2		2					2		2		2			
BARRETT, Charley (Red)			SP					SP			RP				
MARTIN, Freddie	JUMPED TO THE MEXICAN LEAGUE, MAY 23rd.														
ENDICOTT, Bill															
CROSS, Joffre (Jeff)	6	6	6	pr					pr	6	6	6	6	6	6
WILKS, Ted				RP			RP		SP					RP	RP
KRIST, Howie	RP						RP	RP			RP				
SESSI, Walter									ph	ph					
VERBAN, Emil															
KLUTTZ, Clyde				2				2		2	2				2
BRAZLE, Alpha (Al)	RP		RP								SP				
GARAGIOLA, Joe		2			2			ph	2	2	ph		2	2	
LITWHILER, Danny				ph			ph			ph	ph			ph	ph
SCHMIDT, Freddy							RP	RP		RP				RP	
JONES, Vernal (Nippy)															
GRODZICKI, Johnny															
MUNGER, George (Red)															

* May 23-24, Marion refuses to fly from New York to Cincinnati for May 24th game, misses entire Reds series. Rejoins team in Chicago, for game of May 27th.

STL NL

	JUNE	[1]	[2]					[1]	[2]	[1]	[2]				
	8	9	9	10	11	12	15	16	16	17	17	19	20	21	22
	Phl	Phl	Phl	Brk	Brk	Brk	@NY	@NY	@NY	@Bos	@Bos	@Bos	@Bos	@Brk	@Brk
KLEIN, Lou															
MOORE, Terry	8	8	8	ph	8	ph	8	8	8				ph	ph	
MUSIAL, Stan	3	3	3	3	3	3	3	3	3	3	3	3	3	3	3
SLAUGHTER, Enos (Country)	9	9	9	9	9	9	9	9	9	9	9	9	9	9	9
KUROWSKI, George (Whitey)	5	5	5	5	5	5	5	5	5	5	5	5	5	5	5
SISLER, Dick				ph			ph		ph					ph	
MARION, Marty	6	6	6	6	6	6	6	6	6	6	6	6	6	6	6
RICE, Del		2			2		2						2		
BEAZLEY, Johnny	OUT WITH ARM TROUBLE, WON'T REJOIN TEAM TILL JUNE 21st.														
DICKSON, Murry		SP				RP		RP					SP		
ADAMS, Elvin (Buster)	7	7	7	7	7	7	7	7	7	8	8			8	
BRECHEEN, Harry (the Cat)				SP				SP							
DUSAK, Erv		5					h8		8	7	7	7	7	7	7
BURKHART, Ken					SP			SP							
SCHOENDIENST, Al (Red)	4	4	4	4	4	4	OUT WITH INJURED ANKLE.			4			4	4	
DONNELLY, Sylvester (Blix)							RP							RP	
WALKER, Harry (Little Dixie)		8		8	ph	8					8	8	8		8
LANIER, Max															
POLLET, Howie						SP				SP					SP
WILBER, Del															
O'DEA, Ken	2			2	2	2		2					2		
BARRETT, Charley (Red)	SP				RP	SP				SP					
MARTIN, Freddie															
ENDICOTT, Bill														ph	
CROSS, Joffre (Jeff)		6				pr	4	4	46	4	4	4	4	4	
WILKS, Ted			RP				RP		RP		RP		RP		
KRIST, Howie							RP	RP							
SESSI, Walter							ph		ph					ph	
VERBAN, Emil															
KLUTTZ, Clyde								2		2				2	
BRAZLE, Alpha (Al)		SP			RP		SP							SP	
GARAGIOLA, Joe			2			2		2		2		2	2	2	2
LITWHILER, Danny	LITWHILER SOLD OUTRIGHT TO THE BRAVES, JUNE 9th.														
SCHMIDT, Freddy							RP							RP	
JONES, Vernal (Nippy)				h4					4				pr	ph	
GRODZICKI, Johnny															
MUNGER, George (Red)															

NOTE: On June 13th, Klein, Lanier and Martin are each suspended five years, for jumping to the Mexican League.

	JUNE				[1]	[2]	JULY			[1]	[2]			[1]	[2]
	23	25	26	28	30	30	1	2	3	4	4	5	6	7	7
STL NL	@Brk	@Phl	@Phl	@Pts	@Pts	@Pts	Cin	Cin	Cin	Chi	Chi	Chi	Pts	Pts	Pts
KLEIN, Lou															
MOORE, Terry	ph	ph			ph		ph	ph						ph	
MUSIAL, Stan	3	3	3	3	3	3	3	3	3	3	3	3	3	3	3
SLAUGHTER, Enos (Country)	9	9	9	9	9	9	9	9	9	9	9	9	9	9	9
KUROWSKI, George (Whitey)	5	5	5	5	5	5	5	5	5	5	5	5	5	5	5
SISLER, Dick		ph			pr										
MARION, Marty	6	6	6	6	6	6	6	6	6	6	6	6	6	6	6
RICE, Del	2	ph	2		2			2		2				2	
BEAZLEY, Johnny		SP						RP							
DICKSON, Murry			SP				SP						SP	RP	
ADAMS, Elvin (Buster)	8	8	8	8	8		7	8	7	8	8		8	8	8
BRECHEEN, Harry (the Cat)	SP					SP						SP			
DUSAK, Erv	7	7	7	7	7	7	ph	7	75	7	7	7	7	7	7
BURKHART, Ken									SP					SP	
SCHOENDIENST, Al (Red)	4	4	4	4	4	4	4	4	4	4	4	4	4	4	4
DONNELLY, Sylvester (Blix)		RP						RP							
WALKER, Harry (Little Dixie)		h8				8	8	ph	8	8	8	8	8	pr	8
LANIER, Max															
POLLET, Howie				SP			SP				RP				SP
WILBER, Del															
O'DEA, Ken							2								
BARRETT, Charley (Red)					RP						SP				
MARTIN, Freddie															
ENDICOTT, Bill		ph					ph	pr	7	ph			ph		
CROSS, Joffre (Jeff)	pr	pr			pr		pr	ph	6					pr	
WILKS, Ted	RP	RP			RP		RP						RP		
KRIST, Howie		RP							RP						
SESSI, Walter															
VERBAN, Emil															
KLUTTZ, Clyde	ph	2		2	2		2	2						2	2
BRAZLE, Alpha (Al)		RP			SP		RP			SP				RP	
GARAGIOLA, Joe	2	2				2	2	ph	2	ph	2	2	2	2	
LITWHILER, Danny															
SCHMIDT, Freddy							RP								
JONES, Vernal (Nippy)	ph				ph		ph		4						
GRODZICKI, Johnny															
MUNGER, George (Red)															

STL NL	JULY 11 NY	[1] 12 NY	[2] 12 NY	13 NY	[1] 14 Brk	[2] 14 Brk	15 Brk	16 Brk	17 Phl	18 Phl	20 Bos	[1] 21 Bos	[2] 21 Bos	24 @NY	[1] 25 @NY
KLEIN, Lou															
MOORE, Terry	ph		8	8	8	8	8	8	ph	ph		3	3	3	3
MUSIAL, Stan	3	3	3	3	3	3	3	3	3	3	3	3	3	3	3
SLAUGHTER, Enos (Country)	9	9	9	9	9	9	9	9	9	9	9	9	9	9	9
KUROWSKI, George (Whitey)	5	5	5	5	5	5	5	5	5	5	5	5	5	5	5
SISLER, Dick				ph					ph						
MARION, Marty	6	6		6	6	6	6	6	6	6	6	6	6	6	6
RICE, Del	2								2				2	2	
BEAZLEY, Johnny					SP									SP	
DICKSON, Murry						SP					RP	SP			
ADAMS, Elvin (Buster)	8		7	ph		7		7	8	8		8	8		
BRECHEEN, Harry (the Cat)	SP					SP				pr		SP			
DUSAK, Erv	7	7	h4	ph				ph	7	7	7	7	7	7	7
BURKHART, Ken				RP					SP						
SCHOENDIENST, Al (Red)	4	4	46	4	4	4	4	4	4	4	4	4	4	4	4
DONNELLY, Sylvester (Blix)	SOLD TO THE PHILLIES ON WAIVERS, JULY 8th.														
WALKER, Harry (Little Dixie)		8	7	7	7		7		ph	8	8	8	8		8
LANIER, Max															
POLLET, Howie		SP	RP				SP					SP			SP
WILBER, Del															
O'DEA, Ken	SOLD TO THE BRAVES ON WAIVERS, JULY 8th.														
BARRETT, Charley (Red)			RP	RP			RP			SP					
MARTIN, Freddie															
ENDICOTT, Bill			ph	ph											
CROSS, Joffre (Jeff)	ph		6	pr				pr	ph						
WILKS, Ted				SP	RP				RP						
KRIST, Howie	RP								RP						
SESSI, Walter					ph										
VERBAN, Emil															
KLUTTZ, Clyde	ph		2			2		2	ph	2					
BRAZLE, Alpha (Al)			SP	RP						RP					
GARAGIOLA, Joe		2	2	2	2		2				2	2			2
LITWHILER, Danny															
SCHMIDT, Freddy	RP			RP					RP						
JONES, Vernal (Nippy)	OPTIONED TO ROCHESTER, JULY 11th.														
GRODZICKI, Johnny	RP			RP											
MUNGER, George (Red)															

STL NL

	JULY [2]						AUG			[1]	[2]			[1]	[2]
	25	27	28	29	30	31	1	2	3	4	4	7	9	11	11
	@NY	@Bos	@Bos	@Bos	@Brk	@Brk	@Brk	@Phl	@Phl	@Phl	@Phl	@Pts	@Cin	@Cin	@Cin
KLEIN, Lou															
MOORE, Terry	ph	ph	KNEE INJURY SIDELINES MOORE.												
MUSIAL, Stan	3	3	3	3	3	3	3	3	3	3	3	3	3	3	3
SLAUGHTER, Enos (Country)	9	9	9	9	9	9	9	9	9	9	9	9	9	9	9
KUROWSKI, George (Whitey)	5	5	5	5	5	5	5	5	5	5	5	5	5	5	5
SISLER, Dick													7	7	7
MARION, Marty	6	6	6	6	6	6	6	6	6	6	6	6	6	6	6
RICE, Del	2	2					2	2				2			
BEAZLEY, Johnny				SP					SP						SP
DICKSON, Murry	SP					SP				SP				SP	
ADAMS, Elvin (Buster)	8	8				8								8	8
BRECHEEN, Harry (the Cat)		SP					SP					SP			
DUSAK, Erv	7	7	7	7		7	7	7	7	7	7	7	8	7	87
BURKHART, Ken				RP				RP							
SCHOENDIENST, Al (Red)	4	4	4	4	4	4	4	4	4	4	4	4	4	4	4
DONNELLY, Sylvester (Blix)															
WALKER, Harry (Little Dixie)	ph		8	8	8	8	8	8	8	8	8	8	8		
LANIER, Max															
POLLET, Howie					SP		RP				SP		SP		
WILBER, Del															
O'DEA, Ken															
BARRETT, Charley (Red)		RP													
MARTIN, Freddie															
ENDICOTT, Bill				ph	7										
CROSS, Joffre (Jeff)	5	ph								6				6	
WILKS, Ted	RP	RP													
KRIST, Howie															
SESSI, Walter															
VERBAN, Emil															
KLUTTZ, Clyde	2	2				2			2	2				2	
BRAZLE, Alpha (Al)	RP		SP				SP								
GARAGIOLA, Joe			2	2	2	2					2		2		2
LITWHILER, Danny															
SCHMIDT, Freddy	RP														
JONES, Vernal (Nippy)															
GRODZICKI, Johnny															
MUNGER, George (Red)															

STL NL

	AUG 12 @Chi	13 @Chi	14 @Chi	16 Pts	17 Cin	[1] 18 Cin	[2] 18 Cin	19 Cin	20 Bos	21 Bos	[1] 22 Phl	[2] 22 Phl	23 Phl	24 Phl	[1] 25 Brk
KLEIN, Lou															
MOORE, Terry		ph		ph		KNEE PROBLEMS CONTINUE.							ph		ph
MUSIAL, Stan	3	3	3	3	3	3	3	3	3	3	3	3	3	3	3
SLAUGHTER, Enos (Country)	9	9	9	9	9	9	9	9	9	9	9	9	9	9	9
KUROWSKI, George (Whitey)	3	5	5	5							5	5	5	5	5
SISLER, Dick	7		7		7	ph	7	7	7	7	ph	ph		7	7
MARION, Marty	6	6	6	6	6	6	6	6	6	6	6	6	6	6	6
RICE, Del		2		2								2			
BEAZLEY, Johnny						SP							SP		
DICKSON, Murry				SP	RP						SP				
ADAMS, Elvin (Buster)		ph		ph	ph	7	7		7						
BRECHEEN, Harry (the Cat)		SP					SP					SP			
DUSAK, Erv	7	7	7	7	5	5	5	5	5	5	7	7	7	7	7
BURKHART, Ken								SP						SP	
SCHOENDIENST, Al (Red)	4	4	4	4	4	4	4	4	4	4	4	4	4	4	4
DONNELLY, Sylvester (Blix)															
WALKER, Harry (Little Dixie)	8	8	8	8	8	8	8	8	8	8	8	8	8	8	8
LANIER, Max															
POLLET, Howie			SP						SP		RP				SP
WILBER, Del															
O'DEA, Ken															
BARRETT, Charley (Red)					RP										
MARTIN, Freddie															
ENDICOTT, Bill					ph										
CROSS, Joffre (Jeff)															
WILKS, Ted		RP							RP	RP					
KRIST, Howie					RP										
SESSI, Walter					ph										ph
VERBAN, Emil															
KLUTTZ, Clyde		2		2		2					2		2		2
BRAZLE, Alpha (Al)	SP				SP	RP				SP					
GARAGIOLA, Joe	2		2		2		2	2	2	2	2	2		2	2
LITWHILER, Danny															
SCHMIDT, Freddy					RP										
JONES, Vernal (Nippy)															
GRODZICKI, Johnny															
MUNGER, George (Red)															

STL NL

	AUG [2]			[1]	[2]		SEP [1]	[2]	[1]	[2]				
	25	26	27	28	28	29	31	1	1	2	2	4	5	6	7
	Brk	Brk	Brk	NY	NY	NY	@Pts	@Pts	@Pts	@Cin	@Cin	Chi	Chi	Pts	Pts
KLEIN, Lou															
MOORE, Terry	8					8		8	8	8			8	8	8
MUSIAL, Stan	3	3	3	3	3	3	3	3	3	3	3	3	3	3	3
SLAUGHTER, Enos (Country)	9	9	9	9	9	9	9	9	9	9	9	9	9	9	9
KUROWSKI, George (Whitey)	5	5	5	5	5	5	5	5	5	5	5	5	5	5	5
SISLER, Dick	7	7	7	7	7		7			7	7	7			
MARION, Marty	6	6	6	6	6	6	6	6	6	6	6	6	6	6	6
RICE, Del	2								2				2		h2
BEAZLEY, Johnny				SP					SP				SP		
DICKSON, Murry		SP					SP	RP			RP			RP	
ADAMS, Elvin (Buster)	7		ph					ph	ph	7					ph
BRECHEEN, Harry (the Cat)	RP		SP						SP		RP		SP		
DUSAK, Erv	7	7		7		7		7	7	7	7	7	7	7	7
BURKHART, Ken				SP							SP			RP	
SCHOENDIENST, Al (Red)	4	4	4	4	4	4	4	4	4	4	4	4	4	4	4
DONNELLY, Sylvester (Blix)															
WALKER, Harry (Little Dixie)	8	8	8	8	8	8	8	8		8	8	8	8		
LANIER, Max															
POLLET, Howie						SP		RP							SP
WILBER, Del	RECALLED ON SEPTEMBER 8th, BUT NEXT PLAYS FOR CARDINALS IN 1947.														
O'DEA, Ken															
BARRETT, Charley (Red)		RP													
MARTIN, Freddie															
ENDICOTT, Bill			ph				ph								
CROSS, Joffre (Jeff)					pr				pr						ph
WILKS, Ted	RP		RP					RP	RP						RP
KRIST, Howie															RP
SESSI, Walter				ph		ph									
VERBAN, Emil															
KLUTTZ, Clyde				2		2		2	2	2				2	2
BRAZLE, Alpha (Al)	SP				RP		RP			RP	RP				
GARAGIOLA, Joe		2	2		2		2			2	2	2			
LITWHILER, Danny															
SCHMIDT, Freddy			RP				RP								RP
JONES, Vernal (Nippy)	RECALLED AT END OF INTERNATIONAL LEAGUE SEASON, SEPTEMBER 8th.														
GRODZICKI, Johnny															RP
MUNGER, George (Red)	RP		RP				SP			SP					

* On Sep. 8th, Dusak listed at 3B in day-by-day records, but isn't in box score of either game. Assume he's defensive replacement for Kurowski in Game 2, with no AB.

STL NL

	SEP [1] 8 Pts	[2] 8 Pts	10 @Phl	11 @Phl	12 @Brk	13 @Brk	14 @Brk	[1] 15 @NY	[2] 15 @NY	17 @NY	18 @Bos	19 @Bos	21 @Chi	22 @Chi	23 @Chi
KLEIN, Lou															
MOORE, Terry				8	ph	8		8	ph	8			8	8	8
MUSIAL, Stan	3	3	3	3	3	3	3	3	3	3	3	3	3	3	3
SLAUGHTER, Enos (Country)	9	9	9	9	9	9	9	9	9	9	9	9	9	9	9
KUROWSKI, George (Whitey)	5	5	5	5	5	5	5	5	5	5	5	5	5	5	5
SISLER, Dick	7	7	7		7	ph	7		7		7	7		ph	
MARION, Marty	6		6	6	6	6	6	6	6	6	6		6	6	6
RICE, Del		2		2		2		2	2				2		
BEAZLEY, Johnny				SP											
DICKSON, Murry						SP		SP					SP		
ADAMS, Elvin (Buster)	7	7	7	7		ph									
BRECHEEN, Harry (the Cat)			SP			SP					SP				SP
DUSAK, Erv		*5		ph	7	7		7	7	7		7	7		
BURKHART, Ken				RP		RP					RP			RP	
SCHOENDIENST, Al (Red)	4	4	4	4	4	4	4	4	4	4	4	4	4	4	4
DONNELLY, Sylvester (Blix)															
WALKER, Harry (Little Dixie)	8	8	8		8	7	8	r8	8	8	8	8		7	7
LANIER, Max															
POLLET, Howie					SP				RP	SP				SP	
WILBER, Del															
O'DEA, Ken															
BARRETT, Charley (Red)							RP								
MARTIN, Freddie															
ENDICOTT, Bill											ph				
CROSS, Joffre (Jeff)	pr	6				pr				6		6			
WILKS, Ted				RP		RP	RP					RP		RP	
KRIST, Howie															
SESSI, Walter							ph								
VERBAN, Emil															
KLUTTZ, Clyde				2						2					
BRAZLE, Alpha (Al)		SP		RP		RP			SP			RP		RP	
GARAGIOLA, Joe	2		2		2	h2	2		2		2	2		2	2
LITWHILER, Danny															
SCHMIDT, Freddy						RP									
JONES, Vernal (Nippy)					ph		ph	ph							
GRODZICKI, Johnny															
MUNGER, George (Red)	SP					RP			RP			SP			

* September 8th twin bill, Dusak listed at 3B in Official day-by-day records, but appears in box score of neither game. Records don't indicate whether Game 1 or 2. Assume he's a defensive replacement in Game 2, for Kurowski, with no At-Bats.

STL NL	SEP 24 Cin	25 Cin	27 Chi	28 Chi	29 Chi	OCT 1 Brk	3 @Brk	156g
KLEIN, Lou								
MOORE, Terry	8	8	8	8	8	8	8	WS
MUSIAL, Stan	3	3	3	3	3	3	3	WS
SLAUGHTER, Enos (Country)	9	9	9	9	9	9	9	WS
KUROWSKI, George (Whitey)	5	5	5	5	5	5	5	WS
SISLER, Dick		ph	ph	ph				WS
MARION, Marty	6	6	6	6	6	6	6	WS
RICE, Del					ph			WS
BEAZLEY, Johnny								WS
DICKSON, Murry		SP	RP		RP		SP	WS
ADAMS, Elvin (Buster)				7				WS
BRECHEEN, Harry (the Cat)			SP	RP			RP	WS
DUSAK, Erv	7			7	7		7	WS
BURKHART, Ken		RP						WS
SCHOENDIENST, Al (Red)	4	4	4	4	4	4	4	WS
DONNELLY, Sylvester (Blix)								
WALKER, Harry (Little Dixie)		7	7	7		7	h7	WS
LANIER, Max								
POLLET, Howie			SP			SP		WS
WILBER, Del								
O'DEA, Ken								
BARRETT, Charley (Red)								WS
MARTIN, Freddie								
ENDICOTT, Bill								WS
CROSS, Joffre (Jeff)	pr							WS
WILKS, Ted	RP	RP	RP		RP			WS
KRIST, Howie								WS
SESSI, Walter			ph					WS
VERBAN, Emil								
KLUTTZ, Clyde	2				2		2	WS
BRAZLE, Alpha (Al)		RP	RP		RP			WS
GARAGIOLA, Joe		2	2	2		2		WS
LITWHILER, Danny								
SCHMIDT, Freddy								WS
JONES, Vernal (Nippy)	ph	ph	ph	ph	ph			WS
GRODZICKI, Johnny								WS
MUNGER, George (Red)	SP				SP			WS

*PLAYOFFS

* Individual records in Playoff games are counted in each player's season statistics.

WS = eligible for the World Series.

Appendix:
Annotated 1946 Team Rosters

On each team, players are listed in their order of appearance in box scores, from leadoff man on Opening Day through the team's last man to get into the box scores during the season. Date of a player's first appearance this year is noted. Debut dates are indicated, for those who played their first big league game in 1946.

Players with more than one team are listed on the roster of each, with transaction dates and appropriate details included. Each separate position played by outfielders is shown, gleaned from published box scores (this breakdown doesn't appear in any record books, far as I know). Roster dates match those in the Daily Player Use Grids.

Notations are as inclusive as space permits, but most are more fully covered in the foregoing text. Some details cannot be noted on the roster pages at all, due to their overcrowding. Consult the text for details.

For basic research purposes, box scores published in *The Sporting News* and *The New York Times* were used. The "official" box scores are available, somewhere, but out of reach. Consequently, not all games played totals match those in record books such as *The 1947 Baseball Guide* or the various editions of *Mac* and *Total Baseball,* because there are mistakes, typos and misprints in publicly available box scores. They were submitted moments after the end of games, not proofed till a later date, in a more thorough format. After spending a full day trying to reconcile box score totals of Billy Herman's games at third and second base for Brooklyn, with those in my source publications, I've let it lie, leaving that part of the equation up to the reader. You can look it up, in any of a number of sources, to secure the number of games for a player at each of his positions, though, again, they won't always tally up in published box score totals.

Pinch-hit and or pinch-run appearances are included if they seem significant within a particular player's total games played. For a few pitchers, pinch-hitting was a testament to their ability with the bat or speed afoot (or, perhaps, they were better than anybody left on the bench that day). For position players, the minimum number of pinch-hit assignments is ten, though less if a meaningful percentage of just a few total games. These arbitrary criteria are mine.

Mistakes and typos, unless discussed in their context, are mine alone, for which I must apologize and request your help in correcting revisions, in care of the publisher.

BOSTON RED SOX, 1946   104-50   .675   1st place, AL
Joe Cronin, Manager. Del Baker, Larry Woodall, Tom Daly, Tom Carey, coaches.

Total players: 39	Games	Pos	1st game	
DiMAGGIO, Dom	142	cf	Apr 16	
PESKY, Johnny	153	ss	Apr 16	
WILLIAMS, Ted	150	lf	Apr 16	
DOERR, Bobby	151	2b	Apr 16	
YORK, Rudy	154	1b	Apr 16	
METKOVICH, George	86	rf-cf-lf	Apr 16	
ANDRES, Ernie	15	3b	Apr 16 **debut**	May 29 to Buffalo; to Minneapolis June 24.
WAGNER, Hal	117	c	Apr 16	
HUGHSON, Cecil (Tex)	39	p	Apr 16	Out with torn wrist tendons, May 30(2)–June 15.
FERRISS, Dave (Boo)	45	p (ph-5)	Apr 17	
JOHNSON, Earl	29	p	Apr 17	
PYTLAK, Frankie	4	c	Apr 18	Out with arm trouble from Apr 25, released Aug 5.
HARRIS, Mickey	34	p	Apr 18	
DEUTSCH, Mel	3	p	Apr 21(1) **debut**	Optioned to Louisville May 13.
CAMPBELL, Paul	28	1b (ph-14)	Apr 21(1)	
RYBA, Dominic (Mike)	9	p	Apr 21(1)	
RUSSELL, Glen (Rip)	80	3b-2b	Apr 21(1)	
BROWN, Mace	18	p	Apr 21(1)	
DOBSON, Joe	32	p	Apr 21(1)	
BAGBY Jr., Jim	21	p	Apr 21(2)	
HEFLIN, Randy	5	p	Apr 21(2)	Optioned to Louisville, June 18.
CULBERSON, Leon	59	rf-cf-lf-3b	Apr 22	Split finger at 3b May 10, only pr-ph till Jun 8.
PELLAGRINI, Eddie	22	3b-ss	Apr 22 **debut**	Homers first at bat in majors.
STEINER, Ben	3	3b (pr-2)	Apr 23	To Toronto May 30.
DREISEWERD, Clem	20	p	Apr 23	
WILSON, Jim	1	p	Apr 23	Optioned to Louisville, May 8.
McBRIDE, Tom	61	rf-lf-cf (ph-18)	Apr 24	
PARTEE, Roy	40	c	Apr 24	
BUTLAND, Bill	5	p	Apr 24	To Louisville July 10, making room for Gutteridge.
GILBERT, Andy	2	ph-pr	Apr 24	Optioned to Louisville, May 8.
McGAH, Eddie	15	c	Apr 26 **debut**	
LAZOR, Johnny	23	rf-lf (ph-16)	May 16	
HIGGINS, Mike (Pinky)	64	3b	May 22	Bought from Detroit May 19, out spiked Aug 4–10.
KLINGER, Bob	28	p	May 23	Cut by Pts (dnp) May 7, signed by Boston May 9.
WAGNER, Charley	8	p	Jun 06	Wartime illness delays 1st game 7 weeks.
ZUBER, Bill	15	p	Jun 23(2)	Cut by Yanks June 14, signed by Boston June 18.
CAREY, Tom (Scoops)	3	2b	Jun 26(1)	Player-coach, last plays 7/7, full-time coach 7/23.
GUTTERIDGE, Don	22	2b-3b	Jul 25	Toledo manager, bought by Boston July 9.
MOSES, Wally	48	rf-cf	Jul 26	From White Sox on waivers, July 23.

CHICAGO WHITE SOX, 1946   74–80   .481   30 gb   5th place, AL
Jimmie Dykes (10–20) & Ted Lyons, Managers. Red Faber, Mule Haas, Bing Miller, coaches.

Total players: 39	Games	Pos	1st game	
MOSES, Wally	56	rf-cf (ph-19)	Apr 16	Waived to Red Sox, July 23.
BAKER, Floyd	9	3b	Apr 16	To Milwaukee April 28, recalled Sep 8.
JONES, Murrell (Jake)	24	1b	Apr 16	Broken arm May 26(2), out rest of season.
WRIGHT, Taft	115	rf-lf	Apr 16	Tonsillitis & surgery, out May 22 thru June 20.
APPLING, Luke	149	ss	Apr 16	
TROSKY, Hal	88	1b	Apr 16	
KOLLOWAY, Don	123	2b-3b	Apr 16	Hurts shoulder July 24, out till Aug 22 (pr 7/31).
TUCKER, Thurman	121	cf (ph-11)	Apr 16	
TRESH, Mike	80	c	Apr 16	
HODGIN, Ralph	87	lf-rf (ph-29)	Apr 16	
DICKEY, George (Skeets)	37	c	Apr 16	
DIETRICH, Bill	11	p	Apr 16	Line drive breaks finger June 25, out rest of season.
KENNEDY, Bob	113	lf-3b-cf-rf	Apr 16	
RIGNEY, John	15	p	Apr 17	Hurts shoulder, out May 27–Jun 5; Jun 7–Jul 18.
GROVE, Orval	33	p	Apr 17	
LODIGIANI, Dario	44	3b	Apr 20	Fractured elbow surgery, out May 22–July 26.
LOPAT, Ed	30	p	Apr 20	
HAYNES, Joe	32	p	Apr 20	
LYONS, Ted	5	p	Apr 21(1)	Becomes manager May 24, retires as pitcher.
FERNANDES, Ed	14	c	Apr 21(2)	
LEE, Thornton (Lefty)	7	7	Apr 21(2)	Hurts elbow Jun 16, has surgery, out rest of season.
PAPISH, Frank	31	p	Apr 21(2)	
MICHAELS, Cass	91	2b-3b-ss	Apr 21(2)	
SMITH, Eddie	24	p	Apr 22	
PLATT, Mizell (Whitey)	84	lf-cf-rf (ph-17)	Apr 27	From Cubs (dnp there) on waivers, April 20.
CALDWELL, Earl	39	p	Apr 27	
O'NEILL, Emmett	2	p	Apr 28(2)	From Cubs (1 GP), Apr 23; to SF Jun 14.
HAMNER, Ralph	25	p	Apr 28(2) debut	
PERME, Len	4	p	Apr 28(2)	To Milwaukee Jun 14.
WELLS, Leo	45	3b-ss	Apr 28(2)	
CURTRIGHT, Guy	23	rf-lf-cf (ph-8)	Apr 28(2)	
JORDAN, Tom	10	c (ph-8)	Jun 05	Out w/ hurt arm till June 4, sold to Cleveland July 4.
HOLLINGSWORTH, Al	21	p	Jun 09(1)	Bought from Browns, June 6.
KUHEL, Joe	64	1b	Jun 16(2)	Released by Washington, signs with Sox June 13; muscle injury Aug 18 (1), out till Aug 25 (2).
WHITMAN, Frank	17	ss-2b-1b (pr-9)	Jun 30(2) debut	Signs out of Illinois Wesleyan, June 27.
HAYES, Frankie	53	c	Jul 17(2)	Purchased from Cleveland, July 15.
MALTZBERGER, Gordon	19	p	Jul 27	Begins season in Army, reports July 18.
PHILLEY, Dave	17	lf	Sep 10	To Milwaukee May 3, recalled Sep 8.
SMAZA, Joe	2	rf (pr-1) Sep 18(2) debut		From Shreveport Sep 10.

CLEVELAND INDIANS, 1946   68–86   .442   36 gb   4th place, AL
Lou Boudreau, Manager. Oscar Melillo, George Susce, Buster Mills, *coaches.*

Total players: 48	Games	Pos	1st game	
CASE, George	118	lf	Apr 16	Out with back injury, May 20–26; excused Sep 22–29.
LEMON, Bob	55	p-cf (ph-9)	Apr 16	
EDWARDS, Hank	124	rf	Apr 16	
FLEMING, Les	99	1b-rf (ph-17)	Apr 16	Inj. July 9–21; home in TX w/ill son August 8–13.
KELTNER, Ken	116	3b	Apr 16	At father-in-law's funeral, July 31–August 4.
BOUDREAU, Lou	140	ss	Apr 16	
HAYES, Frankie	51	c	Apr 16	Sold to White Sox, July 15.
MACK, Ray	61	2b	Apr 16	
FELLER, Bob	48	p	Apr 16	
WOODLING, Gene	61	cf-lf-rf (ph-23)	Apr 17	
REYNOLDS, Allie	35	p	Apr 17	
SEEREY, Pat	117	rf-lf-cf	Apr 20	
LOLLAR, Sherman	28	c	Apr 20 **debut**	Optioned to Baltimore, July 15.
GROMEK, Steve	37	p (pr-7)	Apr 20	
BLACK, Don	18	p	Apr 20	Sent to Milwaukee, July 17.
CENTER, Pete	21	p	Apr 20	
MONACO, Blas	12	(ph-7, pr-5)	Apr 20	Sold to Seattle May 31.
EMBREE, Charley (Red)	28	p	Apr 24	
MACKIEWICZ, Felix	78	cf	Apr 25	
HEGAN, Jim	88	c	Apr 25	
JOHNSON, Vic	9	p	Apr 25	To Baltimore June 28.
PODGAJNY, Johnny	6	p	Apr 25	Sold to Baltimore May 15.
MEYER, Lambert (Dutch)	72	2b	Apr 25	
BREWSTER, Charlie	3	ss (ph-2)	Apr 25	Sold to Milwaukee June 5.
ROSS, Don	55	3b-rf (ph-11)	Apr 28	
ROCCO, Mickey	34	1b (ph-7)	Apr 28	Hurt till 4/28; to Nashville 6/26, reports July 15.
MILLS, Buster	9	lf	Apr 28	Becomes full-time coach, July 3.
KLIEMAN, Eddie	9	p	May 01	To Indianapolis as part of Becker deal, June 27.
CONWAY, Jack	68	2b-ss-3b	May 02	
FERRICK, Tom	9	p	May 02	Released to Browns, June 24.
KRAKAUSKAS, Joe	29	p	May 05	
HARDER, Mel	13	p	May 07	Injures hand May 22, out till July 1.
BERRY, Joe	21	p	Jul 01	With A's till May 6, bought from Toronto July 1.
WASDELL, Jimmy	32	1b-rf-lb (ph-24)	Jul 02	Released by Phillies, signs as free agent July 1.
WEBBER, Les	4	p	Jul 07(2)	From Dodgers July 2; to Baltimore Aug. 20.
GASSAWAY, Charlie	13	p	Jul 07(2)	Obtained from Oakland, July 1.
JORDAN, Tom	14	c	Jul 07(2)	Purchased from White Sox, July 4.
BECKER, Heinz	50	1b (ph-7)	Jul 16	From Cubs to Nashville, traded for Rocco, reports July 16.
PRICE, Jackie	7	ss (ph-3)	Aug 18(1) **debut**	Acrobatic showman, Veeck favorite, from Oakland Aug 13.
PETERS, Rusty	9	ss	Sep 02(2)	From Army July 31, off NDSL Aug. 8.
SEPKOWSKI, Ted	2	3b	Sep 15(1)	To Ok City 4/27, recalled Sep 8.
MITCHELL, Dale	11	cf	Sep 15(1) **debut**	From Ok City Sep 8.
WEIGEL, Ralph	6	c	Sep 18 **debut**	From Wilkes-Barre Sep 15.
McCABE, Ralph	1	p	Sep 18 **debut**	From Ok City Sep 8.

Total players: 48	Games	Pos	1st game	
MOSS, Howie	8	3b	Sep 19	Reds to Baltimore in May, bought by Cle Sep 16.
ROBINSON, Eddie	8	1b	Sep 19	To Balt. 4/23, recalled Sep 16.
FLANIGAN, Ray	3	p	Sep 20 **debut**	From Baltimore Sep 16.
KUZAVA, Bob	2	p	Sep 21 **debut**	Bought from Wilkes-Barre farm team, Sep 18.

Note: Fleming, Keltner, Embree, Meyer, Ross, Krakauskas, Harder, Berry, Jordan, Becker, Peters— all excused Sep 25–rest of season.

DETROIT TIGERS, 1946   92–62   .597   12 gb   2nd place, AL
Steve O'Neill, Manager. Art Mills, Frank Shellenback & Tommy Bridges, coaches.

Total players: 37	Games	Pos	1st game	
LAKE, Eddie	155	ss	Apr 16	
MAYO, Eddie	51	2b	Apr 16	Collides w/Evers, out.6/3–7/13, 8/7– end of season.
McCOSKY, Barney	25	cf	Apr 16	Traded to Philadelphia for Kell, May 18.
GREENBERG, Hank	142	1b	Apr 16	
WAKEFIELD, Dick	111	lf	Apr 16	Out 5/5–5/9, 5/11–18; bone chips in wrist; in elbow 7/12–27.
MULLIN, Pat	93	rf-cf (ph-16)	Apr 16	Out with dislocated finger, April 22–26.
HIGGINS, Mike (Pinky)	18	3b	Apr 16	Flu May 5–8; sold to Red Sox May 19.
RICHARDS, Paul	57	c	Apr 16	Injured elbow 5/14–18, torn knee ligaments 6/9–7/2.
NEWHOUSER, Hal	37	p	Apr 16	
OUTLAW, Jimmy	92	lf-cf-rf-3b (pr-10, ph-5)	Apr 17	
TEBBETTS, Birdie	87	c	Apr 17	
CULLENBINE, Roy	113	rf-1b-lf (ph-15)	Apr 17	
TRUCKS, Virgil	32	p	Apr 17	
OVERMIRE, Frank	24	p	Apr 17	Falls on pitching hand, out with sprain, 6/4–22, 6/22–7/4.
CASTER, George	26	p	Apr 17	
MOORE, Anselm (Anse)	51	lf-rf (ph-18)	Apr 17 **debut**	
BENTON, Al	28	p	Apr 18	
TROUT, Paul (Dizzy)	40	p	Apr 22	
CRAMER, Roger (Doc)	68	cf (ph-18)	Apr 23	
WEBB, James (Skeeter)	64	2b-ss	Apr 25	
HARRIS, Ned	1	ph	Apr 28	To Portland (PCL) April 29.
SWIFT, Bob	42	c	May 01	Pulled left ankle tendon delays Swift till May 1.
WHITE, Hal	11	p	May 01	
HUTCHINSON, Fred	40	p (ph-12)	May 01	
GENTRY, Ruffus (Rufe)	2	p	May 01	Optioned to Buffalo, May 11.
HITCHCOCK, Billy	3	2b (ph-2)	May 01	Inj. fingers & thumb May 5, sold to Nats May 16.
BRIDGES, Tommy	9	p	May 02	Released September 16.
BLOODWORTH, Jimmy	76	2b	May 14	From NDSL 5/6, reports 5/11.
MANDERS, Hal	2	p	May 15	To Buffalo 6/20, sold to Cubs 8/9.
GRAY, Ted	3	p	May 15 **debut**	From Navy 5/6, to Buffalo 5/24, recalled 9/8.
KELL, George	105	3b-1b	May 19(1)	From A's for McCosky 5/18; inj. 6/8–12, 6/23–7/4.

Total players: 37	Games	Pos	1st game	
EVERS, Walter (Hoot)	81	cf-lf	May 21	Broken ankle & thumb in spring tng, out till 6/21, broken jaw, out Jun 3-21; injured wrist, out July 25-31.
LIPON, Johnny	14	ss-3b	May 22	
GORSICA, Johnny	14	p	Jun 09(2)	
GROTH, Johnny	4	cf	Sep 05 debut	Signed out of Navy, activated 8/11.
HOUTTEMAN, Art	1	p	Sep 25	From Buffalo 9/8.
KRETLOW, Lou	1	p	Sep 26 debut	From Williamsport 9/8.

NEW YORK YANKEES, 1946   87–67   .565   17 gb   3rd place, AL

Joe McCarthy (22–13), Bill Dickey (57–48), Johnny Neun (8–6), Mgrs. Neun, R.Rolfe, J.Schulte, coaches.

Total players: 46	Games	Pos	1st game	
CROSETTI, Frank	28	ss	Apr 16	Pulls calf muscle opening day, inj till June 3.
STIRNWEISS, Snuffy	129	3b-2b-ss	Apr 16	
HENRICH, Tommy	150	rf-1b	Apr 16	Out with spike wound, May 22–28.
DiMAGGIO, Joe	132	cf-lf	Apr 16	Out with knee injury, July 7 till August 2.
ETTEN, Nick	108	1b (ph-24)	Apr 16	
LINDELL, Johnny	102	rf-cf-lf-1b (ph-15)	Apr 16	
DICKEY, Bill	54	c (ph-15)	Apr 16	Quits as Mgr Sep 12, released as player Sep 23.
GRIMES, Oscar	14	ss-2b	Apr 16	Sold to Athletics July 11, making room for Wight.
CHANDLER, Spud	34	p	Apr 16	
GORDON, Joe	112	2b	Apr 17	
ROBINSON, Aaron	100	c	Apr 17	Out with split finger, May 11-28, INS Aug 16-21.
GUMPERT, Randy	33	p	Apr 17	
WIGHT, Bill	14	p	Apr 17 debut	All season with Yankees when option try fails.
ROSER, Emerson (Steve)	4	p	Apr 17	Sold to Braves, May 3.
GETTEL, Al	26	p	Apr 18	
PAGE, Joe	32	p	Apr 19	High life, drinking lead to McCarthy's exit.
KARPEL, Herb	2	p	Apr 19 debut	Released to Newark, April 24.
KELLER, Charlie	150	lf-rf	Apr 19	
STANCEAU, Charley	3	p	Apr 20	Sold to Phillies, June 5.
METHENY, Bud	3	(ph-3)	Apr 20	To Kansas City May 16.
BEVENS, Floyd (Bill)	31	p	Apr 22	
RIZZUTO, Phil	126	ss	Apr 24	Out till April 24, pulled calf muscle; out HBP July 17–29.
MARSHALL, Clarence	23	p	Apr 24 debut	
WADE, Jake	13	p	Apr 24	Sold to Washington August 5.
SILVESTRI, Ken	13	c	Apr 25	Fractured finger May 29, out till June 21.
ZUBER, Bill	3	p	Apr 25	Released June 14, signs with Red Sox June 18.
MAJESKI, Hank	8	3b (ph-6)	Apr 25	Sold to Athletics, June 14.
RUFFING, Charley (Red)	8	p	May 01	Broken kneecap June 29; released Sept. 23.
MURPHY, Johnny	27	p	May 04	
BONHAM, Ernie (Tiny)	18	p	May 05	

Total players: 46	Games	Pos	1st game	
RUSSO, Marius	10	p	May 09	Bone chips in Army wreck career, to Newark 8/5.
DRESCHER, Bill	5	c	May 19(2)	Optioned to Kansas City, June 2.
WEATHERLY, Roy	2	(ph-2)	May 20	Army in April; 1st game May 20, to Indianapolis 6/20.
SOUCHOCK, Steve	47	1b (ph-18, pr-9)	May 25 debut	Discharged from Army in May.
HILLER, Frank	3	p	May 25 debut	Army till May, arm surgery; to Newark June 14.
JOHNSON, Billy	85	3b (ph-11)	May 26(1)	From NDSL 5/6.
NIARHOS, Gus	37	c	Jun 09(1) debut	To Kansas City May 10, recalled June 9.
BYRNE, Tommy	14	p (ph-6, pr-4)	Jun 09(1)	Military veteran, on roster all season.
QUEEN, Mel	14	p	Jun 30	From NDSL till 6/13.
DREWS, Karl	3	p	Sep 08(2) debut	To KC April 24, recalled Sept. 8.
BOCKMAN, Eddie	4	3b	Sep 11 debut	From Kansas City, Sept. 8.
LYONS, Al	2	p	Sep 11	To KC April 24, recalled Sept. 8.
BROWN, Bobby	7	ss-3b	Sep 22(1) debut	To Newark April 13, recalled Sept. 18.
BERRA, Yogi	7	c	Sep 22(1) debut	From Navy to Kansas City to Newark May 12, called up Sept 18.
COLMAN, Frank	5	of	Sep 22(2)	Pirates to Newark June 17, called up Sept. 20.
RASCHI, Vic	2	p	Sep 23 debut	At Binghamton & Newark, called up Sept. 20.

Note: Hal Peck purchased from A's June 19, but ill and unable to play any more this year. Crosetti, Etten, Silvestri, Murphy, Bonham all excused from team, 9/23-29.

PHILADELPHIA ATHLETICS, 1946   49–105   .318   55 gb   8th place, AL
Connie Mack, Manager. Earle Mack, Al Simmons, Earle Brucker, Dave Keefe, coaches.

Total players: 41	Games	Pos	1st game	
GARRISON, Ford	9	lf	Apr 16	To Newark for Derry, May 3.
PECK, Hal	48	rf (ph-13)	Apr 16	Sold to Yankees, June 19.
WALLAESA, Jack	63	ss	Apr 16	To Toronto July 16, recalled Sept. 8.
CHAPMAN, Sam	146	lf-cf	Apr 16	
McQUINN, George	136	1b	Apr 16	
ROSAR, Warren (Buddy)	121	c	Apr 16	
KELL, George	26	3b	Apr 16	Traded to Detroit for McCosky, May 18.
HANDLEY, Gene	89	2b-3b-ss (ph-9, pr-9)	Apr 16 debut	
CHRISTOPHER, Russ	30	p	Apr 16	
FOWLER, Dick	32	p	Apr 16	
KONOPKA, Bruce	38	1b-lf (ph-18)	Apr 16	To S Diego May 15, recalled June 21. To Toronto July 16, recalled September 7.
HARRIS, Lum	34	p	Apr 16	
NEWSOM, Bobo	10	p	Apr 17	Requests release June 3, signs with Nats June 5.
FLORES, Jesse	29	p	Apr 18	
SAVAGE, Bob	40	p	Apr 18	
BESSE, Herm	7	p	Apr 18	Optioned to Toronto, May 23.
VALO, Elmer	108	rf-lf (ph-17)	Apr 18	
KNERR, Luther (Lou)	30	p	Apr 18	

Total players: 41	Games	Pos	1st game	
BERRY, Joe	5	p	Apr 18	To Toronto 5/6, sold by Maple Leafs to Indians 7/1.
VAUGHAN, Porter	1	p	Apr 21(1)	To Kansas City May 2, part of Derry trade.
BENSON, Vern	7	lf (ph-2, pr-4)	Apr 21(2)	To Toronto May 7, to Savannah June 24.
DESAUTELS, Gene	52	c	Apr 21(2)	
HALL, Irv	63	2b-ss (ph-18)	Apr 23	To KC July 17, recalled Sept. 8.
SUDER, Pete	128	ss-3b-2b-1b-rf (ph-12)	Apr 23	
CAULFIELD, Jake	44	ss-3b (pr-9, ph-3)	Apr 24 **debut**	
BROWN, Norm	4	p	Apr 26	Sold to Toronto, May 19.
ARMSTRONG, George	8	c (ph-5)	Apr 26 **debut**	To Savannah July 13.
DERRY, Russ	69	lf-rf-cf (ph-17)	May 01	From Yanks (thru KC) for Garrison, Vaughan, April 30.
STAINBACK, Tuck	91	rf-cf-lf (ph-25)	May 03	Released by Yanks (dnp) 4/29, signed by A's 5/3.
MARCHILDON, Phil	36	p	May 06	Lingering 1945 groin injury plus Garrison knife throwing accident delays season for Marchildon.
KNOTT, Jack	3	p	May 06	Released, May 18.
COOPER, Orge (Pat)	1	p	May 11 **debut**	To Savannah July 11.
McCOSKY, Barney	92	cf-lf	May 22	From Tigers for Kell, May 18.
FAGAN, Everett	20	p	Jun 11(1)	From NDSL, 4/28.
MAJESKI, Hank	78	3b	Jun 19	Purchased from Yankees, June 14.
GRIFFETH, Lee	10	p	Jun 25 **debut**	Signed from Duke U., to Lancaster Aug 13.
GRIMES, Oscar	59	2b-3b-ss	Jul 14(1)	Purchased from Yankees, July 11.
RICHMOND, Don	16	3b	Sep 10	From Toronto, 9/8.
ASTROTH, Joe	4	c	Sep 13(1)	From Lancaster, 9/8.
COLEMAN, Joe	4	p	Sep 15(1)	From Toronto 9/7.
McCAHAN, Bill	4	p	Sep 15(2) **debut**	From Toronto 9/7.

Note: Neither Stainback nor Derry played for Yankees before acquisition by Philadelphia.

ST. LOUIS BROWNS, 1946   66–88   .429   38 gb   7th place, AL
Luke Sewell (58–71), Zack Taylor (13–17), Mgrs. Taylor and Fred Hofman, coaches.

Total players: 44	Games	Pos	1st game	
DILLINGER, Bob	83	3b-ss (ph-19, pr-9)	Apr 16 **debut**	
GRACE, Joe	48	rf	Apr 16	To Senators with LaMacchia for Heath, June 15.
McQUILLEN, Glenn	59	lf-rf (ph-13)	Apr 16	
JUDNICH, Walt (Wally)	142	cf-lf-rf	Apr 16	
BERARDINO, Johnny	144	2b	Apr 16	
CHRISTMAN, Mark	128	3b-ss	Apr 16	
MANCUSO, Frank	87	c	Apr 16	Paratroop back injury sidelines him, Jun 8–July 4.
ARCHIE, George	4	1b (pr-1)	Apr 16	To L.A. April 29.
POTTER, Nelson	23	p	Apr 16	
LUCADELLO, Johnny	87	3b-2b (ph-33)	Apr 17	
ZARILLA, Al	125	rf-lf-cf (ph-18)	Apr 17	
STEPHENS, Vern	115	ss	Apr 17	Injured shoulder, out May 7–June 5 (except 2 ph), again August 15–30 (except 1 ph).

Total players: 44	Games	Pos	1st game	
MILLER, John (Ox)	11	p	Apr 17	Optioned to Toledo, June 24, disallowed June 30, sold outright to Toledo June 30.
FINNEY, Lou	16	lf-rf (ph-8)	Apr 17	To Phils May 29, returned and released, June 13. (DNP Phl)
HELF, Hank	71	c	Apr 17	
STEVENS, Chuck	122	1b	Apr 17	
SHIRLEY, Alvin (Tex)	35	p	Apr 17	
ZOLDAK, Sam	35	p	Apr 17	
GALEHOUSE, Denny	30	p	Apr 18	
FERENS, Stan	34	p	Apr 18	
HOLLINGSWORTH, Al	5	p	Apr 18	Sold to White Sox, June 6.
SEARS, Ken	7	c (ph-3)	Apr 18	Rights dispute W/NY-A till 6/19, to San Antonio 7/11.
LaMACCHIA, Al	8	p	Apr 18	To Senators with Grace, for Heath June 15.
LAABS, Chet	80	rf-lf	Apr 20	
SCHULTE, Len	4	2b-3b (ph-3)	Apr 20	Optioned to Toledo, June 22.
DAHLGREN, Babe	28	1b	Apr 24	From Pirates Apr 23, did not play for Pittsburgh. Released Sept. 28.
KRAMER, Jack	31	p	Apr 24	
MILNAR, Al	4	p	Apr 28(1)	To Phils May 29, returned and released, June 13.
BRADLEY, George	4	cf	Apr 28(2) **debut**	To Toledo May 30, recalled June 15, suspended June 8–Sept. 9, released to San Antonio Sept. 17.
KINDER, Ellis	33	p	Apr 30 **debut**	32-year-old rookie, minors 1939–44, '45 in military.
SCHULTZ, Joe	42	c (ph-25)	Apr 30	Weak arm, okay bat.
SUNDRA, Steve	2	p	Apr 30	Released unconditionally, May 29.
FANNIN, Cliff	27	p	May 12(1)	Sore arm spring training delays first game.
MUNCRIEF, Bob	29	p	May 25	Broken toe in spring training delays first game.
HEATH, Jeff	86	lf	Jun 17	From Senators Jun 15 for Grace & LaMacchia.
BISCAN, Frank	16	p	Jun 23(1)	Arm operation in May, vol. retired list till 6/19.
FERRICK, Tom	25	p	Jun 30(2)	Released by Indians to Browns, June 24.
LEHNER, Paul	16	cf-rf	Sep 10 **debut**	From Toledo, Sept. 8.
WITTE, Jerry	18	1b	Sep 10 **debut**	From Toledo, Sept. 8.
MOSS, Les	12	c	Sep 10 **debut**	From Toledo, Sept. 8.
MARTIN, Boris (Babe)	3	c (ph-1)	Sep 12	From StL to Oakland, to StL, to Toledo, to StL 9/8.
JOHNSON, Chet	5	p	Sep 12 **debut**	From Toledo, Sept. 8.
SANFORD, Fred	3	p	Sep 15(1)	From Toledo, Sept. 8.
SHORE, Ray	1	p	Sep 21(1) **debut**	From Springfield at end of 3-I League season, 9/2.

Note: Mancuso, Potter, Stevens, Laabs, Dahlgren, Martin excused Sep. 24 to let new arrivals play. On Sep. 28, Dahlgren is released.

WASHINGTON NATIONALS, 1946   76–78   .494   28 gb   4th place, AL
Ossie Bluege, Manager. Nick Altrock, Rick Ferrell, Joe Judge, Clyde Milan & Bert Shepard, coaches.

Total players: 36	Games	Pos	1st game	
ROBERTSON, Sherry	74	3b-2b-ss-rf (ph-12)	Apr 16	
LEWIS, John (Buddy)	150	rf-lf-cf	Apr 16	
SPENCE, Stan	152	cf	Apr 16	
TRAVIS, Cecil	137	ss-3b	Apr 16	
HEATH, Jeff	48	lf	Apr 16	To St. Louis for Grace & LaMacchia, June 15.
VERNON, Mickey	148	1b	Apr 16	
PRIDDY, Gerry	138	2b	Apr 16	Torn knee cartilage ends his season, September 11.
EVANS, Al	88	c	Apr 16	
WOLFF, Roger	21	p	Apr 16	
HUDSON, Sid	31	p	Apr 16	
KUHEL, Joe	14	1b	Apr 16	Released by Washington June 12, signs w/White Sox 6/13.
BINKS, George	65	of	Apr 16	
MASTERSON, Walt	29	p	Apr 17	
CURTIS, Vern	11	p	Apr 17	To Buffalo July 22, recalled Sep. 8.
WILSON, Maxie	9	p	Apr 17	To Chattanooga, June 13.
PIERETTI, Marino (Chick)	30	p	Apr 17	
KENNEDY, Bill G.	21	p	Apr 17	
SANFORD, John H.(Jack)	10	1b (ph-4)	Apr 17	To Chattanooga, May 20.
TORRES, Gil	63	ss-3b-2b-p	Apr 18	
SCARBOROUGH, Rae	32	p	Apr 18	
GOOLSBY, Ray	3	lf (ph-2)	Apr 18 debut	To Chattanooga, May 20.
GUERRA, Fermin (Mike)	41	c (ph-10, pr-4)	Apr 18	
HAEFNER, Mickey	33	p	Apr 19	
NIGGELING, Johnny	8	p	Apr 19	Released June 25; signs with Braves July 1.
EARLY, Jake	64	c	Apr 20	
LEONARD, Emil (Dutch)	26	p	Apr 20	
COAN, Gil	59	lf-rf (ph-26)	Apr 27 debut	
MYATT, George	15	3b-2b (ph-5, pr-1)	May 19(1)	Chips ankle in dugout fall, opening day, out till May 19.
HITCHCOCK, Billy	98	ss-3b	May 30(2)	Purchased from Tigers, May 16.
NEWSOM, Bobo	24	p	Jun 07	Released by A's June 3, signs with Nats June 5.
GRACE, Joe	77	lf-rf	Jun 23(1)	With LaMacchia for Heath, June 15.
LaMACCHIA, Al	2	p	Jun 23(2)	With Grace for Heath, June 15, sold to Chattanooga 7/15.
WYNN, Early	25	p (ph-8)	Jul 16	Out of Army July 4, pitches first game July 16.
WADE, Jake	6	p	Aug 08(1)	Purchased from Yankees, August 5
YOST, Eddie	8	3b	Aug 08(1)	Off NDSL 7/25, first game August 8.
CANDINI, Milo	9	p	Aug 25	From NDSL, August 14.

BOSTON BRAVES, 1946   81–72   .529   15.5 gb   4th place, NL
Billy Southworth, Manager. Jake Flowers, Johnny Cooney, Bob Keely, coaches.

Total players: 48	Games	Pos	1st game
RYAN, Connie	143	2b-3b	Apr 16
HOPP, Johnny	129	1b-cf	Apr 16

Total players: 48	Games	Pos	1st game	
HOLMES, Tommy	149	rf-cf	Apr 16	
ROWELL, Carvel (Bama)	95	lf-cf (ph-10)	Apr 16	
McCARTHY, Johnny	2	1b	Apr 16	To Minneapolis, Apr 19.
MASI, Phil	133	c	Apr 16	
ROBERGE, Skippy	48	3b	Apr 16	To Indianapolis June 15, to make room for Herman.
CULLER, Dick	134	ss	Apr 16	Inj leg, out Jun 30–July 3.
SAIN, Johnny	40	p	Apr 16	
SISTI, Sebastian (Sibby)	1	pr	Apr 17	To Indianapolis, Apr 18.
WEST, Max	1	ph	Apr 17	To the Reds for Konstanty & cash, April 19.
WORKMAN, Chuck	25	cf-lf-rf (ph-12)	Apr 17	To Pirates for Johnny Barrett, June 12.
WIETELMANN, Whitey	44	ss-3b-2b-p (ph-15)	Apr 17	
WRIGHT, Ed	36	p	Apr 17	
WALLACE, Jim (Lefty)	27	p	Apr 17	To Indy June 28, returned July 6, waiver mistake.
POLAND, Hugh	4	c (ph-2)	Apr 17	Sold to Seattle, May 8.
SANDERS, Ray	80	1b	Apr 20	HBP 5/5, out til 5/10; ankle inj 6/17–21; broken arm 8/21— .
LEE, Bill	25	p	Apr 20	
GILLENWATER, Carden	99	cf-lf-rf (ph-20)	Apr 21(1)	
FERNANDEZ, Froilan (Nanny)	115	3b-ss-lf	Apr 21(2)	
HUTCHINGS, Johnny	1	p	Apr 21(2)	Released to Indianapolis May 2.
SINGLETON, Elmer	16	p	Apr 21(2)	To Indianapolis August 13.
POSEDEL, Bill	19	p	Apr 22	
WILLIAMS, Bob (Ace)	1	p	Apr 22	Sold to Seattle, May 8.
HENDRICKSON, Don	2	p	Apr 22	Sold to Kansas City, May 3.
COOPER, Mort	28	p	Apr 23	
HOFFERTH, Stew	20	c (ph-5)	Apr 28(1)	To Brk for Herman, Jun 15, vol. retired list 7/9.
JAVERY, Alva	2	p	May 03	Released to Toronto, May 22, returned June 11, optioned to Little Rock June 15, recalled Aug 27, sold to Milwaukee Sept 9.
KONSTANTY, Jim	10	p	May 05(1)	From Reds w/cash for West 4/19; to Toronto 6/15.
ROSER, Emerson (Steve)	14	p	May 07	Bought from Yankees, May 3.
REID, Earl	2	p	May 08 debut	Optioned to Indianapolis, May 25.
JOHNSON, Silas	28	p	May 13	Released by Phils & signed by Braves Apr 29.
WHITE, Ernie	14	p-pr	May 20	Released by Cards (dnp) May 13, signed May 15.
DETWEILER, Bob (Ducky)	1	ph	Jun 01	To Indy 4/26, recalled 5/25, optioned to Rochester 6/14, recalled 8/27, released to Hartford 9/11.
McCORMICK, Mike	59	cf-rf-lf (ph-9)	Jun 04	From Cin 6/3; torn leg ligaments end season 8/31.
LITWHILER, Danny	79	lf-rf-3b (ph-12)	Jun 15	From StL 6/9; HBP 8/31 breaks cheek, out til 9/8.
BARRETT, Johnny	24	cf-rf-lf (ph-8)	Jun 15	From Pts for Workman, Jun 12; inj knee 6/19–8/11.
HERMAN, Billy	75	2b-1b-3b	Jun 16(1)	From Dodgers for Hofferth, June 15.
PADGETT, Don	44	c (ph-18)	Jun 17(1)	Bought from Dodgers, June 12.
SPAHN, Warren	24	p	Jun 17(1)	Discharged from Army, June 11.
BARRETT, Francis (Red)	23	p	Jun 30	Purchased from Louisville, June 28.

Total players: 48	Games	Pos	1st game	
NIGGELING, Johnny	8	p	Jul 06	Cut by Wsh 6/25, signed 7/1; requests release 9/4.
O'DEA, Ken	12	c	Jul 13(1)	From Cards Jul 8, broken finger ends year Aug 6.
DARK, Alvin	15	ss-lf	Jul 14(2) debut	Out of Army, signed as free agent July 4.
BRADY, Bob	3	c (ph-2)	Aug 24 debut	Promoted from Indianapolis, Aug 19 after O'Dea is hurt.
NEILL, Tommy	13	lf	Sep 10 debut	Sou. Assn MVP, bought from Birmingham Sep 7.
MULLIGAN, Dick	4	p	Sep 21	Obtained from Phillies September 18.
PHILLIPS, Damon	2	ph	Sep 21	Discharged from Army, September 10.

BROOKLYN DODGERS, 1946   96–60   .615   2 gb   2nd place, NL

Leo Durocher, Manager. John (Red) Corriden, Charlie Dressen, coaches.

Total players: 45	Games	Pos	1st game	
REESE, Pee Wee	152	ss	Apr 16	Neck injury; misses All-Star Game, out Jul 11–14.
WALKER, Fred (Dixie)	150	rf	Apr 16	Fined $150, suspended May 24–28, brawls w/Cubs.
HERMAN, Billy	47	3b-2b	Apr 16	Traded to Boston Jun 15 for Hofferth (who doesn't report).
WHITMAN, Dick	104	cf-lf (ph-19)	Apr 16 debut	
REISER, Pete	122	lf-cf-3b (ph-11)	Apr 16	[5/19 — hits wall, hurts already-separated shoulder, returns to cf 5/24; 5/28 — hits wall, out 5/29–30, ph only from 6/1–10; 8/1 — hits wall, (and kitchen stove explodes), out till 8/8; 9/1–5 — out with pleurisy; 9/13 — pulls thigh muscle running bases; ph twice, defense once till 9/25; 9/26 — fractured leg ends Reiser's season.]
CASEY, Hugh	46	p	Apr 16	
HERMANSKI, Gene	64	rf-lf-cf (ph-29)	Apr 16	
GRAHAM, Jack	2	1b	Apr 16 debut	Sold to Giants with Rosen, April 28.
FURILLO, Carl	117	cf-lf-rf	Apr 16 debut	
RIGGS, Lew	1	3b	Apr 16	Cut 4/27; signs w/Montreal, 1st game May 19.
ANDERSON, Ferrell	79	c (ph-8)	Apr 16 debut	
ROSEN, Goody	3	cf (ph-2)	Apr 16	Sold to Giants with Graham, April 28.
GREGG, Hal	26	p	Apr 16	Pulled muscle in pitching arm, out May 15–Jun 22, doesn't start again till July 25.
GALAN, Augie	99	lf-rf-3b-1b (ph-13)	Apr 16	
SCHULTZ, Howie	90	1b	Apr 17	
BEHRMAN, Hank	47	p	Apr 17 debut	
STEVENS, Ed	103	1b	Apr 18	Tooth problems keep Stevens out for 1st 2 days.
LOMBARDI, Vic	43	p	Apr 18	
CORRIDEN, Johnny	1	pr	Apr 20 debut	Optioned to Montreal, April 22.
STANKY, Eddie	144	2b	Apr 20	Taken out by Slaughter 7/14, hurts back, sidelined till 7/17.
PADGETT, Don	19	c (ph-12)	Apr 20	Sold to Braves, June 12th.

Total players: 45	Games	Pos	1st game	
ROJEK, Stan	45	ss-2b-3b (ph-13)	Apr 20	
RAMAZZOTTI, Bob	62	3b-2b (ph-18)	Apr 20 debut	With Montreal till 4/20.
HIGBE, Kirby	42	p	Apr 20	
HATTEN, Joe	42	p	Apr 21 debut	
BRANCA, Ralph	24	p	Apr 22	
DAVIS, Otis (Scat)	1	pr	Apr 22 debut	From StL 4/19 (dnp); to Montreal, 5/1.
HEAD, Ed	13	p	Apr 23	No-hitter vs.Bos 4/23, sore arm ends big league career 8/26.
NAYLOR, Earl	3	ph-pr	Apr 26	From StL (dnp) 4/23; to Montreal May 18.
HERRING, Art (Sandy)	35	p	Apr 28(1)	
DAVIS, Curt	1	p	Apr 28(2)	Released May 1, signs with Montreal.
MOULDER, Glen	1	p	Apr 28(2) debut	From NDSL 4/15, to Montreal 5/1.
SANDLOCK, Mike	19	c-3b	Apr 28(2)	To Mobile July 10, later to Montreal & St. Paul.
ROY, Jean-Pierre	3	p	May 05(2) debut	Optioned to Montreal June 15.
WEBBER, Les	11	p	May 05(2)	Sold to Indians, July 2 on waivers.
LAVAGETTO, Cookie	88	3b (ph-16)	May 08	Elbow surgery delays start; plays hurt rest of year.
BARNEY, Rex	16	p	May 30(2)	Joins team after discharge from Army, May 11.
MELTON, Rube	24	p	Jun 05	Joins team 5/22 after Army discharge May 18.
EDWARDS, Bruce	92	c	Jun 23 debut	Called up from Mobile June 21, 1st-stringer upon arrival.
MEDWICK, Joe (Ducky)	41	lf-1b (ph-22)	Jul 01	Free agent, signs with Dodgers June 25.
TEPSIC, Joe	15	lf (pr-9,ph-5)	Jul 12 debut	Signs 7/8, $17,000 bonus, "no-cut" contract.
MIKSIS, Eddie	23	3b-2b	Jul 14(1)	Discharged from Army, joins team July 14.
McLISH, Cal	1	p	Aug 25(2)	With Army in Czechoslovakia, finally discharged, reinstated July 15.
MINNER, Paul	3	p	Sep 12 debut	From Mobile Sept 9, still raw, will be 10-year big leaguer.
TAYLOR, Harry	4	p	Sep 22(1) debut	From St. Paul Sept 3, will go 10–8 for Dodgers next yr.

CHICAGO CUBS, 1946   82–71   .536   14.5 gb   3rd place, NL

Charlie Grimm, Manager. Roy (Hardrock) Johnson, Milt Stock, Richard (Red) Smith, coaches.

Total players: 46	Games	Pos	1st game	
HACK, Stan	92	3b	Apr 16	Thigh inj.5/19, out til 5/28; thumb fracture 8/4, out til 9/12.
JOHNSON, Don	83	2b	Apr 16	Broken hand 8/20 ends Johnson's season.
LOWREY, Peanuts	144	lf-cf-rf-3b	Apr 16	
CAVARRETTA, Phil	139	1b-rf-lf-cf	Apr 16	Injures hand 7/1, out till 7/6.
PAFKO, Andy	65	cf	Apr 16	Slips on ball 6/1, ankle fracture, out till 7/18; broken arm 8/27, out remainder of season.
RICKERT, Marv	111	rf-lf-cf	Apr 16	
LIVINGSTON, Mickey	66	c	Apr 16	5/22, badly sprained ankle, out till 7/7.
GILBERT, Charlie	15	cf-ph-pr	Apr 16	Sold to Phillies, June 14.

Total players: 46	Games	Pos	1st game	
McCULLOUGH, Clyde	95	c	Apr 16	Broken finger Aug 13, out till ph Sept 10.
SCHEFFING, Bob	63	c	Apr 16	
GLOSSOP, Alban (Al)	4	ss-2b	Apr 16	Optioned to Los Angeles, May 11.
MERULLO, Lennie	65	ss	Apr 16	Brawls w/Dodgers, suspended May 24–30, 8 days/$150 fine.
BECKER, Heinz	4	ph	Apr 16	May 27, asks sale to Nashville; later bought by Cleveland.
STRINGER, Lou	80	2b-3b	Apr 16	
STURGEON, Bobby	100	ss-2b	Apr 16	Lacerated finger 9/26, out remainder of season.
PASSEAU, Claude	21	p	Apr 16	Back injury sidelines Passeau 7/21 30, 8/24-rest of season.
WAITKUS, Eddie	113	1b	Apr 16	Bruised elbow, out 5/15–30; fractured finger, out 7/24–8/6.
CHIPMAN, Bob	34	p	Apr 16	
NICHOLSON, Bill	105	rf-ph	Apr 16	
ERICKSON, Paul	14	p	Apr 16	
FLEMING, Bill	14	p	Apr 16	To Los Angeles July 22.
PRIM, Ray	14	p	Apr 16	Inj elbow 4/21, out til 5/4; .inj arm muscle 5/19, on disabled list till 8/19.
WYSE, Hank	40	p	Apr 17	
SCHMITZ, Johnny	42	p	Apr 17	
KUSH, Emil	40	p	Apr 17	
O'NEILL, Emmett	1	p	Apr 17	Sold to White Sox April 23.
BITHORN, Hi	26	p	Apr 18	
BOROWY, Hank	33	p	Apr 20	
DALLESSANDRO, Dom	65	ph-lf-rf	Apr 25	Fractured ankle Aug. 23, out till Sept. 7.
OSTROWSKI, John	64	3b-ph-cf-lf	Apr 26	
SECORY, Frank	33	ph-lf	Apr 26	To Kansas City Aug. 12.
HANYZEWSKI, Eddie	3	p	May 01	To Nashville May 11; 8 GP Tulsa; recall by Cubs 9/14.
JURGES, Billy	82	ss,-3b-2b	May 02	Ill, unable to play till Cubs travel to Cincinnati 4/25.
ADAMS, Charles (Red)	8	p	May 05(2) **debut**	Will be sent to LA 7/3.
MEERS, Russ	7	p	May 29	One gp pre-war, USN vet, ill early-season; to Nashville 8/1.
OLSEN, Vern	5	p	Jun 23(1)	Ill, unable to pitch for first two months of season.
BAUERS, Russ	15	p	Jul 18	Free Agent after 4 yrs in Military, signs July 3.
WILLIAMS, Dewey	4	c-ph	Aug 22	Starts year at Los Angeles, recalled Aug 21.
GARRIOTT, Cecil	6	ph	Sep 04 **debut**	Only season in majors, Army till off NDSL Aug 21.
BLOCK, Seymour (Cy)	6	3b-ph	Sep 12(1)	From Nashville after Sou. Assn season ends 9/8.
PAWELEK, Ted	4	ph-c	Sep 13 **debut**	From Nashville after Sou. Assn season ends 9/8.
MANDERS, Hal	2	p	Sep 13	Ex-Tiger bought from Buffalo, aprx. September 9.
MEYER, Russ	4	p	Sep 13 **debut**	From Nashville 9/8, 1st of 13 yrs in majors.
MADDERN, Clarence	3	lf-ph	Sep 17 **debut**	From Tulsa, approximately September 15.
SCHENZ, Henry	6	3b-pr	Sep 18 **debut**	From Tulsa, approximately September 15.

Total players: 46	Games	Pos	1st game	
LADE, Doyle	3	p	Sep 18 debut	Bought from Shreveport in July, reports Sep 15.

Note: Meers "officially" optioned to Nashville 8/12, but pitches there 8/2.

CINCINNATI REDS, 1946   67–87   .435   30 gb   6th place, NL
Bill McKechnie, Manager. Jimmie Wilson, Hank Gowdy, Gerald (Gee) Walker, coaches.

Total players: 35	Games	Pos	1st game	
CLAY, Dain	121	cf-lf	Apr 16	
FREY, Lonnie	111	2b-lf-rf-cf	Apr 16	Regular 2b on two pennant winners, returns from wartime service at 35, loses job to Adams.
LAMANNO, Ray	85	c	Apr 1	
HATTON, Grady	116	3b-lf	Apr 16 debut	Fractures knee in Crosley concourse fall, out 8/24 for rest of season.
MILLER, Eddie	91	ss	Apr 16	Injured arm, out 7/20–26, 8/2–9/1.
HAAS, Bert	140	1b-3b	Apr 16	
LIBKE, Al	125	rf-p	Apr 16	Starting pitcher last day of season (no decision).
USHER, Bob	92	lf-rf-cf-3b	Apr 16 debut	
LUKON, Eddie	102	lf-rf	Apr 16	
CORBITT, Claude	82	ss	Apr 16	
MUELLER, Ray	114	c	Apr 16	
ZIENTARA, Benny	78	2b-3b	Apr 16	
BEGGS, Joe	28	p	Apr 16	
HEUSSER, Ed	29	p	Apr 16	
ADAMS, Bobby	94	2b-rf-3b	Apr 16 debut	Injures knee in batting practice 5/4, out till 5/28.
VANDER MEER, John	33	p	Apr 17	
GUMBERT, Harry	36	p	Apr 17	
SHOUN, Clyde	27	p	Apr 17	
BLACKWELL, Ewell	33	p	Apr 17	
ANDREWS, Nate	7	p	Apr 18	Released 6/11, signs with Giants 6/16.
WEST, Max	72	lf-cf-rf	Apr 20	From Braves for Jim Konstanty (dnp) 4/19; back infection June 9–15, June 21–July 11.
WALTERS, Bucky	24	p-ph-pr	Apr 20	
SHOKES, Eddie	31	1b	Apr 21(1)	
MOSS, Howie	7	rf	Apr 22	NDSL till 4/22, to Balt 5/16; bought by Indians for Sept delivery.
McCORMICK, Mike	23	cf	Apr 22	Spring training injury delays first game; sold to Braves 6/3.
LAMBERT, Clay	23	p	Apr 22 debut	
VOLLMER, Clyde	9	lf-cf-rf	Apr 24	To Rochester 4/30; recalled @ close of IL season, 9/8.
FOX, Howie	4	p	Apr 24	Appendectomy, out 4/27–6/2; to Syracuse 8/8; in IL playoffs fractures arm, out till next season.
HETKI, Johnny	32	p	Apr 24	
LAKEMAN, Al	23	ph-c	Apr 24	
LAWING, Gerald	2	cf-ph	May 29 debut	NDSL till 5/3, sold to Giants 6/8.
MALLOY, Bob	27	27	May 30(1)	Ex-Red ('43–44), from USN May 8.
DASSO, Frankie	2	2	May 30(1)	Wartime PCL star, sold to Hollywood June 11.
BURPO, George	2	2	Jun 09(1) debut	As in '42 before USN hitch, sent to Syracuse (0–2) on July 12.

Total players: 35	Games	Pos	1st	
GOLDSTEIN, Lonnie	6	ph	Aug 11(2)	Discharged from Army, reports August 9. High-average hitter in Big State League, 1947–53.

NEW YORK GIANTS, 1946   61–93   .396   36 gb   8th place, NL

Mel Ott, Manager. Grover Hartley, Clarence (Bubber) Jonnard, Ralph (Red) Kress, coaches.

Total players: 49	Games	Pos	1st game	
RIGNEY, Bill	110	3b-ss	Apr 16 debut	Out with cold, Aug 23–25.
WITEK, Mickey	82	2b-3b	Apr 16	Pre-war regular 2b, hits wall 4/28, fractures elbow, out til 6/6
OTT, Mel	31	rf-ph	Apr 16	Vision problems May 26–June 2, inactive.
YOUNG, Babe	104	1b-rf-cf-ph	Apr 16	
LOMBARDI, Ernie	88	c	Apr 16	
MARSHALL, Willard	131	cf-lf-rf	Apr 16	
GORDON, Sid	135	lf-3b	Apr 16	Injured April 17–20.
RUCKER, Johnny	95	cf-ph-pr	Apr 16	
KERR, Buddy	145	ss-3b	Apr 16	
VOISELLE, Bill	36	p	Apr 16	Knee injury, out July 25(2) till Aug 11(2).
ADAMS, Ace	3	p	Apr 16	Jumps to Mexican League, April 26.
TRINKLE, Ken	48	p	Apr 16	
MAYNARD, Buster	7	rf-cf-pr	Apr 17	Optioned to Jersey City, April 29.
MIZE, Johnny	101	1b	Apr 17	HBP 8/5, broke hand; out til 9/13, breaks toe, out til 1947.
JOYCE, Bob	14	p	Apr 17	To Minneapolis for Abernathy, July 25.
PIKE, Jesse	16	rf-lf-ph-pr	Apr 18 debut	Optioned to Jersey City, May 22.
FELDMAN, Harry	3	p	Apr 18	Jumps to Mexican League, April 26.
BUDNICK, Mike	35	p	Apr 18 debut	
WARREN, Bennie	39	c-ph	Apr 18	Emergency catcher at Jersey City 6/18, back to NY by 6/30.
BREWER, Jack	1	p	Apr 18	Optioned to Minneapolis, May 18
COOPER, Walker	87	c	Apr 18	Fractured finger 4/25–5/19; broken finger 7/16–28; blood poison left leg 9/15 ends Cooper's season.
KENNEDY, Monte	38	p	Apr 18 debut	
KLUTTZ, Clyde	5	ph-c	Apr 18	To Phils for DiMaggio 5/1, to Cards for Verban same day.
KOSLO, Dave	41	p	Apr 20	
ARNOVICH, Morrie	1	lf	Apr 21	To Jersey City 4/29, returned 6/6, released 6/10.
FISCHER, Rube	15	p	Apr 23	To Minneapolis for Abernathy, July 25.
EMMERICH, Bill	2	p	Apr 23	Optioned to Jersey City May 16.
BARTELL, Dick	5	3b-2b	Apr 24	
CARPENTER, Bob	12	p	Apr 24	Pitching elbow inj. 6/4, pitches 6/29, surgery, out till 8/28.
SCHEMER, Mike	1	ph	Apr 24	Optioned to Jersey City May 29; mgr at Richmond Aug. 11.
ROSEN, Goody	100	cf-rf-lf	Apr 28(1)	From Brk Apr 27, hurt shoulder May 8, out till 30th.
BLATTNER, Buddy	126	2b	Apr 28(1)	
SCHUMACHER, Hal	24	p	Apr 28(1)	
GRAHAM, Jack	100	rf-lf-1b	May 02	From Brooklyn April 27.

Total players: 49	Games	Pos	1st game	
DiMAGGIO, Vince	15	cf	May 03	From Phils for Kluttz May 1. To SF June 8.
THOMPSON, Gene	39	p	May 15	Released by Reds (dnp) April 30, signs with NY May 14; sore arm June 11–29.
KRAUS, "Texas Jack"	17	p	May 18	From Phillies April 23 (dnp for Phils).
CARDEN, John	1	p	May 18 debut	Signed 5/13 out of USMC, to Richmond June 13.
LAWING, Garland	8	ph-lf-pr	Jun 11	Purchased from Reds June 8; to Jersey City July 22.
ANDREWS, Nate	3	p	Jun 16(1)	Released by Reds 6/11, signed by NY 6/16, released 6/26.
KRESS, Red	1	p	Jul 17	Coach, activated July 15–18 when pitchers hurt, released as player Sept 16.
GEE, Johnny	13	p	Jul 17	Voluntary Retired list till June 27.
ABERNATHY, Woody	15	p	Jul 28(2) debut	From Minneapolis July 25.
THOMSON, Bobby	18	3b	Sep 09 debut	From Jersey City 9/9.
GLADD, Jim	4	c	Sep 09 debut	From Jersey City 9/9.
JONES, Sheldon	6	p	Sep 09 debut	From Jacksonville 9/4.
LAJESKIE, Dick	6	2b	Sep 10 debut	From Jersey City 9/9.
GRISSOM, Marv	4	p	Sep 10 debut	From Jersey City 9/9.
GRASSO, Mickey	7	c	Sep 18 debut	From Jersey City 9/9.

PHILADELPHIA PHILLIES, 1946   69–85   .448   28 gb   5th place, NL

Ben Chapman, Manager. Cy Perkins, Benny Bengough, Benny Culp, coaches.

Total players: 49	Games	Pos	1st game	
MURTAUGH, Danny	6	2b	Apr 16	Bat star opening day, to Rochester May 2.
WYROSTEK, Johnny	145	cf-lf	Apr 16	
TABOR, Jim	124	3b	Apr 16	Out with arm injury May 22–June 15.
NORTHEY, Ron	128	rf	Apr 16	Suspended May 5–8.
McCORMICK, Frank	135	1b	Apr 16	Broken rib, June 17 till July 2.
DiMAGGIO, Vince	6	cf	Apr 16	To Giants for Kluttz, 5/1. Kluttz to StL for Verban.
HEMSLEY, Rollie	49	c	Apr 16	Broken wrist 4/30, out till 6/16 (3 games played before diagnosis).
NEWSOME, Skeeter	112	ss-3b-2b	Apr 16	
JUDD, Oscar	46	p	Apr 16	
MULCAHY, Hugh	16	p	Apr 16	
WASDELL, Jimmy	26	ph-rf-lf-1b	Apr 16	Released June 18, signed by Indians July 1.
LOPATKA, Art	4	p	Apr 16	Sold to Louisville July 17, sent back w/sore arm, dnp again.
NOVIKOFF, Lou	17	ph-lf	Apr 16	Novikoff sold to Seattle, June 17.
O'NEIL, John	46	ss	Apr 16 debut	
HOERST, Frank	18	p	Apr 17	
JURISICH, Al	13	p	Apr 17	Sidelined with arthritis, May 26–30. AWOL and suspended, Aug 14–Sept. 18.
MULLIGAN, Dick	19	p	Apr 17	Tonsils out 5/31, out till 7/2, to Braves Sept. 18.
DINGES, Vance	50	1b-ph-lf	Apr 20	To Utica April 25, recalled June 19.
SEMINICK, Andy	124	c	Apr 20	Breaks toe Sep 19, out remainder of season.

Total players: 49	Games	Pos	1st game	
RAFFENSBERGER, Ken	39	p	Apr 20	
KARL, Anton (Andy)	39	p	Apr 20	
HUGHES, Roy	89	ss-3b-2b-1b	Apr 21(1)	
ROWE, Schoolboy	30	p	Apr 21(1)	Pulls groin muscle Aug 4(2), out rest of yr except ph 9/10.
HUGHES, Tommy	29	p	Apr 22	
CRAWFORD, Glen	1	ph	Apr 22	To Portland (PCL) May 7.
RICHARDSON, Ken	6	2b-3b	Apr 23	Sold to Hollywood outright, June 3.
JOHNSON, Si	1	p	Apr 24	April 29, released by Phils, signed by Braves.
PEARSON, Ike	5	p	Apr 24	Sold to Seattle June 14.
ENNIS, Del	141	lf-rf	Apr 28(1) **debut**	
SCHANZ, Charley	32	p	Apr 28(1)	
VERBAN, Emil	138	2b	May 03	From StL for Kluttz, May 1 (see DiMaggio, above)
MAUNEY, Dick	25	p-pr	May 04	
HUMPHRIES, John	10	p	May 05(1)	Optioned to Kansas City Aug 5, doesn't report, suspended, Aug 28 ineligible list.
CHAPMAN, Ben	1	p	May 12	Manager, takes himself off active list, June 11.
RIPPLE, Charlie	6	p	Jun 09(1)	Optioned to Memphis, June 29.
SPINDEL, Hal	1	c	Jun 09(1)	To LA June 18.
BURICH, Bill	3	ph-3b-pr	Jun 09(1)	From Military 5/13, sold to Houston June 11, returned and optioned to Columbus July 5.
MILNAR, Al	1	p	Jun 10	From Browns w/Lou Finney (dnp) 5/29; both sent back 6/10.
STANCEAU, Charley	14	p	Jun 16(2)	Bought from Yankees June 5.
MOORE, Dee	11	c-1b	Jun 16(2)	From NDSL June 10, plays sporadically throughout last season in majors.
GILBERT, Charlie	88	rf-cf-lf	Jun 18	Bought from Cubs June 14.
DONNELLY, Blix	12	p	Jul 25(2)	Purchased from Cardinals July 8.
LETCHAS, Charlie	6	2b	Aug 25(1)	In Military service till August 14.
POSSEHL, Lou	4	p	Aug 25(2)	Ex-GI semi-pro, 20, signs mid-August.
HODKEY, Eli	2	p	Sep 12(2) **debut**	From Utica Sept 4.
HASENMAYER, Don	6	3b-pr-ph	Sep 14	From Utica Sept 4.
GRATE, Don	3	p	Sep 18(2)	14–8 at Utica, reports after EL season, Sept.4.
HAMNER, Granny	2	ss	Sep 28	Only 19, from Military Sept 18, 3rd season in majors.
KOECHER, Dick	1	p	Sep 29 **debut**	Signed out of Temple U, sent to Terre Haute til Sept 4.

PITTSBURGH PIRATES, 1946   63–91   .409   34 gb   7th place, NL

Frankie Frisch (62–89) & Spud Davis (1–2), Mgrs. Davis, Honus Wagner, Del Bissonnette, coaches.

Total players: 43	Games	Pos	1st game	
BROWN, Jimmy	79	ss-2b-3b	Apr 16	
BARRETT, Johnny	32	cf-rf	Apr 16	To Braves for Workman, June 12.
KINER, Ralph	144	lf-cf	Apr 16 **debut**	
ELLIOTT, Bob	140	rf-3b	Apr 16	
FLETCHER, Elbie	148	1b	Apr 16	

Total players: 43	Games	Pos	1st game	
RUSSELL, Jim	146	cf-lf-rf-1b	Apr 16	
COX, Billy	121	ss	Apr 16	
SMITH, Vinnie	7	c	Apr 16	Knee inj 4/27 & surgery 5/10 end big league career.
OSTERMUELLER, Fred	28	p	Apr 16	
COLMAN, Frank	26	rf-lf-1b-ph	Apr 16	Released to Newark June 17 (to Yankees Sept. 22).
BARNHART, Vic	2	pr-ph	Apr 16	Optioned to Albany, April 30.
HEINTZELMAN, Ken	32	p	Apr 16	Sinus operation ends Heintzelman's season Sept. 22.
GABLES, Ken	32	p	Apr 17	
ANDERSON, Alf	2	ph	Apr 17	Sold to Hollywood, April 27; '46 team MVP there.
LANNING, Johnny	27	p	Apr 17	
ALBOSTA, Ed	17	p	Apr 18	
GUSTINE, Frankie	131	2b-ss-3b	Apr 18	Spike wound August 11(2), out till August 28.
STRINCEVICH, Nick	32	p	Apr 18	
GERHEAUSER, Al	37	p-rf	Apr 18	
GIONFRIDDO, Al	64	cf-rf-lf-ph-pr	Apr 20	Appendectomy August 28 ends his season.
CAMELLI, Hank	42	c	Apr 20	To Toronto July 1, recalled Sept. 8.
SEWELL, Rip	26	p	Apr 20	Out with meningitis, May 5(1)–May 26.
HOPPER, Jim	2	p	Apr 21(1) debut	To Columbus of American Association, Jun 7, Birmingham July 8.
GUINTINI, Ben	2	ph-rf	Apr 21(1) debut	Two games in April, to H'wd 5/7, returned; to SDiego 6/14, knee injured, back to Pts (dnp) 8/19, sold to Indianapolis Sept 22.
CLEMENSEN, Bill	1	p	Apr 21(1)	To Columbus of American Assn, Apr 27.
ROE, Preacher	21	p	Apr 21(1)	Basketball knee injury in winter cripples Roe, sent home late summer for rest of '46. Last game 8/9.
SALKELD, Bill	69	c	Apr 21(2)	
HALLETT, Jack	35	p	Apr 21(2)	
VAN ROBAYS, Maurice	59	lf-ph-rf-1b	Apr 21(2)	
HANDLEY, Lee	116	3b-2b	Apr 21(2)	
ZAK, Frankie	21	ss-ph-pr	Apr 26	To Kansas City 6/13, completes Bahr deal in April.
BAKER, Bill	53	c-1b	Apr 26	
WILKIE, Aldon (Lefty)	7	p	Apr 26	To Hollywood, June 14.
COSCARART, Pete	3	ph-ss	Apr 27	To San Diego June 1, balks but signs there June 13.
WHITEHEAD, Burgess	55	2b-3b-ss	May 01	
BAHR, Edson (Ed)	29	p	May 01 debut	From Kansas City approx Apr 30 (see Zak, above).
LOPEZ, Al	56	c	May 19(1)	Breaks hand Apr 20, out till May 19. Foul tip Sept 2(2) injures finger, out remainder of season.
WORKMAN, Chuck	58	rf-ph-pr-lf-3b	Jun 16(1)	From Braves for Barrett, Jun 12.
GORNICKI, Hank	7	p	Jun 17	From Hollywood May 15, w/sore arm.
JARVIS, LeRoy	2	ph-2	Jul 07(2)	Drafted from Brooklyn 1945, in Navy till reinstated from NDSL June 20.
WALSH, Jim (Junior)	4	p	Sep 14 debut	From York at end of Interstate League season, Sept. 8.

Total players: 43	Games	Pos	1st game	
HOWARD, Lee	3	p	Sep 22(1) debut	From York at end of Interstate League season, Sept 15 (after suspension).
TATE, Al	2	p	Sep 27 debut	From Selma at end of Southeastern League season, Sept 1.

St. LOUIS CARDINALS, 1946   98–58   .628   1st place, NL
Eddie Dyer, Manager. Clyde (Buzzy) Wares, Miguel (Mike) Gonzalez, coaches.

Total players: 37	Games	Pos	1st game	
KLEIN, Lou	23	2b	Apr 16	Jumps to Mexican League, May 23.
MOORE, Terry	91	cf-ph	Apr 16	Knee injury July 27–Aug 12.
MUSIAL, Stan	156	1b-lf	Apr 16	New position, 1b, 5/8; June 7–rest of season. MVP
SLAUGHTER, Enos	156	rf	Apr 16	
KUROWSKI, Whitey	142	3b	Apr 16	
SISLER, Dick	83	1b-lf-ph	Apr 16 debut	
MARION, Marty	146	ss	Apr 16	Won't fly from NY to Cin, doesn't play May 24–26; out with arm injury June 4–6
RICE, Del	55	c	Apr 16	
BEAZLEY, Johnny	19	p	Apr 16	Out with arm trouble, June 7 till June 21.
DICKSON, Murry	47	p	Apr 16	
ADAMS, Elvin (Buster)	81	cf-lf-ph	Apr 16	
BRECHEEN, Harry	37	p-pr	Apr 16	
DUSAK, Ervin	100	lf-3b-cf-2b-ph	Apr 16	
BURKHART, Ken	25	p	Apr 16	
SCHOENDIENST, Red	142	2b-3b/ss	Apr 16	Out with injured ankle, June 12–17(2).
DONNELLY, Blix	13	p	Apr 16	Sold to Phillies, July 8.
WALKER, Harry	112	cf-lf-1b-ph	Apr 17	
LANIER, Max	6	p	Apr 17	Jumps to Mexican League, May 23, w/ 6-0 record.
POLLET, Howie	40	p	Apr 18	
WILBER, Del	4	c	Apr 21 debut	To Columbus (AA) May 10; recalled at end of American Assn season, September 8.
O'DEA, Ken	22	c	Apr 21	Sold to Braves, July 8.
BARRETT, Chas.(Red)	23	p	Apr 21	
MARTIN, Freddie	6	p	Apr 21 debut	Jumps to Mexican League, May 23.
ENDICOTT, Bill	20	ph-lf	Apr 21 debut	
CROSS, Joffre (Jeff)	49	ss-2b-3b-pr-ph	Apr 21	
WILKS, Ted	40	p	Apr 23	
KRIST, Howie	15	p	Apr 25	
SESSI, Walter	15	ph	Apr 28(1)	
VERBAN, Emil	1	2b	Apr 28(2)	To Phillies for Kluttz, May 1.
KLUTTZ, Clyde	52	c	May 02	From Giants to Philly to Cards (for Verban), May 1
BRAZLE, Alpha (Al)	37	p	May 16	Discharged by Army, April 24.
GARAGIOLA, Joe	74	c	May 26(1) debut	Discharged by Army, joins team May 15.
LITWHILER, Danny	6	ph	May 27	From Army May 1; sold to Braves June 9.
SCHMIDT, Freddy	18	p	May 30(1)	
JONES, Vernal (Nippy)	16	ph-2b-pr	Jun 09(1) debut	From USMC June 10; optioned to Rochester July 11; recalled at end of IL season, Sept 8.

Total players: 37	Games	Pos	1st game	
GRODZICKI, Johnny	3	p	Jul 11	Wounded war vet has trouble recovering; disabled list May 9 till July 5.
MUNGER, Geo. (Red)	10	p	Aug 25(2)	Discharged by Army, joins team August 20.

Errata

1. *Sporting News* and *New York Times* box scores list pitcher Dave Ferriss, Red Sox, in 44 games, instead of the 45 he is credited with in record books.
2. Boxes credit outfielder Tom McBride, Red Sox, with 62 games, while record books say 61. He is shown pinch-hitting in 14 games in which Ferriss is not in the box score. Any of these could be juxtaposed.
3. Felix Mackiewicz, Indians outfielder, is shown in 77 box scores but credited with 78 games in record books.
4. Two members of the Detroit Tigers are each shown with one more game in box scores than they are credited with in record books. Outfielder-third baseman Jimmy Outlaw is shown 93 times, but records credit him with only 92 appearances; shortstop Skeeter Webb is shown in 65 games but credited with just 64.
5. Outfielder Tuck Stainback of the Athletics can be found in only 90 box scores, records say he played 91 games.
6. Rookie Alvin Dark, Braves, is credited with 16 games played but is found only 15 times in box scores.
7. Three members of the Cincinnati Reds don't match the record books. Outfielder Bob Usher is credited with 92 games but appears in only 91 box scores; outfielder Eddie Lukon is in 101 box scores but should be in 102. Pitcher Ed Heusser should be in 29 box scores, but is only in 28.
8. Two New York Giants are misaligned with the record books. Outfielder Johnny Rucker actually played 95 games, but is in just 94 boxes. Catcher Bennie Warren, credited with 39 games, appears only 38 times in box scores.
9. Pitcher Dick Mauney of the Phillies, credited with 25 games played, shows up only 24 times in boxes.
10. Pitcher Al Gerheauser of the Pirates seems to have appeared in 37 games if you read the box scores, but the record books say he played only 36 games this year.
11. Outfielder Erv Dusak of the Cardinals, credited with 100 games played, can be counted in only 99 box scores.

Perhaps the errors are in my addition, though I've double-checked these totals many times over. It will take a session with the official box scores to make the corrections.

Bibliography

Ace: Phil Marchildon, Canada's Pitching Sensation and Wartime Hero, by Phil Marchildon with Brian Kendall, Toronto: Penguin, 1994; first published by Viking, 1993.
The Alabama Sports Hall of Fame, Bill Legg, director, Birmingham, AL.
The American Association: A Baseball History, 1902–1991, by Bill O'Neal, Austin, TX: Eakin Press, 1991.
The Angels, Los Angeles in the Pacific Coast League 1919–1957, by Richard E. Beverage, Placentia, CA, The Deacon Press, 1981.
Athletes Away: A Selective Look at Professional Baseball Players in the Navy During World War II, by Harrington E. "Kit" Crissey, Jr., SABR, Philadelphia: Archway Press, 1984.
The Ballplayers, Baseball's Ultimate Biographical Reference, ed. by Mike Shatzkin, New York: Arbor House/William Morrow, 1990.
Baseball: A Comprehensive Bibliography, compiled by Myron J. Smith, Jr., Jefferson, NC: McFarland, 1986.
Baseball Between the Lines, by Donald Honig, excerpts printed in *A Donald Honig Reader,* New York: Simon & Schuster, 1988.
The Baseball Encyclopedia, First Edition ("Mac I"): New York/Toronto: Macmillan/Information Concepts, 1969.
The Baseball Encyclopedia, Tenth Edition ("Mac X"): New York: Macmillan, 1996.
The Baseball Register, "the Game's '400,'" compiled by J.G. Taylor Spink, St. Louis: C.C. Spink & Son, 1941; 1942, 1944, 1946, 1947 (after 1942, *Sporting News* publisher Spink shares compilation credits with Paul A. Rikart).
The Baseball Research Journal, #15 (article by Randy Linthurst) 1986, # 21 (article by Alden Mead) 1992, #24 (article by Talmage Boston) 1995, # 26 (articles by John L. Green and Bob Mayer) 1997, Society for American Baseball Research (SABR).
Baseball's Great Experiment: Jackie Robinson and His Legacy, by Jules Tygiel, New York: Vintage Books/Random House, 1983.
The Baseball Timeline, by Burt Solomon, New York: Avon, 1997.
Baseball When the Grass Was Real, by Donald Honig, New York: Coward, McCann & Geoghegan, 1975.
The Boys of the Summer of '48, by Russell Schneider, Champaign, IL: Sports Publishing, 1998.
Branch Rickey: A Biography, by Murray Polner, New York: New American Library, 1982.
Chronology of Major League Baseball Records, compiled by John A. Mercurio, New York: Harper & Row, 1989.
The College Football Hall of Fame, Kent Stephens, director of research, South Bend, IN.
Daguerreotypes, 8th Edition, Craig Carter, ed., St. Louis, MO., *The Sporting News,* 1990.
Distant Drums: The 1949 Cleveland Indians Revisited, by Bruce Dudley, self-published, 1989.
The Encyclopedia of Minor League Baseball, edited by Lloyd Johnson & Miles Wolff, Durham, NC: Baseball America, 1997.
The Encyclopedia of Sports, Sixth Revised Edition, by Frank G. Menke, New York: Doubleday/Dolphin, 1977.
Epic Season: The 1948 American League Pennant Race, by David Kaiser, Amherst: University of Massachusetts Press, 1998.
Even the Browns, by William B. Mead, Chicago, Contemporary Books, 1978. Republished in expanded form as *The 10 Worst Years of Baseball: The Zany, True Story of Baseball in the Forties,* New York: Van Nostrand Reinhold, 1982.
FanPark Encyclopedia, Version 2.00, 1998, Miller Associates, Inc.
Fathers and Sons in Major League History, a report prepared for Father's Day public distribution, Cooperstown, NY: National Baseball Hall of Fame Library, 1997.
Five O'Clock Lightning: Ruth, Gehrig, DiMaggio, Mantle and the Glory Years of the New York Yankees, by Tommy Henrich with Bill Gilbert, New York: Birch Lane Press, 1992.
Football: Facts & Figures, by Dr. L.H. Baker, New York: Rinehart, 1945.
The Glory of Their Times, by Lawrence Ritter, New York: Macmillan, 1966.
Hank Greenberg: The Story of My Life, by Hank Greenberg, edited by Ira Berkow, New York: Times Books/Random House, 1989.

The History of American Football: Its Great Teams, Players and Coaches, by Allison Danzig, Englewood Cliffs, NJ: Prentice-Hall, 1956.
The History of the Texas League of Professional Baseball Clubs 1888–1951, by William B. Ruggles, Dallas: The Texas League, 1951.
Hitter: The Life and Turmoils of Ted Williams, by Ed Linn, New York: Harvest Books/Harcourt Brace, 1993.
H.M.S. Pinafore, from *The Complete Plays of Gilbert and Sullivan*, by W.S. Gilbert and Sir Arthur Sullivan, New York: W.W. Norton, 1976.
The Hollywood Stars: Baseball in Movieland 1926–57, by Richard E. Beverage, Placentia, CA: The Deacon Press, 1984.
The Home Run Heard 'Round the World: The Dramatic Story of the 1951 Giants-Dodgers Pennant Race, by Ray Robinson, New York: HarperCollins, 1991.
I Never Had It Made: An Autobiography, by Jackie Robinson as told to Alred Duckett, Hopewell, NJ: Ecco Press, 1995 (originally published by Putnam, 1972).
The International League: A Baseball History, 1884–1991, by Bill O'Neal, Austin, TX: Eakin Press, 1992.
Joe DiMaggio: A Bio-Bibliography, by Jack B. Moore, New York, Greenwood, 1986.
Leonard Maltin's 1997 Movie & Video Guide, New York: Signet, 1996.
The Little Red Book of Baseball: Baseball's Book of Official Records, compiled by Lester Goodman and Richard Bennett (1969), Seymour Siwoff (1970), New York: Elias Sports Bureau.
Lucky to Be a Yankee, by Jolting Joe DiMaggio (ghost-written by Tom Meany), New York: Rudolph Field, 1946.
Major League Baseball 1946, Facts, Figures and Official Rules, H.G. Salsinger, Harry G. Heilmann, Don H. Black, editors, Racine, WI: Whitman, 1946.
Major League Baseball 1947, Salsinger/Heilmann/Black, eds., New York: Dell, 1947.
Minor League History Journal, article by Richard Thompson, SABR, 1991.
Minor League Stars, vols. I, II, III, Cleveland: Society for American Baseball Research (SABR), 1992.
The National Pastime: A Review of Baseball History, #14 (article by Jay Feldman) 1994, #17 (articles by Phil Bergen and Greg Beston) 1997, # 19 (articles by Kit Crissey, Victor Debs, Jr., and Tom Gallagher) 1999; SABR.
The Negro Leagues Book, ed. by Dick Clark & Larry Laster, Cleveland: SABR, 1994.
The New York Times, daily issues, April 15–September 29, 1946.
Nice Guys Finish Last, by Leo Durocher with Ed Linn, New York: Simon and Schuster, 1975.
Now Pitching, Bob Feller: A Baseball Memoir, by Bob Feller with Bill Gilbert, New York: Birch Lane Press, 1990.
Official Baseball 1946, New York: A.S. Barnes, 1946.
The Official Baseball Guide, Official Rules and Averages 1947, 1948, compiled by J.G. Taylor Spink: St. Louis, C.C. Spink & Son, 1947; 1948.
Official Bulletins, Nos. 6–17, April 18–Sept. 30, 1946. Cincinnati: Office of the Commissioner of Baseball.
The Pacific Coast League: A Statistical History, 1903–1957, by Dennis Snelling, Jefferson, NC: McFarland, 1995.
Professional Baseball Franchises from the Abbeville Athletics to the Zanesville Indians, by Peter Filichia, New York: Facts on File, 1993.
The Professional Baseball Player Database, version 3.0, by Pat Doyle, Old-Time Data, Inc., Baseball Research, 1999.
The Rules and Lore of Baseball, by Richard T. Marazzi, New York: Stein and Day, 1980.
The Sporting News, weekly baseball newspaper, 1946, 1945 and 1942 issues.
The Sporting News 1998 Edition Baseball Guide, Craig Carter & Dave Sloan, ed., St. Louis: *The Sporting News*, 1998.
The Sporting News 1998 Edition Complete Baseball Record Book, Craig Carter, ed., St. Louis: *The Sporting News* Publishing Company, 1998.
The Sports Encyclopedia: Baseball, 17th Edition, by David S. Neft and Richard M. Cohen, New York: St. Martin's, 1997 ("Neft & Cohen XVII").
The Story of Baseball in Words and Pictures, by John Durant, New York: Hastings House, 1947.
Street & Smith's Baseball Year Book 1945, 1946, Charles Moran, ed., New York: Street & Smith, Inc., 1945–46; 1947 version published under auspices of *Pic, the Magazine for Young Men*.
Ted Williams: A Baseball Life, by Michael Seidel, Chicago: Contemporary Books, 1991.
The Texas League 1888–1987: A Century of Baseball, by Bill O'Neal, Austin, TX: Eakin Press, 1987.
Total Baseball V: The Official Encyclopedia of Major League Baseball, edited by John Thorn, Pete Palmer, Michael Gershman and David Pietrusza, New York: Penguin Books, 1997.
USA Today Baseball Weekly, issue of December 29, 1999, article by Bill Carle, of SABR.
Veeck as in Wreck: The Autobiography of Bill Veeck, by Bill Veeck with Ed Linn, New York: Fireside, 1989 (first published in 1962).
We Played the Game: 65 Players Remember Baseball's Greatest Era, 1947–1964, ed. by Danny Peary, New York: Hyperion, 1994.
When the Boys Came Back: Baseball and 1946, by Frederick Turner, New York: Henry Holt, 1996.
Who's Who in Baseball, Clifford Bloodgood, ed., New York: Baseball Magazine, 1946-47-49-51-52-53-54 editions.
Who's Who in the Major Leagues: Photos, Stories and Records of Ball Players in the American and National Leagues, 15th Edition, by John P. Carmichael, Chicago: B.E. Callahan, 1947.
The World Series: Complete Play-by-Play of Every Game, 1903–1978, by Richard M. Cohen, David S. Neft, text by Jordan A. Deutsch, New York: Dial, 1978.
Wrigleyville: A Magical History Tour of the Chicago Cubs, by Peter Golenbock, New York: St. Martin's, 1996.

Index

Abernathy, Woody 81, 251–261, 312–313
Adams, Ace Townsend 313
Adams, Bobby 1, 19, 34, 240–250, 311
Adams, Charles "Red" 24, 34, 69, 229–239, 310
Adams, Elvin "Buster" 87, 112, 284–294, 316
African-Americans/Black Americans/Black trailblazers/Negroes 3–4, 6–7, 26, 41, 69, 75, 77–78
Albany, New York/Senators (Eastern League, class "A" minor league) 37, 274, 315
Albosta, Ed "Rube" 272–283, 315
All-America basketball player 37
All-Rookie team 115
All-Star Game/squads/All-Star Break 3, 25, 32, 38, 57–58, 60, 62, 68, 70–73, 76–77, 79, 103, 124, 134, 146, 157, 168, 178, 190, 200, 211, 222, 233, 244, 255, 266, 277, 288
Altrock, Nick 306
Amarillo, Texas 36
American Association (class "AAA" minor league) 20, 27, 93, 97, 99, 112, 138, 163, 171, 182, 192, 316
American Baseball Guild 4, 30–32, 46, 55, 91
American League All-Star "volunteer" team 111–112
American League lead/pennant 90, 96, 101, 110–111, 128
American Leaguers in military 26
American Legion baseball 59
Anderson, Alfred "Alf" 29, 273–283, 315
Anderson, Ferrell 18, 64, 218–228, 308
Andres, Ernie 19, 57, 119–129, 297
Andrews, Nate 60, 66, 240–261, 311, 313

Appleton, Pete (real name Jablonowski) 15
Appling, Luke 72, 111, 130–140, 299
Archie, George 34, 185–195, 304
Ardizoia, Rinaldo "Rugger" 26
Arkansas Aggies 70
Armstrong, George "Dodo" 27, 79, 174–184, 304
Arnovich, Morris "Morrie" 30, 251–261, 312
Asheville, NC/Blues (Negro Southern League) 71
Astroth, Joe ("Schroft," "Ostroth," "Stroth") 16, 102, 174–184, 304
Athletes Away 17
Atlanta Braves 68
Atlanta, Georgia/Crackers (Southern Association, class "AA" minor league) 16, 55, 66
Bagby, Jim, Jr. 8, 112, 119–129, 298
Bahr, Edson "Ed" 32, 60, 273–283, 315
Baker, Bill 96, 100, 273–283, 315
Baker, Del 298
Baker, Floyd 32–33, 103, 130–140, 299
The Ballplayers 9, 12
Baltimore, Maryland/Orioles (American Association) 110
Baltimore, Maryland/Orioles (American League) 40–41
Baltimore, Maryland/Orioles (International League, class "AAA" minor league) 20, 24, 27, 41–42, 46, 68, 77, 86, 90, 105, 109, 141–142, 145–146, 149, 241, 300–301
Barnes, A. S. (*Official Baseball Guide*) 21
Barnes, Don 95
Barney, Rex 40, 218–228, 309
Barnhart, Clyde 37
Barnhart, Vic 37, 272–283
Barrett, Charles "Red" 9, 112, 284–294, 317

Barrett, Francis "Frank" ("Red") 67, 207–217, 307
Barrett, Johnny "Jack" 58, 62, 207–217, 273–283, 307, 314
Barrow, Ed 25
Bartell, Dick "Rowdy Richard" 73, 109, 251–261, 312
Barthelson, Bob 15
Baseball Writers Association of America (BBWAA) 25
Basketball Association of America 38
Bauers, Russ 69, 229–239, 309
Baumholtz, Frankie 37–38
Beazley, Johnny 56, 112–113, 284–294, 316
Becker, Heinz 49–50, 66, 107, 141–151, 229–239, 300–301, 309
Beggs, Joe 82, 240–250, 311
Behrman, Hank 20, 108, 218–228, 308
Belgium 105
Bengough, Benny 313
Bennett, George E. 14
Benson, Vern 37, 94, 174–184, 304
Benswanger, William E. "Bill" 46, 55
Benton, J. Alton "Al" 152–162, 301
Berardino, Johnny 72, 82, 84, 185–195, 304
Berra, Lawrence "Yogi" 38–39, 47, 49, 52, 96, 106–107, 163–173, 303
Berry, Jonas "Jittery Joe" 35, 68, 107, 141–151, 174–184, 300–301, 304
Besse, Herman "Long Herm" 55, 174–184, 303
betting scandal, Sally League 88
Bevens, Floyd (Bill) 163–173, 302
Biasetti, Hank 94
Big Red Machine 106
Big State League (class "B" minor league) 88, 312
Big Ten Conference 6
Binghamton, New York/

Triplets (Eastern League, class "A" minor league) 107, 163, 303
Binks, George 196–206, 306
Birmingham, Alabama/Barons (Southern Association, class "AA" minor league) 53, 96–97, 102, 207, 273–275, 277, 280, 308, 315
Biscan, Frank 41, 64, 94, 185–195, 305
Bissonnette, Del 314
Bithorn, Hiram "Hi" 229–239, 310
Black, Don 5, 78, 141–151, 300
Black, Lloyd L. (federal judge) 62–63
The Black Babe Ruth (Josh Gibson) 75
Blackwell, Ewell 73, 85–86, 115, 240–250, 311
Blades, Ray 30
Blattner, Robert "Buddy" 30, 82, 115, 251–261, 312
Block, Seymour "Cy" 98, 101, 229–239, 310
Bloodworth, Jimmy 39, 41, 152–162, 301
blooper ball (blooper pitch, eephus pitch) 60, 72
Bluege, Ossie 64, 306
Bockman, Eddie 21, 96, 100, 114, 163–173, 303
Bolling, Jack 20
Bonham, Ernie "Tiny" 1, 107, 163–173, 302–303
Borowy, Hank 82, 94, 229–239, 310
Boston Braves 2, 7–8, 10–11, 13, 16–18, 22, 24–27, 31–38, 40–42, 44, 49, 52–53, 56, 58–59, 61–62, 64–65, 67–68, 70–73, 76, 81–83, 87, 89, 90, 92–95, 97, 99, 102, 104–106, 109–111, 115, 164, 200, 207–217, 219, 221, 240, 242, 262–263, 272–273, 276, 287, 289, 302, 306–308, 311, 313–317
The Boston Globe (newspaper) 25

Index

Boston Red Sox ("Bosox," "Millionaires") 2, 8, 15–16, 19, 22–24, 27, 30, 32–34, 36, 39, 42–43, 46–49, 51, 53–55, 57–58, 65, 67, 70, 72–73, 76, 78–80, 82–85, 87–91, 94, 96, 99–101, 103, 105, 110–115, 119–129, 136, 146, 154, 167, 274, 298–299, 301–302, 317
Bottomley, "Sunny Jim" 82
Boudreau, Lou 64, 72, 76–77, 88, 90, 111, 141–151, 300
Boudreau Shift (also Williams Shift) 76, 113
Bowman, Bob 91
Brady, Bob 93, 207–217, 308
Brady, James 107
Bradley, Alva 63
Bradley, George Washington 64, 106, 185–195, 305
Braganza, Ramon 12
Bramham, W.C., National Association (the minor leagues) president 78, 88
Branca, Ralph 102, 108, 111, 218–228, 309
Brandt, Bill 29
Brannick, Eddie 11
Braves Field, Boston 105
Brazle, Alpha "Al" 22–23, 112, 114, 284–294, 316
Breadon, Sam 9, 11, 18, 45, 62, 71
Brecheen, Harry "The Cat" 107, 112–115, 284–294, 316
Breuer, Marvin "Marv" 21
Brewer, Jack "Buddy" 43, 251–261, 312
Brewster, Charlie 54, 141–151, 300
Bridges, Thomas Jefferson Davis "Tommy" 103–104, 152–162, 301
Briggs Stadium, Detroit 44
Brooklyn Brown Dodgers 6
Brooklyn Bushwicks (semi-pro team) 71, 83
Brooklyn Dodgers ("Dem Bums") 1, 2, 6, 10–12, 14–21, 23–24, 26–30, 33–37, 40–41, 43–44, 46, 49–50, 52–53, 56, 58–61, 64–65, 68–73, 75–77, 82–83, 85–86, 91–95, 99–112, 115, 117, 141, 207, 210, 218–228, 251, 273, 297, 300, 307–310, 312, 315
Brown, Bobby 21, 96, 100, 106, 163–173, 303
Brown, Jimmy 9, 55, 273–283, 314
Brown, Mace 112, 119–129, 298
Brown, Norm 43, 174–184, 304
Brown, Tommy 71, 75, 117
Brucker, Earle, Sr. 303
Budnick, Mike 22, 251–261, 312
Buffalo, NY/Bisons (International League, class "AAA" minor league) 22, 26–27, 33, 35, 38, 57, 62, 80, 88, 98, 102, 105, 108, 121–122, 144, 152–155, 160, 201–202, 204, 229, 235, 239, 298, 301–302, 306, 310
bunions 50, 66
Burdick, Bill 118
Burdt, Dylis 118
Burich, Billy 49, 58, 262–272, 314
Burkett, Jesse "Crab" 25
Burkhart, Ken 112, 284–294, 316
Burpo, George 57, 81, 240–250, 311
Burwell, Bill 20
Butcher, Max 55
Butland, Wilburn "Bill" 54, 73, 119–129, 298
Byrne, Tommy 65–66, 98, 163–173, 303
Byrnes, Milt 21, 74
Caballero, Ralph "Putsy" 62
Caldwell, Earl "Teach" 79, 130–140, 299
Camacho, Gen. Manuel Avila 13
Camelli, Hank 68, 100, 110, 273–283, 315
Campanella, Roy 64, 69, 78, 100
Campanis, Al 23
Campbell, Bruce "Soupy" 15–16, 27
Campbell, Clarence "Soup" 27
Campbell, Paul 27, 112, 119–129, 298
Canadian-American League (Class "C" minor league) 69, 78
Candini, Milo 93, 196–206, 306
Capp, Al 97
Carden, John 2, 40, 43, 50–51, 251–261, 313
Cardoni, Armond "Big Ben" 59
Carey, Tom "Scoops" 80, 119–129, 298
Carmichael, John P. 34
Carpenter, Bob 53, 68, 251–261, 312
Carrasquel, Alejandro "Alex" 12, 44, 130
Carter, Arnold 33
Case, George Washington 8, 48, 76, 107, 141–151, 300
Casey, Hugh 52, 108, 218–228, 308
Caster, George 152–162, 301
Castino, Vince 42
Caulfield, Jake 25, 174–184, 304
Cavarretta, Phil 45, 49, 68, 73, 82, 229–239, 309
Cedars of Lebanon Hospital, Hollywood CA 24
Center, Pete 141–151, 300
Chance, Frank "The Peerless Leader" 25
Chandler, A. B. "Happy" (commissioner of baseball) 6, 10–12, 16, 22, 62, 67, 74, 86, 211
Chandler, Eddie 26
Chandler, Spurgeon "Spud" 72, 104, 163–173, 302
Chapman, Ben 29, 40, 49, 59, 77, 99, 262–272, 313–314
Chapman, Sam 73, 174–184, 303
charity exhibition game 85
Chattanooga, Tennessee/Lookouts (Southern Association, class "AA" minor league) 16, 28–29, 46, 67, 81, 198–199, 201, 204, 306
Chesbro, Jack "Happy Jack" 25
Chicago "Black Sox" (1919 White Sox) 6, 55, 78
Chicago Cubs ("Bruins") 2, 9–10, 13, 15–16, 21, 23–26, 30, 33–35, 37, 40–41, 43–44, 48, 51–54, 56, 59–60, 62–63, 65–66, 68–69, 71, 73, 78, 80, 82–86, 89, 91–98, 101–104, 106–110, 115, 130, 141, 159, 229–239, 262, 299–301, 309–311, 314
Chicago White Sox ("Chisox") 6–8, 12, 16–20, 23–24, 26–28, 30–33, 36, 38, 42, 44, 46–48, 54–56, 58, 60–61, 63, 65, 67, 68, 70, 72–73, 75–77, 79–80, 82–83, 85, 87, 90–91, 99, 102–104, 106–107, 111, 119, 130–141, 146–147, 188, 199–200, 229, 298–300, 305–306, 310
Chipman, Bob 229–239, 309
Christman, Mark 185–195, 304
Christopher, Russ 174–184, 303
Churchill, Winston 4
Cincinnati Reds 1, 8, 11, 16, 19, 21–24, 26–28, 30, 33–34, 36–38, 40–42, 46–52, 55, 57, 60–61, 68, 71, 73, 76, 80–83, 85–90, 92–94, 97–101, 105–109, 111, 115, 207, 240–251, 307, 310–313, 316–317
civilian war work 35, 54
Clark, Allie 98
Class "B" minor league 40, 51
Clay, Dain 240–250, 311
Clemensen, Bill 26, 273–283, 315
Cleveland, B.A.A. (Basketball Association of America) 38
Cleveland Indians 1–3, 5, 8, 13–17, 19, 23, 25–27, 29, 31, 33, 35, 41, 46, 48–50, 52, 54, 58–60, 62–66, 68–70, 72, 74, 76, 78, 80–83, 85–86, 87, 90–91, 96, 98, 101, 103–105, 107, 110–111, 114, 122, 125, 130, 134, 141–151, 167, 185, 222, 266, 299–301, 305, 310–311, 313, 317
Clinton, NC/Blues (Tobacco State League, class "D" minor league) 66
Coan, Gil 28, 64, 196–206, 306
Cole, Mel 65
Coleman, Joseph Howard ("Joe") 103
Coleman, Joseph Patrick ("Joe") 97, 103, 174–184, 304
Collins, Eddie, Jr. 16
Collins, Eddie, Sr. 16
Colman, Frank 61, 107, 163–173, 273–283, 303, 315
Corbitt, Claude 229–239, 311
Columbia, South Carolina/Reds (Sally League, class "A" minor league) 21, 37, 88
Columbus, Georgia/Cardinals (Sally League, class "A" minor league) 88
Columbus, Ohio 87
Columbus, Ohio/Red Birds (American Association, class "AAA" minor league) 7, 10, 17, 26, 29, 42, 53, 67, 74, 98, 207, 266, 270, 273–276, 284–285, 314–316
Comiskey, Dorothy (Rigney) 48
Comiskey Park, Chicago 77
Commissioner's Bulletins (official publication) 36, 40, 80, 118
commissioner's office, Cincinnati, Ohio 62, 70, 93, 95, 118
Communism 4
Connors, Kevin "Chuck" 38
Conroy, Bill 22
Conway, Jack 76, 141–151, 300
Cooney, Johnny 306
Cooper, Mort 9, 73, 90, 110, 207–217, 255, 307
Cooper, Orge "Pat" 39, 74, 174–184, 304
Cooper, Walker 9, 26, 44, 71, 73, 77, 103, 251–261, 312
Corriden, John, Jr. "Johnny" 23, 218–228, 308
Corriden, John, Sr. "Red" 308
Coscarart, Pete 58, 73, 273–283, 315
Country Slaughter's Mad Dash Home 115
Cox, Billy 53, 92, 115, 273–283, 315
Craft, Harry 21
Cramer, Roger "Doc" 152–162, 301
Crawford, Glen 42, 262–272, 314
Crespi, Frank "Creepy" 67, 113
Crissey, Harrington E., Jr. "Kit" 17, 29, 31, 67
Cronin, Joe 51, 79, 91, 105, 113, 298
Crosby, Harry Lillis "Bing" 87
Crosetti, Frankie 19, 46, 78, 107, 163–173, 302–303
Crosley Field, Cincinnati 52, 93, 311
Cross, Harry 25

Index

Cross, Joffre "Jeff" 112, 284–294, 315
Culberson, Leon 39, 112, 114, 119–129, 298
Cullenbine, Roy 152–162, 301
Culler, Dick 68, 207–217, 307
Culp, Benny 313
Curtis, Vern 80, 102, 196–206, 306
Curtright, Guy 79, 130–140, 299
cut-down day 59, 62, 66
Dahlgren, Ellsworth "Babe" 21, 25, 82, 107, 185–195, 273, 305
The Daily Worker (publication) 6
Dallas, Texas/Rebels (Texas League, class "AA" minor league) 26
Dallessandro, Dom "Dim Dom" 92, 229–239, 309
Daly, Tom 298
Daniel, Dan 47
Daniels, Fred 54
Dark, Alvin "Blackie" 70, 76, 207–217, 308, 317
Dasso, Frankie 57, 240–250, 311
Davis, Curt "Coonskin Curt" 29, 112, 218–228, 309
Davis, Otis "Scat" 23, 218–228, 309
Davis, Virgil "Spud" 109, 283, 314
Dean, Jerome Herman "Dizzy" 61
Debs, Victor, Jr. 21
Deininger, Bill 53
de la Cruz, Tomas 11
Demaree, Frank 16
Derry, Russ 20, 174–184, 304
Desautels, Gene 82, 174–184, 304
Detroit Tigers ("Bengals") 1, 2, 8, 11, 13–14, 16–18, 20, 22, 24, 26, 33–36, 38, 41–44, 46, 48, 52–53, 56–57, 59–60, 62, 68, 70, 72, 75, 81–82, 84–86, 88–90, 97–99, 101–105, 107–110, 115, 119, 122, 144, 152–162, 174, 176, 229, 235, 298, 301–302, 306, 310, 317
Detweiler, Bob "Ducky" 32, 52, 207–217, 307
Deutsch, Mel 23, 36, 119–129, 298
Devine, Bing 88
DeWitt, Bill 72
Dickey, Bill 19, 39, 47–48, 54, 72, 74, 100, 107, 163–173, 302
Dickey, George "Skeets" 130–140, 299
Dickson, Murry 112–114, 284–294, 315
Dietrich, Bill "Bullfrog" 65, 90, 130–140, 299
Dillinger, Bob 19, 48, 93, 185–195, 304
DiMaggio, Dominic "Dom" ("The Little Professor")
39, 73, 92, 101, 112, 114, 119–129, 298
DiMaggio, Joe ("Joltin' Joe," "The Yankee Clipper") 1, 3, 8, 12, 17, 19, 39, 44, 48, 71–73, 80, 90, 111, 114, 163–173, 302
DiMaggio, Vince 31, 55–56, 251–272, 312–313
Dinges, Vance 25, 61, 106, 262–272, 312
disabled list 85, 134, 172, 231, 236, 275, 282, 284, 317
Dobson, Joe 39, 111–114, 119–129, 298
Doerr, Bobby 39, 53, 72–73, 83, 101, 109, 112–114, 119–129, 146, 298
Donald, Atley 92
Donnelly, Sylvester "Blix" 18, 71–72, 262–272, 284–294, 314, 316
Dormont team, Greater Pittsburgh League 55
Double-A ball (minor league class "AA") 23, 37, 66
Doyle, Howard "Danny" 33
Dreisewerd, Clem 112, 119–129, 298
Drescher, Bill 54, 163–173, 303
Dressen, Charlie ("Chuck") 101, 308
Drews, Karl 33, 97, 163–173, 303
Dreyfuss, Barney, estate 87
Dreyfuss, Mrs. Barney 63
Drohan, John 46
Dudley, Bruce 96
Durham, North Carolina/Bulls (Piedmont League, class "B" minor league, 1942–1943) 20, 40
Durocher, Leo 7, 12, 52, 54, 77, 101, 106, 108, 308
Dusak, Ervin "Erv" ("Foursack") 84, 92, 107, 112, 114, 269, 284–294, 316–317
Dyer, Eddie 7, 113, 316
Dykes, Jimmie 24, 27–28, 33, 47, 132, 299
Early, Jake 196–206, 306
Eastern League (class "A" minor league) 141, 149, 160, 314
Eastern Shore League (class "D" minor league, 1947) 21
Ebbets Field, Brooklyn 43, 99, 101, 220, 224
Edwards, Bruce 18, 59, 64, 68, 72, 115, 218–228, 309
Edwards, Hank 141–151, 300
Eisenstat, Harry 17
Elias Sports Bureau 118
Elizabethton, Tennessee/Betsy Red Sox (Appalachian League, class "D" minor league) 74
Elliott, Bob 65, 92, 110–111, 273–273, 314
Elliott, Glenn 95
Elysian Fields 1
Embree, Charley "Red" 107, 114, 141–151, 300–301
Emmerich, Bill "Slim" 41–42, 251–261, 312
Enders, Eric 118
Endicott, Bill 23, 112, 284–294, 316
Ennis, Del 4, 29, 73, 115, 262–272, 314
Epperly, Al "Pard" 32–33
Erautt, Eddie 38
Erautt, Joe 38
Erickson, Paul "Li'l Abner" 66, 86, 229–239, 309
Estalella, Bobby 12
Estalella, Roberto 12, 34, 61, 174
Etten, Nick 44, 107, 163–173, 302–303
Evans, Al 196–206, 306
Evansville, Indiana/Braves (Three-Eye [Illinois-Indiana-Iowa] League, class "B") 42
Evers, Johnny "Crab" 25
Evers, Walter "Hoot" 13, 36, 53, 81, 115, 152–162, 302
expansion, major league 1, 46
Eyrich, George 37
Faber, Urban (Red) 299
Fagan, Everett 57, 174–184, 304
Fallon, Charley 53
Fallon, George 16
Fannin, Cliff 40, 185–195, 305
farmhand, farm team, farm system 93, 96, 98–99, 103, 141, 300
Feldman, Harry 27, 61, 251–261, 312
Feller, Bob 9, 12, 19, 24, 28, 31, 72, 75, 79, 83, 87–88, 91–92, 99, 102–104, 110, 141–151, 301
Fenway Park, Boston 51, 72, 79, 90, 94
Ferens, Stan 185–195, 305
Fernandes, Ed 130–140, 299
Fernandez, Froilan "Nanny" 207–217, 307
Ferrell, Rick 306
Ferrell, Wes 89
Ferrick, Tom 65, 68, 141–151, 185–195, 300, 305
Ferriss, David "Boo" 39, 72, 89–90, 101, 104, 112–113, 119–129, 298
Finney, Lou 50, 185–195, 262, 264–265, 305, 314
Fischer, Ruben "Rube" 82, 251–261
Fisher, Don 15
Fitzpatrick, Donald 79
Flair, Al ("Broadway Al") 32
Flanigan, Ray 105, 141–151, 301
Fleming, Leslie Fletchard "Bill" ("Les") 83, 229–239, 309
Fleming, Leslie Harvey "Les" ("Moe") 74, 86, 107, 141–151, 300–301
Fletcher, Elburt "Elbie" 32, 273–283, 314
Flick, Lew 37, 74
Flores, Jesse 174–184, 303
Flowers, D'Arcy "Jake" 306
Forbes Field, Pittsburgh 24, 35, 43, 92
Fort Riley, Kansas, Centuars 67
Fort Worth, Texas/Cats (Texas League, class "AA" minor league) 21, 23, 26, 79, 102, 224
Fowler, Dick 174–184, 303
Fox, Howard "Howie" 27, 52, 88–89, 240–250, 311
Francis, Bill 118
Franklin, Murray 12, 152
Franks, Herman 21
free agents 13–14, 29, 60, 63, 69, 71, 173, 207, 218, 300, 308, 310
Freiberger, Vern 26
Frey, Linus "Lonny" 85, 240–250, 311
Frick, Ford (National League president in 1946; third commissioner in 1951) 25, 62, 82, 111
Frisch, Frankie 19, 109, 283, 314
Fulks, Joe 38
Furillo, Carl 18, 44, 218–228, 308
G. I. Bill of Rights 10, 15, 18
Gables, Ken 273–283, 315
Galan, August "Augie" 82, 218–228, 308
Galaragga, Andres 101
Galbreath, John W. 87
Galehouse, Denny 185–195, 305
Gallagher, Tom 6
Garagiola, Joe 44, 49, 112–113, 284–294, 316
Garbark, Bob 53
Garbark, Mike 53
Gardella, Danny 11, 12, 60–61, 252
Garms, Debs 69
Garriott, Cecil 97, 229–239, 309
Garrison, Ford 20, 36, 174–184, 303
Gas House Gang 109
Gassaway, Charlie 69, 141–151, 301
Gee, Johnny 55, 78, 251–261, 313
Gehrig, Lou 21, 25
Gentry, Ruffus "Rufe" 38, 108, 152–162, 301
Geraghty, Ben 64–65
Gerheauser, Al 106, 273–283, 315, 317
Gettel, Al 163–173, 302
Gettelson, Leonard 110
Gibson, Josh 75
Gilbert, Andy 36, 73, 119–129, 298
Gilbert, Charlie 59, 229–239, 262–272, 309, 314
Gilbert, William S. 7
Gillenwater, Carden 207–217, 307
Gionfriddo, Al 83, 92, 94, 273–283, 315
Gladd, Jim 98, 251–261, 313

Index

Gladu, Roland 41, 219
Glossop, Alban "Al" 37, 229–239, 310
Goldstein, Leslie "Lonnie" 88, 240–250, 312
Golenbock, Peter 45
Gomez, Jose "Chile" 61
Gonzalez, Miguel "Mike" 316
Goodman, Billy 55
Goolsby, Ray 22, 28, 46–47, 196–206, 306
Gordon, Joe 9, 44, 49, 79, 80, 114, 163–173, 302
Gordon, Sid 24, 251–261, 312
Gorman, Thomas Aloysius 14
Gorman, Thomas David "Big Tom" 14
Gornicki, Hank 41, 273–283, 315
Gorsica, Johnny 57, 152–162, 302
Gowdy, Henry "Hank" 311
Grace, Joe 59, 64, 185–206, 304–306
Graham, Jack 18–20, 28, 218–228, 251–261, 308, 312
Grasso, Newton "Mickey" 98, 104, 251–261, 313
Grate, Don "Buckeye" 37, 104, 109, 262–272, 314
Gray, Ted 38, 41, 105, 152–162, 300
Great Lakes Naval Training Station, baseball team 7, 88, 97
Greater Pittsburgh League 55
Greenberg, Hank 1, 57, 72, 82, 108, 111, 152–162, 300
Gregg, Hal 40, 108, 218–228, 308
Griffeth, Lee 65, 86, 174–184, 304
Griffith, Clark "The Old Fox" 25, 31, 47, 50
Griffith Stadium, Washington DC 47, 52, 93
Grimes, Oscar 19, 74, 163–184, 302, 304
Grimm, Charley "Jolly Cholly" 82, 309
Grissom, Lee 98
Grissom, Marvin "Marv" 15, 98, 251–261, 313
Grodzicki, Johnny 38, 74–75, 112, 284–294, 317
Gromek, Steve 141–151, 300
Groth, Johnny 88, 97, 152–162, 302
Grove, Orval 130–140, 299
Guerra, Fermin "Mike" ("Mickey") 196–206, 306
Guintini, Ben 23, 42, 66–67, 273–283, 315
Gumbert, Harry 240–250, 311
Gumpert, Randy 21–22, 163–173, 302
Gustine, Frankie 18, 73, 88, 92, 273–283, 315
Gutteridge, Don 73, 112, 114, 119–129, 298
Haas, Berthold "Bert" 240–250, 311

Haas, George "Mule" 24, 79, 299
Hack, Stan 48, 84, 101, 229–239, 309
Haddix, Harvey 29
Haefner, Milton "Mickey" 65, 111, 196–206, 306
Hall, Irv 79, 107, 174–184, 304
Hallett, Jack 273–283, 315
Hamey, Roy, American Association president 78
Hamner, Granville "Granny" 16, 109, 262–272, 313
Hamner, Ralph 30, 130–140, 299
Hamner, Wesley Garvin 16
Handley, Gene 19, 174–184, 303
Handley, Lee 19, 55, 82, 273–283
Handley Page Halifax bomber 35
Hansen, Andy "Swede" 18
Hanyzewski, Eddie 37, 98, 102, 108, 229–239, 310
Harder, Mel 48, 82, 107, 141–151, 300–301
Harridge, Will, American League President 63, 72
Harris, Luman "Lum" 174–184, 303
Harris, Maurice "Mickey" 39, 72, 101, 112–113, 119–129, 298
Harris, Ned "Bob" 38, 152–162, 301
Harris, Stanley "Bucky" 98–101
Hartford, Conn./Bees (Eastern League, class "A" minor league) 27, 42, 61, 307
Hartley, Grover 311
Hartnett, Charles "Gabby" 96
Hasenmayer, Don 87, 102, 262–272, 314
Hassett, John "Buddy" 31
Hathaway, Ray 36
Hatten, Joe 23, 112, 115, 218–228, 309
Hatton, Grady 19, 93, 97, 115, 240–250, 311
Hausmann, George 14, 252
Hayes, Frank "Frankie" 25, 31, 70, 72, 76–77, 87, 130–151, 299–300
Haynes, Joe 79, 130–140, 299
Hayworth, Myron "Red" 17
Hayworth, Ray 17
Head, Ed 24, 43, 56, 93, 218–228, 309
Heath, Jeff 8, 59, 81, 185–206, 304–306
Heflin, Randy 58, 119–129, 298
Hegan, Jim 70, 141–151, 300
Heintzelman, Ken 108, 273–283, 315
Heitz, Tom 118
Helf, Hank 56, 185–195, 305
Hemsley, Ralston "Rollie" 14, 32, 82, 262–272, 313
Hendrickson, Don 33, 207–217, 307

Henrich, Tom "Tommy" 19, 44, 82, 163–173, 302
Herman, Billy 15, 43, 59, 82, 104, 110–111, 207–228, 297, 307–308
Hermanski, Gene 218–228, 308
Herring, Art "Sandy" 52, 108, 218–228, 309
Hetki, Johnny 110, 240–250, 311
Heusser, Ed 43, 240–250, 311, 317
hidden ball trick 37
Higbe, Kirby 73, 108, 218–228, 309
Higgins, Mike "Pinky" 43, 82, 84, 112, 119–129, 152–162, 298, 301
Hiller, Frank 48, 57, 96, 163–173, 303
Hilligan, Earl J. 110
Hillin, Ash 89
hit by pitch (HBP) 34–35, 78, 85, 207, 215, 257–258, 302, 307, 312
Hitchcock, Billy 34–35, 41, 152–162, 196–206, 301, 306
hobbies of ball players 46
Hodges, Gil 21
Hodgin, Ralph 79, 130–140, 299
Hodkey, Aloysius "Eli" 37, 101, 262–272, 314
Hoerst, Frank 91, 262–272, 313
Hofferth, Stewart "Stew" 59, 72, 207–217, 221, 307
Hofman, Fred 304
Hogue, Bob 26
Holcombe, Ken 26
Hollingsworth, Al "Boots" 56, 130–140, 185–195, 299, 305
Hollywood Stars (Pacific Coast League, class "AAA" minor league) 22, 28, 41–42, 47, 57–58, 62–63, 66, 80, 96, 243, 264, 273–274, 276, 281, 311–314, 316
Holmes, Tommy 207–217, 307
home run title, National League 85
Homestead Grays 41
Hope, Bob 63, 87
Hopp, Johnny 10–11, 73, 81, 207–217, 306
Hopper, Clay 112
Hopper, Jim 23, 53, 273–283, 315
Houma, Louisiana/Indians (Evangeline League, class "D" minor league) 89
Houston Buffs ("Buffalos") (Texas League, class "AA" minor league) 49, 56, 58, 79, 265, 314
Houtteman, Art 98, 108, 152–162, 302
Howard, Lee 22, 102, 106, 273–283, 316
Howell, Homer "Dixie" 28, 33
Howell, Millard "Dixie" 33

Hubbell, Carl 104
Hudson, Sid 24, 196–206, 306
Hughes, Roy 9, 82, 262–272, 314
Hughes, Tommy 262–272, 314
Hughson, Cecil "Tex" 39, 51, 72, 101, 104, 111–113, 119–129, 298
Humphries, John 8, 85, 262–272, 314
Huntington, West Virginia/Aces (Mountain States League, class "D" minor league, 1941) 74
Hutchings, Johnny 33, 207–217, 307
Hutchinson, Fred 152–162, 301
Hyland, Robert F.,. MD 55–56
Indianapolis, Indiana/Indians (American Association, class "AAA" minor league) 15, 20, 32–33, 42, 44, 52, 59, 63, 66–67, 70, 87, 89, 93, 104, 112, 145–146, 167, 207–215, 282, 300, 303, 307–308, 316
ineligible list 6, 13, 169, 174, 186, 218–219, 252, 270
International League (class "AAA" minor league) 6, 20, 23, 33, 46, 69, 77, 88, 96–98, 102, 112, 141, 149, 164, 171, 174, 182, 248, 259, 292, 311, 316
Interstate League (class "B" minor league) 182, 281, 315–316
Irvin, Monte 100
Jacksonville, Florida/Tars (South Atlantic League, class "A") 80, 96, 251, 313
Jacksonville, Texas/Jax (East Texas League 1937, class "C") 89
Jansen, Larry 89
Jarvis, LeRoy "Roy" 71, 273–283, 315
Javery, Alva "Al" ("Bear Tracks") 44, 67, 207–217, 307
Jersey City, New Jersey/Little Giants (International League, class "AAA") 15, 20, 30, 32, 41, 43, 50, 53, 62, 65, 80, 96–98, 251–254, 257–259, 312–313
Johnson, Billy 31, 49, 100, 163–173, 303
Johnson, Chester "Chet" 22, 94, 101, 185–195, 305
Johnson, Donald Spore "Pep" 44, 86, 91, 229–239, 309
Johnson, Earl 22, 39, 112–113, 119–129, 298
Johnson, Roy "Hardrock" 309
Johnson, Silas "Si" 17, 31, 90, 207–217, 262–272, 307, 314
Johnson, Thomas P. 87
Johnson, Vic 8, 68, 141–151, 300

Index

Johnson, Walter 92
Joint Winter Meeting, Annual (major league owners) 10, 73
Jones, Dale 37
Jones, David 118
Jones, Murrell "Jake" 19, 48, 77, 130–140, 299
Jones, Nicholas "Red" 79
Jones, Sheldon "Available" 96–97, 109, 251–261, 313
Jones, Vernal "Nippy" 56, 47, 98, 112, 284–294, 315
Jones, Willie Edward "Puddin' Head" 104
Jonnard, Clarence "Bubber" 312
Joost, Eddie 11
Jordan, Tom 54, 70, 107, 130–151, 299–301
Joss, Addie 87, 92
Joyce, Bob 30, 81–82, 89, 251–261, 312
Judd, Oscar "Ossie" 262–272, 313
Judge, Joe 306
Judnich, Walter "Walt" ("Wally") 93–94, 185–195, 304
Junior World Series 20, 29, 112
Jurges, Billy 13, 24, 82, 229–239, 309
Jurisich, Al 10, 49, 262–272, 313
Kansas City, Missouri/Athletics ("A's") 14
Kansas City, Missouri/Blues (American Association, class "AAA") 20–21, 26, 32–33, 38–39, 54, 57, 60, 64–65, 74, 79, 85, 96–97, 100, 107, 163–166, 169–171, 175, 179, 182, 207–208, 236, 268–269, 273, 276–277, 302–303, 307, 310, 314–315
Kansas City, Missouri/Monarchs (Negro National League) 6–7
Karl, Anton "Andy" 262–272, 314
Karpel, Herb 22, 33, 163–173, 302
Keefe, Dave 303
Keely, Bob 306
Kehn, Chester "Chet" 28
Kell, George 42–43, 56, 83, 126, 152–162, 174–184, 301, 303
Keller, Charley "King Kong" 19, 44, 72, 90, 163–173, 302
Keltner, Ken 48, 72, 76, 83, 107, 141–151, 300–301
Kennedy, Bob 19, 130–140, 299
Kennedy, Montia "Monte" 15, 22, 251–261, 312
Kennedy, William Aulton "Bill" 87
Kennedy, William Gorman "Bill" 87, 196–206, 306
Kerr, John "Buddy" 251–261, 312
Kerr, Paul 25

Keystone combination (shortstop & second baseman) 1, 23
Keystoner (second baseman) 69
Kilroy, Matt 110
Kinder, Ellis 31, 185–195, 305
Kiner, Ralph 4, 19, 29, 85, 115, 273–283, 314
King, Clyde 16
Klein, Lou 45, 61, 284–294, 316
Kleine, Hal 62
Klieman, Eddie 66, 141–151, 301
Klinger, Bob 36, 112, 114, 119–129, 274, 298
Kluszewski, Ted 21, 37
Kluttz, Clyde 31–32, 112, 251–263, 284–294, 312–314, 316
Knerr, Luther "Lou" 174–184, 303
Knickerbocker, Austin 74
Knott, John "Jack" 43, 174–184, 304
knuckleballers 65
Koecher, Dick ("Highpockets") 78, 109, 262–272, 314
Kolloway, Don 80, 103, 130–140, 299
Konopka, Bruce 47, 66, 79, 97, 99, 174–184, 303
Konstanty, Jim 22, 59, 207–217, 240, 307, 311
Koslo, Dave (*Koslowski*) 251–261, 312
Koufax, Sandy 31, 110
Koy, Ernie 49
Krakauskas, Joe 107, 141–151, 300–301
Kramer, John "Jack" 72, 94, 185–195, 305
Kraus, Jack "Tex" ("Texas Jack") 24, 251–261, 313
Kress, Ralph "Red" 1, 77–78, 251–261, 312–313
Kretlow, Lou 14, 108, 152–162, 302
Krist, Howard "Howie" 112, 284–294, 316
Kuhel, Joe 58, 82, 91, 130–140, 196–206, 299, 306
Kurowski, George "Whitey" 1, 18, 35 , 73, 81, 112–114, 284–294, 316
Kush, Emil 229–239, 309
Kuzava, Bob 103, 105–106, 141–151, 301
Laabs, Chet 107, 185–195, 305–306
Lade, Doyle 26, 69, 98, 104, 229–239, 311
Lajeskie, Dick 98, 251–261, 313
Lake, Eddie 8, 41, 48, 152–162, 301
Lakeman, Al 240–250, 311
LaMacchia, Al 59, 81, 185–206, 304–306
Lamanna, Frank 27
Lamanno, Ray 73, 240–250, 311
Lambert, Clay 23, 240–250, 311

Lancaster, Pennsylvania/Red Roses (Interstate League, class "B") 27, 86, 102, 181, 183
Landis, Judge Kenesaw Mountain (first commissioner of baseball) 25, 72
Lang, Don 15
Lanier, Max 35, 45, 61, 86, 284–294, 316
Lanigan, Ernest J. 110
Lanning, Johnny 273–283, 315
Lapihuska, Andy 37
Larsen, Don 54
Lavagetto, Harry "Cookie" 14, 15, 36, 43, 218–228, 309
Lawing, Garland "Butch" 50, 55, 80, 240–261, 311, 313
Lazor, Johnny 112, 119–129, 298
Lazzeri, Toni 82
Lee, Bill 82, 207–217, 307
Lee, Roy 15
Lee, Thornton "Lefty" 83, 130–140, 299
Lefebvre, Bill 15
Lehner, Paul 99, 185–195, 305
Leibold, Nemo 15, 78, 96
Leibowitz, Kerry 118
Lemon, Bob 1, 3, 19, 141–151, 300
Leonard, Emil "Dutch" 22, 53, 65, 196–206, 306
Letchas, Charlie 93, 262–272, 314
Lewis, John "Buddy" 196–206, 306
Libke, Al "Big Al" 86, 109–110, 240–250, 311
Lindell, Johnny 90, 163–173, 302
Linn, Ed 111
Lipon, Johnny 152–162, 302
Little Rock, Arkansas/Travelers (Southern Association, Class "AA") 37, 67, 209, 215, 307
Litwhiler, Danny 49, 56, 95, 97, 207–217, 284–294, 307, 316
Livingston, Thompson "Mickey" 44, 71, 86, 229–239, 309
Lodigiani, Dario 17, 42, 79, 130–140, 299
Lohrke, Jack "Lucky" 65
Lollar, Sherman 23, 25, 77, 141–151, 300
Lombardi, Ernie 251–261, 312
Lombardi, Vic 108, 218–228, 308
Lopat, Eddie (Lopatynski, Edmund) 79, 111, 130–140, 299
Lopatka, Art 16, 67, 78, 262–272, 314
Lopez, Al 18, 23, 48, 96, 100, 273–283, 315
Los Angeles Angels (American League) 110
Los Angeles Angels (Pacific Coast League, class

"AAA") 34, 37, 57, 60, 69, 81, 83, 92, 97, 101–102, 186, 229–230, 233–235, 237, 265, 304, 310, 314
Los Angeles Dodgers 110
Louisville, Kentucky/ Colonels (American Association, class "AAA") 15, 18, 29, 32–33, 36, 40, 73, 78, 96, 112, 120, 123–124, 127–128, 207, 267, 298, 307, 313
Lowrey, Harry "Peanuts" ("P-nuts") 73, 85–86, 229–239, 309
Luby, Hugh 15
Lucadello, Johnny 185–195, 304
Lukon, Eddie 89, 240–250, 311, 317
Lupien, Ulysses "Tony" 63
Lynn, Japhet "Red" 89
Lyons, Al 33, 96, 100, 163–173, 303
Lyons, Ted 47, 68, 79, 90, 130–140, 299
Mack (McGillicuddy), Cornelius "Connie" ("Mister Mack") 2, 5, 25, 35, 52–53, 76, 79, 103, 303
Mack, Earle (McGillicuddy) 303
Mack, Joe 16
Mack, Ray 141–151, 300
Mackiewicz, Felix 141–151, 300, 317
Macmillan Baseball Encyclopedia 18, 24, 29, 36, 43–44, 297
MacPhail, Leland Stanford "Larry" 39, 47, 78, 80, 82–83, 85, 98–101, 114
Maddern, Clarence 98, 102, 104, 229–239, 310
Maglie, Salvatore "Sal the Barber" 14, 2529
Majeski, Hank "Heeney" 58–59, 67, 163–184, 302, 304
Major League draft 65
Major League manager of the year 7
Major League pennants 70
Major League player debuts 18–20, 22–23, 25, 28–29, 34, 36, 41, 48– 49, 50, 56, 64, 68, 70, 76, 93, 96–98, 101–109, 119, 130, 134, 139, 141, 148, 150–153, 160, 162–163, 165–166, 172–175, 178, 183, 185, 194, 196, 207–208, 212, 214, 215, 218–219, 221, 223, 227, 229–230, 237–238, 240, 242, 251–252, 257, 260, 262, 269, 271–273, 282–284, 286–287, 298–310
Malloy, Bob 51, 240–250, 311
Maltzberger, Gordon 73–74, 130–140, 299
Mancuso, Frank 56, 107, 185–195, 304–305
Manders, Hal 62, 102, 152–162, 229–239, 301, 310
Manley, Effa 100

Index

Mapes, Cliff 16
Marchildon, Phil 2, 35, 111, 174–184, 304
Marion, Marty 30, 47–48, 53, 73, 82, 86, 112–114, 284–294, 316
Maris, Roger 25
Marshall, Clarence "Cuddles" 25, 163–173, 303
Marshall, Willard 251–261, 312
Martin, Boris "Babe" 22, 65, 71, 94, 101, 107, 185–195, 305
Martin, Freddie 23, 45, 284–294, 316
Martin, Ray 42
Marty, Joe 37
Masi, Phil 18, 73, 207–217, 307
Masterson, Walter "Walt" 196–206, 306
Mauch, Gene 21
Mauney, Dick 95, 262–272, 314, 317
May, Merrill "Pinky" 42
May, Milt 42
Maynard, Jim "Buster" 30, 251–261, 312
Mayo, Eddie 44, 53, 86, 152–162, 301
Mays, Willie 16, 69
McBride, Tom 112, 119–129, 298, 317
McCabe, Ralph 2, 98, 104, 141–151, 300
McCahan, Bill 16, 97, 103, 174–184, 304
McCarthy, Joe 22, 47, 66, 165, 302
McCarthy, Johnny 26–27, 207–217, 307
McCarthy, Tommy 25
McCormick, Frank 8, 61, 68, 73, 211, 241, 262–272, 313
McCormick, Myron "Mike" 24, 52, 95, 97, 207–217, 240–250, 307, 311
McCosky, Barney 42, 152–162, 174–184, 301, 304
McCoy, Benny 17–18
McCullough, Clyde 89, 229–239, 310
McFarland, Ann 118
McGah, Eddie 27, 39, 51, 112, 119–129, 298
McGinnity, Joe "Iron Man" 25
McKechnie, Bill "Deacon Bill" 100, 106, 111, 311
McKinney, Frank E. 87
McLish, Calvin Coolidge Julius Caesar Tuskahoma 69, 93, 218–228, 309
McMahon, Frank 44
McQuillen, Glenn 185–195, 304
McQuinn, George 5–6, 25, 99, 174–184, 303
Medwick, Joe "Ducky" ("Ducky Wucky") 11, 13–14, 65, 69, 77, 91, 218–228, 309
Meers, Russ 24, 229–239, 310–311

Mele, Sabath "Sam" 32, 54
Melillo, Oscar 299
Melton, Ruben "Rube" 43, 218–228, 309
Memphis, Tennessee/Chicks ("Chickasaws") (Southern Association, class "AA") 67, 266, 270, 314
Meridian, Mississippi/Peps (Southeastern League, class "B") 21
Merkle, Fred 110
Merkle Boner 110
Merullo, Lennie 44–45, 56, 86, 229–239, 248, 310
Metheny, Arthur "Bud" 163–173, 302
Metkovich, George "Catfish" 112, 119–129, 298
Mexican League 9, 11, 13–14, 17, 20, 27, 31, 34–35, 41, 44–45, 54, 58, 60–62, 68, 86, 130, 152, 174, 218–219, 251–252, 263, 277, 286–287, 312, 316
Mexico City Reds club, Mexican League 13
Meyer, Lambert D. "Dutch," "L.D." 107, 141–151, 300–301
Meyer, Russ 98, 102, 229–239, 310
Michaels, Cass (Kwietniewski, Casimir) 130–140, 299
Mierkowicz, Ed 26, 122, 144
Miksis, Eddie 59, 76, 218–228, 309
Milan, Clyde ("Deerfoot Clyde") 306
Miller, Eddie 73, 83, 240–250, 311
Miller, Edmund "Bing" 48, 79, 298
Miller, John Anthony "Ox" 65, 185–195, 305
Miller, John Barney "Dots" 106
Mills, Art 301
Mills, Colonel Buster 70, 141–151, 300
Milnar, Al "Happy" 50, 185–195, 262–272, 305, 314
Milwaukee Braves 36
Milwaukee, Wisconsin/Brewers (American Association, class "AAA") 5, 26, 32, 42, 49, 54, 59, 60, 63, 66, 70, 76, 78, 90, 95, 99, 103, 130–131, 133, 144, 147, 299–300, 307
minimum wage (major league player minimum salary) 4, 32
Minneapolis, Minnesota/Millers (American Association, class "AAA") 15–16, 26–27, 30, 51, 57, 81–82, 122, 127, 207, 251–253, 257–259, 298, 307, 312–313
Minner, Paul 101, 218–228, 309
Minnesota Twins 54
Minor League player of the year 20, 28

minor leaguers in military duty (in 1945) 3
Minor League manager of the year 7, 65
Mississippi River 67
Mitchell, Dale 1, 54, 98, 103, 141–151, 301
Mize, Johnny ("Big Jawn," "Big Cat") 11, 68, 73, 85, 101, 251–261, 312
Mobile, Alabama/Bears (Southern Association, class "AA") 16, 19–20, 23, 59, 64, 72, 101, 218, 221, 223
Mog Mog Island 31
Monaco, Blas 52, 141–151, 301
Monteagudo, René 12, 263
Monterrey, Mexico/Industriales, Mexican League 61
Montreal, Quebec, Canada/Royals (International League, class "AAA") 4, 6–7, 18, 20–21, 23, 26–27, 29–30, 32–33, 36, 40–42, 46, 49, 59, 60–61, 68–69, 71, 77–78, 95, 97, 106, 112, 218–221, 226
Moore, Anselm "Anse" 20, 59, 152–162, 301
Moore, D. C. "Dee" 61, 262–272, 314
Moore, Terry 2, 82–83, 87–88, 112, 114, 284–294
Moses, Wally 79, 80, 101, 112, 119–140, 298–299
Moss, Howard "Howie" 46, 90, 105, 141–151, 240–250, 301, 311
Moss, Les 99, 185–195, 305
Most Valuable Player (MVP) 8–9, 20, 22, 29, 77, 80, 97, 99, 104, 109, 111, 115, 207, 308, 315, 316
Mott, Elisha "Bitsy" 37
Moulder, Glen 29–30, 36, 218–228, 309
Muckerman, Richard C. 95
Mueller, Don 80
Mueller, Ray 25, 86, 240–250, 311
Mueller, Les 33
Mueller, Walter 80
Mulcahy, Hugh 262–272, 313
Mulligan, Dick 51, 106, 207–217, 262–272, 308, 313
Mullin, Pat 1, 24, 152–162, 301
Muncrief, Bob 18, 185–195, 305
Munger, George "Red" 83, 91, 93, 112–113, 284–294, 316–317
Mungo, Van Lingle 15, 66
Murphy, Johnny "Grandma" 35, 82, 107, 163–173, 302–303
Murphy, Robert 30, 32
Murtaugh, Danny 19, 34, 262–272, 313
Musial, Stan 3, 9, 12, 36–37, 56, 73, 112–115, 284–294, 316
Muskogee, Oklahoma 36

Myatt, George 18, 51, 196–206, 306
Napanee, Ontario 104
Nashua, New Hampshire/Dodgers (New England League, class "B") 78
Nashville, Tennessee/Volunteers "Vols" (Southern Association, class "AA") 15, 24, 37, 49–50, 62, 66, 68, 74, 98, 101–102, 108, 145–147, 229–231, 235–237, 300, 310
National Baseball Congress 18, 22
National Baseball Hall of Fame and Museum, Cooperstown, New York 2, 19, 21, 25, 42, 45, 47, 51, 61, 63, 68–69, 75, 85, 106, 110–111, 115, 117–118
National Baseball Library, Cooperstown 117–118
National Basketball Association (NBA) 38
National Basketball League 38
National Defense Service List (NDSL) 130, 141, 152, 163, 174–175, 196, 207, 218, 229, 240, 262, 276, 284, 300–301, 303, 306, 310–311, 314–315
National League pennant race/tie/playoff 85, 95, 101–102, 104–112, 115, 228, 294
The National Pastime (SABR publication) 6, 21
Naylor, Earl 27, 42, 218–228, 309
NCAA (baseball) championship 6
Neft & Cohen (*The Sports Encyclopedia: Baseball*) 196
Negro Leagues 6, 7, 75, 78
Neill, Tommy 97, 207–217, 308
Nelson, Tommy 17, 207, 284
Neun, Johnny 100, 111, 172, 302
New England League 14
New Orleans, Louisiana/Pelicans "Pels" (Southern Association, class "AA") 68, 95, 147, 149
New York Giants 1, 2, 9, 11–16, 18–22, 24, 26–28, 30–32, 37–38, 40–44, 46, 48, 49–53, 55–57, 60, 62, 65–66, 68, 71, 73–74, 76–78, 80–83, 85, 89–90, 92, 94–98, 100–104, 109–110, 115, 218, 242–243, 251–263, 284, 311–313, 316–317
New York Mets 77
New York Times (newspaper) 5, 17, 33–34, 40, 43, 45, 60, 63, 70–71, 75, 78, 83, 107, 177, 297, 317
New York Yankees 1–3, 5, 9–10, 14, 16, 19–22, 25–26, 29–35, 38–39, 44, 46–50, 52–55, 57–61, 63–67, 70,

72, 74, 77–78, 80, 82, 85–86, 88–90, 92–94, 96–101, 103–104, 106–107, 110–112, 119, 141, 163–174, 177–178, 186–187, 196, 207, 258, 262, 298, 302–307, 314–315

Newark, New Jersey/Bears (International League, class "AAA") 20–21, 33, 35, 38–39, 47, 57, 61, 96, 98, 106–107, 112, 163, 166, 171, 174, 276, 302–303, 315

Newcombe, Don 78, 100

Newhouser, Harold "Hal" ("Prince Hal") 2, 30, 72, 82, 104, 109, 111–112, 152–162, 301

Newport News, Virginia/Dodgers (Piedmont League, class "B") 21

Newsom, Louis Norman "Bobo" ("Buck") 2, 52–53, 82, 174–184, 196–206, 303, 306

Newsome, Lamar "Skeeter" 8, 262–272, 313

Niarhos, Constantine "Gus" 38, 54, 57, 163–173, 303

Nicholson, Bill ("Swish") 103, 229–239, 310

Niemec, Al 63

Niggeling, John 65, 97, 196–217, 306, 308

night games, "full slate" 88

no-hitter 5, 24, 31, 40, 52, 93, 103

Norbert, Ted 267

Normandy Invasion (D-Day) 65

Northey, Ron 60, 262–272, 313

Novikoff, Lou 61, 262–272, 313

Oakland, California/Oaks (Pacific Coast League, class "AAA") 16–17, 22, 26, 39, 41, 65, 69, 90, 107, 141, 185, 188, 300, 305

O'Dea, Ken 71, 83, 93, 207–217, 284–294, 308, 316

O'Dea, Paul 13–14

O'Dwyer, William, New York City mayor 85

Oil Bowl 70

Oklahoma City, Oklahoma/Indians (Texas League, class "AA" minor league) 27, 54, 89, 97–98, 103–104, 141, 149, 151, 300

Oklahoma, University of ("Sooners") 54

Old Guard (major league owners & executives) 91

Olmo, Luis 12, 219

Olsen, Vern 24, 229–239, 310

O'Malley, Walter 58

one-hitter 83, 87

O'Neil, John 19, 262–272, 310

O'Neill, Emmett 30, 60, 130–140, 229–239, 299, 310

O'Neill, Steve 301

Oneonta, New York/Indians (Canadian-American League 1941, class "C") 74

Opening Day (Major Leagues) 3, 4, 15, 18–19, 29, 31, 34, 51, 163, 196, 297

Opening Day (Mexican League) 13

Organized Baseball (O.B.) 3, 11, 26, 62–63, 78

Orrell, Forrest "Joe" 26

Ortiz, Roberto 11

Ostermueller, Frederick "Fritz" 273–283, 315

Ostrowski, John 229–239, 310

Ott, Mel "Master Melvin" ("the Little Giant") 2, 11, 18, 49, 73, 81, 251–261, 312

Outlaw, Jimmy 43–44, 152–162, 301, 317

Outlaw league 11, 61, 86

Overmire, Frank "Stubby" 53, 152–162, 301

Owen, Arnold "Mickey" 12, 18, 61, 64, 68, 86, 218

Pacific Coast League (class "AAA" minor league) 39, 60–61, 63, 69, 74, 79–81, 92, 98, 104, 107, 110, 267, 281

Padgett, Don 58, 84, 207–228, 307–308

Pafko, Andy 51–52, 94, 229–239, 309

Page, Joe 47, 85, 163–173, 258, 302

Paige, Leroy "Satchel" 75

Palica, Ervin "Erv" 21

Papish, Frank 130–140, 299

Parade Magazine 107

Parrott, Harold 93

Partee, Roy 39, 112, 119–129, 298

Partlow, Roy 41, 69, 77–78

Pasarella, Art 48

Pasquel, Jorge 11, 13, 45, 61, 68

Pasquel family 11, 12, 17, 34, 59, 86

Passeau, Claude 30, 73, 78, 86, 89, 93, 229–239, 310

Patkin, Max 91

Pawelek, Ted 98, 102, 229–239, 310

Pearson, Isaac "Ike" 61, 262–272, 314

Peary, Danny 29

Peck, Hal 60, 63, 167, 169, 174–184, 303

Pellagrini, Eddie 23–24, 112, 119–129, 298

perfect game 29

performance bonuses (Guild proposal) 32

Perini, Lou 65

Perkins, Ralph "Cy" 313

Perme, Len 60, 130–140, 299

Peruque, Missouri 108

Pesky, Johnny 24, 39, 72, 101, 112–115, 119–129, 298

Peter Principle 111

Peterman, Bill 37

Peters, Forrest (Frosty), American Association umpire 78, 107

Peters, Russell "Rusty" 96, 141–151, 300–301

Pfund, Leroy 16

Philadelphia Athletics 2, 5, 12, 16–17, 20–21, 25, 27, 30, 35–36, 39, 42–43, 47–48, 52–53, 55, 57–58, 59–60, 65–69, 71–76, 79, 81–82, 84, 86, 90–91, 94, 97, 99, 102–103, 106–107, 152, 154, 163, 166–169, 174–184, 186, 196, 300–304, 306, 317

Philadelphia Phillies 4, 8–10, 12, 14–17, 19, 22, 24–25, 27, 29–35, 37, 40, 42, 44, 46, 49, 50–51, 53–54, 56–63, 67–69, 71–73, 77–78, 80, 82, 84–87, 90–93, 95, 97, 99, 101, 102, 104–109, 115, 141, 166, 187–188, 207, 211, 232, 251–252, 262–272, 284–285, 289, 300, 302, 305, 307–309, 312–314, 316–317

Philadelphia Stars 41

Philley, Dave 99, 130–140, 299

Phillips, Damon 99, 207–217, 308

Picciuto, Nick 37

Pieretti, Marino ("Chick") 196–206, 306

Pike, Jesse 22, 43, 251–261, 312

Pittsburgh Pirates ("Buccaneers/Bucs," "Corsairs") 2, 4, 9–10, 18–19, 22–29, 32, 34–38, 41–43, 46, 48–49, 52–55, 58, 60–61, 63, 65–69, 71–73, 76–77, 82–83, 87–89, 91–92, 94, 96, 100, 102, 104–111, 115, 119, 163, 185, 207, 210, 273–283, 227, 298, 303, 305, 307, 314–317

Pittsburgh, Pennsylvania, Post-Gazette (newspaper) 63

Plank, "Gettysburg Eddie" 25

Platt, Mizell "Whitey" 23, 79, 130–140, 229, 299

player pension plan 4, 82

player representatives 82–83

players' bonus prohibition/extra pay for playoffs 111

players' records in NL playoff included in season totals 111

players' share of sale price (proposed by the Guild) 32

players' share of World Series revenue 71, 85

players' union 91

Podgajny, Johnny "Specs" 2, 41, 141–151, 300

Poland, Hugh 2, 42, 207–217, 307

Pollet, Howard "Howie" 73, 104, 111–114, 284–294, 316

Poole, Ray 16

Portland Oregon/Beavers (Pacific Coast League, class "AAA") 38, 42, 153, 263, 301, 314

Posedel, Bill ("Sailor Bill") 207–217, 307, 314

Possehl, Lou 93, 262–272

postseason exhibition series 75

postseason money (World Series shares) 75

postwar housing shortage 18

postwar no-hit pitchers 24

postwar transportation problems, alternatives 46

Potter, Nelson "Nels" 78, 107, 185–195, 304–305

Povich, Shirley 30

Power, Tyrone 25

prewar years 42, 49, 58, 61, 64, 79, 93, 152, 285, 310, 312

Price, Jackie 90–91, 141–151, 300

Priddy, Gerald "Gerry" 102, 196–206, 306

Prim, Ray 23–24, 43, 60, 94, 229–239, 310

protective cap liners 78

Providence Grays (National League, 1884) 110

Providence, Rhode Island/Chiefs (New England League, class "B") 63

Pytlak, Frankie 55, 85, 119–129, 298

Queen, Mel 57–58, 163–173, 303

Quinn, Bob 25

racial integration 4

Radbourne, Charles ("Old Hoss," name also spelled Radbourn) 110

Raffensberger, Ken 262–272, 314

Raleigh, North Carolina/Capitals (Carolina League, class "C") 55

Ramazzotti, Bob 23, 76, 218–228, 309

Raschi, Vic 107, 163–173, 303

Reese, Harold "Pee Wee" 1, 44–45, 55, 71, 73, 218–228, 308

Reid, Earl 36, 44, 207–217, 307

Reiser, Harold "Pete" ("Pistol Pete") 2, 12, 14–15, 43, 50, 52, 56, 73, 77, 101–102, 108, 218–228, 308

Reyes, Napoleon "Nap" 12, 252

Reynolds, Allie 100, 105, 114, 141–151, 300

Reynolds, Danny 54

Rice, Del 38, 112, 284–294, 316

Rice, Grantland 25

Richards, Paul Rapier 2, 57, 152–162, 301

Richardson, Ken 62, 262–272, 314

Richmond, Don 16, 99, 174–184, 304

Richmond, Virginia/Colts (Piedmont League, class "B") 15, 50, 254, 256–259, 312–313

Rickert, Marv 229–239, 309

Rickey, Wesley Branch "Mr. Rickey" ("The Mahatma")

Index

6–7, 11–12, 58–59, 75, 78, 100
Riggs, Lew 29, 218–228, 308
Rigney, Billy 19, 92, 251–261, 312
Rigney, John 7, 48, 55, 67, 79, 130–140, 298
Ripple, Charley 67, 262–272, 314
Rizzo, Johnny 12, 28
Rizzuto, Phil 19, 44, 46, 78, 163–173, 302
Roberge, Al "Skippy" 59, 207–217, 307
Robertson, Sherrard "Sherry" 196–206, 306
Robinson, Aaron 39, 54, 90, 107, 163–173, 302
Robinson, Eddie 20–21, 105, 141–151, 301
Robinson, Jack Roosevelt "Jackie" 3–4, 6–7, 20, 23, 26, 32, 41, 49, 69, 75, 77–78, 95, 112
Rocco, Michael "Mickey" 15, 66, 141–151, 300
Rochester, New York/Red Wings (International League, class "AAA") 11, 19, 34, 38, 74, 98, 210, 215, 241, 248, 263, 284, 289, 307, 311, 313, 316
Rocky Mount, North Carolina/Rocks (Coastal Plain League, class "D") 87
Rodney, Lester 6
Roe, Elwin "Preacher" 100, 273–283, 315
Rojek, Stan 34, 218–228, 309
Rolfe, Robert "Red" 19, 302
Rosar, Warren "Buddy" 72, 174–184, 303
Rosen, Goodwin "Goody" 28, 37, 218–228, 251–261, 308, 312
Roser, Emerson "Steve" 34, 70, 163–173, 207–217, 302, 307
Ross, Chester "Chet" 42
Ross, Don 107, 141–151, 300–301
Ross, Lee "Buck" 16
roster limits/cut-down day 10, 80
Rowe, Lynwood "Schoolboy" 84–85, 262–272, 314
Rowell, Carvel "'Bama" 207–217, 307
Roy, Jean-Pierre 34, 60, 75, 218–228, 309
Royal Canadian Air Force (RCAF) 2, 35
Rucker, Johnny 251–261, 312, 317
Ruel, Herold "Muddy" 86, 95
Ruffing, Charley "Red" 19, 46, 50, 67–68, 107, 163–173, 302
Russell, Glen "Rip" 43, 48, 112, 119–129, 298
Russell, Jim 88, 273–283, 315
Russo, Marius 19, 64, 85, 96, 163–173, 303

Ruth, George Herman "Babe" 12–13, 25, 72
Ryan, Cornelius "Connie" 207–217, 306
Ryan, Nolan 31, 110
Ryba, Dominic "Mike" 112, 119–129, 298
Sacramento, California/Solons (Pacific Coast League, class "AAA" minor league) 19, 22, 37, 92
Sain, Johnny 90, 104, 207–217, 307
St. Joseph Autos 18
St. Louis Browns 2, 5–6, 12–14, 18–19, 22, 25, 27, 30–32, 34–36, 40–41, 46, 48, 50, 56–57, 59–60, 64–66, 68–74, 77–78, 80–82, 84–85, 88–89, 93–96, 99, 101, 103, 106–108, 130, 145, 185–196, 199, 262, 265, 273, 299–300, 304–306, 314
St. Louis Cardinals 2, 7, 9–12, 15–19, 22–23, 27, 30–32, 35, 37–38, 40, 42, 44–49, 52–53, 56, 62, 67, 69–74, 76–77, 80–85, 87–88, 91–95, 98, 101–115, 207, 218, 252, 262, 284–294, 307–308, 313–314, 316–317
St. Paul, Minnesota/Saints (American Association, class "AAA" minor league) 16, 21, 28, 32, 72, 77, 106, 112, 118, 223
Salenger, Oscar 95
Salina, Kansas/Millers (Western Association, 1941, class "C" minor league) 97
Salkeld, Bill 96, 100, 273–283, 315
Sally League (South Atlantic League, Class "A" minor league) 37, 94, 182
San Antonio, Texas/Missions (Texas League, class "AA" minor league) 74, 81, 94, 106, 190, 194, 305
San Diego, California/Padres (Pacific Coast League, class "AAA" minor league) 16, 42, 47, 57–58, 60, 66, 69, 92, 109, 175, 177, 275–277, 280, 315
Sanders, Ray 17, 26, 35, 81, 92, 95, 207–217, 284, 307
Sandlock, Mike 72, 75, 218–228, 309
Sanford, Fred 22, 46, 94, 103, 185–195, 305
Sanford, John Howard "Jack" 46–47, 196–206, 306
Sanford, John Stanley "Jack" 46
San Francisco, California/Mission Reds (Pacific Coast League, class "AAA" minor league) 80
San Francisco Seals (Pacific Coast League, class "AAA" minor league) 15, 31, 39, 56, 60, 71, 89, 92, 107, 133, 254, 260, 313

Sauer, Hank 33
Savage, Bob 17, 174–184, 303
Savannah, Georgia/Indians (South Atlantic League, class "A" minor league) 16, 37, 74, 79, 175, 179
Scarborough, Rae (contemporary spelling of first name; later "Ray") 196–206, 306
Schalk, Ray "Cracker" 55
Schanz, Charley 262–272, 314
Scheffing, Bob 229–239, 310
Schemer, Mike 50, 251–261, 312
Schenz, Henry "Hank" 98, 102, 104, 229–239, 310
Schmidt, Freddie 112, 284–294, 316
Schmitz, Johnny 44, 73, 229–239, 310
Schoendienst, Albert "Red" 45, 56, 73, 112, 284–294, 316
Schulte, Johnny 302
Schulte, Len 64, 94, 185–195, 305
Schultz, Howie 20, 218–228, 308
Schultz, Joe 56, 185–195, 305
Schumacher, Hal ("Prince Hal") 30, 82, 251–261, 312
Schwartz, "Packy" 48, 79
scorekeeper shorthand 117
Scranton, Pennsylvania/Red Sox (Eastern League, class "A" minor league) 54
Sears, John W. "Ziggy" 74
Sears, Ken "Ziggy" 74, 94, 106, 185–195, 305
Seattle Rainiers (Pacific Coast League, class "AAA" minor league) 27, 42, 52, 63, 95, 110, 143, 208, 265, 300, 307, 313–314
second division 28
second or third jobs 46
Secory, Frank 89, 229–239, 310
Seerey, Pat 76, 141–151, 300
Selma, Alabama/Cloverleafs (Southeastern League, class "B" minor league) 109, 276, 316
Seminick, Andy 32, 105, 262–272, 313
semipro ball 93, 262, 314
Sepkowski (Sczepkowski, Scepkowski, Szepkowski) Ted 29, 98, 103, 141–151, 300
Serafini, Mel 39
Sessi, Walter 112, 284–294, 316
Sewell, Luke 19, 59, 95, 304, 315
Sewell, Truett Banks "Rip" 3, 55, 55, 60, 72–73, 82, 91, 273–283
Shawkey, Bob 104
Shea, Frank "Spec" 39
Shellenback, Frank 300
Shepard, Bert 306
Sherman, Texas/Twins (East

Texas League, class "C" minor league) 91
Shirley, Newman "Tex" 82, 93–94, 107, 185–195, 305
Shokes, Eddie 240–250, 311
Shore, Ray 106, 185–195, 305
Shoun, Clyde 240–250, 311
Shreveport, Louisiana/Sports (Texas League, class "AA" minor league) 26, 54, 69, 98, 104, 130, 136, 138, 229, 299
Shupe, Vince 16
Siebert, Dick 5–6, 186
Silver Star 105
Silvestri, Ken 50, 54, 107, 302–303
Simmons, Al (Szymanski, Aloysius) "Bucketfoot Al" 303
Singleton, Elmer 89, 104, 110, 207–217, 307
Sisler, Dick 18–19, 36–37, 112, 284–294, 316
Sisti, Sebastian "Sibby" 20, 207–217, 307
Slaughter, Enos "Country" 3, 73, 76, 112–115, 284–294, 316
Smaza, Joe 104, 130–140, 299
Smith, Don 74
Smith, Edgar "Eddie" 79, 130–140, 299
Smith, Jay B. (Capt., USN, retired) 1
Smith, Richard "Red" 45, 309
Smith, Vincent "Vinnie," ("Vin") 2, 28–29, 273–283, 315
Snelling, Dennis 17
Snider, Edwin "Duke" 79
Society for American Baseball Research (*SABR*) 6, 17
Souchock, Steve 48, 163–173, 303
South Atlantic League (Sally League, class "A" minor league) 21
Southeastern League (class "B" minor league) 280, 316
Southern Association (class "AA" minor league) 47–49, 66, 97, 101, 108, 207, 308, 310
Southpaw 65
Southworth, Billy 7, 306
Spahn, Warren 3, 61, 115, 207–217, 307
Special Committee on the Negro Leagues 75
Spence, Stan 73, 111, 196–206, 306
Spindel, Hal 57, 92, 262–272, 314
Spokane, Washington/Indians (Western International League, class "B" minor league) 64–65
The Sporting News (weekly baseball newspaper, *The Bible of Baseball*, *TSN*) 3–5, 10, 13, 18, 20, 22–23,

26, 29, 32, 36–37, 39, 41–42, 44, 46–47, 49, 51, 54–55, 58–69, 74, 79–80, 86, 89–91, 94–95, 100, 105, 111, 114–115, 127, 146, 161, 175–176, 179, 182–183, 211, 232, 243, 248, 251, 255, 258, 263, 267, 297, 317

The Sporting News Baseball Register (annual publication) 7, 26, 36, 40, 43, 45, 93, 96

Sporting News "Deals of the Week" (weekly feature) 15, 20, 23, 26, 32, 36–37, 42, 46, 54–55, 58, 62, 66, 69, 74, 86, 94

The Sporting News 1942 Dope Book (annual publication) 110

The Sporting News Official 1947 Baseball Guide (annual publication) 29, 107, 297

sports writers 25, 76

spring training 10, 18, 21, 24, 33, 35, 40, 51, 54, 185, 240, 305, 311

Springfield, Illinois/Browns (Illinois-Indiana-Iowa, Three-Eye League, class "B" minor league) 185, 305

Springfield, Ohio/Giants (Ohio-Indiana League, class "D" minor league, 1950) 36

Stainback, Tucker "Tuck" 30, 174–184, 304, 317

Staley, Gerald "Gerry" 92

Stanceau, Charley 54, 163–173, 262–272, 302, 314

Stanky, Eddie 1, 43–45, 59, 76, 218–228, 308

Steengrafe, Milt (Southern Association umpire) 36

Steiner, Ben 53, 119–129, 298

Stephens, Vernon ("Junior") 12, 28, 35, 72, 89, 94, 185–195, 304

Stevens, Chuck 25, 185–195, 305

Stevens, Ed 19–20, 218–228, 308

Stewart, James 91

Stiles, Helen 118

Stirnweiss, George "Snuffy" 44, 49, 72, 111, 163–173, 302

Stock, Milt 309

Stoneham, Horace 14

Stratton, Monty 91

Street & Smith's Baseball Year Book 39

Strincevich, Nick 273–283, 315

Stringer, Lou 109, 229–239, 310

Sturgeon, Bob 109, 229–239, 310

Sturm, Johnny 19, 21

Suder, Peter "Pete" ("Pecky") 174–184, 304

Sundra, Steve 50, 185–195, 305

Surkont, Matthew "Max" 17, 27, 38, 207, 284

Susce, George 300

Sutton, Don 69

Swift, Bob 18, 152–162, 301

Syracuse, New York/Chiefs (International League, class "AAA" minor league) 23, 26, 33, 81, 88, 112, 245–247, 311

Tabor, Jim "Rawhide" 9, 46, 82, 262–272, 310

Tate, Al 109, 273–283, 316

Taylor, Harry 106, 108, 218–228, 309

Taylor, James "Zack" 95, 193, 304, 309

Tebbetts, George "Birdie" 1, 111, 152–162, 301

Tepsic, Joe 71, 75, 218–228, 309

Terre Haute, Indiana/Phillies (Illinois-Indiana-Iowa, Three-Eye League, class "B" minor league) 62, 78, 104, 109, 266, 270, 314

Texas A & M College "Aggies" 40

Texas League (class "AA" minor league) 19, 21, 23, 54, 79, 97–98, 102–104, 108, 141, 149, 237

Thomas, Bill 89

Thompson, Gene "Junior" 26, 40–41, 57, 97, 251–261, 313

Thomson, Bobby "The Staten Island Scot" 98, 251–261, 313

Three-Eye League (Illinois-Indiana-Iowa League, class "B" minor league) 185, 305

Three Rivers, Quebec/Royals (Canadian-American League, class "C" minor league) 40, 77

Tinker, Joe 25

Tipton, Eric 16

Tokyo, Japan 99

Toledo, Ohio/Mud Hens (American Association, class "AAA" minor league) 20, 22, 30, 42, 46, 64–65, 71, 73, 78, 94, 99, 103, 119, 121, 127, 185, 187, 189–190, 192, 298, 305

Torgeson, Earl 95

Toronto, Ontario, Canada/Maple Leafs (International League, class "AAA" minor league) 16, 22, 35, 37, 43–44, 47, 53, 55, 59, 67–68, 77, 79, 94–95, 97, 99–100, 102–103, 121–122, 127, 141, 174–176, 179, 182, 209–210, 277, 281, 298, 307, 315

Torreon, Mexico/Algodoneros club, Mexican League 12, 17, 86

Torres, Gilberto "Gil" 196–206, 306

Tost, Lou 27

Total Baseball 196, 297

trading deadline 59

Travis, Cecil 41, 65, 196–206, 306

Treichel, Al "Li'l Abner" 66

Trenton, New Jersey/Packers (Interstate League, class "B" minor league) 29

Tresh, Mike 79, 130–140, 299

Trinkle, Ken 251–261, 312

Triple-A (minor league class "AAA") 15, 38, 39, 66, 68, 81, 99

Triple Crown, batting 108–109

Triplett, Coaker 88

Triplett, Hooper 88

Trosky, Hal 79, 91, 130–140, 299

Trout, Paul "Dizzy" 111, 152–162, 301

Trucks, Virgil 152–162, 301

Truman, Bess 52

Truman, Margaret 52

Tucker, Thurman 130–140, 299

Tulsa, Oklahoma/Oilers (Texas League, class "AA" minor league) 37, 98, 102, 108, 229, 234, 310

Turner, Ted 68

umpire, American League 48, 79, 94

umpire, National League 14, 29, 74, 89

umpires, minor league 4

unfair labor practices 30

Uniform Player's Contract 12, 79

uniforms 50

Usher, Bob 19, 240–250, 311, 317

Utica, New York/Blue Sox (Eastern League, class "A" minor league) 25, 37, 61–62, 87, 101–102, 104, 262–264, 267, 270, 313

Valdosta, Georgia/Trojans (Georgia-Florida League, class "D" minor league, 1941) 20

Valo, Elmer 174–84, 303

Van Cuyk, Chris 21

Van Cuyk, Johnny 20–21

Vandenberg, Hy 16

Vander Meer, John ("Double No-Hit Johnny") 240–250, 311

Van Meter, Iowa 102

Van Robays, Maurice 273–283, 315

Vaughan, Porter 20, 174–184, 304

Veeck, Bill, Jr. 49, 63–64, 66, 69–70, 72, 90–91, 95, 145

Veeck, William, Sr. 63

Vera Cruz, Mexico/Blues, Mexican League 12–13, 61, 68, 86

Verban, Emil 31–32, 73, 93, 262–272, 284–294, 312, 314, 316

Vernon, James "Mickey" 3, 58, 72, 109, 196–206, 306

Voiselle, Bill 81, 251–261, 312

Vollmer, Clyde 34, 98, 240–250, 311

voluntary retirement status (voluntary retired list) 6, 18, 54–55, 60, 78, 83, 120, 125, 135–136, 168, 185–186, 221, 251, 313

Waddell, George "Rube" 25, 88, 92, 110

Wade, Jake "Whistlin' Jake" 85, 163–173, 196–206, 302, 306

Wagner, Charles "Broadway Charley" 54, 112, 119–129, 298

Wagner, Hal 39, 72, 101, 112, 119–129, 298

Wagner, John Peter "Honus" ("Hans") 314

Waitkus, Eddie 41, 49, 80, 81, 115, 229–239, 310

Wakefield, Dick 34, 44, 75, 152–162, 301

Walker, Fred "Dixie" 6, 45, 56, 73, 82, 218–228, 308

Walker, Gerald "Gee" 311

Walker, Harry "Little Dixie" 1, 87, 112–115, 284–294, 316

Walker, Terry 87

Wallace, Jim "Lefty" 67, 70, 207–217, 307

Wallaesa, Jack 17, 79, 99, 174–184, 303

Walsh, Ed "Big Ed" 25

Walsh, Jim "Junior" 102, 106, 273–283, 315

Walters, Fred 15, 96

Walters, William "Bucky" 82, 108, 240–250, 311

Wares, Clyde "Buzzy" 316

Warren, Bennie 15, 62, 251–261, 300, 317

Wasdell, Jimmy 59, 69, 74, 141–151, 262–272, 300, 313

Washington Nationals ("Nats," "Senators") 1–2, 8, 11, 15, 18, 22, 24–25, 28, 30, 33–35, 41, 44, 46, 51–53, 57–59, 61, 64–65, 67, 70, 72–73, 79–83, 85, 87, 93, 98, 101–105, 108, 130, 153, 169, 177, 185, 188, 196–207, 299, 301–302, 304–306, 308

We Played the Game 29

Weafer, Hal 94

Weatherly, Roy "Stormy" 48, 63, 163–173, 303

Webb, James "Skeeter" 152–162, 301, 317

Webb, Mel 25

Webber, Les 69, 86, 141–151, 218–228, 300, 309

Weigel, Ralph 104, 141–151, 300

Weiss, George 21

Welch, West Virginia/Miners (Appalachian League, class "D" minor league) 55

Wells, Leo 79, 130–140, 299

Wentzel, Stan 110

West, Max 22, 57, 207–217, 240–250, 307, 311

wheelchair race 67

White, Ernie 40, 61, 207–217, 285, 307

White, Hal 152–162, 301

Index

Whitehead, Burgess 273–283, 315
Whitman, Dick 18, 77, 218–228, 308
Whitman, Frank 68, 79, 130–140, 299
Who's Who in Baseball (annual publication) 18, 23–24, 26, 35, 88
Who's Who in the Major Leagues (annual publication) 34
Wietelmann, Wm. "Whitey" 110, 207–217, 307
Wight, Bill 20, 46, 74, 163–173, 302
Wilber, Del "Babe" 23, 42, 98, 284–294, 316
Wiles, Tim 118
Wilkes-Barre, Pennsylvania/Barons (Eastern League, class "A" minor league) 16, 74, 91, 103–104, 141, 149, 300–301
Wilkie, Aldon "Lefty" 58, 273–283, 315
Wilks, Ted 112, 284–294, 316
Williams, Bob "Ace" 42, 207–217, 307

Williams, Dewey "Dee" 92, 229–239, 310
Williams, Ted 3, 9, 12, 27, 39, 60, 72–76, 79, 101, 108–109, 111–115, 119–129, 298
Williams Shift (also Boudreau Shift) 76, 113
Williamsport, Pennsylvania/Tigers (Eastern League, class "A" minor league, 1948) 22, 152, 302
Wilmington, North Carolina/Pirates (Tobacco State League, class "D" minor league) 66, 255
Wilson, Jim 36, 119–129, 298
Wilson, Jimmie 311
Wilson, Maxie 67, 196–206, 306
Wilson Sporting Goods 25
Witek, Nicholas "Mickey" 30, 251–261, 312
Witte, Jerry 20, 99, 185–195, 305
Wolff, Roger 65, 196–206, 306
Wood, Joe "Smoky Joe" 92
Woodall, Larry 298
Woodling, Gene 141–151, 300
Woods, George "Pinky" 15

Workman, Chuck 58, 273–283, 307, 315
World Championship/World Series 5–7, 9–10, 27, 30–31, 36, 47, 49, 52, 54, 58, 62–64, 70–71, 73, 77, 80–81, 85, 89, 91–92, 98, 103, 106, 110–115, 117, 129, 294, 311
World War II 1, 3, 16–17, 19, 21, 27–28, 30–34, 37–39, 44, 48–49, 53–59, 61, 63, 66–69, 72–74, 77, 80–81, 83, 92, 101, 103, 105–107, 115, 117, 130, 284, 298, 311, 317
Wright, Ed 207–217, 307
Wright, John 7, 26, 41, 77–78
Wright, Taft 44, 55, 130–140, 299
Wrigley, Philip K. (Phil, P.K.) 10
Wrigley Field, Chicago 63
Wynn, Early 1, 70, 196–206, 306
Wyrostek, Johnny 10, 262–272, 313
Wyse, Henry "Hank" 229–239, 310

Yankee Stadium, New York 50, 71, 88, 96
Yawkey, Tom 101, 111, 128
York, Rudy 8, 72, 82, 94, 101, 112–113, 119–129, 298
York, Pennsylvania/White Roses (Interstate League, class "B" minor league) 102, 106, 114, 273, 315–316
Yost, Eddie 83, 84, 196–206, 306
Young, Norman "Babe" 251–261, 312
Youngstown Ohio/Bears (National Basketball League) 38
Zabala, Adrian 12, 252
Zak, Frankie 32, 60, 73, 273–283, 315
Zarilla, Al 84, 185–195, 304
Zaslofsky, Max 38
Zientara, Benny 240–250, 311
Zimmerman, Roy 14, 252
Zoldak, Sam 27, 185–195, 305
Zuber, Bill "Goober" 58, 111–112, 119–129, 163–173, 298, 302